BEGINNING KOREAN

BEGINNING KOREAN

by Samuel E. Martin and
Young-Sook C. Lee

with the assistance of
Elinor Clark Horne

Charles E. Tuttle Co.: Publishers
Rutland, Vermont & Tokyo, Japan

Representatives
Continental Europe: BOXERBOOKS, INC., *Zurich*
British Isles: PRENTICE-HALL INTERNATIONAL, INC., *London*
Australasia: BOOKWISE INTERNATIONAL
1 Jeanes Street, Beverley 5009, South Australia

Published by the Charles E. Tuttle Company, Inc.
of Rutland, Vermont & Tokyo, Japan
with editorial offices at
Suido 1-chome, 2-6, Bunkyo-ku, Tokyo, Japan

Library of Congress Catalog Card No. 86-50701
International Standard Book No. 0-8048-1507-0

First Tuttle edition, 1986

PRINTED IN JAPAN

PREFACE

This book aims to teach the essentials of modern spoken Korean in a systematic way. All material is given in the Yale Romanization, from which it is possible to derive by rules (1) the pronunciation, (2) the standard Hankul spelling used in South Korea, and (3) the standard Hankul spelling used in North Korea. At first the Romanization will seem strange to some readers, but they will find it easy to get used to if they listen carefully to the voice of a native speaker and use the Romanized forms primarily as a jog to remembering what their ears have heard. The Romanization makes use of digraphs (two letters treated as a single unit) in order to write a number of Korean sounds without bringing in odd-shaped letters not on the usual typewriter keyboard; thus we imitate the practice of English spelling in writing "ng" (as in sing and singer) for what is a single sound, an "n" made with the back of the tongue instead of the tip. And to take care of the eight vowels distinguished by most speakers of Korean we use the simple vowel symbols for those vowels that are more common (or more basic to the language) and write the other vowels as if they were still pronounced as diphthongs, as they were at an earlier stage of the language. We use the letter i for a sound rather like those in pin or Puccini, e for a sound that resembles both the English sound in son and that in song (a kind of "uh" or "aw" sound), and a for a sound rather like that in father; the letter u is used for a vowel somewhat like that in English cook or coo (provided the words are said with the lips spread in a smile), but to represent the lip-pursed sound that many English speakers have in coo or moo we write wu except after lip sounds (m, p, ph, pp) and after y, where the un-pursed sound does not occur (so that we need not write the w). The English sounds in both met and hay (or hey) resemble the Korean vowel that we write as ey; the English sound in mat resembles the Korean vowel that we write as ay, a sound made with the jaw a bit more open than the sound in English hay or hey.

Although the pronunciation of some of the consonants is difficult at first, the symbols we use should cause little confusion once the student is aware that a single Korean sound unit (a phoneme) may occur in more than one variety, so that what we write as l will sound like a flapped "r" between vowels, what we write as p will sound like an English "b" in some positions, and so on. But one symbol to watch is c, which we use to write a sound that sometimes (as in English cello) sounds like the "ch" sound in churches and sometimes like the "j" sound in judges, but NEVER like the "k" sound of cat or the "s" sound of Cecil! Notice that we use the combination ch for a similar but different sound, a "ch" accompanied by a heavy puff of air from the throat, somewhat like the sound heard in hitchhiker; similar sounds are ph (somewhat like the sound heard in upholster but NEVER like the "f" sound heard in philosophy!), th (somewhat like the sound heard in rathole but NEVER like the fricative sounds heard in either or ether!), and kh (somewhat like the sound heard in cookhouse).

Another characteristic of our Romanization is that, like the usual Hankul spellings, we try to write a word or a part of a word always in the same way, even when the word (or word-part) has two different pronunciations, provided only that the different pronunciations can be automatically predicted from the spelling. This is because changes take place when certain of the sounds are juxtaposed in putting words together. For example, when you add ... man 'just' (or any other element that starts with m or n) to ip 'mouth' (or any other word that ends in p) instead of the expected ...pm... you hear ...mm... But if we wrote 'just the mouth' as im man you wouldn't realize that 'mouth' in many other phrases is pronounced with a p. So the spellings, both in Romanization and in Hankul, tell you MORE than the pronunciation: they tell you the basic shape of the word.

By working carefully through the first section of this book (The Sounds of Korean) you will acquire the principles of the sound system and be able to proceed nicely with the text lessons. Whenever possible, especially in the early stages, work closely with the voice of a native speaker, either in person or on tape. Once you have acquired the sound system and learned to say a good many things in Korean—perhaps after Lesson 5 or Lesson 10—you will want to examine the Hankul writing system. The Hankul symbols are very simple and you can learn to read them by yourself in a very short time; but there are certain subtleties in shaping the symbols so that they join properly in syllable-like blocks, and you would do well to have a Korean help you learn to write some of the sentences in this book. You will find that the Hankul spelling you are taught to follow, whether that in use in South Korea or that preferred in North Korea, will derive quite automatically from the Romanized forms you meet in this book. For futher details on spelling, Romanization, and writing problems, the reader is referred to the introduction to A Korean-English Dictionary by Samuel E. Martin, Yang Ha Lee, and Sung-Un Chang (Yale University Press 1967) and to "A Korean Reference Grammar" by Samuel E. Martin (to appear).

Each lesson has several sections. The BASIC SENTENCES should be practiced until they are memorized, for each one contains important grammatical patterns. You will perhaps notice that a single numbered "sentence" contains several short sentences; occasionally the numbers have been more finely marked by adding a letter (thus: 35a, 36b, 35c). A long stretch of that sort can be learned by memorizing the shorter sentences that make it up, but eventually you should be able to say the entire stretch from memory. Each sentence is accompanied by an English translation and an "amplification"; the amplification explains the individual words that make up the phrases and sometimes it includes a few additional related words that will help you understand the sentence better. The SUPPLEMENTARY VOCABULARY of each lesson contains additional words that you will probably want to know; many of these occur in the later parts of the lesson or in later lessons, but some are included only in order to give you and your Korean tutor greater scope in practicing free conversation. The NOTES explain the grammatical patterns that appear in the sentences and offer more examples of them. The EXERCISES give you a chance to drill on grammatical patterns; the CONVERSATION gives you practice in putting your Korean to work; the VOCABULARY DRILL helps you remember the words; and COMPREHENSION is a chance to listen to see how well you can follow a fair stretch of the language.

Korean, like English, is spoken in many varieties and for certain words we have had to choose among several competing pronunciations; if the student's tutor prefers a different version, he should make the appropriate adjustments. Thus, a word that is often written iyaki is usually pronounced yāyki or yēyki, and we have settled on the latter in most of our sentences. For what we have written as iss.ey yo and ēps.ey yo (and similar cases) many speakers, especially older men, will prefer pronunciations without the first y: iss.e yo, ēps.e yo. We have tried to be consistent in noting the long vowels that are used by older-generation Seoul speakers, but younger speakers largely ignore such distinctions; and we have not marked some vowels that the student may hear pronounced long, notably in words that are given "expressive" or "emphatic" lengthening (as when ani yo 'no' is pronounced āni yo) and in certain verb forms that are abbreviated from longer forms in use at an earlier period, e.g. hay yo 'does' (for which you may hear hāy yo), pwa yo 'sees' (you may hear pwā yo), and wa yo 'comes' (you may hear wā yo). There are a number of common words in which we have omitted marking a long vowel (e.g. yenghwa for yēnghwa 'movies,' komapsup.nita for kōmapsup.nita 'thank you') because even older Seoul speakers seem to use the short vowel.

The heart of this textbook was written in 1952, when Young-Sook Chang (now Mrs. Yang Ha Lee) created the Basic Sentences for each lesson to match a systematic presentation of the essential features of Korean grammar that I had worked out. Part of the exercises were written at that time, together with an outline of grammar notes. The material was originally created for the use of missionaries who were studying Korean at Yale University, and that accounts for the content of at least one of the lessons. The material was put to one side for a number of years while I was busy with other work. When assistance was provided by the Committee on Uralic and Altaic Languages of the American Council of Learned Societies, under a contract with the U.S. Office of Education, Elinor Clark Horne (author of an earlier textbook of spoken Korean) undertook the task of filling out and editing the material; working with Jongsoon Park, Mrs. Horne provided additional examples and much of the practical exercise material. In addition she expanded the grammar notes and added a number of pertinent comments. After that, I went carefully through the manuscript and revised many sections in the light of more recent knowledge of Korean structure and usage; I also tried, as best I could, to make the style of presentation as consistent as possible despite the several hands that had worked on the material at various times.

I am glad that it was possible to incorporate a number of excellent suggestions by Sung-Un Chang, who has taught the lessons, and by Maeng-Sung Lee, who recorded the Basic Sentences and Supplementary Vocabulary of each lesson. I hope that it will be possible in some later edition to incorporate further suggestions by those who use the book, and I would appreciate receiving comments from students and tutors. I offer my apologies that the circumstances of the book's gestation have led to a number of infelicities; in particular, I am sorry that we were unable to institute a rigorous vocabulary control that would both restrict the number of words introduced and make sure that all important common words were included. And I regret that the lessons are uneven in length, so that some will require more time to cover than others, and that the Basic Sentences of a number of the earlier lessons do not comprise a cohesive text with a single theme; both of these faults stem from building the sentences around the careful ordering of the grammar points, a feature that I would be hesitant to forgo. Despite a number of such shortcomings, however, I am confident that this textbook has much to offer the student of Korean, and I hope that he will put it to good use.

August 1968 Samuel E. Martin

In this new printing a number of corrections have been made; for the most part these are based on the careful observations of reviewers such as Yeong-Keun Ko, Seok Choong Song, and E. Sang Yu.

January 1980 S.E.M.

CONTENTS

THE SOUNDS OF KOREAN

Learning to pronounce Korean causes many problems for the student. The following sections give a brief, systematic introduction to the major features of the sound system, as reflected in the Romanization used throughout this book. There are 44 sections, divided into eight groups. The examples are intended to be used as pronunciation drills, they are to be covered thoroughly and should be frequently returned to during the early lessons of the course. The words are given only for the purpose of practicing sounds; you need not memorize their meanings. Vowel length is not marked for the examples which precede Section 36; some of the words have vowels that are etymologically long, but Koreans are used to hearing the length distinctions ignored, so the student need not worry unduly about vowel length in those exercises. The examples of Sections 10, 11, 12, 13, 14, 20, 22, 23, 28, 33, 36, 37, and 38 should be drilled horizontally (from left to right); those of Sections 1, 2, 5, and 19 should be drilled both horizontally and vertically (from top to bottom); the examples of the remaining sections can be drilled vertically. In drilling, always imitate the voice of a native speaker, even when the speaker does not exactly follow the description given in the book; remember that Korean, like English, is spoken in many varieties, and a well-imitated authentic variety is preferable to one you make up yourself.

I. VOWELS

1. The simple vowels. Note that the digraphs ey, ay, wu are to be taken as single units.

	TONGUE FRONT (Smile!)	TONGUE BACK (Smile!)	TONGUE BACK (Purse lips!)
TONGUE HIGH	ki 'flag'	ku 'that'	kwu 'nine'
TONGUE MID	key 'crab'	ke 'that thing(=ku ke)'	ko 'plaster'
TONGUE LOW	kay 'dog'	ka 'edge, brink'	——

Note: Many Koreans have trouble distinguishing ey from ay and u from e, especially when not at the beginning of a word.

2. The vowels with w-. (Purse lips, then relax!)

wi 'above'		
wey 'why (=way)'	wen 'dollar'	——
way 'why'	wa 'come'	——
kwi 'ear'	——	——
kwey 'case, chest'	kwen 'a volume(=chayk-kwen)'	
kway 'divination sign (=phal-kway)'	kwa 'lesson'	——

3. The vowel oy. Some pronounce oy like German [ö], with pursed lips throughout, and some pronounce oy as Korean way; but most Seoul speakers pronounce oy as Korean wey, with pursed lips at the start only.

oy 'cucumber (=oi)'	coy 'sin'
hoy 'meeting, group'	soy 'iron'
noy 'brains'	koy 'guile'

The vowel wi. Some pronounce wi like German [ü], with pursed lips throughout, but it is more common to purse the lips at the start only.

wi 'above'	cwi 'rat'	tan.wi 'unit'
kwi 'ear'	twi 'behind'	

4. The vowel uy. At the beginning of a word, some pronounce uy as Korean ui, with two vowels in a row; others pronounce uy as Korean u (high back unrounded) at the beginning of a word. When not at the beginning of a word uy is pronounced as Korean i, and some speakers use i everywhere.

   uyca [uica or uca] 'chair'
   uymi [uimi or umi] 'meaning'
   huyn ... [hin] 'white ...'
   cwuuy [cwui] 'attention'
   hoyuy [hweyi] 'conference'
   uyuy [uii or ui] 'significance'

   Note: The particle ... uy 'of' is exceptionally pronounced the same as the particle ... ey 'at, to.'

5. The vowels with y-. Note that after a consonant yey is pronounced as Korean ey.

___	___	yun 'gloss'
yey 'yes sir'	ye 'sunken rock'	yo 'mattress'
yay 'hey!'	yak 'medicine'	___
___	___	kyul 'orange'
kyey [key] 'total (=hapkyey)'	kye 'chaff, bran'	kyo 'religion (=congkyo)'
kyay 'that child (=ku ay)'	kyaki 'haughtiness (=kyoki)'	___

II. CONSONANTS

6. The consonants m and n. (Tongue tip touches upper teeth for n!)

mom 'body'	non 'paddy field'
ama 'perhaps'	ani 'no'
sam-man 'thirty thousand'	enni 'older brother of a male, older sister of a female'

7. The consonant -ng. As (usually) in English, the digraph is treated as a unit, a nasal made with the back of the tongue. Unlike English, when followed by a vowel ng begins the syllable. The sound is very weak before i or y, sometimes just nasal quality with no tongue contact at all, like a French nasal vowel.

kong 'ball'	tongyang [to-ngyang] 'Orient'
tong-an [to-ngan] 'interval, while'	kongi [ko-ngi, ko-(ng)i] 'pestle'
sangep [sa-ngep] 'commerce'	
Yenge [ye-nge] 'English'	
kongwen [ko-ngwen] 'park'	

8. The consonant l will sound different to you in different environments:
   (1) Initially (in foreign words only), it is a flap like Japanese or Spanish "r":

latio 'radio'	laymphu 'lamp'	lem 'rum'
leymen or leymon 'lemon'	lotheli 'traffic circle'	lwupi 'ruby'
lingkhu 'link; rink'		

(2) Between vowels (including w/y + vowel) or vowel and h (which often drops), it is also a flap. This is similar to the sound heard in British "berry" and American "Betty."

alay [a-ray] 'below'	ili [i-ri] 'this way'	tele [te-re] 'some'
il-wen [i-rwen] 'one dollar'	halyu [ha-ryu] 'lower reaches of a river'	silhem [sirhem or si-rem] 'experiment'
palhayng [parhayng or pa-rayng] 'publication'		

(3) When double, a long lateral l (as in English "hall light") is heard:

molla 'I don't know'	melli 'far off'	mullon 'of course'
sillyey [silley] 'discourtesy'		

(4) When final before a pause, you will hear a clear lateral l (as in English "feel"):

tal 'moon'	tol 'stone'	kwul 'oyster'

(5) When followed by a consonant, l is often palatalized (as in ly):

talk ita [taly-gi-da] 'it is a chicken'
phal-man [phaly-man] 'eighty thousand'

9. An initial h- is made with friction in the throat, as when blowing to steam up glasses.

hana 'one'	heli 'waist'	hong 'red (= hong-sayk)'
hwu 'afterward'		

But before y or i, the friction may be between the middle-front of the tongue and the hard palate:

hye 'tongue'	him 'strength'	huyn ... [hin] 'white ...'

And between voiced sounds (m, n, l, vowels) the h is weak, and often drops especially when preceded by ng or n and followed by i or y:

sihem [sihem or siem] 'examination'	annyeng hi [an-nye-(ng)i] 'in good health'
	manh.i [ma-ni] 'much, lots'

10. The single s is very weak, something less than an English "s," and often followed by a little puff of local air. The double ss is very strong, something more than an English "s," with tension in the throat and tongue. (Many Koreans distinguish these two sounds poorly, if at all; you will hear them most clearly at the beginning of a word.)

sal 'flesh'	ssal 'hulled rice'
son 'hand'	sson sal 'a shot arrow = a flying arrow'
swul 'wine, liquor'	sswuk 'mugwort'
say 'bird'	sswayki 'wedge'
se yo 'stands'	sse yo 'writes'
use yo 'laughs'	iss.e(y) yo 'stays'

Before i and wi, most speakers palatalize the s (as if it were sy), and it may sound like English "sh" to you. Some speakers do this also for the ss.

si 'poem'	ssi 'seed'
swi 'soon'	mos swinta [mo-sswin-da] 'can't rest'

III. THREE-WAY CONSONANTS

	LIGHT LOCAL RELEASE	HEAVY AIR FROM THROAT	SHARP TIGHT-THROATED RELEASE
11. Three kinds of initial k:			
	kay 'dog'	khay (yo) 'digs out'	kkay 'sesame'
	ki 'flag'	khi 'rudder'	kkini 'meal(time)'
	kun 'catty (weight)'	khun ... 'big ...'	kkun 'string'
	kol 'anger'	kho 'nose'	kkol 'fodder; shape'
	kong 'ball'	khong 'soybean'	kkwum 'dream'
12. Three kinds of initial p:			
	pal 'foot'	phal 'arm'	ppalli 'fast'
	pul 'fire'	phul 'grass'	ppul 'horn'
	pi 'rain'	phi 'blood'	ppi 'with a screech'
	pye 'rice plant'	phyo 'ticket'	ppye 'bone'
13. Three kinds of initial t: (Tongue tip touches upper teeth!)			
	tal 'moon'	thal 'mask'	ttal 'daughter
	tek 'virtue'	thek 'chin'	ttek 'ricecake'
	to 'province'	tho 'earth'	tto 'again'
	tay 'bamboo'	thay 'crack (in plate)'	ttay 'dirt; time'
14. Three kinds of initial c:			
	ca yo 'sleeps'	cha yo 'is cold'	cca yo 'weaves'
	cok 'foreleg (of animal)'	chok 'arrowhead'	ccok 'indigo plant'
	cie yo 'gets defeated'	chie yo 'hits'	ccie yo 'steams'
	cwuwi 'surroundings'	chwuwi 'cold spell'	———

IV. SYLLABLE PROBLEMS

15. When a single consonant, a double consonant that can start a syllable (like pp tt cc kk ss) or a cluster of consonant + h comes between two vowels, it is pronounced as the beginning of the LATER syllable, with a French-like liaison wherever space or hyphen is written.

    mom i [mo-mi] 'body (as subject)' appa [a-ppa] 'Daddy'
    non ey [no-ney] 'in the paddy field' noph.a yo [no-pha-yo] 'is high'
    tal iey yo [ta-ri-ey-yo] 'it is the moon' tan.wi [ta-nwi] 'unit'

    Note that spaces and hyphens (which indicate words and parts of words) are seldom HEARD; Koreans "run their words together." But pauses are often inserted between PHRASES, especially in slow, deliberate speech.

16. When a cluster of two consonants (other than those which can start a syllable) comes between vowels, the first consonant ends the first syllable, and the second begins the next one.

    enni [en-ni] 'older brother of a male, older sister of a female'
    mullon [mul-lon] 'of course'

17. The normally voiceless sounds shown by the single p t c k (which have a light puff of local air when they are at the beginning of a word) are lightly voiced between voiced sounds (vowels, y w, m n ng l) so that they will sound like b d j g to you:

apeci [a-be-ji] 'father'
tat.e yo [ta-de-yo] 'closes it'
ayki [ay-gi] 'baby'
tampay [tam-bay] 'cigarettes, tobacco'
Antong [an-dong] (name of a city)
Cwungkwuk [cwung-gwuk] 'China'
kalpi [kaly-bi] 'ribs'
ancwu [an-jwu] 'snacks to go with drinks'

But these consonants will usually not be voiced if the vowels are whispered (18).

18. In phrases of more than one syllable, many speakers unvoice (= WHISPER) a high vowel (u wu uy i wi) when it occurs with h or s (or consonant + h or s) on one side and a voiceless consonant (p t c k s h) on the other side:

khuta 'it is big'	swi̥sey yo 'rest!'
pu̥chi̥ca 'let's mail it!'	sip-pun 'ten minutes'
khi̥ ka khu̥ta 'is tall'	hu̥ksayk 'black'

Some speakers whisper other vowels in the same places:
hḁksayng or haksayng 'student'
tho̥kki or thokki 'rabbit'

19. Final p t k are unreleased; they are sometimes difficult for an American to hear:

kwup 'hoof'	kwuk 'soup'	kwus [kwut] 'exorcism'
kop 'pus'	ok 'jade'	os [ot] 'garment'
ip 'mouth'	mok 'throat'	mos [mot] 'pond'

20. The only consonants pronounced at the end of a syllable are m n ng l (see above) and p t k. When the basic form of a word ends in something else, the "something else" must be reduced to one of these consonants, unless the word is followed by a particle or ending that begins with a vowel or by ... iey yo 'it is ....'

aph ey 'in front'	aph [ap] 'front'
kaps un 'as for price'	kaps [kap] 'price'
pakk ey 'outside'	pakk [pak] 'outside'
talk iey yo 'it's a chicken'	talk [tak] 'chicken'
puekh iey yo 'it's a kitchen'	puekh [puek] 'kitchen'
os iey yo 'it's a garment'	os [ot] 'garment'
path ey 'in the field'	path [pat] 'field'
nac ey 'in the daytime'	nac [nat] 'daytime'
kkoch iey yo 'it's a flower'	kkoch [kkot] 'flower'

Note: Most cases of noun-final t come from a basic s.

21. The final-reduced forms are used not only when the word is before pause, but also before words beginning with consonants and even before words beginning with vowels, provided the word is not a particle (like the subject particle i or the locative particle ey 'at, to' etc.) or the copula ... iey yo 'it is ....'
talk koki → tak koki [ta-kko-gi] 'chicken (as meat)'
path to → pat to [pa-tto] 'the field too'
path an → pat an [pa-dan] 'inside the field'
os an → ot an [o-dan] 'garment lining'
os to → ot to [o-tto] 'the garment too'

22. Voicing practice:

ip 'mouth'	ip ey 'in the mouth'	ip iey yo 'it's the mouth'
kwuk 'soup'	kwuk ey 'in the soup'	kwuk iey yo 'it's soup'
nac [nat] 'daytime'	nac ey 'in the daytime'	nac iey yo 'it's daytime'
——	——	tat.e yo 'closes it'

23. For Seoul speakers t(h) is pronounced like c(h) before i or y, PROVIDED the i or y begins a particle or ending or iey yo 'it is.'

path [pat] 'field'	path ey [pa-they] 'in the field'	path iey yo [pa-chi-ey-yo] 'it's a field'
kot 'straightway, at once'	kot.a yo [ko-ta-yo] 'is straight'	kot.i [ko-ci] 'straightly'

24. After s and c(h), the semivowel y commonly occurs only as a reduction from the full vowel i, typically at the end of a verb base or some verb form. Many speakers further reduce the sound to nothing at all:
    kacye yo [ka-je-yo] 'possesses'
    pachye yo [pa-che-yo] 'gives to a superior'
    kasye se [ka-sye-se or ka-se-se] '(you) go and then ...'
    kasyess.ey yo [ka-sye-ssey-yo or ka-se-ssey-yo] '(you) went'

    The word syassu 'shirt' was borrowed from Japanese (which got it from English) and it is usually given a Japanese-type pronunciation [syatsu] irregular to the Korean system.

V. AUTOMATIC PHONEME REPLACEMENTS

25. When n is next to l ("n.l" or "l.n") a double ll results:
    il-nyen [il-lyen] 'one year'
    chen-li [chel-li] 'a thousand Korean miles'
    yel neys [yel-leyt] 'fourteen'
    Sin.la [sil-la] (ancient Korean state)

26. When preceded by a consonant other than l or n, the l is pronounced as if n:
    sim.li [sim-ni] 'psychology'
    sang.lyu [sang-nyu] 'upper reaches of a river'

27. When p t k precede m or n (or l pronounced as n), they are pronounced as m n ng.
    hap.nita [ham-ni-da] 'does it' (formal style)
    tat.nunta [tan-nun-da] 'closes it' (plain style)
    mek.nunta [meng-nun-da] 'eats it' (plain style)
    sip-lyuk [sim-nyuk] 'sixteen'
    tok.lip [tong-nip] 'independence'

28. Nasal assimilation practice:

ip iey yo 'it's the mouth'	ip 'mouth'	ip man 'just the mouth'
iph iey yo 'it's a leaf'	iph 'leaf'	iph man 'just the leaf'
puekh iey yo 'it's a kitchen'	puekh 'kitchen'	puekh man 'just the kitchen'
talk iey yo 'it's a chicken'	talk 'chicken'	talk man 'just the chicken'
os iey yo 'it's a garment'	os 'garment'	os nalum iey yo 'it depends on the garment'
kkoch iey yo 'it's a flower'	kkoch 'flower'	kkoch nalum iey yo 'it depends on the flower'

29. Cluster reinforcement: After syllable-final p, t, or k, the single voiceless consonants p t c k s are reinforced so they sound like pp tt cc kk ss:
    yak-pang [yak-ppang] 'drugstore'
    cakta [cak-tta] 'is little' (plain style)
    mekca [mek-cca] 'let's eat' (plain style)
    tepta [tep-tta] 'is warm' (plain style)
    ipca [ip-cca] 'let's wear it' (plain style)
    sip-sam [sip-ssam] 'thirteen'

30. At normal speeds of speech, clusters of three like consonants are not permitted; unless a juncture (pause) intervenes, the first consonant drops.
    sip ppun [si-ppun] 'only ten'
    sip-pun (→ sip-ppun→) [si-ppun] 'ten minutes'
    si ppun 'only the poem'
    os-tan (→ot-ttan→) [o-ttan] 'hem'
    nac.ta (→nat-ta→nat-tta→) [na-tta] 'is low' (plain style)
    mok kkaci [mo-kka-ji] 'up to the neck'
    mek.ki (→mek-kki→) [me-kki] 'eating'

31. Cluster reinforcement practice:

kwuk 'soup'	kwuk pota [kwuk-ppo-da] 'than soup'
	kwuk to [kwuk-tto] 'soup too'
	kwuk cocha [kwuk-cco-cha] 'even soup'
	kwuk sekken [kwuk-sse-kken] 'soup and so on'
	kwuk kwa [kwu-kkwa] 'with soup'
ip 'mouth'	ip pota [i-ppo-da] 'than the mouth'
	ip to [ip-tto] 'the mouth too'
	ip cocha [ip-cco-cha] 'even the mouth'
	ip sekken [ip-sse-kken] 'the mouth and so on'
	ip kwa [ip-kkwa] 'with the mouth'

32. Apical assimilation: Before labial (p pp ph m) or velar (k kk kh) consonants, t and n assimilate in position of articulation (t→p or k, n→m or ng). The cluster reinforcements of 29 and the reductions of 30 then take place, so that tp→tpp→ppp→pp.
    non man [nom-man] 'just the paddy field'
    non pota [nom-bo-da] 'than the paddy field'
    non kwa [nong-gwa] 'with the paddy field'
    os man (→ot-man→on-man→) [om-man] 'just the garment'
    os pota (→ot-pota→ot-ppota→op-ppota→) [o-ppo-da] 'than the garment'
    os kwa (→ot-kwa→ot-kkwa→) [o-kkwa] 'with the garment'

33. Apical assimilation practice:

et.e yo 'gets'	an et.e yo 'doesn't get'	mos et.e yo 'can't get'
ka yo 'goes'	an ka yo 'doesn't go'	mos ka yo 'can't go'
kkakk.e yo 'cuts'	an kkakk.e yo 'doesn't cut'	mos kkakk.e yo 'can't cut'
khie yo 'turns on light'	an khie yo 'doesn't ...'	mos khie yo 'can't ...'
pwa yo 'sees'	an pwa yo 'doesn't see'	mos pwa yo 'can't see'
ppal.e yo 'launders'	an ppal.e yo 'doesn't launder'	mos ppal.e yo 'can't launder'
phal.e yo 'sells'	an phal.e yo 'doesn't sell'	mos phal.e yo 'can't sell' [mo-pha-re-yo, see 34]

34. Clusters of two like consonants are not permitted if followed by h: the first consonant drops unless a juncture (pause) is inserted.

sip-phal [si-phal] 'eighteen'
sik-khal [si-khal] 'kitchen knife'
mos tha yo (→mot-tha-yo→) [mo-tha-yo] 'can't ride'
mos pha yo (→mot-pha-yo→mop-pha-yo→) [mo-pha-yo] 'can't dig'
mos khie yo (→mot-khi-e-yo→mok-khi-e-yo→) [mo-khi-e-yo] 'can't turn on light'

35. Assibilation: Before s(s) the apical stop t becomes s (and that means it becomes s AGAIN, if the t is from a basic s); before c(c) and ch, t becomes c:

mos sa yo 'can't buy': →mot-sa-yo→mot-ssa-yo→mos-ssa-yo→[mo-ssa-yo]
mos ssa yo 'can't wrap': →mot-ssa-yo→mos-ssa-yo→[mo-ssa-yo]
mos ca yo 'can't sleep': →mot-ca-yo→mot-cca-yo→moc-cca-yo→[mo-cca-yo]
mos cca yo 'can't weave': →mot-cca-yo→moc-cca-yo→[mo-cca-yo]
mos cha yo 'can't kick': →mot-cha-yo→moc-cha-yo→[mo-cha-yo]
tat.sup.nita 'closes' (formal style): →tat-ssum-ni-ta→tas-ssum-ni-ta→ ta-ssum-ni-ta = [ta-ssum-ni-da]
iss.sup.nita = iss.sup.nita 'there is' (formal style): →it-sum-ni-ta→ it-ssum-ni-ta→i-ssum-ni-ta = [i-ssum-ni-da]

VI. VOWEL PROBLEMS

36. Long and short vowels: Many Koreans distinguish words by pronouncing a vowel as long or short: il 'one,' īl 'affair, work.' But even for those speakers, vowel length is often suppressed, especially when not at the beginning of a phrase, so that you will often hear short vowels in words that have basically long vowels. What is more, if a one-syllable word ends in a basically short vowel, the vowel is usually lengthened when the word is cited in isolation, so that i 'tooth' sounds like ī 'two'; to hear the difference you have to put the words in a phrase: i ka 'tooth (as subject),' ī ka 'two (as subject).

pam 'evening'	pām 'chestnut'
say cip 'new house'	sāy cip 'bird house'
soli 'sound'	sōli 'small profit'
po to 'dammed pool too'	pōto 'information, report'
swu (ka) 'luck'	swū (ka) 'embroidery; number'
kwul 'oyster'	kwūl 'cave'
yuli 'glass'	yūli 'being profitable'
siqka [si-kka] 'current price'	sīqka [sī-kka] 'market price'
... tul 'group [plural]	tūl 'uncultivated field'
unhayng 'bank'	ūmsik 'food'
wanko 'stubbornness'	wānkwu 'toy'
oykok 'distortion'	ōykwuk 'foreign country'
cwi (ka) 'rat, mouse'	twī (ka) 'behind'

37. Long and short e: Many speakers pronounce long ē with the tongue in a considerably higher position than it is in for the short e. Many speakers hollow the back of the tongue to make the short e so that it sounds rounded like the vowel sound that many people use in English <u>saw</u>, <u>song</u>, <u>dawn</u>.

emi 'mother animal'	ēmi 'suffix'
keli 'street'	kēli 'distance'
sem 'ricebag'	sēm 'island'
cel 'Buddhist temple'	tēl 'less'
ken 'item'	kēn 'key (of piano etc.)'
sekca [sek-cca] 'mesh scoop'	sēk ca [sēk-cca] 'three feet (long)'
yenki 'postponement'	yēnki 'performance, entertainment'
wen 'Korean dollar'	wēn 'desire, request'
phyengqka [phyeng-kka] 'parity'	phyēngq-ka [phyēng-kka] 'valuation'
epta [ep-tta] 'carries piggyback (and then)'	ēps.ta [ēp-tta] 'lacks'
etta 'oh!'	ēt.ta [ē-tta] 'gets (and then)'

38. There are also DOUBLE VOWELS, produced when a word (or part of a word) that ends with a vowel is attached to a word (or part of a word) that begins with the same vowel. Double vowels normally sound the same as long vowels, but they resist suppression, and you may sometimes hear a slight squeeze between the two vowels.

sen 'line'	sēn 'marriage interview'	seen 'preface'
sil 'truth'	sīl 'thread'	siil 'time'
non 'paddy field'	tōn 'money'	koon 'high temperature'
nwun 'eye'	nwūn 'snow'	swuwun 'water transport'
pam 'evening'	pām 'chestnut'	chaap 'legal seizure'
san 'mountain'	sān 'acid'	saan 'private plan'
sok 'sequel'	sōk 'inside'	sōok 'little house'
hom 'groove'	kōm 'bear'	eep 'fishing industry'

VII. REINFORCEMENT PROBLEMS (-q-)

39. When words are put together to build compounds or phrases we expect certain automatic adjustments as called for by the rules given above, e.g. kwuk hako 'with the soup' is pronounced [kwu-kha-go], kwuk man 'just the soup' is pronounced [kwung-man], and kwuk to 'the soup too' is pronounced [kwuk-tto]. But sometimes adjustments are called for which we can not predict so easily from the underlying basic forms. A set of these adjustments that we call REINFORCEMENT is marked by placing a "-q" at the end of the first element. The North Korean orthography uses an apostrophe to represent this "-q"; in the South it is marked (by a final -s) only if the prior element ends in a vowel, but ignored if the prior element ends in a consonant. And in both North and South, people often neglect to mark the reinforcement, especially in Chinese loanwords—where it is automatic in the sequences -l(q)s- and -l(q)c-.

How is -q- to be pronounced?

(1) It doubles a following p t c k s:

twīq path [twī-ppat] 'back field'
sānqpo (→sān-ppo→) [sām-ppo] 'stroll'
namuq kaci [na-mu-kka-ji] 'tree branch'
twīq tali [twī-tta-ri] 'hind leg'
chelqto [chel-tto] 'railroad'
kalqsayk [kal-ssayk] 'brown'
sāqken [sā-kken] 'incident'
kangq ka [kang-kka] 'riverbank'

(2) It is pronounced as a final n before n or m (but the n will sound like m before m, as will any n):

twīq nal [twīn-nal] 'later days'
twīq mun (→twīn-mun→) [twīm-mun] 'back door or gate'

(3) When following a consonant and preceding i- or y-, the q is pronounced as an initial n-:

kūlimq yepse [kū-rim-nyep-sse] 'picture postcard'
yenq-ie [yen-nie-e] 'continually'
sonq-ik.e yo [son-ni-ke-yo] 'is skilled'
sōkq iph (→sōk-nip→) [sōng-nip] 'inner leaf'
pathq ilang (→patq-i-lang→ pat-ni-lang→) [pan-ni-rang] 'field furrow'

(4) When between a vowel and i- or y-, the q is pronounced as -nn-:

twīq il [twīn-nil] 'future affairs'
namuq iph [na-mun-nip] 'tree leaf'
yoq is [yon-nit] 'mattress cover'

VIII. ROMANIZATION PROBLEMS

40. In the Romanization, letters are separated by a DOT for several purposes:

(1) Since ey ay oy uy are digraphs treated as single units, we use a dot to show a sequence of back vowel + ya yay ye yey yo yu:

sa.yang 'declining'	sa.yong 'use'	ce.yuk 'pork'
o.yas 'plum'	he.yeng 'vanity'	hwā.yem 'flames'

But the dot is unnecessary if the first vowel is preceded by y, since the second y can only start the second syllable:

kyōyuk 'education' yūyong 'usefulness'

And there is no need to write a dot when some other break (a space or a hyphen) is shown before the y.

(2) The dot is used to follow the Hankul spelling in showing the morphological divisions (the parts of a word) where these conflict with the spoken syllables, as in iss.ess.ey yo 'was' [i-sse-ssey-yo].

(3) The dot is used to mark boundaries at places that call for automatic reductions or changes in the consonants (other than the cluster reinforcements such as -ps- [pss], -kt- [ktt], etc.):

noph.ta [nop-tta] 'is high'
cōh.ta [cō-tha] 'is good' (explained in a later lesson)
mek.nunta [meng-nun-da] 'eats'
ilk.nunta [ing-nun-da] 'reads'

In this use, the dot conveys no critical information, and you can leave it out: nophta, cōhta, meknunta, ilknunta. But it is a handy reminder to do something about the "impossible cluster."

(4) The dot is also used to mark the reinforcement of certain endings after bases that end in m or n:

kēm.ta [kem-tta] 'is black'
sin.ko [sin-kko] 'wearing (shoes)'

It would be logical to mark this with a -q- (kēmqko, sinqko), but the reinforcement is ignored by the North Korean spelling, as well as the South Korean, so we use a different device to remind you of it.

41. Superscript letters (^{n}, ^{l}, ^{s}, ^{h}, and so on) are used to show certain ways the North Korean spelling differs from the South Korean system. For pronunciation purposes, you can ignore all superscripts. But they will help you find the etymology of many words.

42. An apostrophe is used, as in English, to show abbreviations. The apostrophes are a help for the eye only, since you can't hear them.

43. Spaces are used to show word division, according to a generous notion of what a word is; in pronunciation, however, the words are run together (as they are in French) so you must not expect to hear a hesitation at each space. Junctures (brief hesitations or pauses) are often inserted between phrases, but in fast speech the phrases too are run together without junctures. We have not marked junctures as such, since usually there are several ways to break a given sentence into phrases.

44. The period at the end of a sentence (.) implies a fall of pitch, as in many English statements. The question mark (?) and the comma (,) both imply rises in pitch, the question mark rising higher and longer. Note that in English the punctuation marks are used mostly for LOGICAL purposes, rather than to show intonations, so that all English questions are marked with a final question mark whether they rise or fall in intonation. Koreans often follow this practice when they use punctuation marks in writing Hankul, but in this textbook we mark those questions that FALL in intonation with a period. This helps us distinguish pairs of sentences like these:

    Nwu ka wass.ey yo. 'Who came?' (with falling pitch at the end)

    Nwu ka wass.ey yo? 'Did someone come?' (with rising pitch at the end)

    Other punctuation marks you will run across include the exclamation point (!) used to indicate an abrupt fall of pitch as in Ye' po! 'Hey!' and the triple dot (...) that signals a hesitant dip in pitch (see p. 361—but note that we sometimes use the triple dot just to mark an omission). The double question mark (??) represents a lively dip-and-rise, as in a common version of Ani yo?? 'No.' The double exclamation point (!!) calls for an insistent dip-and-fall, as in Sentence 11 of Lesson 11. The last two intonations are very colloquial and you will hear them most often in sentences that end with -ci (yo) or ... tey (yo).

LESSON 1. SAYING THE RIGHT THING

BASIC SENTENCES

	Korean	English	Amplification
1.	Kim sensayng. Annyeng hasip.nikka?	How are you, Mr. Kim?	Kim (a family name) sensayng 'teacher'; 'Mr.' or 'Mrs.' or 'Miss' Annyeng hasip.nikka? 'Are you peaceful (=well)?' [Some people say Allyeng. . .]
2.	Nēy. Annyeng hasip.nikka?	Fine. How are you (, Mrs. Lee)?	nēy 'yes,' nay 'yep'
3.	Nēy. Komapsup.nita.	Fine, thank you.	=Yes thank you.
4.	Cal cwumusyess.^{s}up.nikka?	Good morning.	=Did you sleep well?
5.	Nēy. Cal cass.^{s}up.nita.	Good morning. [in reply]	=Yes, I slept well.
6.	Cīnci capswusyess.^{s}up.nikka?	Good morning. or Good evening.	=Have you eaten?
7.	Nēy. Mek.ess.^{s}up.nita.	Good morning. or Good evening. [in reply]	=Yes, I've eaten.
8.	Sillyey hayss.^{s}up.nita.	Excuse me (for what I did).	=I have committed a discourtesy.
9.	Sillyey hap.nita.	Excuse me (for what I am doing).	=I am committing a discourtesy.
10.	Sillyey hakeyss.^{s}up.nita.	Excuse me (for what I am about to do).	=I will commit a discourtesy.
11.	Yongse hasipsio.	Excuse me. or Please forgive me.	
12.	Mian hap.nita. or Cōysong hap.nita.	I'm sorry. or Excuse me.	=I feel uneasy
13.	Ani yo?? Kwaynchanh.sup.nita.	Not at all; it's all right.	ani (yo) 'no' (politer with yo) kwaynchanh.sup.nita 'it makes no difference, it doesn't matter, it's OK'
14.	Swūko lul mānh.i kkichyess.^{s}up.nita. or Swūko hayss.^{s}up.nita.	Excuse me for all the trouble I've caused. or Thank you for helping me.	=I've caused a lot of bother.

	Korean	English	Amplification
15.	Chen-man uy māl-ssum ip.nita. or Chen-man ey yo. or Kwaynchanh.sup.nita.	You're welcome. or Not at all.	=It is one of ten million words. [The particle uy is pronounced ey.]
16.	Annyeng hi kasipsio.	Goodbye. [to one who is leaving]	=Go in peace (=health). [Some people say Allyeng . . .]
17.	Annyeng hi kyēysipsio.	Goodbye. [to one who is staying]	=Stay in peace (=health). [Some people say Allyeng . . .]
18.	Tto pōypkeyss.^{s}up.nita.	See you later.	tto 'again' pōypkeyss.^{s}up.nita 'will humbly see or meet = I will see you'
19.	Hana, twūl, sēys, nēys, tases; yeses, ilkop, yetel(p), ahop, yel.	One, two, three, four, five; six, seven, eight, nine, ten.	The word for 'eight' is spelled yetelp but usually pronounced yetel.
20.	Sikan i tā tōyss.^{s}up.nita.	It's time (to begin or stop).	sikan 'time; hour,' sikan i 'time [as subject]' tā 'all, completely' tōyss.^{s}up.nita (or twayss.^{s}up.nita) 'it has become . . .'
21.	Sīcak hapsita.	Let's begin.	
22.	Chayk ul yēsipsio. or Chayk ul phisipsio/phyesipsio.	Please open your book(s).	chayk 'book,' chayk ul 'book [as direct object]' yēsipsio 'please open it'
23.	Chayk ul posipsio.	Please look at your book(s).	posipsio 'please look at it'
24.	Ches pheyici lul posipsio.	Please look at the first page.	ches . . . 'the first . . .' pheyici 'page'
25.	Yeki se puthe sīcak hapsita.	Let's begin here.	yeki 'this place, here,' yeki se puthe '(starting) from here'
26.	Yenge man posipsio.	Just look at the English.	Yenge 'English,' Yenge man 'only English'
27.	Chayk ul posici māsipsio.	Please don't look at your books.	posici māsipsio 'please don't look at it'
28.	Hānkwuk mal ul posici māsipsio.	Please don't look at the Korean.	Hānkwuk or Cosen 'Korea' (Hānkwuk is the term used in South Korea today; Cosen is used in North Korea and was formerly used in all of

Korean	English	Amplification
		Korea and in Japan.) Hānkwuk mal or Cosen mal 'Korean,' Hānkwuk mal ul 'Korean [as direct object]'
29. Taum pheyici lul posipsio.	Please look at the next page.	taum '(the) next'
30. Tut.ki man hasipsio.	Just listen, please.	tut.ki 'the act of listening,' tut.ki man 'only listening' hasipsio 'please do it'
31. Māl hasipsio.	Please say it. or Please talk.	māl 'language; word(s); speech, talking' māl (ul) hasipsio 'please speak; please say it'
32. Āsikeyss.°up.nikka? or Āsip.nikka?	Do you understand?	=Will you know? or Do you know?
33. (Nēy.) Āp.nita.	Yes, I understand.	=I know.
34. (Ani yo??) Molup.nita.	No, I don't understand.	=I don't know.
35. Han pen te māl hay cwusipsio.	Please say it for me again.	han pen 'one time' te 'more,' han pen te 'once again' cwusipsio 'please favor me by doing it = please do it for me'
36. Chēn-chen hi māl hasipsio.	Please say it slowly.	chēn-chen hi 'slowly'
37. Tā kath.i.	All together.	tā 'all; everyone' kath.i [pronounced kachi] or hamkkey 'together'
38. Hānkwuk mal lo hasipsio.	Please say it in Korean.	Hānkwuk mal lo 'in Korean' hasipsio = māl hasipsio 'please say it'
39. Yenge lo haci māsipsio.	Please don't say it in English.	Yenge lo 'in English' haci māsipsio 'please do not do it'; (=māl haci māsipsio) 'please do not say it'
40. Yenge lo nun mues ip.nikka. or Yenge lo mues ila ko hap.nikka.	How do you say it in English? or What is it in English?	Yenge lo nun 'in English (as compared with other languages)' mues 'what,' mues ip.nikka 'what is it?' mues ila ko or mue 'la ko '(saying) that it is what'

Korean	English	Amplification
		mues ila ko (or mue 'la ko) hap.nikka 'what do you say that it is = what do you call it?'
41. Selo iyaki hasipsio.	Please talk to each other.	selo 'mutually, (to) each other' iyaki or yāyki or yēyki 'story, tale; talking, talk'
42. Yeki posipsio.	Please look at me. or Attention, please!	
43. Tāytap'hasipsio.	Please answer.	tāytap 'an answer,' tāytap hasipsio 'please answer'
44. Mul.e posipsio. or Cilmun hasipsio.	Please ask (questions).	mul.e posipsio 'please ask and see (what the answer is)' cilmun 'a question'
45. Twūl(q) tā cōh.sup.nikka?	Are both right?	twūl '(the) two,' tā 'all,' twūl(q) tā 'both (of them)' cōh.sup.nikka [pronounced cōssumnikka] 'is it good? = is it all right?'
46. Tā cōh.sup.nita.	They're all (or both) all right.	cōh.sup.nita [pronounced cōssumnita] 'it is good' = 'it is all right'
47. I ^{l}yēnsup ul ha(si)psita.	Let's do this exercise.	i . . . 'this . . . ,' i ^{l}yēnsup 'this exercise' hasipsita or hapsita 'let's do it'
48. Chayk ul tat.usipsio. or Chayk ul teph.usipsio.	Please close your book(s).	tat.usipsio 'please close it'
49. Cilmun i iss.^{s}up.nikka?	Any questions?	iss.^{s}up.nikka [pronounced issumnikka] 'does there exist? = do we/you have . . .'
50. Cilmun i iss.^{s}up.nita.	I have a question.	iss.^{s}up.nita [pronounced issumnita] 'there exists = we/you have . . .'
51. Mā sensayng hanthey mul.e posipsio.	Please ask Mr. Ma.	ku . . . 'that . . . ,' ku taum 'next to that, after that'
52. Ku taum (or Cikum), sip-pun ccum swīsipsita.	Next (or Now), let's rest for ten minutes.	sip (=yel) 'ten,' pun 'minute,' sip-pun '10 minutes' sip-pun ccum '(about) ten minutes; ten minutes (time)' swīsipsita 'let's rest'

SUPPLEMENTARY VOCABULARY

Kuless.^{s}up.nikka?	Is that so? or Oh? or Really?	Kulay se . . .	And so . . . or And then
Kuless.^{s}up.nita. [formal]	That's so. or That's right. or Yes. or Uh-huh.	Kulay to . . .	Even so . . . or Nevertheless . . .
Kulay yo. [polite]		Ye(ki) posipsio! [formal]	Hey! (on street); Hello! (on telephone or peering into dark house); Waiter! (in restaurant); Clerk! (in store); Dear! (catching attention of husband or wife)
Kulem. [informal]		Ye(ki) posey yo! [polite]	
Kuleh.ci man . . .	But . . . or However . . .	Ye' posio! [informal]	
Kulena . . .	But . . . or Still . . . or Yet . . .	Ye' po! [abrupt]	
Kulen tey . . .	(1) But . . . (2) And then . . . (3) By the way . . .		
Kulem . . .	Well . . . or Now . . . or Then . . .	Swūko hasip.nita.	Hello! [to someone working]
Kulemyen . . .	Then . . . or In that case . . .	Swūko hasipsio.	Goodbye! [to someone working]
Kuliko . . .	And also . . .		

NOTES

1.1. Styles of speech.

Korean is characterized by an intricate system of social styles; you have just had a glimpse of the system in the Supplementary Vocabulary. This characteristic is so pervasive that it is impossible to speak more than a few connected words in Korean without including it; yet there is nothing in English which corresponds to it. In English also, to be sure, the same idea can often be expressed in various styles. Compare, for example, the impersonal or official-sounding "What is your native country?" and the conversational "Where are you from?"; to attract someone's attention, we might say under certain circumstances "Pardon me, Sir!" and under certain others "Hey you!" We can find many examples. But there are few analogies with the Korean system. Every Korean sentence can be adjusted to each of several styles, in a regular and systematic way, and this is done chiefly by changing the endings on the verbs.

Occasionally, stylistic implications in Korean are conveyed in the vocabulary itself: two words denoting the same thing differ in social connotations. But for the most part, the style factors appear not in the words themselves but in verb endings.

Two considerations are significant in the Korean speech styles:

1. the person you are talking TO: certain ways of ending certain words are determined by the social relationship between the speakers; and

2. the person you are talking ABOUT: certain words and parts of words are honorific; they show special respect to the person they refer to (often the person being addressed) and, therefore, are never used by the speaker to refer to himself.

The Basic Sentences of this lesson are FORMAL in style, for the most part, because they are everyday polite formulas. Most of the sentences you will learn in Lessons 2 through 16 will be in the POLITE style, the most useful style for everyday conversation.

‖ 1.2. Word classes.

Korean words, like those of every other language, fall into several different kinds or classes; the words are classified according to the way they are used in sentences.

Korean VERBS (the words at the end of nearly every Basic Sentence in this lesson) are INFLECTED WORDS: they consist of a basic part to which various SUFFIXES are attached, to make them mean different things. For example, you have observed these three sentences:

8. Sillyey hayss.^{s}up.nita. 'Excuse me (for what I did).'
9. Sillyey hap.nita. 'Excuse me (for what I'm doing).'
10. Sillyey hakeyss.^{s}up.nita. 'Excuse me (for what I'm about to do).'

The verb in each case is the same—here, it means 'do'—and its basic part is ha-.

Here are a few sentences of another type:

16. Annyeng hi kasipsio. 'Goodbye [=Go in peace].'
17. Annyeng hi kyēysipsio. 'Goodbye [=Stay in peace].'
23. Chayk ul posipsio. 'Please look at your books.'
30. Tut.ki man hasipsio. 'Just listen, please.'

These sentences all have different verbs, but the verbs all end the same way: -sipsio. This ending (a combination of suffixes) makes each verb express a polite request.

Korean NOUNS, on the other hand, are not inflected; they can be used with no endings attached to them. Instead PARTICLES are optionally added to show the relationship between the noun and the rest of the sentence, much as prepositions are used in English.

The great majority of Korean nouns correspond to English words which are also nouns—chayk 'book,' cilmun 'question,' Yenge 'English,' and so on.

As a vocabulary item, chayk means 'book.' In sentences, however, we translate it variously: 'book, a book, the book, some books, any books, the books, books.' In Basic Sentence 23, it is rendered 'your books.' This is another way of saying that Korean has no words corresponding to a(n), the, some, any, and that Korean nouns may have a plural meaning without any plural marker. To be sure, it is possible to make Korean nouns unambiguously plural (‖ 3.7); but it is not imperative to do so as it is with certain English nouns. Book, for example, is specifically singular or specifically plural every time it is used. The same is not true of such English nouns as money, information, clothing.

‖ 1.3. Korean sentence patterns.

The Basic Sentences of this lesson give you an opportunity to observe, over and over, a basic characteristic of Korean sentences: the verb expression comes at the end. This means, of course, that in a great many cases the order of things in a Korean sentence is different from the English order. Translated directly, Sentence 5, for example [Nēy. Cal cass.^{s}up.nita.] is 'Yes. Well [I] slept'; Sentence 35 [Han pen te māl hay cwusipsio] is 'Once again please say it for me'; and so on.

In Korean sentences, the order of the various parts is determined not by grammatical function, as it is in English, but by importance: the closer a word is to the end of a Korean sentence, the more important it is. At the very end comes the one element which is indispensable—the verb.* Many Korean sentences contain nothing but a verb:

Mek.ess.^{s}up.nita. 'I've eaten.'

This verb says in a formal way that someone ate, past tense; that is all it specifies. But the sentence is grammatically complete. It would not be wrong to add a subject (and/or an object), but it would be superfluous.

Aside from commands, it is a rare English sentence which has no subject. Telegram style and post-card or diary style are special cases: Arrive 9 a.m. Monday. Will bring George. Saw a movie last night. Having a wonderful time. Even commands not uncommonly have subjects: You stop that! You boys get out of here!

As a general rule, the nearer the beginning of a Korean sentence a word or phrase appears, the less essential it is—the more readily expendable. The order of such elements as subject, object, time, place, is determined by the emphasis assigned to each; and one thing that makes them less necessary is earlier mention in a context. A conversation beginning with some such sentence as John bought a new suit could continue in Korean without further mention of either John or the suit. (Notice that in English both of these must reappear, as pronouns if not in their original form: When did HE buy IT? and so on; the Korean equivalent could say simply When bought? and still be complete.) In other words, old information, if repeated at all, comes at or near the beginning of a Korean sentence, while newly supplied information clusters near the verb. If subject and object both offer new information, the object is more likely to come next to the verb.

‖ 1.4. Korean names.

This phrase appeared in Basic Sentence 1:

Kim sensayng 'Mr. Kim'

It illustrates another example of difference in English and Korean word order: the title is used AFTER the name.

Kim 'Kim' is a family name. As a general pattern, a Korean has two names: the family name is followed by a personal or given name. Most of the family names have one syllable, but an occasional name has two syllables: for example, Hwangpo. If the family name has one syllable, the personal name most commonly has two: ^{L}I Sungman 'Syngman Rhee,' Kim Ilqseng 'Ilsung Kim.' If the family name has two syllables, the personal name has only one, so that either way there are usually three syllables in the full name. There are exceptions to this pattern, and a number of Korean names have only two syllables: He Wung, Payk Chel, Kim Kwu, etc.

A title used with a full name comes at the very end:

Kim Poktong sensayng 'Mr. Poktong Kim'

---

*But occasionally a Korean switches the expected order of a sentence by saying the last part and then adding the first part as an afterthought: Posipsio—chayk ul 'Look at it—the book.' Sīcak hapsita—yeki se puthe 'Let's start—from here.'

Sensayng is a title of respect honoring the person whose name it accompanies: you should use this title with the names of people to whom you wish to show courtesy; and you should NOT use it with your own name. When you introduce yourself, for example, simply give your name—'My name is Adams' or 'I'm Helen Baker'—with no title.

When otherwise unspecified, the title sensayng is usually translated 'Mr.,' but sometimes the context tells you that 'Mrs.' or 'Miss' would be more appropriate. To say specifically 'Mrs.' or 'Miss' you have to say something like 'Mr. Kim's wife' (Kim sensayng puin) or 'Mr. Kim's daughter' (Kim sensayng tta' nim). If the Kims are parents, an informal way of saying 'Mrs. Kim' is to refer to her as the eldest child's mother, e.g. Poktong-i emeni (or eme' nim) 'Mrs. Kim (who is Poktong-i's mother),' and similarly Mr. Kim may be referred to as Poktong-i apeci (or ape' nim) 'Mr. Kim (who is Poktong-i's father).' Foreigners sometimes mistranslate 'Mrs. Kim' as Kim puin (rather than Kim sensayng puin), but that is apt to be misinterpreted as 'Mr. Kim's lady-friend (i.e. mistress),' so it should be avoided. In Seoul shops you will often hear samo nim used for 'Mrs.' or 'Madam' (instead of puin or . . . sensayng puin); samo is an elegant word that means 'one's teacher's wife.'

There are a number of ways to say 'you' in Korean, and the most polite way is by using a title or name-plus title. As your study of the language proceeds, you will notice that Korean is in many respects less direct than English. Basic Sentence 1 is an example of such indirectness; it seems to say 'How is Mr. Kim?' but it means 'How are you, Mr. Kim?'

As a classroom convenience, the Korean teacher should assign Korean names to the students and address them that way during the class hours. Here are some suggested names to correspond to American names:

Andrews, Anderson	An
Benson	Pyen
Black [because of meaning]	Hyen
Banks	Pang
Bailey	Pay
Chase	Choy
Cooper	Kwu
Cornell, Cowgill	Ko
Harris, Harvey	Ha
Hamilton, Hammond	Ham
Hanson, Hanley, Henderson	Han
Horne	Hong
Johnson	Ceng *or* Cang
Jones	Cen
Kelly, Keller	Kil
Kimball, Kimberley, McKim; Gold [because of meaning]	Kim
King [because of meaning]	Wang
Lee, Leigh	^{1}Ī
Lawrence, Lawson	^{1}No
Mann, Mansfield, Manning	Māyng
Martin, Marshall, Marlow, Mac . . .	Mā
Moore, Morris, Morgan	Mo
Nelson	^{1}Na
O'Brien, O' . . .	O
O'Connor, O'Connell	Ok
Park, Parks, Parker	Pak
Pond [because of meaning]	Ci
Simpson, Singer	Sin
Shaw, Shea	So
Smith	Se
Swanson	Sung
White [because of meaning]	Payk
[for sound]	He
Williams, Wilson	Wi
Wood(s) [because of meaning]	^{1}Im
Wright, Wooster	Wu
Young	^{1}Yang

As you can see, most of the Korean names are selected to sound something like the American names, but in some cases the resemblance in meaning of the Korean name is used, instead. Perhaps your Korean tutor will want to give you a personal name, too, either one suggested by your English name or one whose meaning fits your personality in some fashion.

EXERCISES

I

Which response—or responses—are appropriate to the sentence given? Read aloud first the sentence itself, then all the responses given; finally, the one or ones you choose.

1. Sillyey hap.nita.
   a. Yongse hasipsio.
   b. Ani yo?? Kwaynchanh.sup.nita.
   c. Chen-man uy māl-ssum ip.nita.

2. Āsikeyss.^{s}up.nikka?
   a. Nēy.
   b. Nēy. Cal cass.^{s}up.nita.
   c. Ani yo?? Molup.nita.

3. Sikan i tā tōyss.^{s}up.nita.
   a. Kulemyen, sīcak hapsita.
   b. Kuleh.sup.nikka?
   c. Cikum, sip-pun ccum swīsipsita.

4. Mian hap.nita.
   a. Swūko lul mānh.i kkichyess.^{s}up.nita.
   b. Chēn-chen hi māl hasipsio.
   c. Tut.ki man hasipsio.

5. Cilmun i iss.^{s}up.nikka?
   a. Nēy.
   b. Ani yo??
   c. Iss.^{s}up.nita.

6. Cīnci capswusyess.^{s}up.nita.
   a. Nēy. Mek.ess.^{s}up.nita.
   b. Ani yo?? Kwaynchanh.sup.nita.
   c. Nēy. Cal cass.^{s}up.nita.

7. Annyeng hi kasipsio.
   a. Annyeng hi kasipsio.
   b. Annyeng hi kyēysipsio.
   c. Tto pōypkeyss.^{s}up.nita.

8. Twūl(q) tā cōh.sup.nikka?
   a. Ani yo??
   b. Nēy.
   c. Twūl(q) tā cōh.sup.nita.

9. Cilmun i iss.^{s}up.nita.
   a. Tāytap hasipsio.
   b. Kim sensayng hanthey mul.e posipsio.
   c. Tā cōh.sup.nita.

10. Swūko lul mānh.i kkichyess.^{s}up.nita.
    a. Chen-man uy māl-ssum ip.nita.
    b. Kwaynchanh.sup.nita.
    c. Sikan i tā tōyss.^{s}up.nita.

II

Match each sentence in the left-hand column with an appropriate response from the right-hand column. Don't use a response unless you need it; use it more than once if you need to.

a. Komapsup.nita.
b. Cīnci capswusyess.^{s}up.nikka?
c. Twūl(q) tā cōh.sup.nikka?
d. Annyeng hasip.nikka?
e. Cilmun i iss.^{s}up.nikka?
f. Sillyey hayss.^{s}up.nita.
g. Āsikeyss.^{s}up.nikka?
h. Kuless.^{s}up.nikka?
i. Annyeng hi kyēysipsio.
j. Mian hap.nita.
k. Sillyey hap.nita.
l. Cal cwumusyess.^{s}up.nikka?
m. Swūko lul mānh.i kkichyess.^{s}up.nita.
n. Annyeng hi kasipsio.

1. Annyeng hi kasipsio.
2. Yenge lo haci māsipsio.
3. Nēy.
4. Nēy. Cal cass.^{s}up.nita.
5. Ani yo?? Kwaynchanh.sup.nita.
6. Tā kath.i.
7. Chen-man uy māl-ssum ip.nita.
8. Tāytap hasipsio.
9. Nēy. Iss.^{s}up.nita.
10. Nēy. Mek.ess.^{s}up.nita.
11. Tā cōh.sup.nita.
12. Nēy. Komapsup.nita.
13. Kuless.^{s}up.nita.
14. Ani yo??

CONVERSATION

Even with the very limited material contained in Lesson 1, you can carry on brief conversations in Korean.

1. Talk with a friend on the street: greet each other, exchange a few amenities, and take your leave.

2. Take the part of a teacher and conduct a brief class hour, directing the other students, making sure they understand, and insisting that they do as you say; don't let them break out in English, or peek at the books at the wrong time. Give them a ten-minute break when you feel they deserve it.

VOCABULARY DRILL

The vocabulary items you have learned at this point are not easy to separate from the short sentences in which they appear. One way you can drill yourself on the words is to make use of a technique which in fact will be valuable throughout the lessons:

After you have completed the job of memorizing the Basic Sentences, copy each one on a 3" x 5" card or slip or paper—the Korean on one side, the English on the other—one sentence to a card. Shuffle the cards thoroughly, then arrange them so that you see only the Korean side; run through them as rapidly as you can, reading aloud the Korean and immediately calling off the English equivalent. Reshuffle and repeat: looking only at the English, see whether the Korean comes instantly to your mind.

By this method, you can be your own judge of whether you have completed your work on Lesson 1.

COMPREHENSION

Actions speak louder than puzzled looks. A sure way of testing your comprehension at this point is to listen while your Korean speaker calls off classroom commands. If you respond as you should, you are ready for Lesson 2. If you close your book when you were asked merely to refrain from looking at it, your ear needs a little more practice.

LESSON 2. WHAT'S WHAT AND WHO'S WHO

BASIC SENTENCES

Korean	English	Amplification
1. I kes i mues iey yo.	What's this?	i . . . 'this' . . . kes or ke 'thing, object' i kes or i ke 'this thing, this' i kes i or i key 'this (thing)' [as subject] mue(s) or mwe(s) or me(s) 'what thing?, what?' mues iey yo or mue 'ey yo 'what is it? what are they?'
2. Ku kes un chayk iey yo.	That's a book.	ku . . . 'that . . . (near you)' ku kes or ku ke 'that thing (nearby), that (aforementioned) thing, it' ku kes un or ku ke n' 'that (thing)' [as topic] . . . iey yo 'it is; they are (the same thing as . . .)'
3. I kes i musun chayk iey yo.	What sort of book is this?	musun . . . 'what (kind of) . . .' musun chayk 'what kind of book?'
4. Hānkwuk mal chayk iey yo.	It's a Korean book.	Hānkwuk mal chayk 'Korean language book'
5. Kim sensayng (uy) chayk iey yo?	Is it Mr. Kim's book?	Kim sensayng uy . . . 'Mr. Kim's . . .' Kim sensayng chayk 'Mr. Kim's book'
6. Ani yo?? Nay chayk iey yo.	No, it's my book.	nay = na uy 'my, of me'
7. Ce kes un chayk i ani 'ey yo.	That thing over there isn't a book.	ce . . . 'that . . . (over there)' ce kes 'that thing, that (over there)' ce kes un or ce ke n' 'that (over there)' [as topic] ani 'ey yo 'it or they are not (the same thing as)' chayk i ani 'ey yo 'is not a book'
8. Capci 'ey yo.	It's a magazine.	capci 'magazine'

	Korean	English	Amplification
9.	Nwukwu (uy) capci 'ey yo.	Whose magazine is it?	nwukwu 'who?' nwukwu uy . . . 'whose . . .' nwukwu uy capci 'whose magazine?'
10.	Kim sensayng uy kes iey yo, tangsin uy kes iey yo.	Is it Mr. Kim's, or is it yours?	Kim sensayng uy kes 'Mr. Kim's thing, a thing of Mr. Kim' tangsin 'you' tangsin uy kes 'your thing, a thing of yours'
11.	Nay kes iey yo.	It's mine.	nay kes 'my thing, mine'
12.	Etten kes i capci 'ey yo. <u>or</u> Enu kes i capci 'ey yo.	Which one is a magazine?	etten . . . <u>or</u> enu . . . 'which? etten ke(s) <u>or</u> enu ke(s) 'which thing?, which one?, which?' etten kes i <u>or</u> enu kes i 'which?' [as subject]
13.	I kes iey yo, ce kes iey yo.	Is it this one, or that one over there?	
14.	Ce kes i capci 'ey yo.	That one over there is a magazine.	ce kes i <u>or</u> ce key 'that (thing) (over there)' [as subject]
15.	Nwu' ka sensayng iey yo.	Who's the teacher?	nwu' ka 'who?' [as subject]
16.	Sensayng nim i sensayng iey yo.	You are the teacher.	sensayng nim 'esteemed teacher; you; esteemed Mr. (Mrs., Miss)'
17.	Hānkwuk mal sensayng i nwukwu 'ey yo.	Who is the Korean teacher?	Hānkwuk mal sensayng 'Korean language teacher' Hānkwuk mal sensayng i 'Korean language teacher' [as subject] nwukwu 'ey yo 'who is it?'
18.	Hānkwuk mal sensayng un Kim sensayng iey yo.	The Korean teacher is Mr. Kim.	Hānkwuk mal sensayng un 'Korean language teacher' [as topic]
19.	Nwu' ka haksayng iey yo.	Who is the student?	haksayng 'student, pupil'
20.	Nay ka haksayng iey yo.	I'm the student.	nay ka 'I' [as subject]
21.	Sensayng (nim) i nwukwu 'sey yo.	Who are you?	. . . 'sey yo (=isey yo) someone esteemed is
22.	Na nun haksayng iey yo.	I'm a student.	na nun 'I' [as topic]
23.	Na nun Kim Poktong iey yo.	I'm Poktong Kim.	

Korean	English	Amplification
24. Hānkwuk mal haksayng i na 'ey yo.	I'm the Korean student.	(=The Korean language student is me.) na 'I, me' na 'ey yo 'it is me'
25. Na nun Hānkwuk mal haksayng iey yo.	I'm a Korean student.	
26. Sensayng (nim) un enu/etten/musun nalaq salam isey yo.	What nationality are you?	sensayng (nim) un 'you' [as topic] nala 'country, land' sālam 'man, person (people)' . . . nalaq salam 'a man of . . . country'
27. Na nun Mikwuk salam iey yo.	I'm an American.	Mikwuk 'America' Mikwuk salam 'an American'
28. Ku sālam un Mikwuk salam i ani 'ey yo.	He is not an American.	ku sālam 'that person (nearby or aforementioned), he, she' ku sālam un 'that person' [as topic] Mikwuk salam i 'American' [as subject]
29. Hānkwuk salam iey yo.	He's a Korean.	Hānkwuk (or Cosenq) salam 'Korean' [Korean person]
30. Kim moksa uy chinkwu 'ey yo.	He's Reverend Kim's friend.	moksa 'minister, pastor' Kim moksa 'Reverend Kim; Mr. Kim, who is a minister' Kim sinpu 'Father Kim; Mr. Kim who is a priest' Kim moksa uy 'Reverend Kim's . . .' chinkwu 'friend'
31. Wuli nun tā kwun.in iey yo.	All of us are servicemen.	wuli 'we, us' wuli ta 'all of us, we all' kwun.in 'servicemen'

SUPPLEMENTARY VOCABULARY

uysa	doctor, physician	cāngkyo	officer
pyēnho-sa	lawyer	sōwi	2d lieutenant; ensign
senkyo-sa	missionary	cwungwi	1st lieutenant; lieutenant JG
pyengceng	soldier	tāywi	captain; (full) lieutenant
swupyeng	navy enlisted man, sailor	hakca	scholar
sen.wen	crewman, sailor	sil.ep-ka or sāmu-ka	businessman
hāykwun	navy		
'yuk.kwun	army	sangin	merchant
kongkwun	air force	kaceng puin	housewife

nongpu	farmer	[1]Nosea	Russia
[1]īpal(q)-sa	barber	[1]Nosea mal	Russian (language)
kēnchwuk-ka	architect	[1]Noseaq salam	Russian (person)
namphyen or cwuin	husband	Solyen or (in N. Korea) Ssolyen	Soviet Union
puin	your/his wife		
anay or [North Korea] anhay	my wife	kong-chayk	notebook
		yenphil	pencil
Ilpon	Japan	mānnyen-phil	fountain pen
Ilpon mal	Japanese language	congi	paper
Ilponq salam	Japanese (person)	payk.muk	chalk
Cwungkwuk	China	chilphan	blackboard
Cwungkwuk mal	Chinese language	sinmun	newspaper
Cwungkwuk salam	Chinese (person)	tāmpay	cigarette(s)
Yengkwuk	England	sengnyang	match(es)
Yenge	English	pheyn	a pen
Yengkwuk salam	English (person)	ingkhu	ink
		cay-ttel.i	ash tray

NOTES

2.1. Sentence subjects and topics.

As you have seen, Korean nouns commonly appear in particle-marked phrases, and the particle after a noun sometimes has no translatable meaning but rather assigns a grammatical function to the noun.

Two such particles are the SUBJECT PARTICLE, which indicates that the noun before it is the subject, and the TOPIC PARTICLE, which marks its noun as the sentence topic.

Some particles have two pronunciations or shapes: one when they come after a word which ends with a consonant, the other after words ending with vowels. Except for the reversed order of things, this is completely analogous to the English indefinite article a/an:

Shape before Consonant	Shape before Vowel
a man	an apple
a sandwich	an orphan
a headache	an idea

The subject and topic particles are both TWO-SHAPE PARTICLES. The subject particle is pronounced i when it comes after a consonant and ka when it comes after a vowel:

Shape after Consonant	Shape after Vowel
chayk i 'book'	capci ka 'magazine'
puin i 'wife'	an(h)ay ka 'wife'
tangsin i 'you'	nay ka 'I'
mues i 'what?'	nwu' ka 'who?'
yenphil i 'pencil'	congi ka 'paper'

(Na 'I' and nwukwu 'who?' have altered shapes when they come before the subject particle i/ka: nay ka, nwu' ka.) Remember that i and ka are the same word: it is a word with two pronunciations.

The same is true of the topic particle, which is pronounced un after consonants and nun after vowels:

Shape after Consonant	Shape after Vowel
chayk un 'book'	capci nun 'magazine'
puin un 'wife'	an(h)ay nun 'wife'
tangsin un 'you'	na nun 'I'
yenphil un 'pencil'	congi nun 'paper'
sengnyang un 'matches'	tāmpay nun 'cigarettes'

A Korean sentence subject (noun plus the particle i/ka) usually corresponds to an English sentence subject. So, often, does a Korean topic (noun plus the particle un/nun). But they are by no means interchangeable.

When you first mention a subject—when it is "new information"—you usually attach i/ka, the subject particle, to it. Thereafter in the same context, if you repeat the subject at all, it has become "old information" and usually has the particle un/nun. Basic Sentences 1 and 2 form a context of this sort:

1. I kes i mues iey yo. 'What's this?'
2. Ku kes un chayk iey yo. 'That's a book.'

Basic Sentences 3 through 6 form another context. Sentence 3 mentions the subject (i kes i 'this'); the same thing, a book, which is discussed in Sentences 4, 5, and 6, is not mentioned again at all, but if it were, it would be as a topic—followed by the particle un/nun.

As these examples demonstrate, un/nun is a particle of DEEMPHASIS. The word or phrase in front of it refers to the least unknown ingredient in your communication—the part you would be most likely to drop if you wanted to make your sentence briefer. For this reason, the topic phrase nearly always comes at the very beginning of the sentence. As you have learned, the important things in a Korean sentence tend to accumulate toward the end, near the verb—the single indispensable element. The dispensable things—what the other person is most likely to know already—are put closer to the beginning, where they are missed the least if they are dropped out altogether.

You can lessen the emphasis on any element in the sentence (except the verb!) by pulling it out of place, saying it first, and making a topic out of it. Here, to give you the feel of this deemphasis, is a single English sentence showing how each element might appear as the topic of a Korean sentence, and the emphasis of the resulting order:

That student is studying Korean at school now.

a. That student un/nun, is studying Korean at school now. [The important information is the nature of his activity—NOT who is doing it.]
b. Now un/nun, that student is studying Korean at school. [Talking about what's happening now . . . that student is studying Korean at school.]
c. At school un/nun, that student is now studying Korean (there). [To mention what's going on at school . . .]
d. Korean un/nun, that student is studying [it] at school now. [What I want to say about the Korean language is . . .]

Another kind of reduced emphasis occurs when each of two parallel statements begin with a topic. The two noun expressions are deemphasized and the contrast between them is pointed up:

Kim sensayng un uysa 'ey yo. Kuleh.ci man, na nun pyēnho-sa 'ey yo. 'Mr. Kim (—he) is a doctor. But (me—) I'm a lawyer.'

(Confusingly enough, English speech habits make us give a heavy accent to BOTH pairs of elements; in the example here, we stress Mr. Kim, doctor, I, and lawyer.)

The subject particle i/ka, on the other hand, does not deemphasize the noun it follows. It appears most often with subjects which have not been mentioned previously in the context.

Certain words, by the very nature of their meaning, almost never appear in Korean topics, but frequently in subjects. These are words which ask for new information—such as nwukwu 'who?,' musun . . . 'what (kind of) . . . ?,' mues 'what?,' etten . . . and enu . . . 'which. . . ?' By the same token, when you answer a question having one of these words, you use a subject to supply the new information, rather than a topic. You observed this pattern in Basic Sentences 12 and 14, 15-16, and 19-20:

Etten kes i capci 'ey yo. Ce kes i capci 'ey yo. 'Which one is a magazine?' 'That one over there is a magazine.'

Nwu' ka sensayng iey yo. Sensayng nim i sensayng iey yo. 'Who is the teacher?' 'You are the teacher.'

Nwu' ka haksayng iey yo. Nay ka haksayng iey yo. 'Who is the student?' 'I am the student.'

Of course, if the question word occurs outside of the subject or topic, then the subject and topic positions in the sentence are handled as described above: the subject upon its first mention will have i/ka and if mentioned thereafter, un/nun. Here are the examples you have seen of this sort of sequence (Basic Sentences 1-2, 3-4, 17-18):

I kes i mues iey yo. Ku kes un chayk iey yo. 'This thing is what?' '(That thing) is a book.'

I kes i musun chayk iey yo. Hānkwuk mal chayk iey yo. 'This thing is what kind of book?' '—is a Korean book.'

Hānkwuk mal sensayng i nwuku 'ey yo. Hānkwuk mal sensayng un Kim sensayng iey yo. 'The Korean teacher is who?' '(The Korean teacher) is Mr. Kim.'

2.2. The copula; equational sentences.

Each of the Basic Sentences in this lesson ends with a special verb called the COPULA. The copula is pronounced iey yo after consonants but generally shortened to 'ey yo after vowels:

After consonants:	After vowels:
sensayng iey yo 'it is a teacher'	uysa 'ey yo 'it is a doctor'
chayk iey yo 'it is a book'	capci 'ey yo 'it is a magazine'
yenphil iey yo 'it is a pencil'	congi 'ey yo 'it is paper'
sengnyang iey yo 'it is a match'	tāmpay 'ey yo 'it is a cigarette'

(The shape 'ey yo is just an abbreviation of iey yo and sometimes you will hear the full form, even after a vowel.)

The copula is different from other verbs in this respect: it cannot make a complete sentence by itself, but must always have something in front of it—nearly always a noun expression. It is pronounced as though it were part of its preceding word, like a suffix, and your voice should not pause or hesitate between the noun expression and the copula.

The copula translates the English verb to be (am, are, is) when it means 'it equals' or 'it is (the same thing as).' For this reason sentences ending with the copula are called EQUATIONAL SENTENCES.

The copula is made negative by the word ani, followed generally by the abbreviated form which is normal after vowels: ani 'ey yo.

The noun expression before the negative (not the affirmative!) copula may be a subject—i.e. may have the particle i/ka after it—as in Basic Sentences 7 and 28:

Chayk i ani 'ey yo. 'It isn't a book.'
Mikwuk salam i ani 'ey yo. 'He is not an American.'

Negative equational sentences thus can accommodate two subjects, the second of which corresponds to the English complement.

Nwu' ka kwun.in i ani 'ey yo. 'Who is not a serviceman?'
Musun chayk i nay chayk i ani 'ey yo. 'Which book isn't mine?'
Kim sensayng i Ilponq salam i ani 'ey yo. 'Mr. Kim isn't Japanese.'
I kes i Yenge ka ani 'ey yo. 'This isn't English.'

‖ 2.3. Alternative questions.

10. Kim sensayng uy kes iey yo, tangsin uy kes iey yo. 'Is it Mr. Kim's, or is it your?'

11. I kes iey yo, ce kes iey yo. 'Is it this one, or that one over there?'

An ALTERNATIVE QUESTION asks which of two alternatives is true. In English, the alternatives are separated by the conjunction or; but in Korean you simply use two contrasting sentences, one after the other.

Neither of the Basic Sentences quoted above contains a subject or topic. Most alternative questions share a common situational element—perhaps one which does not appear in the sentence itself because it is a contextual carryover. The included sentences of Basic Sentence 10, for example, share the carryover topic ce kes un 'that thing over there' which appeared first in Basic Sentence 7; and for Sentence 13, capci 'magazine,' carried over from the preceding sentence, is the unexpressed topic.

ADDITIONAL EXAMPLES

1. Sensayng nim i Cwungkuk salam iey yo, Ilponq salam iey yo.	Is the teacher Chinese or Japanese?
2. Ce salam i Kim sensayng iey yo, Pak sensayng iey yo.	Is that Mr. Kim or Mr. Pak?
3. I kes i yenphil iey yo, mānnyen-phil iey yo.	Is this a pencil or a fountain pen?
4. I kes i sensayng nim uy yenphil iey yo, Kim sensayng uy yenphil iey yo.	Is this your pencil or Mr. Kim's?

‖ 2.4. Nouns.

It was pointed out in ‖ 1.2 that Korean nouns usually, but not always, correspond to English nouns.

An instance of non-correspondence is the English pronouns, which in Korean are a kind of noun:

na . . . . I, me
wuli . . . . we, us
tangsin . . . . you

Other English pronouns have no direct Korean equivalent, but only phrases:

ku sālam . . . . . that (aforementioned) person = he, him; she, her; they, them
ku kes . . . . that (aforementioned) thing = it

Correspondence of vocabulary is one thing, and correspondence of sentence patterns is another. Korean sentences in general are less specific than English sentences. A key spot where this difference shows up is in what strikes us as "omission of pronouns" from Korean sentences, particularly as subject and topic. It is especially important to be cautious about addressing the second person, i.e. saying 'you.' The person you are addressing may be called, respectfully, sensayng nim, or Kim sensayng, or Kim sensayng nim; or you may use a professional title—moksa nim 'you (who are a minister)' or Kim moksa 'you (Rev. Kim)' or Kim moksa nim. (All of these also can be used for the THIRD person, so that a given sentence containing such an expression is, out of its context, ambiguous.)

You should use as few "pronouns" in Korean as you can possibly manage—omit more than you think you can do without, in the beginning, and see what happens. Observe carefully your native Korean teacher, or, better yet, listen in while two Koreans are talking together. You will not hear many cases of na, and you will hear tangsin rarely, if at all; and yet each of the speakers clearly understands what the other one is talking about.

Korean nouns are used in sentences in one of the following four positions.

1. Before particles:

A particle after a noun shows its grammatical relationship to the rest of the sentence.

2. Before the copula:

A noun (call it N) plus the copula means 'is (the same thing as) N' in the formula X is N or It is N.

3. Before another noun:

Nouns are used to modify or describe other nouns. Such noun-noun phrases as Kim sensayng and Kim Poktong are quite familiar to you. Names of nations (Mikwuk 'America,' Hānkwuk 'Korea') combine in such phrases as these:

Mikwuk salam 'America' [America-person]
Hānkwuk mal 'Korean' [Korea-language]

You have seen instances of the latter phrase, Hānkwuk mal, in turn being used to modify a third noun:

Hānkwuk mal chayk (sensayng, haksayng) 'Korean language book (teacher, student)'

Some nouns, actually, are used more frequently as modifiers of other nouns than by themselves. Commonly used in this way are i 'this,' ku 'that (aforementioned),' and ce 'that (over there).'

A special group of nouns is used ONLY before other nouns. These are PRE-NOUNS, and you have learned some interrogative ones in this lesson:

musun [chayk] 'what kind of [book]?'
etten (or enu) [kes] 'which [thing]?'

Another special group of nouns are used only after such pre-nouns (or after other modifying elements); these we can call QUASI-FREE NOUNS, since they seem to be free to do everything except start a sentence: [ku] kes '[that] thing.'

4. By itself (absolute):

Finally, Korean nouns are sometimes used by themselves, with nothing but a pause after them, in absolute position—usually at the beginning of a sentence, like a topic. You will learn more about this in Lesson 4.

‖ 2.5. The subordinating particle uy.

5. Kim sensayng uy chayk iey yo? 'Is it Mr. Kim's book?'
9. Nwukwu uy capci 'ey yo. 'Whose magazine is it?'
10. Kim sensayng uy kes iey yo, tangsin uy kes iey yo. 'Is it Mr. Kim's or is it yours?'

The particle that is spelled uy (but pronounced ey!) is a ONE-SHAPE particle: it is always the same, whether it comes after a vowel or a consonant.

The function of this particle is to link noun expressions together in such a way that the first one modifies, or describes, or limits the meaning of, the second one. The instances you have observed in the Basic Sentences of this lesson illustrate the POSSESSIVE meaning of uy: it corresponds to the English suffix -'s: John's . . . , Mr. Cooper's . . . . (English pronouns, of course, are made possessive in other ways: I–my, you–your, he–his, and so on. Even who plus 's undergoes a spelling alternation: whose.) Nay 'my' is actually a combination of na 'I' and the possessive particle uy, run together.

A possessive meaning is present in such phrases even when there is no uy, as is often the case:

tangsin chayk 'your book'
Kim sensayng tãmpay 'Mr. Kim's cigarettes'

An important difference between English and Korean is that Korean sentences do not usually end with possessive phrases of this kind, as English sentences sometimes do, for the particle uy must have another noun expression after it. This may be the unspecific quasi-free noun kes 'the thing, the one,' which in this usage corresponds to the English possessives in such sentences as 'This is the teacher's.' and 'Where is Mr. Dewey's?'.

ADDITIONAL EXAMPLES

1. I chayk i sensayng nim uy chayk iey yo?	Is this book yours?
2. I kes i Ilpon mal sensayng uy yenphil iey yo.	This is the Japanese teacher's pencil.
3. Ce sinmun i nwukwu uy sinmun iey yo. —Nay kes iey yo.	Whose newspaper is that?—It's mine.

EXERCISES

I

To practice making a quick choice of shapes when using two-shape particles, say each of the following words aloud (together with its English meaning), then say it again with the subject particle i/ka after it; then with the topic particle un/nun after it. Finally add iey yo/'ey yo so that you have a sentence 'It is . . . .' Do you remember what each word means?

an(h)ay	Hānkwuk mal	namphyen	sensayng
cāngkyo	hāykwun	[1]Noseaq salam	sinmun
capci	Ilponq salam	payk.muk	S(s)olyen
chayk	kes	puin	tāmpay
chilphan	ku sālam	pyēnho-sa	tangsin
congi	mānnyen-phil	sālam	uysa
Cwungkwuk mal	moksa	sengnyang	Yenge
haksayng	na	senkyo-sa	yenphil

II

A. Say the following sentence in Korean, completing it with each of the expressions in the list below. Repeat the entire sentence each time. Then say each one again, making it negative.

That person over there (a) is ---, (b) is not --

1. Japanese.
2. a serviceman.
3. an American doctor.
4. Mr. Kim's wife
5. my wife.
6. an air force officer.
7. a Korean missionary.
8. a Russian student.
9. a sailor.
10. my friend.
11. my husband.
12. an English teacher.

B. Now, fill in the blanks of the following two pattern sentences with each of the expressions below, again repeating the entire sequence each time.

1. This is not a ---. Then what is it?
2. This is (a) ---. Whose --- is it?

1. blackboard
2. chalk
3. Chinese newspaper
4. cigarettes
5. fountain pen
6. Japanese magazine
7. magazine
8. matches
9. newspaper
10. paper
11. pencil
12. Russian book

C. Complete this sentence by using each of the following expressions, of course repeating the whole sentence every time.

This newspaper is ---.

1. Doctor Ma's.
2. His.
3. Mine.
4. My friend's.
5. My husband's.
6. My wife's.
7. Poktong Kim's.
8. Rev. Ma's wife's.
9. That lawyer's.
10. Your husband's.
11. Your wife's.
12. Yours.

(More natural English calls in some of these cases for the expression <u>This</u> <u>news-paper</u> <u>belongs</u> <u>to</u> . . . .)

III

Build alternative questions in Korean around each of the following pairs of alternatives.

1. Yours or mine?
2. A book or a magazine?
3. A Chinese magazine or a Japanese magazine?
4. My Japanese book or your Japanese book?
5. Your Japanese book or your Korean book?
6. A soldier or a sailor?
7. A pencil or chalk?
8. Mr. Kim's pencil or Mr. Ma's pencil?
9. Mr. Ma's pencil or Mrs. Ma's pencil?

IV

Translate these sentences into Korean:

1. Is that Mr. Kim's notebook?
2. No, that's not Mr. Kim's.
3. Then, whose notebook is it?
4. It's mine.
5. Is Mr. Kim a missionary?
6. No. Mr. Kim is not a missionary. He's a Korean pastor.
7. But, Mr. Kim's friend is a missionary.
8. Is that friend an American?
9. No. He's not an American. He's an Englishman.
10. Are these your cigarettes?
11. No. They're not mine.
12. Well, whose cigarettes are these? Are they Mr. Kim's cigarettes?
13. No. They are that soldier's cigarettes.
14. Who is that soldier?
15. That soldier is a Korean (language) student. He's an air force officer.

CONVERSATION

The following conversation should be repeated until each member of the class has taken every A role and every B role.

I

A: What is this?
(B replies.)

A: (Is it your ---?
(B replies.)

A: Then which one is mine? <u>or</u>
Then whose is it?
(B replies.)

II

A: What is that?
(B replies that it's a book.)

A: Is it a --- (language) book?
(B replies that it isn't.)

A: Then what kind of book is it?
(B replies.)

III

A: Are you a teacher or a student?
(B replies that he's a student.)

A: Then who is the teacher?
(B replies.)

A: Is (s)he an English teacher or a Russian teacher?
(B replies.)

IV

A asks B about his nationality and occupation; when B has replied, A asks B the same questions about C, who is B's friend.

VOCABULARY DRILL

Each of the following sets of words contains a misfit—a word whose meaning does not fit in with that of the rest. Spot the misfit, and be sure you know why it does not belong. (This drill is best done orally and rapid-fire.)

1. pyēnho-sa, moksa, cāngkyo, sinmun
2. congi, kaceng puin, payk.muk, yenphil
3. Ilpon, Yenge, S(s)olyen, Mikwuk
4. tāywi, sōwi, cwungwi, congi
5. sensayng, haksayng, hakca, hāykwun
6. Cwungkwuk mal, Ilpon mal, Yenge, Hānkwuk
7. na, tangsin, senkyo-sa, wuli
8. nongpu, [l]īpal(q)-sa, sengnyang, sangin
9. kongkwun, kong-chayk, hāykwun, [l]yuk.kwun
10. namphyen, puin, an(h)ay, chilphan

LESSON 3. WHERE THINGS ARE

BASIC SENTENCES

Korean	English	Amplification
1. Yeki ka eti 'ey yo.	What place is this (place)?	yeki 'this place, here' eti 'what place? where?'
2. Yeki nun hak.kyo 'ey yo.	This (place) is a school.	hak.kyo 'school'
3. Wuli nun cikum eti iss.ey yo.	Where are we now?	cikum 'now' iss.e(y) yo 'exist(s), there is or are; am or are or is (in a place)'
4. Kyōsil an ey iss.ey yo.	We're in the classroom.	kyōsil 'classroom' an 'the inside (of something rather empty)' [cf. ‖ 3.5] kyōsil an 'the inside of the classroom, the classroom's inside' kyōsil an ey '(in the) inside (of) the classroom'
5. Ku kapangq sōk ey mues i iss.ey yo.	What's in that briefcase? or What have you got in that briefcase?	kapang 'bag, case, handbag, briefcase' sōk 'the inside (of something rather full); the insides, the content' [cf. ‖ 3.5] sōk ey '(in the) inside (of)'
6. Sōk ey nun, mues i iss.ey yo.	What's inside of it?	
7. Chayk hako, kong-chayk hako, yenphil i iss.ey yo.	There's [or I've got] a book, a notebook, and some pencils.	hako 'and' [cf. ‖ 3.4]
8. Cēki, ce yuli chang pakk ey, mues i iss.ey yo.	What's outside that window over there?	cēki '(that place) over there; (over) there' yuli 'glass' (as a substance)' chang 'window' yuli chang '(glazed) window' pakk 'the place outside, the outside' yuli chang pakk ey '(in the) outside (of) that window'
9. Keki, namu tul hako phul i iss.ey yo.	There are trees and grass there.	keki 'that place; there (aforementioned)' namu 'tree; plant = shrub'

Korean	English	Amplification
		namu tul 'trees' phul 'grass; plant'
10. Ku namu wi ey nun, sāy ka iss.ey yo?	Are there any birds on top of that tree [or those trees]?	wi [in N. Korea wu] 'the place above; the top; high place' wi ey '(in the place) above; on top; in or on (a high place)' ku namu wi ey nun '(talking about) on top of that tree' sāy 'bird'
11. Ani yo?? Sāy nun ēps.ey yo. Talam-cwi ka iss.ey yo.	No. there aren't any birds. There are some squirrels.	ēps.e(y) yo 'doesn't exist, there isn't or aren't; am or are or is not (in a place)' cwi 'rat' talam-cwi 'squirrel'
12. Ku namu mith ey nun mues i iss.ey yo.	What's under the tree?	mith 'the place underneath) (beneath, below); (at) the bottom' namu mith ey '(in the place) under (beneath, below) the tree; at the bottom of the tree'
13. Kkoch namu hako pitwulki ka iss.ey yo.	There's a flowering tree and some pigeons.	kkoch 'flower' kkoch namu 'flower(ing) tree' pitwulki 'pigeon'
14. Ce cip mun aph ey mues i iss.ey yo.	What's in front of the door of that house over there?	cip 'house' tayk 'house (of an esteemed person), your house' mun 'door' cip mun 'door of the house (house's door)' aph 'the place in front; the front' mun aph '(the place in) front of the door' aph ey 'in (the place in) front' mun aph ey 'in front of the door'
15. Kāy hako kwāyngi ka iss.ey yo.	There's a dog and a cat.	kāy 'dog' kwāyngi or ko.yangi 'cat'
16. Cip twī ey ttul un ēps.ey yo?	Isn't there a yard in back of the house?	twī 'the place behind or in back; the back'

Korean	English	Amplification
		twī ey '(in the place) behind; in back' cip twī ey 'behind or in back of the house (in the house's place-behind)' ttul 'yard, grounds'
17. Iss.ey yo. Ku ttul an ey kkoch path hako chāyso path i iss.ey yo.	There is (a yard). In the yard there is a flower garden and a vegetable garden.	ku 'that, the aforementioned' ku ttul an ey 'in(side) the aforementioned yard' path 'field, garden' path i [pron. pachi] 'the garden' [as subject] kkoch path [pron. kkoppat] 'flower garden' chāyso 'vegetable' chāyso path 'vegetable garden, vegetable patch'
18. Kuliko, ku cip cwuwi ey nun swuph i iss.ey yo.	And around the house there is a forest.	cwuwi 'the place surrounding or around' cip cwuwi ey '(in the place) surrounding or around the house' cip cwuwi ey nun 'around the house—guess what?' swuph 'forest, woods'
19. Tangsin(q) yeph ey nwu' ka iss.ey yo.	Who is beside you?	yeph 'the place next to or beside' [occasionally pron. nyeph after a consonant: tangsinq yeph = /tangsinnyep/] tangsin(q) yeph ey 'next to you, beside you (in your place-beside)'
20. Ōyn phyen ey nun Pak sensayng i iss.ey yo. Palun phyen ey nun Kim sensayng i iss.ey yo.	On the left is Mr. Pak. On the right is Mr. Kim.	
21. Pak sensayng taum ey nun mues i iss.ey yo. Uyca ka iss.ey yo.	What is next to Mr. Pak? There's a chair (there).	taum '(what is) adjacent, next' Pak sensayng taum ey 'next (adjacent) to Mr. Pak'
22. Na nun eti iss.ey yo.	Where am I?	

Korean	English	Amplification
23. Sensayng nim un Pak sensayng palun phyen, O sensayng ōyn phyen ey iss.ey yo.	You are to the right of Mr. Pak and to the left of Mr. O.	O [a family name]
24. Chayk-sang un i kyōsil an eti (ey) iss.ey yo.	Where is the desk in this classroom?	sang 'table' chayk-sang ("book-table" =) 'desk, table' i kyōsil an eti 'where in this classroom (in what place of this classroom)?'
25. Ku kes un i kyōsil an, chilphan aph ey iss.ey yo.	It's in front of the blackboard in this classroom.	chilphan 'blackboard' chilphan aph ey 'in front of the blackboard'
26. Chilphan mac.un phyen ey mues i iss.ey yo. Mun i iss.ey yo.	What's across from the blackboard? There's a door.	mac.un '. . . which is facing, opposite' mac.un phyen ey 'in the opposite or facing direction, across from' mun 'door'
27. I yuli chang hako ce yuli chang sai ey mues i iss.ey yo.	What is (there) between this window and that window?	sai or sāy 'intervening space; interval' sai ey 'in the intervening space; between' A hako B sai ey 'between A and B (in A and B's intervening space)'
28. Pyek i iss.ey yo. Pyek wi ey nun kūlim i iss.ey yo. Pata uy kūlim iey yo.	There's a wall. On the wall, there's a picture. It's a picture of the sea.	pyek 'wall' pyek wi ey '(up) on the wall' kūlim 'picture' pata 'sea, ocean' pata uy kūlim 'picture of the sea'
29. Kūlimq sōk ey pay nun ēps.ey yo?	Isn't there a boat in the picture?	kūlimq sōk ey 'in(side) the picture' pay '(small) boat'
30. Nēy. Ēps.ey yo.	No, there isn't.	'Yes, there isn't.'
31. Ani yo?? Iss.ey yo.	Yes, there is.	'No, there is.'
32. Pay nun ku kūlimq sōk mul wi ey iss.ey yo.	The boat is on the water in that picture.	mul 'water' mul wi ey 'on (top of) the water'
33. I kyōsil an ey, tto eti kūlim i iss.ey yo.	Where else in the classroom have we pictures?	tto 'and, too, also, again' tto eti '(also where =) where else?'

Korean	English	Amplification
34. Chilphan wi, pyek ey iss.ey yo.	We have one (or some) on the wall above the blackboard.	
35. Palo chenceng mith ey (or Chenceng palo mith ey) iss.ey yo.	It's right below the ceiling.	palo . . . or palwu . . . 'right, just, directly'
36. Chilphan māyn wi ey iss.ey yo.	Is it way above the blackboard?	māyn . . . 'way, far' (opposite of palo)

SUPPLEMENTARY VOCABULARY

cwāwu (phyen) ey	on left and right; on both sides	miswul-kwan	art gallery
pang	room	^{l}yekwan	hotel
sāmu-sil	office	cengke-cang, yek	railroad station
malwu	floor	kongcang	factory
sang, chayk-sang, theyipul	table	cik.kong	factory worker
chīm-sang, chīmtay	bed	^{l}notong ca	worker
cang	chest (for storage)	sangcem	store
chayk-cang	book-case	yak	medicine, drug
sangca	box	yak-pang	drugstore, pharmacy
pyenso, twīq-kan	toilet	chayk-pang, secem, chayk-sa	bookstore
twī-ci (twīq congi) pyensoq congi	toilet paper	cwumeni	bag, purse; pocket
^{l}yeypay-tang, kyōhoy	church	ho-cwumeni, phokheythu or phokheys	pocket
tose-kwan	library (building)	swunkyeng or kyeng(chal)-kwan	policeman
tose-sil	library (room)	ai (āy) or elin ai/ay/i	child
yenghwa	movies, cinema, films	ayki (aki)	baby
yenghwa-kwan	movie theater	sōnyen	boy
kukcang	theater	sōnye	girl
tāysa	ambassador	namca	man (= male)
tāysa-kwan	embassy	^{n}yeca	woman; girl
Mikwuk tāysa-kwan	American embassy	kwa	lesson
pak.mul-kwan	museum	swukcey	homework
		pul	a light; fire
		mo-thwungi	corner

NOTES

‖ 3.1. Iss.ey yo and ēps.ey yo: existence and location.

The English word be (am, are, is) has a variety of meanings; these are expressed in Korean by a variety of vocabulary items.

One—be in the sense that something "equals" or is (the same thing as) something else—corresponds to the Korean copula iey yo/'ey yo (above, ‖ 2.2).

Be in the sense that something is located somewhere or is existing, on the other hand, is iss.ey yo. The negative is a separate word, ēps.ey yo 'does not exist, is not located.' These words also mean 'there is or are' and 'there isn't or aren't' respectively.

Here are some pairs of sentences which contrast the meanings of these verbs with that of the copula.

1. Chayk iey yo. 'It's a book.' 'They're books.'
   Chayk i iss.ey yo. 'There's a book (somewhere).' 'There are some books (somewhere).' '(Someone) has got a book.'
   Chayk (i) ani 'ey yo. 'It's not a book.' 'They aren't books.'
   Chayk i ēps.ey yo. 'There isn't any book (somewhere).' 'There aren't any books (somewhere).' '(Someone) hasn't got a book.'

2. Hak.kyo 'ey yo. 'It's a school.' 'They are schools.'
   Hak.kyo ey iss.ey yo. 'It's at school.' 'They are at school.' OR: 'There's (one) at school.' 'There are (some) at school.' 'They've got one at school.'
   Hak.kyo (ka) ani 'ey yo. 'It's not a school.' 'They aren't schools.'
   Hak.kyo ey ēps.ey yo. 'It's not at school.' 'They aren't at school.' OR 'There isn't or aren't (any) at school.'

3. Yeki ka eti 'ey yo. 'What is this (place)?' [lit. This place is what place?]
   Yeki (ey) eti iss.ey yo. 'Where in this place is it?' OR: 'Where in this place is there (one)?'

Basic Sentence 28 contains both constructions:

. . . kūlim i iss.ey yo. Pata uy kūlim iey yo. 'There's a picture . . . It's a picture of the sea.'

The copula, then has one meaning, which we can label IDENTITY.

The verb iss.ey yo and its negative ēps.ey yo have meanings we can label EXISTENCE ('there is[n't] or are[n't]') and LOCATION ('is[n't or are[n't] in a place'). A third meaning for these—POSSESSION—is discussed in the following section.

ADDITIONAL EXAMPLES

1. Haksayng i yeki iss.ey yo.	The student is here.
2. Chīm-sang wi ey chayk i ēps.ey yo.	There aren't any books on the bed.
3. Kyōsil an ey kūlim i iss.ey yo?— Nēy. Iss.ey yo.—Ani yo?? Ēps.ey yo.	Are there any pictures in the classroom?—Yes, there are.—No, there aren't.
4. [1]Yekwan i eti iss.ey yo.—Cēki iss.ey yo.	Where is the hotel?—It's over there.
5. Pyenso ka eti iss.ey yo.—Ōyn phyen ey iss.ey yo.	Where is the toilet?—It's to your left.
6. Yeki yenghwa-kwan i iss.ey yo?— Ēps.ey yo.	Is there a movie theater here?—(No) there isn't.
7. Nay chayk un yeki ēps.ey yo.	My book isn't here.
8. Kkoch path i cip cwāwu (phyen) ey iss.ey yo.	There are flower gardens on both sides of the house.

‖ 3.2. Iss.ey yo and ēps.ey yo: possession.

As you have just observed, iss.ey yo is in one way more limited than its English counterpart: it is equivalent to be (am, are, is) in only ONE of its meanings.

At the same time, iss.ey yo is too broad in scope for a single English equivalent. It is the normal Korean way of expressing possession, as conveyed by English 'has (have)' and 'has got (have got)':

Chayk i iss.ey yo?
EITHER: 'Is there a book (in some place)?'
OR: 'Have you a book?'

Yenphil i ēps.ey yo.
EITHER: 'There aren't any pencils (in some place).'
OR: 'I haven't got a pencil.'

These two meanings seem quite distinct to people who are accustomed to English vocabulary patterns, but Koreans do not ordinarily draw the distinction. The context usually makes it clear which English translation is more suitable in each instance.

It is not unusual for a Korean sentence of this type to have two subjects—one naming the possessor of an object, the other naming the object possessed—as follows:

Nay ka ayki ka iss.ey yo. 'I have a baby.'
Ku salam i chayk i iss.ey yo? 'Has he a book?'
Nay ka yak i ēps.ey yo. 'I haven't any medicine.'
Kim sensayng i congi ka ēps.ey yo. 'Mr. Kim hasn't got any paper.'

(Another kind of sentence that can have two subjects, you recall, is a negative copular sentence: Ku kes i nay kes i ani 'ey yo. 'That isn't mine.')

ADDITIONAL EXAMPLES

1. Sengnyang i iss.ey yo?— Iss.ey yo.	Have you got a match? (Yes), I have.
2. Yenphil i ēps.ey yo.	I haven't any pencil.
3. Kkoch path i iss.ey yo?— Nēy. Iss.ey yo.	Have you a flower garden?— Yes, we have.
4. I pang ey nun, chayk-sang i ēps.ey yo.	I haven't got any desk in this room.

‖ 3.3. Location particle ey 'in/at.'

You have observed the use of the particle ey, meaning 'in, at, on,' in nearly every Basic Sentence of this lesson:

Kyōsil an ey iss.ey yo. 'We're in the classroom.'
Hak.kyo ey ēps.ey yo. 'He's not at school.'

This particle conveys the meaning carried by several English prepositions—general location. Perhaps the hardest thing to get used to in Korean is placing the particle AFTER the noun, to correspond to what in English appears BEFORE the noun.

After certain nouns that end in -i, -ey, or -ay, the particle ey is often not heard. This can happen for example in the expression eti ( ) issey yo '(in) what place is it?' (Basic Sentences 3, 22, 26) and Keki ( ) . . . '(In) that place' (Basic Sentence 9). But this is not true in every case: cf. sai ey 'between' (Basic Sentence 27) and wi ey 'on top of' (Basic Sentence 28, 32).

‖ 3.4. The particle hako 'and.'

Another single vocabulary item in English—the connective 'and'—is translated variously in Korean, depending on its usage.

Between Korean NOUNS, the word for 'and' is hako, as you have seen e.g. in Basic Sentence 7:

chayk hako, kong-chayk hako, yenphil 'a book and a notebook and a pencil'

It is natural for English speakers to pause (if at all) BEFORE the 'and'; but the Koreans pause AFTER hako. This is because hako is a particle, and particles are pronounced as part of the word they follow, like a suffix rather than a separate word (‖ 1.2.)

Until you learn Korean equivalents for 'and' in other uses, such as to join sentences, you can use two separate sentences and begin the second with kuliko or tto.

‖ 3.5. Place nouns.

You have seen in this lesson a number of nouns denoting specific place relationships. With ey 'in, at, on' after them, they mean 'in [a certain place relationship].' Here is a list:

an ey 'inside'
sōk ey 'inside'
pakk ey 'outside'
wi ey 'above, over, on (top); upstairs'
mith ey 'at the bottom, below under(neath)'
alay (ey) 'below, lower, down; downstairs'
aph ey 'in front'
twī ey 'in back; behind'
cwuwi ey 'around'
yeph ey 'next to, beside'
. . . phyen (or ccok) 'side, direction'
ōyn phyen/ccok ey 'on the left'
palun phyen/ccok ey 'on the right'
mac.un phyen/ccok ey 'across from, opposite'
taum ey 'adjacent (next) to'
sai ey 'between'

These are PLACE NOUNS. They are most frequently used in phrases with other nouns (cf. above ‖ 2.4. noun use 3), as:

mun aph ey 'in front of the door'
sang taum ey 'next to the table'

It is important to put these nouns in the right order. If the place noun comes BEFORE the other noun, the meaning is changed—the place noun modifies:

mun aph ey 'in front of the door'
aph mun 'the front door'
path twī ey 'in back of the garden'
twīq path 'the back garden'

pang taum 'next to the room'
taumq pang 'the next room'

Other place nouns are also used in this way.

The place noun sai (sai ey 'between') by the nature of its meaning usually requires two nouns before it; these are linked with hako 'and':

hak.kyo hako cip sai ey 'between the school and the house'

Some place nouns also are used as time nouns: sai can refer to an interval of time as well as of space; aph can refer ahead in time (to the future); an can mean 'within (a certain time),' and taum most commonly means 'next (in order or time).'

Two place nouns — an and sōk — have the same English translation, 'inside.' An is used for the inside of loosely filled spaces — a room, a building, a garden, for example — things which generally have more air than substance filling their interior. Sōk, on the other hand, means the inside of things which are normally well filled, or which are easily filled up — a suitcase, a drawer, etc.

Corresponding to such English expressions as 'where in this room' — requests for more specific locations — there are Korean phrases like these:

i kyōsil an eti ('in what place of this classroom's inside?' =) 'where in this classroom?'
chayk-sang wi eti 'where on (top of) the desk?'

You may have noticed the relationship between a certain set of place nouns with the set of noun-modifying nouns you learned in Lesson 2:

i 'this'	yeki 'this place, here'
ku 'that (nearby, aforementioned)'	keki 'that place, there (nearby; aforementioned)'
ce 'that (over there)'	cēki 'that place, (over) there'

You will hear these words occasionally pronounced yo, ko, co; yoki, koki, coki. These are what we call **LIGHT ISOTOPES** of the words; they add a connotation of smallness or cuteness ("this li'l") or of deprecation ("this ole"). See ‖ 11.5 for further discussion.

ADDITIONAL EXAMPLES

1. Ku sang wi ey nun, musun chayk i iss.ey yo.	What kind of books are there on that table?
2. Hak.kyo aph ey mues i iss.ey yo.	What is there in front of the school?
3. Mun pakk ey nwu' ka iss.ey yo.	Who's outside the door?
4. I cip an ey sālam i iss.ey yo.	Is there anybody in(side of) this house?

‖ 3.6. More about the topic particle un/nun.

The Basic Sentences of this lesson offer more examples of the topic particle in its capacity for reducing the emphasis of what goes before it. We can put these uses under three general headings:

1. Stage setting. The topic particle sets the stage for what the sentence is going to be about; it comes after a noun expression and sets it aside as what we're going to talk about. This is the usage we see in Basic Sentence 6:

Sōk ey nun, mues i iss.ey yo. 'Talking about the inside— what have we got (what is there) there?'

2. Contrast. Two noun expressions or other phrases, about which you want to make contrasting statements or offer differing information, are set aside at the beginning of their respective clauses and each is followed by the particle un/nun— to reduce their emphasis so that the way is cleared for the important contrasting statements. You have seen this usage in Basic Sentence 20:

Ōyn phyen ey nun . . . . Palun phyen ey nun . . . .
'On the left [guess what?!—]. . . . . [and] on the right [guess what?!—]

3. Repetition of a subject. The first time a subject is mentioned in context, its newness calls for emphasis in the shape of the subject particle i/ka after it. Then, if this subject reappears in the conversation, it comes under the heading of Old Business— it appears with the particle un/nun, which relegates it to the realm of reduced emphasis. In fact, it often happens that the subject disappears altogether, as you have seen before.

‖ 3.7. The specific index of plurality: tul.

Korean nouns, as you know, are not specific with respect to number. Basic Sentence 7 of this lesson conveys information which might correspond to several English sentences:

Chayk hako, kong-chayk hako, yenphil i iss.ey yo.	I've got a book, a notebook, and a pencil. OR
	I've got some books, a notebook, and a pencil. OR
	I've got some books, a notebook, and some pencils. OR
	I've got some books, some notebooks, and a pencil.

And so on— till the mathematical possibilities are exhausted. But if it is really necessary, or if he feels like it, a Korean speaker can make his nouns specifically plural. (Without using numerals, he cannot make them specifically singular.) He does this by placing tul, a word meaning something like 'group,' after them:

sensayng	'teacher or teachers'
sensayng tul	'teachers'

Particles to be used with the plural phrase come after the tul, which corresponds to the English plural suffix that we write -s etc. (The word tul is uniquely versatile; it may pop up just about anywhere in a Korean sentence and it need not always refer to the words near it. Only the most common uses are shown in this book.)

‖ 3.8. Answering negative questions.

If you want to answer a Korean question with 'yes' or 'no,' you do it just as you would in English— so long as the question is an affirmative one.

But if the QUESTION is NEGATIVE, you use the Korean word for 'yes' to agree with the NEGATIVENESS, and the Korean word for 'no' to DISAGREE with the negativeness; the resulting usage is the opposite from the English. Expanded, the translations of Basic Sentences 30 and 31 can be thought of like this:

[Kūlimq sōk ey pay nun ēps.ey yo? 'Isn't there a boat in the picture?]
30. Nēy. Ēps.ey yo. 'Yes, I agree with your words: there isn't a boat.'
31. Ani yo?? Iss.ey yo. 'No, you have a mistaken impression: there IS a boat.'

(Occasionally there are exceptions, as when the question is put in the negative form just to be polite.)

ADDITIONAL EXAMPLES

1. I sālam i Mikwuk salam i ani 'ey yo?—Nēy. Yengkuk salam iey yo.	Isn't this man an American?—No, he's English.
2. I chayk i Kim sensayng uy chayk i ani 'ey yo?—Ani yo?? Kim sensayng uy chayk iey yo.	Isn't this Mr. Kim's book?—Yes, it's Mr. Kim's.
3. Panana ka ēps.ey yo?—Nēy. Ēps.ey yo.	Have we no bananas? Yes, we have no bananas.

EXERCISES

I

Make Korean sentences on the following outlines, completing them in any way you choose. Practice saying them aloud until you feel sure of them.

1. Mr. Kim is
   a. next to
   b. to the left of
   c. across from
   d. between
   e. to the right of

2. My book is
   a. on
   b. under
   c. near
   d. between
   e. inside of

3. The flower garden is
   a. near
   b. in front of
   c. between
   d. across from
   e. behind

4. There's a forest
   a. around
   b. near
   c. in back of
   d. to the left of
   e. outside of

II

Now, fill in the blanks of the following sentences with an expression which begins with each of the five place expressions listed; express them in Korean and practice them aloud.

1. There are children ________ the house.
   a. in
   b. outside
   c. in front of
   d. near
   e. in back of
2. Is your notebook ________ your briefcase?
   a. on top of
   b. in
   c. near
   d. under
   e. to the right of
3. Is Mr. Kim's wife ________ (the) school?
   a. at
   b. behind
   c. near
   d. in front of
   e. outside

III

Translate these sentences into Korean, and practice them until you can say them fluently.

1. Where are my cigarettes?
2. Are they inside your briefcase?
3. In my briefcase I've got some books, some papers, and a fountain pen.
4. But I don't have any cigarettes.
5. Here, I have some cigarettes. Have you got a match?
6. The matches are on the desk.
7. I'm sorry. There aren't any matches on the desk.
8. Are they under the desk? Are they on the floor?
9. There aren't any matches on the floor. Are there any on the bookcase next to the desk? Aren't there some under that picture?
10. There aren't any. However, I have some in the next room. Excuse me.
11. Here are some matches. They are Korean matches.
12. Are your cigarettes Korean cigarettes?
13. No. They're American (ones).
14. There isn't any light. Where is my chair? Is this my chair?
15. No. That's not your chair. That chair over there next to Mr. Han is yours.
16. Oh? Who's across from me? Is it Mrs. Kim?
17. No. Mrs. Kim is between Mr. Pak and Mrs. Pak.
18. Well, then, who is that over there beside the window?
19. It's my friend. It's Mrs. Ma.
20. Who's Mrs. Ma? Is she the school teacher? Is she the missionary's wife?
21. What's outside the window? Is that a bird?

22. No. It's a squirrel. Now the squirrel is in front of the window. Now the squirrel is under the tree. Now the squirrel is up on the tree.
23. There's a cat behind the squirrel. There's a dog behind the cat.
24. Is it your dog, (or) is it my dog?
25. It's the minister's dog. It's Reverend Kim's. Where is Reverend Kim now?
26. He's at church.
27. Where is Reverend Kim's church?
28. It's across from the library, to the left of the movie theater. It's next to the school.
29. There's grass all around the church.
30. And, in front of the door there is a flower garden.

CONVERSATION

Each student should bring to class a large picture, cut from a magazine, showing the inside of a room. The larger, more detailed, and more colorful, the better. He should then lead a discussion session centered around his picture. He may ask members of the class to name the thing he is pointing out, and to say where it is in relation to the other things. He must keep on his toes and correct any misstatement he hears.

Then, everyone also bring an outdoor picture, showing buildings and landscape features, and conduct a discussion like the one above.

VOCABULARY DRILL

Complete the following sentences by inserting into them, one by one, each of the words listed below them. Repeat the entire sentence aloud in Korean each time.

1. Is (are) there ________ near the table?

a book-case	a pen	a notebook
a handbag	some windows	a bird
some pencils	any pictures	a desk
a door	a cat	a table
some chairs	a blackboard	a wall
a chest	any medicine	a light
a child	some toilet paper	a baby
a bag	a photograph	a box

2. Isn't (aren't) there ________ near your house?

a school	a forest	a tree
any squirrels	any grass	flowers
pigeons	a dog	a yard
a vegetable garden	the sea	a boat
a movie theater	a drugstore	a hotel
any water	a factory	a church
a railroad station	factory workers	any stores
a bookshop	an embassy	a library

COMPREHENSION

Listen carefully while your teacher says to you, in Korean, a numer of true-false statements. These statements will be of the sort The table is between the window and the door. and There's a factory outside the school. It's up to you to answer Nēy. if the statement is true and Ani yo?? if it is false. The faster this drill can speed along, the more valuable it will be to you as a means of developing your understanding of spoken Korean.

LESSON 4. GETTING THINGS DONE

BASIC SENTENCES

Korean	English	Amplification
1. Wuli nun cikum mues ul hay yo.	What are we doing now?	cikum 'now' mues ul or mue l' 'what [as direct object]' hay yo 'does, is doing'
2. Hānkwuk mal ul kongpu hay yo.	We're studying Korean.	Hānkwuk mal ul 'Korean language [as direct object]' kongpu (lul) hay yo 'studies, is studying'
3. Hānkwuk mal sikan ey nun, Hānkwuk mal lo hay yo. Yenge lo an hay yo.	In Korean period, we talk Korean; we don't talk English.	Hānkwuk mal(q) sikan 'Korean time, Korean hour or period' Hānkwuk mal lo 'by means of Korean, in Korean' Hākwuk mal lo hay yo 'speaks or says (in) Korean' an hay yo 'doesn't speak or say or do' Yenge lo an hay yo 'doesn't speak (in) English'
4. Hānkwuk mal ul cal hasey yo?	Do you speak Korean well?	Hānkwuk mal ul hay yo 'speaks the Korean language, speaks Korean' cal 'well, nicely' hasey yo 'someone esteemed does or is doing'
5. Acik cal mōs hay yo.	I can't speak well yet.	acik 'still, yet' mōs hay yo 'cannot do, definitely does not'
6. Hānkwuk mal ul mues ulo paywusey yo.	What do you use to learn Korean?	= "With what do you learn Korean" mues ulo 'with or by means of what?, from what?' paywusey yo '(someone esteemed) learns'
7. Hānkwuk mal chayk ulo paywe yo.	We learn it from a Korean book.	Hānkwuk mal chayk ulo 'with a Korean book' paywe yo 'learns'
8. Nwukwu hanthey paywusey yo?	From whom do you learn it?	nwukwu hanthey 'to or by whom, who to or by'

	Korean	English	Amplification
9.	Kim sensayng hanthey paywe yo.	We learn it from Mr. Kim.	
10.	Hānkwuk mal haksayng tul i manh.e yo?	Are there lots of Korean students?	= "Are the Korean students many or numerous?" mānh.e yo 'there's a lot, there are many'
11.	Ani yo?? Cham cek.e yo.	No, there are very few.	cek.e yo 'there are few' cham 'very; real(ly)'
12.	Cikum tayk ey nwukwu wa kath.i sāsey yo.	Who are you living with at home now?	tayk 'house, home [of someone esteemed]' tayk ey 'at (your) home' nwukwu wa 'with whom?; who with?' kath.i [pron. kachi] 'together' sāsey yo '[someone esteemed] lives, resides'
13.	Pumo nim hako, kāy han mali hako kath.i sal.e yo.	I'm living with my parents and a dog.	pumo 'parents' pumo nim 'esteemed parents' pumo nim hako 'with esteemed parents' kāy 'dog' han mali 'one [animal]' kāy han mali 'one dog, a dog' kāy han mali hako kath.i 'together with one dog' sal.e yo 'lives, resides'
14.	Ape' nim un nul cip ey se chayk ul ilk.usey yo.	Father is always reading at home.	apeci 'father' ape' nim 'esteemed father' nul 'always' cip ey se '(happening) at home' chayk ul 'book [as direct object]' ilk.usey yo '[someone esteemed] reads'
15.	Ōhwu ey nun ttul uy phul ul kkakk.usey yo.	In the afternoons he cuts the grass in the yard.	ōhwu 'afternoon' ōhwu ey 'in the afternoon(s)' ttul uy phul 'the grass (of=) in the yard' phul ul 'grass [as direct object]' kkakk.usey yo '[someone esteemed] cuts (=mows)'

Korean	English	Amplification
16. Cenyek ey nun eme' nim kwa kath.i kongwen ey se sānqpo hasey yo.	In the evenings, he takes a walk in the park with Mother.	cenyek 'evening' cenyek ey 'in the evening(s)' emeni 'mother' eme' nim 'esteemed mother; Mother' eme' nim kwa 'with Mother' kongwen 'public park' kongwen ey se 'in the park' sānqpo 'a walk, a stroll' sānqpo (lul) hay yo 'takes a walk' sānqpo hasey yo '[someone esteemed] takes a walk'
17. Na wa kāy nun cip ey se nol.a yo.	The dog and I play at home.	na wa kāy 'I and the dog' nol.a yo 'plays, has fun, amuses oneself'
18. Na nun latio lul tul.e yo. Kāy to na kath.i latio lul tul.e yo.	I listen to the radio. The dog listens to the radio too, like me.	latio <u>or</u> laytio <u>or</u> leytio 'radio' latio lul 'radio [as direct object]' tul.e yo 'hears, listens to' na kath.i 'like me, similar to me'
19. Kāy nun nay yeph ey anc.e yo.	The dog sits beside me.	anc.e yo 'sits, sits down'
20. Wuli cip kāy nun acik mōs cic.e yo.	Our dog can't bark yet.	wuli 'we, us' wuli (uy) cip 'our house; our family' wuli cip kāy 'the dog (of=) at our house; our (family) dog' cic.e yo 'barks' mōs cice yo 'cannot bark'
21. Kulena, honca mun ul yel.e yo. Kuliko, tto honca tat.e yo.	But he opens the door by himself; and what's more, he closes it by himself too.	honca 'alone, by oneself' mun 'door' mun ul 'door [as direct object]' yel.e yo 'opens it' tat.e yo 'closes it'
22. Ku kāy nun na chelem koki lul cal mek.e yo. Mul un cal an masye yo.	The dog eats a lot of meat, like me. Water, he doesn't drink much.	na chelem 'like me, similar to me' koki 'meat' koki lul 'meat [as direct object]' cal 'a lot, many, much' <u>or</u> 'often' <u>or</u> 'well' mek.e yo 'eats'

Korean	English	Amplification
		mul 'water' mul un 'when it comes to water' masye yo 'drinks' an masye yo 'doesn't drink'
23. Na nun pōthong Kum-yoil cenyek ey nun chinkwu wa kath.i yenghwa kwūkyeng ul ka yo.	On Friday evenings I usually go to (see) the movies with some friends.	pōthong 'usual, ordinary, regular' pōthong (ulo) 'as (a) usual (thing), usually' Kum-yoil 'Friday' Kum-yoil(q) cenyek ey 'on Friday evening(s)' chinkwu 'friend' chinkwu wa 'with friend(s)' chinkwu wa kath.i '(together) with friend(s)' yenghwa 'movie, motion picture' kwūkyeng 'a viewing, watching, looking at; a show' ka yo 'goes' kwūkyeng (ul) ka yo 'goes to see (something interesting); looks at (with pleasure)'
24. Tho-yoil ōhwu ey nun chinkwu tul hanthey phyēnci lul sse yo.	On Saturday afternoons I write letters to my friends.	Tho-yoil 'Saturday' Tho-yoil ōhwu ey 'on Saturday afternoon(s)' phyēnci 'letter' phyēnci lul 'letter [as direct object]' sse yo 'writes'
25. Na nun chinkwu ka mānh.e yo.	I have lots of friends.	= "As for me friends are many."
26. Nwu' ka tangsin eykey tōn ul cwue yo. Apeci ka cwue yo.	Who gives you your money? Father gives it to me.	tangsin eykey 'to you' tōn 'money' tōn ul 'money [as direct object]' cwue yo 'gives'
27. Apeci hanthey tōn i mānh.e yo.	Father has lots of money.	= "To Father, money is much; to Father, there is much money."
28. Apeci nun nwukwu hanthey se tōn ul pat.usey yo.	Who does your father get the money from?	nwukwu hanthey se 'from whom?, who from?' pat.usey yo '[someone esteemed] receives, gets'

Korean	English	Amplification
29. Unhayng ey se tōn ul pat.e yo. Unhayng ey se īl ul hay yo.	He gets the money from the bank. He works at the bank.	unhayng 'bank' unhayng ey se 'at the bank' pat.e yo 'receives, gets' īl 'work, task, job' īl (ul) hay yo 'works, does some work'
30. Unhayng un etteh.key ka yo. = Unhayng un eti lo ka yo.	How do you get to the bank?	etteh.key 'how? in what way? or how come?' eti lo 'toward where'
31. Wuli cip aph ey se palun phyen ulo ka yo.	From in front of our house you go to the right.	aph ey se 'from the front' palun phyen ulo 'to(ward) the right'
32. Eti se osey yo. Wuphyen-kwuk ey se wa yo.	Where are you coming from? I'm coming from the post office.	eti se 'from where?' osey yo '[someone esteemed] comes' wuphyen-kwuk or wuchey-kwuk 'post office' wuphyen-kwuk ey se 'from the post office' wa yo 'comes'
33. Eti (ey) ka yo. Unhayng ey ka yo.	Where are you going? I'm going to the bank.	eti or eti ey '(to) where?' unhayng ey 'to the bank'

SUPPLEMENTARY VOCABULARY

capswusey yo	[someone esteemed] eats	chac.e yo	looks for or finds; looks up, visits
ca yo or cam (ul) ca yo	goes to bed, sleeps	chac.usey yo	[someone esteemed] looks for or finds; looks up, visits
cwumusey yo	[someone esteemed] goes to bed, sleeps	chac.e wa yo	comes visiting, comes on a visit
il.e na yo	gets up		
il.e nasey yo	[someone esteemed] gets up	kaluchye yo [pron. kaluche yo]	teaches
manna yo	meets or sees (a person)	kaluchisey yo	[someone esteemed] teaches
mannasey yo	[someone esteemed] meets or sees (a person)	phiwe yo or phie yo or phyē yo	smokes
		phi(wu)sey yo	[someone esteemed] smokes
pwa yo, poa yo	sees, looks at; reads		
posey yo	[someone esteemed] sees or looks at or reads	kkakk.e yo	cuts = trims, mows, peels, pares; sharpens (pencil)
		pēy yo	cuts (into, off, or out)
kitalye yo	waits for, waits	pēysey yo	[someone esteemed] cuts
kitalisey yo	[someone esteemed] waits for, waits	cōh.a yo [pron. cōa yo or cwā yo]	is good, is nice; is all right, is OK; has a good one

cōh.usey yo [pron. cōusey yo or cōsey yo]	[someone esteemed] is good; has a good one
nappe yo	is bad; has a bad one
nappusey yo	[someone esteemed] is bad; has a bad one
khe yo	is large or big (in size)
khusey yo	[someone esteemed] is large or big; has a large one
mānh.e yo	is much, are many; has much or many
mānh.usey yo	[esteemed people] are many; [an esteemed person] has much or many
cak.e yo	is little or small (in size); has a small one
cak.usey yo	[someone esteemed] is little; has a little one
cek.e yo	is small (in quantity), are few (in number); has little or few
iss.ey yo	stays; is, exists; has got
kyēysey yo	[someone esteemed] stays, is, exists
iss.usey yo	[someone esteemed] has got

mānh.i	lots, much, a great deal
com or cokum (or cokom or cokuman)	a little (bit), some
ppalli	fast; right away
chēn-chenhi [pron. chēncheni]	slowly
mence	first, to begin with, before anything else
ilccik(i)	early
nuc.key	late
way	why? (cf. etteh.key 'how come?')
ēncey	when?
achim	morning; breakfast
nac	daytime
pam	night(time)
onul	today
yoil	day of the week
musun yoil	what day of the week?
Wel-yoil	Monday
Hwā-yoil	Tuesday
Swu-yoil	Wednesday
Mok-yoil	Thursday
Kum-yoil	Friday
Tho-yoil	Saturday
Il-yoil	Sunday
Cwuil (nal)	Sunday, the Sabbath
ūmsik	food
mas	taste, flavor

NOTES

‖ 4.1. Verbs: polite style.

The Korean sentences of this lesson end with VERBS of various kinds. Notice that the verbs you have learned (including iss.ey yo 'is, exists,' ēps.ey yo 'isn't, doesn't exist,' and the copula iey yo 'is') end with yo, and that before this yo there is a vowel sound. Verbs that end this way are in the POLITE STYLE of speech.

As you have seen earlier, the social relationship between two speakers determines what style they use when speaking to each other—i.e. what endings they will use with the verbs at the end of their sentences. If they are educated people who respect each other and yet do not feel stiff or formal together, they are apt to use the polite style most of the time.

The polite-style ending is the same regardless of whether it is used with a verb which asks a question or one which makes a statement: it is usually the speaker's tone of voice, rather than the actual syllables he utters, that indicate this sort of meaning, in the same way that you can turn such a sentence as You're not going into either a question or an announcement. Verbs in the polite style can make suggestions (Let's . . .) or even gentle commands (Why don't you . . . or How about . . . -ing?)—all with the same verb form, ending in a vowel sound plus yo.

‖ 4.2. Verbs: honorific, polite style.

When a Korean speaker uses a verb to describe the action of a person he specially esteems (or honors), he makes the verb form HONORIFIC. Esteemed (honored) people in Korea include parents and other older relatives; older people in general; high officials; people of education—teachers, doctors, other professional people. Often, of course, the esteemed person is the listener ('you') as in Basic Sentence 6:

Hānkwuk mal ul mues ulo paywusey yo. 'What do you learn Korean from?'

In Basic Sentence 14, a parent is spoken of in honorific terms:

Ape' nim . . chayk ul ilk.usey yo. 'Father . . . is reading a book.'

Just as important as showing esteem for others is to avoid showing it for yourself: Koreans never use honorific verb forms to describe their own actions. Compare the question and the answer in Basic Sentences 4 and 5:

Hānkwuk mal ul cal hasey yo? 'Do you speak Korean well?'
Acik cal mōs hay yo. 'I can't speak well yet.'

Ordinarily, a verb is made honorific by changing -e or -a to -usey or just adding -sey (when the verb base ends in a vowel—or a vowel + an extending -l-) before attaching the polite particle yo:

'looks for'	chac.e yo [polite]
	chac.usey yo [honorific polite]
'meets'	manna yo [polite]
	mannasey yo [honorific polite]

In a few cases, the word itself is different:

'eats'	mek.e yo [polite]
	capswusey yo [honorific polite]

Here is a list of all the verbs you have learned, in the polite style and the honorific style (arranged alphabetically according to the English).

	Polite	Honorific Polite
is bad	nappe yo	nappusey yo
barks	cic.e yo	cic.usey yo
is big	khe yo	khusey yo
closes it	tat.e yo	tat.usey yo
comes	wa yo	osey yo
cuts	pēy yo	pēysey yo
cuts (= mows)	kkakk.e yo	kkakk.usey yo
does	hay yo	hasey yo
drinks	masye yo	masisey yo / capswusey yo
eats	mek.e yo	capswusey yo
exists see is; has (got)		

are few	cek.e yo	cek.usey yo
finds	chac.e yo	chac.usey yo
gets up	il.e na yo	il.e nasey yo
gives	cwue yo	cwusey yo
goes	ka yo	kasey yo
goes to bed	ca yo	cwumusey yo
good	cōh.a yo	cōh.usey yo
has (got)	iss.ey yo	iss.usey yo
has not (got)	ēps.ey yo	ēps.usey yo
hears	tul.e yo	tul.usey yo
it is [copula]	iey yo	isey yo
(there) is; is (there)	iss.ey yo	kyēysey yo
(there) isn't; isn't (there)	ēps.ey yo	an kyēysey yo
is large	khe yo	khusey yo
learns	paywe yo	paywusey yo
listens	tul.e yo	tul.usey yo
is little (in size)	cak.e yo	cak.usey yo
is/has little (in quantity)	cek.e yo	cek.usey yo
lives	sal.e yo [sā-l-]	sāsey yo
looks at	pwa yo	posey yo
looks for	chac.e yo	chac.usey yo
are/has many	mānh.e yo	mānh.usey yo
meets	manna yo	mannasey yo
is/has much	mānh.e yo	mānh.usey yo
opens it	yel.e yo [yē-l-]	yēsey yo
plays	nol.a yo	nōsey yo
reads	ilk.e yo	ilk.usey yo
reads, sees	pwa yo, poa yo	posey yo
receives	pat.e yo	pat.usey yo
sees [someone], meets	manna yo	mannasey yo
sees [general]	pwa yo, poa yo	posey yo
sits	anc.e yo	anc.usey yo
sleeps	ca yo	cumusey yo
is small	cak.e yo	cak.usey yo
smokes	phie yo, phyē yo	phisey yo
stays	iss.ey yo	kyēysey yo
teaches	kaluchye yo	kaluchisey yo
waits for	kitalye yo	kitalisey yo
writes	sse yo	ssusey yo

As this list shows, a verb is typically made honorific by the suffix -<u>usey</u> or -<u>sey</u> before the ending <u>yo</u> (as in the words for 'learns'). But in a few cases, the word itself is different: see the words meaning 'eats,' 'goes to bed; sleeps,' 'has (got)' and 'stays.'

The ending -<u>(u)sey yo</u> is often written (and sometimes pronounced) -<u>(u)sye yo</u> [also pronounced -<u>(u)se yo</u>]. The verbs <u>iss.ey yo</u> and <u>ēps.ey yo</u> are often written (and pronounced) <u>iss.e yo</u> and <u>eps.e yo</u>. The versions with the extra -<u>y</u> before <u>yo</u> are more modern and colloquial.

Verbs with the vowel a in them (like tat.e yo) are often written with the ending -a yo ("tat.a yo") but they are usually pronounced -e yo.

The honorific part of a verb has no connection whatever with the social style being used. All the verbs in this lesson are in the polite style; some of them are honorific, and some are not. Verb forms in any of the Korean social styles can either be made honorific or left as they are, without respect to the suffixes which show the social level on which the speakers are conversing. This means that the honorific suffix can be put before the endings of ANY social style—not just the polite style—when the speaker uses the verb for the actions of an especially esteemed person.

‖ 4.3. Verbs: short negative.

To put a verb into the short negative form, you place before it one of the two negative words an and mōs. But a DESCRIPTIVE verb (translated 'is . . .') can not take the short negative with mōs in this way; instead you must use the long form that is optional for the other verbs. (The long negative form is discussed below, ‖ 7.3.)

An is an abbreviation of ani 'no'; the full form is used before the copula (ani 'ey yo 'it isn't') and before the particle yo (ani yo 'no'). It is a simple negative word meaning 'not.'

Mōs is more emphatic: it means either 'not possibly, cannot' or 'emphatically (definitely, absolutely) not; not at all.' When a verb begins with i- or y- it is usual for mōs to pick up a final -q, and the rule for -sq i- (or -sq y-) makes you pronounce it -nni- (-nny-). So when you want to say 'can't read; doesn't read at all' the form is mōsq ilk.e yo [pronounced monnilke.yo] and when you want to say 'can't open it; doesn't open it at all' the form is mōsq yel.e yo [pronounced mōnnyele.yo]. But iss.ey yo is an exception; 'can't stay' is mōs iss.ey yo [pronounced mōtisseyyo]. You may occasionally hear exceptional versions of the other verbs: mōs ilk.e yo [mōtilke.yo], mōs yel.e yo [mōtyele.yo].

Here are some examples of an and mōs:

1. Wuli ayki nun cal an ca yo.	My baby doesn't sleep well.
2. Ku kāy nun pap ul mōs mek.e yo.	The dog doesn't eat at all.
3. Nay (or Wuli) an(h)ay nun īl ul cal mōs hay yo.	My wife can't do much work.
4. I kkoch ey mul ul an cwusey yo?	Don't you water these flowers?
5. Phyēnci ka Hānkwuk ey se an wa yo.	There is no letter from Korea.
6. Poktong-i ka cip ey iss.ey yo, ēps.ey yo.	Is Poktong-i at home or isn't he?
7. Way na hako kath.i unhayng ey mōs ka yo.	Why can't you go to the bank with me?
8. Tose-kwan ey se sinmun ul mōsq ilk.e yo.	I don't read newspapers at the library.
9. Onul un sangcem ul ilccik an tat.e yo.	We don't close the store early today.
10. Ku tōn un chayk-sang mith ey se mōs chac.e yo.	You can't (=won't) find that money under the desk.
11. Haksayng tul i ku kwa lul an paywess.ey yo.	The students haven't learned that lesson.
12. Kim sensayng nim i onul an wa yo.	Mr. Kim doesn't come today.

13. Onul un swukcey ka ēps.ey yo.	There is no homework today.
14. Etteh.key yeki mōs anc.e yo? Uyca ka ēps.ey yo?	How come we can't sit here? Aren't there any chairs?
15. Pam ey kāy ka cal cic.e yo. Kulay se (cam ul) cal mōs ca yo.	At night the dog barks a lot. So I can't get much sleep.
16. An(h)ay ka ilccik an il.e na yo. Nuc.key il.e na yo.	My wife doesn't get up early. She gets up late.
17. Way i pang an ey mōs iss.ey yo?	Why can't we stay in this room?
18. Co sensayng nim i i hak.kyo se an kaluchisey yo. Eti se kaluchisey yo?	Mr. Co doesn't teach in this school. Where does he teach?
19. Yeki (ey) se to tāmpay lul mōs phiwe yo?	Can't we smoke here, either?
20. Wuli elin ay ka ce cip ai tul hako an nol.a yo.	My child doesn't play with the children of that house.
21. I kwa to ku kwa to an paywe yo.	We don't learn either this lesson or that lesson.
22. I mun ul cal mōs tat.e yo.	I can't get this door closed very well.
23. O sensayng puin ul cal mōs manna yo. Kulay se ku puin hanthey phyēnci lul cal sse yo.	I don't get the chance to see Mrs. O very much. So I write her letters quite a bit.

§ 4.4. Kinds of verbs.

Korean verbs are either PROCESSIVE or DESCRIPTIVE. Processive verbs usually mean 'does (it),' i.e. performs an action; descriptive verbs, sometimes called ADJECTIVES, usually mean 'is [a certain way],' i.e. has some characteristic. Sometimes descriptive verbs mean 'has one that is [a certain way]' as in Chayk i mānh.e yo 'I have lots of books.'

There are grammatical differences between processive and descriptive verbs, but in most ways they are alike. One of the differences is that you can use the processive verbs as commands ('do it!') and suggestions ('let's do it!'), but the descriptive verbs are limited to statements ('it is') and questions ('is it?'). To say 'let's be good' in Korean you have to turn the sentence into one that means 'let's behave nicely.' The verb iss.ey yo is peculiar: when it means 'stays' it is treated as a processive verb, but when it means 'there is' or 'has got' it is treated as a descriptive verb.

Descriptive verbs can have a SUBJECT, and sometimes two subjects: Nwu' ka chayk i iss.ey yo 'Who has the book?' Nwu' ka meli ka aphe yo 'Who has a headache?' (also said as Nwukwu uy meli ka aphe yo 'Whose head is aching?') Nay ka i kes i cōh.a yo 'I like this.' Ūmsik i mas i cōh.a yo 'The food has a good flavor = tastes good.'

Many processive verbs, on the other hand, can take a DIRECT OBJECT as well as a subject: pap ul mek.e yo 'eats one's food (or rice),' chayk ul pwa yo 'looks at (or reads) the book,' sensayng ul manna yo 'meets (up with) the teacher.' These verbs are called "transitive single-object verbs." In addition, some processive verbs can take an indirect object, marked by the particle hanthey (or eykey) for people and the particle ey for things or institutions: emeni hanthey tōn ul cwue yo 'gives one's mother some money, gives money to one's mother,' phyēnci lul unhayng ey ponay yo 'sends a letter to the bank,' chinkwu hanthey phyēnci lul sse yo 'writes a letter to a friend,' sensayng hanthey Hānkwuk mal ul paywe yo 'learns Korean from the teacher' [note the translation!]. But a few processive verbs take an indirect object with the double particle hanthey se (or eykey se) for people and the double particle ey se for things or institutions: emeni hanthey se tōn ul pat.e yo 'receives money from one's mother,' phyēnci lul unhayng ey se pat.e yo 'gets a letter from the bank,' chinkwu hanthey se phyēnci lul pat.e yo 'gets a letter from a friend.' All these verbs can be called "transitive double-object verbs."

Some processive verbs will not take a direct object; any object that may be in the English translation must be represented as a subject: tōn i iss.ey yo 'has money,' chinkwu ka ēps.ey yo 'lacks friends.' Some of them can take an indirect object, and they are called "one-object intransitive verbs": uyca ey anc.e yo 'sits on a chair,' yeki ey iss.ey yo 'stays here.' Others can take two indirect objects; typical cases of these "two-object intransitive verbs" are words for going and coming (the two objects are 'to. . .' and 'from . . .' in either order): Na hanthey emeni hanthey se phyēnci ka wa yo 'A letter comes from Mother for me.' Unhayng ey se hak.kyo ey ka yo 'It (or He etc.) goes from the bank to the school.'

The copula is a special kind of descriptive verb; it has a number of grammatical peculiarities all its own. For example, it is made negative with ani (and the Korean writing system usually treats ani 'ey yo as a single verb, the negative copula) and it never occurs with mōs, either in short or long negative constructions.

‖ 4.5. The direct object particle ul/lul.

The DIRECT OBJECT PARTICLE ul/lul is another two-shape particle, like the subject particle i/ka and the topic particle un/nun: it is pronounced ul after consonants and lul after vowels. Here are some examples:

ul after Consonant		lul after Vowel	
chayk ul	'book'	chinkwu lul	'friend'
cip ul	'house'	koki lul	'meat'
yenphil ul	'pencil'	tāmpay lul	'cigarettes'

After a vowel lul is often abbreviated to just l' especially in common expressions like na l' 'me,' i ke l' 'this thing.'

Remember that the Koreans pronounce most particles as though they were part of the preceding word, like suffixes, without hesitating—just as you pronounce sandwich-es or boy-s without stopping between the word and its suffix. If you need to pause and think what particle to use, it is better to do so before you begin to say the noun, not after you have said it. But if you find you must pause, once you have found the right particle, go back and start from the noun again: chinkwu . . . , chinkwu . . . , chinkwu lul . . .

Again like the subject and topic particles, ul/lul has no English translation. Rather, it marks a grammatical function: the noun before it is the direct object of the verb, the 'IT' of 'does IT.'

Since the subject and object particles mark their nouns as such, the order in which these expressions come along in a Korean sentence is not crucial, as it is in corresponding English sentences, where word order alone marks grammatical functions so that Mother sees Baby does not mean the same thing as Baby sees Mother:

Emeni ka ayki lul pwa yo }
Ayki lul emeni ka pwa yo } 'Mother sees Baby.'

Emeni lul ayki ka pwa yo }
Ayki ka emeni lul pwa yo } 'Baby sees Mother.'

In spoken Korean either subject or object particle may drop out, and if both are omitted the sentence may become ambiguous: Emeni ayki pwa yo and Ayki emeni pwa yo can both have two opposite meanings 'Mother sees Baby' and 'Baby sees Mother,' since Korean does not use simple order to signal subject-object relations. If only one particle drops, of course, the sentence is not ambiguous: Emeni ka ayki pwa yo and Emeni ayki lul pwa yo can only mean 'Mother sees Baby.'

A word of caution: not all English direct objects correspond to Korean direct objects. Observe these sentences:

a. Hānkwuk mal lo hay yo.
b. Hānkwuk mal ul hay yo.

Both mean 'We speak Korean,' but only the second contains a direct object in Korean; the first could be translated more literally as 'speaks in (or by means of) Korean.'

Many English verbs take objects by way of a linked preposition: sālam ul kitalye yo 'waits for a person = awaits a person.' So you can't always count on a one-to-one correspondence between transitive verbs in Korean and what are called "transitive" verbs in English.

In certain kinds of Korean sentences, as you have learned, a verb can have two subjects, i.e. two different nouns with the particle i/ka. But there is usually only one direct object to a verb. (If you find more than one, the particle ul/lul is functioning as a colloquial synonym for some other particle such as ey.)

Most often, a direct object is similar in meaning to English direct objects: chayk ul pwa yo 'reads a book,' phyēnci lul sse yo 'writes a letter.' But sometimes the particle ul/lul is used as an equivalent of ey to indicate the direction of an action: unhayng ul ka yo = unhayng ey ka yo 'goes to the bank.' And sometimes a verbal noun (i.e. a noun showing action) is used with ul/lul + a verb of going to mean 'goes for the purpose of, goes to do': kwūkyeng ul ka yo 'goes (in order) to see.' This can be regarded as an abbreviation of kwūkyeng ul hale ka yo 'goes to see' using the purposive form of hay yo 'does' to be learned in Lesson 24 (see ‖ 24.9). Another unusual type is cam ul ca yo 'sleeps (a sleep)' (see ‖ 26.3).

‖ 4.6. Verbal nouns (processive and descriptive).

The verb hay yo, as you have observed in the Basic Sentences of this lesson, is a versatile word. First of all, it means 'does' or 'performs an action,' as in the first sentence:

Wuli nun cikum mues ul hay yo. 'What are we doing now?'

Secondly, it means 'says, speaks':

3. . . . Hānkwuk mal lo hay yo. Yenge lo an hay yo. '. . . we speak (in) Korean; we don't speak (in) English.'
4. Hānkwuk mal ul cal hasey yo? 'Do you speak Korean well?'
5. Acik cal mōs hay yo. 'I can't speak well yet.'

And sometimes it means 'thinks, intends' [see ‖ 14.5 -ulq ka hay yo; ‖ 19.1; ‖ 14.9 -ulye hay yo].

There is a group of VERBAL NOUNS which form phrases with hay yo. You have now learned four of these:

2. kongpu 'study(ing)': kongpu (lul) hay yo 'studies [i.e. performs studying]'
16. sānqpo 'a walk or stroll': sānqpo (lul) hay yo 'takes [i.e. does] a walk'

23. kwūkyeng '(sight)seeing, viewing': kwūkyeng (ul) hay yo 'views, watches, sees [i.e. does (sight)seeing or viewing]'
29. īl 'work, job': īl (ul) hay yo 'works [i.e. performs work, does a job]'

The verbal noun may be the direct object of the verb hay yo or it may precede it directly, with little difference in meaning:

kwūkyeng hay yo 'watches, views'
kwūkyeng ul hay yo 'does watching/viewing = watches, views'

If the verbal noun itself is a direct object (i.e. has the particle ul/lul after it), there can be no other direct object, since, as you have just seen, a Korean sentence can ordinarily have only one. But when the verbal noun is not marked as the direct object of hay yo (e.g. kwūkyeng hay yo), the whole expression as a unit may have a direct object. This means that either of two combinations is possible:

'sees a movie'
yenghwa kwūkyeng ul / hay yo [does / movie-viewing]
yenghwa lul / kwūkyeng hay yo [watches / a movie]

'studies Korean'
Hānkwuk mal ul / kongpu hay yo [studies / Korean]
Hānkwuk mal kongpu lul / hay yo [does / Korean studies]

There are also DESCRIPTIVE verbal nouns in which hay yo means 'is' rather than 'does': kkaykkus hay yo 'is clean, neat,' chēn-chen hay yo 'is slow,' annyeng hay yo 'is at peace = well,' mian hay yo 'is uneasy.' Many of these have a special form, the DERIVED ADVERB, with hi (or its abbreviation 'i) in place of hay yo: kkaykkus 'i 'neatly,' chēn-chen hi 'slowly,' annyeng hi 'at peace = in good health.' Some descriptive verbs have the derived adverb form, too; it is usually made by detaching -(e) yo and adding -i. You have had mānh.i 'lots' from mānh.e yo 'is much / are many'; the word ppalli 'fast' comes from an adjective ppalle yo 'is fast,' and the word kath.i 'like; together' comes from the adjective kath.e(y) yo 'is similar.' Sometimes a derived adverb ends in -wu (or -o); cacwu (or caco) 'often' comes from the adjective cac.e yo 'is frequent' and palo (or palwu) 'right, directly' comes from the adjective palle yo 'is right.' Since these are derived forms, you are not free to make them; use only the ones you have heard.

4.7. Absolute use of nouns: adverbs.

The four ways in which Korean nouns are used are:

1. before particles;
2. before the copula;
3. before another noun; and
4. by themselves (absolute).

Now, in this lesson, you have some examples of the ABSOLUTE, or ADVERBIAL, use of nouns. Nouns used in absolute position are complete sentence segments by themselves, without being a part of another construction. Adverbs are nouns that typically appear in this position and never serve as subjects or objects.

The adverbs in the Basic Sentences and Supplementary Vocabulary of this lesson are:

acik 'still, yet'
cal 'well; often, a lot'
cham 'very'

cikum 'now'
com, cokum, cokom 'a little (bit)'
honca 'alone, by oneself'
hamkkey 'together'
ilccik(i) 'early'
mence 'first of all, to begin with'
nul 'always; often'

In addition to the adverbs listed above, there are a number of DERIVED ADVERBS that were mentioned at the end of the preceding note. mānh.i 'lots,' ppalli 'fast,' kath.i 'like; together,' kkaykkus i 'neatly,' chēn-chen hi 'slowly,' annyeng hi 'at peace = in good health'; cacwu 'often,' palo (or palwu) 'right, directly.'

Some of the adverbs overlap in meaning. Notice, for example, that 'like' is expressed by the particle chelem and also by kath.i; but 'together' is only kath.i (or else its synonym, the adverb hamkkey). Again, cal and mānh.i share the meaning 'many, much, a lot' but only cal means 'well' and 'often' in addition (and 'often' is also expressed by the adverb cacwu).

The adverb mānh.i and the descriptive verb mānh.e yo should not be confused with each other. The verb means 'there is much, there are many' or '[someone] has much/many'; it is equivalent to mānh.i iss.ey yo:

Chayk i mānh.e yo. = Chayk i mānh.i iss.ey yo. 'There are a lot of books.'
Chinkwu ka mānh.e yo. = Chinkwu ka mānh.i iss.ey yo. 'He has lots of friends.'

The opposite of mānh.e yo is cek.e yo 'there is little, there are few' or '[someone] has little/few.' But cek.e yo is sometimes used as a "heavy isotope" synonym of cak.e yo 'is small, little' (the opposite of khe yo 'is big, large'): Ayki ka cak.e yo only means 'She has a small baby' (or 'The baby is small') but Ayki ka cek.e yo means both that and (more commonly) 'She has few babies' (or 'The babies are few').

‖ 4.8. Particles of direction and location.

Corresponding to English 'to' are the particle ey for places and hanthey (or the less colloquial eykey) for persons:

unhayng ey 'to the bank'
kongwen ey 'to the park'
nay chinkwu hanthey (or nay chinkwu eykey) 'to my friend'
Kim sensayng hanthey (or Kim sensayng eykey) 'to Mr. Kim'

'From' is expressed by the same particles with se after them (for 'from a place' you can often say simply se):

unhayng ey se (or unhayng se) 'from the bank'
kongwen ey se (or kongwen se) 'from the park'
nay chinkwu hanthey se (or nay chinkwu eykey se) 'from my friend'
Kim sensayng hanthey se (or Kim sensayng eykey se) 'from Mr. Kim'

For places, other particles also mean 'to.' Besides ey, the particle ulo/lo sometimes also has a directional meaning (below ‖ 4.9), as does kkaci (‖ 6.4); you may hear the sequences ey lo and (especially) hanthey lo or eykey lo when the 'to' implies movement: Emeni hanthey lo ka yo 'He goes to his mother.' And sometimes the direct-object particle ul/lul is used with the meaning 'to,' either by itself or following ey: hak.kyo (ey) lul ka yo 'goes to school.' When both ey and lul are used together, more emphasis is directed toward the word representing the goal (here 'school'). The combination is often abbreviated: hak.kyo ey l' ka yo.

Corresponding to English 'in, at, on,' as you learned in Lesson 3, is the particle ey '(being) at,' with or without some specific word of location in front of it. This is a particle of STATIC location: something IS in (at, on) a place. For DYNAMIC location, when something HAPPENS in (at or on) a place, Koreans use the particle se '(happening) at' or the combination ey se. These particles have the same English translation as ey but are used when the verb denotes an action. Here are some examples:

Cip ey iss.ey yo. 'He is at home.'
Cip ey se mek.e yo. 'He eats at home.'
Kim sensayng i hak.kyo ey kyēysey yo. 'Mr. Kim is at school.'
Kim sensayng i hak.kyo (ey) se kaluchisey yo. 'Mr. Kim teaches at school.'

With some verbs either ey or (ey) se is used: Sewul ey sal.e yo, Sewul (ey) se sal.e yo 'lives in Seoul.' But with most verbs only one of the alternatives is possible: iss.e yo 'is, stays' and anc.e yo 'sits' take only ey.

Notice that (ey) se also means 'from': hak.kyo (ey) se wa yo 'comes from school.' Traditional Korean grammars treat ey se as one word (eyse) and consider se (in these uses) as an abbreviation of eyse. Our treatment is based on the analogy with hanthey se (or eykey se) 'from a person': emeni hanthey se wa yo 'comes from one's mother.' You may be interested to know that se comes from an old Korean form sye (infinitive of an old verb si-/isi-) equivalent to modern Korean iss.e (infinitive of the verb iss-). In bookish Korean today you will sometimes see ey-iss.e for ey se.

4.9. More new particles: kwa/wa (= hako), ulo/lo, and chelem.

Kwa/wa means 'with' or 'and,' just like the more colloquial particle hako; but hako is a one-shape particle and kwa/wa is a two-shape particle which is pronounced kwa after consonants and wa after vowels:

After consonants	After vowels
chayk kwa 'and a book'	congi wa 'and paper'
ku sālam kwa 'and him'	nay chinkwu wa 'and my friend'
sensayng kwa 'and the teacher'	wuli wa 'and us'

Like other particles, it is pronounced as though it were part of the word before it. This means that if you are going to pause between nouns linked by kwa/wa, you pause AFTER the word for 'and' instead of BEFORE it as we do in English:

congi wa . . . chayk kwa . . . yenphil 'paper . . . and books . . . and a pencil'

Once two or more nouns have been linked with this particle, the group as a whole is followed by whatever particle is necessary to show its relation to the rest of the sentence. For example:

yenphil kwa congi nun 'pencil and paper [as topic]'
ape' nim kwa eme' nim i 'father and mother [as subject]'
sangcem kwa [l]yekwan ul 'the store and the hotel [as object]'

But sometimes kwa/wa is added after the last noun before putting on the relational particle: yenphil kwa congi wa nun. The adverb kath.i (or hamkkey) means 'together' or 'like'; when it follows noun-plus-kwa/wa or noun-plus-hako, the whole phrase means 'together with [so-and-so]' or simply 'with [so-and-so].' The noun in these expressions usually denotes a person or other living being:

ape' nim kwa kath.i or ape' nim hako hath.i '(together) with Father'
nay chinkwu wa kath.i or nay chinkwu hako '(together) with my friend'
kāy wa kath.i or kāy hako kath.i '(together) with the dog'

'With' a person, then, is kwa/wa or hako. In English, when we say 'with' plus the name of an object, we are often using 'with' in a different sense, namely 'by' or 'by means of': I wrote this with a pencil. This 'with' is the Korean particle ulo/lo. You have also seen ulo/lo with the names of languages, to mean 'in [i.e. by means of] that language'—Hānkwuk mal lo 'in Korean,' Yenge lo 'in English.' This is a two-shape particle which is pronounced ulo after all consonants except l, but lo after l:

After most consonants	After vowels and l
chayk ulo 'with a book'	congi lo 'with paper'
mues ulo 'with what'	mue lo 'with what' [also muel lo]
payk.muk ulo 'with chalk'	yenphil lo 'with a pencil'
sengnyang ulo 'with matches'	Yenge lo 'in English'

The particle ulo/lo has a variety of meanings:

1. MANNER: '-ly, with, as'	Yelqsim ulo kongpu lul hay yo. 'He studies with zeal (= zealously).'
2. FUNCTION: 'as, for, in the capacity of'	Senkyo-sa lo Hānkwuk e iss.ey yo. 'He is in Korea as a missionary.'
3. DIRECTION: 'toward, to, in the direction of'	Palun phyen ulo kasipsio. 'Go to the right.'
	Eti lo kasey yo. 'Where are you headed?'
4. MEANS: 'with, by, by means of'	I phyēnci lul yenphil lo sse yo. 'I'm writing this letter with a pencil.'
	Pihayng-ki lo kasey yo? 'Are you going by plane?'

And there are a number of other meanings you will learn later (see ‖ 19.8).

The particle chelem means 'like': na chelem 'like me,' sensayng chelem 'like the teacher.' The word kath.i, in addition to meaning 'together' also means 'like': na kath.i = na chelem, sensayng kath.i = sensayng chelem. Why, then, isn't kath.i called a "particle?" Because it is a special form, the derived adverb from the descriptive verb kath.e(y) yo 'is similar, is like'; you can say Na nun sensayng kath.ey yo 'I am like the teacher' and Sensayng i na kath.usey yo 'The teacher is like me.' We treat this as an abbreviation of . . . kwa/wa kath.e(y) yo, for that form occurs in less colloquial speech. Thus we treat na kath.i as an abbreviation of na wa kath.i; the latter can have two meanings in less colloquial speech, 'together with me' (= na wa hamkkey) and 'like me' (= na chelem), but it usually means only 'together with me' in more colloquial usage.

‖ 4.10. The particle to.

The particle to [often pronounced twu] has only one shape regardless whether it follows a vowel or a consonant. You have seen this particle in Basic Sentence 18:

. . . Kāy to . . . latio lul tul.e yo. 'The dog listens to the radio too.'

To means 'too, also, indeed, even.' It reinforces the emphasis on the word before it, with reference to something earlier in the context: in Basic Sentence 18, for example, 'I listen to the radio' is followed by the statement that 'the dog too listens to the radio.'

The English words that correspond to the particle to fall most naturally at the end of the sentence, so that they may be widely separated from the word they belong with, as in the example above, and as in this one:

Ku haksayng to cikum hak.kyo se Hānkwuk mal ul kongpu hay yo. 'That student is studying Korean in school now too.'

In a negative sentence, English substitutes 'either' for 'too':

Yenphil i iss.ey yo. Chayk to iss.ey yo. 'I have a pencil; I have a book too.'
Yenphil i ēps.ey yo. Chayk to ēps.ey yo. 'I haven't got a pencil; I haven't got a book either.'

The natural position of 'too' and 'either' frequently results in ambiguity: the sentence I gave Mr. Kim a book too can be interpreted in three ways:

1. I, too, gave Mr. Kim a book [and so did someone else].
2. I gave a book to Mr. Kim [as well as giving one to Mr. Han].
3. I gave Mr. Kim a book [in addition to giving him something else].

Korean sentences are not open to this kind of ambiguity, however, since the particle to immediately follows the phrase to which it refers:

1. Na to Kim sensayng hanthey chayk ul cwue yo. 'I, too, am giving Mr. Kim a book.'
2. Na nun Kim sensayng hanthey to chayk ul cwue yo. 'I'm giving a book to Mr. Kim also.'
3. Na nun Kim sensayng hanthey chayk to cwue yo. 'I'm giving Mr. Kim a book too.

Negative sentences work the same way:

1. Na to Kim sensayng hanthey chayk ul an cwue yo. 'I'm not giving Mr. Kim a book either.'
2. Na nun Kim sensayng hanthey to chayk ul an cwue yo. 'I'm not giving a book to Mr. Kim either.'
3. Na nun Kim sensayng hanthey chayk to an cwue yo. 'I'm not giving Mr. Kim a book either.'

When you use the particle to with a noun, you do not use the particles that would mark that same noun as topic, subject, or direct object; notice how to takes the place of those particles:

Na nun Mikwuk salam iey yo. 'I'm an American.'
Na to Mikwuk salam iey yo. 'I'm an American too.'

Yenphil i iss.ey yo? 'Have you a pencil?'
Yenphil to iss.ey yo? 'Have you a pencil too?'

Chayk ul ilk.e yo. 'I read books.'
Chayk to ilk.e yo. 'I read books too.'

This means that some sentences with to are ambiguous out of context: Ayki to pwa yo can mean either 'The baby sees it [or her etc.] too' or '[She etc.] sees the baby too.' You can clear up the ambiguity by adding context: Emeni ka ayki to pwa yo 'The mother sees the baby too,' Emeni lul ayki to pwa yo 'The baby sees the mother too.' You can, however, use to after any of the other particles. For example, hak.kyo ey se to means 'at school also' or 'from school also'; Kim sensayng hanthey to means 'to Mr. Kim'; and so on.

Two occurrences of to in the same Korean sentence often correspond to English 'both . . . and . . .' or, in a negative sentence, '[not] either . . . or . . .':

Yenphil to congi to iss.ey yo. 'There are both pencils and paper.'
Yenphil to congi to ēps.ey yo. 'There aren't any pencil or (any) paper (either).'
Achim ey to pam ey to īl hay yo. 'I work both in the morning and at night.'
Achim ey to pam ey to īl an hay yo. 'I don't work either in the morning or at night.'
Yenphil lo to mānnyen-phil lo to an sse yo. 'I don't write either with a pencil or with a pen.'
Mikwuk ey se to Ilpon ey se to wa yo. 'They come both from America and from Japan.'
Mikwuk ey se to Ilpon ey se to an wa yo. 'They don't come either from America or from Japan.'
Cip to path to iss.ey yo. 'I have both a house and a garden.'
Cip to path to ēps.ey yo. 'I have neither a house nor a garden.'

English 'both,' of course, is limited to two, so that if a Korean sentence has more than two cases of to, we no longer translate the first one with 'both'; we may use 'all' with the last one (or 'none' in a negative sentence):

Kim sensayng to, Pak sensayng to, Cang sensayng to wa yo. 'Mr. Kim and Mr. Pak and Mr. Chang are all coming.'
Kim sensayng to, Pak sensayng to, Cang sensayng to an wa yo. 'Mr. Kim isn't coming, and neither is Mr. Pak or Mr. Chang.'
Chayk-sang to uyca to chilphan to iss.ey yo. 'There's a table and a chair and a blackboard (all three).'
Chayk-sang to uyca to chilphan to ēps.ey yo. 'There isn't any table or chair or blackboard (none of them).'

This particle should not be confused with the adverb tto; see ‖ 7.6.

‖ 4.11. Particle sequences.

A topic in a Korean sentence (i.e. a phrase ending with the particle un/nun) is most often a noun or noun phrase. But it may also be another particle phrase—an expression of time, place, manner and so on—such as achim ey 'in the morning,' hak.kyo ey se 'from (or at) school,' mānnyenphil lo 'with a pen,' yenphil lo 'with a pencil,' etc. When such a phrase becomes a topic, the result is a sequence (or string) of particles, the last one being the topic particle un/nun:

Achim ey nun, kongpu hay yo. 'In the mornings, I study [as contrasted with what I do the rest of the time].'
Hak.kyo ey se nun, Hānkwuk mal ul kongpu hay yo. 'At school, we study Korean.' [Talking about what happens at school . . . we study Korean there.]
Mānnyen-phil lo nun, phyenci lul sse yo. 'With a pen, I write letters.' [in answer to the question 'What do you do with a pen?']

These phrases, like other topics, are DEEMPHASIZED. They are set aside at the beginning; the fact that they have un/nun at the end means that the important part of the sentence is elsewhere. They act either (1) as stage setting—announcing the time, place, etc., of the rest of the sentence; (2) as repetition, for clarity, of something mentioned earlier in the context; or (3) to emphasize a contrast, since playing down the topic highlights the importance of the contrasting feature following it.

Other particle sequences you have observed end with to in much the same way; for to, the particle of reinforced emphasis, is directly opposite in meaning to un/nun, the particle of deemphasis.

Particles which do NOT enter into sequences with to or with un/nun are i/ka the subject particle and ul/lul the direct-object particle. A subject or object which is being deemphasized simply has the topic particle.

Hānkwuk mal ul kaluchye yo?—Ani yo?? Hānkwuk mal un Kim sensayng i kaluchye yo. 'Do you teach Korean?—No, it's Mr. Kim who teaches Korean.' [Do you teach Korean?—No, if it's Korean, Mr. Kim (is the one who) teaches it.]

Pam ey nun mues ul hay yo.—Chayk ul pwa yo.—Phyēnci nun an sse yo? 'What do you do in the evenings?—I read books.—How about letters: don't you write (any)?'

Similarly, to appears INSTEAD OF i/ka or ul/lul, not in combination with them:

Chayk i iss.ey yo?—Nēy, iss.ey yo.—Yenphil to iss.ey yo? 'Have you a book? —Yes. I have.—Have you a pencil too?'

Chayk ul pwa yo.—Sinmun to pwa yo? 'I read books.—Do you read newspapers too?'

This means that some sentences with deemphasized elements (. . . un/nun) and reemphasized elements (. . . to) are ambiguous, like sentences in which the subject (i/ka) or direct object (ul/lul) particle is dropped: Emeni ayki pwa yo 'The mother, the baby—someone looks at someone,' Emeni nun ayki nun pwa yo 'The mother, guess-what; the baby, guess-what—SOMEONE LOOKS AT SOMEONE,' Emeni to ayki to pwa yo 'The mother too, the baby too—someone looks at someone' (1. Both mother and baby look at someone; 2. Someone looks at both mother and baby; 3. The mother, too, looks at the baby, too; 4. The baby, too, looks at the mother, too). Ambiguity can usually be cleared up by marking either the subject or the object with what remains understood as the unmarked one; but it is not possible in Korean to specify the subject or object and at the same time reemphasize or deemphasize it.

EXERCISES

I

Fill in the following blanks with the noun-plus-particle expressions indicated below each sentence. Say the complete Korean sentence out loud

1. Every evening I read ____.
   - a magazine
   - the newspaper
   - both a magazine and the newspaper
   - letters
   - a Chinese book
   - an English newspaper and a Russian newspaper
   - some American magazines

2. My mother gives me ______.
   - a radio
   - a bookcase
   - some meat
   - both cigarettes and matches
   - a notebook
   - some money
   - pencils and paper

3. In the afternoons I see ______.
   - both the garden and the park.
   - the doctor and his wife
   - a movie
   - both Mrs. Kim and Mrs. Pak
   - the teacher
   - my friends
   - a lot of students

II

Here is a list of phrases. Express each one in Korean, then build a complete Korean sentence around it; practice your sentences aloud.

1. to the movies
2. from Rev. Pak
3. in the house
4. at the railroad station
5. on the floor
6. with a fountain pen
7. to my friend
8. from school
9. in the morning
10. at home
11. on Tuesdays
12. with my parents
13. to the park
14. from my father
15. in this room
16. at a hotel
17. on the blackboard
18. with chalk
19. to the drugstore
20. in the garden

III

Here is an English sentence with two blanks in it. Express the sentence in Korean 14 times, each time using one of the verb expressions from the list below in the blanks—the same verb in both blanks, speaking honorifically of course when you refer to the other person's actions.

Father is ______ and I'm ______ too.

1. closing windows
2. drinking some water
3. getting some money
4. getting up
5. going to the store
6. learning English
7. listening to the radio
8. looking at a magazine
9. playing with the baby
10. seeing a movie
11. smoking a cigarette
12. speaking Korean
13. waiting for the doctor
14. working

Now, proceed in the same way with this sentence:

The teacher isn't ______ and I'm not ______ either.

1. going to school
2. eating breakfast

3. giving books to the students
4. going to bed
5. living with his parents
6. meeting a friend
7. mowing the lawn
8. opening the door
9. reading the newspaper
10. sitting in a chair
11. staying home
12. taking a walk in the park
13. teaching Russian
14. writing letters
15. opening the window

IV

Translate the following sentences into Korean.

1. What are you doing now?
2. I'm looking at a picture. In the picture there's a dog.
3. Well, what's the dog doing?
4. It's listening to the radio. It's sitting beside a child. The child is listening to the radio too.
5. Have you a dog? Where is it now? What's it doing?
6. My dog is playing in the park. He plays by himself. He comes home by himself too. He's very good.
7. Is your dog big, (or) is he small?
8. He's little. He still can't bark. But he eats lots of meat. He drinks water a lot, too.
9. I'm waiting for my dog. But he is (comes) late.
10. I'm going to the park. I'll look for the dog.
11. I'll go to the park with you. I'll look for the dog too.
12. How do you get to the park?
13. From in front of our house you go left. The park is across from the post office.
14. My father works at the post office. He gets lots of letters.
15. But he doesn't write letters at all.
16. And on Sundays he stays at home.
17. What does he do at home? Does he mow the lawn? Does he play with you and the dog?
18. No. He just reads. What does your father do?
19. He is a school teacher. He teaches English.
20. Sunday morning he goes to church. And Sunday evenings he goes to the park for a walk.
21. Who does he walk in the park with?
22. He walks with (my) mother. She looks at the flowers.
23. At our house there's a student living with us now.
24. He gets up early. And he goes to bed late.
25. He studies hard (well). He learns a lot.

CONVERSATION

Hold brief conversations, two by two, along the following outlines. Don't be shy about making up answers; sometimes a fictional situation is more interesting than a real one. Just keep your fictional situation consistent.

1. A asks B what he customarily does at various times of the day, beginning with 'What do you do in the mornings?' and ending by asking whether he goes to bed

early or late. A should find out also whether B does these same things on Saturdays and Sundays as well as on weekdays, and B should tell what he does differently on the weekends.

2. C asks D whether he is working now and D says no he's going to school. By further questioning, C learns what languages D is studying, whether or not he can speak them well yet, who the teacher is, where he studies, whether he studies alone, etc. etc.

3. E asks F for directions around the city: how to get to various public buildings, where the parks, stores, movie houses are, and so on. F gives clear and exact replies to every question and supplies all the helpful information he can. Use the blackboard to draw maps and diagrams if necessary. The word for map is cito: Cito lul sse cwusipsio means 'Please draw me a map.' The word for 'street' or 'road' is kil. The word for 'corner' is mo-thwungi, but sometimes nēy-keli 'cross-roads, intersection' is a better word to use in giving directions.

VOCABULARY DRILL

Express the sentences below in Korean, filling in the blank space with each of the expressions listed beneath the sentence. Say the complete sentence aloud each time. Rearrange or add words if you can make better sentences by doing so.

1. I _____ in the mornings.

can't study	get some money	play with the cat
can't take walks	go to the bank	read the paper
come home	go to the park	read my letters
don't go to the movies	get up early	stay home
don't mow the lawn	learn Russian	speak English
don't eat meat	listen to the radio	study with my friend
don't smoke cigarettes	look for my dog	teach Chinese
drink lots of water	meet my friends	work at the post office
eat breakfast	open the window	

2. I write letters _____.

at night	late	Saturdays
early	on Friday mornings	Tuesday afternoons
fast	on Sundays	Thursday evenings
first	slowly	usually
in the afternoon	Monday mornings	Wednesday afternoons
in the daytime		

COMPREHENSION

Listen carefully while your Korean teacher reads the following conversation aloud to you—two or three times. Make sure you understand the meaning of every sentence. Then, with your teacher reading the part of Mr. Pak, supply Mr. Kim's answers. You are not expected to commit these answers to memory, but only to supply sentences which are sensible, and in correct Korean.

Pak sensayng. Kim sensayng eti ka yo?
Kim sensayng. Hak.kyo ey ka yo.

Pak sensayng. Hak.kyo ey se mues ul hay yo?
Kim sensayng. Hānkwuk mal ul kongpu hay yo.

Pak sensayng. Hānkwuk mal kongpu nun ōhwu ey hay yo?
Kim sensayng. Ani yo?? Achim ey hay yo.

Pak sensayng. Achim ey ilccik il.e na yo?
Kim sensayng. Nēy. Achim ey cham ilccik il.e na yo.

Pak sensayng. Pōthong ōhwu ey nun mues ul hay yo?
Kim sensayng. Kongwen ey se sānqpo lul hay yo.

Pak sensayng. Ku taum, cip ey wa yo?
Kim sensayng. Ani yo?? Cip ey nun cenyek nuc.key wa yo.

Pak sensayng. Pam ey nun mues ul hay yo.
Kim sensayng. Pōthong chinkwu wa kath.i yenghwa lul kwūkyeng hay yo.

Pak sensayng. Nul yenghwa kwūkyeng ul hay yo?
Kim sensayng. Ani yo?? Cwuil nal pam ey nun chayk ul pwa yo.

Pak sensayng. Phyēnci nun an sse yo?
Kim sensayng. Pōthong ulo an sse yo.

Pak sensayng. Ilcciki cwumusey yo?
Kim sensayng. Nēy. Ilcciki ca yo.

LESSON 5. REVIEW

I. VOCABULARY REVIEW

A. In each of the following groups of six Korean words, five have meanings which are related to each other, while there is one which doesn't belong. Read aloud all the words in each group; then name the misfit.

1. na
   nwukwu
   tangsin
   an(h)ay
   wuli
   ku sālam

2. capci
   chayk
   congi
   kong-chayk
   cikum
   sinmun

3. chinkwu
   nwukwu
   etten kes
   mues
   eti
   enu kes

4. onul
   mence
   Wel-yoil
   yoil
   Mok-yoil
   Cwuil

5. yeki
   mith ey
   palun phyen
   sai ey
   cēki
   pyek

6. Yenge
   Hānkwuk mal
   Mikwuk salam
   Cwungkwuk mal
   Ilpon mal
   [1]Nosea mal

7. cik.kong
   swupyeng
   pyēnho-sa
   uysa
   moksa
   namphyen

8. cwi
   pitwulki
   kwāyngi
   kāy
   pay
   sāy

9. chayk-sang
   sangcem
   swunkyeng
   sang
   kūlim
   chayk-cang

10. paywe yo
    kongpu hay yo
    sānqpo hay yo
    sse yo
    kaluchye yo
    ilk.e yo

11. mul
    sōk
    pakk
    wi
    an
    aph

12. cip
    [1]yeypay-tang
    [1]yekwan
    yak
    hak.kyo
    kongcang

13. congi
payk.muk
hako
mānnyen-phil
yenphil
chilphan

14. namu
phul
ttul
kkoch
chāyso
swuph

15. pumo
puin
apeci
ai
eme' nim
tā

B. Now, here are some groups of three Korean words each—all of similar meanings. Your task is to supply two or three additional Korean words for each group which match the meanings of the words in the original group.

1. sensayng
senkyo-sa
kwun.in

2. cengke-cang
unhayng
hak.kyo

3. ōhwu
achim
nac

4. mun
yuli chang
malwu

5. cwuwi
twī
taum

6. Yengkwuk
Solyen
Mikwuk

7. an(h)ay
ayki
apeci

8. Kum-yoil
Tho-yoil
Hwā-yoil

9. ca yo
il.e na yo
mek.e yo

II. PARTICLE REVIEW

A. Here are 15 sentences with all the particles replaced by blank spaces. Say each sentence aloud, putting in the particles that are appropriate for each blank. (Remember that when you pause in your speech to think what particle to use, pause before you say the noun—not between noun and particle!) You will find that some sentences can be completed in more than one appropriate way.

1. Hak.kyo _____ Hānkwuk mal _____ kongpu hay yo.
2. Na _____ Tho-yoil _____ kongwen _____ sānqpo _____ hay yo.
3. Nwu(kwu) _____ sensayng iey yo. Ce sālam _____ sensayng iey yo.
4. Cwuil nal _____ sensayng nim _____ ilcciki il.e na yo?
5. Cenyek _____ cip _____ mues _____ hay yo. Pōthong _____ phyēnci _____ sse yo.
6. Cip _____ mues _____ posey yo? Sinmun _____ capci _____ pwa yo.
7. Onul achim _____ na _____ cip _____ kongpu _____ hay yo.

8. Ku sālam _____ nac _____ pam _____ chayk _____ ilk.e yo.
9. Cenyek _____ phyēnci _____ sse yo, capci _____ pwa yo?
10. Tho-yoil _____ chinkwu _____ phyēnci _____ wa yo.
11. I yenphil _____ Kim sensayng _____ yenphil iey yo, ku puin _____ yenphil iey yo? [ku puin = ku (sālam) uy puin 'his wife']
12. Unhayng _____ ape' nim _____ musun īl _____ hay yo.
13. Kim sensayng _____ hak.kyo _____ Hānkwuk mal _____ kaluchye yo.
14. Ku phyēnci _____ Kim sensayng _____ sse yo, ku puin _____ sse yo?
15. I uyca _____ nwukwu _____ uyca 'ey yo.

B. Here is a list of noun-plus-particle phrases. Build a Korean sentence around each phrase, and practice saying your sentence aloud so it comes out smooth and fast. The exercise will do you more good if you write nothing down.

apeci hanthey se
chinkwu wa
yenphil lo
chayk-sang ey
ce sālam uy
cāngkyo wa
Cwungkuk mal lo to
Cwuil nal ey nun
chinkwu hanthey to
eme' nim uy
hak.kyo ka
Ilpon mal lo
i kyōsil ey
i congi nun
kyōsil ey se
ku sālam un
kūlim to sacin to
ku pang ey se nun
kkoch hako
kyōhoy to
koki lul
kongcang to yak-pang to
mues i
Pak sensayng uy

mānnyen-phil lo nun
Mikwuk salam i
ˡNoseaq salam hanthey
namu mith ey se
namu mith ey
nay chinkwu hanthey se
namu lul
pumo nim kwa
pul un
Pak sensayng to Kim sensayng to
phyēnci lul
sengnyang hako
sensayng nim eykey se to
sinmun ul
sāmu-sil ey se
sinmun to
uysa hanthey
wuphyen-kwuk ey to
Yengkwuk salam eykey
yak to
ˡyeypey-tang ey se to
yenghwa-kwan ey se nun
yuli chang ey se

III. VERB REVIEW

A. Express each of the following brief questions aloud in Korean; then answer your own question negatively. Assume in each case that the person you are talking about is someone for whom you wish to show special respect. The first one, for example, will be the Korean equivalent of: Is he studying English? No, he's not studying English.

Is he studying English?
Is he sleeping?
Is he learning Russian?
Is he looking for his book?
Is he at home?

Is he waiting for his friend?
Is he living along?
Are there many Koreans here?
Is he sitting on the bed?
Is he watching a movie?

Is he a doctor?
Does he get many letters?
Is he speaking Japanese?
Is he staying here?
Does he take walks in the park?
Does he listen to the radio much?
Does he work in the post office?
Is he mowing the lawn?
Is he a minister?
Is he reading his letters?
Is he at the office now?

B. Now, ask and answer the following group of questions aloud in Korean <u>without</u> showing special respect for the person you are referring to.

Is he listening to the radio?
Does he play with his children?
Does he get up early?
Is he at home now?
Is he Korean?
Is he studying Chinese?
Does he usually get lots of letters?
Does he usually go to bed late?
Is he learning English?
Is he looking for his fountain pen?
Does he meet his friend in the park?
Is he waiting for his wife?
Does he live with his parents?
Does he go to the movies much?
Is he sitting in the classroom?
Does he close the windows in the morning?
Is he a lawyer?
Is he reading a book?
Is he at the bank now?
Does he come home early?
Does he usually go to work late?

C. Repeat the ANSWERS to the questions in A and B above, making them mean '<u>can't</u> do so-and so' whenever possible.

D. Express the following group of questions aloud in Korean and answer them by using a verb of different or opposite meaning: for example, <u>Is it large? No, it's small. Is he reading? No, he's writing.</u>

Is the classroom large?
Are there many students?
Are you teaching Korean?
Is he getting up?
Is that child good?
Is he reading the newspaper?
Is he working?
Is he opening the door?
Is he giving Mrs. Kim some money?
Is he eating meat?
Is he going home
Does he listen to the teacher('s words)?
Does he usually stay home?

E. Now repeat the sentences of D above — questions and answers — changing them so that they refer to someone highly esteemed.

IV. SENTENCE REVIEW

A. <u>Korean-English</u> — Here are 50 Korean sentences, using the vocabulary and constructions you have learned in the first four lessons. Read each one aloud, then translate it into English. In your English, convey the meaning of the Korean but without necessarily making a word-for-word translation.

1. Sikan i tā tōyss.ˢup.nita. Sīcak hapsita.
2. Onul un Hwā-yoil iey yo.
3. Ku sālam un sensayng iey yo? Ani yo?? Haksayng iey yo.
4. Cikum mues ul hasey yo? Sinmun ul pwa yo.

5. I kong-chayk i nwukwu uy kong-chayk iey yo? Nay kong-chayk iey yo.
6. Eti se Hānkwuk mal kongpu lul hasey yo? I kyōsil ey se hay yo.
7. Eti kasey yo? Hak.kyo ey ka yo.
8. Cenyek ey nun sānqpo lul hasey yo? Nēy. Hay yo.
9. Yenge lo hasipsio. ¹Nosea mal lo haci masipsio.
10. Na nun cham nuc.key il.e na yo. Tto nuc.key ca yo.
11. Hak.kyo ey an kasey yo? Nēy, onul un mōs ka yo.
12. Ku yenphil i Ilpon mal sensayng uy yenphil iey yo.
13. Pōthong ilcciki cwumusey yo? Nēy. Pōthong ilcciki ca yo.
14. Cenyek ey nun kongpu lul an hay yo.
15. Ilpon mal lo haci māsipsio. Cwungkwuk mal lo hasipsio.
16. Ōhwu ey mues ul hasey yo. Pōthong un capci lul namu mith ey se ilk.e yo.
17. Mues ul pwa yo. Pyek ul pwa yo.
18. Ce sālam i Mikwuk salam i ani 'ey yo? Nēy. Yengkwuk salam iey yo.
19. Achim ey ku sangcem ey se sinmun ul pwa yo.
20. I mānnyen-phil i ¹Nosea mal sensayng uy mānnyen-phil i ani 'ey yo?
21. Hānkwuk mal ul kaluchye yo? Ani yo?? Yenge lul kaluchye yo.
22. Eti se kaluchye yo? Hak.kyo ey se kaluchye yo.
23. Wuli cip pakk ey nun kkoch path kwa chāyso path i iss.ey yo.
24. Māyn twī(q) pang ey se nwu' ka cwumusey yo?
25. Taum(q) pang i kyōsil iey yo, sāmu-sil iey yo?
26. Pōthong ulo kongpu lul hak.kyo ey se hay yo, cip ey se hay yo. Cip ey se hay yo.
27. Kāy ka iss.ey yo? Nēy, iss.ey yo. Kwāyngi to iss.ey yo.
28. Cikum ape' nim i tayk ey kyēysey yo? Nēy, kyēysey yo.
29. Cip aph ey se ai tul i nol.a yo.
30. Mok-yoil ey nun nay ka yenghwa kwūkyeng ul mōs ka yo.
31. Eti se phyēnci lul sse yo? Pōthong cip ey se sse yo.
32. Ce uyca nun Hānkwuk mal sensayng uy uyca 'ey yo.
33. Chayk un nac ey pwa yo, pam ey pwa yo. Pam ey pwa yo.
34. Yuli chang kwa mun sai ey nun mues i iss.ey yo. Kūlim i iss.ey yo.
35. Chilphan i sāmu-sil ey iss.ey yo, kyōsil ey iss.ey yo. Kyōsil ey iss.ey yo.
36. Kyōsil ey nun payk.muk to iss.ey yo.
37. Cip an ey nwu' ka iss.ey yo? Eme' nim i kyēysey yo. Ai to iss.ey yo?
38. Hak.kyo ey se kongpu hasey yo? Nēy. Cip ey se to hay yo.
39. Cwuil nal un pōthong ilcciki il.e nasey yo? Ani yo?? Cwuil nal un nuc.key il.e na yo.
40. Chayk-sangq sōk ey mues i iss.ey yo. Yenphil hako congi ka iss.ey yo.
41. Ku sang wi ey nun musun chayk i iss.ey yo.
42. Cikum nwukwu lul kitalisey yo. Ape' nim hako eme' nim ul kitalye yo.
43. Pōthong ulo hak.kyo ey se palo cip ey ka yo.
44. Kum-yoil ōhwu ey nun wuphyen-kwuk aph ey se chinkwu lul manna yo.
45. Pōthong yeki se haksayng tul ul kitalisey yo, hak.kyo ey se kitalisey yo.
46. Ce chayk-sangq sōk ey nun congi ka cham mānh.i iss.ey yo.
47. Chayk-sang palo mith ey chayk i ēps.ey yo?
48. Kim sensayng kwa Pak sensayng sai ey nwu' ka anc.e yo. Mā sensayng i anc.e yo.
49. Cenyek ey nuc.key cip ey osey yo? Ani yo?? Nuc.key an wa yo. Pōthong ilcciki wa yo.
50. Cwuil nal achim ey namu mith ey se chayk ul ilk.e yo.

B. English-Korean — Now, here are 50 English sentences for you to put into Korean. Practice them aloud until you can say each one smoothly.

1. Please don't look at your books; just listen.
2. Excuse me, I don't understand. Please say it again.
3. What's that in front of you? It's my book.
4. Where's the Korean teacher? She's in the office.
5. Are you American or English? I'm English.
6. What are you doing here? I'm waiting for my friend.
7. Whose pencil is that next to the notebook? It's mine.
8. Are there pencils and chalk in the classroom? Yes, there are.
9. There is also a blackboard and some paper.
10. Is your wife going to Korea with you? Yes, she is.
11. Who's sitting in front of you? My friend Mr. Ma.
12. What's that thing way over there? It's a tree.
13. Why are you learning Japanese? I'm going to Japan.
14. Have you any cigarettes? Yes, there are both cigarettes and matches on my desk.
15. Just to the left of the window there's a bookcase.
16. Do you read magazines or books in the evening? I usually read the newspaper first.
17. There are doors in the room; but there aren't any windows.
18. Do you live with your parents? No, I live with a friend.
19. Have you got a pen? I'm sorry, I haven't either a pen or a pencil.
20. Where is your vegetable garden? It's way back of the house.
21. Is the flower garden in front of the house or beside it?
22. There are both flower gardens and vegetable gardens around the house.
23. Don't speak English, speak Korean.
24. What are you doing? I'm looking for my dog.
25. Mr. Kim doesn't smoke either at home or at his office.
26. I can't go to the movies with you this evening.
27. I stay home in the evenings. And I go to bed early.
28. Are there many flowering trees in Korea? Yes, a great many. But there aren't many in England.
29. Mr. Kim teaches Korean in the United States. And Mr. Pak teaches English in Korea.
30. Are you learning Japanese at school? No, I'm learning Chinese; but I can't speak it well yet.
31. Have you got any paper in your briefcase? Yes, here's some.
32. I haven't got either matches or cigarettes. Have you got (any)?
33. Is your house large? No, it's not large at all; it's very small.
34. But there are many trees, both to the right and to the left of the house.
35. What kind of trees are they? They're flowering trees.
36. I always go to bed late. And I always get up early.
37. There are woods around our house. In the woods there are many birds and squirrels.
38. Have you got a cat? No, we haven't got either a dog or a cat.
39. I work at a factory daytimes, and at night I read books at the library.
40. I meet my friend in front of this store on Friday evenings. Then we go to the movie.
41. Dogs and cats are both big.
42. Dogs are big; but squirrels are small.

43. Squirrels are small; and birds are small too.
44. Neither birds nor squirrels are big.
45. Do you usually go for walks in the park by yourself? No, I usually go with a friend of mine (= 'my friend').
46. My dog is little. He can't bark yet. Cats can't bark either!
47. I cut the grass early in the mornings. There is a lot of grass around our house.
48. I eat breakfast very early (in the morning). Then I cut the grass.
49. I drink a lot of water. But I don't eat much meat.
50. Time's up; let's rest for ten minutes.

V. PERSONAL SKETCH

Give, orally, a personal sketch of yourself in Korean—as full as possible with the vocabulary and constructions you have learned. Tell who you are, where you live and with whom, what your profession is, what sorts of things you do during the course of an average week.

You should prepare your talk by practicing aloud; you should not write it out in Korean. If you want to make notes, jot them down in English to remind yourself of what you are planning to say.

Remember that these exercises are just for practice; if you want to embroider a bit—or even create an entirely fictional new personality for yourself,—go ahead and string the class along as far as they will let you.

VI. KOREAN CONVERSATION

Practice the following conversations aloud, taking turns with the roles. Speak them as naturally and easily as you can; sound as much like a native Korean speaker as you can. Make sure you know what each sentence means.

I

Sensayng. Annyeng hasip.nikka?

Haksayng. Nēy. Komapsup.nita.

Sensayng. Sikan i tā tōyss.ˢup.nita. Sīcak hapsita.

Haksayng. Nēy. Sīcak hapsita.

Sensayng. Onul un Yenge lo haci māsipsio. Hānkwuk mal lo hasipsio.

Haksayng. Nēy? Mian hap.nita. Han pen te māl hay cwusipsio.

Sensayng. Hānkwuk mal lo hasipsio. Āsikeyss.ˢup.nikka?

Haksayng. Nēy. Āp.nita.

Sensayng. I chayk i nwukwu uy chayk iey yo. Tāytap hasipsio.

Haksayng. Kim sensayng uy chayk iey yo.

Sensayng. Cōh.sup.nita. Ce kong-chayk i Kim sensayng uy kong-chayk iey yo?

Haksayng. Ani yo?? Ku kong-chayk un ce haksayng uy kong-chayk iey yo.

Sensayng. I hak.kyo sensayng i nwukwu 'ey yo. Yengkwuk salam tul iey yo?

Haksayng. Ani yo?? Tā Mikwuk salam iey yo.

Sensayng. Cōh.sup.nita. Sikan i tā tōyss.ˢup.nita. Sip-pun ccum swīsipsita.

Haksayng. Tto pōypkeyss.ˢup.nita.

II

Kim sensayng. Pak sensayng eti kasey yo.

Pak sensayng. Hak.kyo ey ka yo.

Kim sensayng. Hak.kyo ey se mues ul hay yo.

Pak sensayng. Hānkwuk mal ul kongpu hay yo.

Kim sensayng. Achim ey ilcciki il.e na yo?

Pak sensayng. Nēy. Achim ey cham ilcciki il.e na yo.

Kim sensayng. Hānkwuk mal kongpu nun ōhwu ey to hay yo?

Pak sensayng. Ani yo?? Ōhwu ey nun kongwen ey se sānqpo lul hay yo. Pōthong ulo cip ey nuc.key ka yo.

Kim sensayng. Pam ey nun mues ul hay yo. Yenghwa kwūkyeng ul kasey yo?

Pak sensayng. Ani yo?? Pōthong ulo cip ey iss.ey yo. Chayk hako capci lul pwa yo.

III

Kim sensayng. Cikum eti lul ka yo.

Pak sensayng. Wuphyen-kwuk ey ka yo.

Kim sensayng. Wuphyen-kwuk ey se īl ul hay yo?

Pak sensayng. Nēy. Na nun wuphyen-kwuk ey se īl hay yo. Ōhwu ey to wuphyen-kwuk ey se īl hay yo.

Kim sensayng. Tayk ey nuc.key kasey yo?

Pak sensayng. Ani yo?? Pōthong ilcciki wa yo. Cip ey se kongpu lul hay yo.

Kim sensayng. Musun kongpu lul cip ey se hay yo.

Pak sensayng. Hānkwuk mal ul kongpu hay yo.

Kim sensayng. Pam ey nun mues ul hasey yo.

Pak sensayng. Pōthong ulo capci lul pwa yo.

Kim sensayng. Sinmun to posey yo?

Pak sensayng. Sinmun un achim ey pwa yo.

Kim sensayng. Phyēnci lul an sse yo?

Pak sensayng. Pōthong un an sse yo.

IV

Kim sensayng. Sensayng nim i hak.kyo ey se mues ul kaluchye yo.

Pak sensayng. Cwungkwuk mal ul kaluchye yo. Sensayng nim un mues ul kaluchye yo?

Kim sensayng. Na nun Ilpon mal ul kaluchye yo.

Pak sensayng. Eti se kaluchye yo?

Kim sensayng. Hak.kyo ey se kaluchye yo.

Pak sensayng. Na to hak.kyo ey se kaluchye yo. Kyōsil ey se haksayng tul ul manna yo.

Kim sensayng. Cikum na nun chinkwu lul kitalye yo. Wel-yoil achim ey yeki se kitalye yo.

Pak sensayng. Ku chinkwu nun nwukwu 'ey yo?

Kim sensayng. Mā sensayng iey yo. Mā sensayng to hak.kyo ey se kaluchye yo.

Pak sensayng. Cēki ce sālam i sensayng nim uy chinkwu 'ey yo?

Kim sensayng. Nēy. Cēki Mā sensayng i wa yo.

VII. FREE CONVERSATION

1. Assume the role of a stranger in a roomful of students. Get acquainted with them by explaining who you are and what you are doing there, and asking each person in turn who he is and what his profession is. Find out what each person is studying, and where he studies.

2. Draw up a list of Korean true-false questions—at least half a dozen—about the layout of your classroom. (For example: The window is opposite the door. Mrs. X sits between Mr. A and Mr. B.) Ask each student in turn a question, to which he will answer either 'Yes' or 'No,' preferably with a full sentence. While you keep score on your fellow students, your teacher will keep score on you.

3. Draw a simple sketch of a house with its surrounding buildings and natural features. Without letting anyone see it, describe it in Korean to the other members of the class and have them reproduce your sketch simply through hearing your statements of what is to the right and to the left of what else, where this building is in relation to that building, etc., etc. When you have finished, the correspondence between your original drawing and those of the other class members will be an indication of your own speaking and the others' comprehension.

LESSON 6. COUNTING THINGS

BASIC SENTENCES

Korean	English	Amplification
1. Ēncey osyess.ey yo.	When did you get here?	ēncey 'when?' osyess.ey yo '[someone esteemed] came'
2. Meychil cen ey wass.ey yo.	I got here several days ago.	meychil or myechil 'how many days; some (several) days' cen 'before' meychil cen 'several days ago or back (earlier)' wass.ey yo 'came'
3. Tāyhak ey se Hānkwuk mal ul paywe yo.	I'm studying Korean at the University.	tāyhak 'university, college'
4. Hānkwuk mal ul ēncey puthe sīcak hasyess.ey yo.	When did you start Korean?	ēncey puthe 'from when?' hasyess.ey yo '[someone esteemed] did' sīcak hasyess.ey yo '[someone esteemed] began or started'
5. Cīnan cwuil puthe sīcak hayss.ey yo.	I began last week.	= I started from last week cīnan . . . 'last . . . , the past . . .' cwuil 'week' sīcak hayss.ey yo 'started, began'
6. Achim mata meych si ey hak.kyo ey kasey yo.	What time do you go to school every morning?	. . . mata 'each (every). . .' achim mata 'every morning' meych or myech 'how many?; several, some a certain number' . . . si 'hour, o'clock' meych si '[how many o'clocks? =] what time?' meych si ey '(at) what time?'
7. Nal mata yetelq si ccum ka yo. Yetelq si sip-pun ey kongpu lul sīcak hay yo.	I go around eight o'clock. At 8:10 we begin the class ('the study').	nal mata or māyil 'every day' yetel(p) 'eight' yetelq si 'eight o'clock' yetelq si ccum 'about eight o'clock'

		sip (=yel) 'ten' pun 'minute' yetelq si sip-pun '[8 o'clock 10 minutes=] 8:10'
8. Meych si ey kongpu ka kkuth na yo.	What time is class over?	kkuth 'end, termination' na yo 'it comes/goes out, it is produced' kkuth na yo 'it ends, comes to an end, stops, is over'
9. Ōhwu sēy si cēngkak ey kkuth na yo.	It's over at three o'clock sharp.	sēys, sēy . . . 'three' sēy si 'three o'clock' . . . cēngkak 'exactly on the hour' sēy si cēngkak 'three o'clock sharp, exactly three o'clock'
10. Ōcen yetelq si puthe ōhwu sēy si kkaci hak.kyo ey iss.ey yo.	We're in school from eight a.m. to three p.m.	ōcen 'morning, forenoon' yetelq si puthe 'from eight o'clock . . . kkaci '(all the way up) [a time or place]; until, till [a time]' sēy si kkaci 'until three o'clock'
11. Kulem, halwu ey meych sikan ssik ina hak.kyo ey se kongpu lul hasey yo.	Then, about how many hours a day do you study at school?	halwu 'one day, a day' sikan 'hour('s time); time' . . . ssik 'each . . . . apiece' . . . ina 'it is but [is it?]' = 'about/approximately . . . ; . . . or the like' meych sikan 'how many hours?' meych sikan ssik 'how many hours (each)?' meych sikan ssik ina 'about how many hours (each)?' meych ina '(about) how many; several'
12. Phyengkyun tases sikan ssik kongpu lul hay yo.	On the average I study about five hours each (day).	phyengkyun '(on) the average' tases 'five' tases sikan 'five hours' tases sikan ssik 'five hours apiece'
13. Cikum meych si 'ey yo.	What time is it now?	

	Korean	English	Amplification
14.	Cikum ōhwu twū si pān iey yo. Pān sikan hwū ey kongpu ka kkuth na yo.	It's 2:30 in the afternoon now. In half an hour the class is over.	twūl, twū . . . 'two' twū si 'two o'clock' pān (. . .) 'half' . . . pān 'and a half' twū si pān '2:30' twū sikan pān 'two and a half hours' pān sikan 'half an hour' hwū 'after' pān sikan hwū ey '[after=] in half an hour'
15.	Nal mata hak.kyo ey kasey yo?	Do you go to school every day?	
16.	Ani yo?? Wel-yoil puthe Kum-yoil kkaci man hak.kyo ey ka yo. Tho-yoil kwa Il-yoil ey nun an ka yo.	No. I go to school just from Monday to Friday. On Saturday and Sunday I don't go.	. . . man 'only/just . . .' Kum-yoil kkaci man 'only until Friday'
17.	Hānkwuk mal haksayng tul i meych salam ina iss.ey yo.	How many Korean students are there?	= The Korean students are about how many people? meych salam 'how many people; several (some) people'
18.	Han yel myeng iss.ey yo.	There are around ten.	han . . . 'about approximately . . .' yel 'ten' . . . myeng '(counted persons)'
19.	Hānkwuk mal sensayng i meych ina iss.ey yo.	How many Korean (language) teachers have you?	
20.	Hānkwuk mal sensayng un nēys i iss.ey yo.	We have four Korean teachers.	nēys, nēy . . . 'four'
21.	Ēncey kkaci yeki se Hānkwuk mal ul kongpu hasey yo.	Till when do you study Korean here?	ēncey kkaci 'till when?'
22.	Elmaq tong-an yeki se Hānkwuk mal ul kongpu hasey yo.	(For) how long will you study Korean here?	elma 'how much' tong 'a period, an interval' tong-an 'length <u>or</u> duration of time' elmaq tong-an '[how much (length of) time?=] how long?'
23.	[1]Naynyen Ō-wel kkaci kongpu hay yo.	We'll study till next May.	[1]naynyen 'next year' kumnyen 'this year' cak.nyen 'last year'

Korean	English	Amplification
		Ō-wel(q tal) '[fifth month =] May' [1]naynyen Ō-wel 'may of next year'
24. Ecey ka musun yoil iess.ey yo.	What day (of the week) was yesterday?	ecey 'yesterday' yoil 'day of the week' . . . iess.ey yo 'it was . . .'
25. Ecey nun Il-yoil iess.ey yo. Kulay se, cip ey se swiess.ey yo.	Yesterday was Sunday; so I rested at home.	swie yo 'rests' swiess.ey yo 'rested'
26. Onul i meychil iey yo.	What day (of the month) is today?	meychil 'how many days' or 'what (numbered) day? how many-eth day? what date?'
27. Onul un Sī'-wel sam-il iey yo.	Today's the third of October.	Sī'-wel(q tal) '[tenth month =] October' sam (=sēys) 'three' sam-il 'day number three, third day'
28. [1]Nayil un Sī'-wel sā-il iey yo. Nay sayngil iey yo.	Tomorrow is October 4th. It's my birthday.	[1]nayil 'tomorrow' sā (=nēys) 'four' sā-il 'fourth day, day number four' sayngil 'birthday'
29. Cenyek yeses si ey wuli cip ey osey yo.	Please come to my house at six o'clock.	yeses 'six' yeses si 'six o'clock' yeses si ey 'at six o'clock' osey yo 'an esteemed person comes; come!'
30. Son nim i han yelq salam wa yo.	About ten guests are coming.	=Guests, about ten people are coming. son (nim) 'guest' yel 'ten' yelq salam 'ten people' han yelq salam 'about ten people'
31. Han cwukan un meychil iey yo.	A week is how many days?	hana, han . . . 'one' cwukan 'week' han cwukan 'one week, a week'
32. Han cwukan un iley 'ey yo.	A week is seven days.	iley 'seven days'
33. Il-nyen un meych tal iey yo.	A year is how many months?	il (= hana) 'one' il-nyen 'one year, a year' tal 'month' meych tal 'how many months?'

Korean	English	Amplification
34. Il-nyen un yelq twū tal iey yo.	One year is 12 months.	yelq twūl, yelq twū . . . 'twelve' yelq twū tal '12 months'
35. Ī-nyen cen ey catong-cha lul sass.ey yo.	I bought a car two years ago.	ī (= twūl) 'two' ī-nyen 'two years' cen 'before' ī-nyen cen ey '[before two years =] two years ago <u>or</u> back' catong-cha 'automobile, car' sa yo 'buys' sass.ey yo 'bought'

SUPPLEMENTARY VOCABULARY

	PRIMARY NUMERALS		SECONDARY NUMERALS
	Ordinary Pronunciation	Pronunciation before Nouns	
'1'	hana	han	il
'2'	twūl	twū	ī
'3'	sēys	sēy/sēk	sam
'4'	nēys	nēy/nēk	sā
'5'	tases	[same]	ō
'6'	yeses	[same]	ˈyuk
'7'	ilkop	[same]	chil
'8'	yetel(p)	yetel(q)	phal
'9'	ahop	[same]	kwu
'10'	yel	yel(q)	sip
'11'	yel hana	yel han	sip-il
'12'	yelq twūl	yelq twū	sip-i
'13'	yelq sēys	yelq sēy/sēk	sip-sam
'14'	yel nēys	yel nēy/nēk	sip-sa
'15'	yelq tases	[same]	sip-o
'16'	yel yeses	[same]	sip-ˈyuk [simnyuk]
'17'	yel ilkop	[same]	sip-chil
'18'	yel yetel(p)	yel yetel(q)	sip-phal
'19'	yel ahop	[same]	sip kwu
'20'	sumul	sumu	ī-sip
'21'	sumul hana	sumul han	ī-sip il
'22'	sumulq twūl	sumulq twū	ī-sip ī
'23'	sumulq sēys	sumulq sēy/sēk	ī-sip sam
'24'	sumul nēys	sumul nēy/nēk	ī-sip sā
'30'	selun	[same]	sam-sip
'33'	selun sēys	selun sēy/sēk	sam-sip sam
'40'	mahun	[same]	sā-sip
'44'	mahun nēys	mahun nēy/nēk	sā-sip sā
'50'	swīn	[same]	ō-sip

'55'	swīn tases	[same]	ō-sip ō
'60'	yeyswun	[same]	^{l}yuk-sip
'66'	yeyswun yeses	[same]	^{l}yuk-sip ^{l}yuk [yukssimnyuk]
'70'	ilhun	[same]	chilq-sip
'77'	ilhun ilkop	[same]	chilq-sip chil
'80'	yetun	[same]	phalq-sip
'88'	yetun yetel(q)	[same]	phalq-sip phal
'90'	ahun	[same]	kwu-sip
'99'	ahun ahop	[same]	kwu-sip kwu
'100'	—		payk; il(q)-payk
'200'	—		ī-payk
'300'	—		sam-payk
'400'	—		sā-payk
'500'	—		ō-payk
'600'	—		^{l}yuk-payk
'700'	—		chil-payk
'800'	—		phal-payk
'900'	—		kwu-payk
'1,000'	—		chen; il-chen
'10,000'	—		mān; il-man
'60,000'	—		^{l}yuk-man
'100,000'	—		sip-man
'1,000,000'	—		payk-man

Counters Used with Primary Numerals

si	o'clock
sikan	hours
tal*	months
hay	years
sal	years of age
salam	people
pun	esteemed people
myeng	persons, people (impersonal)
kwen	bound volumes
mali	animals, fish, birds
pen	times
cang*	flat objects, newspapers, sheets, pages, leaves
can*	cupfuls
chay	buildings
tay	vehicles, mounted machines
kay	items, units, objects
kaci	kinds, varieties, abstract things

Counters used with Secondary Numerals

(-)pun	minutes
(-)il	days

---

* When the primary numerals for 3 and 4 are used with these counters they are pronounced sēk and nēk respectively.

(-)kaywel	months(' time or duration)
(-)^{n}yen/-nyen	years
(-)wel(q tal)	month names
(-)chung	floors (of a building)
(-)wen	money unit: dollar, wen, yen
(-)cen	money unit: cent, sen
(-)^{l}i	Korean mile ('li') = 1/3 US mile

Counting Days

meych nal, meychil	'how many days?'
halwu	1 day
ithul	2 days
sahul	3 days
nahul	4 days
tas-say	5 days
yes-say	6 days
iley	7 days
yetuley	8 days
ahuley	9 days
yelhul	10 days
yel halwu	11 days
yel ithul	12 days
yelq sahul	13 days
yel nahul	14 days
yelq tas-say	15 days
yel yes-say	16 days
yel iley	17 days
yel yetuley	18 days
yel ahuley	19 days
sumu nal	20 days

Above 20, the secondary numerals are more common:

ī-sip il '20 days'
ī-sip il-il '21 days' etc.

Below 20, the secondary numerals are also used, but usually only for dates:

ō-il 'the 5th day of the month' etc.

Counting Weeks

cwuil	week
cwukan	week('s time)

Weeks are counted with either primary or secondary numerals:

han cwuil or ilq-cwuil	one week
twū cwuil or ī-cwuil	two weeks
sēy cwuil or sam cwuil	three weeks
han cwukan or ilq-cwukan	one week('s time)
twū cwukan or ī-cwukan	two weeks(' time)
sēy cwukan or sam-cwukan	three weeks(' time)

Counting Months

meych tal <u>or</u> meych kaywel	how many months?
han tal <u>or</u> il-kaywel	one month
twū tal <u>or</u> ī-kaywel	two months
sēk tal <u>or</u> sam-kaywel	three months
etc.	etc.

Naming Months

musun tal <u>or</u> meych wel	what month?
Il-wel(q tal) <u>or</u> Cengwel	January
Ī-wel(q tal)	February
Sam-wel(q tal)	March
Sā-wel(q tal)	April
Ō-wel(q tal)	May
Yu'-wel(q tal)	June
Chil-wel(q tal)	July
Phal-wel(q tal)	August
Kwu-wel(q tal)	September
Sī'-wel(q tal)	October
Sip.il-wel(q tal)	November
Sip.i-wel(q tal) <u>or</u> Sēt-tal	December

Counting Years

meych hay <u>or</u> meych nyen	how many years
han hay	one year
twū hay	two years
sēy hay	three years
nēy hay	four years
tases hay	five years
yeses hay	six years
ilkop hay	seven years
yetelp hay [yetelphay]	eight years
ahop hay	nine years
yel hay	ten years
sumu hay	twenty years
payk hay	100 years
payk sumu hay	120 years

Counting or Naming Years

meych nyen	what year? (e.g. 1970)
musun/enu hay	what year? (e.g. the Year of the Dragon)
il-nyen	one year; Year One
ī-nyen	two years; Year Two
sam-nyen	three years; Year Three
sā-nyen	four years; Year Four
ō-nyen	five years; Year Five
[l]yuk-nyen	six years; Year Six
chil-nyen	seven years; Year Seven
phal-nyen	eight years; Year Eight
kwu-nyen	nine years; Year Nine

sip-nyen	ten years; Year Ten
ī-sip nyen	twenty years; Year Twenty
payk-nyen	100 years; Year 100
payk ī-sip nyen	120 years; Year 120

NOTES

6.1. Numbers and counting.

The Koreans have two sets of numerals. One of these (il, ī, sam . . .) they borrowed from the Chinese; the other set is native (hana, twūl, sēys . . .).

Up to 99, both sets are used. For units of 100 and above, only the Chinese set is used; but in compound numbers (like 121) you will hear both (payk ī-sip il and payk sumul hana).

In general, the numerals above 10 are combinations of the first ten: 11 is 10 + 1 (yel hana; sip-il), 12 is 10 + 2 (yelq twūl; sip-i), and so on. The Korean numerals 20, 30, 40, etc., are special words, but in the Chinese system, 20 is 2 × 10 (ī-sip), 30 is 3 × 10 (sam-sip), etc.

Each of the Korean numerals from 1 to 4 (hana, twūl, sēys, nēys) and 20 (sumul) is peculiar in this respect: when used right before the word it is counting, the numeral drops its last sound. Here are some common examples:

hana 'one'	han salam 'one person'
	han kay 'one object'
	han si 'one o'clock'
twūl 'two'	twū salam 'two people'
	twū kay 'two objects'
	twū si 'two o'clock'
sēys 'three'	sēy salam 'three people'
	sēy kay 'three objects'
	sēy si 'three o'clock'
nēys 'four'	nēy salam 'four people'
	nēy kay 'four objects'
	nēy si 'four o'clock'
sumul 'twenty'	sumu salam 'twenty people'
	sumu kay 'twenty objects'

In place of twū . . . 'two' you will sometimes hear ˈyāng . . . 'both,' especially with things that ordinarily come in pairs.

You may wonder why we link some of the secondary numerals together (with other secondary numerals or with counters) by a hyphen, when the corresponding primary numerals are written separately with a space. This is just a convention we follow, based in part on a general trend of words borrowed from Chinese: one-syllable words tend to be bound (that is, limited in their combinations). Han . . . 'one . . .' can occur in front of thousands of nouns, but il- . . . 'one. . .' is limited to a few counters and special noun compounds (Cf. mono- and uni- in English). The conventions will be clear from these examples:

sip-wen	'10 wen'
sam-sip wen	'30 wen'
sam-sip sam-wen	'33 wen'
payk-wen	'100 wen'
payk sip-wen	'110 wen'

payk sam-sip wen '130 wen'
payk sam-sip sam-wen '133 wen'

In English we can say either two cows or two head of cattle; but if we are counting, say, dogs, we have but one choice: two dogs. Koreans use both types of construction widely, but they often prefer the latter type: kāy twū mali 'two dogs.' The word mali is a special kind of COUNTER that we call a CLASSIFIER, because it classifies nouns for counting purposes according to some common characteristic: things counted with mali are non-human living beings, things counted with cang are thin flat sheet-like things, and so on.

Other kinds of counters are MEASURES, used to tell how much there is of something that can be measured out by the cupful, the kilogram or pound, the mile (of distance), the dollar or wen (of money), etc. English has measures, like Korean, and also a few classifiers (such as 'head' for cattle), but Korean has more of these than English has. That is why there is no ready English equivalent for the classifiers in chayk sēy kwen 'three [volumes of] books,' cip sēy chay 'three [buildings of] houses.'

As the list in the Supplementary Vocabulary shows, there are some counters which go with the Korean numerals and others which require the Chinese numerals. The distinction is sometimes crucial, as in the case of pun:

han pun 'one esteemed person'	il-pun 'one minute'
twū pun 'two esteemed people'	ī-pun 'two minutes'
sēy pun 'three esteemed people'	sam-pun 'three minutes'

When you are using particles with numerical expressions, you enjoy a certain amount of freedom as to where you can put the particle in the sentence. By NUMERICAL EXPRESSION we mean either a numeral by itself or a numeral plus a classifier. Another way of stating this is to say that numerical expressions have the same four usages as other noun expressions:

1. They modify other nouns:
   Twū chayk i iss.ey yo. 'There are two books.'
   Twū kwen (uy) chayk i iss.ey yo. 'There are two (volumes of) books.'
2. They have particles after them:
   Chayk twūl i iss.ey yo. 'There are two books.'
   Chayk twū kwen i iss.ey yo. 'There are two (volumes of) books.'
   Twūl i iss.ey yo. 'There are two.'
   Twū kwen i iss.ey yo. 'There are two (volumes).'
3. They are used as adverbs (cf. ‖ 4.7):
   Chayk i twūl iss.ey yo. 'There are two books.'
   Chayk i twū kwen iss.ey yo. 'There are two (volumes of) books.'
4. They are used before the copula:
   Chayk i twūl iey yo. '[The books are two =] There are two books.'
   Chayk i twū kwen iey yo. '[The books are two volumes =] There are two books.'

Here are some examples of numerical expressions in sentences:

1. I pang an ey nun yuli chang ilkop kay ccum iss.ey yo. — There are about seven windows in this room
2. Ce chayk-sang wi ey chayk nēy kwen kwa capci sēy kwen i iss.ey yo. — There are four books and three magazines on that desk.

3. Nay ka wuphyen-kwuk aph ey se catong-cha yeses tay lul pwass.ey yo.	I saw six cars in front of the post office.
4. Sinmun ul sēk cang sass.ey yo.	I bought three newspapers.
5. Kongwen taum ey sangcem i twūl (or twū chay) iss.ey yo.	There are two stores next to the park.
6. Catong-cha han tay man iss.ey yo.	We have only one car.
7. Ilpon pyengceng nēy salam ul pwass.ey yo.	I saw four Japanese soldiers.
8. Kyōsil ey uyca ka meych kay 'na iss.ey yo.	How many chairs are there in the classroom?
9. Sēk tal hwū ey Yengkwuk ey ka yo.	I'm going to England in ['after'] three months.
10. Ku secem i meych chung iey yo.	How many floors is the bookshop? or Which floor is the bookshop?
11. Chāyso sēy kaci cwusey yo.	Please give me three [kinds of] vegetables.

6.2. Numerals in time expressions.

To tell time in Korean, you use the primary numerals followed by si 'o'clock':

han si	'one o'clock'
tases si	'five o'clock'
yelq twū si	'twelve o'clock'

To say 'half past . . .' you put . . . pān '. . . and a half' AFTER this expression:

han si pān	'1:30'
tases si pān	'5:30'
yelq twū si pān	'12:30'

A specific number of minutes after the hour is expressed by the SECONDARY numerals with (-)pun 'minute' after the expression:

han si sip-pun	'1:10' [one o'clock 10 minutes]
tases si sip-o pun	'5:15' [five o'clock 15 minutes]
yelq twū si ī-sip sam-pun	'12:23' [twelve o'clock 23 minutes]

To express the number of minutes BEFORE the hour, you use the same expression but add cen 'before' at the end:

han si sip-pun cen	'10 minutes to one' [one o'clock 10 minutes before]
tases si sip-o pun cen	'quarter to five' [five o'clock 15 minutes before]

For a.m. and p.m., you use achim or ōcen 'morning,' ōhwu 'afternoon,' or pam 'night' at the BEGINNING of the expression.

ōcen sēy si (or achim sēy si)	'three o'clock in the morning'

ōhwu nēy si — 'four o'clock in the afternoon'
pam ahop si pān — 'half past nine in the evening'

Si means 'hour' only in the sense of a POINT in time, an 'o'clock.' For length or DURATION of time, sikan 'hour' is used (as you know, sikan also means 'time in general'):

Yeses sikan īl hayss.ey yo. — 'I worked (for) six hours.'
Meych sikan īl hayss.ey yo. — 'How many hours did you work?'
Nal mata tases sikan pān ssik kongpu hay yo. — 'I study for five and a half hours every day.'

As explained in the Supplementary Vocabulary, weeks are counted with either set of numerals.

Dates are given in Korean by proceeding from the longest to the shortest time element; we do the opposite in English. For example:

Chen kwu-payk ō-sip ī-nyen, Sī'-wel sip-il, Kum-yoil, ōhwu sēy si sip-o pun '3:15 p.m., Friday, 10 October 1952.' This breaks down to:

Chen | kwu-payk | ō-sip | ī-nyen '1952' [thousand | nine-hundred | fifty | two-year]

Sī'-wel | sip-il '10 October' [October | ten-day]

Kum-yoil 'Friday'

ōhwu | sēy si | sip-o pun '3:15 p.m.' [afternoon | three o'clock | fifteen minutes]

As you can see in the lists, there are irregular forms for counting days. The word meychil is not, as you might think made up of meych + -il (the bound Chinese element meaning 'day') but rather of meych + a variant of -hul, an old Korean bound element meaning '(counted) day' which you will find at the end of ithul 'two days,' sahul 'three days,' nahul 'four days,' and yelhul 'ten days.'

6.3. Some particles often used in connection with numbers.

a. Mata 'each, every'

Mata is a particle that means 'each' or 'every.'

Achim mata sinmun ul sa yo. 'I buy a paper every morning.'
Sensayng mata achim ey ilccik-i il.e na yo? 'Does every teacher get up early in the morning?'

With time expressions, mata is more normally expressed in English by the indefinite article 'a(n)': nal mata yetelq sikan '[every day eight hours =] eight hours a day.' (But to say 'three days a week' han cwuil ey sahul is more natural than cwuil mata sahul.)

b. Man 'only; just'

Man, on the other hand, restricts the noun expression it follows. It limits the meaning of the noun to 'no more than' what is specified:

I kes man iss.ey yo. '[There is only this =] This is all there is.'
Na man ka yo. '[Only I am going =] I'm the only one who's going.'

(Be careful not to use tā to translate 'all' in a sentence like the first example.)

When man follows a noun, the subject, topic, and object particles (i/ka, un/nun, ul/lul) are not normally used with the same expression:

Chayk man iss.ey yo. 'There are only books.'
Kim sensayng man wa yo. 'Only Mr. Kim is coming.'
Kongpu man hay yo. '[I am doing only studying=] I'm only studying.'

But occasionally you will run across such combinations as . . . man i, . . . man ul, and . . . man un. And man may be used at the end of other noun-plus-particle expressions, as follows:

Wuphyen-kwuk ey man ka yo. 'I'm going only to the post office.'
Hānkwuk mal lo man hasipsio. 'Speak only in Korean.'
Kongwen ey se man sānqpo lul hay yo. 'I only take walks in the park.'
Kim sensayng hanthey se man phyēnci ka wa yo. 'Letters come only from Mr. Kim.'

When man is used in sentences with numerical expressions, its meaning is to limit the amount to what is specified. Here are some examples:

Twū sikan man kongpu hayss.e yo. 'I studied for two hours.'
[Man limits the time to two hours: 'Two hours is the length of time I studied.' 'I studied for two hours but not longer.']
Chayk yelq kwen man sass.e yo. 'I bought ten books.' [Man indicates that ten is exactly the number of books bought.]

In this latter sense, man represents a shade of meaning which usually goes unexpressed in English; it contrasts in meaning with the particles ina/'na and ccum, discussed below.

c. Ssik 'each, apiece'

The particle ssik is readily translatable as 'each' or 'apiece'; but this is another common particle which is very often unexpressed in corresponding English sentences:

Pam mata yetelq sikan ssik ca yo. '[Every night I sleep eight hours each=] I sleep eight hours a night.'

Ssik is used at the end of numerical expressions, but it refers back to some other element in the sentence. This may be a subject or object; it may be a time expression generalized with mata:

Nal mata sēy sikan ssik kongpu hay yo. 'I study for three hours every day [apiece].'
Unhayng ey se nal mata meych sikan ssik ina īl hay yo? 'How many hours [apiece] a day do you work at the bank?'

d. Ina/'na 'about, approximately'

Koreans are often less precise about numbers than speakers of English are. Thus, such words as ina (usually pronounced 'na after vowels) are often used with numerical expressions to make them sound vaguer and hence less abrupt:

Nal mata meych sikan ssik ina īl ul hay yo? '(About) how many hours a day do you work?'

Ina comes from a form of the copula iey yo, but it behaves much like a particle. When used after an interrogative word (nwukwu 'who?,' mues 'what?,' and other words that ask questions) ina removes the interrogative meaning and generalizes the scope of the word, as follows:

nwukwu 'who?'	nwukwu 'na 'anyone, everyone'
mues 'what?'	mues ina 'anything; everything'
ēncey 'when?'	ēncey 'na 'any time; all the time'
elma 'how much?'	elma 'na 'some amount; any amount'
meych 'how many?'	meych ina 'some number; any number'
eti 'where?'	eti 'na 'anywhere; everywhere'
etten . . . 'what . . .?'	etten [chayk] ina 'some [book]; any [book]'
enu . . . 'which . . .?'	enu [phyen] ina 'either [way]'

The combination ssik ina, commonly used after numerical expressions, means 'about [so-and-so many] each': meych sikan ssik ina 'about how many hours each?' For other uses of ina, see ‖ 18.3.

e. Ccum 'about, approximately; by'

The particle ccum is used with time expressions. When the time expression refers to a POINT in time, ccum means 'at about [that time]':

meych si ccum '(at) about what time?'
yelq si pān ccum '(at) about ten-thirty'

With expressions referring to DURATION of time, ccum means 'by [that time]' or 'for about [that length of time]':

nēy sikan ccum '(for) about four hours'
ˈnayil ccum 'by tomorrow'

It is not unusual for the Koreans to reinforce the indefiniteness of their numerical expressions by doubling up the particles ccum and ina:

meych si ccum ina 'at about what time?'
meych sikan ccum ina 'for about how many hours?'

Han . . . 'about, approximately' used at the BEGINNING of a numerical expression has the same meaning as ina and/or ccum at the END of it as in Basic Sentence 18:

Han yel myeng iss.ey yo. 'There are about ten people.'

Be careful not to confuse this han . . . , which is ALWAYS FOLLOWED BY A NUMERICAL EXPRESSION, with han . . . the short form of hana 'one' which is ALWAYS FOLLOWED BY A NOUN OR A COUNTER.

Han 'about, approximately' is often used in combination with a particle of the same meaning, reinforcing the imprecise character of the expression:

Eceyq pam han ī-sip myeng ccum wass.ey yo. 'About twenty people were here [came] last night.'

Han twū si ccum wuli cip ey wa yo. 'He comes to our house about two o'clock.'

‖ 6.4. The particles puthe 'from' and kkaci 'to.'

You have learned ways of saying 'from' (ey se) and 'to' (ey), and this lesson introduces others: the particles puthe 'from' and kkaci 'to.'

Puthe 'from' is used with either TIME or PLACE expressions, but with place words it must be preceded by ey se:

tases si puthe 'from 5 o'clock'
cip ey se puthe 'from home'

Ey se 'from' or '(happening) at,' on the other hand, is used only in PLACE expressions: cip ey se 'from home' or '(happening) at home.' Puthe is often used to translate 'at' in time expressions with 'begin' (though ey may be used in these expressions): Yelq si puthe/ey sīcak hay yo. 'We begin at 10 o'clock.' Kkaci, also used with both TIME and PLACE expressions, means 'to' in the sense 'as far as' or 'up to' or 'until.' Ey with time expressions, you recall, means 'AT or IN that time': cenyek ey 'in the evening,' pam ey 'at night'; and with place expressions it means either '(being) IN, AT, ON that place'—static location, as in cip ey iss.ey yo 'he's at home,' uyca ey anc.e yo 'sits on the chair,' kongwen ey iss.ey yo 'it's in the park'—or 'TO that place': hak.kyo ey ka yo 'goes to school.' When referring to people, you will recall, 'to' is hanthey or eykey and 'from' is hanthey se or eykey se: Chinkwu hanthey se sensayng hanthey phyēnci ka wass.ey yo. 'A letter came to the teacher from a friend.'

Here are some more examples of puthe and kkaci in sentences:

1. Na nun Hānkwuk ey se (puthe) Cwungkwuk kkaci ka yo.	I'm going from Korea to China.
2. Hak.kyo ey se nun ˡnayil puthe sīcak hay yo.	[At school, we start from tomorrow=] School starts tomorrow.
3. Unhayng ey se nun achim ahop si puthe īl ul sīcak hay yo.	I start work at the bank every morning at nine o'clock.
4. Twū si puthe nēy si kkaci sāmu-sil ey se kongpu hayss.ey yo.	I studied in the office from two o'clock till four o'clock.
5. Achim puthe pam kkaci īl ul hay yo.	I work from morning till night.

‖ 6.5. Verbs: past tense, polite style.

Korean verb forms, as you know, are made up of bases with endings on them. The present-tense forms you have learned are all in the POLITE STYLE and have the particle yo at the end to mark the style. If you remove this yo (and change any final -ey to -e), the part that remains is what we call the INFINITIVE of the verb. The Korean infinitive has a great many uses of its own (discussed below in Lesson 8), and in addition it is what the PAST TENSE is based on.

Here is an alphabetical list of all the verbs you have learned, in the infinitive form:

anc.e	'sits'	chac.e	'looks for; finds'
ca	'goes to bed; sleeps'	cic.e	'barks'
cac.e	'is frequent'	cōh.a	'is good'
capswusye	'[someone esteemed] eats'	cwumusye	'[someone esteemed] goes to bed'
cak.e	'is little'	cwue	'gives'
cek.e	'is small, are few'	ēps.e	'is nonexistent'

hay	'does' [IRREGULAR]	palle	'is right'
il.e na	'gets up'	ppalle	'is fast'
ilk.e	'reads'	pat.e	'receives, gets'
iss.e	'is, exists; stays, has got'	paywe	'learns'
		pēy	'cuts'
ka	'goes'	phi(w)e or phyē	'smokes'
kaluchye	'teaches'		
kyēysye	[someone esteemed] is, stays'	pwa [<poa] or p'a	'looks at, sees; reads'
khe	'is large, big'	sa	'buys'
kitalye	'waits (for)'	sal.e	'lives'
kkakk.e	'cuts (= mows)'	se	'stands'
kkuth na	'stops, ends, is over'	sse	'writes'
mānh.e	'is much; are many'	swie	'rests'
manna	'meets/sees (a person)'	tat.e	'closes it'
masye	'drinks'	tul.e	'hears; listens to'
mek.e	'eats'	wa [<oa]	'comes'
nol.a	'plays'	yel.e	'opens it'

If you glance down the list, you will see that all of the infinitives end in a vowel, -e or -a. (Hay is irregular.) The vowel at the end is in some cases an ENDING (to mark the infinitive), while in others it belongs to the basic part of the verb (its BASE) and the infinitive is represented by a zero ending—that is, by nothing at all. You may wonder why we translate the infinitives by English forms like 'does' instead of 'to do'; that is because the Korean forms can be used as sentences just as they stand: When you remove the polite-style particle yo you have sentences in the INTIMATE style, about which we will learn more later. The word "infinitive" (like many grammar terms) doesn't mean the same thing when we talk about Korean as when we talk about English.

Bases of Korean verbs are classified into two main types: CONSONANT BASES and VOWEL BASES. Consonant-base verbs typically have the infinitive ending -e and their infinitives consist of the base + this vowel ending. If the last vowel of the base is o (and in written Korean often a) then the ending is -a instead of -e

Here is a list of consonant bases and infinitives:

anc-	'sits'	anc.e	'sits'	[often written anc.a]
cac-	'be frequent'	cac.e	'is frequent'	[often written cac.a]
cāk-	'be little'	cak.e	'is little'	[often written cak.a]
cēk-	'be small/few'	cek.e	'is small; are few'	
chac-	'look for; find'	chac.e	'looks for; finds'	[often written chac.a]
cic	'bark'	cic.e	'barks'	
cōh-	'be good'	cōh.a	'is good'	
ēps-	'be nonexistent'	ēps.e	'is nonexistent'	
ilk-	'read'	ilk.e	'reads'	
iss-	'be, exist; stay'	iss.e	'is, exists; stays; has got'	
kkakk-	'cut (= mow)'	kkakk.e	'cuts'	[often written kkakk.a]
mānh-	'be much/many'	mānh.e	'is much; are many'	[often written manh.a]
mek-	'eat'	mek.e	'eats'	
pat-	'receive, get'	pat.e	'receives, gets'	[often written pat.a]
tat-	'close it'	tat.e	'closes it'	[often written tat.a]
tul-	'listen to; hear'	tul.e	'listens to; hears'	

Vowel-base verbs are somewhat more complex:

1. In one group, the infinitive is the same shape as the base. The ones you have had all end in a or ey but those ending in ay and oy belong here too, as you will see later. Here is a list of the ones you have had:

ca-	'go to bed; sleep'	ca	'goes to bed; sleeps'
il.e na-	'get up'	il.e na	'gets up'
ka-	'go'	ka	'goes'
kkuth na-	'end'	kkuth na	'it ends'
manna-	'meet'	manna	'meets'
sa-	'buy'	sa	'buys'
pēy-	'cut'	pēy	'cuts'

2. In another group, the base ends in i and the infinitive ending -e is added, but the sequence ie is abbreviated to ye for bases of more than one syllable (and in fast speech to yē for many bases of one syllable):

capswusi-	'eat'	capswusye [<capswusie] '[someone esteemed] eats'
cwumusi-	'sleep'	cwumusye [<cwumusie] '[someone esteemed] sleeps'
kaluchi-	'teach'	kaluchye [<kaluchie] 'teaches'
kitali-	'wait'	kitalye [<kitalie] 'waits'
masi-	'drink'	masye [<masie] 'drinks'
. . .i-	'be [COPULA]	. . .ie 'it is'
phi-(= phiwu-)	'smoke'	phie [>phyē] 'smokes'
swī-	'rest'	swie 'rests'

All of the honorific forms belong to this group:

kasi- 'go,' kasye [<kasie] '[someone esteemed] goes'; osi- 'come,' osye [<osie] '[someone esteemed] comes'

3. A similar group consists of the bases that end in wu; they add the ending -e and the sequence wue abbreviates to we for bases of more than one syllable (and in fast speech to we for many bases of one syllable):

paywu-	'learn'	paywe [<paywue] 'learns'
phiwu-	'smoke'	phiwe [<phiwue] 'smokes'
cwu-	'give'	cwue [>cwe] 'gives'

4. Vowel bases that end in o add the infinitive ending as -a and the sequence oa is shortened to wa for both long and short bases:

o-	'come'	wa [<oa] 'comes'
po-	'look at, see'	pwa [<poa] 'looks at, sees'

Since Koreans frequently drop w after a consonant, especially a sound made with the lips like p, you will hear pwa pronounced p'a in fast or sloppy speech.

5. Most vowel bases that end in u drop the u before adding the infinitive ending -e:

khu-	'be large'	khe	'is large'
su-	'stand'	se	'stands'
ssu-	'write'	sse	'writes'

6. But most vowel bases that end in lu not only drop the u but double the l before adding the appropriate infinitive ending (normally -e but -a when the vowel of the preceding syllable is o or, in written Korean, often also a):

palu-	'be right'	palle	'is right' [often written palla]
ppalu-	'be fast'	ppalle	'is fast' [often written ppalla]

These are called L-doubling vowel bases.

7. Another common kind of vowel base is one which looks at first glance like a consonant base: it ends in a vowel in the most basic form but picks up an l before certain endings, one of which is the infinitive:

nō-l-	'play'	nol.a	'plays'
sā-l-	'live'	sal.e	'lives' [often written sal.a]
yē-l-	'open it'	yel.e	'opens it'

These are called L-extending vowel bases; later you will see how they differ from consonant bases that end in l- (like tul- 'hear,' tul.e 'hears').

There are a few other kinds of verb bases that you will learn about later. The important verb ha- 'do' has an irregular infinitive: hay (literary form ha.ye) 'does.'

The past tense is made by adding ss to the infinitive: anc.ess-, cass-, kitalyess-, cwuess-, wass-, ssess-, ppalless-, nol.ass-. To the past tense formed in this way you add a verb ending. If you are speaking in the polite style you add the polite ending -e yo or (more colloquially) -ey yo: anc.ess.e(y) yo 'sat,' cass.e(y) yo 'went to bed, slept,' cwuess.e(y) yo 'gave,' wass.e(y) yo 'came,' ssess.e(y) yo 'wrote,' ppalless.e(y) yo 'was fast,' nol.ass.e(y) yo 'played.' If you remove the particle yo you are left with the PAST INFINITIVE, about which you will learn more later.

It may be helpful to know that in origin the past tense is an abbreviation of the infinitive -e + the verb iss-, so that anc.ess.e(y) yo 'sat' was once the same form as anc.e iss.e(y) yo 'is seated.' But the two forms today have slightly different meanings, and that is why we do not write the past tense forms as abbreviations "anc.e 'ss.e(y) yo" etc.

The HONORIFIC BASE of a verb is its base + the honorific marker, pronounced -usi- after consonants and -si- after vowels. Honorific present-tense polite forms end in -(u)sey yo; this is the usual pronunciation of what is sometimes written -(u)sye yo, the HONORIFIC INFINITIVE + the particle yo. The honorific infinitive consists of the honorific marker -(u)si- + the infinitive ending -e, with the expected abbreviation of -(u)sie to -(u)sye; since most speakers do not distinguish sy from s, the ending -(u)sye is pronounced as if spelled -(u)se or -(u)s'e.

BASE	HONORIFIC BASE	HON. INFINITIVE	HON. POLITE
ka- 'go'	kasi-	kasye	kasey yo
o- 'come'	osi-	osye	osey yo
paywu- 'teach'	paywusi-	paywusye	paywusey yo
anc- 'sit'	anc.usi-	anc.usye	anc.usye yo
kkakk- 'cut'	kkakk.usi-	kkakk.usye	kkakk.usey yo
ilk- 'read'	ilk.usi-	ilk.usye	ilk.usey yo
ppalu- 'be fast'	ppalusi-	ppalusye	ppalusey yo
nō-l- 'play'	nōsi-	nōsye	nōsey yo

As the last example shows, when you have an L-extending vowel base you attach the honorific marker to the UNEXTENDED BASE. Note how differently you treat consonant bases that end in l:

tul- 'listen to; hear'	tul.usi-	tul.usye	tul.usey yo

To make honorific forms past tense, you add the past-tense marker -ss- to the HONORIFIC INFINITIVE and complete the form by adding a polite-style ending:

BASE	HON. BASE	HON. INF.	HON. PAST	HON. PAST INF.	HON. PAST POLITE
ka-	kasi-	kasye	kasyess-	kasyess.e	kasyess.ey yo
o-	osi-	osye	osyess-	osyess.e	osyess.ey yo
anc-	anc.usi-	anc.usye	anc.usyess-	anc.usyess.e	anc.usyess.ey yo
ilk-	ilk.usi-	ilk.usye	ilk.usyess-	ilk.usyess.e	ilk.usyess.ey yo
nō-l-	nōsi-	nōsye	nōsyess-	nōsyess.e	nōsyess.ey yo

Here is a list of the verbs you have learned so far, in the polite past and the honorific polite past:

BASE	POLITE PAST	HONORIFIC POLITE PAST
anc- 'sit'	anc.ess.e(y) yo 'sat'	anc.usyess.e(y) yo '[someone esteemed] sat'
ca- 'sleep'	cass.e(y) yo 'slept'	[SEE cwumusi-]
[SEE mek-]	[SEE mek-]	capswusyess.e(y) yo '[someone esteemed] ate'
cāk- 'be small'	cak.ess.e(y) yo 'were small'	cak.usyess.e(y) yo '[someone esteemed] was small or had a small one'
cēk- 'be little/few'	cek.ess.e(y) yo 'was little; were few'	cek.usyess.e(y) yo '[esteemed persons] were few, [an esteemed person] had little/few'
chac- 'look for; find'	chac.ess.e(y) yo 'looked for; found'	chac.usyess.e(y) yo '[someone esteemed] looked for or found'
cōh- 'be good'	cōh.asse(y) yo 'was good'	cōh.usyess.e(y) yo '[someone esteemed] was good or had a good one'
[SEE ca-]	[SEE ca-]	cwumusyess.e(y) yo '[someone esteemed] went to bed'
cwu- 'give'	cwuess.e(y) yo 'gave'	cwusyess.e(y) yo '[someone esteemed] gave'
ēps- 'be non-existent'	ēps.ess.e(y) yo '(there) wasn't; hadn't got	ēps.usyess.e(y) yo '[someone esteemed] hadn't got, lacked' an kyēysyess.e(y) yo '[someone esteemed] wasn't, or didn't stay'
ha- 'do'	hayss.e(y) yo 'did'	hasyess.e(y) yo '[someone esteemed] did'
i- 'it is'	iess.e(y) yo 'it was'	isyess.e(y) yo '[someone esteemed] was'
il.e na- 'get up'	il.e nass.e(y) yo 'got up'	il.e nasyess.e(y) yo '[someone esteemed] got up'
ilk- 'read'	ilk.ess.e(y) yo 'read'	ilk.usyess.e(y) yo '[someone esteemed] read'
iss- 'be, exist; have; stay'	iss.ess.e(y) yo 'was; had; stayed'	iss.usyess.e(y) yo '[someone esteemed] had' [see also kyēysi-, ēps-]
ka- 'go'	kass.e(y) yo 'went'	kasyess.e(y) yo '[someone esteemed] went'
kaluchi- 'teach'	kaluchyess.e(y) yo 'taught'	kaluchisyess.e(y) yo '[someone esteemed] taught'
kyēysi- 'be, exist; stay'	[SEE iss-, ēps-]	kyēysyess.e(y) yo '[someone esteemed] was (in a place) or stayed'
khu- 'be big'	khess.e(y) yo 'was big'	khusyess.e(y) yo '[someone esteemed] was big or had a big one'
kitali- 'wait (for)'	kitalyess.e(y) yo 'waited'	kitalisyess.e(y) yo '[someone esteemed] waited'

BASE	POLITE PAST	HONORIFIC POLITE PAST
kkakk- 'cut (= mow)'	kkakk.ess.e(y) yo 'cut'	kkakk.usyess.e(y) yo '[someone esteemed] cut'
kkuth na- 'stop, end, be over'	kkuth nass.e(y) yo 'it stopped, came to an end, was over'	kkuth nasyess.e(y) yo '[something pertaining to someone esteemed] stopped'
mānh- 'are much/many'	mānh.esse(y) yo 'there was much or were many; had much/many'	mānh.usyess.e(y) yo 'there were many [esteemed persons]; [an esteemed person] had much/many'
manna- 'meet, see (a person)'	mannass.e(y) yo 'saw or met (a person)'	mannasyess.e(y) yo '[someone esteemed] saw or met (a person)'
masi- 'drink'	masyess.e(y) yo 'drank'	masisyess.e(y) yo '[someone esteemed] drank'
mek- 'eat'	mek.ess.e(y) yo 'ate'	[SEE capswusi-]
nō-l-	nol.ass.e(y) yo 'played'	nōsyess.e(y) yo '[someone esteemed] played'
o- 'come'	wass.e(y) yo 'came'	osyess.e(y) yo '[someone esteemed] came'
pat- 'receive, get'	pat.ess.e(y) yo 'received got'	pat.usyess.e(y) yo '[someone esteemed] received or got'
paywu- 'learn'	paywess.e(y) yo 'learned'	paywusyess.e(y) yo '[someone esteemed] learned'
phi(wu)- 'smoke'	phi[w]ess.ey yo or phyēss.ey yo 'smoked'	phi(wu)syess.e(y) yo '[someone esteemed] smoked'
po- 'look at, see; read'	p(w)ass.e(y) yo 'saw, looked at; read'	posyess.e(y) yo '[someone esteemed] saw or looked at or read'
sa- 'buy'	sass.e(y) yo 'bought'	sasyess.e(y) yo '[someone esteemed] bought'
sā-l- 'live'	sal.ess.e(y) yo 'lived'	sāsyess.e(y) yo '[someone esteemed] lived'
ssu- 'write'	ssess.e(y) yo 'wrote'	ssusyess.e(y) yo '[someone esteemed] wrote'
swī- 'rest'	swiess.e(y) yo 'rested'	swīsyess.e(y) yo '[someone esteemed] rested'
tat- 'close it'	tat.ess.e(y) yo 'closed it'	tat.usyess.e(y) yo '[someone esteemed] closed it'
tul- 'listen to; hear'	tul.ess.e(y) yo 'listened to; heard'	tul.usyess.e(y) yo '[someone esteemed] listened to or heard'
yē-l- 'open it'	yel.esse(y) yo 'opened it'	yēsyess.e(y) yo '[someone esteemed] opened it'

The past tense is usually translated by the English 'did' ('was') or 'had done' ('had been'), but for verbs of going and coming a result is implied: kass.ey yo means 'he went (and is still gone); he's gone/left' and wass.ey yo means 'he came (and is still here); he's here.' To say 'he went (but is back now)' and 'he came (but left again so he isn't here any more),' there is a special PAST-PAST form (-ess.ess-): kass.ess.ey yo 'he was here (but he's left again).' See ‖ 24.2. Notice that there are two ways to look at such English expressions as 'he's here/there': 1. simple location (Yeki/Cēki ey iss.ey yo); 2. the result of movement from another place (Wass.ey yo / Kass.ey yo). When you can paraphrase 'he's here' by 'he's arrived, here he comes/is' the second version is appropriate.

EXERCISES

I

A. Each of the following sentences means 'I do or did something.' Change the topic and the verb form so that the meaning is 'do (or did) you, sir, do something?' Say or write out the changed sentence and then translate it. For example, the first will be:

Sensayng nim un hak.kyo ey kasey yo? 'Are you going to school?'

1. Na nun hak.kyo ey ka yo.
2. Na nun wuphyen-kwuk ey se īl hay yo.
3. Na nun onul achim ey kongpu lul mānh.i hayss.ey yo.
4. Na nun pam mata chayk ul ilk.e yo.
5. Na nun Hānkwuk ey se Yenge lul kaluchye yo.
6. Na nun meychil cen ey kongwen ey se kāy wa kath.i nol.ass.ey yo.
7. Na nun ku ai hanthey tōn ul cwuess.ey yo.
8. Na nun ōhwu mata chinkwu eykey phyēnci lul sse yo.
9. Na nun tose-kwan aph ey se hak.kyo sensayng ul mannass.ey yo.
10. Na nun Mikwuk se wass.ey yo.
11. Na nun tōn ul mānh.i mōs pat.e yo.
12. Na nun onulq pam ey cip ey iss.ey yo.
13. Na nun ku chinkwu lul chac.e yo.
14. Na nun Tho-yoil mata phul ul kkakk.e yo.
15. Na nun i uyca ey anc.ess.ey yo.
16. Na nun mānh.i mōs mek.e yo.
17. Na nun ku sālam uy māl ul tul.ess.ey yo.
18. Na nun emeni lul kitalye yo.
19. Na nun tāmpay lul mōs phi(w)e yo.
20. Na nun pam mata ilccik ca yo.
21. Na nun Yeyil [Yale] Tāyhak ey se Hānkwuk mal ul paywess.ey yo.
22. Na nun yeki (se) sal.e yo.
23. Na nun ku sāy lul pwass.ey yo.
24. Na nun Hānkwuk salam iey yo.
25. Na nun sikan mata sip-pun ccum swie yo.

B. Each of the following sentences means 'someone DOES something.' Change the verb form so that the meaning is 'someone DID something.' Then translate the sentence. For example, the first will be:

Sensayng nim un mues ul hasyess.ey yo. 'What did you do?'

1. Sensayng nim un mues ul hasey yo.
2. Sensayng nim un ku yenghwa lul kwūkyeng ka yo?
3. Na nun chinkwu tul hanthey phyēnci lul mānh.i sse yo.
4. Kāy ka cikum mun ul yel.e yo.
5. Na nun tōn i cek.e yo.
6. Kuleh.ci man, chinkwu ka mānh.e yo.
7. Kāy nun koki lul mānh.i mōs mek.e yo.
8. Emeni ka ku chayk ul ilk.e yo.
9. Ku yenghwa ka cōh.a yo?
10. Apeci ka na hanthey tōn ul mānh.i cwue yo.
11. Na nun kongwen ey se ai wa kath.i nol.a yo.

12. Sensayng nim to kongwen ey kasey yo?
13. Na nun unhayng ey se wa yo.
14. Nwu' ka wuli lul pwa yo.
15. Apeci ka cip ey kyēysey yo.
16. Ku kāy nun cham khe yo.
17. Na nun Yeyil Tāyhak-(hak)sayng iey yo.
18. Na nun New York ey (se) sal.e yo.
19. Nay yenphil i yeki iss.ey yo.
20. Chayk-sang wi ey nun tāmpay ka ēps.ey yo.

II

A. Count quickly in Korean from one to twelve, putting the following words after each number, in order: one table, two minutes, three people, and so on. Repeat, from 13 to 24; from 25 to 36; from 37 to 48; from 49 to 60; and so on up to 96.

1. tables [no counter!]
2. minutes
3. people
4. years
5. cats
6. days
7. months
8. years old
9. dollars
10. weeks
11. floors
12. Korean miles
13. books

B. Say the following things in Korean, completing each sentence in several ways:

1. I got up this morning at _____.
   7:00
   8:15
   7:05
   6:55
   6:30

2. I usually go to bed around _____.
   11:00
   10;45
   11:15
   9:30
   12:00

3. I worked at the office for _____.
   two hours
   five days
   fourteen days
   eight and a half hours
   ten minutes

4. I ate breakfast at _____.
   8:17
   8:47
   7:53
   7:25
   exactly 7:00 on the hour

5. I saw _____.
   six people
   nine magazines
   three squirrels
   eleven buildings
   four cars

6. I have _____.
   only two dollars
   three newspapers
   ten books
   two dogs
   fifteen pieces of paper

7. I stayed there for _____.
   two days
   ten days
   two weeks
   three months
   six years

C. Answer these questions in Korean (short answers only!):

1. ^{l}Naynyen un meych nyen iey yo.
2. Onul un meychil iey yo.
3. "Christopher Columbus" un ēncey Ameylikha ey wass.ess.ey yo.
4. "George Washington" uy sayngil i ēncey 'ey yo.
5. Enu tal (or musun tal) ey Sēngthan-cel ("Christmas") i iss.ey yo.
6. Ēncey Hānkwuk Cēncayng ("Korean War") i sīcak hayss.ey yo.
7. Tangsin sayngil i ēncey 'ey yo.
8. Enu nal i "Columbus Day" iey yo.
9. Ēncey Mikwuk uy "Civil War" ka sīcak hayss.ey yo.
10. Na nun achim yetelq si pān ey īl ul sīcak hayss.ey yo. Cenyek tases si kkaci an kkuth na yo. Kulemyen, meych sikan ina īl hayss.ey yo.
11. Musun tal ey say hay ("New Year") ka sīcak hay yo.
12. Na nun chen kwu-payk ō-sip ō-nyen ey īl ul sīcak hayss.ey yo. Kulemyen, meych nyen ina īl hayss.ey yo.
13. Mikwuk hak.kyo sensayng un hay mata meychil ina swie yo.
14. Unhayng ey se nun myech si puthe īl ul sīcak hay yo.
15. "Pearl Harbor Day" nun ēncey iess.ey yo.
16. Ōcen han si puthe ōhwu yelq twū si kkaci nun meych sikan ina iss.ey yo

III

Here are some Korean sentences with some of the particles missing. Read each sentence aloud and fill in the blanks with appropriate particles you have learned in this lesson.

1. Nal mata meych sikan _____ _____ kongpu lul hay yo?
2. Hak.kyo ey se nun ^{l}nayil _____ sīcak hay yo.
3. Swu-yoil _____ ['every'] cip ey se swie yo?
4. Ku sang wi ey nun chayk _____ ['only'] iss.ey yo.
5. Onul achim cip ey se twū si _____ sēy si pān _____ kongpu lul hayss.e yo.
6. Pam _____ meych sikan _____ cwumusey yo?
7. Sāmu-sil ey se yetelq si pān _____ nēy si pān _____ īl ul hay yo.
8. Achim _____ meych si _____ _____ il.e na yo?
9. Sāmu-sil ey se nun achim ahop si _____ sīcak hay yo.
10. Achim _____ meych si _____ hak.kyo ey kasey yo? Achim _____ yelq si _____ ka yo.

CONVERSATION

1. Beginning with 6 o'clock in the morning, divide up an entire working day—say Wednesday—hour by hour, and have each student tell how he spends that hour. Student A says in Korean, "From 6 to 7 a.m. I _____ "; Student B tells what he does from 7 to 8; and so on, till midnight.

2. Following the same general procedure as above, Student A asks Student B what he did yesterday (or the most recent day off) from 6 to 7; Student B replies, and in turn asks Student C what he did that day from 7 to 8; and so on, till midnight.

3. Each student should make up a list of questions on the analogy of those in Exercise II, Part C, above—enough to ask two of each member of the class. Then each student takes turns asking his questions, and checks carefully on the accuracy of the answers he receives.

VOCABULARY DRILL

Rapid-fire Drill.—Call off the Korean for each group below. Use numeral and counter, and, if appropriate, a noun.

1. One person, one building, one o'clock.
2. Two months, two years, two days.
3. Three honored people, three o'clock, three years old.
4. Four dollars, four dogs, four newspapers.
5. Five miles, five days, five houses.
6. Six cents, six floors, six years old.
7. Seven months, seven books, seven years.
8. Eight hours, eight cars, eight minutes.
9. Nine times, nine days, nine cats.
10. Ten cents, ten people, ten o'clock.
11. One o'clock, two o'clock, three o'clock.
12. Two years old, three years old, four years old.
13. Three years, four years, five years.
14. Four people, five people, six people.
15. Five days, six days, seven days.
16. Six sheets of paper, seven sheets of paper, eight sheets of paper.
17. Seven magazines, eight magazines, nine magazines.
18. Eight days, nine days, ten days.
19. Nine floors, ten floors, eleven floors.
20. Ten times, eleven times, twelve times.
21. Eleven cents, twelve cents, thirteen cents.
22. Twelve squirrels, thirteen squirrels, fourteen squirrels.
23. Thirteen days, fourteen days, fifteen days.
24. Fourteen years old, fifteen years old, sixteen years old.
25. Fifteen months, sixteen months, seventeen months.
26. Sixteen minutes, seventeen minutes, eighteen minutes.
27. Seventeen cars, eighteen cars, nineteen cars.
28. Eighteen years, nineteen years, twenty years.

COMPREHENSION

I

Your Korean speaker will call off to you several dozen pairs of numerical expressions like the ones listed below. Your task is to listen and then repeat the one expression from each pair which was GREATER than the other. In the first example below—nahul, ahuley '4 days, 9 days'—you of course name ahuley.

4 days — 9 days	2 1/2 hours — 7 hours
3 cars — 4 cars	21 years old — 31 years old
8:30 — 10:45	etc.

II

Here is a little conversation between two Korean speakers. Read it and make sure you understand it all. Taking turns with the roles, practice it aloud with your fellow students, making your speech sound as natural and easy as you can.

Kim: Mian hap.nita. Tose-kwan un eti 'ey yo.

Pak: Ce sam-chung cip ōyn phyen ey iss.ey yo.

Kim: Yeki se elma 'na ka yo.

Pak: Han ī-pun ccum ka yo. Na to cikum ku ccok ulo ka yo. Na hako kath.i kasipsio.

Kim: Komapsup.nita. Tose-kwan un meych si ccum ey yel.e yo.

Pak: Cwukan ey nun ōcen yetelq si pān puthe ōhwu tases si sam-sip pun kkaci yel.e yo. Kulena, Tho-yoil ey nun achim nēy sikan man yel.e yo.

Kim: Kulemyen Il-yoil man swie yo?

Pak: Ani yo?? Il-wel il-il kwa Chil-wel sā-il kwa Sip.i-wel ī-sip ō-il to swie yo.

Kim: Kulen tey chayk un mānh.e yo?

Pak: Kulay yo. Han phal-man kwen ccum ina iss.ey yo.

Kim: Sālam tul to mānh.i wa yo?

Pak: Nēy. Han sikan ey to phyengkyun ō-sip myeng ssik ina wa yo.

Kim: Sensayng nim un eti (ey) se īl hasey yo.

Pak: Unhayng ey se ilq-cwuil ey sahul ssik man īl hay yo. Kulena cak.nyen kkaci nun tas-say tā īl hayss.ey yo.

Kim: Ku kes cham cōh.sup.nita. Na nun Hānkwuk mal ul paywe yo. Kulena acik cal mōs hay yo.

Pak: Kuleh.sup.nikka? Ca tā wass.ey yo.* Yeki iey yo.

Kim: Komapsup.nita.

Pak: Chen-man ey yo. Kulem, yongse hasey yo.

---

* 'Well, we've come all the way = we've arrived.'

LESSON 7. MEET THE FAMILY

BASIC SENTENCES

	Korean	English	Amplification
1.	Sik.kwu ka meych iey yo.	How many are there in your family?	sik.kwu 'family member' = Your family members are how many?
2.	Nēy sik.kwu 'ey yo.	There are four.	= [They] are four family members.
3.	Apeci hako, emeni hako, oppa hako, na (hako) 'ey yo.	There's my father, my mother, my older brother, and me.	oppa 'a male's older brother'
4.	Enni nun an kyēysey yo?	You haven't any older sisters?	enni 'a female's older sister; a male's older brother'
5.	Enni ka iss.ci man, wuli hako kath.i sālci anh.e yo.	I have an older sister, but she doesn't live with us.	iss.ci man 'there is, but' sālci anh.e yo 'doesn't live'
6.	Enni nun ō-nyen cen ey kyelhon hayss.ey yo.	My older sister got married five years ago.	kyelhon 'marriage' kyelhon (ul) hay yo 'marries, gets married'
7.	Namphyen un hak.kyo sensayng iey yo. Pelsse ttal hana atul hana ka iss.ey yo.	Her husband is a school teacher. They now have a daughter and a son.	pelsse 'already; by now' ttal 'daughter' atul 'son'
8.	Ai tul i tā ttok-ttok hay yo?	Are the children both bright?	ttok-ttok hay yo 'is bright, smart, clever'
9.	Ttal un ttok-ttok haci man, atul un ttok-ttok haci mōs hay yo.	The daughter is bright, but the son isn't bright at all.	ttok-ttok haci man 'is bright, but' ttok-ttok haci anh.e yo 'isn't bright' ttok-ttok haci mōs hay yo 'isn't bright at all'
10.	Tongsayng un ēps.ey yo?	You haven't any younger brothers or sisters?	tongsayng 'younger brother and/or sister, younger sibling'
11.	Tongsayng un ēps.ey yo. ^{n}Ye-tongsayng to, nam-tongsayng to ēp.sey yo. Cey ka 'mak-nay 'ey yo.	I haven't any younger siblings. I have neither younger brother nor younger sisters. I'm the baby of the family.	^{n}ye-tongsayng 'younger sister' nam-tongsayng 'younger brother' ce 'I, me' [FORMAL]

Korean	English	Amplification
		cey ka 'I [as subject]' macimak 'the end' 'mak . . . 'the last' 'mak-nay 'the lastborn, the youngest of the family'
12. Oppa to kyelhon hayss.ey yo?	Is your older brother married too?	= Has your older brother also married?
13. Ani yo?? Oppa nun kyelhon haci anh.ess.ey yo. Oppa nun mān-nyen tāyhak-sayng iey yo.	No, my older brother isn't married. He's a perpetual college student.	kyelhon haci anh.ess.ey yo 'has not married' mān-nyen tāyhak-sayng '10,000-year college student'
14. Oppa nun "yeca lul cōh.a haci anh.e yo.	My older brother doesn't like girls.	"yeca 'girl' cōh.a hay yo 'likes' cōh.a haci anh.e yo 'doesn't like'
15. Oppa nun toksin saynghwal ul cōh.a hay yo.	He likes single life.	toksin 'solitary, alone, single' saynghwal 'life'
16. Na nun kaceng saynghwal i coh.a yo.	I like family life.	= "As for me, family life is good" kaceng 'the home (as center of domestic life)'
17. Oppa nun swulq cip ey to, ttaynsu-hol ey to an ka yo.	My brother doesn't go either to bars or to dance halls.	swul 'wine, liquor' swulq cip 'wine house, bar' (t)taynsu-hol 'dance hall'
18. Oppa nun um.ak-hoy ey cal ka yo.	He goes to concerts a lot.	um.ak 'music' hōy 'meeting' um.ak-hoy 'concert'
19. Oppa to cal kaci man, na to cal ka yo.	He goes a lot, ['but' =] and so do I.	kaci man 'goes, but'
20. Ape' nim kkey se nun, mues ul hasey yo.	What does your father do?	. . . kkey 'to [an esteemed person]' . . . kkey se 'from [an esteemed person]; [oblique subject]' . . . kkey se nun '[deemphasized oblique subject]' ape' nim kkey se nun 'your esteemed father [as deemphasized oblique subject]'
21. Apeci kkey se nun tāyhak kyōswu 'syess.ci man, cikum	My father was a university professor, but now he just writes books at	kyōswu 'professor' . . . (i)syess.ci man '[someone esteemed] was, but'

Korean	English	Amplification
un cip ey se pam-nac chayk man ssusey yo.	home all the time.	pam-nac 'night and day; all the time'
22. Ape' nim uy ^{n}yensey ka mānh.usey yo?	Is your father very old?	^{n}yensey 'esteemed age' ^{n}yensey ka mānh.usey yo '[someone esteemed] is old, has many years (of age)'
23. Nēy. Apeci kkey se nun nai nun mānh.usici man, maum un tāytan hi celm.usey yo.	Yes, my father is quite old, but his heart is extremely young.	nai 'age' nai ka mānh.e yo '[age is much = has much age =] is old' mānh.usici man '[someone esteemed] has many/ much' maum 'mind, heart, spirit' tāytan hi 'very, extremely' celm.e yo '[an adult] is young' celm.usey yo '[an esteemed adult] is young' elye yo '[a child] is young'
24. Onulq cenyek ey yenghwa kwūkyeng ul kaci anh.usey yo?	Aren't you going to the movies this evening?	kaci anh.e yo 'doesn't go' kaci anh.usey yo '[some-one esteemed] doesn't go'
25. Na nun um.ak-hoy nun cōh.a haci man, yenghwa nun cōh.a haci anh.e yo.	I like concerts, but I don't like movies.	cōh.a haci man 'likes it, but . . .'
26. I pen kaul ey na nun han pen to yenghwa-kwan ey kaci anh.ess.ey yo.	I haven't been to a single movie this fall.	= This (time) fall, I haven't gone to a movie theater even one time. kaul 'fall, autumn' i pen 'this time' i pen kaul 'this autumn' han pen to 'even one time, even once' kaci anh.ess.ey yo 'didn't go, hasn't gone'
27. Tto nun, um.ak-hoy ey to kaci anh.ess.ey yo. Kulena, ce pen ey kāngyen-hoy ey kass.ess.ey yo.	Nor have I been to any concerts either. But I went to a lecture the other day.	ce pen (ey) 'the other day' kāngyen(-hoy) 'lecture' kass.ess.ey yo 'went (but is no longer there)'
28. Wuli tongsayng un um.ak-hoy nun cōh.a haci anh.ci man, yenghwa nun cōh.a hay yo.	[Our =] My younger brother doesn't like concerts, but he does like movies.	cōh.a haci anh.ci man 'doesn't like it, but'

Korean	English	Amplification
29. Na nun kāngyen i cōh.ci man, nay yak.hon-ca nun kāngyen ul silh.e hay yo.	I like lectures, but my fiancée hates them.	kāngyen 'lecture' cōh.ci man 'is good, but' yak.hon 'engagement, getting engaged' yak.hon-ca 'fiancé(e)' silh.e hay yo 'hates, dislikes' [pron. /sile/ or /silye/]
30. Hal-apeci nun kkoch kwūkyeng ul cōh.a haci anh.usici man, hal-'meni nun cōh.a hasey yo.	My grandfather doesn't like flower viewing, but my grandmother likes it.	hal-apeci 'grandfather' kkoch kwūkyeng 'flower viewing' cōh.a haci anh.usici man '[someone esteemed] doesn't like it, but . . .' hal-'meni 'grandmother' cōh.a hasey yo '[someone esteemed] likes'
31. Na nun ku yēyki ka silh.e yo.	I don't like that story.	= As for me, that story is disliked. yēyki, yāyki, iyaki 'story'
32. Kulemyen, tut.ci māsey yo.	Then don't listen.	tul.usey yo '[someone esteemed] listens; listen!' tut.ci māsey yo 'don't listen!'

SUPPLEMENTARY VOCABULARY

Kinship Terms.—In the following list, honorific kinship terms are given in capital letters. (See ‖ 7.8 for the use of honorific words.)

1. Relatives for which the terms differ according to the sex of the person related:

A male's . . .	A female's . . .	
cāngin	si-apeci; SI-APE'NIM	father-in-law
cāngmo	si-emeni; SI-EME'NIM	mother-in-law
an(h)ay; PUIN	namphyen; NAMPHYEN, CWUIN	spouse
hyengcey	(oppa tul kwa nam-tongsayng tul)	brothers
nammay (or hyengcey)	nammay; hyengcey	brothers and sisters
camay	camay	sisters
enni; HYENG (NIM)	oppa; OLAPENI(M)	older brother
nwūna; NWŪ'NIM	enni; HYENG (NIM)	older sister
tongsayng [adult term] / awu [childish term]	tongsayng	younger sibling
tongsayng [adult] / awu [childish]	nam-tongsayng (or tongsayng)	younger brother

"ye-tongsayng nwui-tongsayng (or tongsayng)	tongsayng	younger sister

2. Relatives for which the terms do NOT differ according to the sex of the person related:

co-pumo; CO-PUMO NIM	grandparents
hal-apeci, HAL-APE' NIM: copu, COPU NIM	grandfather
hal-'meni, HAL-'ME' NIM: como, COMO NIM	grandmother
pumo; PUMO NIM	parents
apeci; APE' NIM	father
emeni: EME' NIM	mother
ai/ay (tul)	child(ren)
atul; ATU' NIM	son
ttal; TTA' NIM	daughter
soncwu, soncwu ai	grandchild(ren)
sonca	grandson
sonnye	granddaughter
sawi	son-in-law
myenuli, meynuli	daughter-in-law
yak.hon-ca	fiancé(e)
sā-chon	cousin
acessi	uncle
acumeni	aunt
cokha	nephew
cokha ttal	niece

3. Other useful words

kacok, cip-an, cip	family

NOTES

‖ 7.1. Verbs: suspective form -ci.

Korean verbs with the suffix -ci attached to them are in the SUSPECTIVE FORM. Suspectives can be present or past; that is, the suffix can be added directly to the base and make a present-tense form, or to the past (-ess- etc.) to make a past-tense form. As usual, the honorific marker (-usi-/-si-) can be attached to the base before the final suffix is added, so that you can make up four different forms:

Suspective (present)	-ci
Honorific suspective (present)	-(u)si.ci
Past suspective	-ess.ci
Honorific past suspective	-(u)syess.ci

The suspective suffix is a ONE-SHAPE ENDING: it is always -ci, regardless of the kind of base it is attached to. In this respect it differs from the honorific marker, for example, which is a TWO-SHAPE ENDING attached in the shape -usi- (-usy-) to consonant bases but -si- (-sy-) to vowel bases. When one-shape endings that begin with a consonant are attached to bases that end in a consonant, clusters of consonants result that sometimes must be simplified. A Korean SYLLABLE can only end in one of the consonants p t k m n ng l, so that any other consonants or clusters at the end of the BASIC SHAPE of a word or base must first be reduced to one of these: ēps- reduces to /ēp-/, chac- reduces to /chat-/, kkakk- reduces to /kkak-/, and so on. It is to this reduced form that you then add the one-shape ending: /ēp-/ + /-ci/, /chac-/ + /-ci/, /kkak-/ + /-ci/. In pronouncing the resulting form you have to follow the usual rules of sound change (/ēpcci, chacci, kkakcci/) so that the final form AS SPOKEN involves two sets of operations on the basic form AS WRITTEN:(1) reduction of the base to a "pronounceable" syllable, and (2) automatic sound changes required when the final consonant of one element comes in contact with the initial consonant of another. In addition there are a few special peculiarities to note.

When a base ends in a vowel or n or l followed by h (as in cōh-, mānh-, and silh- 'be disliked') the h leap-frogs over a following voiceless consonant (c, t, k) so that cōh.ci is pronounced /cōchi/, mānh.ci is pronounced /mānchi/ and silh.ci is pronounced /silchi/.

When a base ends in lm (like celm- 'be young') it reduces to m (/cem-/), and when a base ends in nc (like anc- 'sit') it reduces to n (/an-/). Together with bases that end in a simple m or n (such as sīm- 'plant' and sin- 'wear shoes' [both Lesson 8]), these bases have an unexpected strengthening effect on a following voiceless consonant (c → /cc/, t → /tt/, k → /kk/) so that celm.ci is pronounced /cemcci/ and anc.ci is pronounced /ancci/. You will recall that we put our dot in the romanization always to remind you of something: when it is between two consonants it reminds you that certain automatic changes have to take place in the pronunciation. You may wonder why the dot is necessary in anc.ci: it represents the fact that -ci is not simply added to the basic form anc- as it stands, for first you have to reduce anc- to an- and then attach -ci which then follows the same rule of reinforcement (doubling) that it follows after simple n: sin.ci is pronounced /sincci/ and here the dot is used to remind you of the UNEXPECTED nature of the reinforcement. It is unexpected because both /nc/ and /ncc/ are pronounceable clusters in Korean, and the latter automatically replaces the former only at a point where an ending attaches to a base. The noun sīnca 'believer' [Lesson 17] has no dot so it is pronounced as you would expect with /nc/; but sin.ca 'let's put on our shoes' [Lesson 19]—following the pattern of sin.ci /sincci/—is pronounced /sincca/.

In Standard Korean L-extending vowel bases attach the suspective ending (and all other one-shape endings that begin with c, t, or k) to the EXTENDED shape: yē-l- 'open' has the suspective yēlci. In contrast, the CONSONANT bases that end in l do something rather peculiar: the l changes to t and this is shown in the spelling as well as in the pronunciation, so the suspective form of tul- 'listens' is tut.ci pronounced (by automatic change) /tucci/. Since Korean grammarians usually take the plain literary present (which ends in -ta) as the form in which to cite verbs in dictionaries, they consider these verbs as "irregular T verbs" (with the t changing to l rather than the other way round) and contrast them with "regular T verbs" such as tat- 'close' which has the suspective form tat.ci pronounced (by automatic sound change) /tacci/.

You can see that when special rules for verb forms are added to the usual automatic sound changes, the process of making up and pronouncing forms can get quite complex. It may be easier for you just to learn the forms for common verbs you run across; then you will find yourself extending the underlying rules to new verbs without worrying too much about them.

Here is a list of the -ci forms for most of the verbs you have learned with the pronunciation (when different) shown between slant lines:

BASE	SUSPECTIVE	HON. SUSP.	PAST SUSP.	HON. PAST SUSP.
anc- 'sit'	anc.ci /ancci/	anc.usici	anc.ess.ci /ancecci/	anc.usyess.ci /ancusecci/
ca- 'sleep'	caci	[cwumusici]	cass.ci /cacci/	[cwumusyess.ci] /cwumusecci/
cāk- 'be small'	cākci /cākcci/	cak.usici	cak.ess.ci /cakecci/	cak.usyess.ci /cakusecci/
cēk- 'be little or few'	cēkci /cēkcci/	cek.usici	cek.ess.ci /cekecci/	cek.usyess.ci /cekusecci/
chac- 'find'	chac.ci /chacci/	chac.usici	chac.ess.ci /chacecci/	chac.usyess.ci /chacusecci/
cōh- 'be good'	cōh.ci /cōchi/	cōh.usici /cō(h)usici/	cōh.ass.ci /cō(h)acci/	cōh.usyess.ci /cō(h)usecci/
cwu- 'give'	cwuci	cwusici	cwuess.ci /cw(u)ecci/	cwusyess.ci /cwusecci/
ēps- 'lack'	ēps.ci /ēpcci/	ēps.usici /epssusici/	ēps.ess.ci /epssecci/	ēps.usyess.ci /epssusecci/
ha- 'do'	haci	hasici	hayss.ci /haycci/	hasyess.ci /hasecci/
. . . i- 'be'	. . . ici	. . . isici	. . . iess.ci /iecci/	. . . isyess.ci /isecci/
il.e na- 'get up'	il.e naci	il.e nasici	il.e nass.ci /ilenacci/	il.e nasyess.ci /ilenasecci/
ilk- 'read'	ilk.ci /ikci/	ilk.usici	ilk.ess.ci /ilkecci/	ilk.usyess.ci /ilkusecci/
iss- 'have got' 'stay'	iss.ci /icci/	iss.usici kyēysici /kēysici/	iss.ess.ci /issecci/	iss.usyess.ci /issusecci/ kyēysyess.ci /kēysecci/
khu- 'be big'	khuci	khusici	khess.ci /khecci/	khusyess.ci /khusecci/
kitali- 'wait'	kitalici	kitalisici	kitalyess.ci /kitalyecci/	kitalisyess.ci /kitalisecci/
kkakk- 'cut (= mow)'	kkakk.ci /kkakcci/	kkakk.usici	kkakk.ess.ci /kkakkecci/	kkakk.usyess.ci /kkakkusecci/
mānh- 'be much or many'	mānh.ci /mānchi/	mānh.usici /mān(h)usici/	mānh.ess.ci /mān(h)ecci/	mānh.usyess.ci /mān(h)usecci/
manna- 'meet'	mannaci	mannasici	mannass.ci /mannacci/	mannasyess.ci /mannasecci/
masi- 'drink'	masici	masisici	masyess.ci /masecci/	masisyess.ci /masisecci/
mek- 'eat'	mekci /mekcci/	capswusici /capsswusici/	mek.ess.ci /mekecci/	capswusyess.ci /capsswusecci/
nō-l- 'play'	nōlci	nōsici	nol.ass.ci /nolacci/	nōsyess.ci /nōsecci/
o- 'come'	oci	osici	wass.ci /wacci/	osyess.ci /osecci/
pat- 'get'	pat.ci /pacci/	pat.usici	pat.ess.ci /patecci/	pat.usyess.ci /patusecci/

BASE	SUSPECTIVE	HON. SUSP.	PAST SUSP.	HON. PAST SUSP.
paywu- 'learn'	paywuci	paywusici	paywess.ci	paywusyess.ci
			/paywecci/	/paywusecci/
pēy- 'cut'	pēyci	pēysici	pēyss.ci	pēysyess.ci
			/pēycci/	/pēysecci/
phi(wu)- 'smoke'	phi(wu)ci	phi(wu)sici	phi(w)ess.ci	phi(wu)syess.ci
			/phi(w)ecci/	/phi(wu)secci/
po- 'look at'	poci	posici	pwass.ci	posyess.ci
			/p(w)acci/	/posecci/
sa- 'buy'	saci	sasici	sass.ci	sasyess.ci
			/sacci/	/sasecci/
sā-l- 'live'	sālci	sāsici	sal.ess.ci	sāsyess.ci
			/salecci/	/sāsecci/
silh- 'be disliked'	silh.ci	silh.usici	silh.ess.ci	silh.usyess.ci
	/silchi/	/sil(h)usici/	/sil(h)ecci/*	/sil(h)usecci/
ssu- 'write'	ssuci	ssusici	ssess.ci	ssusyess.ci
			/ssecci/	/ssusecci/
swī- 'rest'	swīci	swīsici	swiess.ci	swīsyess.ci
			/swiecci/	/swīsecci/
tat- 'close it'	tat.ci	tat.usici	tat.ess.ci	tat.usyess.ci
			/tatecci/	/tatusecci/
tul- 'listen'	tut.ci	tul.usici	tul.ess.ci	tul.usyess.ci
	/tucci/		/tulecci/	/tulusecci/
yē-l- 'open it'	yēlci	yēsici	yel.ess.ci	yēsyess.ci

* Also pronounced /silyecci/.

7.2. Uses of the suspective: with man 'but.'

5. Enni ka iss.ci man, . . . 'I have an older sister, but . . .'
9. Ttal un ttok-ttok haci man . . . 'The daughter is bright, but . . .'
19. Oppa to cal kaci man . . . 'My brother goes often, too, and . . .'
21. . . . tāyhak kyōswu 'syess.ci man . . . '[He] used to be a college professor, but . . .'
23. . . . nai nun mānh.usici man . . . 'He's old, but . . .' [his age is much, but . . .']
25. . . . um.ak-hoy nun cōh.a haci man . . . 'I like concerts, but . . .'
27. . . . um.ak-hoy nun cōh.a haci anh.ci man . . . '[He] doesn't like concerts, but . . .'
29. Na nun kāngyen i cōh.ci man . . . 'I like lectures, but . . .
30. . . . kkoch kwūkyeng ul cōh.a haci anh.usici man . . . '[Someone esteemed] doesn't like flower viewing, but . . .'

Phrases consisting of a suspective form plus man mean '(so-and-so) but.' The particle man, like other particles, is pronounced as though it were part of the preceding word (the -ci form, in this case) though in English the pause comes BETWEEN the equivalents of these words; and not infrequently the English equivalent of such phrases requires the separation of the verb from the word 'but' (see, for example, basic sentences 5, 21, 25, 27, 29, and 30, quoted above).

We can retain the Korean phrasing by using 'though, although':

'Although I have an older sister . . .'

'Though the daughter is bright . . .'

The translation 'but,' of course, is much more natural, and conveys the Korean more realistically.

In some instances, man in this construction may be interpreted by some such wording as 'but then again,' which is fairly close to English 'and,' as in Basic Sentence 19. See ‖ 7.5.

The special phrase kuleh.ci man, literally meaning 'it is so, but . . . ,' is used at the beginning of Korean sentences in the same way that we use 'however' or 'on the other hand, on the contrary.'

The expression -ci man, then, is a device to put together two sentences that could be said separately, with the second introduced by Kuleh.ci man . . .

‖ 7.3. Uses of the suspective: long negatives.

5. . . . wuli hako kath.i sālci anh.e yo. 'She doesn't live with us.'
9. . . . atul un ttok-ttok haci mōs hay yo. 'The son isn't bright at all.'
13. . . . Oppa nun kyelhon haci anh.ess.ey yo . . . 'My brother isn't [hasn't] married.'
14. . . . ⁿyeca lul cōh.a haci anh.e yo. 'He doesn't like girls.'
24. . . . yenghwa kwūkyeng ul kaci anh.usey yo? 'Won't you go to the movies?'
25. . . . yenghwa nun cōh.a haci anh.e yo. 'I don't like movies.'
26. . . . yenghwa-kwan ey kaci anh.ess.ey yo. 'I haven't gone to a movie theater.'
28. . . . um.ak-hoy nun cōh.a haci anh.ci man . . . '[He] doesn't like concerts, but . . .'
30. . . . kkoch kwūkyeng ul cōh.a haci anh.usici man . . . '[Someone esteemed] doesn't like flower viewing, but . . .'

The short negative forms that you have learned to make by prefixing verbs and adjectives with an and mōs (‖ 4.3) are less common in actual use than a more complex type of negative made with -ci suspective forms.

The LONG NEGATIVE is a phrase which consists of a present-tense -ci followed by a negative element. The -ci form names the verb; the element following it carries the other meanings for the phrase—negativeness and tense, as well as the meaning carried in its ending (polite style, etc.).

The element following the -ci suspective form in long negative phrases is a negative form of the auxiliary base ha-, that is, a form of an ha-; the polite-style present-tense form at the end of a sentence is of course an hay yo:

kaci | an hay yo 'doesn't go'
tut.ci | an hay yo 'doesn't listen'
anc.ci | an hay yo 'doesn't sit down'

Most often, this is shortened to anh.e yo—in effect, a verb with the base form anh-, which makes up into different forms in the same way as the base mānh- '(there are) many.'

The past tense of a long negative is made by putting an ha- or anh- into the past tense; the -ci suspective form remains unchanged:

kaci | anh.ess.e(y) yo 'didn't go'
tut.ci | anh.ess.e(y) yo 'didn't listen'
anc.ci | anh.ess.e(y) yo 'didn't sit down'

The long negative differs from the SHORT NEGATIVE (the one you have been using up till now) only in that it is a phrase rather than a single word; the meaning of each corresponding form is the same. Here is a group of examples. Every verb has both forms except for the copula, which has only the form ani 'ey yo.

	Short Negative	Long Negative	Meaning
Present Tense			
anc- 'sit'	an anc.e yo	anc.ci anh.e yo	'doesn't sit'
ca- 'sleep'	an ca yo	caci anh.e yo	'doesn't sleep'
cōh- 'be good'	an cōh.a yo	cōh.ci anh.e yo	'isn't good'
ilk- 'read'	an ilk.e yo	ilk.ci anh.e yo	'doesn't read'
mānh- 'be much/many'	an mānh.e yo	mānh.ci anh.e yo	'isn't much/ aren't many'
mek- 'eat'	an mek.e yo	mekci anh.e yo	'doesn't eat'
o- 'come'	an wa yo	oci anh.e yo	'doesn't come'
sā-l 'live'	an sal.e yo	sālci anh.e yo	'doesn't live'
ssu- 'write'	an sse yo	ssuci anh.e yo	'doesn't write'
Past Tense			
anc- 'sit'	an anc.ess.e(y) yo	anc.ci anh.ess.e(y) yo	'didn't sit'
ca- 'sleep'	an cass.e(y) yo	caci anh.ess.e(y) yo	'didn't sleep'
cōh- 'be good'	an cōh.ass.e(y) yo	cōh.ci anh.ess.e(y) yo	'wasn't good'
ilk- 'read'	an ilk.ess.e(y) yo	ilk.ci anh.ess.e(y) yo	'didn't read'
mānh- 'be much or many'	an mānh.ess.e(y) yo	mānh.ci anh.ess.e(y) yo	'wasn't much or weren't many'
mek- 'eat'	an mek.ess.e(y) yo	mekci anh.ess.e(y) yo	'didn't eat'
o- 'come'	an wass.e(y) yo	oci anh.ess.e(y) yo	'didn't come'
sā-l- 'live'	an sal.ess.e(y) yo	sālci anh.ess.e(y) yo	'didn't live'
ssu- 'write'	an ssess.e(y) yo	ssuci anh.ess.e(y) yo	'didn't write'

In rapid speech -ci anh.e yo is often run together and shortened to -c'anh.e yo.

Long negatives with the STRONG NEGATIVE mōs 'cannot, emphatically not' rather than an 'not' are made in the same way except that there is no shortening of mōs ha-.

Base	Short Strong Neg.	Long Strong Neg.	Meaning
anc- 'sit'	mōs anc.e yo	anc.ci mōs hay yo	'can't sit'
	mōs anc.ess.e(y) yo	anc.ci mōs hayss.e(y) yo	'couldn't sit'
cōh- 'be good'		coh.ci mōs hay yo	'is no good'
		coh.ci mōs hayss.e(y) yo	'was no good'
mek- 'eat'	mōs mek.e yo	mekci mōs hay yo	'can't eat'
	mōs mek.ess.e(y) yo	mekci mōs hayss.e(y) yo	'couldn't eat'
ssu- 'write'	mōs sse yo	ssuci mōs hay yo	'can't write'
	mōs ssess.e(y) yo	ssuci mōs hayss.e(y) yo	'couldn't write'
tul- 'hear'	mōs tul.e yo	tut.ci mōs hay yo	'can't hear'
	mōs tul.ess.e(y) yo	tut.ci mōs hayss.e(y) yo	'couldn't hear'

The short negative with an occurs for processive verbs (an ka yo 'doesn't go'), less commonly for adjectives (an cak.e yo 'is not small'), and in a slightly different form for the copula (chayk i ani 'ey yo 'it is not a book'). But the short STRONG negative with mōs occurs only for processive verbs (mōs ka yo 'can't go; definitely doesn't go'): there is no corresponding form for descriptive verbs (= adjectives) or the copula, so that you will never hear *mōs cak.e yo or *chayk i mōs iey yo.

On the other hand, we find long negatives with mōs for both processive verbs (kaci mōs hay yo 'can't go; definitely doesn't go') and descriptive verbs (cākci mōs hay yo 'definitely isn't small'), though not for the copula: there are no long negatives for the copula, so there is no strong negative for the copula at all.

In the examples listed above the long negatives have the polite-style endings that are used at the end of a sentence. Other endings are also possible, when you want to put the negative into some larger sentence; for example, you can put a negative sentence into the construction with -ci man discussed in ‖ 7.2.

anc.ci an haci man = anc.ci anh.ci man = an anc.ci man 'doesn't sit but'
anc.ci an hayss.ci man = anc.ci anh.ess.ci man = an anc.ess.ci man 'didn't sit but'
cōh.ci mōs haci man 'is no good but'

This means that the phrase has two -ci endings: the first, attached to the base of the main verb, is needed to form the complex negative, and the second is needed to form the -ci man 'but' construction. You have seen examples of this usage in Basic Sentences 28 and 30, quoted at the beginning of this Note.

In speaking about an esteemed person, you can add the honorific element in any of several ways:

1. You can make the verb honorific (ka ya → kasey yo) and then build the negative on this: kasici anh.e yo. This is the most common way.
2. You can make the verb negative (ka yo → kaci anh.e yo) and then build the honorific on that: kaci anh.usey yo. This is also fairly common.
3. You can make the verb honorific (ka yo → kasey yo), build a negative on this (kasey yo →: kasici anh.e yo) and build a further honorific on that: kasici anh.usey yo. Most of the time such "double" honorifics would seem to be overdoing things, and you would do well to avoid them.

The strong negative behaves in the same way: kasici mōs hay yo, kaci mōs hasey yo, and kasici mōs hasey yo all mean '[someone esteemed] can't/won't go.'

‖ 7.4. Uses of the suspective: negative commands.

32. Kulemyen, tut.ci māsey yo. 'Then, don't listen.'

You have noticed that the polite forms can be used as a statement, (Ka yo. 'I'm going.'), a question (Kasey yo? 'Are you going?'), a command (Kasey yo! 'Please go!'), and occasionally even a suggestion (Ka yo! 'Let's go!'). The negative forms can be used as statements (An ka yo. or Kaci anh.e yo. 'I'm not going.' Mōs ka yo. or Kaci mōs hay yo. 'I can't go.') and as questions (An kasey yo? or Kasici anh.e yo? 'Aren't you going?' Mōs kasey yo? or Kasici mōs hay yo? 'Can't you go?'), but not as commands or suggestions. Instead, you make negative commands (that is, "prohibitions") and negative suggestions (that is, "dissuasions") with another auxiliary verb mā-l- 'avoid' added to the suspective -ci: Anc.ci māsey yo! 'Don't sit down!' Poci māsey yo! (or Posici mal.e yo! or Posici māsey yo!) 'Don't look!'

You have already seen examples of negative commands in a different style, the formal style, which puts a special command ending -(p)sio on bases as in Annyeng hi kasipsio! 'Go in good health!' where -psio is added to the honorific base kasi- of the verb ka-. The examples of prohibitions that you had in Lesson 1 were:

27. Hānkwuk mal ul posici māsipsio. 'Please don't look at the Korean.'
37. Yenge lo haci māsipsio. 'Please don't say it in English.'

Another way of making such forms is to put the honorific only on the verb (posici) and add the command ending -sio directly to the unextended base of mā-l-: Posici māsio! = Poci māsipsio! = Posici māsipsio! 'Please don't look!'

There is also a special ending for suggestions in the formal style, with the shape -(u)psita as you learned in Sīcak ha(si)psita! 'Let's begin!' To make negative suggestions you add this ending to the unextended base of mā-l- and produce the form māpsita (or honorific māsipsita) to use after the suspective -ci: Chayk ul po(si)ci mā(si)psita! 'Let's not look at our books!' The honorific element can be inserted with either, or both, verbs. You may think it odd to use an honorific way of speaking about an act that you yourself are involved in, but suggestions involve the persons you are speaking to as well, and the honorific refers to them: 'You whom I esteem and me, let's . . .' If your tutor prefers not to use honorifics with suggestions, follow his preferences.

7.5. The particle to: agreement of noun expressions.

11. . . . ⁿYe-tongsayng to, nam-tongsayng to ēps.ey yo . . . 'I have neither younger brothers nor younger sisters.'

17. Oppa nun swulq cip ey to, ttaynsu-hol ey to an ka yo. 'My brother doesn't go either to bars or to dance halls.'

19. Oppa to cal kaci man, na to cāl ka yo. 'My brother goes there a lot, and so do I.'

As you know, the particle to often occurs twice in a sentence, showing a kind of tandem agreement between noun phrases ('both A and B do so-and-so'; neither X nor Y does so-and-so'); more examples of this construction occur in the basic sentences of this lesson. In AFFIRMATIVE sentences, the to's mean 'both . . . and'; when the verb is NEGATIVE, they mean 'neither . . . nor.' The literal wordings both . . . and and neither . . . nor are actually somewhat formal in English, and in conversational style some other phraseology is more usual.

For affirmative agreement, for example, we often use some such construction as 'I have some pencils and (I have) some paper too' or 'I have some pencils, and also some paper' or simply 'I have pencils AND paper (saying the word and louder than the rest). All these correspond to the Korean sentence Yenphil to congi to iss.ey yo.

For negative agreement, actual use of the words neither . . . nor is quite rare in informal speech; we usually prefer some such wording as 'I haven't any pencils and I haven't any paper either' or 'I haven't any pencils or any paper either' or simply 'I haven't any pencils OR paper' (pronouncing the word or louder than the other words.

The translations given here for to . . . to, then, as 'both . . . and' and 'neither . . . nor' should be considered as dictionary definitions, subject to adjustment in the expression of corresponding English meanings.

Notice that the phrases with to must AGREE with each other—that is, you are saying the same thing about both of them. To say DIFFERENT things about two noun expressions, you do not use to; cf. Basic Sentence 9:

Ttal un ttok-ttok haci man, atul un ttok-ttok haci mōs hay yo. 'The daughter is bright, but the son isn't bright at all.'

If both—or neither—was bright, you would use the particle to with each:

Ttal to ttok-ttok haci man, atul to ttok-ttok hay yo. 'The daughter is bright, but then so is the son.'

Ttal to ttok-ttok haci anh.ci man, atul to ttok-ttok haci anh.e yo. 'The daughter isn't bright, and the son isn't either.'

In sentences having two clauses linked by -ci man 'but' (as discussed in ‖ 7.2 above), to . . . to means the same thing: 'not only A, but also B' — that is, 'both A and B.' (See Basic Sentence 19, quoted above.) If the sentence is negative, the expression means 'not only does A not (do so-and-so) — B doesn't either':

Oppa to cal kaci anh.ci man, na to cal kaci anh.e yo. 'My brother doesn't go there much, and neither do I.'

‖ 7.6. The adverb tto, the particle to, and the pseudo-particle ina/'na.

The adverb tto has the same general type of meaning as the particle to: 'and, again, too.' However, since tto is an adverb it is independent and does not have to be attached to a noun expression, unlike the particle. Tto at the beginning of a sentence means 'and also' or 'and further(more)'; you have also had Kuliko in this meaning, and you can start a sentence with both of them: Kuliko tto . . . 'And moreover . . . .'

Notice the similarity between to the particle and tto the adverb in such sentences as the following:

Congi to | iss.ey yo. 'There's paper, too.'
Congi (nun) | tto iss.ey yo. 'There's still some more paper.'

An occasional accident of sound change may even make to and tto sound the same in some environments:

Chayk to iss.ey yo. 'There are books, too.'
Chayk (|) tto iss.ey yo. 'There are still some (more) books.' } /chayktto/

The words to and ina/'na are alike in some ways, too. You learned ina/'na in Lesson 6 with meaning 'about, approximately' and as a generalizer of the meaning of an interrogative word (nwuku 'na 'anybody at all'). Both to and ina/'na can be used twice in a sentence — to to show tandem agreement, and ina/'na to show freedom or indifference of choice:

kong-chayk to yenphil to . . . 'both notebooks and pencils' or 'neither notebooks nor pencils . . .'
kong-chayk ina yenphil ina . . . 'both notebooks and pencils' or 'either notebooks or pencils . . .'

The particle to is definite, while ina/'na is vague or unspecific:

I kes to ce kes to cōh.a yo. 'Both this one and that one are all right.'
I kes ina ce kes ina cōh.a yo. 'Either this one or that one is all right.'

The pseudo-particle ina/'na, then, when it is used after each of two (or more) comparable noun expressions, means '(either) . . . or (. . . or).' The adverb-particle phrase tto nun means 'or (else)' BETWEEN NOUN EXPRESSIONS: yenphil | tto nun mānnyen-phil 'a pencil or (else) a fountain pen.'

At the beginning of a sentence, the phrase tto nun also has this contrastive idea, as you have seen in Basic Sentence 27 of this lesson:

Tto nun, um.ak-hoy ey to kaci anh.ess.ey yo. '[I haven't been to a single movie this fall, disliking them as I do.] Nor (on the other hand) have I been to any concerts either [and I DO like concerts].'

Tto nun and ina/'na thus both mean 'or'; but ina/'na accepts either choice indifferently where tto nun excludes one of the choices, by contrasting it with the accepted choice.

7.7. Kinship terms.

The Korean names for relatives can be divided into two types: those for which some of the words differ according to the sex of the person related (that is, whether you are speaking for example about a MAN'S brother or a WOMAN'S brother), and those for which the words are the same regardless of the sex of the person related.

You have noticed also that the Koreans cannot speak of their brothers and sisters without specifying whether that person is older or younger than the person related.

The words for 'grandfather' and 'grandmother' are also used to mean 'old man' and 'old woman'; similarly, the words for 'uncle' and 'aunt' are used to mean '(older) man' and '(older) lady,' particularly in expressions used by children, or in speaking to children, such as 'Say hello to the MAN, dear' or 'The LADY who lives next door.'

The word cip (TAYK) 'house' is also used in the way we use the word 'family': Wuli cip i khe yo 'Our house [family] is large.' Sik.kwu — literally, 'mouths to feed' — means 'members of the family.' To ask — or tell — how many people there are in someone's family, you can use a form of either iss- '(there) are' or i- (the copula):

Sik.kwu ka | meych iey yo? 'Your family members | are how many (people)?'
Sik.kwu ka | meych i iss.ey yo? 'Your family members | how many of them are there?

You have noticed that Koreans often referred to 'we/us' where Americans would say 'I/me': wuli kāy 'my dog.' This is extended even to cases where the explanation given earlier ('belonging to our family') is not so convincing: wuli namphyen is the usual way of saying 'my husband,' and wuli an(h)ay 'my wife.'

7.8. Honorifics.

When you are talking in Korean about someone who has relatively high social status — a government official, a foreign guest, a minister, a teacher — you use some special forms called HONORIFICS. (Remember that when you are talking TO someone of high status, you use either the polite style or the formal style — a matter of which endings you put on the verbs at the end of sentences.) Honorifics are also used frequently to refer to the second person; this is a way of honoring your listener, as well as showing that you mean 'YOU' without actually using a pronoun.

There are several kinds of honorifics.

1. Nouns

Some English nouns are translated by two different Korean nouns, one neutral and the other honorific:

cip 'house; home'	TAYK '(esteemed) house or home'
nai '(years of) age'	"YENSEY '(years of) age (of an esteemed person)'
sālam 'person'	PUN '(esteemed) person'

Some terms for relatives also have separate honorific forms: see the Supplementary Vocabulary of this lesson.

2. Verbs

Similarly, a few verbs come in pairs: a neutral and an honorific one.

ca yo 'sleeps'	cwumusey yo '[someone esteemed] sleeps'
iss.ey yo 'stays'	kyēysey yo '[someone esteemed] stays'
mek.e yo 'eats'	capswusey yo '[someone esteemed] eats'

But for most verbs you just add the honorific marker -(u)si- [or its abbreviated form -(u)sy-] to the base:

anc.e yo 'sits'	anc.usey yo '[someone esteemed] sits'
hay yo 'does'	hasey yo '[someone esteemed] does'
wa yo 'comes'	osey yo '[someone esteemed] comes'
tul.e yo 'hears'	tul.usey yo '[someone esteemed] hears'

3. Particles

The particle kkey is honorific; it means the same thing as eykey and hanthey — 'to [a person]' — but is used only after nouns denoting a specially honored person:

ape' nim kkey 'to [esteemed] father'

The combination kkey se is the honorific equivalent of eykey se 'from [a person]':

moksa nim kkey se 'from the [esteemed] minister'

These phrases meaning 'from,' both the honorific and the neutral one, have a special use as subject markers, either alone or followed by the deemphasizing particle nun:

eykey se or eykey se nun [neutral — rarely used]
kkey se or kkey se nun [honorific]

You saw an example of this in Basic Sentence 20:

Ape' nim kkey se nun, mues ul hasey yo. 'What does your father do?'

This OBLIQUE SUBJECT is used only for persons, and is another example of characteristic Korean 'softness' — more polite because it is less direct and abrupt. For institutions ("the bank sent it," "the school gave him money," etc.) you use ey se (nun) or se (nun) as a similar sort of indirect subject or topic.

Here are some more examples of honorifics and oblique subjects used in sentences:

1. Hal-'me' nim kkey phyēnci lul ssess.ey yo.	I wrote Grandmother a letter.
2. Sensayng nim kkey se uy phyēnci lul pat.ess.ey yo.	I received a letter from the teacher.
3. Hal-ape' nim kkey se catong-cha ka ēps.usey yo.	Doesn't your grandfather have a car?
4. Ape' nim i tayk ey an kyēysey yo?	Isn't your father at home?
5. Wuli kyōhoy (ey) se Pak moksa nim kkey phyēnci lul ssess.ey yo.	Our church wrote a letter to Reverend Pak.

An important thing to remember about honorifics is that YOU NEVER USE HONORIFICS TO REFER TO YOURSELF OR TO A RELATIVE YOUNGER THAN YOURSELF. This principle makes a conversation between 'you' and 'me' quite clear without using anything corresponding to the English pronouns:

Eti kasey yo?	Where are you going?

Hak.kyo ey ka yo.	I'm going to school.
Tayk ey kyēysey yo?	Are you at home?
Cip ey iss.ey yo.	I'm at home.
Eti se osyess.ey yo.	Where have you come from?
Wuphyen-kwuk ey se wass.ey yo.	I've come from the post office.

Notice also the following examples:

Olapenim i kongpu lul hasey yo.	My older brother is studying.
Nam-tongsayng i kongpu lul hay yo.	My younger brother is studying.

But it is not obligatory to use honorifics for older members of the family:

Nwūna ka [or Nwū' nim i] cip ey se īl ul hay yo [or hasey yo] 'My older sister works at home.'

When you address older members of your family, you usually call them by title: Nwū' nim, eti kasey yo. 'Where are you going [Older] Sister?' But you normally address younger relatives by given name: Ok.huy, eti ka. 'Where are you going, [younger sister] Ok.huy?' (The polite particle yo usually drops when you are speaking to younger relatives.)

‖ 7.9. Meanings for cōh.a yo and related words.

Cōh.a yo—a descriptive verb—has the meanings (1) 'is good or fine or all right' and (2) 'is liked.' In the first meaning, only one noun phrase is involved, but in the second meaning, it often has two subjects, or else a topic and a subject:

1. I kes i cōh.a yo. 'This is good.'
2. Nay ka [or Na nun] i kes i cōh.a yo. 'I like this.' [= As for me, this is liked.]

The phrase cōh.a hay yo, a processive verb, means 'finds it good' or 'likes it' and takes direct objects:

Nay ka i kes ul cōh.a hay yo. 'I like it.'

This phrase also has the emotional connotation '[someone] is happy (or glad)—commonly used in speaking of someone else, but sometimes for special emphasis to mean 'I am happy (or glad).'

Notice the negative forms of each of these:

cōh.ci anh.e yo '[something] isn't good; [something] isn't liked'
cōh.a haci anh.e yo '[someone] doesn't like [something]'

The antonyms are comparable expressions:

cōh.a yo 'is liked' . . . . silh.e yo 'is disliked' [base silh-]
cōh.a hay yo 'likes' . . . . silh.e hay yo 'dislikes'

Both of these appeared in the basic sentences of this lesson:

31. Na nun ku yēyki ka silh.e yo. 'I don't like that story.' [= As for me, that story is disliked; the thing disliked is the SUBJECT]

29. . . . nay yak.hon-ca nun kāngyen ul silh.e hay yo. 'My fiancée dislikes lectures.' [The thing disliked is the DIRECT OBJECT]

Notice that in English the meanings of the negative phrase cōh.a haci anh.e yo 'doesn't like' and the affirmative phrase silh.e hay yo 'dislikes' usually fall together as the phrase 'do(es)n't like.' The Korean cōh.a haci anh.e yo implies simple absence of fondness, without actual aversion; silh.e hay yo, on the other hand, implies an active or positive dislike. You can, of course, make a negative out of the 'dislike' phrases too: silh.ci anh.e yo 'I don't dislike it,' silh.e haci anh.e yo 'he doesn't dislike it.'

‖ 7.10. Words for 'young' and 'old.'

To say someone is 'old' (meaning he has lived for many years) you use the verb nulk.e yo 'gets old'; in its modifier form (‖12.1) this is nulk.un . . . '. . . who is old,' and the expression nulk.un i = nulk.un salam means 'an old person, an oldster.' To say someone is '(still) young,' though an adult, you use the expression celm.e yo; the modifier form is celm.un . . . , and celm.un i = celm.un sālam 'a young person, a young adult.' To refer to a child as being 'young' you use a different expression elye yo (eli-); the modifier form is elin . . . , so elin i (or elin ai) means 'a young one, a child.'

But when you want to say someone is 'oldER' or 'youngER' than someone else, you do not ordinarily use these expressions; they are, as it were, absolute—not relative. When you want to speak of relative age, you use the word for 'age' (nai): nai ka wi 'ey yo 'the age is above (= higher),' nai ka alay 'ey yo 'the age is below (= lower).' So you can ask Nwu' ka nai ka wi 'ey yo 'Who is the older (or oldest)?' To say 'He is older THAN me' you have to use the particle pota 'than' (‖ 21.7): Ku sālam i na pota nai ka wi 'ey yo. To say 'How old are you?' you say Meych sal iey yo 'How many years-of-age is it?' or Meych sal ul mek.ess.ey yo 'How many years-of-age did you "eat up?"' Nai lul mek.e yo means 'acquires age' (literally 'eats age up').

The word 'old' has two meanings in English; we have been talking about the meaning that is the opposite of 'young' and has to do with people. But 'old' is also the opposite of 'new' and can have to do with things as well as people. In that case, the Korean word is nalk.e yo; the modifier form is nalk.un . . . so that nalk.un kes means 'old things, things that have been around for a long time.' But instead of nalk.un you often find hēn . . . '. . . that is worn (out) with age,' the modifier form from hel.e yo 'gets worn (out), suffers from age and use': hēn kes 'old (used) things,' hēn catong-cha 'an old car,' hēn os 'old clothes.' The opposite of hēn . . . is say . . . 'new': say kes 'new things,' say catong-cha 'a new car,' say os 'new clothes.' But say, like i 'this,' functions as a pre-noun; to say 'it is new' you have to use a special form say-lowa yo (suspective form say-lopci); or you can say say kes iey yo 'it is a new one.'

EXERCISES

I

Each of the following Korean sentences means '[someone] does something.' Change the verb expression so that the meaning is '[someone] DOESN'T DO something,' using the longer way of saying 'does not do.' Then translate the sentence. For example, the first will be: Kim puin uy hyeng nim un ku hak.kyo se kongpu lul haci anh.ess.ey yo. 'Mrs. Kim's older sister did not study at that school.'

1. Kim sensayng puin uy hyeng nim un ku hak.kyo se kongpu lul hayss.ey yo.
2. Kim sensayng puin uy si-ape' nim un tōn i mānh.e yo.
3. Kim sensayng uy cāngin un tōn i cek.e yo.
4. Sensayng nim to Kim sensayng uy chayk ul ilk.ess.ey yo?
5. Na nun Ilpon se wass.ey yo.
6. Enni nun way na lul kitalyess.ey yo.
7. Hal-apeci nun tāmpay lul cal phiwe yo.
8. Na nun Hānkwuk mal ul Hānkwuk se paywess.ey yo.
9. Acessi nun ku sinmun ul pwa yo.
10. Atul un phul ul kkakk.ess.ey yo.
11. Ape' nim un hal-ape' nim kkey se phyēnci lul pat.usyess.ey yo.
12. Cokha atul un nay yeph ey anc.ess.ey yo.
13. Soncwu ai tul un nal mata hak.kyo ey ka yo.
14. Ku sawi nun cāngmo lul cōh.a hay yo.
15. Cang sensayng un oppa wa kath.i latio lul tul.e yo.
16. Tho-yoil ey nun na nun cal swie yo.

II

Each of the following items includes two sentences, the second beginning with Kuleh.ci man 'but . . . .' Link the two sentences into one by changing the verb expression of the first to mean 'does, but . . .' and dropping the kuleh.ci man. Then translate the combined sentence that results. For example, the first will be: Na nun yenghwa kwūkyeng ul cal kaci man, tongsayng un cal kaci anh.e yo. 'I often go to the movies, but my younger brother [sister] doesn't go much.'

1. Na nun yenghwa kwūkyeng ul cal ka yo. Kuleh.ci man, tongsayng un cal kaci anh.e yo.
2. Na nun tōn i cek.e yo. Kuleh.ci man, chinkwu ka mānh.e yo.
3. Kim moksa nun camay ka ēps.ey yo. Kuleh.ci man, hyengcey ka twūl iss.ey yo.
4. Oppa nun ilcciki wass.ey yo. Kuleh.ci man, tongsayng un nuc.key wass.ey yo.
5. Ku ape' nim un wuphyen-kwuk ey se īl ul hasey yo. Kuleh.ci man, phyēnci lul mānh.i an ssusey yo.
6. Na nun ku cen ey nun pyengceng iess.ey yo. Kuleh.ci man, cikum un senkyo-sa 'ey yo.
7. 'Mak-nay nun elye yo. Kuleh.ci man, pumo nim un celm.usici anh.e yo.
8. Nay yak.hon-ca nun na hanthey kkoch ul cwuess.ey yo. Kuleh.ci man, na nun kkoch ul cōh.a haci anh.e yo.
9. Acwumeni nun Pusan ey sal.e yo. Kuleh.ci man, Sam-welq tal mata Sewul ey wa yo.
10. Kāy nun nay yeph ey anc.e yo. Kuleh.ci man, latio lul mōs tul.e yo.
11. Wuli cip un khuci anh.e yo. Kuleh.ci man, cōh.a yo.
12. Na nun cal caci anh.ess.ey yo. Kuleh.ci man, ilcciki il.e nass.ey yo.
13. Na nun Yenge lul kaluchye yo. Kuleh.ci man, Yengkwuk salam i ani 'ey yo.
14. Na nun phul ul kkakk.e yo. Kuleh.ci man, tōn ul pat.ci anh.e yo.
15. Na nun eceyq pam ey cal kongpu hayss.ey yo. Kuleh.ci man, onul achim ilcciki il.e na se com te paywess.ey yo.
16. Haksayng tul un mānh.e yo. Kuleh.ci man, hak.kyo nun cak.e yo.

III

Here are some English sentences. Express each one in Korean TWICE: the first time insert 'my younger brother' as the subject, and the second time use 'my father' as the subject.

1. He reads his newspaper under the tree in the garden.
2. He went to bed early last night, but he didn't get up early this morning.
3. He doesn't eat much meat and he doesn't drink much water either.
4. He's old, but his heart is young.
5. He's a factory worker.
6. He bought cigarettes at the drugstore, but he didn't buy any matches.
7. He doesn't like magazines, but he likes books.
8. He gets some money from the bank every Wednesday morning.
9. He wasn't home yesterday afternoon, but he's home now.
10. He works hard in the daytime. At night, he rests.
11. He taught English at the University last year, but he doesn't teach there now.
12. He waited at the hotel for an hour, but his friend didn't show up.
13. He doesn't cut the grass every week.
14. He gave my little sister some money yesterday.
15. He listened to the radio for two hours last night.

IV

Translate the following conversation into Korean. Mr. Kim and Mr. Pak are talking.

1. My family ['house'] is big. There are many members ['members are many'].
2. How many brothers and sisters do you have, Mr. Kim?
3. I have four younger brothers and one younger sister.
4. You don't have any older brothers or sisters?
5. That's right, I haven't. I have neither older brothers nor older sisters.
6. Who is the youngest in your family?
7. My younger sister is the baby of the family. She is nine years old.
8. Are you married, Mr. Kim?
9. Yes, I'm married, but my wife and I ['I and my wife'] live at (my) father's house.
10. I'm married too. But I don't live with my folks. I live with my in-laws [an(h)ay uy pumo].
11. Is your father-in-law nice, Mr. Pak? Is your mother-in-law nice? Do you like your parents-in-law?
12. Both my father-in-law and my mother-in-law are nice. I like them both. Your in-laws don't live in Seoul, Mr. Kim?
13. That's right. They don't live in Seoul. They live in Phyengyang.
14. When did your wife come to Seoul, Mr. Kim?
15. She came to ˡIhwa College a few years ago. She was a student. She studied English. I taught English at ˡIhwa College. So, we got married.
16. My father was a university professor too, but he is very old now. He doesn't teach at the university now. He just writes books at home.
17. He likes students, but he hasn't been to the University once this fall.
18. Do you have children, Mr. Pak?
19. Yes, we now have a son and a daughter. (And) you, Mr. Kim?
20. I still have neither son nor daughter.

VOCABULARY DRILL

Say each of the following sentences in Korean five different times—each time using in the blank space one of the expressions listed below it.

1. I got a letter from my—.
   spouse
   older brother
   nephew
   grandmother
   mother-in-law

2. My—gave me some money.
   father
   aunt
   older sister
   parents
   grandfather

3. My friend is sitting next to his—.
   younger brother
   older brother
   father-in-law
   nephew
   spouse

4. My friend lives with—.
   older brother
   parents
   father-in-law
   grandchildren
   aunt

5. My younger sister is reading a book to her—.
   cousin
   spouse
   sisters
   brothers
   children

COMPREHENSION

I

Your Korean teacher, referring to the Supplementary Vocabulary, will call off pairs of words for relatives, then ask you to name the one from each pair which is normally older than the other. If the first pair, for example should be

acessi
cokha

you will of course name <u>acessi</u>, since an uncle is normally older than a nephew or niece.

II

Your Korean teacher will talk to you for five or ten minutes about himself and the other members of his family: who and how many they are, their ages, what sort of work they do, their likes and dislikes, their habits. Listen carefully, and jot things down if you like. Then at the end, the teacher will ask you questions about what he has told you, to find out how well you have followed the narrative. It might be worth while for the teacher to run through the story again after the questions have been asked and answered.

LESSON 8. DAILY ACTIVITIES

BASIC SENTENCES

Korean	English	Amplification
1. Na nun sēyswu hako myēnto hay yo.	I get washed up and shaved.	sēyswu hay yo 'washes (oneself) up' sēyswu hako 'washes up and . . .' myēnto hay yo 'shaves oneself'
2. Os ul ipko, meli lul pis.e yo.	I get dressed and comb my hair.	os 'clothing' ip.e yo 'puts on; wears (clothing)' ipko 'puts on (wears) and . . .' os ul ipko 'gets dressed and . . .' meli 'the head; (= meli thel) hair (on the head)' pis.e yo 'combs'
3. Na nun neykthai lul māyko iss.ey yo.	I am wearing a necktie.	neykthai 'necktie' māy yo 'ties; puts on, wears [tie, shoelaces, etc.]' māyko iss.ey yo 'is tying; is putting on, is wearing'
4. Moca lul ssuko iss.ey yo.	I am wearing a hat.	moca 'hat' sse yo 'puts on, wears (on or over the head)' ssuko iss.ey yo 'is putting on, is wearing (on the head)'
5. Say kwutwu lul sin.ko siph.e yo.	I want to wear my new shoes.	say . . . 'new' kwutwu 'shoe(s)—esp. Western type' sin.e yo 'puts on, wears (footgear)' siph.e yo 'wants to; would like to' sin.ko [sinkko] siph.e yo 'wants (would like) to put on <u>or</u> wear (footgear)'
6. Say cāngkap ul kkiko siph.e yo.	I want to wear my new gloves.	cāngkap 'glove(s)' kkie yo, kkyē yo 'puts on <u>or</u> wears (gloves)'

Korean	English	Amplification
		kkiko siph.e yo 'wants to put on or wear (gloves)'
7. Sangcem ey ka se, sin ul sa yo.	I'm going to the store and buy some shoes. (or Let's go to the store and buy some shoes!)	ka se 'goes and (then) . . . ; goes (in order) to . . .' sin 'shoe(s)—esp. Korean type'
8. Say sin ul sa se, cōh.a yo.	I'm glad I bought new shoes.	sa se 'buys, and (so) . . .' = I bought new shoes, so I'm glad.
9. Na nun tōn i mānh.ci anh.e to, nul mulken ul sa yo.	Even though I haven't much money, I'm always buying things.	mānh.ci anh.e to 'even though there isn't much' mulken 'things, goods'
10. Sangcem i mel.e to, cacwu ka yo.	Even though the stores are a long way off, I go there often.	mel.e yo [mē-l-] 'is far, distant, a long way (off)' mel.e to 'even though [it] is far' cacwu 'often'
11. Wuli hal-apeci nun tōn i cokum to ēps.ess.e to, nul kippe hayss.ey yo.	My grandfather was always happy, even though he had no money at all.	cokum to 'even a little bit' ēps.ess.e to 'even though (there) wasn't; even though [he] hadn't' kippe yo 'is happy or glad' kippe hay yo 'is happy or glad'
12. Onul say os ul ip.e to cōh.a yo?	Is it all right for me to [= May I] wear my new clothes today?	ip.e to 'even though [I] wear' ip.e to cōh.a yo? 'may [I] wear? is it all right if [I] wear?'
13. Say sin ul sin.e to kwaynchanh.e yo?	May I wear my new shoes?	sin.e to 'even though [I] wear (footgear)' kwaynchanh.e yo 'it's all right, it doesn't matter, it makes no difference' sin.e to kwaynchanh.e yo? '(even though I wear, does it matter? =) may [I] wear? is it all right if [I] wear?'
14. Onulq pam ey cip ey nuc.key tol.a wa to kwaynchanh.e yo?	Is it all right for me to [= Do you mind if I] come (back) home late tonight?	tol.a yo 'turns' tol.a wa yo 'comes back, returns, comes home' tol.a wa to 'even if [I] come back'

Korean	English	Amplification
15. Onul(q) cenyek ey chinkwu lul manna ya hay yo.	This evening I have to meet a friend.	manna ya 'only if I meet' manna ya hay yo 'have to meet or must meet (a person)'
16. Nuc.e to yeses si cen ey nun ku chinkwu cip ey ka ya hay yo.	At the latest, I've got to get to ['that'=] my friend's house by six o'clock.	nuc.e yo 'is late; gets late' nuc.e to 'even though it is (or gets) late; at the latest' ka ya hay yo 'has to go, must go'
17. Catong-cha lul thako ka yo, kel.e ka yo.	Are you going to drive or walk?	= Are you going riding in a car, or going walking? catong-cha 'car, automobile; (= thayksi) taxi, cab' catong-cha lul tha yo 'gets in or rides [in] a car' catong-cha lul thako ka yo 'goes riding [in] a car = goes by car, drives' kel.e yo [kēl-] 'walks' kel.e ka yo 'goes [somewhere by] walking, goes on foot'
18. Nuc.e se, catong-cha lul thako ka ya hay yo.	It's late, so I'll have to go by car.	nuc.e se 'it's late, so . . .' thako ka ya hay yo 'has to go by riding, has to ride'
19. Catong-cha han tay lul ppalli pulle cwusipsio.	Please call a ['car'=] cab for me right away.	catong-cha han tay '[car, one vehicle=] a car' pulle yo [pulu-] 'calls, hails' cwusipsio 'please give me!' pulle cwusipsio '[please give me (the act of) calling=] please call for me'
20. Kuleh.ci man, yeki se catong-cha lo nun cek.e to sam-wen un tul.e yo.	But from here by car, it will cost at least 3 wen.	cek.e to 'even though it's small, even though (there are) few; at least' tul.e yo [tu-l-] 'cost'
21. Ani yo?? Amman mānh.e to, ī-wen ō-sip cen pakk-ey nun an tul.e yo.	No, at the very most, it will cost only 2.50 wen.	amman 'however much' [< āmu man] mānh.e to 'even though (there are) many; at most' . . . pakk-ey an tul.e yo '[outside of or except for . . . it won't cost=] it will only cost'

Korean	English	Amplification
22. Tōn sip-wen man cwusey yo.	Let me have 10 wen, please.	tōn sip-wen man '10 wen (of money)' cwusey yo 'please give'
23. Catong-cha hōysa ey cēnhwa lul kel.e posey yo.	Give the cab company a call (and see . . .).	hōysa 'company, firm' cēnhwa 'telephone (call)' (. . . ey/eykey) cēnhwa lul kel.e yo [kē-l-] or hay yo 'telephone (to . . .), calls (. . .) on the telephone' cēnhwa lul hay posey yo 'try telephoning; telephone and see (what results)'
24. Chayk man ilk.ci mālko, catong-cha hōysa lul ese cēnhwa lo pulle yo.	Don't just [sit there and] read a book—go on and call the cab company on the phone.	ilk.ci mālko 'don't read, [and] . . . ' ese 'right away; please' cēnhwa lo pulle yo 'calls by phone'
25. Tto han pen cēnhwa lul hay pwa yo.	Try calling again.	cēnhwa lul hay pwa yo 'tries telephoning; telephones (to see what will happen)'
26. Na nun wuli chinkwu ka kongpu lul cal hay se, cōh.a yo.	I'm glad our friend is studying hard [or doing well in his studies].	hay se . . . 'does, and (then) . . . ; does, (and) so . . .' hay se cōh.a yo '[he does, so it's good =] am glad he does'
27. Sensayng to, (wuli chinkwu ka kongpu lul cal hay se) cōh.a hasey yo.	The teacher's glad (he's studying hard or doing well) too.	hay se cōh.a hasey yo '[someone esteemed] is glad [he] does'
28. Na nun ku chinkwu chelem kongpu lul cal hako siph.e yo.	I want to study hard, like ('that' =) my friend.	kongpu (lul) hako siph.e yo 'would like to study, wants to study'
29. Ku chinkwu nun na lul [or nay īl ul] mānh.i towa cwue yo.	('That' =) My friend helps me [or me in my affairs] a lot.	īl 'things, affairs, circumstances, situation; job, work' towa yo 'helps' towa cwue yo '[gives (the act of) helping =] helps [someone]'
30. Thukpyel hi wuli pumo nim ul nul towa tulye yo.	Especially, he's always helping my parents.	thukpyel 'special, particular' thukpyel hay yo 'is special' thukpyel hi '(e)specially, particularly'

Korean	English	Amplification
		tulye yo 'gives [to someone esteemed]' towa tulye yo '[gives help to =] helps [someone esteemed]'
31. Na to mullon ku chinkwu lul towa cwuko, ku uy pumo nim ul towa tulye yo.	Of course I help him and (help) his parents, too.	mullon 'of course' towa cwuko 'helps and . . . [gives help and . . .]'
32. Ku chinkwu nun cīnan cwuil na hanthey chayk han kwen ul sa cwuess.ko, emeni hanthey kkoch ul sa tulyess.ey yo.	Last week he bought ['one' =] a book for me and (bought) some flowers for my mother.	sa cwue yo '[gives (the act of) buying =] buys (for someone)' sa cwuess.e(y) yo '[gave (the act of) buying =] bought (for someone)' sa cwuess.ko 'bought (for someone), and . . .' sa tulyess.e(y) yo 'bought (for someone esteemed) [= gave to someone esteemed (the act of) buying]'
33. Ku chayk ul ilk.ko siph.e hasey yo?	Would you like to read the book?	ilk.ko 'reads, and . . .' ilk.ko siph.e yo 'would like to read, wants to read' ilk.ko siph.e hasey yo '[someone esteemed] would like to read or wants to read'
34. Kim sensayng un anc.e iss.ko, Pak sensayng un se iss.ey yo.	Mr. Kim is sitting (down), and Mr. Pak is standing (up).	anc.e iss.ey yo 'is seated' anc.e iss.ko . . . 'is sitting and . . .' se yo [su-] 'stands' il.e se yo 'stands up' se iss.ey yo 'is standing'

SUPPLEMENTARY VOCABULARY

ille yo [ilu-]	is early	na ka yo	goes out
kakkawe yo [kakkaw-]	is near(by), close	nah.a yo [pron. naa yo]	gives birth to
tul.e yo [tu-l-]	enters		
tul.e wa yo	comes in	tte yo	becomes detached; leaves; floats
tul.e ka yo	goes in		
na yo	emerges, exits, leaves; is produced, is born	tte-na yo	leaves, departs, goes away
		nwuwe yo [nwuw-]	lies down
na wa yo	comes out	nwuwe iss.ey yo	is lying down, is recumbent

māycem	a shop, a stand
cēm.wen	a (store) clerk
sāmu-wen	a clerk (in an office), an office worker
phal.e yo [pha-l-]	sells
sse yo [ssu-]	uses; spends (money)
cēncha	streetcar; electric train
kicha	(steam or diesel) train
(p)pesu	bus
thayksi	taxi, cab
hapsung (thayksi)	jitney (cab)
chacang	conductor
son	hand
phal	arm
pal	foot
tali	leg
i(q-pal)	teeth
chi-sol, iq-sol	toothbrush
takk.e yo	polishes, shines
i lul takk.e yo	brushes one's teeth
kwutwu lul takk.e yo	shines one's shoes
ssis.e yo	washes (anything)
kam.e yo [kā-m-]	washes (one's hair or body)
mok.yok	bathing
mok.yok (ul) hay yo	takes a bath
mok.yok-thong	bathtub
syawa, syawe	shower
pinwu	soap
swūken	towel
sonq swuken	handkerchief
sēyswuq tayya	wash basin
chan mul	cold water
tewun mul	hot water
el.um mul	ice water
waisyassu, syassu [usually pron. s(y)atsu]	shirt

paci	trousers
cokki	vest
yangpok	suit; dress (Western style)
chima	skirt
cekoli	Korean jacket or blouse
nāypok, nāyuy, sōk os	underwear
yangmal	(Western-style) socks, stockings
pesen, posen	(Korean) socks, stockings
ōythwu	overcoat
tanchwu, taynchwu	button
tanchwu lul kkie yo or chaywe yo [chaywu-]	buttons a button
os ul tanchwu lo chaywe yo or os tanchwu lul chaywe yo	buttons clothing
panci	ring (for the finger)
panci lul kkie yo	puts on or wears a ring
phin	pin
phin ul kkoc.a yo	puts on or wears a pin
tti	belt
tti lul ttie yo	puts on or wears a belt
ānkyeng	(eye)glasses
ānkyeng ul sse yo [ssu-]	puts on or wears glasses
sin kkun	shoelaces, shoestrings
sin kkun ul māy yo	puts on or wears ('ties') shoelaces
wūsan, yangsan	umbrella
wūsan ul sse yo [ssu-]	carries an umbrella, walks under an umbrella
wūsan ul pat.e yo	opens (carries) an umbrella
wūsan ul tat.e yo	closes an umbrella
wūsan ul cep.e yo	folds up (or furls) an umbrella
os ul pes.e yo	removes a garment, takes off clothes, gets undressed

NOTES

8.1. Expressions for 'only.'

21\. . . . ī-wen ō-sip cen pakk-ey nun an tule yo. 'It will only cost 2.50 wen.'

22\. Tōn sip-wen man cwusey yo. 'Let me have 10 wen, please.'

The particle man plus an AFFIRMATIVE verb means 'only.' The quasi-particle pakk-ey (derived from the place noun pakk 'outside' + the particle ey) plus a NEGATIVE verb arrives at the same meaning by a more circuitous route. For example:

Il-wen pakk-ey ēps.ey yo. 'I have only a dollar.' [= Except for or outside of a dollar, I haven't (anything); or I haven't (anything) but a dollar.]

Here are some more examples of this quasi-particle:

1. Na nun ai hana pakk-ey ēps.ey yo. — I have only one child.
2. Yenphil pakk-ey ēps.ey yo. — I have nothing but a pencil.
3. Eceyq pam yenghwa-kwan ey na pakk-ey an kass.ey yo. — I was the only one who went to the movies last night.
4. Koki pakk-ey mōs mek.ess.ey yo. — I could only eat meat.

Remember that with numerical expressions man 'only' or 'just' has no English equivalent: it means 'no more, no less' or 'exactly [the number specified].' See Basic Sentence 22.

8.2. Directional expressions.

The particle ulo/lo 'with, by (means of)' is used with vehicles when the verb is ka yo 'goes' or wa yo 'comes':

cēncha lo ka yo 'goes by streetcar, goes on a streetcar'
kicha lo wass.e yo 'came by train, came on the train'

The verb tha yo 'gets on (a vehicle, a horse); rides,' on the other hand, takes a direct object:

cēncha lul thako . . . 'riding [on] a streetcar'
kicha lul thako oci anh.e yo 'doesn't come (riding) [on] the train'

Kel.e yo 'walks' resembles tha yo 'rides' in that it is not used alone in sentences implying purposeful direction. It too joins in phrases with ka yo 'goes' or wa yo 'comes' but in its infinitive form:

kel.e kass.ey yo 'went walking' = 'walked [there]
kel.e oci anh.e yo 'doesn't come walking' = 'doesn't walk [here]

8.3. Verbs: gerund form -ko.

Korean verbs with the ending -ko are in the GERUND form. This is a one-shape ending, like the -ci suspective form; it is the same regardless of whether it comes after a vowel or a consonant.

(Two connective words you have learned come from gerund verb forms: these are hako 'and' and kuliko 'and, then, and then.')

There are tenseless gerunds, made by attaching the ending -ko to the base of the verb (ka- 'go': kako), and past-tense gerunds, made by attaching -ko to the past-tense base with the automatic sound change -ss.k- → -t.k- → -kk-.

Base:	ka- 'go'
Past-tense base:	ka-ss-
Past-tense gerund:	kass.ko [kakko] 'went and . . . '

In actual speech, however, past-tense gerunds are uncommon; they appear only in the first usage described below (‖ 8.4) in the meaning '. . . and . . .' to anticipate a past-tense verb at the end of the sentence; even here, they are used only in long sentences and could still be replaced, just as correctly, by a plain gerund.

To make honorific gerunds, you add -ko to the honorific base ending in -si-:

Base:	ka- 'go'
Honorific base:	ka-si-
Honorific gerund:	kasiko '[someone esteemed] goes, and . . .'

In the past tense, you add -ko to the past honorific base:

Base:	ka- 'go'
Honorific past base:	ka-syess-
Honorific past gerund:	kasyess.ko [kasekko] '[someone esteemed] went, and . . .'

The Korean gerund has three different meanings, depending on how it is used in the sentence:

1. does or is [so-and-so], and . . .
2. doing or being [so-and-so]
3. to do or to be [so-and-so]

These uses are described in ‖ 8.4–6 below.

Now, how do you go about forming the gerund? One-shape endings that begin with voiceless consonants (t, s, c, k) all attach to bases in much the same way, so that the -ko gerund is formed very much like the -ci suspective. Here are some rules to help you with the spelling and the pronunciation:

1. In all cases, both nouns and verbs alike, the sequences that we spell pk, pc, kp, kc (etc.) are pronounced /pkk, pcc, kpp, kcc/ (etc); because these sound changes are automatic they are ignored in our spelling:

ip-	'wear'	→ ipko /ipkko/
		→ ipci /ipcci/
mek-	'eat'	→ mek.ko / mekko/
		→ mekci / mekcci/

2. The sequences -t.k- and -t.c- are pronounced /-kk-/ and /-cc-/ respectively:

tat-	'close'	→ tat.ko /takko/
		→ tat.ci /tacci/

3. Consonant-base verbs that end in l change the final consonant to t before another consonant, and the t (as in 2 above) is pronounced as /k/ before k or /c/ before c:

tul-	'listen'	→ tut.ko /tukko/
		→ tut.ci /tucci/
kēl-	'walk'	→ kēt.ko /kēkko/
		→ kēt.ci /kēcci/

4. Consonant bases that end in s, ss, c, or ch (such as coch- 'follows' which you haven't had yet) change their final consonants to an interim t—along the way, as it were:

pes- 'removes' → pes.ko (→pet.ko) /pekko/
→ pes.ci (→pet.ci) /pecci/
iss- 'there is' → iss.ko (→it.ko) /ikko/
→ iss.ci (→it.ci) /icci/
cic- 'bark' → cic.ko (→cit.ko) /cikko/
→ cic.ci (→cit.ci) /cicci/
coch- 'follow' → coch.ko (→cot.ko) /cokko/
→ coch.ci (→cot.ci) /cocci/

This includes ALL past-tense gerunds:

-ess.ko (→ -et.ko) /-ekko/, -ass.ko (→ -at.ko) /-akko/, -ss.ko (→ -t.ko) /-kko/, hayss.ko (→ hayt.ko) /haykko/

5. Consonant bases that end in w change the w to p before another consonant:

kakkaw- 'be near' → kakkapko /kakkapkko/
(kakkawe yo) → kakkapci /kakkapcci/
tōw- 'help' → tōpko /tōpkko/
(towa yo) → tōpci /tōpcci/

6. For bases that end with more than one consonant (other than nh and lh—see Rule 8) you pronounce only one of the consonants when you attach an ending that starts with a consonant:

ēps- 'there isn't' → ēps.ko (→ēp-ko) /ēpkko/
→ ēps.ci (→ēp-ci) /ēpcci/
siph- 'want to' → siph.ko (→sip-ko) /sipkko/
→ siph.ci (→sip-ci) /sipcci/
takk- 'polish' → takk.ko (→tak-ko) /takko/
→ takk.ci (→tak-ci) /takcci/
celm- 'be young' → celm.ko (→cem-ko) /cemkko/ (7)
→ celm.ci (→cem-ci) /cemcci/ (7)
anc- 'sit' → anc.ko (→an-ko) /ankko/ (7)
→ anc.ci (→an-ci) /ancci/ (7)
ilk- 'read' → ilk.ko (→il-ko) /ilkko/ (7)
or (→ik-ko) /ikko/
→ ilk.ci (→il-ci) /ilcci/ (7)
or (→ik-ci) /ikcci/

7. Bases that end in m (including lm), n (including nc) and an l that is a reduction of a cluster (like lk above) double a following voiceless consonant:

sin- 'wear on feet' → sin.ko /sinkko/
→ sin.ci /sincci/
anc- 'sit' → anc.ko (→an-ko) /ankko/
→ anc.ci (→anc-ci) /ancci/
sīm- 'plant' → sīm.ko /sīmkko/
→ sīm.ci /sīmcci/
celm- 'be young' → celm.ko (→cem-ko) /cemkko/
→ celm.ci (→cem-ci) /cemcci/

8. The sequence (vowel, n, l +) -h.k- is pronounced /kh/, -h.c- is pronounced /ch/:

cōh- 'be good' cōh.ko /cōkho/
cōh.ci /cōchi/

mānh-	'is much'	mānh.ko /mānkho/
		mānh.ci /mānchi/
silh-	'be disliked'	silh.ko /silkho/
		silh.ci/ silchi/
nah-	'give birth to'	nah.ko /nakho/
		nah.ci /nachi/

This does not, of course, apply to -ph.k- and -ph.c-, -th.k- and -th.c-, -ch.k- and -ch.c-, -kh.k- and -kh.c-; these sequences would have already lost the "h" by Rule 6: siph- 'want to' → siph.ko (→sip-ko) /sipkko/.

9. The gerund ending -ko, like the suspective -ci, is attached to the EXTENDED bases of L-extending vowel verbs:

pha-l-	'sell'	→ phalko
		→ phalci
yē-l-	'open it'	→ yēlko
		→ yēlci
tō-l-	'turn round'	→ tōlko
		→ tōlci
tu-l-	'cost; enter'	→ tulko
		→ tulci

For the double ll in pulless.ko (the past gerund of pulu- 'call'), see below ‖ 8.7, on infinitives.

‖ 8.4. Uses of the gerund: 'and.'

When a gerund is used in the middle of a sentence, we have a situation that is common in Korean: a word or phrase which is a compact unit in Korean corresponds to things which in English may be separated from each other. For example, a noun with the particle to must be pronounced as a unit—na to 'I, too'—though the English equivalent may place these parts at opposite ends of the sentence: 'I [do so-and-so] too.' Another example is the -ci man construction you learned in Lesson 7: kaci man 'goes, but . . . ,' for example, is an indivisible unit in Korean, which may however be translated in widely separated English equivalents: 'He goes to the movies every evening in the week, but . . .'

The same is true of Korean gerund forms and, as you will see, it is true also of nearly every other Korean verb form that is used in the middle of sentences.

A -ko gerund form is a way of breaking a sentence into parts and linking the parts with 'and.' The implication may be that the separate actions happen more or less alongside each other ['. . . and also'], or necessarily in sequence, as in Basic Sentence 32:

. . . na hanthey . . . chayk . . . ul sa cwuess.ko, emeni hanthey kkoch ul sa tulyess.ey yo. 'He bought a book for me and also bought some flowers for my mother.'

Or it may imply that one happens later than the other ['. . . and then'], as in Basic Sentences 1 and 2:

Na nun sēyswu hako, myēnto hay yo. 'I get washed up and (then) shaved.'
Os ul ipko, meli lul pis.e yo. 'I get dressed and (after that) comb my hair.'

The gerund has no tense of its own; it shares the tense of some other verb. In this construction, it gets its tense meaning from the next verb in the sentence that carries any tense—often the verb at the end of the sentence:

Achim mek.ko hak.kyo ey kass.ey yo. 'I ate breakfast, and went to school.'
Nal mata achim mek.ko, hak.kyo ey ka yo. 'Every day I eat breakfast, and go to school.'

In a similar way, a final command or suggestion usually carries through any preceding gerunds:

Achim mek.ko, hak.kyo ey kapsita! 'Let's eat our breakfast and go to school!'

To make a gerund negative, you attach the -ko ending to the negative verb (or you use the short form):

sako 'buys, and . . .'	saci anh.ko or an sako 'doesn't buy, and . . .'
	saci mōs hako or mōs sako 'can't buy, and . . .'
phalko 'sells, and . . .'	phalci anh.ko or an phalko 'doesn't sell, and . . .'
	phalci mōs hako or mōs phalko 'can't sell, and . . .'
tōn i mānh.ko 'has lots of money, and . . .'	ton i mānh.ci anh.ko 'hasn't much money, and . . .'
nay chayk iko 'It is my book, and . . .'	nay chayk i ani 'ko 'it is not my book and (nor) . . .'

Negative gerunds in this usage have rather flexible English equivalents:

Kongpu haci anh.ko, capci lul ilk.ess.ey yo.	I didn't study—(but) I read a magazine instead.
or:	Instead of studying, I read a magazine.
or:	I read a magazine without doing my studying.

If the final verb is to be a command or proposition, you use the gerund of the auxiliary mal.e yo 'desists': Saci mālko, phasey yo! 'Don't buy; [instead] sell!' Phalci mālko sapsita! 'Let's not sell; [instead] let's buy!' You have seen this double-command usage in Basic Sentence 24:

Chayk man ilk.ci mālko, catong-cha hōysa lul . . . pulle yo. 'Don't just read —call the cab company!'

Here are some more sentences showing this 'and' usage of gerunds.

1. Cenyek ey nun chayk ul ilk.ko, ca yo.	In the evenings, I read books and then go to sleep.
2. Mayil achim mek.ko, hak.kyo ey kasey yo?	Do you eat breakfast every morning and then go to school?
3. Kongpu lul tā hako cip ey kass.ey yo.	I did all my studying and then went home.
4. Cenyek ey meych sikan ccum ina kongpu hako cwumusey yo.	How long do you study at night before you go to bed? [= At night, how many hours do you study and then go to bed?]
5. Sensayng un sāmu-sil ey kyēysiko, haksayng un kyōsil ey iss.ey yo.	The teacher is in the office and the students are in the classroom.
6. Wuphyen-kwuk ey to kako unhayng ey to kass.ey yo.	I went both to the post office and to the bank.
7. Os to ēps.ko, tōn to ēps.ey yo.	I have no clothes and no money.

8. Na nun hak.kyo ey kaci anh.ko, cip ey iss.ey yo. — I'm not going to school—I'm going to stay home.

8.5. Uses of the gerund: 'is [do]ing.'

3. Na nun neykthai lul māyko iss.ey yo. 'I am wearing a necktie.'
4. Moca lul ssuko iss.ey yo. 'I am wearing a hat.'

A phrase consisting of a gerund and a form of iss- 'is, stays' corresponds to English verb phrases like 'is writing, is eating, is buying' as opposed to simple forms like 'writes, eats, buys.' This correspondence is by no means one hundred per cent, however, we say 'is going' where the Korean uses the single verb ka yo. For most cases of -ko iss.ey yo you can substitute a simple verb, so that (for example) mek.e yo 'eats' covers about the same ground as mek.ko iss.ey yo 'is eating.' This does not work in the other direction, though. You may NOT automatically substitute a -ko iss.ey yo phrase for every simple verb form.

To show tense, you change the verb iss.ey yo: ssuko iss.ey yo 'is writing' becomes ssuko iss.ess.ey yo 'was writing.' For other sentence types you also make the change on the last verb, as you can see in ssuko iss.ci man 'is writing, but . . .' and ssuko iss.ko 'is writing, and . . . .' For honorific expressions you substitute kyēysey yo for iss.ey yo, so that ssuko iss.ey yo becomes ssuko kyēysey yo (or ssusiko kyēysey yo) to mean '[someone esteemed] is writing.'

But the NEGATIVE can be made either on the underlying verb or on the expression as a whole, with slightly different meanings. If you merely want to deny an assertion you can say ssuko iss.ci anh.e yo 'is not writing,' but if you want to imply that the subject goes along nicely without the activity you say ssuci anh.ko iss.ey yo 'is not writing [for the time being, these days, etc.]' or 'gets along (manages to get by) without writing' or 'keeps away from one's typewriter.' Both kinds of negative can be put into the various other sentence types, so that for the meaning 'isn't writing, but . . .' you will hear both ssuko iss.ci anh.ci man (or ssuko iss.ci mōs haci man)—usually as a denial of an assertion—and ssuci anh.ko iss.ci man (or ssuci mōs hako iss.ci man). In fact, you may even run across some DOUBLE NEGATIVES: Na nun ssuci anh.ko iss.ci anh.e yo means something like 'It isn't true that [= I want to deny the assertion that] I am going along without writing.'

Here are some more examples of this construction.

1. Pak sensayng i taum pang an ey se kongpu hako iss.ey yo. — Mr. Pak is studying in the next room.
2. Emeni nun acik to capswusiko kyēysey yo. — Mother is still eating.
3. Ku haksayng i kitaliko iss.ey yo. — That student is waiting for you.
4. Tongsayng i acik cako iss.ey yo. — My little brother is still asleep.
5. Say os ul ipko iss.ess.ey yo. — She was wearing [or had on] a new dress.
6. Kāy ka cic.ci anh.ko iss.ey yo. — The dog is keeping quiet.
7. Sinmun ul poci mōs hako iss.ey yo. — I can't be bothered with newspapers.
8. Acik ku ay lul chac.ci mōs hako iss.ey yo. — We still can't find that child.

‖ 8.6. Uses of the gerund: 'wants to.'

5. Say kwutwu lul sin.ko siph.e yo. 'I want to wear my new shoes.'
6. Say cāngkap ul kkiko siph.e yo. 'I want to wear my new gloves.'
28. Na nun . . . kongpu lul cal hako siph.e yo. 'I want to study hard.'
33. Ku chayk ul ilk.ko siph.e hasey yo? 'Would you like to read the book?'

The verb siph.e yo means 'I want or would like' and siph.e hay yo means 'you, he, she, they want or would like.' A gerund combined with one of these forms means 'wants to do [what is specified in the gerund]':

ssuko siph.e yo 'wants to write'
kkoch kwūkyeng kako siph.e yo 'would like to go flower viewing'

The expression -ko siph.e yo is ordinarily used only of one's own desires; for other people's hankerings, you use the expression -ko siph.e hay yo (‖ 8.10). But you can occasionally use the simpler form even for other people, especially when asking a question: Kako siph.e yo? 'Would you like to go?' In such cases you can make either verb or both verbs honorific: Kasiko siph.e yo? Kako siph.usey yo? Kasiko siph.usey yo? (Cf. remarks on honorifics with the long negative at the end of ‖ 7.3.)

The particle which follows the object of a transitive verb with -ko siph.e yo can either be retained as ul/lul or changed to the subject particle i/ka, since siph.e yo is an auxiliary descriptive verb meaning 'it is desired.' Here are some more examples of the construction:

1. Onul ōhwu ey na wa kath.i sānqpo hako siph.e yo?	Would you like to take a walk with me this afternoon?
2. Kwūkyeng ul com te hako siph.e yo.	I'd like to do a little more sightseeing.
3. Emeni lul poko siph.ci man cip i nemu mel.e se, mōs ka yo.	I want to see my mother, but home is too far away, so I can't go.
4. Cenyek ul mek.ko siph.ci anh.e yo.	I don't want to eat supper.
5. Hak.kyo ey kako siph.ci anh.ci man ka ya hay yo.	I don't want to go to school, but I have to go.
6. Onul to swīko siph.ko nayil to swīko siph.e yo.	I want to rest today and tomorrow too.
7. Yenge lul paywuko siph.e se i chayk ul sass.ey yo.	I want to learn English, so I bought this book.
8. Um.ak-hoy ey kako siph.ci anh.ko tose-kwan ey kako siph.e yo.	I don't want to go to the concert, but I want to go to the library.
9. Kongpu hako siph.ci anh.e se, cip ey ilccik wass.ey yo.	I didn't want to study, so I came home early.
10. Kim sensayng nim un Mikwuk ey kyēysiko siph.e hasey yo?	Does Mr. Kim want to stay in the United States?
11. Nēy. Mikwuk ey iss.ko siph.e haci man, Yenge lul mōs hay yo.	Yes, he wants to stay in the United States, but he does not speak any English at all.
12. Pak sensayng un īl ul hako siph.e haci anh.e yo?	Doesn't Mr. Pak want to work?
13. Nēy. Pak sensayng un īl hako siph.e haci anh.ci man, tōn i cokum to ēps.e se, hay ya hay yo.	No, he doesn't want to work, but he hasn't got any money, so he has to work.
14. Kim sensayng un swul ul masiko siph.e hako, Pak sensayng un tāmpay lul phiko siph.e hayss.ey yo.	Mr. Kim wanted to drink wine, and Mr. Pak wanted to smoke.

15. Ku "yeca ka ku panci lul kkiko siph.e hay se, cwuess.ey yo. — She wanted to wear that ring, so I gave it to her.

‖ 8.7. Verbs: infinitive form.

(Note: In this discussion a few verbs are introduced that you have not had; they are starred.)

Korean INFINITIVES are nearly always the same as the polite-style present-tense form with the yo particle removed:

1. Consonant-base verbs usually have the infinitive ending -e added to the base:

pis- 'comb'	pis.e
mek- 'eat'	mek.e
ip- 'wear'	ip.e
cic- 'bark'	cic.e
tul- 'listen'	tul.e
nwuw- 'lie down'	nwuwe
sin- 'wear shoes'	sin.e
ilk- 'read'	ilk.e

But if the last vowel of the base is o, the ending is a:

kkoc- 'pin it'	kkoc.a
cōh- 'be good'	cōh.a (often pronounced co[w]a)
tōw- 'help'	towa

And if the last vowel of the base is a, Koreans often write the ending as -a even though they say it as -e:

tat- 'close'	tat.e (often written tat.a)
anc- 'sit'	anc.e (often written anc.a)
takk- 'polish'	takk.e (often written takk.a)

2. L-extending vowel bases add the infinitive ending to the extended base (with the l) in the same way as consonant bases add the ending: as -a if the last vowel of the base is o, otherwise as -e (though often spelled -a if the last vowel is a):

yē-l- 'open'	yel.e
sā-l- 'live'	sal.e (often written sal.a)
nō-l- 'play'	nol.a

3. Some vowel-base verbs (those ending in a, ay, ey) have infinitives of the same shape as the base:

ka- 'go'	ka
māy- 'tie'	māy (sometimes written maye)
pēy- 'cut'	pēy (sometimes written peye)

Vowel-bases ending in oy usually have an infinitive of the same shape as the base (though pronounced with a long vowel and sometimes written oye) but often this is spelled—and occasionally pronounced—way:

*toy- 'become'	tōy (toye, tway)

4. Vowel bases of more than one syllable that end in i reduce this to y and add -e:

kitali- 'wait for'	kitalye
kaluchi- 'teach'	kaluchye (pronounced /kaluche/)

And even one-syllable verbs are often pronounced with the i shortened to y before the -e (but usually they are written out in full); and the e is often lengthened to ē:

tti- 'wear belt'	ttie (ttyē)
*chi- 'hit'	chie (chyē /chē/)
swī- 'rest'	swie (often pronounced sōy or swēy)

5. Those vowel verbs which end in wu add -e and often shorten the wu to w (though those with but one syllable are usually written out in full):

*nanwu- 'divide'	nanwe
cwu- 'give'	cw(u)e

Vowel bases which end in o change the o to w and add a:

o- 'come'	wa

But after a labial (such as p) the sound w often drops:

po- 'look at'	p(w)a

6. Those vowel verbs which end in -u (other than wu) drop the u and add -e:

su- 'stand' (often written se-)	se
ssu- 'write'	sse

If the last vowel left when the u drops is o, the ending is attached as -a:

*mou- 'gather'	moa

7. There are a few verbs with bases ending in -lu-; most of them form their infinitives by changing the -lu- to -lle (that is, by dropping the u as in 6, and then doubling the l before attaching the ending -e):

pulu- 'call'	pulle

If the -lu- is preceded by o (and in Korean writing also often a) the infinitive is added in the shape -a:

*molu- 'don't know'	mōlla [The long ō is an irregularity.]
*malu- 'get dry'	malle (often written malla)

8. When you remove the yo from a polite-style ending and -ey remains, the infinitive drops the final y:

Present Polite	Infinitives
. . . iey yo 'is [copula]'	. . . ie
iss.ey yo '(there) is'	iss.e
ēps.ey yo '(there) isn't'	ēps.e

The PAST INFINITIVE is thus formed by dropping the y:

Past Polite	Past Infinitive
kitalyess.ey yo 'waited'	kitalyess.e
mek.ess.ey yo 'ate'	mek.ess.e
wass.ey yo 'came'	wass.e

Past Honorific Polite	Past Hon. Inf.
hasyess.ey yo '[someone esteemed] did'	hasyess.e
tul.usyess.ey yo '[someone esteemed] listened'	tul.usyess.e
phasyess.ey yo '[someone esteemed] bought'	phasyess.e

From honorific present-tense forms, to find the HONORIFIC INFINITIVE, you change -ey to -ye:

Honorific Present Polite	Hon. Inf.
anc.usey yo '[someone esteemed] sits'	anc.usye
hasey yo '[someone esteemed] does'	hasye
ilk.usey yo '[someone esteemed] reads'	ilk.usye

Another way of looking at all this is to say that the infinitive -e picks up a -y (that is changes from -e to -ey) before the final particle yo. And there are some people who say (and more people who write) such things as hasye yo for hasey yo, wass.e yo for wass.ey yo, and iss.e yo for iss.ey yo.

‖ 8.8. Uses of the infinitive: polite style.

POLITE-STYLE verb forms, those forms you use at the end of your sentences when speaking with someone you are on 'polite-style terms' with, are based on the infinitive.

The present tense polite style is the plain infinitive with yo added to it, with those few exceptions noted just above when the -e ending picks up a -y.

The past tense polite style is the past infinitive (with added -y), plus yo.

‖ 8.9. Uses of the infinitive: with the particle se.

7. Sangcem ey ka se, sin ul sa yo. 'I'm going to the store and buy some shoes.'
18. Nuc.e se, catong-cha lul thako ka ya hay yo. 'It's late, so I'll have to go by car.'

In the middle of a sentence, the particle se after an infinitive (or, sometimes an infinitive all by itself, with no se) has the general meaning 'so.' There is usually a cause-and-result flavor to such sentences. The first part, ending with -e se, gives a cause, and the second half gives a result:

CAUSE: Tōn i ēps.e se . . . 'I have no money . . .
RESULT: . . . kaci mōs hay yo. . . . so I can't go.'

With verbs of direction, the se takes on a meaning of 'so as to . . .'—a purpose-and-result flavor:

PURPOSE: Sangcem ey ka se . . . 'I went to the store . . .
RESULT: . . . tāmpay lul sass.ey yo. . . . (so as) to get some cigarettes.'

This purpose-result situation is most often expressed in English by 'and':

I went to the store AND got some cigarettes.

But this 'and' is of course different from the kind of 'and' linkage expressed by a Korean gerund (above, ‖ 8.4): the -ko form means '. . . and (then afterwards)' or '. . . and (also, in addition).'

Here again we are faced with a unified Korean construction that corresponds to a separate English construction: sometimes the 'so' or 'and' is separated from the verb only by a slight pause, and sometimes a number of words may intervene:

Nuc.e se, catong-cha lo kass.ey yo. 'It was late, so I went by car.'
Nal mata sangcem ey ka se, tāmpay lul sa yo. 'I go to the store every day and buy some cigarettes.'

Now, what about these sentences that you have seen:

8. Say sin ul sa se, cōh.a yo. 'I'm glad I bought new shoes.'
26. . . . kongpu lul cal hay se, cōh.a yo. 'I'm glad [he]'s studying hard.'

There is a special English translation when -e se is followed by cōh.a yo in the second half of the sentence. Such sentences, which mean literally '[so-and-so happens], so it's good,' are generally rendered by some such English pattern as 'I'm glad (that) . . .' or 'It's a good thing (that) . . . .'

For example:

Kim sensayng i wa se cōh.a yo. 'It's nice that Mr. Kim is here.' or 'I'm glad Mr. Kim came.'

Kim sensayng i wa se na nun cōh.a yo. 'I'm glad Mr. Kim is here.' [= Mr. Kim came, so, as for me, it's good.]

In the se constructions described above, it is not generally necessary to use a past-tense infinitive; if the verb at the end of the sentence is past, the infinitive also usually carries a past-tense meaning. (Gerunds are the same way, you remember, in this respect.) You use a past-tense infinitive only if there is genuine ambiguity without it, or if the sentence is a very long one.

The similarity in sound between certain infinitives and the particle se is likely to lead to some confusion, so that it is important to distinguish between plain infinitives and infinitives with se after them. Bases that end in s, for example, have infinitives ending in -s.e:

pis-	'comb'	inf.	pis.e

All honorific infinitives end in -sye (which is pronounced -se):

ka-	'go'	hon. inf.	kasye /kase/

All past infinitives end in -ss.e:

ka-	'go'	past inf.	kass.e
		hon. past inf.	kasyess.e /kasesse/

In the infinitive-plus-se construction, then, it is important not to confuse the infinitive ending itself with the particle:

	Inf.	Inf. + se
pis- 'comb'	pis.e	pis.e se 'combs, so . . .'
honorific:	[ha]sye	hasye se '[someone esteemed] does, so . . .'
past tense:	[hay]ss.e	hayss.e se 'did, so . . .'
honorific past tense	[ha]syess.e	hasyess.e se '[someone esteemed] did, so . . .'

Here are some more examples of infinitives with se in sentences.

1. Nal mata sangcem ey ka se, mulken ul sa yo.	He goes to the store every day and buys things.
2. Enni ka hak.kyo ey ka se, ēps.ey yo.	My older brother isn't home—he's gone go school. [= My older brother has gone to school, so he isn't (here).]
3. Khe se cōh.a yo.	I'm glad it's big.
4. Hak.kyo ey wa se, kongpu lul hayss.ey yo.	I came to school and studied.
5. Mānnyen-phil hana sa se, Kim sensayng eykey tulyess.ey yo.	I bought a fountain pen and gave it to Mr. Kim.
6. Sikan i ēps.e se, capci lul ilk.ci mōs hay yo.	I can't read the magazine—I haven't time. [= There isn't time, so I can't . . .]
7. Sensayng nim i an kyēysye se, kongpu lul mōs hayss.ey yo.	The teacher wasn't there, so we couldn't [study =] have our class.
8. Kongpu lul mōs hay se, mian hap.nita.	I'm sorry I couldn't study. [= I couldn't study, so I'm sorry.]
9. Kkoch ul cwue se, komapsup.nita.	Thank you for the flowers. [= You gave me flowers, so I am grateful.]
10. Eme' nim i cek.e to sip-wen ccum un cwusye se, komawe yo.	I am thankful that my mother gave me at least ten dollars.
11. Nuc.e to ˡnayil kkaci nun wa se, ttul uy phul ul kkakk.e ya hay yo!	You must come at the latest by tomorrow to cut the grass in my yard.
12. Ku (p)pesu ka nuc.e se, pihayng-ki lul mōs thass.ey yo.	The bus was late, so that I missed the airplane.

8.10. Uses of the infinitive: turning descriptive verbs into processive verbs (-e hay yo).

11. . . . nul kippe hayss.ey yo. 'He was always happy.'
27. Sensayng to . . . cōh.a hasey yo. 'The teacher is glad too.'
33. . . . ilk.ko siph.e hasey yo? 'Would you like to read [it]?'

Korean people do not ordinarily presume to state flatly what another person feels or thinks: such inner processes can be known only at second hand, and the Koreans are likely to use an indirect means of referring to them.

One way of doing this is to combine descriptive verbs that refer to emotions like 'dislikes' and 'is glad' with hay yo. This combination externalizes the emotion and, in grammar, changes the descriptive verb into a processive one. Here is a list of such expressions:

cōh.a yo 'is good; is liked'
  cōh.a hay yo 'likes'
silh.e yo 'is disliked'
  silh.e hay yo 'dislikes'
siph.e yo 'wants to, would like to'
  siph.e hay yo '[someone else] wants to or would like'
kippe yo 'is happy or glad'
  kippe hay yo '[someone else] is happy or glad'
komawe yo 'is thankful or grateful'
  komawe hay yo 'is grateful for, is thankful about; [someone else] is thankful or grateful'

So far you have met this verb only as Komapsup.nita, a sentence meaning 'thank you.' It is a consonant-base verb like towa yo 'helps.' The base is komaw-, the infinitive komawe (often written komawa), the gerund komapko, and the suspective komapci.

All of these expressions except siph.e hay yo are TRANSITIVE: they can take as direct objects a noun expression with the particle ul/lul. Siph.e hay yo occurs only after the -ko gerund.

Here is an illustration of the difference in usage between describing your own emotions and those of someone else:

Kim sensayng i wa se, cōha yo. 'It's nice that Mr. Kim has come.' OR 'I'm glad that Mr. Kim is here.'
Kim sensayng i wa se, cōh.a hay yo. '[Someone else] is glad that Mr. Kim has come.' OR 'Mr. Kim is glad to be here.'
Kim sensayng i wa se, na nun cōh.a yo 'I'm glad Mr. Kim is here.'
Kim sensayng i wa se, Poktong-i nun cōh.a hay yo. 'Poktong(-i) is glad that Mr. Kim is here.'

These emotion expressions are made honorific by changing hay yo to hasey yo: cōh.a hasey yo, silh.e hasey yo, kippe hasey yo, komawe hasey yo, siph.e hasey yo. From the expression -ko siph.e yo you can make the honorifics in two different ways (-usiko siph.e yo or -ko siph.usey yo) and from the expression -ko siph.e hay yo you also have both possibilities: -usiko siph.e hay yo or -ko siph.e hasey yo, but the latter is more common. And it is even possible to have a double-honorific form (like -usiko siph.usey yo): -usiko siph.e hasey yo.

To make the emotion-expression negative you change hay yo to haci anh.e yo: cōh.a haci anh.e yo, silh.e haci anh.e yo, kippe haci anh.e yo, komawe haci anh.e yo, -ko siph.e haci anh.e yo.

To make the expression both negative and honorific you can apply either the negative first (cōh.a haci anh.usey yo), or the honorific first (cōh.a hasici anh.e yo), or you can take the latter expression and re-apply the honorific (cōh.a hasici anh.usey yo) for a somewhat over-honorific effect. In the case of -ko siph.e hay yo, you actually find all these possibilities:

1. -ko siph.e haci anh.usey yo
2. -ko siph.e hasici anh.usey yo
3. -ko siph.e hasici anh.e yo
4. -usiko siph.e haci anh.e yo
5. -usiko siph.e haci anh.usey yo

6. -usiko siph.e hasici anh.e yo
7. -usiko siph.e hasici anh.usey yo

See if you can figure out just what went into the building of each of these expressions, and the order of application. (The last example, triply honorific, is a bit too fancy for everyday use.)

‖ 8.11. Uses of the infinitive: compound verb expressions.

The expressions discussed in ‖ 8.10 just above—cōh.a hay yo 'liked,' komawe hay yo 'is grateful for,' and so on—are COMPOUND VERB EXPRESSIONS. They are made by joining to an infinitive—a verb which names the action—some form of another verb (hay yo 'does' in these two cases) which does the rest of the work: it shows the tense, and whether the expression is affirmative or negative, question or statement, etc. This pattern, as you are aware by this time, is a general one with Korean verb expressions: the MAIN VERB merely tells what action or quality is under discussion— 'goes, eats, walks; is good, is large, is late' —and is otherwise frozen; the AUXILIARY VERB completes the expression and fits it into the sentence with appropriate endings. The honorific and negative expressions are usually built on the auxiliary verb, not on the infinitive.

Some of the compound expressions you have learned in the Basic Sentences of this lesson involve the verbs ka yo 'goes (from us/here/now)' and wa yo 'comes (to us/here/now)' used as auxiliaries to show direction:

With tō-l- 'turn (round)':	tol.a ka yo 'goes back' tol.a wa yo 'comes back'
With tu-l- 'enter':	tul.e ka yo 'goes in' tul.e wa yo 'comes in'
With na- 'exit':	na ka yo 'goes out' na wa yo 'comes out'
With kēl- 'walk':	kel.e ka yo 'walks (there)' kel.e wa yo 'walks (here)'

Other expressions involve the verb iss.ey yo 'is, stays' used as an auxiliary to show resultant state:

With anc- 'sit':	anc.e iss.ey yo 'is seated' anc.e iss.ci anh.e yo 'is not seated'
With nwuw- 'lie down':	nwuwe iss.ey yo 'is recumbent, is lying down' nwuwe iss.ci anh.e yo 'is not recumbent, is not lying down'
With su- 'stand up':	se iss.ey yo 'is standing, is upright' se iss.ci anh.e yo 'is not standing, is not upright'

Here are some more examples of these expressions in sentences:

1. Ape' nim i [l]nayil Mikwuk ey se tol.a osey yo.	Father is returning from the United States tomorrow.
2. Cang sensayng nim un ēncey Hankwuk ulo tol.a kasyess.ey yo.	When did Mr. Chang go back to Korea?
3. Na nun ku [n]yeca pang ey tul.e kaci anh.ess.ey yo.	I didn't go into her room.

4. Kulen tey, ku ^{n}yeca ka nay pang ey tul.e oko siph.e hay yo.	But she wants to come into my room.
5. Na nun catong-cha ka ēps.e se hak.kyo ey kel.e kaci man, tangsin un way kel.e kako siph.e hasey yo.	I don't have a car, so I walk to school, but why do you want to walk?
6. Na nun nwuwe iss.ci to anc.e iss.ci to anh.ess.ey yo. Se iss.ess.ey yo.	I was neither lying down nor sitting. I was standing.
7. Ku yenghwa-kwan an ey sālam i nemu mānh.e se, na oko siph.ess.ci man sip-pun te iss.ess.ey yo.	There were too many people in that movie-theater, so I wanted to come out, but I stayed for another ten minutes.
8. Swulq cip ey to tul.e kako siph.ci anh.ci man, cip ey to tol.a kako siph.ci anh.e yo.	I don't want tc go to the bar, but I don't want to go home, either.
9. Ppalli kel.e kaci anh.e to cōh.a yo.	You don't have to walk so fast.
10. Na nun han-talq tong-an ina pakk ey na kaci anh.ess.ci man, sālam tul i poko siph.ci anh.e yo.	I haven't been out for a month, but I don't want to see anybody.

‖ 8.11.1. Infinitive compounds with pwa yo 'sees.'

23. Catong-cha hōysa ey cēnhwa lul hay posey yo. 'Try making a call to the cab company.'

25. Tto han pen cēnhwa lul hay pwa yo. 'Make another call (and see . . .).'

The verb pwa yo ordinarily means 'looks, sees, reads.' As an auxiliary verb, however, it means 'tries doing'—NOT 'tries to do' but 'tries doing'—'samples the act to see what it's like,' 'does it to see (just how it will be, how it will turn out, etc.)' This exploratory construction is often used with 'going' and 'coming.' [The expression 'tries to do (but maybe fails)' is expressed in several ways: -ulye hay yo 'intends to' (‖ 24.9, 27.2), -ki ey him sse yo 'endeavors to' (‖ 13.11) are common translations.]

Here are some more examples:

1. Hānkwuk mal lo phyēnci lul sse pwass.ey yo.	I tried writing a letter in Korean.
2. Ilpon sinmun ul pwa pwass.ey yo.	I took a look at a Japanese newspaper.
3. Yengkwuk ey ka posyess.e yo?	Have you ever been to England [to see how you'd like it]?
4. Say chayk ul ilk.e pwa yo.	I'm reading a new book.
5. Han pen mek.e pwass.e yo.	I tasted it. [= I tried eating it once.]

6. Say os ul ip.e pwa yo.	I'm trying on some new clothes.
7. Say sin ul sin.e pwa yo.	I'm trying on some new shoes.
8. Say moca lul sse pwa yo.	I'm trying on a new hat.
9. Nay chinkwu ka ^{1}nayil i kongwen ey wa pwa yo.	My friend is coming to (see) this park tomorrow.
10. Wuphyen-kwuk ey ka pwass.ci man, phyēnci nun oci anh.ess.ey yo.	I went to the post office (to see whether there was any letter), but no letter had come.
11. Ce moca lul sako siph.ci (nun) anh.ci man, sse poko siph.e yo.	I want to try that hat on, even if I don't want to buy it.
12. Cwungkwuk ey se sal.e poko siph.ci man, cikum un ku nala ey mōs tul.e ka yo.	I wish I could live in China sometime (to see what it would be like), but we are not able to enter that country now.
13. Kāngyen un tul.e poko siph.ci anh.ci man, cōh.un um.ak un tul.e poko siph.e yo.	I don't want to listen to any lecture, but I would like to listen to some good music.

‖ 8.11.2. Infinitive compounds with cwue yo (tulye yo) 'gives.'

19. Catong-cha . . . lul . . . pulle cwusipsio. 'Call me a cab.'
29. Ku chinkwu nun na lul mānh.i towa cw(u)e yo. 'That friend helps me a lot.'
30. . . . pumo nim ul nul towa tulye yo. 'He's always helping my parents.'
31. Na to mullon ku chinkwu lul towa cwuko, ku uy pumo nim ul towa tulye yo. 'Of course I help him and (help) his parents too.'
32. Ku chinkwu nun cīnan cwuil na hanthey chayk han kwen ul sa cw(u)ess.ko, emeni hanthey kkoch ul sa tulyessey yo. 'Last week he bought a book for me and (bought) some flowers for my mother.'

To tell about a favor done for someone, you use a compound consisting of the infinitive, plus a word for 'give'—either cw(u)e 'gives (to anyone)' or tulye yo 'gives to someone esteemed.' The person FOR whom the favor is done is the INDIRECT OBJECT and takes the particle hanthey (or eykey) or its honorific equivalent kkey.

Sometimes the action verb itself can take an indirect object; if there are two hanthey-phrases, the one nearest the verb of action goes with it: Poktong-i ka awu hanthey chinkwu hanthey phyēnci lul sse cwue yo. 'Poktong-i writes a letter FOR his little brother TO a friend.'

Here are some more examples of this construction.

1. Yēyki lul hay cwusey yo.	Tell me a story.
2. Mānnyen-phil lo sse cwusey yo.	Please write it with a pen.
3. Kim puin un uli ai com pwa cwuko iss.ey yo.	Mrs. Kim is looking (after) my child for me.
4. Ku phyēnci lul ilk.e tulyess.ey yo.	I've read the letter for him.
5. Ku ^{n}yeca eykey kkoch ul sa cwuko siph.ci man, acik	I want to buy her some flowers, though I can't (bring myself to) speak to her.

māl hay poci mōs hayss.ey yo.	
6. Hal-ape' nim i ku chayk ul ilk.e poko siph.e hasye se, Kim sensayng nim i ponay tulyess.ey yo.	My grandfather wanted to read that book, so Mr. Kim sent it to him.
7. Ku īl ul cal mōs hasyess.ey yo? Kulemyen nay ka towa tulikeyss.ey yo.	Did you have trouble with that task? Then I will help you.
8. Acessi uy kwutwu lul takk.e tuliko siph.ess.ey yo.	I wanted to polish my uncle's shoes.
9. Achim mata tongsayng uy tanchwu lul chaywe cwuko siph.ci anh.e yo.	I don't want to button my brother's clothes for him every morning.
10. Co sensayng(q) tayk ttul uy phul ul kkakk.e tuliko siph.ess.ci man, ku pun un tōn ul cwuci anh.e yo.	I wanted to cut the grass in Mr. Cho's yard, but he doesn't pay for it.
11. Ku sālam ul kitalye cwuko siph.ci anh.ess.ci man, com te iss.e cwuess.ey yo.	I didn't want to wait for him, but I did stay for a little while.
12. Emeni nun hal-'me' nim uy ānkyeng ul chayk-sang mith ey se chac.e tulyess.ey yo.	My mother found my grandmother's glasses underneath the desk.
13. Hyeng nim un ku "yeca eykey os ul sa cwuko siph.e haci anh.ess.ey yo.	My brother didn't want to buy a dress for her.
14. Ku sālam un il-pun to na lul kitalye cwuci anh.ess.ey yo.	He didn't even wait for me a minute.
15. Choy sensayng nim i wa cwusye se, tāytan hi komapsup.nita.	I am very glad that Mr. Choy has come for us.
16. Ayki lul pwa cwuci anh.ess.ci man, ku emeni nun tōn ul com cwusyess.ey yo.	Even though I didn't look after the baby, his mother gave me some money (anyway).
17. Apeci nun Pak sensayng uy yēyki lul tul.e tuliko siph.e haci anh.usyess.ci man, emeni nun tul.e poko siph.e hasyess.ey yo.	My father didn't want to listen to Mr. Pak's story, but my mother wanted to.

‖ 8.12. Uses of the infinitive: with the particle ya.

15. Onul(q) cenyek ey chinkwu lul manna ya hay yo. 'I have to meet a friend this evening.'

16. . . . ku chinkwu cip e ka ya hay yo. 'I have to go to that friend's house.'
18. Nuc.e se, catong-cha lul thako ka ya hay yo. 'It's late, so I'll have to go (riding) in a car.'

To express obligation— 'have to, must, should, ought to'—you use an infinitive for the main verb, and attach to it the particle ya 'only if' plus a form of hay yo; -e ya hay yo adds the meaning 'have to' [etc.] to the main verb.

Occasionally -e ya is followed by some verb other than the auxiliary hay yo: Payk-wen iss.e ya tul.e ka yo. 'You have to have 100 wen to get in.' Sensayng hanthey mul.e pwa ya al.e yo. 'We will only find out by asking the teacher.' = 'We won't find out unless we ask the teacher.'

Be careful about trying to use negatives for this type of expression. The genuine opposite of these, in English, is 'doesn't have to; needs not.' But the Korean opposites are made by an altogether different construction, discussed in the next note (‖ 8.13).

'Must not'—which appears on the surface to be the negative of 'has to'—is actually a denial of permission; it is the opposite of 'may,' which gives permission. The denial of permission, again, is an entirely different Korean construction which will not be taken up until Lesson 9 (‖ 9.5).

Here are some more examples of -e ya:

1. Amman nuc.e to onulq pam kkaci nun i kwa lul kongpu hay ya hay yo.	At the latest, I must study this lesson tonight.
2. Na nun nuc.e to ōhwu tases si kkaci nun cenyek ul mek.e ya hay yo.	At the latest, I have to eat my supper by five p.m.
3. I say catong-cha nun cek.e to ī-chen wen un cwusye ya hayss.ci anh.e yo? (or . . . haci anh.ess.ey yo?)	Didn't you have to pay at least two thousand dollars for this new car?
4. Hakkyo ey amman nuc.e to achim un mek.e ya hay yo.	You must eat your breakfast, no matter how late for school you will be.
5. Cōh.un koki nun ku sangcem ey achim ilccik ka ya sa yo.	You will get good meat only by going to that shop early in the morning.

‖ 8.13. Uses of the infinitive: with the particle to.

An infinitive with the particle to has the basic meaning 'even though [so-and-so happens],' as you have seen in these Basic Sentences from this lesson:

9. Na nun tōn i mānh.ci anh.e to, nul mulken ul sa yo. 'Even though I haven't much money, I'm always buying things.' [= As for me, my money, even though there isn't much . . .]
10. Sangcem i mel.e to, cacwu ka yo. 'Even though the stores are far away, I go there often.'
11. . . . tōn i cokum to ēps.ess.e to, nul kippe hayss.ey yo. 'Even though he hadn't any money at all [= money, even a little bit], he was always happy.'

Again, with this construction, it is not necessary to use a past-tense infinitive before the to, even when the meaning is past, unless ambiguity would otherwise result; the past-tense verb at the end does all the work.

Notice the basic similarity between this construction and the -ci man 'but, although' construction you learned in Lesson 7. Both constructions mean 'though [so-and-so happens] . . .'; but -e to is stronger. It means 'even though . . .' or 'in spite of the fact that . . .'; if we want to switch its force to the next part of the sentence, we can give it some such translation as '. . . but even so':

I haven't much money, but even so I'm always buying things.
The stores are a long way off, but in spite of this I go there a lot.
He had no money at all, but even so he was always happy.

Constructions with -ci man 'although . . .' or '. . . but' are not this strong; but the fundamental meaning is similar.

Here are some more examples:

1. Ku hal-apeci nun sonca ka mānh.e to han salam to towa tuliko siph.e haci anh.e yo.	Even though the grandfather (or that old man) has many grandsons, not one of them wants to help him.
2. Na nun selun tases sal ie to kyelhon hako siph.ci anh.e yo.	Even though I am 35 years old, I still don't want to get married.
3. Na nun māyil cengke-cang ey se īl ul hay to kicha lul han pen to tha poci mōs hayss.ey yo.	I work at the railroad station every day. but (even so) I have never ridden on a train.
4. Ce chacang un nai nun mānh.e to māyil yetelq sikan ssik īl hay yo.	That conductor is old, but he still works eight hours every day.
5. Eceyq pam ey pi ka wass.e to ku um.ak-hoy ey nun cek.e to sam-payk myeng ccum son nim i wass.ey yo.	Even though it was raining last night, at least 300 guests came to the concert.

‖ 8.13.1. Asking and giving permission.

12. Onul say os ul ip.e to cōh.a yo? 'Is it all right for me to [= May I] wear my new clothes today?
13. Say sin ul sin.e to kwaynchanh.e yo? 'May I wear my new shoes?' [= Even though I wear . . . does it make no difference?]
14. Onulq pam ey cip ey nuc.key tol.a wa to kwaynchanh.e yo? 'Is it all right for me to [= Do you mind if I] come home late tonight?'

To ask for permission in Korean you use a construction with the literal meaning 'even though I [do it], is it all right?' or 'even if I [do it], does it matter or make any difference?' This corresponds to English 'may or can I [do it]' or, much more closely, 'is it all right if I [do it]?'

‖ 8.13.2. Giving negative permission ('doesn't have to . . .'; denial of obligation).

To say 'I have to . . .' in Korean, you use the construction -e ya hay yo (above ‖ 8.12). The negative of this— 'I don't have to . . .'—is a permission construction, meaning literally 'even though I don't [do it], it's all right' or 'it doesn't matter if I don't [do it].'

Here are some examples of this:

1. Ilccik tol.a osici anh.e to kwaynchanh.e yo.	You don't have to come back early. [= Even though you don't come back early, it doesn't matter.]
2. Hak.kyo ey an ka to cōh.a yo.	You don't have to go to school.
3. I chayk ul poci anh.e to kwaynchanh.e yo.	You don't need to read this book.
4. Onul unhayng ey ka to cōh.ko, an ka to cōh.a yo.	It doesn't matter whether I go to the bank today or not. [= If I go to the bank today it's all right, and if I don't go it's all right.]
5. Ku phyēnci nun cikum ssuci anh.e to cōh.ci man, i phyēnci nun sse ya hay yo.	That letter doesn't have to be written now, but this letter I have to write.

8.13.3. Special maximum-minimum expressions.

There are a few descriptive-verb infinitives with the particle to that have a special maximum-minimum meaning (alongside their usual meaning, in other contexts, of 'even though it's . . .') like these three you learned in the Basic Sentences:

16. nuc.e to 'at the latest' [even though it's late]
20. cek.e to 'at least' [even though it's few or small]
21. mānh.e to 'at (the) most' [even though it's much or many]

Another example is ille to 'at the earliest' from the descriptive verb ilu- 'be early' [from which the adverb ilccik(i) is derived]. Other examples of this sort are khe to 'at the largest,' ppalle to 'at the fastest,' mel.e to 'at the farthest,' kakkawe to 'at the nearest.'

Here are some examples of these:

1. Ku phyēnci nun ille to 'nayil ey 'na wa yo.	That letter will come tomorrow at the earliest.
2. Ku sakwa nun khe to sip-cen ssik pakk-ey an tul.e yo.	At their largest, those apples only cost 10 cents apiece.
3. Tangsin (catong-)cha nun ppalle to han sikan ey phalq-sip mail pakk-ey mōs ka yo.	At the fastest, your car won't do over eighty miles an hour.
4. Mel.e to sip-li man kel.e ka to cōh.a yo.	At the farthest, we only have to walk 10 li (about 4 miles).
5. Kakkawe to ō-li 'na kel.e ka ya sinmun ul sa yo.	At the nearest, we have to walk about 5 li (2 miles) to buy a newspaper.

These maximum-minimum expressions are often preceded by amman 'however much' to mean 'at the very (most, least, latest, etc.)'

EXERCISES

I

Each of the following sentences mean 'someone DOES something.' Change the verb expression in each so that the meaning is 'someone WANTS TO DO something.' Then translate the sentence. For example, the first will be: Na nun say catong-cha lul sako siphe yo. 'I want to buy a new car.'

(Remember to use -ko siph.e yo of the first person only; for the second and third person, use -ko siph.e hay yo.)

1. Na nun catong-cha lul sa yo.
2. Na nun i neykthai lul māy yo.
*3. Ai nun phul ul kkakk.ci anh.e yo.
4. Nay chinkwu nun catong-cha lul pulle yo.
5. Sensayng nim un hak.kyo ey cēnhwa lul kel.e yo?
*6. Wuli ttal un i lul takk.ci anh.ess.ey yo.
7. Na nun Hānkwuk salam hanthey phyēnci lul ssess.ey yo.
8. Na nun Cwungkwuk mal to paywe yo.
9. Kāy nun ayki wa kath.i nol.a yo.
10. Ku haksayng un yuli chang ul yel.e yo.
11. Na nun mun ul tat.e yo.

*[These will end up . . . -ko siph.e haci anh- . . . , the negative going with the auxiliary.]

II

In verb exercise II of Lesson 7, each item includes two sentences. In doing that exercise, you linked the two sentences together so that the meaning was 'someone DOES something BUT [something else happens].' Now take each of the items in that exercise and link the two sentences together so that the meaning is 'EVEN THOUGH someone DOES something [something else happens].' Then translate the sentence. For example, the first will be: Na nun yenghwa kwūkyeng ul cal ka to, tongsayng un cal kaci anh.e yo. 'Even though I go to the movies a lot, my younger brother doesn't go much.' [If this were to be said in two sentences, it would be: Na nun yenghwa kwūkyeng ul cal ka yo. Kulay to, tongsayng un cal kaci anh.e yo.]

Notice how similar the expressions with -e to [or -e yo. Kulay to] are in meaning to the expressions with -ci man [or -e yo. Kuleh.ci man].

NOTE: For sentences 6, 12, and 15, it is necessary to use the PAST infinitive before to; in the others, the ordinary infinitive is used, regardless of the tense of the verb called for when the meaning is conveyed by two sentences.

III

Each of the following sentences mean 'someone DOES or DID something.' Change each so that it means I'M GLAD someone DOES or DID something.' For example, the first sentence will be: Sensayng nim i osye se, (na nun) cōh.a yo. 'I'm glad the teacher came.' Be sure to translate the complete sentence. It is not necessary to include the na nun to mean 'I am glad' but without it the sentence might also be translated 'It's good that . . .' or 'It's nice that . . . .'

1. Sensayng nim i osyess.ey yo.

2. Apeci ka mulken ul phal.ess.ey yo.
3. Ku chinkwu ka na hanthey phyēnci lul ssess.ey yo.
4. Na nun eceyq pam ey yetelq sikan ccum cass.ey yo.
5. Chinkwu ka sēy si kkaci kitalyess.ey yo.
6. Ayki ka ku ūmsik ul cal mek.ess.ey yo.
7. Kāy ka wuli lul pwa to cic.ci anh.e yo.

IV

Now take each sentence of exercise III and make it mean 'Mr. Kim is glad that someone does or did something.' For example, the first will be: Sensayng nim i osye se, Kim sensayng un cōh.a hay yo (or cōh.a hasey yo).

V

Each of the following sentences means 'someone DOES something.' Change each so that it means 'IT'S ALL RIGHT FOR someone TO DO something' or 'someone MAY DO something.' Or, if the sentence is negative, make it mean 'someone NEED NOT DO something' or 'IT'S ALL RIGHT IF someone DOESN'T DO something, someone DOESN'T HAVE TO DO something.' For example, the first sentence will be Hānkwuk ey se to i kwutwu lul sin.e to coh.a yo? 'Is it all right (for me) to wear these shoes in Korea too?'

1. Hānkwuk ey se to i kwutwu lul sin.e yo?
2. Nay ka ayki hanthey i ūmsik ul cwue yo?
3. Ai tul i kāy wa kath.i nol.a yo.
4. Kim sensayng uy chinkwu ka onulq cenyek ey wa yo.
5. Moksa nim i wuli ttul ey se sānqpo hasey yo.
6. Ku mun ul tat.ci anh.e yo?
7. Cikum cēnhwa haci anh.e yo?

VI

Each of the following sentences means 'someone HAS TO DO something, someone MUST DO something.' Change each one so that it means 'someone NEED NOT DO something, someone DOESN'T HAVE TO DO something.' In some of your sentences, use cōh.a yo and in others use kwaynchanh.e yo for 'it's all right.' Then translate the sentence. For example, the first will be: [1]Nayil achim un wuli ka ilccik il.e naci anh.e to, coh.a yo (OR kwaynchanh.e yo). 'We don't have to get up early tomorrow morning.'

1. [1]Nayil achim un wuli ka ilccik il.e na ya hay yo.
2. Atul i say kwutwu lul takk.e ya hay yo.
3. Na nun i chayk ul ilk.e ya hay yo.
4. Ttal i nay yeph ey anc.e ya hay yo.
5. Yeki se mul ul masye ya hay yo.
6. Wuli nun sip-pun ccum swie ya hay yo.
7. Catong-cha lul pulle ya hay yo.

VII

Each of the following sentences means 'someone NEED NOT DO something, someone DOESN'T HAVE TO DO something.' Change each one so that it means 'someone HAS TO DO something, someone MUST DO something.' Then translate the sentence. For example, the first will be: Wuli nun chinkwu lul kitalye ya hay yo. 'We have to wait for our friends.'

1. Wuli nun chinkwu lul kitalici anh.e to cōh.a yo.
2. [1]Nayil achim ey hak.kyo lul an ka to, kwaynchanh.e yo?
3. Na nun Hānkwuk mal ul cal paywuci anh.e to cōh.a yo.
4. Emeni nun ayki wa kath.i mānh.i nōlci anh.e to cōh.a yo.
5. Sensayng nim un i uyca ey anc.usici anh.e to cōh.a yo.
6. Ku haksayng i hak.kyo sensayng ul mannaci anh.e to kwaynchanh.e yo.
7. Ku ai nun honca mun ul yēlci anh.e to cōh.a yo.

VIII

Each of the following sentences means 'someone DOES or DID something'; change each so that the meaning is 'someone TRIES or TRIED DOING something; someone DID something TO SEE (HOW IT WOULD BE).' For example, the first will be Kim sensayng i Ilpon ey ka pwass.ey yo. 'Mr. Kim tried going to Japan. Mr. Kim went to Japan to see. Mr. Kim went to see Japan.' Be sure you know what each of your sentences means.

NOTE: Be careful to make the changes in the FIRST verb expression, not in the auxiliary verb. For example, don't change anh.e yo or siph.e yo or ya hay yo or kwaynchanh.e yo.

1. Kim sensayng i Ilpon ey kass.ey yo.
2. Na nun Hānkwuk ūmsik ul mek.ess.ey yo.
3. Na nun Sewul ey kicha lul thako kako siph.e yo.
4. [1]Nayil achim un ku haksayng i hak.kyo ey ilccik okeyss.ey yo.
5. Kāy nun latio lul tut.ko siph.e hay yo?
6. Na nun i chayk ul ilk.e ya hay yo.
7. Sensayng nim un Hānkwuk os ul ipci anh.e to, kwaynchanh.e yo.
8. Na nun ku kūlim tul ul kwūkyeng hako siph.e yo.

CONVERSATION

I

Talking in Korean two at a time, discuss your classmates' wearing apparel: let A tell what each lady is wearing, alternating with B, who tells what the men have on. (If you want to inject a personal note and comment on anyone's clothing, so much the better for the Korean practice it will afford.)

II

Again chatting two by two, discuss your ambitions in life—either serious or whimsical, long-range or short-range. Ask the other person what he'd like to do or be; listen while he answers. When it's your turn to reply, do so as fully as you can. Would you like to travel? If so, where (and where else and when) would you like to go? Why (way or etteh.key) can't you, or why don't you? What profession would you like to pursue? Why? Or are you happy right now, doing what you are doing? Would you like to eat lunch in a different place tomorrow—at a restaurant instead of eating at home, say? Would you like most of all to buy a new hat? Is getting married what you want to do? How about the latest best seller: would you like to read it? Or would you rather write one of your own? Let your imagination rove. Then tell why you can't do all the things you want to do.

VOCABULARY DRILL

Here are a number of short sentences, each having a blank space. Express the sentence in Korean five times each—filling the blank each time with one of the expressions listed below the sentence.

1. He's glad that ___.
   a. he studied hard.
   b. his friend is coming.
   c. he doesn't have to go to school.
   d. it's all right for him to stay home.
   e. it's Sunday.

2. He has on ___.
   a. a necktie.
   b. glasses.
   c. new socks.
   d. his ring.
   e. Korean clothes.

3. I walked ___.
   a. to the store.
   b. in the park.
   c. under an umbrella.
   d. back home.
   e. from the post office to the bank.

4. I have to ___.
   a. brush my teeth.
   b. button my jacket.
   c. wash.
   d. get undressed.
   e. shave.

5. He's trying on ___.
   a. some shoes.
   b. his shirt.
   c. overcoats.
   d. his new suit.
   e. new glasses.

6. She ___ for me.
   a. looked after my children.
   b. bought a hat.
   c. called the clerk
   d. buttoned my dress
   e. bought some soap and towels

7. It's all right not to ___.
   a. have much money.
   b. go on the streetcar.
   c. call me on the telephone tonight.
   d. take off your overcoat now.
   e. wear a pin on that blouse.

8. You must ___ now.
   a. put on your belt
   b. comb your hair
   c. put on your socks
   d. get dressed
   e. tie your shoes

9. He ___ for my parents.
   a. bought some food
   b. went to the bank and got some money
   c. called a cab
   d. opened the umbrella
   e. wrote some letters

10. I'd like to ___.
   a. buy lots of hats.
   b. sell clothing in a clothing shop.
   c. go home now.
   d. see Japan and Korea.
   e. go to Seoul on the train.

COMPREHENSION

Your Korean teacher will say a number of sentences rapidly in Korean about Mr. Kim, based on the things you have learned in this lesson. Your task is to listen carefully, and, when the sentence is over, raise your RIGHT hand if the sentence said Mr. Kim DID something and your LEFT hand if it says he DID NOT do something. Here, for example, are some 'RIGHT-hand' sentences:

Mr. Kim is sitting in that chair.
Mr. Kim has to work hard.

Mr. Kim is putting on his socks and shoes.
Mr. Kim likes to read.
Mr. Kim would like to buy a new suit.
Mr. Kim tied his shoelaces.
Mr. Kim took off his glasses and lay down.

This kind of sentence calls for the LEFT hand:

Mr. Kim didn't have to go to the office this morning.
Mr. Kim doesn't like to brush his teeth.
Mr. Kim doesn't want to ride on the streetcar.
It's all right if Mr. Kim doesn't polish his shoes today.

Now, listen while your Korean teacher makes a number of statements he has prepared: you say kulay yo 'yes' if the statement is generally true, or sensible; otherwise, you say kuleh.ci anh.e yo 'No.'

Here are some 'yes-es,' for example:

You get up in the morning and then get dressed and have breakfast.
You don't have to buy new shoes every day.

These would be 'no':

Ladies always wear shirts and trousers.
You often go to bed with your clothes on.

[In doing this exercise your teacher will proceed from relatively simple sentences to quite complicated ones. Listen very carefully to any long sentence, and ask to hear it again if you are not sure you got it.]

LESSON 9. WEATHER AND OTHER CONDITIONS

BASIC SENTENCES

Korean	English	Amplification
1. Path ey nun mues ul sim.usikeyss.ey yo?	What are you going to plant in your garden?	sim.e yo [sīm-] 'plants it' sim.usikeyss.ey yo '[someone esteemed] will plant or is going to plant'
2. Path ey nun yele kaci kkoch to sīm.ko, chayso to sīm.keyss.ey yo.	We're going to plant all kinds of flowers and (plants) vegetables.	kaci 'kind, variety' yele kaci 'all kinds (of)' sīm.ko /sīmkko/ 'plants, and . . .' sīm.keyss.ey yo /sīmkkeyssey yo/ 'will plant, is going to plant'
3. Pi ka omyen, kkoch kwa phul i cal cala yo.	When it rains, the flowers and grass grow nicely.	pi 'rain' pi ka wa yo '[rain comes=] it rains' omyen 'if or when it comes' pi ka omyen 'if or when it rains' cala yo [cala-] '[something] grows'
4. I kwāyngi ka ippuci man, kiluci nun anh.keyss.ey yo.	This cat is cute, but I'm not going to keep [= raise] it.	ippe yo [ippu-], yeyppe yo [yeyppu-] 'is cute, lovable, precious' kille yo [kilu-] 'raises [animals], grows [plants]' kiluci anh.keyss.ey yo 'will not raise/grow it'
5. Palam un pūlci man, nal un chwupci anh.keyss.ey yo.	The wind is blowing, but [the weather] it probably isn't cold.	palam 'wind' pul.e yo [pū-l-] 'blows' nal 'day'; (= nal-ssi) 'weather' chwuwe yo [chwuw-] 'is cold or cool' chwupci anh.e yo 'isn't cold' chwupci anh.keyss.ey yo 'will not be cold; probably is not cold'
6. Pi ka omyen se (to), hay ka na yo.	(Even) while it's raining, the sun is shining.	pi ka omyen se 'while it rains' pi ka omyen se to 'even while it rains'

	Korean	English	Amplification
			hay 'sun' hay ka na yo '[the sun emerges=] the sun shines'
7.	Pom i kaci anh.umyen, cōh.keyss.ey yo.	I wish it would stay spring. [=If spring would not go, it would be good.]	pom 'spring' kaci anh.umyen 'if it doesn't go (away)' cōh.keyssey yo 'it will <u>or</u> would be good'
8.	Nal mata, nac imyen tewe ciko, pam imyen chwuwe cye yo.	Every day, it warms up in the daytime and cools off at night. [=Every day, when it's daytime, it gets warm, and when it's night, it gets cold.]	nac imyen 'if <u>or</u> when it's daytime' tewe yo [tēw-] 'is warm <u>or</u> hot' tewe cye yo [ci-] 'gets warm <u>or</u> hot' tewe ciko 'gets warm, and . . .' pam imyen 'if it's night' chwuwe cye yo 'gets cold; cools off'
9.	I kkoch ul cwusimyen, komapkeyss.ey yo.	I'd love to have you give me these flowers. [=If you give me these flowers, I'll be grateful.]	cwusimyen 'if <u>or</u> when [someone esteemed] gives' komapkeyss.ey yo 'will be thankful <u>or</u> grateful'
10.	Nal i hulye cici anh.umyen, na nun pakk ey na ka se, sānqpo lul hakeyss.ey yo.	If the weather doesn't cloud up, I'll go outside and take a walk.	hulye yo [huli-] 'is cloudy' hulye cye yo 'gets cloudy, clouds up' hulye cici anh.e yo 'doesn't get cloudy, doesn't cloud up' hulye cici anh.umyen 'if it doesn't get cloudy <u>or</u> cloud up' hakeyss.ey yo 'will (=is going to) do' sānqpo lul hakeyss.ey yo 'will (=is going to) take a walk'
11.	Onul ōhwu ey nal i cōh.umyen, sānqpo hasikeyss.ey yo?	If it's nice this afternoon, are you going to take a walk?	nal i cōh.a yo '[the weather is good=] it's nice, it's a nice day' nal i cōh.umyen 'if it's (a) nice day, if the weather is good' hasikeyss.ey yo '[someone esteemed] will <u>or</u> is going to do'

Korean	English	Amplification
12. Nemu mānh.i kel.umyen, phikon hay yo.	If I walk too much, I [am=] get tired.	nemu 'too, excessively' nemu mānh.i 'too much, too many' kel.umyen 'if [I] walk' phikon hay yo 'is tired'
13. Pi ka omyen, cip ey iss.keyss.ey yo.	If it rains, I'll stay home.	iss.keyss.ey yo '(there) will be; will (=is going to) stay'
14. Na nun achim mek.umyen se, sinmun ul ilk.keyss.ey yo.	I'll read the paper while I eat breakfast.	pap 'cooked rice; a meal' [honorific: cīnci] achim(q pap) mek.e yo [honorific: achim(q cinci) capswusey yo] 'eats breakfast' achim(q pap) mek.umyen se 'while eating' ilk.keyss.ey yo 'will read, is going to read'
15. Um.ak ul tul.umyen se, kōhyang ul sayngkak hayss.ey yo.	I was thinking of home while I listened to the music.	tul.umyen se 'while listening (to)' kōhyang 'home, home town' sayngkak 'a thought, an idea' sayngkak hay yo 'thinks'
16. Nolay lul hamyen se, chwum ul chwue yo.	They dance and sing at the same time.	nolay 'song' nolay (lul) hay yo 'sings' nolay lul hamyen se 'while singing' chwum 'a dance' chwum (ul) chwue yo [chwu-] 'dances'
17. Na nun cip ey iss.ci anh.ko, sangcem ey ka se, chayk ul sakeyss.ey yo.	I'm not going to stay home—I'm going to the store and buy some books.	sakeyss.ey yo 'will buy, is going to buy'
18. I chayk i cōh.ci man, pissa se, saci anh.keyss.ey yo.	This book is good, but it's expensive, so I'm not going to buy it.	pissa yo 'is expensive' pissa se 'is expensive, so . . .' saci anh.keyss.ey yo 'won't buy, isn't going to buy'
19. (Mān-il) i chayk i ssamyen, sālam tul i mānh.i sakeyss.ey yo.	If this book were cheap(er), lots of people would buy it.	mān-il '[one in 10,000=] if, in the event that' ssa yo 'is inexpensive, cheap' ssamyen 'if it's cheap' sakeyss.ey yo 'will buy; would buy'

Korean	English	Amplification
20. Wēn hasimyen, nay chayk ul pillye tulikeyss.ey yo.	If you like, I'll lend you my copy.	wēn hay yo 'wants' wēn hasimyen 'if [someone esteemed] wants'
21. Pillye to kwaynchanh.e yo?	May I borrow it?	pillye yo [pilli-] 'borrows' pillye cwue yo 'lends' pillye tulikeyss.ey yo 'will lend [as a favor for someone esteemed]'
22. I chayk ul ilk.umyen, an tōy yo.	It won't do for you to read this book. or You must [or may] not read this book.	ilk.umyen 'if [someone] reads' tōy yo [toy-] 'becomes; is; happens satisfactorily' an tōy yo 'isn't; doesn't become; is not satisfactory'
23. Keli ey kamyen, an tōy yo.	You shouldn't go to town.	= If you go to town, it won't do. keli 'downtown streets; downtown, the town' kamyen 'if [one] goes'
24. Kongpu lul an hamyen an tōy yo.	You ought to study.	= If you don't study, it isn't satisfactory. an hamyen 'if [one] doesn't do'
25. Oppa nun nul nōlmyen se (to), kongpu lul cal hay yo.	While [it's true that] my brother is always having fun, he [also] studies a lot.	nōlmyen 'if [someone] plays' nōlmyen se 'while [someone] plays' nōlmyen se to 'even while playing'
26. Ama cikum ccum un yeph pang haksayng tul i ku kongpu lul pelsse tā hayss.keyss.ey yo.	By now the students in the next room have probably already studied that whole lesson.	ama 'perhaps, maybe; probably' cikum ccum (un) 'by now' pelsse 'already; before this, by now' tā 'all; all the way' hayss.keyss.ey yo 'will have done; have probably done, must have done'
27. Moley ccum un wuli to ku kongpu lul machikeyss.ey yo.	We will finish that lesson by the day after tomorrow, too.	moley 'day after tomorrow' moley ccum (un) 'by day after tomorrow' machye yo [machi-] 'finishes it' machikeyss.ey yo 'will finish it'

Korean	English	Amplification
28. Nay tongmu ka ku kongpu lul kucekkey hayss.ess.ey yo.	My pal studied that lesson the day before yesterday.	tongmu or pes 'comrade, friend, pal' kucekkey 'day before yesterday' hayss.ess.ey yo 'had done; did (earlier)'
29. Hānkwuk mal ul cal hamyen cōh.keyss.ey yo.	I hope I speak Korean well. or I wish I spoke Korean well.	hamyen 'if [one] does' cōh.keyss.ey yo 'it will (or would) be good' [= If I speak/spoke Korean well, it will/would be good.]
30. Eti kasyess.ess.ey yo.	Where have you been?	kasyess.ess.ey yo '[someone esteemed] had gone or went and came back'
31. Keli ey kass.ess.ey yo.	I've been to town [and come back].	kass.ess.ey yo 'had gone; went and came back'
32. Na nun cīnan cwuil ey Sewul ey wass.ey yo.	I came to Seoul last week [and am still here]. or I've been in Seoul since last week.	Sewul 'Seoul' [capital of South Korea]
33. Ese pānghak i omyen, cōh.keyss.ey yo.	I hope vacation will be here soon. or I wish vacation would get here soon.	ese 'quickly, soon' pānghak 'vacation (from school)' [= If vacation comes/came quickly, it will/would be good.]

SUPPLEMENTARY VOCABULARY

pom	spring	senul hay yo	is cool
yelum	summer	chwuwe yo [chwuw-]	is cold
kaul	fall, autumn	cha yo [cha-]	is cold (to the touch)
kyewul	winter	kunul	shade
nwūn	snow	kwulum	cloud
nwūn i wa yo	it snows	kos	place
ttattus hay yo [= tewe yo]	is warm or hot	i kos (= yeki)	this place
ttukewe yo [ttukew-]	is hot	enu kos (= eti)	what place; some place
etwuwe yo [etwuw-]	is dark	wuyu	(cow's) milk
		sēnmul	gift, present

NOTES

‖ 9.1. Verbs: future.

The basic sentences of this lesson contain a number of verbs in the FUTURE FORM. The marker for the future is -keyss-; it is a one-shape marker which is attached to the bases of verbs in the same way as the gerund ending -ko.

Here are a few examples:

ka- 'go'	kakeyss- 'going to go'
kitali- 'wait'	kitalikeyss- 'going to wait'
ssu- 'write; use; wear'	ssukeyss- 'going to write or use or wear'
pulu- 'call'	pulukeyss- 'going to call'
cwu- 'give'	cwukeyss- 'going to give'
po- 'see'	pokeyss- 'going to see'
ip- 'wear'	ipkeyss- /ipkkeyss-/ 'going to wear'
pat- 'get'	pat.keyss- /pakkeyss-/ 'going to get'
chac- 'look for; find'	chac.keyss- /chakkeyss-/ 'going to look for (find)'
pis- 'comb'	pis.keyss- /pikkeyss-/ 'going to comb'
iss- 'stay; have'	iss.keyss- /ikkeyss-/ 'going to stay/have'
mek- 'eat'	mek.keyss- /mekkeyss-/ 'going to eat'
takk- 'polish'	takk.keyss- /takkeyss-/ 'going to polish'
ēps- 'be lacking'	ēps.keyss- /ēpkkeyss-/ 'going to be lacking'
ilk- 'read'	ilk.keyss- /ilkkeyss-/ or /ikkeyss-/
sīm- 'plant'	sīm.keyss- /sīmkkeyss-/ 'going to plant'
celm- 'be young'	celm.keyss- /cemkkeyss-/ 'going to be young'
sin- 'wear (shoes)'	sin.keyss- /sinkkeyss-/ 'going to wear (shoes)'
anc- 'sit down'	anc.keyss- /ankkeyss-/ 'going to sit down'
mānh- 'be much/many'	mānh.keyss- /mānkheyss-/ 'going to be much/many'
cōh- 'be good'	cōh.keyss- /cōkheyss-/ 'going to be good'
nwuw- 'lie down'	nwupkeyss- /nwupkkeyss-/ 'going to lie down'
tul- 'hear'	tut.keyss- /tukkeyss-/ 'going to hear'
tu-l- 'enter; cost'	tulkeyss- 'going to enter or cost'

To make honorific future forms, you simply add -keyss- to the honorific base:

ka- 'go' → kasi- → kasikeyss-
pat- 'get' → pat.usi- → pat.usikeyss-

A future base is not a complete word by itself; it needs an ending. To make it polite style, you add -ey yo:

ka- 'go' → ka(si)keyss.ey yo 'will go'
pat- 'get' → pat.(usi)keyss.ey yo 'will get'

You can make a future suspective by adding -ci to -keyss-:

ka- 'go' → ka(si)keyss.ci man 'will go, but . . .'
pat- 'get' → pat.(usi)keyss.ci man 'will get, but . . .'

For long negatives in the future, you use a plain -ci suspective and make the auxiliary anh- future:

ka- 'go' → kaci anh.keyss.ey yo 'won't go'
pat- 'get' → pat.ci anh.keyss.ey yo 'won't get'

As usual, the -ci form merely says what action is performed, while the negative word anh- carries the other meanings of the phrase. Also, as usual, either word —or both—may be honorific if the phrase refers to someone esteemed:

ka- 'go'	kaci anh.usikeyss.ey yo	
	kasici anh.keyss.ey yo	'[someone esteemed] won't go'
	kasici anh.usikeyss.ey yo	

When it comes to meaning, Korean future forms have a variety of corresponding English expressions, and in order to understand the Korean future fully, it is necessary to have a careful look at the meanings of certain similar English words.

1. 'Will, is going to':

Simple future action is expressed in English by 'will' and 'is going to.' These have slightly different connotations, but both are covered by the Korean future:

ilk.kess.ey yo 'will read, is going to read'

2. 'Would':

In certain conditional ('if') sentences, the Korean future corresponds to English 'would [do so-and-so].' These are discussed below.

Koreans often prefer to use the future for verbs of knowing: ālkeyss.ey yo 'I know' or 'I understand' where we would expect al.e yo, molukeyss.ey yo 'I don't know' or 'I don't understand' where we would expect mōlla yo. The present forms are also used, but the future form has a suggestion of tentativeness (like English 'I wouldn't know') and perhaps for that reason seems more polite, especially in questions: Āsikeyss.ey yo 'Do you know?' or 'Do you understand?' (compare English 'Would you happen to know?')

3. 'Is willing to, wants to':

In both English and Korean, a future verb form may mean 'will' in the sense 'is willing to' or 'wants to [do so-and-so].' In this sense, the future is much like -ko siph.e yo 'wants to':

Sānqpo hasikeyss.ey yo? 'Would you like to take a walk? [or Are you willing to take a walk? or Will you take a walk? or Are you going to take a walk?']

4. 'Probably; must':

The words 'probably' and 'must' are alike in adding the same flavor to English sentences in a certain usage. In this connection, it is necessary first to distinguish between the two kinds of English 'must.' One 'must' expresses OBLIGATION:

It's raining—you must wear your raincoat.
I simply must get my work finished.

This kind of 'must,' as you know, is expressed by the Korean construction -e ya hay yo (‖ 8.12).

The other 'must' expresses PROBABILITY or LIKELIHOOD:

That girl with Bill must be his fiancée.
It's raining— it must be getting cooler.

It is this second kind of 'must' which is sometimes conveyed by the Korean future. [In British English, the future is sometimes used in this Korean way. For example, you might describe a certain building to a Londoner and ask him what it is, and receive the reply 'That will be St. Paul's.' Americans sometimes use 'would' in this way: 'That would be the RCA Building.'] In the same sentence with such a future form, there often appears the adverb <u>ama</u>, which means 'probably' or 'likely' and strengthens the connotation of the future verb form.

You will learn a fifth usage for the future in Lesson 11 (¶ 11.12).

Here are a few more examples of Korean sentences with future verbs.

1.	Phyēnci nun ssukeyss.ci man, cēnhwa nun an hakeyss.ey yo.	I'll write a letter, but I won't telephone.
2.	Kongpu lul hako, cakeyss.ey yo.	I'm going to study and then go to bed.
3.	Wuli eykey kūlim (tul) ul cwusikeyss.ey yo?	Will you give us some pictures?
4.	Sinmun i chayk-sang wi ey acik to iss.keyss.ey yo.	The newspaper is still probably [= must still be] on the desk.
5.	Īl un hakeyss.ci man, tōn un an pat.keyss.ey yo.	I'll do the job, but I won't ['receive' =] take any money (for it).
6.	Nayil wuli cip kwūkyeng osikeyss.ey yo?	Would you like to come and see our house tomorrow?
7.	Ēncey ccum machikeyss.ey yo.	(By) when will it be finished?
8.	I chayk ul Kim sensayng eykey tulikeyss.ey yo?	Are you going to give [= Will you give] this book to Mr. Kim?
9.	^{1}Nayil hak.kyo ey haksayng tul i ēps.keyss.ey yo?	Won't the students be at school tomorrow?
10.	Na nun i īl un hakeyss.ci man, ce īl un an hakeyss.ey yo.	I'll do this, but I won't do that.
11.	^{1}Nayil un sangcem ey chayk i mānh.keyss.ey yo.	There will be lots of books at the store tomorrow.
12.	Mues ul hasikeyss.ey yo?	What are you going to do?
13.	Tases sikan ccum ina kongpu hako, cakeyss.ey yo.	I'm going to study for about five hours and then go to bed.
14.	Pakk ey com te anc.e iss.keyss.e yo.	I'm going to sit outside for a little longer.
15.	Sensayng nim un cikum ccum pihayng-ki lul thako kyēysikeyss.ey yo.	The teacher must be on the plane by now.
16.	Emeni to han pen yenghwa kwūkyeng ul ka poko siph.usikeyss.ey yo.	Mother might sometimes want to go see the movies too.
17.	Wuli ai to say os ul ip.e poko siph.e hakeyss.ey yo.	My child may like to try on some new clothes too.
18.	Cikum ce kos ey kasye to nuc.ci anh.usikeyss.ci man, ^{1}nayil achim ilccik kasipsio.	Even though it is not too late to go there now, (you better) go tomorrow morning early.
19.	Ōhwu yeses si pān kkaci oci anh.umyen te kitaliko iss.ci anh.keyss.ey yo.	I am not going to wait for you if you don't come by 6:30 p.m.
20.	Ku māl i chayk ey sse iss.ci anh.keyss.ey yo?	Wouldn't it ['those words'] be written in the book?
21.	Wuli ayki lul pwa poci anh.keyss.ey yo?	Won't you look after my baby?
22.	Hal-apeci uy cwumeni lul chac.e tulikeyss.ey yo.	I will find my grandfather's purse for him.
23.	Nay yak.hon-ca (uy) sayngil ey kkoch ul sa cwuci anh.keyss.ey yo.	I am not going to buy any flowers for my fiancée on her birthday.

‖ 9.2. Verbs: past-future and past-past.

There is a PAST-FUTURE verb form which is made by attaching the FUTURE marker -keyss- to the PAST BASE of any verb—either the plain past base or the honorific past base—like this:

Base	Past Base	Past-Future Base	
ka- 'go'	kass-	kass.keyss-	/kakkeyss-/
kasi-	kasyess-	kasyess.keyss-	/kasekkeyss-/
pat- 'get'	pat.ess-	pat.ess.keyss-	/patekkeyss-/
pat.usi-	pat.usyess-	pat.usyess.keyss-	/patusekkeyss-/

Since all past bases, either plain or honorific, end with the past marker ss (which is pronounced like t before a one-shape ending), all future perfect bases end in -ss.keyss- (→ -t.keyss-) → -kkeyss-. To this base, you then attach whatever ending is appropriate for the sentence.

You have seen an example of a past-future perfect verb in the basic sentences of this lesson:

26. Ama . . . ku kongpu lul hayss.keyss.ey yo. 'They have probably already studied [it].'

The past marker gives to the form the same meaning as the English auxiliary verb 'has' or 'have,' while the future marker gives it one of the future meanings listed in ‖ 9.1 just above—'probably.'

When you are listening to a Korean person speaking, your only clue to the difference between a future verb form and a past-future verb form is very small—sometimes only the difference between /k/ and /kk/:

kakeyss.ey yo /kakeyssey yo/ 'will go'
kass.keyss.ey yo /kakkeyssey yo/ 'will have gone'

Another problem in fine distinctions comes in PAST-PAST verb forms, which are made by attaching the past tense marker -ess- to the past base of any verb, either honorific or plain, forming in effect a double past base:

	Past Base	Past-Past Base
ha- 'do'	hayss-	hayss.ess-
hasi-	hasyess-	hasyess.ess-

The form is made complete by adding an appropriate ending.

The past-past, then, is distinguished from the past by being longer:

Past:	hayss.ey yo 'did'
Past-Past:	hayss.ess.ey yo 'did (earlier)'

Before a one-shape ending, this is a little more difficult to detect:

Past:	hayss.ci man 'did, but . . .' /haycci/
Past-Past:	hayss.ess.ci man 'did (earlier), but . . .' /haysecci/

You have met with three examples of the past-past in the basic sentences of this lesson:

28. Nay tongmu ka ku kongpu lul kucekkey hayss.ess.ey yo. 'My pal studied that lesson the day before yesterday.'

30. Eti kasyess.ess.ey yo. 'Where have you been?'
31. Keli ey kass.ess.ey yo. 'I've been to town [and come back].'

These forms do not correspond to any single English word; in general, they mean about the same thing as regular past-tense forms, except that they have the feeling of a more definitely completed action (as in Basic Sentence 28) or a comparatively remote past action.

But there is one area of meaning where a real difference exists: if an action has come full circle, you use the past-past; for a similar action which has not yet come full circle, you use the plain past. (You will see further examples of this in Lesson 11, Basic Sentences 32 and 33.) This distinction is common in verbs meaning 'come' and 'go' and is illustrated by Basic Sentences 30 and 31, quoted just above. Compare sentence 32, in which the traveler has not yet returned to his point of origin:

Na nun cīnan cwuil ey Sewul ey wass.ey yo. 'I came to Seoul last week [and, as you can see, I am still here].'

'Come' and 'go' in the past-past may be literally translated, respectively, as 'come and return' and 'go and come back'; in the past they mean, respectively, '(came and) is here' and '(went and) is gone.'

Thus, you will not be surprised to find that a person who says (pap) mek.ess.ey yo 'I've eaten' is full, but a person who says (pap) mek.ess.ess.ey yo 'I ate [but got hungry again]' is ready for another meal.

‖ 9.3. Verbs: conditional form.

Verbs with the ending -umyen/-myen are in the CONDITIONAL form. The conditional ending is a two-shape ending: you attach it to consonant bases as -umyen and to vowel bases as -myen; L-extending vowel bases attach -myen to the extended base (with the l). Honorific conditionals are made by attaching the ending to the honorific base: -usi-myen/-si-myen.

Base	Conditional	Honorific conditional
Vowel-base verbs:		
ka- 'go'	kamyen	kasimyen
ippu- 'be cute'	ippumyen	ippusimyen
po- 'see'	pomyen	posimyen
cwu- 'give'	cwumyen	cwusimyen
su- 'stand up'	sumyen	susimyen
pulu- 'call'	pulumyen	pulusimyen
L-extending:		
pha-l- 'sell'	phalmyen	phasimyen
yē-l- 'open it'	yēlmyen	yēsimyen
nō-l- 'play'	nōlmyen	nōsimyen
tu-l- 'enter; cost'	tulmyen	tusimyen
Consonant-base verbs:		
ip- 'wear'	ip.umyen	ip.usimyen
siph- 'want to'	siph.umyen	siph.usimyen
ēps- 'be lacking'	ēps.umyen	ēps.usimyen
pat- 'get'	pat.umyen	pat.usimyen
pes- 'removes (clothes)'	pes.umyen	pes.usimyen
iss- 'have'	iss.umyen	iss.usimyen

chac- 'looks for; finds'	chac.umyen	chac.usimyen
mek- 'eat'	mek.umyen	mek.usimyen
kkakk- 'cut'	kkakk.umyen	kkakk.usimyen
ilk- 'read'	ilk.umyen	ilk.usimyen
tul- 'listen; hear'	tul.umyen	tul.usimyen
sīm- 'plant'	sim.umyen	sim.usimyen
celm- 'be young'	celm.umyen	celm.usimyen
sin- 'wear (shoes)'	sin.umyen	sin.usimyen
anc- 'sit down'	anc.umyen	anc.usimyen
cōh- 'be good'	cōh.umyen	cōh.usimyen
mānh- 'be much/many'	mānh.umyen	mānh.usimyen
silh- 'be disliked'	silh.umyen	silh.usimyen
tōw- 'help'	towumyen	towusimyen

There is a past conditional, formed by adding -umyen to the -ss- of the past base to produce -ess.umyen (etc.), but it is fairly uncommon in Seoul; the meaning 'if [one] had done [so-and-so]' is likely to be conveyed instead by a more complicated construction which you will learn later: -(ess.)tula 'myen, ‖ 24.1. Still, you will occasionally run across sentences like Ku sālam ul mannass.umyen cōh.keyss.ey yo (or cōh.ass.keyss.ey yo) 'If I had met him it would be good = I wish I had met him.'

‖ 9.4. Uses of the conditional.

The basic meaning of the conditional ending is 'if [so-and-so happens]' or 'when(ever) [so-and-so happens].' This meaning is illustrated by Basic Sentence 12 of this lesson:

Nemu mānh.i kel.umyen, phikon hay yo. 'If I walk too much, I get tired.' or 'When I walk too much, I get tired.' or 'Whenever I walk too much, I get tired.'

Here are a few more examples:

1. Pi ka omyen kaci mōs hakeyss.ey yo.	I won't be able to go if it rains.
2. Onul ōhwu ey nal i cōh.umyen, sangcem ey kakeyss.ey yo.	If it's nice this afternoon, I'll go to the store.
3. Pi ka omyen, cip ey iss.ess.ey yo.	Whenever it rained, we stayed home.
4. Phikon hamyen, com swīpsita.	If you're tired, let's rest a bit.
5. Na kath.umyen, i kos ey se īl ul hako siph.ci anh.keyss.ey yo.	[If it be like me =] If it were me, I wouldn't want to work in this place.

Most of these sentences—if the context called for it—could go into English in a slightly different tense form:

1. I wouldn't be able to go if it rained.
2. If it were nice this afternoon, I would go to the store.
3. If it rained, we would stay home.

There are a couple of special uses for the conditional which lead to English translations quite different from word-for-word versions of the Korean. These are discussed below.

‖ 9.4.1. Uses of the conditional: -umyen cōh.a yo.

A conditional sentence ending with some form of cōh.a yo 'is good or nice' may correspond to an English sentence expressing a HOPE or a WISH, as you have seen in several of the basic sentences:

7. Pom i kaci anh.umyen, cōh.keyss.ey yo. 'I wish it would stay spring.' [= If spring didn't go away, it would be good.]
29. Hānkwuk mal ul cal hamyen cōh.keyss.ey yo. 'I hope I speak Korean well.' or 'I wish I spoke Korean well.' [= If I speak/spoke Korean well, it will/would be good.]
33. Ese pānghak i omyen, cōh.keyss.ey yo. 'I hope/wish vacation will/would get here soon.'

If the sentence is a question, the corresponding English may contain SHALL WE . . . ?:

Musun sangcem ey kamyen cōh.keyss.ey yo. 'Which store SHALL WE go to?' [= If we went to which store, would it be good?]

These sentences shade into expressions of MILD OBLIGATION, as follows:

I sangcem ey kamyen cōh.keyss.ey yo? 'Shall [or Should] we go to this store?' [= Would it be good if we went to this store?]

Kongpu lul com te hamyen cōh.keyss.ey yo. 'You should study a little more.' [= It would be good if you'd study a little more.]

Cikum cip ey kamyen cōh.keyss.ey yo. 'We'd better go home now.' [= It will be good if we go home now.]

‖ 9.4.2. Uses of the conditional: -umyen komawe yo (indirect requests).

A conditional verb followed by the future form komapkeyss.ey yo means literally 'if you do so-and-so, I will be grateful,' or komawe hakess.ey yo '. . . [someone else] will be grateful.' This is a polite and somewhat oblique way of saying 'please do so-and-so.' You observed this construction in Basic Sentence 9:

I kkoch ul cwusimyen, komapkeyss.ey yo. 'I'd like you to give me these flowers.' or 'May I ask you to give me these flowers?'

Of course there is nothing in the Korean to convey the abruptness of the most nearly literal English corresponding to this construction (I'll thank you to leave me alone); on the contrary, its indirectness gives it a flavor of greater courtesy in Korean.

Here are some more examples:

1. Ilccik com osimyen komapkeyss.ey yo.	I'd appreciate it if you'd come a little early. [= If you'd come a little early, I'd be thankful.]
2. Tōn ul com cwusimyen, komapkeyss.ey yo.	Would you give me a little money?
3. I īl ul hasimyen komawe hakeyss.ey yo.	He'd like you to do this work.

The foregoing discussion may leave you feeling that the meaning of the Korean conditional is somewhat vague and difficult to pin down; and you are quite right. In terms of their real meaning—what they actually convey—Korean conditional sentences are likely to have English equivalents quite far afield from the word-for-word renditions. As a tag translation of the forms "if or when" will do.

‖ 9.5. Other uses of the conditional: mild obligation; denial of permission.

Two more oblique constructions with the conditional involve the use of the verb tōy yo, which in this case means something like 'is permitted or allowed'; in the negative, 'it won't do; it isn't allowed or permitted.' Notice that An tōyss.ey yo is the usual way to say 'That's too bad; that's a shame [= I'm sorry to hear that]; that's no good'; Tōyss.ey yo means 'It's OK; That's all right.'

A double negative expression consisting of the negative conditional followed by the negative form an tōy yo results in an affirmative indication of OBLIGATION:

24. Kongpu lul an hamyen an tōy yo. 'You ought to study.' [= If you don't study, it won't do.]

The obligation this construction expresses is milder than the rather stern meaning conveyed by -e ya hay yo 'has to—' or 'must—' yet stronger than -umyen cōh.keyss.ey yo meaning literally 'it would be good if—' that is, 'I'd better—' etc.

If the only negative verb is an tōy yo, then the sentence DENIES PERMISSION: it means 'you may not . . .' or 'you must not . . .':

22. I chayk ul ilk.umyen, an tōy yo. '[If you read this book, it won't do.=] You may [or must] not read this book.'
23. Keli ey kamyen, an tōy yo. '[If you go to town, it isn't permissible.=] You mustn't or may not or shouldn't go to town.'

Here are more examples of these constructions.

1. Cip ey iss.ci anh.umyen an tōy yo.	We ought to stay at home.
2. Sensayng uy māl ul an tul.umyen an tōy yo.	You must do as the teacher says. [You must listen to the teacher's words.]
3. Onulq cenyek ey kongpu lul an hamyen an toykeyss.ey yo.	I've got to study tonight. [If I don't study tonight, it will not do.]
4. Koki lul nemu mānh.i mek.umyen an tōy yo.	You mustn't eat too much meat. [If you eat too much meat, it won't do.]
5. Nemu ilcciki il.e namyen an tōy yo.	You shouldn't get up too early.
6. Ku chayk-sang aph ey se kyēysimyen an tōy yo.	You mustn't stand in front of that desk.
7. Cikum na lul poko iss.umyen an tōy yo.	You mustn't look at me now.
8. Yun sensayng puin ul kitaliko iss.ci anh.umyen an tōy yo.	I ought to stay here and wait for Mrs. Yun.
9. Ku kes ul poko siph.e hamyen an tōy yo.	You mustn't yearn to see that.
10. I tāmpay lul phiwe pomyen an tōy yo.	You mustn't smoke (or try) this cigarette.
11. Ku yenghwa lul ka poci anh.umyen an tōyss.ey yo.	I had to go see that movie.
12. Han sikan man i chayk-sang wi ey se iss.ci anh.umyen an tōy yo.	You are to stand on this desk for an hour.
13. Yelum ey nun ttul uy phul ul kkakk.ci anh.umyen an tōy se, silh.e yo.	I have to mow the yard in the summer, so I don't like summer.

14. Onulq pam ey nun cip ey ēps.umyen an tōy yo.	You ought to stay at home tonight.
15. Ape' nim un pang an ey man pam-nac kyēysimyen an tōy yo.	Father, you shouldn't stay in your room all the time.
16. Sālam tul i mun an tul.e kamyen an toyci man, sensayng nim un tul.e kasye to tōy yo.	People aren't allowed to enter this door, but you may enter it.
17. Onul nay tōn ul cwuci anh.umyen an tōyss.ci man, nuc.e to ˡnayil kkaci nun cwusye ya hap.nita.	You were supposed to give (or pay) me back my money today, but you must give it to me by tomorrow at the latest.
18. Say os ul ipci anh.umyen an tōy se, an kakeyss.ey yo.	I have to have new clothes in order to go there, so I am not going.

‖ 9.6. Conditional forms with the particles se and se to.

A conditional form plus the particle se means 'while doing so-and-so'; whatever action is named in the clause following is done (1)at the same time and(2) by the same person as the -umyen se action. For this reason there is usually only one subject expressed for the two actions.

14. Na nun achim mek.umyen se, sinmun ul ilk.keyss.ey yo. 'I'll read the paper WHILE I EAT BREAKFAST.'
15. Um.ak ul tul.umyen se, kōhyang ul sayngkak hayss.ey yo. 'I was thinking of home WHILE AT THE SAME TIME I was listening to the music.'
16. Nolay lul hamyen se, chwum ul chwue yo. 'THEY dance WHILE SINGING SIMULTANEOUSLY.'

If the particle to is added to this construction, it contributes its usual meaning 'though' or 'even':

25. Oppa nun nul nōlmyen se to, kongpu lul cal hay yo. '[My brother, even while always playing, studies a lot.=] While it's true that my brother is always having fun, he studies a lot too.'

But sometimes the meaning is 'although' even without the particle to; notice how the English word while (it is true that . . .) sometimes means 'although,' too.

These -umyen se to clauses differ from -e to clauses ('even though . . .') in this respect: the latter may have different subjects or topics for the two clauses, while -umyen se to sentences have the same subject or topic for both.

Here are some more examples of these constructions:

1. Pap ul mek.umyen se, chayk ul ilk.keyss.ey yo.	I read a book while I was eating.
2. Onul achim ey kicha lul thako omyen se, kongpu lul hayss.ey yo.	I studied while I was coming on the train.
3. Eceyq cenyek ey nun latio lul tul.umyen se īl ul hayss.ey yo.	Last night I listened to the radio while I worked.
4. Tōn un ēps.umyen se to, cal sse yo.	Though I haven't got any money, I spend a lot.

5. Ku ⁿyeca nun emeni 'myen se (to) hak.kyo sensayng iey yo.
   She is a school teacher and a mother at the same time.
6. Ku kicha nun ppalumyen se (to) cōh.a yo.
   The train is fast and nice, too.
7. Emeni nun īl hako kyēysimyen se (to) ayki lul posey yo.
   My mother looks after the baby while she works.
8. Sensayng nim un wuli lul posici anh.umyen se māl-ssum hasey yo.
   The teacher doesn't look at us while he talks. [He talks without looking at us.]

‖ 9.7. The conditional for oblique topics.

Basic Sentence 8 illustrates another conditional usage: the conditional copula after nouns as an oblique substitute for the topic particle un/nun 'as for . . . ,' to state a topic for CONTRAST:

> Nal mata, nac imyen tewe ciko, pam imyen chwuwe cye yo. 'Every day it warms up in the daytime and cools off at night.' [Every day, if it be daytime it becomes warm, and if it be night it becomes cold.]

Here are some more examples of this:

1. Sāy tul un māynyen pom imyen chac.e oko, kaul imyen tol.a ka yo.
   The birds come to visit us every spring, and go back in the fall.
2. Emeni 'myen cip ey se īl hako, apeci 'myen pakk ey se īl hay yo.
   Mother works at home, and father works outside.
3. Kāy 'myen nwūn ul cōh.a hako, kwāyngi 'myen silh.e hay yo.
   The dog likes snow and the cat dislikes it.
4. Wuli 'myen mun ul yēlko, wuli chinkwu 'Yu sensayng imyen yēlci mal.e yo.
   Open the door if it is us, and don't if it is our friend, Mr. 'Yu.
5. Sinmun imyen ape' nim kkey tuliko, capci 'myen c(e) eykey cwusey yo.
   Give it to father if it is a newspaper, and give to me if it is a magazine.
6. Yeki ka Hānkwuk imyen cōh.keyss.ey yo.
   I wish this was Korea.
7. Hānkwuk i yeki 'myen cōh.keyss.ey yo.
   I wish Korea was here.
8. Mikwuk imyen yangpok ul ip.e ya hay yo.
   In America you ought to wear a (Western style) suit.
9. Sewul imyen cikum chwup.keyss.ey yo.
   It must be cold in Seoul now.

‖ 9.8. The auxiliary verb cye yo [ci-].

8. Nal mata, nac imyen tewe ciko, pam imyen chwuwe cye yo. 'Every day, it gets warm in the daytime and gets cool at night.'

10. Nal i hulye cici anh.umyen . . . 'If it doesn't get cloudy . . .'

The auxiliary verb cye yo (an abbreviation of cie yo from the base ci-) means 'begins to be . . .' or 'gets (to be) . . . .' It follows the infinitives of descriptive verbs (adjectives) to form processive verb compounds, like these:

chwuwe yo 'is cold'	chwuwe cye yo 'gets cold, cools off'
cōh.a yo 'is good'	cōh.a cye yo 'gets better'
hulye yo 'is cloudy'	hulye cye yo 'gets cloudy, clouds up'
nappe yo 'is bad'	nappe cye yo 'gets worse'
phikon hay yo 'is tired'	phikon hay cye yo 'gets tired'
tewe yo 'is hot'	tewe cye yo 'gets hot, warms or heats up'

(Notice that natural English often uses a phrase to translate such compounds: warms UP, cools OFF, etc.)

Verb phrases with the auxiliary descriptive verb siph.e yo 'wants to, would like to' can also enter into such compounds:

[ha]ko siph.e yo 'wants to [do]'	[ha]ko siph.e cye yo 'gets so that one wants to [do]'

As is usual for compound expressions, the infinitive remains changeless. It is the auxiliary ci- which adjusts to fit the sentence by adding an appropriate ending:

tewe cye yo 'gets hot'
tewe cyess.ey yo 'got hot'
tewe cikeyss.ey yo 'will get hot'
tewe cici man 'gets hot, but . . .'
tewe cimyen 'if it gets hot'
tewe cici anh.umyen 'if it doesn't get hot'

The auxiliary ci- is usually inseparable from the infinitive; it is tacked right on to the -e in pronunciation. You will recall that the letter y (here, as so often, an abbreviation of i) is usually not heard after s, ss, c, or ch, so -e cye yo is pronounced /-ece.yo/.

Here are more examples of these expressions:

1. Nal i chwuwe cyess.ey yo.	It has turned cold.
2. Īl ul nemu mānh.i hamyen, phikon hay cye yo.	If you work too hard, you get tired.
3. Um.ak i cōh.a cyess.ey yo.	I've come to like music.
4. Kyewul i omyen, kkoch tul un tā ēps.e cikeyss.ey yo.	All the flowers will die ['become non-existent'] in the winter.
5. Cikum un mulken i tā pissa cye yo.	Everything's getting expensive nowadays.

‖ 9.9. Verb forms: summary.

Any Korean verb form used in a Korean sentence has two parts to it: a BASE and an ENDING. A base is not complete, ready for use, until it is finished off with an ending; and obviously, an ending must be attached to something before it can be put into a sentence (just as you don't use the English endings -ing or -ed in mid-air).

When we summarize verb forms, then, we can most conveniently split our discussion into the two large categories BASES and ENDINGS.

‖ 9.9.1. Verb bases.

Each verb has a SIMPLE BASE which is the source of all its changes. Some simple bases end with vowels, others with consonants. Some of the vowel-base verbs are L-extending: they add an l before certain markers and endings. A few of the vowel-base verbs end in -<u>lu</u>- which changes to -<u>ll</u>- before adding the infinitive ending -<u>e</u> (or -<u>a</u>).

The INFINITIVE of a verb is its base plus an infinitive ending. The infinitive ending has so many shapes, however, that it is perhaps harder to learn rules for adding the ending than it is to memorize the form outright for each verb.

Here is a complete list of all the verbs that have appeared so far in these lessons, classified according to type (vowel base, consonant base) and listed alphabetically by base within each classification. Variant forms are in parentheses; if otherwise unmarked, they mostly represent fast speech forms. The numbers following the gloss tell which lesson the verb first appeared in. [Subsequent lists in this section are representative of the following complete list, in that they contain a base of each type, to act as a pattern for all the others of that type: a base ending in each of the vowels together with the slightly irregular base <u>ha</u>-; an L-extending base and an L-doubling base; and one base each ending in the consonants p, t, s, c, k, l, h, w, together with a few bases ending in double consonants.]

Base	Infinitive
Vowel-base verbs	
ca- 'go to bed' (1)	ca
cala- 'grow' (9)	cala
capswusi- 'eat' (1)	capswusye
chaywu- 'fasten' (8)	chaywe
chwu- 'dance' (9)	chwue (chwe)
. . . ci- 'get (to be) . . .' (9)	. . . cye
cwu- 'give' (1)	cwue (cwe)
eli- 'be young' (7)	elye
ha- 'do' (1)	hay
huli- 'be cloudy' (9)	hulye
. . . i- 'be' [copula] (1)	. . . ie (ye)
il.e na- 'get up' (4)	il.e na
il.e su- 'stand up' (8)	il.e se
ippu- 'be cute, lovable' (4,9)	ippe
ka- 'go' (1)	ka
kaluchi- 'teach' (4)	kaluchye
khu- 'be large' (4)	khe
kippu- 'be happy' (8)	kippe
kitali- 'wait for' (4)	kitalye
kki- 'put on [gloves]' (8)	kkie (kkyē)
kkichi- 'cause [trouble]' (1)	kkichye
kkuth na- 'end' (6)	kkuth na
kyēysi- 'be, stay' (1)	kyēysye
machi- 'finish [it]' (9)	machye
manna- 'meet' (4)	manna
masi- 'drink' (4)	masye
māy- 'tie' (8)	māy
na- 'leave, exit' (8)	na
nappu- 'be bad' (4)	nappe [often spelled nappa]
o- 'come' (4)	wa
paywu- 'learn' (4)	paywe
pēy- 'cut' (4)	pēy [often spelled peye]
phi(wu)- 'smoke' (4)	phi(w)e, (phyē)
pilli- 'borrow' (9)	pillye

pissa- 'be expensive' (9)	pissa
po- 'look at, see' (1)	pwa (pa)
yē-l- 'open it' (1)	yel.e
L-doubling vowel-base verbs	
ilu- 'is early' (8)	ille
kilu- 'raise, grow it' (9)	kille
molu- 'doesn't know or understand' (1)	mōlla [long ō irregular]
pulu- 'call' (8)	pulle
Consonant-base verbs	
anc- 'sit' (4)	anc.e [often spelled anc.a]
anh- 'don't.' (7)	anh.e [often spelled anh.a]
cāk- 'be small' (4)	cak.e [often spelled cak.a]
cēk- 'be little/few' (4)	cek.e
celm- 'be young' (7)	celm.e
cep- 'fold, furl (8)	cep.e
chac- 'look for; find' (4)	chac.e [often spelled chac.a]
chwuw- 'be cold' (9)	chwuwe
cic- 'bark' (4)	cic.e
cōh- 'be good' (1)	cōh.a
ēps- 'be lacking' (3)	ēps.e
etwuw- 'is dark' (9)	etwuwe
ilk- 'read' (4)	ilk.e
ip- 'wear' (8)	ip.e
iss- 'exist; stay; have'	iss.e
kakkaw- 'be near(by)' (8)	kakkawe [often spelled kakkawa]
kēl- 'walk' (8)	kel.e
kkakk- 'cut' (4)	kkakk.e [often spelled kkakk.a]
sa- 'buy' (6)	sa
ssa- 'be inexpensive, cheap' (9)	ssa
ssu- 'write' (4)	sse
ssu- 'wear [on head]' (8)	sse
ssu- 'use; spend' (8)	sse
su- 'stand' (8) [often spelled se-]	se
swī- 'rest' (1)	swie (sōy, swēy)
tha- 'ride' (8)	tha
toy- 'become; be satisfactory'	tōy (tway)
tte na- 'leave, depart' (8)	tte na
tti- 'wear [belt]' (8)	ttie (ttyē)
tuli- 'give [to someone esteemed]' (8)	tulye
L-extending vowel-base verbs	
ā-l- 'know, understand' (1)	al.e [often spelled al.a]
kē-l- 'call [on phone]' (8)	kel.e
. . . mā-l- 'avoid; don't!' (1)	. . . mal.e [often spelled mal.a]
mē-l- 'is far, distant' (8)	mel.e
nō-l- 'have fun' (4)	nol.a
pha-l- 'sell' (8)	phal.e [often spelled phal.a]
pū-l- 'blow' (9)	pul.e
sā-l- 'live' (4)	sal.e [often spelled sal.a]

tō-l- 'turn' (8)	tol.a
tu-l- 'cost; enter' (8)	tul.e
kkoc- 'pin it' (8)	kkoc.a
komaw- 'be thankful' (1)	komawe [often spelled komawa]
kwaynchanh- 'do not matter, be all right' (1)	kwaynchanh.e [often spelled kwaynchanh.a]
mānh- 'be much/many' (4)	mānh.e [often spelled manh.a]
mek- 'eat' (1)	mek.e
mul- 'ask' (1)	mul.e
nuc- 'be late' (8)	nuc.e
nwuw- 'lie down' (8)	nwuwe
pat- 'receive' (4); 'unfold, unfurl' (8)	pat.e [often spelled pat.a]
pes- 'remove, take off' (8)	pes.e
pis- 'comb'	pis.e
pōyw- 'see <u>or</u> meet [someone esteemed]' (1)	pōywe
silh- 'be disliked' (7)	silh.e [often pronounced silye]
sīm- 'plant' (9)	sim.e
sin- 'wear [on feet]' (8)	sin.e
siph- 'want to' (8)	siph.e
takk- 'shine, polish' (8)	takk.e [often spelled takk.a]
tat- 'close [something]' (1)	tat.e [often spelled tat.a]
tēw- 'be hot, warm' (9)	tew.e
tōw- 'help' (8)	towa
ttukew- 'be hot' (9)	ttukew.e
tul- 'listen (to), hear' (1)	tul.e

The simple base of a verb, then, is the verb reduced to its minimum form: nothing can easily be taken away from the simple base, because it has only one part. But a variety of things can be added to it, still without making it a complete verb form—that is, without putting on an ending. A simple base with further base-forming things attached to it is a COMPLEX BASE.

One kind of complex base is an HONORIFIC BASE—the simple base + the honorific marker:

<u>Base</u>	<u>Honorific base</u>
manna- 'meet'	mannasi-
su- 'stand'	susi-
kitali- 'wait for'	kitalisi-
po- 'look at'	posi-
paywu- 'learn'	paywusi-
ha- 'do'	hasi-
ā-l- 'know'	āsi-
molu- 'do not know'	molusi-
anc- 'sit'	anc.usi-
cōh- 'be good'	coh.usi-
cāk- 'be small'	cak.usi-
kēl- 'walk'	kel.usi-
sīm- 'plant it'	sim.usi-
sin- 'wear [on feet]'	sin.usi-
ip- 'wear'	ip.usi-

pes- 'remove'	pes.usi-
tat- 'close'	tat.usi-
tōw- 'help'	towusi-
celm- 'be young'	celm.usi-
ēps- '(there) isn't'	ēps.usi-

Nearly every Korean verb form is subject to the dichotomy of plain and honorific, so that when we speak of any form of a verb—gerund, suspective, past tense, etc., let's keep in mind the fact that each form comes in two varieties: one, the general variety; and two, the variety which we must not use for ourselves or younger members of our family.

Remembering, then, that each kind of verb form comes in these two varieties, here are the other kinds of complex bases you have learned about, illustrated by ha- 'do', first shown with its infinitives:

INFINITIVES (base + infinitive ending):

hay	hasye

PAST BASES (infinitive + the past marker -ss-):

hayss-	hasyess-

FUTURE BASES (base + the future marker -keyss-):

hakeyss-	hasikeyss-

PAST-PAST BASES (past base + the past marker -ess-):

hayss.ess-	hasyess.ess-

PAST-FUTURE BASES (past base + future marker -keyss-):

hayss.keyss-	hasyess.keyss-

All complex bases, however many ingredients may go into them, share this feature with one another and with simple bases: none are complete until they are finished off with an ENDING.

9.9.2. Verb endings.

Endings, added to bases, make the verb form complete. In addition to this function, they often perform another job at the same time: they tell whether or not you have come to the end of a sentence.

Any form of a verb ends a CLAUSE in Korean. Some clauses are FINAL: the verb at the end completes a sentence. Some are NONFINAL: the verb form does not complete a sentence: in this category are the infinitive (-e etc.), the suspective (-ci), the gerund (-ko), and the conditional (-umyen/-myen) endings. [In the intimate style, which you will learn later, the infinitive and the suspective can end a sentence.] You have learned to use only one final ending so far: the polite-style ending -e(y) yo which consists of the infinitive (-e, -a, etc.—often with y-extension after ss, ps, the honorific infinitive -usye, etc.) + the polite particle yo. This ending typically finishes a sentence, whether it is a present-tense form (attached to a base), a past-tense form (attached to a past base), or a future form (attached to a future base):

hay yo 'does'	hasey yo '[someone esteemed] does'
hayss.ey yo 'did'	hasyess.ey yo '[someone esteemed] did'
hakeyss.ey yo 'will do'	hasikeyss.ey yo '[someone esteemed] will do'

When you use this ending at the end of your sentence, it implies that you are on informal, though dignified, terms with the person you are talking to.

Endings are either ONE-SHAPE ENDINGS or TWO-SHAPE ENDINGS.

One-shape endings are much the same, regardless whether they are attached to a vowel base or a consonant base.

Two-shape endings have one shape which attaches to vowel bases and another which attaches to consonant bases.

For purposes of attaching endings, the group of vowel bases includes not only simple bases (like ka-, su-, kitali-, po-, paywu-, etc.) but also ALL honorific bases since each one ends in i regardless of the simple base on which it is built:

Base	Honorific base
ka- 'go'	kasi-
pat- 'get'	pat.usi-

Similarly, all past bases and future bases are consonant bases, regardless of what sort of base you began with:

Base	Past base	Future base
ka- 'go'	ka(sye)ss-	ka(si)keyss-
pat- 'get'	pat.(usy)ess-	pat.(usi)keyss-

Here are all the nonfinal endings you have learned, grouped according to whether they have one shape or two shapes. (For purposes of combining parts of verbs, it is convenient to consider the honorific marker, the past marker, and the future marker along with other endings, since they too are of either one shape or two shapes and follow the same rules.)

ONE-SHAPE ENDINGS		TWO-SHAPE ENDINGS		
			After vowel	After consonant
[past marker]	-ss-	[honorific marker]	-si-	-usi-
[suspective]	-ci	[conditional]	-myen	-umyen
[gerund]	-ko			
[future marker]	-keyss-			

The only special feature about two-shape endings is that the conditional ending -myen is attached to the EXTENDED base of L-extending bases:

ā-l- 'know'	ālmyen 'if [someone] knows'
mē-l- 'be far'	mēlmyen 'if [it]'s far'
nō-l- 'play'	nōlmyen 'if [someone] plays'
pū-l- 'blow'	pūlmyen 'if [it] blows'

Several peculiarities, however, must be mentioned about one-shape endings. (The past marker -ss- is omitted here because it is attached to infinitives rather than directly to other bases and so does not follow the same rules.)

1. The base capswusi- 'eat' often abbreviates to capswus- before one-shape endings:

capswusiko → capswus.ko '[someone esteemed] eats, and . . .'
capswusici man → capswus.ci man '[someone esteemed] eats, but . . .'
capswusikeyss.ey yo → capswus.keyss.ey yo '[someone esteemed] will eat'

2. One-shape endings are attached to the EXTENDED BASES of L-extending verbs:

ā-l- 'know'	ālci man 'knows, but . . .'
	ālko 'knows, and . . .'
	ālkeyss.ey yo 'knows' or 'will know'

3. When a one-shape ending that begins with t, c, or k is attached to a consonant base that ends in h, the strings -h.t-, -h.c-, and -h.k- are pronounced -th-, -ch-, and -kh-:

cōh- 'be good'	cōh.ci /cōchi/
	cōh.ko /cōkho/
	cōh.keyss- /cōkheyss-/

This is true also of nh and lh:

mānh- 'be much/many'	mānh.ci /mānchi/
	mānh.ko /mānkho/
	mānh.keyss- /mānkheyss-/
silh- 'be disliked'	silh.ci /silchi/
	silh.ko /silkho/
	silh.keyss- /silkheyss-/

If the ending begins with some other consonant—the only common case is n—the final h after a vowel is pronounced as if it were t: Cōh.ni? 'Is it good? [to a child]' (‖ 22.3) is pronounced /cōnni/, just as Pat.ni? 'Do you get it? [to a child]' is pronounced /panni/. The clusters nh and lh reduce to n and l: mānh.ni is pronounced /mānni/, silh.ni is pronounced /silli/.

4. When a one-shape ending is attached to a consonant base that ends in w, the w changes to p:

tōw- 'help'	tōpci /tōpcci/
	tōpko /tōpkko/
	tōpkeyss- /tōpkkeyss-/
	[tōp.ni? /tōmni/]

If it were not for the other forms (towa, towumyen, towusi-) we would not know that such bases are different from the usual bases ending in p, like ip- 'wear': ipci, ipko, ipkeyss-; ip.e, ip.umyen, ip.usi-. In traditional Korean grammar, the w-verbs are called "irregular p-verbs."

5. When a one-shape ending is attached to a consonant base that ends in l, the l changes to t:

tul- 'hear'	tut.ci /tucci/
	tut.ko /tukko/
	tut.keyss- /tukkeyss-/
	[tut.ni? /tunni/]

Notice the difference between the behavior of these bases and the L-extending vowel bases: tu-l- 'enter; cost' has the forms tulci, tulko, tulkeyss-, [tuni?]. The infinitives are the same; both tu-l- and tul- come out as tul.e.

But the conditional forms are different: tulmyen is from tu-l-, tul.umyen is from tul-. And the honorific forms are also different: tusimyen is from tu-l-, tul.usimyen is from tul-. In traditional Korean grammar, the consonant bases that end in l are called "irregular t-verbs": note that a regular t-verb like tat- 'close it' will have similar forms when attaching most one-shape endings (tat.ci, tat.ko, tat.keyss-) but different forms when attaching two-shape endings (tat.umyen, tat.usi-) or forming the infinitive (tat.e).

6. The usual automatic sound changes take place when a base ending in a consonant attaches an ending shape that begins with a consonant. First, if the base ends in a consonant or cluster other than p, t, k, m, n, l, in pronouncing the resulting form you reduce the consonant or cluster to one of those: ps and ph are treated like p; kk and usually lk are treated like k; lm is treated like m, nc is treated like n; s, ss, c, and ch are all treated like t.

Next, there are a number of automatic adjustments between the syllable-final consonant at the end of the base and the syllable-beginning consonant at the start of the ending:

1. Voiceless consonants are doubled (reinforced) after a voiceless consonant, so that -pt- is pronounced /ptt/, -pc- /pcc/, -ps- /pss/, -pk- /pkk/; -kt- is pronounced /ktt/, -kc- /kcc/, -ks- /kss/; -k.k-, however comes out just /kk/ (since you don't get the same consonant repeated more than once). And after -t, the following consonant is doubled but the t usually drops: -tk- is pronounced /kk/ (/tkk/ only in very slow reading pronunciations), -tc- sounds like /cc/, and ts- sounds like /ss/.

2. After verb-base final m or n (or an l that is reduced from a cluster—simple l changes to t), you reinforce (= double) a t, c, s, or k that begins an ending. Since the Korean spelling does not show this doubling, we have reminded you of it with a dot in our orthography:

sīm- 'plant it'	sīm.ci /sīmcci/
	sīm.ko /sīmkko/
	sīm.keyss- /sīmkkeyss-/
sin- 'wear [on feet]'	sin.ci /sincci/
	sin.ko /sinkko/
	sin.keyss- /sinkkeyss-/

‖ 9.10. Glossary of verb constructions.

Knowing how to put Korean verb forms together is one thing; learning to use these completed forms in sentences—knowing what they mean—is something else, equally important.

Here, to summarize the constructions you have learned, is an English-Korean glossary list. (For ha- 'do/be,' of course, you substitute whatever verb you want.) The numbers refer to the section containing the complete discussion of each construction.

all right to [do] (giving permission)
  [hay] to cōh.a yo, [hay] to kwaynchanh.e yo ‖ 8.13
although
  [ha]ci man ‖ 7.5
although [= even while (do)ing]
  [ha]myen se to ‖ 9.6
am [do]ing
  [ha]ko iss.ey yo ‖ 8.5
and (also)
  [ha]ko ‖ 8.4
and (at the same time [does])
  [ha]myen se ‖ 9.6
and [= but then on the other hand]
  [ha]ci man ‖ 7.5
and: goes for the purpose of [doing]
  ka se [ha-] ‖ 8.9
and (then afterwards)
  [ha]ko ‖ 8.4; [hay] se ‖ 8.9

are [do]ing
  [ha]ko iss.ey yo ‖ 8.5
begins to [be]
  [hay] cye yo ‖ 9.8
better [do] (mild obligation)
  [ha]myen cōh.a yo ‖ 9.4
but
  [ha]ci man ‖ 7.2
but (instead)
  [ha]ci anh.ko/mālko ‖ 8.4
can't [do]
  mōs [hay] yo ‖ 4.3
  [ha]ci mōs hay yo ‖ 7.3
[do] and see . . .
  [hay] pwa yo ‖ 8.11
[do] for someone
  [hay] cwue yo ‖ 8.11
[do] for someone esteemed
  [hay] tulye yo ‖ 8.11
don't . . . !
  [ha]ci māsey yo ‖ 7.4
even though [someone does]
  [hay] to ‖ 8.13
even though [= even while (do)ing]
  [ha]myen se to ‖ 9.6
for someone
  [hay] cwue yo ‖ 8.11
for someone esteemed
  [hay] tulye yo ‖ 8.11
gets to be . . .
  [hay] cye yo ‖ 9.8
glad that . . .
  [hay] se cōha (hay) yo ‖ 8.9
going to [do]
  [ha]keyss- ‖ 9.1
had [done]
  [hay]ss.ess- ‖ 9.2
has to [do] (mild obligation)
  an [ha]myen an tōy yo ‖ 9.5
has to [do] (strong obligation)
  [hay] ya hay yo ‖ 8.12
hope that . . .
  [ha]myen cōh.a yo ‖ 9.4
if
  [ha]myen ‖ 9.4
if it be [NOUN]
  [NOUN] imyen ‖ 9.7
if: only if [hay] ya ‖ 8.12
in spite of the fact that . . .
  [hay] to ‖ 8.13
instead of [do]ing
  [ha]ci anh.ko/mālko ‖ 8.4
is [do]ing
  [ha]ko iss.ey yo ‖ 8.5
it's all right to [do] (giving permission)
  [hay] to cōh.a yo, [hay] to kwaynchanh.e yo ‖ 8.13
it's nice/good that . . .
  [hay] se cōh.a (hay) yo ‖ 8.9
may [do] [= has permission]
  [hay] to cōh.a yo, [hay] to kwaynchanh.e yo ‖ 8.13
may not [do] (denying permission)
  [ha]myen an tōy yo ‖ 9.5
must [do] (mild obligation)
  an [ha]myen an tōy yo ‖ 9.5
must [do] (strong obligation)
  [hay] ya hay yo ‖ 8.12
must [do/be] (probability, likelihood)
  [ha]keyss- ‖ 9.1
must have [done]
  [hay]ss.keyss- ‖ 9.2
must not [do] (denying permission)
  [ha]myen an tōy yo ‖ 9.5
need not [do]
  [ha]ci anh.e to cōh.a yo, [ha]ci anh.e to kwaynchanh.e yo ‖ 8.13
nice that . . .
  [hay] se cōh.a (hay) yo ‖ 8.9
not [do]
  an [hay] yo ‖ 4.3
  [ha]ci anh.e yo ‖ 7.3
not [do] at all
  mōs [hay] yo ‖ 4.3
  [ha]ci mōs hay yo ‖ 7.3
not [be] at all [ha]ci mōs hay yo ‖ 7.3
not have to [do]
  [ha]ci anh.e to cōh.a yo, [ha]ci anh.e to kwaynchanh.e yo ‖ 8.13
only if [does]
  [hay] ya ‖ 8.12
or
  [alternative questions] ‖ 2.3
ought not to [do] (denying permission)
  [ha]myen an tōy yo ‖ 9.5
ought to [do] (mild obligation)
  an [ha]myen an tōy yo ‖ 9.5
  [ha]myen cōh.a yo ‖ 9.4
ought to [do] (strong obligation)
  [hay] ya hay yo ‖ 8.12
please [do]
  [ha]myen komapkeyss.ey yo ‖ 9.4
probably [does/is]
  [ha]keyss- ‖ 9.1

see (how it comes out)
  [hay] pwa yo ‖ 8.11
shall we [do]?
  [ha]myen cōh.a yo? ‖ 9.4
should [do] (mild obligation)
  an [ha]myen an tōy yo ‖ 9.5
  [ha]myen cōh.a yo ‖ 9.4
should [do] (strong obligation)
  [hay] ya hay yo ‖ 8.12
should not [do] (denying permission)
  [ha]myen an tōy yo ‖ 9.5
so
  [hay] se ‖ 8.9
though [= but]
  [ha]ci man ‖ 7.2
though [= even though]
  [hay] to ‖ 8.13
though [= even while doing/being]
  [ha]myen se to ‖ 9.6
to [do]: goes for the purpose of [doing]
  ka se [ha-] ‖ 8.9
tries [do]ing
  [hay] pwa yo ‖ 8.11
wants to [do]
  [ha]ko siph.e yo ‖ 8.6
  [ha]keyss- ‖ 9.1

when(ever)
  [ha]myen ‖ 9.4
while [do]ing (simultaneously)
  [ha]myen se ‖ 9.1
will [do]
  [ha]keyss- ‖ 9.1
will have [done]
  [hay]ss.keyss- ‖ 9.2
willing to [do]
  [ha]keyss- ‖ 9.1
wish that . . .
  [ha]myen cōh.a yo ‖ 9.4
without [do]ing
  [ha]ci anh.ko/mālko ‖ 8.4
would [do]
  [ha]keyss- ‖ 9.1
would have [done]
  [hay]ss.keyss- ‖ 9.2
would like some to [do]
  [ha]myen komapkeyss.ey yo, [ha]myen komawe hakeyss.ey yo ‖ 9.4
would like to [do]
  [ha]ko siph.e yo ‖ 8.6

EXERCISES

I

Each of the following sentences means 'someone DOES/IS something.' Make each one mean 'someone WILL DO/BE something'; then translate the sentence. For example, the first will be Na nun wuphyen-kwuk ey kakeyss.ey yo. 'I'm going to the post office.'

1. Na nun wuphyen-kwuk ey ka yo.
2. Ku haksayng un yenphil ul kkakk.e yo.
3. Sensayng nim un mues ul hasey yo.
4. Kāy nun cic.ci man, apeci nun tut.ci anh.e yo. [Make both verbs future.]
5. [1]Nayil kongpu ka mānh.e yo.
6. Moley kongpu ka cēkci anh.e yo.
7. Onulq pam ey son nim i cēncha lul thako wa yo.
8. Na nun Hānkwuk ey se Yenge lul kaluchye yo.
9. Sensayng un ku mun ul yel.e yo?
10. Kim sensayng un catong-cha lul pulle yo?
11. [1]Nayil achim puthe nwūn i wa yo.
12. Na nun i pen kaul ey nun Ilpon ey ka pwa yo.
13. Hal-'me' nim hanthey musun sēnmul ul cwusey yo.

II

Each of the following sentences means 'someone DOES/IS something.' Make each one mean 'someone PROBABLY DOES/IS something'; then translate the sentence. For example, the first will be: Cang sensayng un kongpu hako kyēysikeyss.ey yo. 'Mr. Cang is probably studying.'

1. Cang sensayng un kongpu hako kyēysey yo.
2. Na nun onulq pam ey yenghwa kwūkyeng ka to, cōh.a yo.
3. Pakk i chwuwe cye yo.
4. Wuli ka nuc.key camyen an tōy yo.
5. Haksayng tul i ilccik hak.kyo ey an kamyen, an tōy yo.
6. Ku ai ka elye yo.
7. Kuleh.ci man, ku pumo nim tul i celm.usici anh.e yo.
8. Ku sangcem i kakkawe yo.
9. Yenghwa-kwan un nemu mel.e yo.
10. Ku [1]yeypay-tang ey kamyen, say os ul ipci anh.e to kwaynchanh.e yo.
11. Hānkwuk ey se īl hamyen, Hānkwuk mal ul paywe ya hay yo.
12. Sensayng nim uy yak.hon-ca nun kkoch ul cōh.a hasey yo.
13. Say moksa ka Mikwuk salam ici man, Hānkwuk mal ul hay yo. [Change both verbs.]
14. Say moksa ka Mikwuk salam i ani 'e to, Yenge lul hay yo.
15. Sensayng nim uy kōhyang i mel.e yo.

III

Each of the following sentences means 'someone DOES/IS something.' Make each mean 'I HOPE someone DOES/IS something'; then translate the sentence. For example, the first will be: Ku sālam i wuli chinkwu ka toymyen cōh.keyss.ey yo. 'I wish he would become our friend; I hope he will become our friend.'

1. Ku sālam i wuli chinkwu ka tōy yo.
2. Na nun tōn ul mānh.i pat.e yo.
3. Ku chinkwu ka na hanthey cēnhwa lul kel.e yo.
4. Palam i pūlci anh.e yo.
5. Ku sangcem uy mulken i ssa yo.
6. Ai tul i mānh.i kel.e ya haci man, phikon hay cici anh.e yo.
7. Emeni ka ku ai to sayngkak hasey yo.
8. Ku ai to emeni lul sayngkak hay yo.
9. Emeni ka nay sayngkak to hay yo.
10. Hak.kyo ey kel.e ka to cōh.a yo.
11. Say kwutwu lul sin.ci anh.e to kwaynchanh.e yo.

IV

Each of the following sentences means 'someone MAY DO something.' Change each so that it means 'someone MAY NOT or MUST NOT DO something'; then translate the sentence. For example the first will be: Ai tul i kāy wa kath.i nōlmyen an tōy yo. 'The children mustn't play with the dog.'

1. Ai tul i kāy wa kath.i nol.a to cōh.a yo.
2. Wuli atul i ku kwāyngi lul kille to cōh.a yo.
3. Na nun say os ul sa to cōh.a yo.

4. Tangsin i ayki eykey ūmsik ul cwue to kwaynchanh.e yo.
5. [1]Yeypay-tang ey se chwum ul chwue to kwaynchanh.e yo.
6. Kongpu sikan ey nolay lul pulle to cōh.a yo.
7. Tōn i ēps.umyen se cal sse to cōh.a yo.
8. Yeki se os ul pes.e to cōh.a yo.
9. (Tangsin un) nay chayk ul phal.e to kwaynchanh.e yo.
10. Ku cēm.wen i i mulken ul phal.e to cōh.a yo.
11. Mikwuk ey se chacang hanthey tōn ul cwue to cōh.a yo.

V

Each of the following sentences means 'someone DOESN'T HAVE TO or NEED NOT DO something.' Make each mean 'someone OUGHT TO DO something'; then translate the sentence. For example, the first will be: Sensayng nim un i chayk ul an posimyen (or posici anh.umyen), an tōy yo. 'You ought to read this book. You should read this book.'

1. Sensayng nim un i chayk ul posici anh.e to kwaynchanh.e yo.
2. Atul i phul ul kkakk.ci anh.e to cōh.a yo.
3. Mul ul mānh.i an masye to kwaynchanh.e yo.
4. Wuli ka sip-pun ccum swīci anh.e to cōh.a yo.
5. Catong-cha hōysa ey cēnhwa lul kēlci anh.e to kwaynchanh.e yo.
6. Hak.kyo ey catong-cha lul thako an ka to cōh.a yo.
7. Sensayng nim un ku sālam ul mannaci anh.e to kwaynchanh.e yo.
8. Wuli ka Sewul ey sālci anh.e to cōh.a yo.
9. Onulq pam ey wuli atul i neykthai lul an māy to kwaynchanh.e yo.
10. Wuli ka ku yenghwa lul kwūkyeng haci anh.e to kwaynchanh.e yo.
11. Onulq pam ey wuli ka latio lul tut.ci anh.e to cōh.a yo.

VI

Each of the following sentences means 'you do something.' Make each mean 'I WISH YOU WOULD do something for me, I'D LIKE YOU TO do something for me'; then translate the sentence. For example, the first will be: Catong-cha hōysa ey cēnhwa lo pulle cwusimyen, komapkeyss.ey yo. 'I'd like you to call the cab company for me.'

1. Catong-cha hōysa ey cēnhwa lo pulusey yo.
2. I yenphil ul kkakk.usey yo.
3. Kongwen ey kasimyen, keki se wuli kāy lul chac.usey yo.
4. Hānkwuk mal ul kaluchisey yo.
5. Tta' nim hanthey i sēnmul ul cwusey yo.
6. Māyil achim ahop si pān ey na hanthey cēnhwa lul kēsey yo.

VII

Each item below contains two sentences. Link the two together, so that they mean 'WHILE someone DOES something, AT THE SAME TIME he does the other'; then translate the sentence. For example, the first will be: Kāy nun ku sālam ul pomyen se, cic.ess.ey yo. 'The dog barked while looking at him.'

1. Kāy nun ku sālam ul pwass.ey yo. Cic.ess.ey yo.
2. Na nun onulq pam ey latio lul tut.keyss.ey yo. Kongpu hakeyss.ey yo.

3. Wuli nun kongwen ey ka se, sānqpo hakeyss.ey yo. Kkoch ul kwūkyeng hakeyss.ey yo.
4. Apeci nun sinmun ul ilk.e yo. Um.ak ul tul.e yo.
5. Na nun cip sayngkak ul hayss.ey yo. Emeni hanthey phyēnci lul ssess.ey yo.
6. Ku haksayng i cenyek ul mek.e yo. ˡNayilq kongpu lul hay yo. [ˡNayilq kongpu = ˡnayil uy kongpu 'the lesson for tomorrow']

CONVERSATION

I

Pair off two by two and converse in Korean. Center your conversation around plans for an outing you hope to take: a flower viewing excursion, a trip to another city, dinner out and then a movie, or whatever appeals to you (within your vocabulary range). Discuss the plans in minute detail: what you will each wear if it rains or snows or is nice (compare notes and show interest in the other person's ideas); what time you will do each part of the planned outing; by what means you will get to where you are going, and how you will return; things you must be sure NOT to do (getting there too late, not bringing your umbrella, having too little money, or whatever); and so on. Make it sound as lively and interesting as possible.

II

Have the class take the part of a family at breakfast: a father and/or mother and several young adults. Have each of the young people ask for permission to do various things (at the table, in the course of the day, the following day, or in the future). Try to make your requests interesting. The "parent(s)" should be very strict about granting or denying permission, but they should give reasons whenever possible.

VOCABULARY DRILL

Here is a list of English questions; answer them IN KOREAN with an appropriate verb, or noun-verb expression (such as 'the wind is blowing'), taken from the new vocabulary introduced in Lesson 9. For example, the first would be the Korean equivalent of 'plant.'

1. What do you do with flowers?
2. What do rain and sunshine make plants do well?
3. What would happen if you stayed awake for 24 consecutive hours?
4. What is Enrico Caruso famous for?
5. What is the winter temperature like in your home town?
6. Why doesn't every woman own a mink coat?
7. What should be happening while you "make your hay"?
8. Why do baby animals appeal to us so much?
9. What is the outstanding climatic feature of March?
10. What is the outstanding climatic feature of April?
11. What is the outstanding climatic feature of August?
12. If your best friend needed money desperately, what would you do?

13. What does a ballerina do?
14. What does the sky look like when it's about to pour?
15. What are you supposed to do to your studying before you go to the movies?
16. What's it like outdoors at night?
17. Under what conditions might you buy a yacht?
18. What kind of weather is it usual to hope for at Christmas time in the United States?
19. How do you characterize autumn weather?
20. What do farmers do to pigs?

COMPREHENSION

I

Let your teacher talk briefly in Korean about the climate in his home town, and what activities he and his friends engage in under various weather conditions. Take notes if you wish. When he has finished, he will ask you questions about what he has said, to find out how well you have followed him.

II

Your teacher will ask you a number of true-false questions using the verb constructions of this lesson:

hakeyss.ey yo
hamyen
  hamyen . . . cōh.a yo
  hamyen . . . an tōy yo
  an hamyen . . . an tōy yo
  hamyen se
  hamyen se to
hay cye yo

You might hear the Korean equivalent of such sentences as these:

You mustn't talk and eat at the same time.
If it rains, the flowers don't grow.
It gets hot in summer.
It's dark in the daytime.

It's up to you to say 'yes' (kulay yo!) if the statement is reasonable, or generally true, otherwise, 'no' (kuleh.ci anh.e yo!). Don't split hairs.

LESSON 10. REVIEW

I. KOREAN-ENGLISH TRANSLATION

Translate the following Korean passage into English.

Onul un Sā-wel samsip-il, Il-yoil iey yo. Achim ey com ilccik ile-na se sēyswu hako meli lul cal pis.ess.ey yo. Kuliko apeci hako emeni hanthey ka se "Annyeng hi cwumusyess.^{s}up.nikka?" hako, tongsayng tul kwa kath.i pakk ey na kass.ey yo. Ecey kkaci nal mata pi man oko chwuwess.ey yo. Kulena, onul un palam to an pūlko ttattus hay yo. Chāyso path un nay kes iko kkoch path un nwū' nim kes iey yo. Chāyso nun swuph aph ey sim.ess.ko, kkoch un yuli chang mith ey sim.ess.ey yo. Onul achim ey nun yele kaci kkoch i ipp.e yo. Apeci nun pelsse ttul ey se phul ul kkakk.ko kyēysyess.ey yo.

Ōhwu ey nun, unhayng twī uy tose-kwan ey kass.ey yo. Ku tose-kwan un khuko senul hako cōh.a yo. Pōthong nal ey nun ōcen ahop si sip-o pun cen ey yēlko ōhwu nēy si pān ey tat.e yo. Il-yoil un ōhwu han si puthe tases si kkaci yel.e yo. Keki ey nun chayk i mānh.i iss.ko Yenge chayk to Hānkwuk mal chayk to iss.ey yo. Tto capci 'na sinmun to iss.ey yo. Kulay se, haksayng to oko uysa to oko pyēnho-sa to nwukwu 'na wa yo. Mikwuk salam to mānh.e yo. Na nun acik apeci chelem chayk ul ppalli ilk.ci mōs hako chēn-chen hi ilk.e yo. Chayk un tose-kwan an ey se man ilk.ci anh.e to cōh.a yo. Han pen ey sēy kwen ccum ina pillye na wa to cōh.a yo. Kulena yelq kwen ssik un an tōy yo. Tōn un an cwue to kwaynchanh.e yo. Chayk ul cal mōs chac.keyss.umyen sāmu-wen hanthey mul.e pwa to cōh.a yo.

Han sēy sikan ccum kongpu hako, chayk ul sēy kwen pillye nāy wass.ey yo. Wuli cip ey nun chayk i mānh.i ēps.ey yo. Cenyek ey nun etwuwe cimyen se pi ka oki sīcak hayss.ey yo. Latio ey se "Nayil un nal i huliko tēpkeyss.ey yo." hay yo. Yelq si ey cako siph.ess.ci man, ku cen ey hyeng nim eykey phyēnci lul han cang ssess.ey yo. Hyeng nim un wuli wa kath.i sālci anh.e yo. Yengkwuk tāyhak ey se sam-nyen cen puthe kongpu lul hako kyēysey yo. Hyeng nim i poko siph.e yo. Na to yeki se kongpu lul cal hamyen hyeng nim kath.i Yengkwuk ey ka se kongpu hay pokeyss.ey yo.

II. VOCABULARY REVIEW

A. Matching synonyms.

Here are two columns of Korean expressions. For each expression in the left-hand column, there appears in the right-hand column an expression of similar meaning. Call out the left-hand word, then find its matching right-hand word; now translate, and explain any difference between the words (by example, if possible). You may want to say Kkok kath.ey yo 'They are exactly alike' or Com talle yo 'They are a little different'; your tutor may want to ask Etteh.key talle yo 'How are they different?'

cīnci	cako siph.e yo
cōh.a yo	hak.kyo
cwue yo	iley
han cwukan	kwaynchanh.e yo
il-nyen	māyil
ilk.e yo	pap
kongpu hay yo	keki
kyōswu	paywe yo
māycem	pwa yo
sam-myeng	sēy salam
nal mata	sangcem
phikon hay yo	sensayng
tāyhak	tulye yo
tewe yo	ttukewe yo
ku kos	yelq-twū tal

B. Matching antonyms.

Now, here are two more columns of Korean expressions; this time, you are to pick from the right-hand column the expression of opposite meaning to match each of the expressions in the left-hand column. Use the two expressions in sentences; if possible, put them both into one sentence.

cen	anc.e yo
chwuwe yo	atul
hay ka na wa yo	ecey
īl hay yo	enni
ille yo	hulye yo
il.e na yo	hwū
kaul	kakkawe yo
kyelhon	kyewul
mel.e yo	machye yo
moley	nac
na wa yo	nam-tongsayng
nwūna	nuc.e yo
ōcen	nwuwe yo
oppa	ōhwu
pam	phal.e yo
sa yo	pissa yo
se yo	pom
sīcak hay yo	senul hay yo
sonca	sonnye

ssa yo	swie yo
tewe yo	toksin
ttal	tongsayng
yelum	ttukewe yo
^{n}ye-tongsayng	tul.e ka yo
yēyki hay yo	tul.e yo

C. Picking the misfits.

Here are eight groups of Korean expressions—five to a group. Four expressions in each group have meanings which are grouped around the same subject matter; one does not. You are to pick the misfit; then speaking Korean, try to show why it is a misfit.

1. hay ka na wa yo
   kāy ka na wa yo
   nwūn i wa yo
   pi ka wa yo
   ttukewe cye yo

2. pal
   paci
   phal
   tali
   son

3. catong-cha lo ka yo
   cēncha lo wa yo
   kicha lul tha yo
   cēnhwa lul kel.e yo
   kel.e ka yo

4. camay
   nammay
   sawi
   soncwu
   tanchwu

5. palam i pul.e yo
   hulye yo
   senul hay yo
   ttattus hay yo
   ttok-ttok hay yo

6. ip.e yo
   kkie yo
   sim.e yo
   sin.e yo
   sse yo

7. sēyswu hay yo
   kippe hay yo
   myēnto hay yo
   os ul ip.e yo
   meli lul pis.e yo

8. kwulum
   cāngkap
   sin
   yangmal
   chima

III. PARTICLE REVIEW

The new particles, and new uses for old particles, that you have learned in Lessons 6 through 9 are listed here, together with the sections where they were discussed:

ccum	'about, approximately' ‖ 6.3
ina/'na	'about, approximately' ‖ 6.3
	'either . . . or . . .' ‖ 7.6
kkaci	'to, up to, as far as; until' ‖ 6.4
kkey	'to <u>or</u> for [someone esteemed]'; kkey se 'from [someone esteemed]' ‖ 7.8
man	'only, just' ‖ 6.3
	(with suspective -<u>ci</u> <u>man</u>) 'but' ‖ 7.2
mata	'every' ‖ 6.3
pakk-ey	'outside of, except for; only' ‖ 8.1

puthe 'from' ‖ 6.4
se (with infinitive -e se) 'so; (in order) to' ‖ 8.9
(with conditional -umyen se) 'while . . .ing'; -umyen se to 'even while . . .ing' ‖ 9.6
ssik 'each, apiece' ‖ 6.3
to 'both . . . and . . .; neither . . . nor . . .' ‖ 7.5
(with infinitive -e to) 'even though; but' ‖ 8.13
ul/lul thako 'by [a vehicle]' ‖ 8.2
ulo/lo 'by [a vehicle]' ‖ 8.2
ya (with infinitive -e ya) 'only by doing/being; have to' ‖ 8.12

Now, here are 25 English sentences. Express them in Korean, and make sure you use in each at least one of the particles in the list. Notice what a lot of Korean translations the English word 'get' has: pat- (= 'receive'), ka- (= 'go'), sa- (= 'buy'), iss- (= 'have got') -e ci- (= 'become') -e ya ha- (= 'have got to, must').

1. You have to walk to town, even though you don't want to.
2. Isn't it all right for me to go on the train?
3. Either the train or the streetcar is all right.
4. I haven't any clothes except these.
5. Even if they're expensive, I have to get [= buy] some new clothes.
6. I need both socks and shoes.
7. Also, I should get either a coat or an umbrella.
8. All together, my new clothes will probably cost (just) $50.
9. (About) how many books do you own?
10. I read the paper while I have breakfast every morning.
11. It doesn't get very cold here in the winter, and it doesn't get very hot in the summer (either).
12. How long does it take to get [= go] from Seoul to Pusan on the train?
13. I got a letter from my father yesterday, and today I wrote to him.
14. I have to ride on a streetcar at least once a day.
15. It costs $2 a week.
16. Even if it rains today, I'm going down town and see a movie.
17. How much time have we got? Only about 10 minutes.
18. I've eaten nothing but meat today.
19. I telephoned the minister twice, but he wasn't home.
20. I want to watch the trees and flowers while I'm riding in the car.
21. How many times a year do you go to concerts?
22. I worked from 8 a.m. till 10 p.m. today, so I'm very tired.
23. I got [= received] these books from a professor at the University in my home town.
24. It didn't snow yesterday and it didn't rain, either.
25. It got cloudy and cold, so we couldn't go to see the flowers.

Now, just to tighten your hold on these particles, run quickly through the list and make up a Korean sentence using each of them.

IV. REVIEW OF NUMBERS

Here are 10 brief sentences, each with something missing. Say each sentence aloud, in Korean, 5 times—inserting one after another the number expressions listed below it. (Watch out for changes in meaning that might call for a shift in one of the basic words of the sentence.)

1. Yesterday I worked ___.
   for 6 hours
   from 10 o'clock till 4 o'clock
   for only 40 minutes
   from quarter till 7 till quarter after 1
   for $3\frac{1}{2}$ hours

2. I saw ___ in Seoul last week.
   3 friends
   4 movie theaters
   10 American soldiers
   5 factories
   about 10,000 people

3. There are ___ in the classroom.
   3 newspapers
   about 50 books
   40 students
   3 teachers
   6 windows and 2 doors

4. I studied Chinese ___.
   for 3 years
   for only 5 weeks
   for several months
   in 1957
   from February till June

5. My brother is ___.
   2 years old
   10 months old
   19 days old
   40 years old
   6 weeks old

6. I began studying Korean ___.
   in 1959
   at 9:20 this morning
   3 months ago
   on September 15th
   in March 1958

7. There are ___ in front of the post office.
   12 cars
   4 dogs
   5 air-force officers
   about 45 pigeons
   2 streetcars

8. I was born ___.
   21 years ago
   on April 1, 1940
   on September 30, 1936
   on January 14, 1945
   on May 27, 1928

9. I will finish my work ___.
   in 45 minutes
   in 14 more days
   in 3 years
   in 5 weeks
   in 8 hours

10. The train leaves ___.
    at 6:18 p.m.
    at 4:42 a.m.
    at 7:37 p.m.
    at 5:05 p.m.
    at 1:19 a.m.

B

Your teacher will tell you about a (presumably imaginary) shopping trip he has taken recently. He will tell you in Korean about the things he bought, and ask you to work out the arithmetic involved in his purchases—this kind of thing:

1. I bought some socks for $1.75 and some gloves for $3.50. How much did I have to give the clerk?
2. I bought $4.17 worth of things and gave the clerk $10.00. How much did the clerk give back to me?
3. I bought 3 shirts for $7.50. How much did each one cost?
4. They had neckties for $3.25 apiece, and I bought 4. How much did they cost altogether?

After three or four rounds of this, your teacher will ask you to take turns asking each other the same kinds of questions. Here you will have to evaluate the answers your fellow students give you: did they do the arithmetic right, and did they transfer their results into Korean properly? Insist on correct answers. (Use a scratchpad to help keep track of the arithmetic—or, better yet, learn how to use an abacus, the way Koreans do.)

V. VERB REVIEW

Turn to the list of verb constructions in ‖ 9.10, pp. 167 to 169, and make up two Korean sentences to illustrate each of the constructions. (Because of the multiplicity of English translations, there are duplications; just use each construction once.) In order to avoid using the same few verbs over and over, plan to use each verb ONLY ONCE. You can refer to the lists on pp. 161–3, to remind you of verbs you have learned.

Make your sentences as varied and interesting as possible. One way of doing this is to change off frequently between past, present, and future. Another is to vary the subjects and objects of the verbs. Make some of your sentences honorific; make some of them negative; make some of them questions.

VI. REVIEW OF HONORIFICS

Here is the bare outline of a story—in English. Embroidering on this outline, and changing details as you wish to, tell the story—in Korean—TWICE. The first time, use as the central character (called only 'he' in the outline) your younger brother or sister, or a close friend, or some other person for whom it is not normal to use honorifics. At the second telling, weave your story around a highly esteemed person—your father, a teacher who is also a good friend, some other elderly relative, etc.—for whom you must use honorific speech.

Practice your story aloud ahead of time, so that you can tell it smoothly, with a minimum of pausing for thought.

> He's [not] very old. He's ___ years old. He lives in Seoul. His house is not large, but it's very nice. He usually eats his meals and sleeps at home, but sometimes he has to go to town and stay there for several days. He gets up early every day and works hard; when he gets too tired, I help him. On Sundays, he takes it easy ['rests']. If it's nice weather, he goes flower viewing or to the park; if it's raining, he stays home and reads. He owns a great many books. He smokes and reads the newspaper every evening. He doesn't like radio music so he doesn't listen much, but he often goes to concerts. I telephone him several times a week. When he's not at home, I usually get a letter from him. Sometimes he gives me books or clothes. He likes family life. There are six people in his family. He lives with his wife and children, and he often takes walks with them and plays with them.

VII. AUTOBIOGRAPHY

During your last review, you were asked to give an autobiographical sketch. You are now in a position to continue this narrative, adding a sizable amount of detailed information to it. Figures, for example: dates—of your birth and other significant events in your life; ages—of your close relatives and friends. You can also tell about the sort of things you do all day, on typical days—and how your activities change according to the weather; what you like and why; what you may do and must do. And you might tell something about your home town.

Plan a five-minute talk in Korean along the lines of this scanty outline, and get firm enough control of it so that your speech will be mostly talk—very little silence. Don't write out every word you are going to say—just jot down an outline of what you want to say and reminders of the expressions you will need to say it; at home, practice making up the right sort of sentences to express what you want to say. But instead of memorizing the sentences, make them up again—with spontaneous variations—when you speak to the class.

LESSON 11. I GUESS YOU KNOW

BASIC SENTENCES

[Two ladies, Mrs. A. and Mrs. B., are talking.]

	Korean	English	Amplification
A.1.	I kes i mues ici yo? ^{1}Yuseng-ki 'ci yo??	What do you suppose this is? It's a phonograph, isn't it?	mues ici yo? 'what would it be, what is it, do you think' ^{1}yuseng-ki or chwuk.um-ki or cēnchwuk or lekhōtu 'phonograph, record player' ^{1}yuseng-ki 'ci yo?? 'it's a record player, isn't it?'
B.2.	Nēy. Ku kes un ^{1}yuseng-ki 'ey yo.	Yes, it's a record player.	
A.3.	Mikwuk ^{1}yuseng-ki ci yo??	I guess it's an American record player, isn't it?	
B.4.	Nēy. Mikwuk ^{1}yuseng-ki 'ey yo. Cham cōh.ci yo??	Yes, it's an American record player. It's quite nice, don't you think?	cōh.ci yo?? 'it's nice, isn't it?, isn't it nice?'
A.5.	Nēy. Kaps i pissaci yo??	Yes. I suppose it's expensive?	kaps 'price, cost' pissaci yo?? 'it's expensive, isn't it, it's expensive, don't you think so?' [The price is expensive = it has an expensive price.]
B.6.	Kuleh.key pissaci anh.e yo. Ssa yo.	It isn't so expensive. It's cheap.	kuleh.key 'like that, in that way, so'
A.7.	Mikwuk ey nun ^{1}yuseng-ki ka mānh.ci yo??	I suppose there are lots of record players in America.	mānh.ci yo?? 'I suppose there are many; there are many, aren't there?'
B.8.	Nēy. Mānh.e yo.	Yes, there are (lots).	
9.	Incey ^{1}yuseng-ki (lul) com tut.ci yo.	Suppose we listen to the record player now.	incey 'now; starting now, from now on' [cf. cikum 'right now,' pelsse 'already (now)'] tut.ci yo 'let's listen; suppose we listen'

Korean	English	Amplification
A.10. Ecey ku ^{n}yeca son nim i nwukwu 'yess.ci yo??	Who was that lady caller yesterday, I wonder?	^{n}yeca 'woman, lady, girl, female' ^{n}yeca son nim 'lady guest' nwukwu 'yess.ci yo?? 'who might it have been; who was it, do you suppose?'
11. Acwumeni 'ci yo!!	I bet it was your aunt, wasn't it.	acwumeni 'ci yo!! 'it's your aunt, isn't it; I suppose it's your aunt?'
B.12. Nēy. Nay acwumeni 'ey yo.	Yes, it [is=] was my aunt.	
A.13. Meych nyen cen ey Sewul Tāyhak ey tanisyess.ci yo??	She went to Seoul University a few years ago, didn't she.	tanye yo [tani-] 'go (regularly, back and forth)' tanisyess.ey yo '[someone esteemed] went (regularly)' tanisyess.ci yo?? '[someone esteemed] went, didn't he/she?'
14. Kuliko Mikwuk se cīnan pom ey tol.a osyess.ci yo??	And then, she returned from [a trip to] America last spring—isn't that right?	cīna yo 'passes, goes by' cīnan pom 'last spring, the past spring' osyess.ci yo?? '[someone esteemed] came, didn't she?'
B.15. Nēy. Etteh.key kuleh.key cal āsey yo.	Yes—how come you know [her or about her] so well?	etteh.key 'how, in what way?' kuleh.key cal 'that well, so well'
A.16. Ku ^{n}yeca nun wuli emeni (uy) chinkwu 'ci yo.	(I know because) she's a friend of my mother's.	chinkwu 'ci yo 'is a friend, you know!'

Korean	English	Amplification
A.17. I īl ul nwu' ka hakeyss.ey yo.	Who's going to do this (job)?	
B.18. Ama enni ka hasikeyss.ci yo.	I guess probably my older sister will do it.	hasikeyss.ci yo 'I guess or suppose or presume [someone esteemed] will do'
A.19. Enni ka sikol se ēncey osey yo.	When is your older sister coming from the country?	sikol 'country [as opposed to city], rural area'
B.20. Cal molukeyss.ey yo. Ama onulq cenyek ey nun osikeyss.ci yo.	I don't know for sure [= well]. I suppose she'll probably be here by this evening.	osikeyss.ci yo '[someone esteemed] will probably come, I guess'

Korean	English	Amplification
A.21. Enni kkey se ku īl ul cal hasikeyss.ci yo?	Do you suppose your older sister will do the job well?	hasikeyss.ci yo? '[someone esteemed] will probably do, won't he, [he] will do, do you suppose or guess or presume?'
B.22. Mullon cal hasikeyss.ci yo.	Of course she'll do it well, I presume.	hasikeyss.ci yo 'I suppose or guess or presume [he] will do'
A.23. Eti se ku sōsel chayk ul sasyess.ey yo.	Where did you buy that novel?	sōsel 'fiction' sōsel chayk 'a novel [= book of fiction]'
24. Chayk-pang ey ku sōsel chayk i ēps.keyss.ci yo??	They don't [or wouldn't] have that novel at the bookshop, you know!	chayk-pang 'bookshop' ēps.keyss.ci yo?? 'They wouldn't have it, would they? They wouldn't have it, you know!'
A.25. Kulay, Kim sensayng(q) cip i ettay yo.	Well, what's Mr. Kim's house like?	ettay yo 'how is it?'
B.26. Khuko cōh.keyss.ci yo.	Oh, it's nice and big.	cōh.keyss.ci yo 'it's nice, you know!'
A.27. Sewul(q) kwūkyeng (ul) cal hasyess.ey yo?	Did you see a lot of Seoul?	[= Did you sight-see Seoul well?]
28. Sewul ey sālam i cham mānh.keyss.ci yo??	There are a lot of people in Seoul, you know!	mānh.keyss.ci yo?? '(there are) many, you know!'
29. Kim sensayng uy acessi ka Sewul se nass.ci yo.	Mr. Kim's uncle was born in Seoul, you know.	na yo [na-] 'emerges, is produced, gets born' [also 'occurs'] nass.ci yo 'was born, you know!'
B.30. Kim sensayng puin i swii ayki lul nah.keyss.ci yo??	Mrs. Kim is going to have a baby soon, isn't she?	swii, swī 'soon' nah.a yo [nah-] 'gives birth to, produces' nah.keyss.ci yo?? 'will give birth to, won't she?'
A.31. Na nun na(h.a) se, han pen to pyēng i an nass.ey yo.	In all my life I've never been sick even once.	(. . . i/ka) na se 'was born and (then)' = (. . . ul/lul) nah.a se 'she bore [him/me/etc.] and (then)' pyēng 'sickness, illness' pyēng i na yo '[sickness happens=] gets sick, becomes ill'

Korean	English	Amplification
32. Kulena, eceyq cenyek ey, nemu mānh.i mek.e se pyēng i nass.ci man, swii nās.keyss.ci yo.	However, last night I ate so ['too'] much I got sick; but I'll be better soon.	pyeng i nāss.ci man 'got sick [and has not recovered] but' [PAST] naa yo [nā(s)-] 'recovers, gets better; is better, is well (after having been sick)'
B.33. Nay atul i pyēng i nass.ess.ci man, cikum un tā naass.ey yo.	My son got sick, but he's all well now.	pyēng i nass.ess.ci man 'got sick but [has recovered]' [PAST-PAST]
A.34. Wuli cip talk i pyēng i nass.ci man, al un cal nah.a yo.	Our chicken got sick, but still it's laying eggs all right.	talk 'chicken' al 'egg'; talkyal, kyeylan 'chicken eggs' al ul nah.a yo /alulla(h)a.yo/ 'lays [produces] eggs' cal nah.a yo /calla(h)a.yo/ 'produces nicely'
35. Talk uy pyēng un naass.ci man, acik al un mōs na yo.	The chicken got well, but it's still not laying eggs.	['The chicken's illness got better but . . .']

SUPPLEMENTARY VOCABULARY

ˡyuseng-ki/chwuk.um-ki phan, umphan, leykhōtu (phan)	phonograph record
ⁿyensey [HONORIFIC = nai]	age
ⁿyenkap [OLD-FASHIONED HONORIFIC = nai]	age
chwunchwu [HIGHBROW, FANCY = nai]	age
ⁿyen.lyeng [IMPERSONAL = nai]	age
sēngham [HONORIFIC = ilum]	name
sēngmyeng [IMPERSONAL = ilum]	name
chwulqsayng-ci	birthplace
poncek(-ci)	ancestral home
ponkwuk	homeland, native country
cwuk.e yo [cwuk-]	dies
tol.a kasey yo [HONORIFIC]	dies, passes away
samang hay yo [IMPERSONAL]	dies, deceases
Kim Yengho samang	the deceased K.Y.
kō Kim Yengho	the late K.Y.
thānsayng hay yo [LITERARY]	(a saint) is born
chwulqsayng hay yo [IMPERSONAL]	is born
thān(sayng)-il	birthday of a king or saint
nāy yo [nāy-]	puts out; pays, contributes
puchye yo [puchi-] <u>or</u> nāy yo [nāy-]	mails
kyōkwa-se	textbook

NOTES

‖ 11.1. Uses of the suspective: casual polite style.

The Basic Sentences of this lesson offer a number of examples of suspective (-ci) forms with the polite-style particle yo after them. This is the CASUAL POLITE STYLE. Quoted here are examples of a past, a present, and a future casual polite sentence:

14. . . . Mikwuk se . . . tol.a osyess.ci yo?? 'She came back from America, didn't she?'

5. Kaps i pissaci yo?? 'I suppose (the price) is expensive?'

18. Ama enni ka hasikeyss.ci yo. 'I guess probably my big brother will do it.'

Casual-style verb forms cannot be assigned any single translation; they correspond to a number of English expressions of this type:

Haci yo.	I guess he does it.
	I presume he does it.
	I suppose he does it.
	Doesn't he, though!
	He does, you know (or you see).
Hayss.ci yo.	I guess he did it.
	I presume he did it.
	I suppose he did it.
	Didn't he, though!
	He did, you know (or you see).
Hakeyss.ci yo.	I guess he'll do it.
	I presume he'll do it.
	I suppose he's going to do it.
	Won't he, though!
	He will, you know (or you see).

These are statements. With a rising intonation (such as we use in English yes-or-no questions like Is it raining? Are you coming with me?), they ask questions:

Pissaci yo? 'I suppose it's expensive?'
Kkoch ul cōh.a hasici yo? 'I imagine you like flowers?'

When casual statements are pronounced with the same dipping and rising intonation you usually hear with Ani yo?? 'No!' they are livelier, and often the speaker is inviting confirmation or agreement:

Kim sensayng puin isici yo?? 'It's Mrs. Kim, isn't it?'
Kass.ci yo?? 'He's gone, isn't he?'

Our -ci yo sentences can also convey casual suggestions or commands, as in Basic Sentence 9:

Incey 'yuseng-ki lul com tut.ci yo. 'How about listening to the record player now?'

(In this meaning, of course, just as with English, there are no pasts or futures.)

You usually do not answer questions about yourself with this casual form; instead, use the regular polite style.

Here are some more examples:

1. Yeki com swie to cōh.ci yo? It will be all right to rest here a bit, won't it?

2. Mul com masici yo? — Let's have a drink of water.
3. Yeki anc.usici yo. — Please sit here.
4. Yenghwa lul posici yo? — How about seeing a movie?
5. Sensayng nim i kkoch kwūkyeng ul cōh.a hasici yo? — I suppose you like flower-viewing?
6. Kim sensayng i Pusan se sālci yo. — Mr. Kim lives in Pusan, you know.
7. Ku sālam i Hānkwuk salam ici yo?—Mullon ici yo! — Is that person Korean?—Of course!
8. I phyēnci lul nāyko (or puchiko) siph.ci man, eti kamyen cōh.keyss.ci yo. — I want to mail this letter; where should I go?
9. Nay ka tōn ul nāyci yo! — I'll pay! (or: Let me pay!)

NOTE: In pronouncing the ending -ci yo, be careful not to drawl it out; Koreans usually run these two short syllables together -c(i)yo and you may sometimes hear it just as -co. Notice how mek.e yo sounds a little longer than mekc' yo = mekci yo.

‖ 11.2. Uses of the future: lively present.

24. Chayk-sa ey ku sōsel chayk i ēps.keyss.ci yo?? 'They don't have that novel at the bookstore!!'
26. Khuko cōh.keyss.ci yo. 'Oh, it's nice and big.'
28. Sewul ey sālam i cham mānh.keyss.ci yo?? 'What a lot of people there are in Seoul!'

These sentences illustrate future -ci yo sentences to convey PRESENT meanings in a lively and enthusiastic tone.

Such sentences should not be confused with genuine future sentences in casual style—sentences like these, which have FUTURE meanings:

30. Kim sensayng puin i swii ayki lul nah.keyss.ci yo?? 'Mrs. Kim is going to have a baby soon, isn't she?'
32. . . . swii nās.kess.ci yo 'I'll be better soon.'

Compare the use of the future with verbs of knowing, mentioned earlier: Āsikeyss.ci yo? 'Do you understand?' Molukeyss.ey yo 'I don't get it [= understand].'

‖ 11.3. The adverb com.

The adverb com has two meanings. In Basic Sentence 9, for example, it means 'just' or 'only,' limiting the action of the verb in much the same way the particle man limits the scope of a noun:

Incey ˡyuseng-ki lul com tut.ci yo. 'Suppose we (just) listen to the record player now.'

In other sentences, it may mean '[do so-and-so] a little bit':

Pap com te cwusipsio. 'Please give me a little more rice.'

Here are some more examples.

1. Com kitalisici yo. — Wait just a bit.
2. Yenphil ul com cwusipsio. — (Just) give me a pencil, please.
3. Hānkwuk mal com hay yo. — I speak a little Korean.
4. Na to ku sinmun com ilk.ci yo. — How about me (just) reading the paper, too?
5. Com swie to cōh.ci yo? — Can we rest a bit?

‖ 11.4. Descriptive gerund followed by cōh.a yo.

26. Khuko cōh.keyss.ci yo. 'Oh, it's nice and big.'

The sequence khuko [or any other appropriate descriptive gerund] cōh.a yo means 'it's big and (in addition) it's nice.' Both clauses—(1)khuko and(2) cōh.a yo—refer to the same subject.

This construction should not be confused with the similar construction which uses khe se [or any other appropriate descriptive infinitive + se] cōh.a yo:

Khe se cōh.a yo. 'I'm glad it's big.' [Because it's big, that's nice; It's nice that it's big.]

The two clauses of this second construction have different subjects: (Ku kes i) khe se, (nay ka) cōh.a yo.

‖ 11.5. Abbreviated verbs of manner.

There is a set of Korean place words corresponding to the basic set of words you learned back in Lesson 2:

i	'this'	yeki	'here; this place'
ku	'that [nearby; aforementioned]'	keki	'there; that place'
ce	'that [remote]'	cēki	'over there'
enu	'what (one)'	eti	'where; what place'

There is also a corresponding set of verb expressions. The verbs, in their full form, are:

ile hay yo	'does or is like this'
kule hay yo	'does or is like that [nearby; aforementioned]'
cele hay yo	'does or is like that [remote]
ecci hay yo	'does like what?; does how (or why)?'
ette hay yo	'is like what?; is how?'

Most often, however, they are used in an abbreviated form. As processive (action) verbs, they are vowel-base verbs ending in e- but with irregular infinitives like that of ha-:

ile-,	ilay yo	'does [it] this way'
kule-,	kulay yo	'does [it] that [nearby or aforementioned] way'
cele-,	celay yo	'does [it] that [remote] way'
ecce-,	eccay yo	'does it how (or why)?'

As descriptive verbs (adjectives) they are a special class of base we can call AMBIVALENT or H-DROPPING. They have consonant bases ending in eh before one-shape endings only, but vowel bases ending in e before two-shape endings, and their infinitives are irregular like that of ha-:

ile(h)-,	ilay yo	'is like this'
kule(h)-,	kulay yo	'is like that'
cele(h)-,	celay yo	'is like that [remote]'
ette(h)-,	ettay yo	'is like what? is how?'

Since these forms are all abbreviations, we might want to use an apostrophe and write kul' 'ay yo, kule 'myen, etc. But they are in such common use that we will write them as single words, following the Korean practice.

Here is a table showing the forms for each of these verbs:

	Base	Inf.	Present Polite	Past Base	Future Base	Honorific Base	Gerund	Sus-pective	Condi-tional
'does like this' 'is like this'	ile- ile(h)-	ilay	ilay yo	ilayss-	ilekeyss- ileh.keyss-	ilesi-	ileko ileh.ko	ileci ileh.ci	ilemyen
'does like that' 'is like that'	kule- kule(h)-	kulay	kulay yo	kulayss-	kulekeyss- kuleh.keyss-	kulesi-	kuleko kuleh.ko	kuleci kuleh.ci	kulemyen
'does like that (there)' 'is like that (there)'	cele- cele(h)-	celay	celay yo	celayss-	celekeyss- celeh.keyss-	celesi-	celeko celeh.ko	celeci celeh.ci	celemyen
'does how?' 'is how?'	ecce- ette(h)-	eccay ettay	eccay yo ettay yo	eccayss- ettayss-	eccekeyss- etteh.keyss-	eccesi- ettesi-	ecceko etteh.ko	ecceci etteh.ci	eccemyen ettemyen

There are two corresponding sets of adverbs:

ileh.key	'like this, in this way'	ili	'this way'
kuleh.key	'like that, in that way'	kuli	'that way'
celeh.key	'like that (there), in that way'	cēli	'that way over there'
etteh.key	'how? in what way?; how come? why?'	ecci	'what way? how? why?'

Adverbs of the first set (-key, the regular adverbative, ‖ 17.3) usually refer to manner; the second set (-i, derived adverbs) usually refer to direction and are often followed by the particle lo, but they are sometimes used with the same meaning as adverbs of the first set. You will occasionally run across the processive verbs ili/kuli/cēli hay yo 'does this/that way' as well as ecci hay yo 'does what way?' In writing, some people would prefer to use ile/kule/cele hay yo only as descriptive verbs 'is like this/that'; for such people we can say that ile-/kule-/cele- are abbreviations from ili/kuli/celi ha- just as ecce- is an abbreviation from ecci ha-, whereas ile(h)-/kule(h)-/cele(h)- are abbreviations from ile/kule/cele ha-. For the processive verbs, these people would use etteh.key/ileh.key/kuleh.key/celeh.key hay yo or the abbreviations etteh.ke'/ileh.ke'/celeh.ke' ('y) yo. You may notice that some people in Seoul normally pronounce ha- as he-.

Here are sentences to illustrate some of these words:

1. Wuli cip un ilay yo. Tayk un ettay yo.	Our house is like this. What's yours like?
2. Tongsayng un nul kulay yo.	My little brother is always doing that.
3. Etteh.key kuleh.key cal hasey yo.	How come you do it so well?
4. Ili osipsio.	Please come this way.
5. Cēli (lo) kamyen, pata ka pōy yo.	If you go that way over there, you can see the sea.
6. Kuli ka to kwaynchanh.e yo?	May I come over where you are?
7. Way ku kos ey kako siph.e hasey yo?	Why do you want to go to that place?

All of these words except the question forms occur in variant shapes called LIGHT ISOTOPES: yole 'like this,' kole 'like that,' cole 'like that (there)'; yoli 'this way,' koli 'that way,' coli 'that way over there.' The latter are especially common in the directional meanings. Compare the place nouns (‖ 3.5) yeki/yoki = i/yo kos 'here, this place,' keki/koki = ku/ko kos 'there, that place (just mentioned or near you),' cēki/coki = ce/co kos 'there, that place (previously mentioned or over there).'

‖ 11.6. Three confusing verbs.

Basic Sentences 29 through 35 illustrate the use of three verbs which sound very much alike; two of them have related meanings, but are separate words:

a. na yo [na-] 'emerges, comes/goes out; is produced; gets born; happens, occurs'
b. nah.a yo [nah-] 'gives birth to, "has" [a baby]'
c. naa yo [nā(s)-] 'recovers, gets better; is well [again, after having been ill]'

Here again are the pertinent Basic Sentences, with each of these verbs identified as either a, b, or c:

29. Kim sensayng uy acessi ka Sewul se nass.ci yo (a).	Mr. Kim's uncle was born in Seoul, you know.
30. Kim sensayng puin i swi(i) ayki lul nah.keyss.ci yo?? (b)	Mrs. Kim is going to have a baby soon, isn't she?
31. Na nun na se (a), han pen to pyēng i an nass.ey yo (a).	In all my life I've never been sick even once.
32. Kulena, eceyq cenyek ey nemu mānh.i mek.e se pyēng i nass.ci man (a), swii nās.keyss.ci yo (c).	However, last night I ate so much I got sick; but I'll be better soon.
33. Nay atul i pyēng i nass.ess.ci man (a), cikum un tā naass.ey yo (c).	My son got sick, but he's all well now.
34. Wuli cip talk i pyēng i nass.ci man (a), al ul cal nah.a yo (b).	Our chicken got sick, but now it's laying eggs all right.
35. Talk un pyēng un naass.ci man (a), acik al un mōs nah.a yo (b).	The chicken got well, but it's still not laying eggs.

Here, for reference, are the forms of these three verbs:

	(a) 'emerges; gets born; happens'	(b) 'gives birth to'	(c) 'gets/is well'
Base:	na-	nah-	nā(s)-
Infinitive:	na	nah.a /naa/	naa
Present Polite:	na yo	nah.a yo	naa yo
Past Base:	nass-	nah.ass- /naass-/	naass-
Future Base:	nakeyss-	nah.keyss- /nakheyss-/	nās.keyss- /nākkeyss-/
Honorific Base:	nasi-	nah.usi /nausi-/	nausi-
Gerund:	nako	nah.ko /nakho/	nās.ko /nākko/
Suspective:	naci	nah.ci /nachi/	nās.ci /nācci/
Conditional:	namyen	nah.umyen /naumyen/	naumyen

The confusion in pronunciation (where aa and a are pronounced alike and often reduced to just a so that naa yo 'gets better' and na yo 'exits' may sound the same) is compounded by the fact that -h- is usually not pronounced between vowels so that the infinitive nah.a from nāh- sounds identical with the infinitive naa from nā(s)-. Verbs like nah- are simply consonant verbs that end in h; in pronunciation such verbs behave somewhat like our ambivalent H-dropping verbs ile(h)-, kule(h)-, etc., but they lack irregular infinitives like ilay, kulay, etc., and they are written as if the h never dropped. Verbs like nā(s)- can be called "S-dropping consonant verbs": they drop the s before an ending that begins with a vowel (such as the infinitive -e or -a or the appropriate -umyen shape of the conditional). Note that the infinitive is added as -a rather than the expected -e when the vowel preceding the (droppable) s or h is a as well as when it is o. [For ordinary consonant verbs the ending is usually PRONOUNCED as /a/ only when the last vowel of the base is o, though Koreans often WRITE the ending as a when the last vowel of the base is a too.]

Because the meanings of na yo 'gets born' and nah.a yo 'gives birth to' are so similar, Koreans often get confused about the two verbs and write nah.a yo for both. The distinction becomes obvious only when the subject and object are made explicit: Emeni ka ayki lul nah.a yo. 'The mother gives birth to the baby.' but Ayki ka na yo. 'The baby is born.' The expressions na se 'from the time I was born' and nah.a se 'from the time my mother bore me,' after all, add up to the same thing.

EXERCISES

I

Each of the following sentences is in the polite style (-e yo). Change each one to the casual polite style (-ci yo). Then translate the sentence. For example, the first will be: Pap ul nemu mānh.i mek.umyen pyēng i naci yo. 'If you eat too much you'll get sick, you know.'

1. Pap ul nemu mānh.i mek.umyen pyēng i na yo.
2. Wuli talk un al ul māyil nah.ci man, Swunnam-i (uy) talk un ithul ey han kay man nah.a yo.
3. Poktong-i uy hal-ape' nim un ⁿyensey ka mānh.usey yo?
4. Hal-'me' nim un pelsse sam-nyen cen ey tol.a kasyess.ey yo.
5. Nay ka silh.umyen māl haci mal.e yo!
6. Enni nun wuli wa kath.i sālci anh.e yo.
7. Kōhyang ey tol.a kako siph.e yo.
8. Ku sālam eykey nun sālam tul i tōn ul pillye cwuko siph.e haci anh.e yo.
9. Ku ˡīpal(q)-sa nun tongsayng uy meli lul kkakk.e cwuko siph.e hay yo.
10. Ku sālam un cikum swīko iss.keyss.ey yo.
11. Cikum ccum un sinmun i wa iss.keyss.ey yo.
12. Cang sensayng nim un ku yēyki lul ālko kyēysici anh.keyss.ey yo?
13. Yenge lo mul.e poci anh.ess.ey yo.
14. Hānkwuk mal lo kaluchye cwuci anh.e yo.
15. Tongsayng os ey phin ul kkoc.a cwukeyss.ey yo?
16. Sip-li nun te kel.e kaci anh.umyen an tōy yo?
17. Ku sālam ul māyil manna poko siph.e hamyen an tōy yo.
18. Pang an ey se wūsan ul sse pomyen an tōy yo?
19. Pānghak i kkuth na to hak.kyo ey kako siph.ci anh.keyss.ey yo.
20. Way oppa nun kōhyang ul tte na iss.ci anh.umyen an tōy yo.

II

Here are a series of sentence pairs. The first sentence ends in -ci yo and the second begins with Kuleh.ci man . . . ; put the sentences together into one sentence with -ci man 'but.' Then translate the new sentence. For example, the first will be Say yangpok ul ip.e pwass.ci man say sin ul sin.e poci anh.ess.ey yo. 'I tried on my new suit but I didn't try on my new shoes.'

1. Say yangpok un ip.e pwass.ci yo. Kuleh.ci man say sin un sin.e poci anh.ess.ci yo.
2. Ayki nun caci yo. Kuleh.ci man emeni nun cwumusici anh.ci yo.

3. Kāngyen-hoy ey nun kaci anh.ci yo. Kuleh.ci man um.ak-hoy ey nun kaci yo.
4. Nay nai ka yetun sal (or phalqsip-sey) 'ci yo. Kuleh.ci man ōsip-nyen man te sal.e poko siph.ci yo.
5. Ōcen cwung ey machimyen toyci yo. Kuleh.ci man ōhwu kkaci nun nemu nuc.e se an toyci yo.
6. Se iss.umyen an toyci yo. Kuleh.ci man anc.e iss.umyen tōy yo.
7. Cikum capci lul poko iss.umyen an toyci yo. Kuleh.ci man Hānkwuk mal kyōkwa-se lul ilk.ko iss.umyen cōh.ci yo.
8. Pang an ey se nun moca lul pes.e ya haci yo. Kuleh.ci man kwutwu nun sin.ko iss.ci anh.umyen an toyci yo.
9. Cak.nyen ey nun kōhyang ey tol.a ka se emeni lul pwass.ci yo.
10. Sensayng nim ul towa tuliko siph.ci yo. Kuleh.ci man sikan i ēps.ey yo.

III

Here are a series of sentences that end in -ci yo. Make each sentence (1) negative (-ci anh.ci yo), (2) desiderative (-ko siph.ci yo or -ko siph.e haci yo), (3) negative desiderative (-ko siph.ci anh.ci yo or -ko siph.e haci anh.ci yo). Be sure you can translate each resulting sentence. For example, the first will be (1) Cip ey tol.a kaci anh.ci yo. 'I guess I won't go home,' (2) Cip ey tol.a kako siph.ci yo. 'I think I'd like to go home,' (3) Cip ey tol.a kako siph.ci anh.ci yo. 'I don't want to go home, you see.'

1. Cip ey tol.a kaci yo.
2. Tongsayng i ku chayk ul ilk.ci yo.
3. Ayki ka cēki se cako iss.ci yo.
4. Sensayng nim un Kim sensayng ul chac.usici yo?
5. Poktong-i ka i lul takk.ci yo.
6. Cip an ey se ōythwu lul pes.ci yo.
7. Wuli ka phul wi ey anc.e iss.ci yo.
8. Na nun i congi ey ilum ul ssuci yo.
9. Pak sensayng puin un sikol ey se ayki lul nah.usici yo.
10. Wuli elin ay nun kongwen ey se nōlci yo.
11. Sāy ka sāy cip an ulo tul.e kaci yo.
12. Kāy ka cic.umyen na nun tut.ci yo.
13. Na nun um.ak ul tul.umyen se kongpu lul haci yo.
14. Emeni ka sangcem ey ka se mulken ul saci yo.
15. Wuli atul un nal mata mok.yok ul haci yo.
16. Tta' nim un meli lul ileh.key pis.usici yo?
17. (Tangsin un) Hānkwuk os ul ip.usici yo?
18. Sensayng nim un wuli aph ey kyēysici yo.
19. Moksa nim un ¹yeypay-tang(q) yeph ey sāsici yo?
20. Ape' nim un unhayng ey cēnhwa lul kēsici yo?
21. Na nun catong-cha lul kot puluci yo.

IV

Take each of the sentences of Exercise III and make it PAST in each of the forms. For example, the first will be (0) Cip ey tol.a kass.ci yo. 'I went home, you see,' (1) Cip ey tol.a kaci anh.ess.ci yo. 'I didn't go home, you see,' (2) Cip ey tol.a kako siph.ess.ci yo. 'I wanted to go home, you see,' (3) Cip ey tol.a kako siph.ci anh.ess.ci yo. 'I didn't want to go home, you see.'

V

Now take each of the sentences of Exercise III and make it FUTURE in each of the forms. For example, the first will be (0) Cip ey tol.a kakeyss.ci yo. 'I guess I will go home,' (1) Cip ey tol.a kaci anh.keyss.ci yo. 'I guess I won't go home,' (2) Cip ey tol.a kako siph.keyss.ci yo. 'I will want to go home, you know,' (3) Cip ey tol.a kako siph.ci anh.keyss.ci yo. 'I bet I won't want to go home.'

VI

Say the following things in Korean; you need not translate literally, just get the idea across.

1. You like concerts, don't you?—Yes; I don't like lectures, but I like concerts.
2. Then how about going to a concert with me tonight?—Fine.
3. I wonder what time it is.—I don't know.
4. Isn't it a beautiful day! Suppose we take a walk in the park.
5. How did you learn that song?—I heard it on the radio.
6. It snowed a lot last night, didn't it?
7. Did you buy that record at the bookshop?—No! They don't sell records at the bookshop!
8. What a lot of stores there are in this city!
9. Will the train get here soon, I wonder?—Of course!
10. I guess we'd better listen to the radio instead of (listening to) the record player.

VOCABULARY DRILL

Here is a list of Korean words. Read each one aloud and then call off half a dozen other Korean words that are suggested to you by the given one—the old psychological game of "free association." You need not stick to one kind of word; a noun might suggest other nouns, or it might indicate a couple of nouns and a couple of verbs. The word baby, for example, might suggest such things as name, birthplace, gives birth, gets born, father and mother, Mrs. Kim (who just had a baby), etc. If you play the game in class, other members of the class can challenge any item for its relevance, and you must explain why you are reminded of it (for example, by using both words in a Korean sentence).

ayki	pyēng	kōhyang
cōh.a yo	sōsel chayk	sēnmul
Hānkwuk	talk	chīm-sang
pissa yo	um.ak	kyōkwa-se
pom	^{n}yeca	

Each member of the class should keep a list of the words he has trouble remembering from earlier lessons: Test each other on these words by using them to play the Free Association game with.

CONVERSATION

Assume for a moment the role of a Korean census taker who is gathering data and needs to know the names, ages, and birthplaces of each person in the classroom, as well as when each of their children was born. The information you request should be given cheerfully but need not be strictly factual, so long as it is reasonable.

Then, assume by turns the role of a friendly but inquisitive neighbor who wishes to ascertain the same type of information but of course goes about it in a more casual fashion.

COMPREHENSION

Listen while your teacher gives you a brief account of a recent illness undergone by himself of a member of his family (real or imaginary). The teacher will then question you to see whether you have been able to follow the progress of the illness properly, and what the present condition of the patient is.

You can then play 'Pass It On': One student whispers an interested sentence to his neighbor who passes it on to HIS neighbor and so on until the sentence comes back to the first student who then reveals what the original was and how badly it got garbled in going around the class.

LESSON 12. A CONCERT-GOER

BASIC SENTENCES

Korean	English	Amplification
1. Cham cōh.un um.ak-hoy 'ci yo??	Isn't it a fine concert?	um.ak-hoy ka cōh.a yo 'the concert is good' cōh.un um.ak-hoy 'a concert that is good = a good concert'
2. Celm.un um.ak-ka ka mānh.ci yo!!	My, what a lot of young musicians!	um.ak-ka 'musician' um.ak-ka ka celm.e yo 'the musician is young' celm.un um.ak-ka 'a musician who is young = a young musician'
3. Ecey sinmun ey nan ku sengak-ka ka palo ce sālam iey yo.	The singer who appeared in yesterday's paper is that very person over there.	sengak-ka '(classical) singer, vocalist' sengak 'vocal music' kaswu 'singer (of classical or popular music)' sengak-ka ka sinmun ey nass.ey yo 'the singer['s name] appeared in the newspaper' sinmun ey nan (ku) sengak-ka 'the (that) singer who[se name] appeared in the newspaper' palo . . . 'right, just . . .' palo ce sālam 'just that person, that very person'
4. Cikum tokchang hanun pun i yūmyeng han sengak-ka 'ey yo.	The person who is singing a solo now is a famous singer.	tokchang 'vocal solo' tokchang (ul) hay yo 'sing a solo' tokchang hanun pun 'the esteemed person who is singing a solo' (sengak-ka ka) yūmyeng hay yo '(a singer) is famous' yūmyeng han sengak-ka 'a singer who is famous = a famous singer'

Korean	English	Amplification
5. Caycwu wa myengseng un iss.e to tōn un ēps.nun sālam ici yo.	He's a person who, though he has talent and fame, has no money.	caycwu, caykan 'talent' myengseng 'fame' A nun iss.e to B nun ēps.e yo 'has A but lacks B' A nun iss.e to B nun ēps.nun sālam 'a person who has A but lacks B'
6. Phiano pancwu hanun sālam un ku uy an(h)ay 'ey yo.	The person accompanying him on the piano is his wife.	phiano 'piano' phiano pancwu 'piano accompaniment' phiano pancwu (lul) hay yo 'play a piano accompaniment' phiano pancwu hanun sālam 'person who is playing a piano accompaniment'
7. Ileh.key cōh.un nolay lul tul.un īl i iss.ey yo?	Have you ever heard such fine singing?	ileh.key cōh.un nolay 'song that is this good = such a good song, such good singing' īl i iss.ey yo? 'does the event (<u>or</u> experience) exist?' nolay lul tul.ess.ey yo 'I (have) heard singing' tul.un īl i iss.ey yo? 'has [someone] ever heard it' [= does a having-heard experience exist?]
8. Ani yo?? Ileh.key cōh.un nolay lul tul.un īl un han pen to ēps.ey yo.	No, I've never heard singing this good (even once).	tul.un il un . . . ēps.ey yo 'has never heard it' [= a having-heard experience does not exist]
9. I um.ak-hoy ka kkuth nan hwū ey, na nun ku sengak-ka lul manna pokeyss.ey yo.	After this concert is over, I'm going to see (meet) that singer.	um.ak-hoy ka kkuth nass.ey yo 'the concert (has) ended' um.ak-hoy ka kkuth nan hwū ey 'after the concert has come to an end (= is over)'
10. Ku pun ul mannan twī ey, ku pun kwa kath.i tapang ey kakeyss.ey yo.	After I meet him I'll go to a teashop with him.	ku pun ul mannass.ey yo 'I (have) met him' ku pun ul mannan twī ey 'after meeting him' tapang, chaq cip 'teahouse, teashop'
11. Tapang ey ka pon īl i iss.ey yo?	Have you ever been to a teashop?	tapang ey ka pwass.ey yo 'I went to a teashop'

Korean	English	Amplification
		ka pon īl 'experience of having tried going' ka pon īl i iss.ey yo 'has ever tried going'
12. Nēy. Sim-sim hamyen kakkum tapang ey kanun īl i iss.ci yo.	Yes; I sometimes go to a teashop when I'm [feeling] bored.	sim-sim hay yo 'is bored; is lonely' kakkum 'sometimes' tapang ey ka yo 'I go to a teashop' kanun īl 'the experience of going' kanun īl i iss.ey yo '[there exists the experience of going =] sometimes goes'
13. Wuli nun cikum cha lul masinun cwung ici yo.	We are now (in the middle of) drinking our tea.	cha, hong-cha 'tea' cwung 'middle, midst' masinun cwung 'in the [midst=] act of drinking' masinun cwung iey yo '[someone] is in the act of drinking'
14. Cha han can masin taum ey nun, mues ul hakeyss.ey yo.	What are you going to do after you drink a cup of tea?	cha han can 'a [one] cup of tea' masyess.ey yo 'drank it' masin taum ey '(next) after having drunk'
15. Tapang yuli chang ey se nun san i pōy yo.	You can see mountains from the teahouse windows.	san 'mountain' pōy yo [pōy-] = po.ye yo [poi-] 'is visible, can be seen'
16. Hānkwuk ey nun noph.un san i mānh.e yo.	There are many high mountains in Korea.	noph.a yo 'is high or tall' san i noph.a yo 'the mountains are high; has high mountains' noph.un san 'mountains that are high = high mountains'
17. San ey nun nac.un namu ka museng hay yo.	Low trees are thick on the mountains.	nac.e yo 'is low or short' namu ka nac.e yo 'the trees are low; has low trees' nac.un namu 'trees that are low = low trees' museng hay yo 'is rich (with verdure), grows thickly'

Korean	English	Amplification
18. Cen ey [or Ku cen ey] nun, san ey phulun so'-namu ka museng hayss.ci yo.	Before [the War] green pine trees were thick on the mountains.	(ku) cen ey 'before that' sol, so'-namu 'pine(tree)' phulule yo 'is green or blue' [phulu-; the infinitive phulule is irregular]
19. Wuli nun tapang ey iss.nun tong-an, yēyki hayss.ey yo.	While we were in the teashop, we talked. [During our time in the teashop . . .]	tong-an '(duration of) time; interval' tapang ey iss.ey yo 'we are/stay at the teashop' tapang ey iss.nun tong-an 'while we are at the teashop'
20. Ku sengak-ka ka han yēyki ka caymi iss.ey yo.	I was interested in what the singer had to say. or The story the singer told was interesting.	han yēyki 'the story [one] told; the things [one] said' caymi 'interest' caymi (ka) iss.ey yo 'is interesting' [= there is interest, it has interest]
21. Nay ka cikum hanun yēyki ka, ku sengak-ka ka han, palo ku yēyki 'ey yo.	The story I'm telling now is the very story the singer told [me].	nay ka cikum hanun yēyki 'the story I am telling now' ku sengak-ka ka han yēyki 'the story that singer told' palo ku yēyki 'just that story, that very story'
22. Caymi iss.nun yēyki 'ci yo??	Isn't it an interesting story?	yēyki ka caymi iss.ey yo 'the story is interesting' caymi iss.nun yēyki 'a story that is interesting = an interesting story'
23. Kath.un yēyki 'ey yo?	Is it the same story?	kath.e(y) yo [kath-] 'is the same; is like or similar to' kath.un yēyki 'the same (or a like) story'
24. Ani yo?? Talun yēyki 'ey yo.	No; it's a different story.	talle yo [talu-] 'is different (from), other' talun yēyki 'a different story, another story'
25. Wuli ka cha lul masiko yēyki hanun tong-an, sēy sikan i cīna kass.ey yo.	While we have been drinking tea and talking, three hours have gone by.	cha lul masiko yēyki hay yo 'we drink tea and talk' masiko yēyki hanun tong-an 'while drinking and talking' cīna ka yo 'goes by'

Korean	English	Amplification
26. Incey cip ey kamyen cōh.keyss.ey yo.	We'd better go home now.	
27. Nēy. Sikan i nemu nuc.ess.ey yo. Cip ey kanun kes i cōh.keyss.ci yo.	Yes; [the hour =] it has gotten late. It would be best to go home.	nemu 'overly, too' nuc.e yo 'is late; gets late' cip ey kanun kes 'the act [= thing] of going home' [= . . . going home would be good.]
28. Nay ka um.ak-hoy ey kan sai ey, cip ey totwuk i tul.ess.ey yo.	While I was at the concert, a burglar got into the house.	um.ak-hoy ey kass.ey yo 'I went to the concert' kan sai ey 'while [I] was away [= in the having-gone interval]' totwuk (nom) 'burglar, thief, robber'
29. Sik.kwu tul i canun sai ey, totwuk i mānh.un mulken ul kacye kass.ey yo.	While the family was asleep, the burglar took a lot of stuff.	sik.kwu tul i ca yo 'the family is sleeping' canun sai ey 'while [someone] is sleeping [= in the sleeping interval]' mulken i mānh.e yo 'things are numerous' mānh.un mulken 'many things' kacye yo [kaci-] 'takes in one's hand, carries; has, owns, possesses' kacye wa yo 'brings HERE' [comes carrying] kacye ka yo 'takes AWAY' [goes carrying] kaciko wa yo 'BRINGS here' kaciko ka yo 'TAKES away'
30. Totwuk i kum sikyey totwuk cil hanun tāysin ey, un sikyey lul hwumchye kass.ey yo.	Instead of stealing a gold watch, the burglar swiped a silver watch (and went).	kum 'gold' sikyey 'clock, watch' . . .cil (hay yo) '(engages in) the behavior of . . .' totwuk cil hay yo 'steals, burglarizes' tāysin 'stead, lieu; substitute, representative' tāysin ey 'instead (of); in substitution' totwuk cil hanun tāysin ey 'instead of stealing' un 'silver' hwumchye yo [hwumchi-] 'wipes; swipes (= steals); ransacks'

Korean	English	Amplification
31. Totwuk i tāymun ulo na kanun tāysin ey, yuli chang ulo na kass.ey yo.	Instead of leaving by the gate, the thief went out through a window.	tāymun '(front) gate' na kanun tāysin ey 'instead of going out'
32. Mun kwa chang ul cal tat.ci anh.un kkatalk ey, totwuk i tul.e wass.ey yo.	The burglar got [came] in because we didn't close the doors and windows (very) well.	tat.ci anh.ess.ey yo 'we didn't close it' kkatalk 'reason, cause' kkatalk ey/ulo 'by reason, because' tat.ci anh.un kkatalk ey/ulo 'because of not closing'
33. Tangsin i um.ak-hoy ey kan kkatalk ey totwuk ul mac.ess.ey yo.	You had a burglar because you went to the concert.	kan kkatalk ey 'because [one] went' mac.e yo [mac-] 'meets up with, faces, confronts, has, gets, suffers, receives'
34. Kulay yo. Nay ka um.ak-hoy ey kan kkatalk ici yo.	That's right; I guess it's because I went to the concert.	kan kkatalk iey yo 'it is because [one] went'
35. Kuleh.ci man, na nun um.ak-hoy lul kacang cōh.a hanun kkatalk ulo, kkok ka(ss.e) ya hayss.ci yo.	But because I like concerts better than anything else, I simply had to go, you see.	kacang, ku-cwung 'most of all' kacang cōh.a yo 'I like most of all (better than anything else)' cōh.a hanun kkatalk ulo 'by reason of liking' kkok 'exactly, just, for sure, without fail'
36. Um.ak-hoy (ey) teyliko ka se komapsup.nita.	Thank you for taking me to the concert.	teylye yo [teyli-] 'escorts, accompanies' teyliko wa yo 'brings [a person]' teyliko ka yo 'takes [a person]' mōsye yo [mōsi-] 'escorts, accompanies [someone esteemed]; waits upon, attends [a superior]' mōsiko wa yo 'brings [an esteemed person]' mōsiko ka yo 'takes [an esteemed person]'

SUPPLEMENTARY VOCABULARY

soli	noise, sound; (= māl) words	yēncwu-hoy	concert; recital
tokchang-hoy	vocal recital	phiano tokcwu-hoy	a piano recital

sāngyen	performance	ipcangq-kwen	admission ticket
phiano	piano	ipcang-lyo	admission price, fee
phiano (lul) chie yo (or hay yo)	plays the piano	kakuk, opheyla	opera
		sophulano, koum	soprano
paio(l)lin; cey-kum	violin	a(y)ltho, cēum	alto
paio(l)lin (ul) khie yo (or hay yo)	plays the violin	theyne	tenor
		peysu, passo	bass, basso
kyohyang-ak or simphoni	symphony (music)	chaq pang	1. pantry (in a house) 2. teashop (= tapang)
kyohyangak-tan	symphony orchestra	micang-wen	beauty parlor
		(p)pesu thanun kos	bus stop
hapchang	chorus	phyēnci neh.nun kos	mail box (to mail letters in)
īcwung-chang, pyēngchang	(vocal) duet	tāyse	(= tāyphil) writing on behalf of another; (= tāyse-in) a letter writer (for the uneducated), a scrivener
samcwung-chang	(vocal) trio		
sācwung-chang	(vocal) quartet		
īcwung-cwu	(instrumental) duet		
samcwung-cwu	(instrumental) trio	tāyse lul hay yo	performs as a letter writer; writes for others
sācwung-cwu	(instrumental) quartet		
cihwi-ca	director	tāyse-so	a scrivener's (office)
cihwi hay yo	directs		
mūtay	stage	kum-unq pang	jewelry shop
chengcwung	(listening) audience	yanghwa-cem	shoe store
		tosi	city
kwancwung	(viewing) audience; spectators	cēncayng	war
		tomuci	(not) at all; all in all, totally
leykhōtu um.ak	recorded music		
nolay lul pulle yo [pulu-]	sings a song	pantusi	by all means, without fail; be sure to
cwāsek, cali	seat	kiph.e yo [kiph-]	is deep
phyo	ticket	yath.e yo [yath-]	is shallow

NOTES

‖ 12.1. Modifiers.

Korean has a way to take a simple sentence and turn it into a clause that modifies some noun or noun phrase. This is done by changing the final verb to a MODIFIER form and putting the sentence in front of the noun to be modified (which may or may not be lifted from the original sentence). The Basic Sentences of this lesson contain a number of verbs and adjectives in two of the MODIFIER forms.

One kind of modifier has the two-shape ending -<u>un</u>/-<u>n</u>, pronounced /un/ after consonants and /n/ after vowels (and added to the UNEXTENDED form of L-extending vowel bases):

After consonant	After vowel
anc.un [sit]	mannan [meet]
cōh.un [be good]	sun [stand]
cek.un [be little/few]	kitalin [wait]

After consonant	After vowel
kel.un [walk]	pon [see]
sim.un [plant]	paywun [learn]
sin.un [wear on feet]	han [do]
ip.un [wear]	cwun [give]
pes.un [take off]	ān [know]
tat.un [close it]	nōn [play]
towun [help]	tun [enter]
celm.un [be young]	molun [not know]

This simple modifier has two different meanings, as follows.

With ADJECTIVES and the COPULA, it means 'which is [ADJECTIVE]; which is or equals [NOUN]':

khun cip 'house which is large' (← cip i khe yo 'the house is large')
moksa (i)n Kim sensayng 'the Mr. Kim who is a minister' (← Kim sensayng i moksa 'ey yo 'Mr. Kim is a minister.')

With PROCESSIVE (action) verbs, it has a past meaning— 'which did or has done' OR 'which [someone] did or has done.'

mek.un sālam 'person who ate or who has eaten' (← sālam i mek.ess.ey yo 'the person ate')
ssun phyēnci 'the letter which [I] wrote or have written' (← phyēnci lul ssess.ey yo 'wrote the letter')

‖ 12.2. Processive modifiers.

In addition to the simple forms just described, processive verbs have another modifier form made with the one-shape ending -nun (added directly to consonant and vowel bases and to the UNEXTENDED form of L-extending vowel bases):

manna-	'meet'	mannanun
su-	'stand'	sunun
kitali-	'wait for'	kitalinun
po-	'look at'	ponun
ka-	'go'	kanun
cwu-	'give'	cwunun
molu-	'not know'	molunun
ā-l-	'know'	ānun
nō-l-	'play'	nōnun
yē-l-	'open it'	yēnun
tu-l-	'enter; cost'	tunun
tul-	'listen'	tut.nun /tunnun/
pat-	'get'	pat.nun /pannun/
chac-	'look for'	chac.nun /channun/
pes-	'remove (garment)'	pes.nun /pennun/
nā(s)-	'get better'	nās.nun /nānnun/
nah-	'give birth to'	nah.nun /nannun/
anc-	'sit'	anc.nun /annun/
sin-	'wear on feet'	sinnun
sīm-	'plant'	sīmnun
ip-	'wear'	ip.nun /imnun/
tōw-	'help'	tōp.nun /tōmnun/

mek-	'eat'	mek.nun /mengnun/
takk-	'polish'	takk.nun /tangnun/
ilk-	'read'	ilk.nun /ingnun/

This ending is not used with adjectives (descriptive verbs), only with processive verbs. Iss.ey yo and ēps.ey yo are peculiar in that they sometimes behave like processive verbs (especially iss.ey yo) and sometimes behave like descriptive verbs (especially ēps.ey yo). With respect to the processive modifiers, they both usually behave like processive verbs:

chayk i iss.ey yo 'has a book' → iss.nun chayk 'the book that [one] has'
chayk i ēps.ey yo 'lacks a book' → ēps.nun chayk 'the book that [one] lacks'

The processive modifier ending -nun has a present meaning— 'which is doing' or 'which [someone] is doing':

mek.nun sālam 'the person who is eating'
ilk.nun sinmun 'the newspaper which [he] is reading'

After DESCRIPTIVE verbal nouns, hay yo is a descriptive verb and has only the modifier form han:

(ku) sālam i yūmyeng hay yo 'the man is famous' → yūmyeng han sālam 'a man who is famous = a famous man'

namu ka museng hay yo 'the trees are luxuriant' → museng han namu 'trees that are luxuriant = luxuriant trees'

After PROCESSIVE verbal nouns, hay yo is a processive verb and has the processive modifier form hanun ('. . . which [one] does') as well as the ordinary han ('. . . which [one] did')

kongpu hay yo 'studies'
kongpu hanun sālam 'the person who is studying'
kongpu hanun chayk 'the book [we] are studying'
kongpu han chayk 'the book [we] studied'

sānqpo hay yo 'takes a walk'
sānqpo hanun sālam 'the person who is taking a walk'
sānqpo han sālam 'the person who took a walk'

kwūkyeng hay yo 'sees, watches'
kkoch kwūkyeng hanun sālam 'the person who is looking at the flowers'
kwūkyeng han kkoch 'the flowers we saw'

Notice that hay yo as an auxiliary verb may be either descriptive or processive, depending on the other words it is used with. When used with verbal nouns, hay yo takes whatever modifier forms would be appropriate to the grammar of the verbal noun. That is, each verbal noun is either descriptive ('being . . .') or processive ('doing . . .') just like each verb.

‖ 12.3. Modifier clauses.

Modifier clauses are used, in general, in the same way we use relative clauses in English. The only complication is the order of things: in Korean, the modifying clause always comes BEFORE the noun expression it modifies. In English, modifying VERBS usually come after the word and modifying ADJECTIVES, before; though in the case of adjectives we have a choice.

English order	Korean order
green TREES TREES which are green	green TREES
a nice, large ROOM A ROOM which is nice and large	nice-and-large ROOM
THE MAN who came to dinner	came-to-dinner MAN
THE PLAY we saw last night	we-saw-it-last-night PLAY
THE FRIEND OF MINE who took a trip to America last year	took-a-trip-to-America-last-year MY FRIEND
THE RICE I'm eating	I'm-eating-it RICE
THE MAN who is eating rice	is-eating-rice MAN

Any Korean sentence can be made into a modifier by using one of the modifier endings, and then placing a noun after it. You start with a complete sentence (long or short), put a modifier ending on the verb, and add a noun; the new result is a noun expression—no longer a sentence. The newly made noun expression then becomes a subject, or object, or whatever, just like any other noun expression.

HE
MR. KIM
THAT NICE LADY
THE BOY WEARING THE BLUE SHIRT
THE MAN WHO IS SITTING BETWEEN MR. KIM AND MRS. PAK } is my friend.

Descriptive verbs are easy because for the most part they are just like English:

cak.un cip 'a small house'
chwuwun nal 'cold weather'

The exceptions here are iss.ey yo and ēps.ey yo:

yenphil i iss.nun sālam 'the person who has a pencil'
chayk i ēps.nun sālam 'the person who has no book'

Processive verbs are more complicated, because (a) they can be either present or past; (b) in Korean they come BEFORE the noun instead of in the usual English order AFTER the noun; and (c) they can include direct objects. The noun modified may come from either the SUBJECT or the OBJECT of the modifying verb; it is usually clear from the context which function is intended:

With modified noun as original SUBJECT:

mek.nun sālam 'the person who is eating'
mek.un sālam 'the person who ate'

cikum tul.e onun sālam 'the person who is coming in now'
ecey on sālam 'the person who came yesterday'

With modified noun as original OBJECT:

tat.nun mun 'the door which [someone] is closing'
tat.un mun 'the door which [someone] closed'

ilk.nun sinmun 'the newspaper that [someone] is reading'
ilk.un sinmun 'the newspaper that [someone] has read'

Particles, of course, will make the meaning unambiguous:

Kim sensayng ul pon sālam 'the person who saw Mr. Kim'
Kim sensayng i pon sālam 'the person Mr. Kim saw'

Now, here is an example of a sentence turned into a modifier twice: in the first switch, the modified noun is the SUBJECT of the modifier clause; in the second, it is the OBJECT.

Ku sālam i tose-kwan ey se chayk ul pillyess.ey yo. 'That person borrowed a book from the library.'

1. Tose-kwan ey se chayk ul pillin (ku) sālam i nwukwu yess.ey yo? 'Who was the PERSON WHO BORROWED a book from the library?'
2. Ku sālam i tose-kwan ey se pillin chayk i musun chayk iess.ey yo? 'What was THE BOOK that person BORROWED from the library?'

Instead of coming from the subject or object of the underlying sentence, the noun modified may be the PLACE at/from/to which the action applies, or the TIME, or some other ingredient of the situation:

Ku sālam i chayk ul pillin tose-kwan i musun tose-kwan iess.ey yo. 'Which LIBRARY was it THAT HE BORROWED the book FROM?'

Ku sālam i tose-kwan ey se chayk ul pillin nal i Swu-yoil iess.ey yo. 'THE DAY THAT HE BORROWED the book from the library was Wednesday.'

Here are some more sentences illustrating the use of modifiers. To help you over the hump of transferring these clauses from one language to the other, the modifier clauses, plus the nouns they modify, are printed in large letters.

1. HULIN NAL un hay ka naci anh.e yo.	The sun doesn't come out on CLOUDY DAYS.
2. Ku sālam kwa na nun TĀYTAN HI KAKKAWUN CHINKWU 'ey yo.	He and I are VERY CLOSE FRIENDS.
3. Ku catong-cha wa kicha nun KKOK KATH.UN SIKAN ey wass.ey yo.	The car and the train got here at EXACTLY THE SAME TIME.
4. Ku sangcem ey se PISSAN MULKEN to phalko, SSAN MULKEN to phal.e yo.	They sell both EXPENSIVE THINGS and CHEAP THINGS at that store.
5. Kim sensayng uy cip i KHUKO CŌH.UN CIP iey yo.	Mr. Kim's house is A NICE LARGE HOUSE.
6. TTUKEWUN NAL ey nun cip ey se chayk ul pwa yo.	On HOT DAYS I read books at home.
7. Tōn i mānh.ci anh.e se, NEMU PISSACI ANH.UN MULKEN ul sass.ey yo.	I didn't have much money, so I just bought THINGS THAT WEREN'T VERY EXPENSIVE.
8. SINMUN UL PONUN SĀLAM ul mannass.ey yo?	Did you see A MAN READING A NEWSPAPER?
9. KIM SENSAYNG I PON SĀLAM ul na to pwass.ey yo.	I, too, saw THE MAN MR. KIM SAW.
10. KUKCANG EY KAKO SIPH.UN SĀLAM i iss.ey yo?	Is there ANYBODY here [= A PERSON] WHO WANTS TO GO TO THE THEATER?
11. KUKCANG EY KAKO SIPH.CI ANH.UN SĀLAM i iss.ey yo?	Is there ANYBODY here WHO DOESN'T WANT TO GO TO THE THEATER?
12. ACHIM ILCCIKI IL.E NANUN SĀLAM un pam ilcciki ca ya hay yo.	PEOPLE WHO GET UP EARLY have to go to bed early.

13. KU TOSI EY SE NAN SENSAYNG i kyēysey yo.	There's A TEACHER here WHO WAS BORN IN THAT CITY.
14. Ku sālam i MĀYIL KONGWEN EY SE SĀNQPO HANUN SĀLAM iey yo.	That man is THE MAN WHO TAKES A WALK IN THE PARK EVERY DAY.
15. Ku ai ka PHULUN SYASSU lul ipko iss.ey yo.	That child is wearing a BLUE SHIRT.
16. KU PHULUN SYASSU LUL IP.UN AI ka nwukwu 'ey yo.	Who is THAT CHILD WHO IS WEARING A BLUE SHIRT?
17. KU PHULUN SYASSU LUL IP.UN AI HAKO NŌLKO ISS.NUN AI ka wuli atul iey yo.	THE CHILD WHO IS PLAYING WITH THE CHILD WEARING THE BLUE SHIRT is my son.
18. Yeki ka WULI TUL I MĀYIL KONGPU HANUN PANG iey yo.	Here's THE ROOM WHERE WE STUDY EVERY DAY.
19. ECEY NAY KA LATIO LO TUL.UN CAYMI ISS.NUN NOLAY lul Kim sensayng to tul.ess.ey yo?	Did you(, too,) hear THE INTERESTING SONG I HEARD YESTERDAY ON THE RADIO, Mr. Kim?
20. ECEY KICHA EY SE MANNAN SĀLAM i wuli kyōhoy moksa 'ey yo.	THE MAN SAW ON THE TRAIN YESTERDAY is the minister of our church.

‖ 12.4. Modifier clauses for experiences: 'ever, never, sometimes.'

The noun īl, which means 'work,' also means 'event, act, experience.' The phrase īl i iss.ey yo means 'the event or experience exists' and īl i ēps.ey yo means 'the event or experience does not exist.'

With modifiers from processive verbs, there are four uses to which you can put these expressions.

1. -un īl i iss.ey yo 'has ever done'
   Hānkwuk ey kan īl i iss.ey yo? 'Have you ever gone/been to Korea?' [= Does having-gone-to-Korea exist? or Is there such a thing as (your) having gone to Korea? or Has it ever happened that you went to Korea?]
   Nēy. Hānkwuk ey kan īl i iss.ey yo. 'Yes, I've been to Korea.' [Notice that in affirmative statements—as differentiated from questions—we do not use the word 'ever' in English.]

2. -un īl i ēps.ey yo 'has never done'
   Hānkwuk ey kan īl i ēps.ey yo? 'Haven't you ever been to Korea?' [= Does having-gone-to-Korea not exist? or Isn't there such a thing as (your) having gone to Korea? or Hasn't it ever happened that you went to Korea?]
   Hānkwuk ey kan īl i ēps.ey yo. 'I've never been to Korea.'

3. -nun īl i iss.ey yo 'ever does; sometimes does'
   Kongwen ey kanun īl i iss.ey yo? 'Do you ever go to the park?' [= Do events of going exist? Does it ever happen that you go to the park?]
   Kongwen ey kanun īl i iss.ey yo. 'We sometimes go to the park.' [= Events of going to the park exist. It (sometimes) happens that we go to the park.]

4. -nun īl i ēps.ey yo 'never does'
   Kongwen ey kanun īl i ēps.ey yo? 'Don't you ever go to the park?' [= Does going-to-the-park not exist? Does it never happen that you go to the park?]

Kongwen ey kanun īl i ēps.ey yo. 'We never go to the park.' [= Going-to-the-park does not exist. It never happens that we go to the park.]

Notice that we have kept iss.ey yo and ēps.ey yo constant through these expressions, letting the time be expressed in the modifiers. But you can change the tense of the final verb and get expressions like these:

pon īl i iss.ess.ey yo 'had (once) seen'
pon īl i ēps.ess.ey yo 'had never seen'
ponun īl i iss.ess.ey yo 'used to see, had been seeing (sometimes)'
ponun īl i ēps.ess.ey yo 'never used to see, hadn't been seeing (ever)'

And you can use the future, especially with tentative meaning:

Kulen kes ul pon īl i ēps.keyss.ci yo. 'I don't suppose you've ever seen such a thing.'
Sānqpo kanun īl i iss.keyss.ey yo. 'They probably take walks (at times).' or 'We will be taking walks (at times).'

If you want to make the expression honorific you can make either or both verbs honorific:

Phyēnci lul ssusinun īl i iss.ey yo? or . . . ssunun īl i iss.usey yo? or . . . ssusinun īl i iss.usey yo? Do you ever write letters?
Phyēnci lul ssusici anh.nun (ssuci anh.usinun, ssusici anh.usinun) īl i iss.ey yo? or . . . iss.usey yo? or Phyēnci lul ssuci anh.nun īl i iss.usey yo? 'Does it ever happen that you don't write letters [but instead telephone etc.]?'

In place of īl you may find cek 'time, experience': -nun cek i iss.ey yo (ēps.ey yo), etc.

Here are some more examples:

1. Cwungkwuk ūmsik ul mek.un īl i ēps.ey yo?	Haven't you ever eaten Chinese food?
2. Ku tāyhak ey se kongpu han īl i iss.ey yo.	I've studied at that college.
3. Kim moksa lul manna pon īl i ēps.ey yo.	I've never met Mr. Kim, the minister.
4. Tāmpay lul phinun īl i iss.ey yo.	I sometimes smoke cigarettes.
5. Apeci ka koki lul capswus(i)nun īl i ēps.ey yo.	My father never eats meat.
6. Meli lul pis.un īl i ēps.nun ^{n}yeca nun micang-wen ey kan īl to ēps.keyss.ci yo.	A woman who has never combed her hair would surely never have been to a beauty parlor either.
7. Sewul ey kan īl i iss.nun sālam imyen, Nam Tāymun to pon īl i iss.keyss.ci yo.	If he is someone who has been to Seoul, surely he will/would have seen South Gate.
8. Hānkwuk ey iss.un īl i iss.e ya kulen īl to tā al.e yo.	You would have to have [stayed =] lived in Korea to understand all about such things.
9. Yēncwu-hoy ey cacwu taninun īl i iss.e ya, ku ^{n}yeca lul mannanun īl i iss.ey yo.	To have the experience of sometimes seeing that woman you have to go to concerts often.
10. Pesen ul sin.e poko siph.usin īl i iss.usey yo?	Do you ever have an urge to try wearing Korean socks?

11. Kyelhon han īl i iss.e to cōh.a yo.	It's all right to have been married.
12. Wuli namphyen un han pen to pyēng i nan īl i ēps.e se cōh.a yo.	I'm glad my husband has never once been ill.
13. Kul ul sse pon īl i ēps.umyen tāyse lul mōs hay yo.	If you've never tried writing letters, you can't be a letter writer for others.
14. Cīnan cwuil ey nun halwu to nal i hulye cin īl i ēps.ey yo.	Last week it didn't get cloudy a single day.
15. Ku ⁿyeca uy nolay lul tul.un īl i ēps.umyen, ˡnayil ku tokchang-hoy ey kkok kasey yo.	If you've never heard her sing, be sure to go to her recital tomorrow.
16. Kulen kos ey ka pon īl i iss.ey yo?	Have you been to such a place?

‖ 12.5. Modifier clauses: 'after.'

An expression made up of a modifier clause plus hwū ey 'after,' twī ey 'in back of, behind,' or taum ey 'next (after)' means 'after (something) happens or happened or has happened.' The modifiers in these expressions are from processive verbs and have the regular ending -un/-n.

A word of caution: You do NOT use a similar construction with cen ey 'before'; instead you use an entirely different verb form (-ki cen ey), which you will learn in the next lesson.

Here are some more examples of the 'after' construction.

1. Cip ey tol.a on hwū ey, kongpu lul hayss.ey yo.	After I got home, I studied.
2. Pi ka kkuth nan hwū ey, hay ka na wass.ey yo.	After it stopped raining, the sun came out.
3. Wuli ka um.ak ul tul.un twī ey, tapang ey ka se, cha lul han can masyess.ey yo.	After listening to the music, we went to a teashop and drank a cup of tea.
4. Khun taum ey nun te cōh.un os ul sa se cwukeyss.ey yo.	After you're big[ger], I'll buy (and give you) better clothes.

In the last example, khe yo (usually a descriptive verb 'is big') is used as a processive verb 'gets big(ger), grows.' You have had several bases which function either as descriptive ('is . . .') or processive ('becomes . . .'): nuc.e yo 'is/becomes late,' naa yo [nā(s)-] 'is/gets better,' hulye yo [huli-] 'is/gets cloudy.' But you must not assume that every descriptive verb can be converted in this way: usually you have to use the infinitive + auxiliary expression -e cye yo as shown by cak.e cye yo 'it gets small(er).' You can, of course, use this expression with descriptive verbs that are also used as processives: khe cye yo = khe yo 'gets big(ger).'

‖ 12.6. Modifier clauses: 'while.'

To say 'while (something) is happening' you use a PROCESSIVE modifier (-nun) followed by cwung 'middle, midst' or tong-an or sai (often shortened to sāy) 'interval.' This may or may not have the particle ey after it:

kongpu hanun { cwung / tong-an / sai } (ey) 'while studying, in the middle of studying'

If you want to say 'is (in the middle of) doing,' a form of the copula follows the noun:

· Kongpu hanun cwung iey yo (tong-an iey yo, sai 'ey yo). '[He] is in the midst of studying.'

Occasionally you will find a processive verb in the simple modifier form (-un/-n) before tong-an or sai (but not before cwung):

kan sai/tong-an ey '(in the interval) while we were (in the state resulting from having gone) away'

tul.e on sai/tong-an ey 'while (in the state resulting from having come) inside'

And there are a few descriptive verbs that occur with -(u)n cwung: pappusin cwung ey 'in the midst of your being busy' (pappe yo, pappu- 'is busy').

Here are some more examples of this construction:

1. Na nun cikum kongpu hanun cwung ici man, kongpu lul han hwū ey yenghwa kwūkyeng ka to cōh.a yo.	I'm in the middle of my studying now, but after I've studied it'll be all right to go to the movies.
2. Kim sensayng i pap ul mek.nun tong-an, nay ka sinmun ul pwass.ey yo.	While Mr. Kim ate, I read the newspaper.
3. Tāyhak ey iss.nun tong-an, tose-kwan ey mānh.i kamyen cōh.a yo.	It's a good idea to go to the library a lot while you're at the university.
4. Apeci ka sānqpo hasinun sai ey, son nim i cip ey osyess.ey yo.	While you were out walking, Father, we had a caller.
5. Īl hanun tong-an, sālam kwa yēyki hamyen an tōy yo.	You mustn't talk to (other) people while they're working!
6. Wuli ka tapang ey iss.nun tong-an, pakk ey nwūn i mānh.i wass.ey yo.	While we were in the teashop, it snowed a lot outside.
7. Sensayng i iyaki lul hako iss.nun tong-an na nun phikon hay se cass.ey yo.	I was so tired I fell asleep while the teacher was talking.
8. Latio lul tul.umyen se pap ul mek.ko iss.nun sāy, totwuk nom i wa se wuli catong-cha lul hwumchyess.ey yo.	When we were eating while listening to the radio, a thief came and stole our car.

‖ 12.7. Modifier clauses: 'instead of.'

The noun tāysin means 'a substitute' or 'a representative.' Tāysin ey means 'instead of.' A processive modifier plus tāysin ey means 'instead of doing': kongpu hanun tāysin ey 'instead of studying.' This construction means about the same thing as the -ci anh.ko construction you have learned, but emphasizes the substitution of one action for the other.

A descriptive modifier with tāysin ey means 'instead of being': chwuwun tāysin ey 'instead of being cold.' Ku tāysin (ey) means 'instead of that' or 'on the contrary, on the other hand.'

Here are more examples of this construction:

1. Cip ey iss.nun tāysin ey, sānqpo lul hayss.ey yo.	Instead of staying home, I took a walk.

2. Sānqpo hanun tāysin ey, cip ey iss.ess.ey yo.	Instead of taking a walk, I stayed home.
3. Cīnan pam ey kongpu hanun tāysin ey cass.ey yo.	Last night I went to bed instead of studying.
4. Na nun kwun.in in tāysin ey, kēnchwuk-ka yess.umyen cōh.keyss.ey yo.	I wish I were an architect instead of a soldier.
5. Wuli ai nun phiano lul chinun tāysin ey, nolay lul hako siph.e hay yo.	My boy wants to sing rather than play the piano.
6. Apeci nun wuli hako kath.i sāl.ci anh.nun tāysin ey, tal mata tōn kwa sēnmul ul mānh.i cwusey yo.	Instead of his living with us, Father sends us money and presents every month.
7. Khun soli lo ilk.nun tāysin ey (or ilk.ci mālko) com cak.un soli lo ilk.e cwusey yo.	Instead of reading in a ["big sound"=] loud voice, read in a ["small sound"=] soft(er) voice.

‖ 12.8. Modifier clauses: 'because of.'

A processive modifier (-nun) + kkatalk 'reason, cause' + a particle ey or ulo means 'because [someone] does' [= by reason of the fact that (someone) does]:

kongpu hanun kkatalk ey 'because [he] is studying'
mek.nun kkatalk ulo 'because [he] is eating'

A processive verb with the simple -un/-n modifier ending in this construction has the usual past meaning:

kongpu han kkatalk ey 'because [he] studied'
mek.un kkatalk ulo 'because [he] ate'

Descriptive modifiers with kkatalk ey or kkatalk ulo mean 'because [something] is':

chwuwun kkatalk ey 'because it's cold'
cōh.un kkatalk ulo 'because it's good'

If kkatalk is followed by a form of the copula instead of by a particle, the meaning is 'It's because . . .':

Kongpu hanun kkatalk iey yo.	'It's because I'm studying.'
Chwuwun kkatalk iess.ey yo.	'It was because it was cold.'

All these expressions are more common in writing than in speech, where the more informal construction -ki ttaymun (‖ 13.9) is used instead. More examples:

1. Pi ka nemu mānh.i onun kkatalk ey, sānqpo kaci mōs hay yo.	We can't go walking because it's raining too much.
2. Kel.e wa ya han kkatalk ulo nuc.key osyess.ey yo.	They got here late because they had to walk.
3. Tōn i ēps.nun kkatalk ey oci anh.un sālam i cey chinkwu ey yo.	The person who didn't come because he lacked the money is my friend.
4. Seng.ak ul cōh.a hanun kkatalk ey ku tokchang-hoy ey kanun "yeca ka ku seng.ak-ka lul mannako siph.e hay yo.	The woman going to that recital because she likes vocal music wants to meet the singer.

5. Kongwen ey kanun īl i ēps.nun kkatalk ey ku sālam ul manna pon īl ēps.ey yo.	I've never run into him because I never go to the park.
6. Hānkwuk ey ka pon īl i iss.nun kkatalk ulo Sewul ul com ālci yo.	I know Seoul a bit because I have been to Korea, you know.
7. Cāngkap ul kacye oci anh.un kkatalk ey chwuwe yo.	I'm cold because I came without my gloves (= forgot to bring my gloves).
8. Pak sensayng ul cikum mannako siph.ci man, sāmu-sil ey ēps.nun kkatalk ey, Wel-yoil ey tto chac.e okeyss.ey yo.	I want to see Mr. Pak but since he isn't in his office I'll come to see him again on Monday.
9. Ku sangcem uy moca lul sse pwass.ci man, nemu pissan kkatalk ulo saci mōs hayss.ey yo.	I tried wearing hats from that store, but I didn't buy any because they are too expensive.
10. Emeni lul manna poko siph.un kkatalk ulo, kōhyang ey tol.a wass.ey yo.	I returned to my home town because I wanted to see my mother.
11. Chayk sēy kwen ul pilliko siph.un kkatalk ulo, tose-kwan ey kakeyss.ey yo.	I'm going to (go to) the library because I want to borrow three books.
12. Ape' nim i Sewul ey kasici anh.umyen an toysinun kkatalk ey, kwutwu lul takk.e tulyess.ey yo.	Because Father had to go to Seoul, I shined his shoes for him.
13. I kongwen i namu ka phuluko cōh.un kkatalk ey, sālam i mānh.i sānqpo wa yo.	Because this park has such nice green trees, lots of people come to it for walks.
14. Mikwuk salam in kkatalk ey Yenge cal haci yo.	He speaks English well because he is an American, I guess.
15. Nac i ani 'n kkatalk ulo etwuwe yo.	It is dark because it isn't day(time).
16. Pakk ey se sālam tul i khun soli lo iyaki hako iss.nun kkatalk ulo cam ul mōs cako iss.ey yo.	They are making such a racket all the time outside that I can't sleep very well.
17. Mul i kiph.ci anh.un kkatalk ulo khun pay ka tul.e oci mōs hay yo.	Big ships can't enter because the water isn't deep.

EXERCISES

I

Here are 12 two-sentence groups. Each group of two has the same subject. You are to combine the sentences into one, in such a way that the first is incorporated into the second as a modifier. For example, the first pair means: 'The person is reading a magazine in the next room. When did that person get here?' Your job is to combine these so that they mean: 'When did the person who is reading a magazine in the next room get here?' Your sentence should be: Yeph pang ey se capci lul ponun (ku) sālam i ēncey wass.ey yo.

1. Sālam i yeph pang ey se capci lul pwa yo. Ku sālam un ēncey wass.ey yo.
2. Ai ka ecey achim ey cip aph ey se kāy wa kath.i nol.ass.ey yo. Ku ai nun taum cip atul iey yo. [Retain the adverb kath.i in the combined sentence.]
3. Sensayng i yeki se Yenge lul kaluchye yo. Ku sensayng un Yengkwuk salam i ani 'ey yo.
4. Son nim i eceyq pam ey wass.ey yo. Ku son nim un nwukwu yess.ey yo.
5. Phyēnci ka nal mata wa yo. Ku phyēnci nun mānh.e yo.
6. Catong-cha ka khe yo. Ku catong-cha nun Kim sensayngq kes iey yo?
7. Ku cip i khuko cōh.a yo. Ku cip un Pak sensayng(q) cip ici yo??
8. Ai tul i latio lul tul.e yo. Ku ai tul un wuli cokha 'ey yo.
9. Ayki ka elye yo. Ku ayki nun wuyu ['milk'] man mek.e yo.
10. Ku hak.kyo ka mel.e yo. Ku hak.kyo nun cōh.a yo.
11. Sālam i tāmpay lul phi(wu)ko iss.ey yo. Ku sālam un wuli hyeng nim iey yo.
12. Ai ka pam mata ilcciki cako siph.e hay yo. Ku ai nun cōh.a yo.

II

Here again are some two-sentence groups. Combine each group into one sentence in such a way that the first sentence becomes the modifier of the direct object of the second. Your first sentence, for example, should be: Nay ka ku īl ul han (ku) sālam ul mannass.ey yo. 'I saw the man who did that work.'

1. Sālam i ku īl ul hayss.ey yo. Nay ka ku sālam ul mannass.ey yo.
2. Ai ka nay kwutwu lul takk.ess.ey yo. Nay ka ku ai lul chac.ko iss.ey yo.
3. Neykthai ka chayk-sang wi ey iss.ey yo. Nay ka ku neykthai lul māyko siph.e yo.
4. Moca ka chīm-sang wi ey iss.ess.ey yo. Nay ka ku moca lul ssess.ey yo.
5. Wuli atul i cēki anc.ess.ey yo. Nay ka wuli atul ul pulless.ey yo.
6. Ku kwāyngi ka ippe yo. Nay ka ku kwāyngi lul poko siph.e yo.
7. Hānkwuk salam han salam i cēki se sal.e yo. Nay ka ku sālam ul sayngkak hayss.ey yo.
8. Kāy ka cal cic.e yo. Kim moksa ka ku kāy lul cōh.a haci anh.e yo.
9. Ūmsik i nappe yo. Wuli ka ku ūmsik ul mek.umyen an tōy yo.
10. Apeci ka namu lul sim.ess.ey yo. Wuli ka ka se ku namu lul poci yo!
11. Kkoch i ippe yo. Chinkwu ka na hanthey ku kkoch ul cwuess.ey yo.

III

This time, combine the two sentences so that the first one becomes the modifier of the same noun in the second. Number 1, for example, has the subject ai 'child'; make it into a modifier for ai (in the phrase ai hanthey) of the second. Your completed sentence should be: Na nun phul ul kkakk.un ai hanthey tōn ul cwuess.ey yo. 'I gave some money to the boy who mowed my lawn.'

1. Ai ka phul ul kkakk.ess.ey yo. Na nun ai hanthey tōn ul cwuess.ey yo.
2. Ku yenghwa-kwan i kakkawe yo. Ku yenghwa-kwan ey kako siph.e yo.
3. Ku yenghwa ka caymi iss.ey yo. Ku yenghwa lul kwūkyeng hamyen cōh.keyss.ey yo.
4. Ku sangcemq kaps i pissa yo. Kim sensayng un ku sangcem ey se mulken ul sako siph.e haci anh.keyss.ci yo.
5. Mikwuk i mel.e yo. Mā sensayng un Mikwuk se wass.ey yo.
6. Tose-kwan i hak.kyo yeph ey iss.ey yo. Na nun ku tose-kwan ey se cwuil mata capci lul ilk.e yo.

7. Ku namu ka khuko phulule yo. Ku namu wi ey nun sāy ka iss.ci yo??
8. Ku haksayng i Hānkwuk se wass.ey yo. Wuli ka ku haksayng kwa kath.i cha han can masici yo!
9. Ku sālam i unhayng ey se īl ul hay yo. Na nun ku sālam uy cip ey se sal.e yo.
10. Haksayng i na hanthey chayk ul cwuess.ey yo. Na nun ku haksayng hako kath.i māl hako iss.ess.ey yo.
11. Kim moksa ka wuli cip ey se sālko iss.ey yo. Na nun (ku) Kim moksa hanthey sayngil sēnmul ul cwukeyss.ey yo.

IV

In each of the sentence pairs below, the first sentence contains a direct object. Combine each pair into one sentence so that the first sentence modifies the direct-object word. For example, your first sentence should be: Kim sensayng i ponun chayk i Hānkwuk mal chayk ikeyss.ci yo. 'I guess the book Mr. Kim is reading is a Korean (language) book.'

1. Kim sensayng i chayk ul pwa yo. Ku chayk un Hānkwuk mal chayk ikeyss.ci yo.
2. Nay ka catong-cha lul kacyess.ey yo. Ku catong-cha nun khuko cōh.a yo.
3. Nay ka sōsel chayk ul sass.ey yo. Ku sōsel chayk un caymi iss.e se cōh.a yo.
4. Wuli ai ka os ul pes.ess.ey yo. Ku os un eti iss.ey yo.
5. Wuli atul i say sin ul sin.ess.ey yo. Ku sin un cham ippuci yo??
6. Nay ka ku kes ul masyess.ey yo. Ku kes un mul i ani yess.ci yo!!
7. Moksa ka tōn ul pat.e yo. Ku tōn un cēkci yo??
8. Cang sensayng i phyēnci lul sse ya hay yo. Ku phyēnci nun Hānkwuk mal phyēnci 'keyss.ci yo??
9. Kongpu sikan cen ey nay ka chayk ul ilk.e ya hayss.ey yo. Ku chayk un Hānkwuk mal chayk iess.ey yo.
10. Nay ka catong-cha lul sako siph.e yo. Ku catong-cha nun kaps i nemu pissa se, saci mōs hakeyss.ey yo.
11. Nay ka nal mata cēncha lul tha yo. Ku cēncha nun palo hak.kyo ey ka yo.

V

Each of the following pairs of sentences, again, has a noun common to both. In this case, the first sentence is to become a clause modifying the direct object of the second. For example, the first one should be: Kim sensayng i ponun chayk ul na to pwass.ey yo. 'I (too) have read the book that Mr. Kim is reading.'

1. Kim sensayng i chayk ul pwa yo. Na to ku chayk ul pwass.ey yo.
2. Nay ka mun ul tat.ess.ey yo. Ku mun ul yel.e cwusikeyss.ey yo?
3. Nay ka sōsel chayk ul sass.ey yo. Ku chayk ul ilk.ko siph.e hasey yo?
4. Kim sensayng i ku yenghwa lul cōh.a hay yo. Kim sensayng puin to ku yenghwa lul cōh.a hay yo.
5. (Sensayng nim i) sālam ul mannasyess.ey yo. Ku sālam ul nay ka cal al.e yo.
6. Hyeng nim i neykthai lul māyko iss.ey yo. Ku neykthai lul na to han pen māyss.ey yo.
7. Apeci ka na hanthey sēnmul ul cwuess.ey yo. Ku sēnmul ul posyess.ey yo.

8. Emeni ka ku sālam ul cēnhwa lo pulless.ey yo. Ku sālam ul apeci to han pen pulless.ci yo.
9. Nay ka ūmsik ul mekci anh.ess.ey yo. Ku ūmsik ul kāy ka mek.ess.ey yo?
10. Wuli ka ūmsik ul mekci anh.e yo. Ku ūmsik ul kāy hanthey cwue to cōh.keyss.ey yo?
11. Kāy ka honca mun ul yel.e yo. Ku mun ul ayki to honca yel.e yo.
12. Nay ka nolay lul pulle yo. Ku nolay lul sensayng nim to āsikeyss.ci yo??
13. Atul i tōn ul ssess.ey yo. Ku tōn ul nwukwu hanthey se pat.ess.ci yo?
14. Wuli ka Hānkwuk se um.ak ul tul.ess.ey yo. Ku um.ak ul kakkum sayngkak hasey yo?

VI

In the following groups, the noun common to both sentences has a particle after it in the second. Combine the sentence so that the first modifies the noun (+ particle) of the second. The first combination will be: Cang sensayng i kaluchin kwa puthe sīcak hasici yo! 'Let's begin with the lesson that Mr. Cang taught.'

1. Cang sensayng i ku kwa lul kaluchyess.ey yo. Ku kwa puthe sīcak hasici yo!
2. Emeni ka mun ul yel.e yo. Ku mun aph ey nwu' ka iss.ey yo.
3. Nay ka onul achim ey tose-kwan ul kwūkyeng hayss.ey yo. Ku tose-kwan ey se haksayng tul i kongpu lul hay yo?
4. Nay ka eceyq pam ey moksa lul mannass.ey yo. Ku moksa uy cip ey se sensayng nim i sālko iss.ey yo?
5. Nay ka cēncha lul tha yo. Ku cēncha lo tangsin to hak.kyo kkaci kakeyss.ci yo.
6. Kim sensayng i chinkwu lul mannass.ey yo. Ku chinkwu hako kath.i ūmsik ul mek.ess.ey yo.
7. Oppa ka onul achim ey hak.kyo lul pwass.ey yo. Ku hak.kyo ey nay ka ka yo.
8. Nay ka ku hak.kyo lul sayngkak hayss.ey yo. Ku hak.kyo ey phyēnci lul ssess.ey yo.

VII

These sentences, like the preceding ones, have a noun in common; when the noun first occurs, it is followed by a location particle (in the first one tose-kwan ey se 'at the library'). Combine the sentences in such a way that the first sentence modifies the shared noun of the second. The first one will be: Nay ka capci lul ponun (ku) tose-kwan un kakkawe yo. 'The library where [at which] I read magazines is nearby.'

1. Nay ka tose-kwan ey se capci lul pwa yo. Ku tose-kwan un kakkawe yo.
2. Nay ka nal mata hak.kyo ey ka yo. Ku hak.kyo nun mel.e yo.
3. Wuli ka ku cip ey sal.e yo. Ku cip un cak.e yo.
4. Nay ka ku tosi ey se sal.e yo. Ku tosi nun Pusan iey yo.
5. Nay ka ku ai hako kath.i nol.ass.ey yo. Ku ai nun cip ey tol.a wass.ey yo. [Retain kath.i in the combined sentence.]
6. Nay ka ku yenphil lo i phyēnci lul ssess.ey yo. Ku yenphil un eti iss.ey yo.
7. Yenghwa ka ku sikan puthe sīcak hay yo. Ku sikan un nuc.ci yo??
8. Kim sensayng i ku sālam hanthey cēnhwa lul kel.ess.ey yo. Ku sālam un nwukwu yess.ci yo.
9. Chayk tul i ku pang ey iss.ey yo. Ku pang un taum pang iey yo.

VIII

In the following pairs, the noun which is common to both sentences has in the first sentence a particle after it meaning 'at, on in, to, from, or with.' Combine the two, again, so that the first sentence modifies the shared noun of the second. The first should be: Wuli ka kyelhon ul han (ku) [1]yeypay-tang ul Han sensayng i kwūkyeng hakeyss.ey yo. 'Mr. Han is going to have a look at the church where we got married.'

1. Wuli ka ku [1]yeypay-tang ey se kyelhon ul hayss.ey yo. Ku [1]yeypay-tang ul Han sensayng i kwūkyeng hakeyss.ey yo.
2. Nay ka ku chayk ulo Hānkwuk mal ul paywess.ey yo. Ku chayk ul posyess.ey yo?
3. Nay ka ku tāyhak ey se kongpu lul hay yo. Ku tāyhak ul kwūkyeng hasikeyss.ey yo?
4. Hyeng nim i ku cip ey sal.e yo. Ku cip ul cal al.e yo.
5. Palam i ku tosi ey se cal pul.e yo. Ku tosi lul cōh.a hasey yo?
6. Nay ka cwuil mata [1]yeypay-tang ey ka yo. Ku [1]yeypay-tang ul Se sensayng i mōs chac.usyess.ey yo?
7. Nay ka Kim sensayng ul ku um.ak-hoy ey se mannass.ey yo. Ku um.ak-hoy lul tangsin to tul.ess.ey yo?

IX

Combine the following pairs into one sentence each. As before, the first sentence is to be made into a modifier of one of the nouns in the second—the noun which appears in both. The first: Nay ka sānun tosi ey se cēncha chacang hanthey tōn ul cwuci anh.e yo. 'In the town where I live, you don't give your money to the streetcar conductor.'

1. Nay ka ku tosi ey se sal.e yo. Ku tosi ey se cēncha chacang hanthey tōn ul cwuci anh.e yo.
2. Wuli ka ku sālam hako kath.i sal.e yo. Ku sālam uy ilum un Kim Poktong iey yo.
3. Wuli ka Hānkwuk mal ul ku chayk ulo paywess.ey yo. Ku chayk an ey say māl i mānh.ess.ey yo.
4. Yenghwa ka ku sikan puthe sīcak hay yo. Ku sikan kkaci mues ul hasici yo.
5. Ayki ka ku pang an ey iss.ey yo. Ku pang an ey se nōlmyen an tōy yo.
6. Wuli ka ku [1]yeypay-tang ey se caymi iss.nun yāyki lul mānh.i tul.ess.ey yo. Ku [1]yeypay-tang yeph ey iss.nun cip un [1]yeypay-tang moksa cip iey yo.

X

In each of the following pairs, the second sentence starts with Ku hwū/taum/twī ey . . . 'After that . . .' and the first sentence ends with -ess.ey yo 'did' or the like. Combine the two sentences into one. For example, the first will be: Cenyek ul cal mek.un hwū ey sānqpo lul hayss.ey yo. 'After eating a good dinner, I took a walk.'

1. Cenyek ul cal mek.ess.ey yo. Ku hwū ey sānqpo lul hayss.ey yo.
2. Tose-kwan ey ka se chayk ul han kwen pillyess.ey yo. Ku taum ey cip ey tol.a ka se ku chayk ul ilk.ess.ey yo.

3. Sensayng nim un tapang ey se cha han can masyess.ey yo. Ku twī ey eti lo kasyess.ey yo?
4. Apeci ka unhayng ey se tōn ul mānh.i pat.ess.ey yo. Ku taum ey khun catong-cha lul sass.ey yo.
5. Um.ak-hoy ka kkuth nass.ey yo. Ku twī ey wuli ka kongwen ey ka se chinkwu tul ul mannass.ey yo.
6. Hal-apeci ka sinmun ul pwass.ey yo. Ku hwū ey hak.kyo ey cēnhwa lul kel.ess.ey yo.
7. Poktong-i ka meli lul pis.ess.ey yo. Ku twī ey moca lul ssuko na kass.ey yo.
8. Acwumeni ka kulus ul ssis.ess.ey yo. Ku taum ey ayki lul teyliko sangcem ey ka se mulken ul sass.ey yo.
9. Acessi ka cip ul phal.ess.ey yo. Ku hwū ey wuli nun pat.un tōn ul wuli unhayng ey kacye wass.ess.ey yo.
10. Kāy ka cic.ess.ey yo. Ku taum ey ayki ka caci mōs hayss.ey yo.
11. Hal-'meni ka pyēng i nass.ey yo. Ku twī ey pata lo ka se swiess.ey yo.

XI

In each of the following pairs, the second sentence starts with Ku tong-an/sai (ey) 'During that . . .' and the first ends with a verb. Combine the two sentences into one. For example, the first will be: Na nun i lul takk.nun tong-an tongsayng uy yēyki lul tut.ci mōs hayss.ey yo 'While I was brushing my teeth I couldn't hear what my little brother was saying.'

1. Na nun i lul takk.e yo. Ku tong-an ey tongsayng uy yēyki lul tut.ci mōs hayss.ey yo.
2. Hānkwuk mal ul kongpu hay yo. Ku sai Yenge lo māl hamyen an toyci yo.
3. Caymi iss.nun chayk ul poko iss.ey yo. Ku tong-an ey cako siph.e haci anh.keyss.ci yo.
4. Ippun "yeca hako yēyki lul hako kyēysici yo. Ku sai ey sikyey lul an posikeyss.ci yo!
5. Nay ka malwu wi ey nwuwess.ey yo. Ku sai cēnhwa ka wass.ey yo.
6. Totwuk nom i cip ey iss.ey yo. Ku tong-an wuli kāy ka cic.e yo.

XII

In each of the following pairs, the second sentence starts with Ku tāysin ey 'Instead of that . . .' and the first ends with a negative verb. Combine the two sentences into one. For example, the first will be: Say os ul ip.nun tāysin ey hēn kes ul ipkeyss.ci yo 'Instead of wearing my new clothes I guess I'll put on my old ones.' (Note that the negative has to change to positive.)

1. Say os ul ipci anh.e yo. Ku tāysin ey hēn kes ul ipkeyss.ci yo.
2. Nal i chwuwe cici anh.e yo. Ku tāysin ey com tewe cyess.ci yo.
3. Na nun cha lul masici mōs hay yo. Ku tāysin ey wuyu lul masiko siph.e yo.
4. Wuli ka moksa nim ul mannaci anh.keyss.ci yo. Ku tāysin ey ku puin ul mannass.ci yo.
5. Nay ka tangsin hako mōs ka yo. Ku tāysin ey honca kakeyss.ci yo.
6. Yenphil kkakk.ci anh.e yo. Ku tāysin ey mānnyen-phil lo ssukeyss.ey yo.
7. Sewul ul cal moluci yo. Ku tāysin ey Pusan ul cal ālci yo. [Remember that molu- is the negative form of ā-l-.]
8. Tōn i ēps.e yo. Ku tāysin ey ai tul i mānh.i iss.ey yo. [Remember that ēps- 'lack' is the negative of iss- 'have.']

CONVERSATION

Play several brisk rounds of pass-it-on (A asks B a question in Korean; B answers, then asks C a question; C replies and then questions D; and so on), along the following lines.

I

A asks B, 'Have you ever done so-and-so?' and B gives a truthful, or at least reasonable, answer in a full sentence ('Yes, I've done so-and-so' or 'No, I've never done so-and-so'). If the situation is interesting enough to discuss it a bit (three or four more sentences), fine. Here are a few suggestions:

Have you ever eaten Korean/Japanese/Chinese/etc. food?
seen a Korean/Japanese/Chinese/etc. movie?
met Mr./Mrs./Miss So-and-So?
been to So-and-So's house?
read [a current best seller]?
bought anything at [a certain store]?
taken a train/car/streetcar to [some interesting place]?
etc., etc.

II

A tells B something in Korean—a sentence with a direct object. B questions A about this object. Some suggestions:

I'm reading a bood.—What kind of book are you reading?
—Is the book you're reading interesting?
I saw a movie last night.—
I bought a car last week.—
I went to see some friends yesterday.—
I have a new dress/suit.—
etc., etc.

VOCABULARY DRILL

Say each of the following sentences in Korean five times—each time filling the blank with a different expression, as listed below the sentence.

1. I'd like to listen to a ___.
singer
piano recital by Mrs. Kim
symphony orchestra
vocal trio
piano

2. The person sitting over there is ___.
the very person who sang at the concert
the same man who played the violin
a bass
the person we saw in the audience
a conductor

3. Have you ever heard ___?
a piano duet
that famous soprano
an opera
a symphony
a vocal duet

4. I'm right in the middle of ___.
buying a ticket for the concert
playing the piano
listening to some recorded music
looking at the mountains from the tea-house windows
reading my textbook

5. I've never owned ___.
   a gold watch
   many things
   a violin
   a record player
   a silver cup

6. While I was in Seoul, I saw ___.
   an opera
   a thief stealing some money
   a chorus singing on the stage
   a famous man drinking tea
   a lot of high mountains and green trees

COMPREHENSION

Your Korean teacher will make up a number of incomplete statements (in Korean) containing modifier clauses, and say them to you to finish. Some suggestions:

The person who is sitting next to A (or between B and C) is ___.
The thing on top of that table over there is ___.
The person who's wearing a blue necktie/a new dress/an overcoat/etc. is ___.
The person who just opened his book is ___.
The person who just closed the door/window is ___.
The thing you can see from the window is ___.
A place where you go and drink a cup of tea is a ___.
A building where you get money is a ___.
A place where you go to mail letters is a ___.
A building where teachers teach and students learn is a ___.
A book that you study from is a ___.
And so on, and so on . . .

LESSON 13. SCHOOL DAYS

BASIC SENTENCES

Korean	English	Amplification
1. Mōtun kes ul tā cal haki (ka) elyewe yo.	It's hard to do everything well. [= The act of doing everything well is difficult.]	mōtun . . . 'all . . .' mōtun kes 'all things, everything' haki 'the act of doing' swiwe yo [swiw-] 'is easy' elyewe yo [elyew-] 'is hard, difficult'
2. Achim ey ilcciki il.e naki silh.e yo.	I hate (the act of) getting up early in the morning.	il.e naki 'the act of getting up'
3. Tāychey lo wuli cip sik.kwu tul un achim ey ilcciki il.e naki lul silh.e haci yo.	The members of my family generally hate to get up early in the morning, you know.	tāychey '(in) outline; generally' tāychey lo 'in general, by and large, on the whole'
4. Hak.kyo ey kaki cen ey, tewun copan ul mek.e yo.	Before I go to school, I eat a hot breakfast.	kaki 'the act of going' kaki cen ey 'before going' copan 'breakfast'
5. Swukcey lul machyess ey yo?	Have you finished your homework?	swukcey 'homework'
6. Ani yo?? Kongpu sikan i toyki cen ey machye ya hay yo.	No; I have to finish it before (it gets to be) class (time).	tōy yo [toy-] 'becomes, gets to be; is' kongpu sikan i tōy yo 'it gets to be class time' kongpu sikan i toyki cen ey 'before it gets to be class time'
7. Na to i swukcey lul machiki ey āy (lul) ssuci man, nay chinkwu to āy lul sse yo.	Both my friend and I are trying to finish this homework. [= I too am doing my best to finish this homework, but then my friend is trying his best too.]	machiki 'the act of finishing' āy 'one's reservoir of strength' [< 'guts'] āy (lul) sse yo [ssu-] '[uses one's guts =] tries, endeavors, takes pains, does one's best' machiki ey āy (lul) sse yo '[uses one's guts to(ward) finishing =] tries one's best to finish'

	Korean	English	Amplification
8.	Etteh.key onul achim to tto hak.kyo ey nuc.ess.ey yo.	How come you're late for school again this morning?	
9.	Sikyey ka ēps.ki ttaymun ey nuc.key wass.ci yo.	I'm late because I haven't any watch. [= I came late by reason of the fact that I haven't a watch.]	ēps.ki 'the state of not having' ttaymun 'cause, reason' ēps.ki ttaymun 'the reason of not having' ēps.ki ttaymun ey 'by reason of not having, because [one] has not'
10.	Swukcey lul mōs machyess.ki ttaymun ey tulici mōs hay yo.	I can't hand in my homework because I couldn't get it finished.	machyess.ki 'the act of having finished' mōs machyess.ki ttaymun ey 'because of not having been able to finish' tulye yo [tuli-] '[gives to someone esteemed=] hands in, submits'
11.	Swukcey nun taum sikan ey pachiki lo hay yo.	I've decided to hand in my homework next hour.	pachye yo [pachi-] 'presents, submits, gives, hands over' pachiki lo hay yo 'decides or agrees to hand it over'
12.	Way i chayk ul ilk.ci anh.e yo?	Why aren't you reading this book?	way 'why?'
13.	I chayk ul ilk.ki nun haci/ilk.ci man, ttus ul mōlla yo.	I AM reading this book, but I don't know what it means [= I don't know or understand the meaning].	ilk.ki 'the act of reading' ilk.ki nun haci man or ilk.ki nun ilk.ci man 'is (indeed) reading, but . . .' ttus 'meaning, significance'
14.	Molunun māl ul kong-chayk ey ssess.ey yo?	Did you write the words you don't understand in your notebook?	molunun māl 'the word [one] doesn't know or understand'
15.	Kong-chayk ey ku māl ul ssuki nun hayss.ci/ssess.ci man, cal mōs ssess.ci yo.	I DID write the words in my notebook; but I didn't write them properly.	ssuki nun hayss.ci man or ssuki nun ssess.ci man 'did (indeed) write, but . . .'
16.	Yeph ey anc.un haksayng un kongpu man hay yo.	The student who sits next to me does nothing but study.	
17.	Ku haksayng un pucilen haki to haci yo!	He sure is a hard worker!	pucilen hay yo 'is diligent, hard-working' pucilen haki to hay yo 'is really or decidedly hard-working'

Korean	English	Amplification
18. Na poki ey nun (or Nay sayngkak ey nun) ku haksayng i wuli pan ey se kacang pucilen hay yo.	The way I see it, he's the hardest worker in our class.	poki 'the act of seeing or looking at; view, opinion; appearance' na poki ey nun 'the way I look at [it]; in my view' . . . (uy) sayngkak ey nun 'in the opinion of . . . , to the mind of . . . ' pan 'class'
19. Ku haksayng uy thāyto to poki (ka) cōh.ci man, elkwul to poki (ka) cōh.ci yo.	You see, not only is his attitude pleasant (but) his face is nice to look at too.	thāyto 'attitude' poki (ka) cōh.a yo 'is good to look at, is pleasant-looking or good-looking' elkwul 'face'
20. Talun sālam poki ey nun, nay ka kacang keyuluci yo.	The way other people look at it, I guess I'm the laziest.	keyulle yo [keyulu-] 'is lazy'
21. Na nun kongpu sikan ey caki man hay yo.	In class (time) I do nothing but sleep.	caki 'the act of sleeping' caki man 'only the act of sleeping' caki man hay yo 'does only the act of sleeping'
22. Kongpu man haki ka him tul.ki to hay yo.	It's really hard to do nothing but study.	kongpu man haki 'the act of doing only studying' him 'strength, power' him (i) tul.e yo 'takes strength = is difficult, hard, onerous' him tulki 'the state of being difficult or hard' him tulki to hay yo 'is really difficult, is decidedly hard'
23. Na nun pon.lay nōlki ka cōh.a yo.	Basically, I like to have fun.	pon.lay 'basically, fundamentally' nōlki 'the act of playing'
24. Na man kulen ka yo?	And I'm not the only one!	na man 'only I/me' kulen ka yo? 'is it like that?!' [rhetorical question]
25. Nay tongsayng to nōlki lul cōh.a hay yo.	My younger brother likes to fool around too.	
26. Sāsil māl hamyen, na nun nōlki wi hay se hak.kyo ey tanici yo.	To tell the truth, I just go to school for the sake of playing.	sāsil 'truth; fact' sāsil māl hamyen 'if [I] speak the truth' sāsil un 'in reality, in fact'

Korean	English	Amplification
		. . . ul wi hay yo 'does for the good (sake, benefit) of . . . , does in favor (on behalf, in the interest) of' . . . ul wi hay se 'for the sake of' -ki lul wi hay se 'for the sake of [do]ing' nōlki (lul) wi hay se 'for the sake of playing'
27. Nay hak.kyo kongpu nun nōlki lul wi han kongpu 'ey yo.	My school work is study for the sake of playing.	nōlki lul wi han kongpu 'study (which is) for the sake of playing'
28. Yo say nun nal i cōh.ko ttattus hay se, pakk ey se nōlki ka cham cōh.a yo.	Lately the weather has been nice and warm, so it's been very nice to play outside [= the act of playing outside is very nice].	yo = i 'this/these' sāy = sai 'interval' yo say (nun) 'lately, nowadays, these days'
29. Wuli pumo nim un nay ka kongpu lul cal haki lul palako kyēysici yo.	My parents are hoping I'll study hard, I suppose.	pala yo 'hopes for; looks forward to' haki 'the act of doing' pala pwa yo 'scrutinizes, looks at (something distant); looks on (from the sidelines); expects' haki lul pala yo 'hopes for (the act of) doing; hopes [someone] does, will do'
30. Kuliko, nay sengcek i cōh.ki lul palasici yo.	And also, I guess they hope my grades will be good.	sengcek 'records (of one's achievements); (school) grades' sengcek i cōh.a yo 'has good grades' cōh.ki 'the state of being good' sengcek i cōh.ki lul pala yo 'hopes for the grades to be good'
31. Kulay se, cīnan cwuil puthe yelqsim ulo kongpu haki lul sīcak hayss.ey yo.	So, (starting from) last week I began to study like mad.	yelqsim = yel.uy 'earnestness, enthusiasm' yelqsim ulo = yelqsim hi 'earnestly, enthusiastically, assiduously' yelqsim hay yo 'is enthusiastic'

Korean	English	Amplification
		haki (lul) sīcak hay yo 'begins to do' kongpu haki lul sīcak hayss.ey yo 'began to study'
32. Na nun yo say cōh.un sengcek ul nāyki ey him ul sse yo.	I've been trying lately to make a good record.	sengcek ul nāy yo '[puts out=] makes a record' sengcek ul nāyki ey 'to(ward) the act of making a record' him 'strength, power' him (ul) sse yo '[uses strength=] tries, makes an effort'
33. Nay tongsayng to him sse kongpu hamyen, cōh.un cemqswu lul et.keyss.ci yo.	My younger brother will get good marks too, if he studies hard.	him sse (se) 'with effort (endeavor), hard, energetically' cemqswu 'marks, grades' et.e yo 'receives, gets'
34. Nay sāchwun un kongpu lul swīpkey cal hay yo.	My cousin studies well with no effort.	swīpkey 'easily, effortlessly'
35. Ku ay nun kongpu to hako, nōlki to hay yo.	That boy studies and plays around too.	[= . . does studying, and also does playing]
36. Tto Tho-yoil hako Il-yoil ey nun wūntong to hako, sānqpo to ka yo.	Moreover, on Saturdays and Sundays he goes out for sports as well as going for walks.	wūntong 'sport, athletics' wūntong (ul) hay yo 'engages in sports, goes out for sports'
37. Yo say nun sihem ttay ka tōy se (wuli nun) puncwu (haki) to hako phikon (haki) to hay yo.	It's exam time these days, so we're both busy and tired.	sihem 'test, examination' ttay 'time, occasion' sihem ttay ka tōy yo 'it is <u>or</u> has become examination time' puncwu hay yo <u>or</u> pappe yo [pappu-] 'is busy' puncwu haki to hako phikon haki to hay yo <u>or</u> puncwu to hako phikon to hay yo 'is both busy and tired'
38. Na nun sihem ul cal chi(lu)ki to hako, mōs chi(lu)ki to hay yo.	Some exams I come through well, and some I can't get through.	chi(l)e yo [chi(lu)-] 'takes or gets through [a test]' chi(lu)ki 'the act of taking <u>or</u> getting through [a test]' cal chi(lu)ki to hako, mōs chi(lu)ki to hay yo 'there happens getting-through-well and there happens can't-getting-through'

SUPPLEMENTARY VOCABULARY

chile yo [chilu-]*	disburses, settles (a bill); takes, gets through (a test)
sihem ul hay yo	gives a test
sihem ul pwa yo	takes a test
mūncey	problem, topic, question
col.ep	graduation
col.ep (ul) hay yo	graduates
col.ep-sayng	alumnus, graduate
col.ep-cang	diploma
swuep-lyo or welqsa-kum	tuition
kwuk.min hak.kyo or sō-hak.kyo or pōthong hak.kyo	elementary school
cwung-hak.kyo	junior high school, middle school
kotung hak.kyo	(senior) high school

tokse-sil	reading room, study hall
tose-sil	library (room)
tose-kwan	library (building)
secay	one's study, (home) library
ūmsik-cem or ^{l}yoli-cem or ^{l}yoliq cip or leysutholang	restaurant
pyēl	star
tal	moon or month
mukewe yo [mukew-]	is heavy
kapyewe yo [kapyew-]	is light (in weight)
(A lul B lo) pakkwe yo [pakkwu-]	exchanges (A for B)
kel.e yo [kē-l-]	hangs it (up), (cēnhwa lul~) makes a phone call

*Note that the infinitive does not double the l, unlike most verbs that end in lu; cf. pulle yo [pulu-] 'calls.' This is because the form derives from an abbreviation of the obsolete form chilwe [chilwu-]. A common modern variant is chie yo [chi-].

NOTES

‖ 13.1. More about verbal nouns.

Since you first learned about verbal nouns (Lesson 4; ‖ 4.6), a number of new ones have appeared in the Basic Sentences. All of them are listed here:

Processive Verbal Nouns

Intransitive

cēnhwa hay yo 'telephones'
chwulqsayng hay yo 'is born'
col.ep hay yo 'graduates'
īl hay yo 'works'
kyelhon hay yo 'marries'
myēnto hay yo 'shaves'
nolay hay yo 'sings'
pyelqsey hay yo 'dies'
samang hay yo 'dies'
sānqpo hay yo 'takes a walk'
sēyswu hay yo 'washes up'
sihem hay yo 'gives a test'
sillyey hay yo 'commits a discourtesy'
thānsayng hay yo 'is born'
tokchang hay yo 'sings a solo'
wūntong hay yo 'engages in sports'
yēyki hay yo 'talks; tells a story'

Transitive

kongpu hay yo 'studies'
kwūkyeng hay yo 'watches'
māl hay yo 'says; speaks'
sayngkak hay yo 'thinks (of)'
sīcak hay yo 'begins'
tāytap hay yo 'answers'
totwuk cil hay yo 'steals'
wi hay yo 'does for the sake of'
yongse hay yo 'forgives'

Descriptive Verbal Nouns

mian hay yo 'is sorry'
museng hay yo 'is rich, thick, verdant'
phikon hay yo 'is tired'
pucilen hay yo 'is diligent'
puncwu hay yo 'is busy'
senul hay yo 'is cool'
sim-sim hay yo 'is lonely'
ttattus hay yo 'is warm'
ttok-ttok hay yo 'is smart'
yūmyeng hay yo 'is famous'

Two-syllable processive verbal nouns whether transitive or intransitive can usually be separated from hay yo by the direct object particle ul/lul (or some substitute for it such as the particle of reduced emphasis un/nun or the particle of reinforced emphasis to): sānqpo lul hay yo 'takes a walk,' kyelhon ul hay yo 'gets married.' Of course, if the verbal noun is transitive and the object is expressed, the verbal noun is usually followed directly by hay yo: emeni lul sayngkak hay yo 'thinks of mother,' yenghwa lul kwūkyeng hay yo 'sees a movie.' Often you can, instead, let the object modify the verbal noun and put the direct-object particle after the resulting noun phrase: emeni sayngkak ul hay yo '[does mother-thinking=] thinks about mother,' yenghwa kwūkyeng ul hay yo '[does movie-viewing=] sees the movie.' But this option is not available if the object is modified by a clause (nor, usually, if by such words as ku 'that,' say 'new,' etc., or noun phrase + uy 'of'): Poktong-i uy emeni lul sayngkak hay yo 'thinks of Poktong-i's mother,' caymi iss.nun yenghwa lul kwūkyeng hay yo 'sees an interesting movie.' On the other hand, if you want to modify the verbal noun itself, it has to become the object and the phrase can no longer take another object: ku kongpu lul hay yo 'does that studying,' kulen kwūkyeng ul hay yo 'does that kind of sightseeing.' When the verbal noun is marked as object (with ul/lul) it can, like any other object, be separated from the verb (in this case hay yo) by intervening material: ku kongpu lul ecey hayss.ey yo 'did that studying yesterday,' kwūkyeng ul meych si puthe meych si kkaci hakeyss.ey yo 'from what time to what time will we do our sightseeing?'

Some one-syllable verbal nouns can also be separated from hay yo, for example īl ul hay yo 'does the job'; a few others that you have not had, for example sok hay yo 'belongs (to)' can not be separated. Separable verbal nouns can be used freely like most other nouns—as subject, or to modify a noun, or before the copula iey yo, etc.

A few of the DESCRIPTIVE verbal nouns can be used as free nouns, but even they are usually not separated from hay yo except for an occasional intrusion of the particles to 'also' man 'only,' un/nun (deemphasis): yūmyeng to hay yo = yūmyeng haki to hay yo 'is famous too,' yūmyeng man hamyen = yūmyeng haki man hamyen 'if only I were famous,' yūmyeng un haci man = yūmyeng haki nun haci man 'he's famous all right but . . . .'

‖ 13.2. Verbs: nominative form -ki.

A number of verbs in this lesson have appeared in the NOMINATIVE form—that is, with the ending -ki attached to them.

The one-shape ending -ki is attached to bases in exactly the same way as is the gerund ending -ko (above, ‖ 8.3.). You can make past forms by attaching it to past bases, and future forms by attaching it to future bases:

Present	haki
Past	hayss.ki /haykki/
Future	hakeyss.ki /hakeykki/

The resulting forms are noun-like words; they mean 'the act of doing' if processive, and 'the state of being' if descriptive. Past forms mean 'the act of having done, the state of having been,' and future forms mean 'the act of going-to-do; the state of going-to-be.' Sometimes the forms translate 'to do/be.'

These noun-like forms are used in all of the four positions that regular nouns are used in—most commonly, these three:

1. Followed by a particle (‖ 13.3, 4, 6, 8, 10, and 11 below);
2. Modifying a following noun (‖ 13.9 and 13 below);
3. In absolute (adverbial) position—in constructions where a particle has optionally been dropped (‖ 13.15).

It is rarer to find a -ki form in the remaining noun use:

4. Before the copula. Ileh.key haki 'ey yo. '(It is [a matter of] doing it this way=) Let's decide to do it this way. Other constructions of this type involve quotations, which you will learn to handle later.

Theoretically, you can use a nominative form of any verb and make it the direct object of hay yo 'does':

caki (lul) hay yo 'does sleeping'
kitaliki (lul) hayss.ey yo 'performed the action of waiting'

In actual use this is rare, however, since the meaning is the same as that of the verb alone:

ca yo 'sleeps [= does the action of sleeping]'
kitalyesse.y yo 'waited [= performed the act of waiting]'

Nominative verb forms enable you to take an entire sentence and turn it into the subject, object, or some other part of a larger sentence.

Kongpu lul hay yo. 'I study.'→ Kongpu lul haki lul silh.e hay yo. 'I hate to study.'

This sentence neatly contains two direct objects: one within the -ki clause, and one which is the -ki clause itself. You can, of course, drop either particle (l)ul—or both of them:

Kongpu haki lul silh.e hay yo.
Kongpu lul haki silh.e hay yo.
Kongpu haki silh.e hay yo.

‖ 13.3. Nominative forms with the particle to.

1. 'indeed':

17. . . . pucilen haki to hay yo. 'He's really hard-working.'
22. . . . him tulki to hay yo. 'It's really hard.'

A -ki form with to hay yo after it means 'really does/is' or 'does/is indeed.'

Tēpki to hay yo. 'It certainly is hot.'
Mukepki to hay yo. 'It's really heavy!'
Mānh.i oki to hayss.ey yo. 'There sure are a lot of them (come) here!'
Pissaki to hakeyss.ci yo. 'I guess it must be expensive indeed!'

Note that the past and future elements, as usual, attach to the auxiliary verb hay yo. The honorific, also, usually attaches to the final auxiliary:

Kako siph.e haki to hasey yo. 'He really wants to go (badly).'

2. 'also':

38. . . .cal chiluki to hako, mōs chiluki to hay yo. 'Some I get through, some I don't.'

If there are two instances of -ki to hay yo right together (either descriptive or processive), the meaning is 'does/is both x and y.' Here are some more examples:

Cōh.ki to hako, nappuki to hay yo. 'It's both good and bad.'— 'It has its good points and its bad points.'
Chwupki to hako, tēpki to hay yo. 'It [e.g. a country] is both cold and hot.'— 'There are cold parts and hot parts.'
Chwupki to hako, palam to pul.e yo. 'It's both cold and windy.'
Ālki to hako, moluki to hay yo. 'Some of it I know and some I don't.'

Notice that this construction is used for comparing actions or descriptions that are expressed by VERBS. For comparing actions expressed by VERBAL NOUNS (as well as other nouns), it is the nouns which have to after them, as in Basic Sentence 36:

36. . . . wūntong to hako, sānqpo to ka yo. 'He both engages in sports and takes walks.'

But it is somewhat more natural to use haki (to hay yo) after DESCRIPTIVE verbal nouns, as shown in Sentence 37:

37. . . . puncwu (haki) to hako, phikon (haki) to hay yo. 'We're both busy and tired.'

You can have a verbal noun in one part of the construction and a verb in the other part as in Sentence 35:

35. . . .kongpu to hako, nōlki to hay yo. 'He both studies and plays around.'

13.4. Nominative forms: -ki nun haci man.

13. I chayk ul ilk.ki nun haci/ilk.ci man, ttus ul mōlla yo. 'I AM reading this book, but I don't understand it.'
15. Kong-chayk ey ku māl ul ssuki nun hayss.ci/ssess.ci man, cal mōs ssess.ey yo. 'I DID write the words in my notebook; but I didn't write them properly.'

A -ki form followed by either itself or ha- in the suspective (-ci) form plus man means 'does/is, to be sure, but . . .':

Ku kes ul mek.ki nun mek.ess.ci/hayss.ci man, mas i ēps.ess.ey yo. 'I DID eat it, all right, but it had no flavor.'

Notice that the past or future markers attach only to the -ci form in this construction—not to the -ki form, which remains constant.

13.5. Nominative forms: 'begins to.'

31. . . . kongpu haki lul sīcak hayss.ey yo. 'I began to study.'

To say 'begins to do' or 'begins doing' you use a -ki form (with or without the direct object particle lul) and sīcak hay yo 'begins.'

Pi ka oki sīcak hay yo. 'It's beginning to rain.'
Pyēl i naki sīcak hayss.ey yo. 'The stars had started to come out.'
Cikum mek.ki (lul) sīcak haci yo?? 'Let's begin eating, shall we?'

This construction is used with processive verbs only. For adjectives— 'begins to BE'—you use an infinitive (-e) with the auxiliary verb cye yo 'begins [to be]' (‖ 9.8).

Tewe cye yo. 'It's getting hot.' [= It's beginning to be hot.]

You can take the -e cye yo expression and use it, like any processive expression, in this construction:

Tewe ciki (lul) sīcak hayss.ey yo. 'It started getting hot.'
Mūncey ka elyewe ciki sīcak hay yo. 'The problems are beginning to get (more) difficult.'

‖ 13.6. Nominative forms with the particle man.

21. . . . caki man hay yo. 'I do nothing but sleep.'

The construction . . . -ki man hay yo means 'does nothing but . . .' or 'only . . .s' [= does only . . .-ing]:

mek.ki man hay yo 'only eats; does nothing but eat'
nōlki man hay yo 'fools around all the time; does nothing but play'
kulen soli man hay yo 'does nothing but make that sort of noise; only says things like that'
mūncey ka elyepki man hay yo 'the problems are all difficult'
Ayki ka mek.ko caki man haci yo. 'Babies do nothing but eat and sleep, you know.'

Notice that in theory, English I read only books and I only read books are different; similarly, in Korean Chayk man ilk.e yo (= 'Books are all I read') is theoretically different from Chayk ul ilk.ki man hay yo (= 'All I do is read books'). But in both languages, this distinction is often ignored.

With verbal nouns, you can omit haki: Kongpu (haki) man hay yo 'I do nothing but study.' Somewhat similar are cognate objects (‖ 26.3) as in cam ul ca yo 'sleep (a sleep)': you can say either cam ul caki man hay yo or cam man ca yo for 'does nothing but sleep (one's sleep).'

‖ 13.7. Nominative forms: 'wants to, likes to, dislikes to.'

2. Achim ey ilcciki il.e naki silh.e yo. 'I hate to get up early in the morning.'
3. . . . wuli cip sik.kwu tul un achim ey ilcciki il.e naki lul silh.e hay yo. 'My family hates to get up early in the morning.'
23. . . . nōlki ka cōh.a yo. 'I like to play.'
25. . . . nōlki lul cōh.a hay yo. 'He likes to play.'

Processive verbs in the -ki form can be used as direct objects of such verbs as these:

wēn hay yo 'wants (to do)'
cōh.a hay yo 'likes (to do)'
silh.e hay yo 'dislikes (doing)'

Here are examples:

Cip ey tol.a kaki lul wēn hay yo. 'I want to go home.'

I chayk ul ku chayk ulo pakkwuki wēn hasey yo? 'Do you want to exchange this book for that one?'

Na kaki lul silh.e hay yo. 'He hates to go out.'

Nay tongsayng un chwum chwuki lul cōh.a hay yo. 'My sister likes to dance.'

To mean 'I like (or dislike) doing,' you make the -ki form the SUBJECT—not object—of the verbs cōh.a yo or silh.e yo:

Na nun nolay haki ka cōh.a yo. 'I love to sing.'

Ilcciki il.e naki ka silh.e yo. 'I hate getting up early.'

‖ 13.8. Nominative forms with the particle ey.

A -ki nominative form plus the particle ey has three uses:

1. '(in the process of) doing':

Īl haki ey puncwu hay yo. 'I'm busy (in or at) working.'

2. 'as, in accordance with':

nay ka sayngkak haki ey (nun) 'as I think; in accordance with what I think'

nay ka tut.ki ey (nun) 'according to what I hear'

na poki ey (nun) 'the way I look at it; in my view'

talun sālam poki ey (nun) 'the way other people look at it; in the view of others'

The use of poki in the last two examples should not be confused with its use in Basic Sentence 19:

poki (ka) cōh.a yo 'is good-looking, nice to look at'

3. 'as, because, by reason of' [cf. also ‖ 13.9]:

Chayk i ssaki ey han kwen ul sass.ey yo. 'As the book was cheap, I bought a copy.'

Ku āy nun pam-nac caki ey, talun īl ul mōs hay yo. 'That child sleeps all the time, so he can't do anything else.'

Nal i cōh.ki ey, sānqpo na kass.ci yo. 'Since it was a nice day, I went out for a walk.'

Nemu nuc.key il.e nass.ki ey kicha lul mōs thass.ey yo. 'I got up so late I missed [= couldn't get on] the train.'

Pi ka okeyss.ki ey, wūsan ul kaciko wass.ey yo. 'I expected rain, so I came with umbrella.'

‖ 13.9. Nominative forms: 'because.'

9. Sikyey ka ēps.ki ttaymun ey nuc.key wass.ey yo. 'I'm late because I haven't any watch.'

10. Swukcey lul mōs machyess.ki ttaymun ey tulici mōs hay yo. 'I can't hand in my homework because I couldn't get it finished.'

A -ki form followed by ttaymun ey 'by reason of, because of' means 'because [one] does/is.' This is like the third meaning for -ki ey, just discussed in the preceding note. The construction means about the same thing as a modifier plus kkatalk ey/ulo (‖ 12.8), but is less formal. When the "because" sentence has nemu 'overly, too' + adjective it is sometimes better to translate it with 'so [ADJECTIVE] that':

I moca ka nemu cōh.ki ttaymun ey sass.ey yo. 'This hat was so [= too] nice that I bought it.' [= Because this hat was so nice, I bought it.]

Kim sensayng tayk i nemu mēlki ttaymun ey cēncha lo ka ya hayss.ey yo. 'Mr. Kim's house was so far away that I had to go [there] on the streetcar.'

Nal i nemu cōh.ki ttaymun ey, sālam tul i mānh.i wass.ey yo. 'It was such a nice day that lots of people came.'

Notice that a somewhat weaker form of 'because' is expressed by -e se: Nemu pissa se mōs sass.ey yo. 'It was so expensive I couldn't buy it.'

‖ 13.10. Nominative forms: 'decides to (do).'

11. Swukcey nun taum sikan ey pachiki lo hay yo. 'I've decided to hand in my homework next hour.'

Processive verbs in the -ki form plus lo hay yo mean 'decides to do' or 'agrees to do' or 'promises to do.' Notice that the -ki form remains fixed; it is the form of hay yo which contains any past or future markers.

Yoli-cem ey ka se mek.ki lo hayss.ey yo. 'I decided to go eat at a restaurant.'
Yelq si pān ey mannaki lo hayss.ey yo. 'I agreed to meet him at 10:30.'
Cip ey iss.ki lo hayss.ey yo. 'I decided to stay home.'
Ku kūlim ul yeki ey kēlki lo hayss.ci man, etteh.keyss.ci yo?? 'We've decided to hang the picture here, but how do you think that would be?'
Tōn ul cwusiki lo hayss.ey yo. 'He promised to give me some money.'
Tol.a kaki lo hasyess.ey yo? 'Have you decided to go home?'
Kim sensayng un taum Wel-yoil na wa kath.i Pusan ey kasiki lo hasyess.ey yo. 'Mr. Kim agreed to go to Pusan with me next Monday.'

The honorific marker, as shown by the last three examples, can be inserted in either part of the expression, or in both parts.

‖ 13.11. Nominative forms: 'tries to (do).'

7. Na to i swukcey lul machiki ey āy (lul) ssuci man, nay chinkwu to āy lul sse yo. 'Both my friend and I are trying to finish this homework.'

32. . . . cōh.un sengcek ul nāyki ey him ul sse yo. 'I've been trying to make a good record.'

Two expressions mean 'tries (hard), endeavors': āy (lul) sse yo and him (ul) sse yo—both literally 'exerts strength.'

There are two ways to use these in sentences:

1. As infinitives, followed by the main verb:

Na nun āy/him sse paywe yo. 'I'm trying to learn it.'
Phyēnci lul āy/him sse sse yo. 'I'm trying to write a letter.'
Chayk ul āy/him sse ilk.e yo. 'I'm trying to read a book.'

2. As the main-verb construction of the Korean sentence, with what translates the English main verb appearing as a -ki form plus the particle ey:

Paywuki ey āy (lul) sse yo. 'I'm trying hard to learn it.'
Phyēnci lul ssuki ey him (ul) sse yo. 'I'm trying to write a letter.'
Chayk ul ilk.ki ey him (ul) sse yo. 'I'm trying to read a book.'
Towa cwuki ey āy (lul) sse yo. 'I'm trying to help him.'

The meaning emphasizes putting in EFFORT ('tries hard') rather than mere attempt; for the latter, see -ulye (‖ 24.9). Notice, too, the construction -e pwa yo 'tries (out) doing, does to see (how it will be).' We can, perhaps, differentiate three kinds of "try" in this world: (1) EFFORT, (2) ATTEMPT, (3) SAMPLING.

‖ 13.12. Nominative forms: 'hopes (that).'

29. Wuli pumo nim un nay ka kongpu lul cal haki lul palako kyēysici yo. 'My parents are hoping I'll study hard, I suppose.'
30. Kuliko, nay sengcek i cōh.ki lul palasey yo. 'Also, I guess they hope my grades will be good.'

The verb pala yo means 'hopes, looks forward to.' The hoped-for action appears in Korean in the -ki form as a direct object. This construction is used with either processive or descriptive verbs.

[1]Nayil un nal i cōh.ki lul pala yo. 'I hope it will be a nice day tomorrow.'
Na nun Kim sensayng i oki lul pala yo. 'I hope Mr. Kim will come.'

You have already had one way to say 'hopes, wishes': -umyen cōh.keyss.ey yo (‖ 9.4), literally translatable 'it would be nice if . . . .' A literal translation of -ki lul pala yo is 'I am looking forward [hopefully] to the doing/being.' For most cases of English 'hope,' the former expression (-umyen cōh.keyss.ey yo) is more appropriate.

Here are more examples:

1. Hal-'meni ka i kkoch ul posiko kippe hasiki lul palaci yo.	You know, I hope Grandmother is delighted when she sees the flowers.
2. Ppalli Hānkwuk ey tol.a kaki lul pala yo.	I hope they will return to Korea soon.
3. Sewul ey pi ka an oki lul pala yo.	I hope it won't be raining in Seoul.
4. Emeni lul [1]naynyen ey nun pōypki lul pala yo.	I hope to see Mother next year.
5. Ku tōn ul Pak sensayng eykey cwuki lul pala yo.	I hope you gave that money to Mr. Pak.
6. Ku koki lul mek.ko siph.e haci anh.ess.umyen cōh.keyss.ey yo.	I had hoped they wouldn't want to eat that meat.
7. Incey tol.a kamyen cōh.keyss.ey yo.	I hope we're going home now.
8. I cwung Mikwuk ey ka pon īl i iss.nun sālam i iss.umyen cōh.keyss.ey yo.	I hope among these people there is a person who has been to America.
9. Tal i na oci anh.umyen cōh.keyss.ey yo.	I hope the moon doesn't come out.
10. Kapang i kapyewumyen cōh.keyss.ey yo.	I hope the briefcase (or bag) is light.
11. Mukepci anh.umyen cōh.keyss.ey yo.	I hope it isn't heavy.

‖ 13.13. Nominative forms: 'before.'

4. Hak.kyo ey kaki cen ey, tewun copan ul mek.e yo. 'Before I go to school, I eat a hot breakfast.'

6. . . . Kongpu sikan i toyki cen ey machye ya hay yo. 'I have to finish it before (it gets to be) class (time).'

Processive verbs in the -ki form enter into phrases with cen ey 'before' to mean 'before [someone] does.' Regardless of the time of the English— 'before [he] does' or 'before [he] did' or 'before [he] will do'—the Korean -ki form remains constant, so that the meaning of the phrase is 'before doing . . .':

Na kaki cen ey pap ul mek.e yo. 'He eats before he goes out.'
Na kaki cen ey pap ul mek.ess.ey yo. 'He ate before he went out.'
Na kaki cen ey pap ul mek.keyss.ey yo. 'He's going to eat before he goes out.'
Sangcem ey kaki cen ey unhayng ey mence ka ya hay yo. 'I have to go to the bank (first) before I go to the store.'

‖ 13.14. Nominative forms: direct quotations.

The pattern for quoting directly what someone says is as follows:

[Ku sālam i] māl haki lul, ". . ." hayss.ey yo. '[That person] said ". . . ," his words.'

It is more common for Koreans to quote indirectly ("He said that . . . ," "He asked us to . . . ," "I suggested that we . . . ," "She told me to . . ."); you will learn how to do this in Lesson 19.

‖ 13.15. Nominative forms: other noun-like uses.

1. Mōtun kes ul tā cal haki (ka) elyewe yo. 'It's hard to do everything well.'
19. Ku haksayng uy thāyto to poki (ka) cōh.ci man, elkwul to poki (ka) cōh.a yo. 'His attitude is good, and he's nice-looking too.'
22. Kongpu man haki ka him tulki to hay yo. 'It's really hard to do nothing but study.'
26. . . .nōlki wi hay se hak.kyo ey tanye yo. 'I go to school for the sake of playing.'
27. Nay hak.kyo kongpu nun nōlki lul wi han kongpu 'ey yo. 'My school work is study for the sake of playing.'
28. . . .pakk ey se nōlki ka cham cōh.a yo. 'It's very nice to play outside.'

Sentences 26 and 27 illustrate the use of -ki forms before wi hay yo 'does for the sake of.'

In each of the six sentences just quoted, a -ki form appears as subject or object; and in each case, the subject or object particle (as usual) is optional, so that the -ki form without the particle is left in an absolute, or adverbial, construction. Another case of this type is the construction with sīcak hay yo 'begins' (‖ 13.5) in which the -ki form is, optionally, the direct object of the phrase sīcak hay yo.

Here are some more examples of this kind of sentence.

1. Hānkwuk mal paywuki (ka) swiwe yo?	Is it easy to learn Korean?
2. Hānkwuk mal paywuki (ka) cham elyepkeyss.ci yo.	I guess it must be very hard to learn Korean.
3. Chayk ul ilk.ki (ka) caymi iss.ey yo.	It's fun to read books.
4. Sewul ey se sālki nun ettay yo.	What's it like to live in Seoul?
5. Sālki nun cōh.a yo.	It's nice living [there].

6. Sālam tul i tā īl ul yelqsim hi hako siph.e haki ka swīpci anh.e yo.	It isn't easy for everyone to want to work with enthusiasm.
7. Nal i ttattus hay se namu lul sīm.ki (ka) coh.a yo.	The weather is warm, so it would be nice to plant trees.
8. Ayki nun calaki ka ppaluki to hay yo.	The baby is really growing fast!
9. I cip ey nun pang i hana pakk-ey ēps.nun kkatalk ey, sālki ka swīpci anh.ci yo.	It isn't easy to live in this house, because it has only one room.
10. Tut.ki silh.un soli man hasey yo.	You keep saying such unpleasant things (to hear).
11. Hal-'meni nun nemu māl-ssum ul mānh.i hasye se, tut.ki silh.e yo.	Grandmother talks so much I hate to listen.

The last expression Tut.ki silh.e yo 'I hate to listen' is often used where we would say things like 'Ugh!,' 'I don't want to hear about it!,' 'Must you say such things?!,' 'What an awful thing (to hear)!'

EXERCISES

I

Each of the following items contains two sentences, the second beginning with Kuleh.ki ttaymun ey 'because it's like that.' Combine them into a single sentence meaning 'Because [this] happens, [that] happens.' For example, the first will be: Kim sensayng i ilcciki oci anh.ess.ki ttaymun ey, na nun Kim sensayng ul mōs mannass.ci yo. 'I couldn't see Mr. Kim, because he didn't get there early.'

1. Kim sensayng i ilcciki oci anh.ess.ey yo. Kuleh.ki ttaymun ey, na nun Kim sensayng ul mōs mannass.ci yo.
2. Na nun tōn i cek.e yo. Kuleh.ki ttaymun ey, chayk ul mānh.i saci mōs hay yo.
3. Ecey nal i nemu chwuwess.ey yo. Kuleh.ki ttaymun ey na nun cip ey iss.ess.ey yo.
4. Yak.hon-ca ka kkoch ul cōh.a hay yo. Kuleh.ki ttaymun ey, na nun kkoch ul mānh.i sa se cwuess.ey yo.
5. Na nun ku yenghwa ka cōh.a yo. Kuleh.ki ttaymun ey, twū pen kwūkyeng kakeyss.ey yo.
6. Ku chayk i pissa yo. Kuleh.ki ttaymun ey, na nun mōs sass.ey yo.
7. Wuli ka [1]nayilq pam ey kongpu haci anh.e to kwaynchanh.e yo. Kuleh.ki ttaymun ey, um.ak-hoy ey ka se um.ak ul tut.keyss.ci yo.
8. Onul ōhwu ey pi ka okeyss.ey yo. Kuleh.ki ttaymun ey, hak.kyo ey wūsan ul kaciko wass.ci yo.
9. [1]Nayil nal i cōh.keyss.ey yo. Kuleh.ki ttaymun ey, ōythwu lul ipci anh.e to cōh.keyss.ci yo.
10. [1]Nayilq pam ey son nim i okeyss.ey yo. Kuleh.ki ttaymun ey, emeni ka ūmsik ul cal hamyen ['make, fix'] komapkeyss.ey yo.
11. [1]Nayil achim ey kongpu ka yetelq si puthe sīcak hay yo. Kuleh.ki ttaymun ey, wuli ka ilcciki il.e na ya hakeyss.ey yo.

II

Now link sentences 1 through 6 above with -un kkatalk ey or -nun kkatalk ey. The translation will be the same.

III

Each of the following sentences means '[this] happens AFTER [that].' Change them so that they mean '[this] happens BEFORE [that].' For example, the first will be: Na nun Kim sensayng ul mannaki cen ey, kongwen ey se sānqpo lul com hayss.ey yo. 'I took a little walk in the park before I saw Mr. Kim.'

1. Na nun Kim sensayng ul mannan hwū ey, kongwen ey se sānqpo lul com hayss.ey yo.
2. Kim sensayng puin i on hwū ey, Kim sensayng i wass.ci yo.
3. Ai tul i pap ul mek.un hwū ey, kongpu lul hayss.ey yo.
4. Wuli sensayng i pang ey se na kan hwū ey, ku haksayng hako kath.i iyaki hayss.e yo.
5. Na nun yenphil ul kkakk.un hwū ey, congi lul chac.keyss.ey yo.
6. Kongpu sikan i kkuth nan twī ey, Yenge lo māl hamyen an tōy yo.
7. Cha han can ul masin taum ey, nolay lul com pulle yo??
8. Cip an ey tul.e kan hwū ey, emeni wa kath.i yēyki lul com hay cwusey yo.
9. Os ul ip.un hwū ey, sēyswu lul an hamyen an tōy yo.
10. Na nun os ul pes.un hwū ey kāy ka cic.nun kes ul tul.ess.ey yo.
11. Apeci ka cip ey tol.a osin hwū ey, na nun cal kongpu hayss.ey yo.

IV

Each of the following sentences means '[someone] does [this].' Change it to mean '[someone] does only [this]—does nothing but [this].' For example, the first will be: Wuli kāy ka nul cic.ki man hay yo. 'My dog just barks all the time.'

1. Wuli kāy ka nul cic.e yo.
2. Emeni ka latio lul tul.e yo.
3. Atul i pakk ey na kaci anh.ko, cip ey iss.ey yo.
4. Hal-apeci ka nal mata sinmun ul pwass.ey yo.
5. Ku namca ka tāmpay lul phi(w)e yo.
6. Wuli chinkwu ka māl haci anh.ko, anc.e iss.ey yo.
7. Ku āy ka nul kwutwu lul takk.ci yo.
8. Ayki ka mek.e yo.
9. Tangsin un nul swie yo.
10. Tangsin un nul nol.a yo.

V

Each of the following sentences means 'someone DOES or IS . . . .' Change it to mean 'someone REALLY DOES or REALLY IS . . . .' For example, the first will be: Na nun ku kkoch i cōh.ki to hayss.ey yo. 'I certainly did like those flowers!'

1. Na nun ku kkoch i cōh.ass.ey yo.
2. Na nun yenghwa kwūkyeng ul kako siph.e yo.
3. Wuli ka tōn i ēps.ci yo.
4. Atul i tōn ul ssess.ey yo.

5. Hak.kyo ka cip ey (se) kakkawe yo.
6. Wuphyen-kwuk i [l]yeypay-tang ey se mel.e yo.
7. Ku sālam un phyēnci (lul) ssuki lul cōh.a hay yo.
8. Ku ayki ka elye yo.
9. Wuli moksa nim i celm.usey yo. [Most common to make just hay yo honorific.]
10. Na nun eceyq pam ey cal cass.ci yo.
11. [l]Nayil nal i chwupkeyss.ey yo.
12. I phyēnci ka mukewe yo.

VI

The next three exercises are designed to give you some more practice on the modifiers you learned in Lesson 12.

Each of the following sentences means 'someone IS DOING . . .' Change it to mean 'someone IS IN THE MIDST OF DOING . . .' For example, the first will be: Na nun Hānkwuk malq kongpu lul hanun cwung iess.ey yo. 'I was in the midst of doing my Korean lesson.' [Of course, it would be possible to say . . . hako iss.nun cwung . . . instead of . . . hanun cwung . . . ; but the meaning is clear without the -ko iss- because of the force of cwung.]

1. Na nun Hānkwuk malq kongpu lul hako iss.ess.ey yo.
2. Ai tul i [l]yuseng-ki lul tut.ko iss.ey yo.
3. Ku sālam i sōsel ul ilk.ko iss.ey yo?
4. Ce twū salam i keli kwūkyeng ul hako iss.keyss.ey yo.
5. Atul i phul ul kkakk.ko iss.ess.ci yo?
6. An(h)ay ka mulken ul sako iss.ey yo.

VII

Each of the following items contains two sentences. The first means 'someone IS DOING [this]'; the second, beginning with Kulenun cwung ey, means 'In the midst of that happening.' Combine the two sentences into a single one meaning 'in the midst of someone's doing [this], [that] happens.' For example, the first one will be: Nay ka kongpu hanun (or hako iss.nun) cwung ey, son nim i osyess.ey yo. 'While I was in the middle of studying, guests dropped in.'

1. Nay ka kongpu hako iss.ess.ey yo. Kulenun cwung ey son nim i osyess.ey yo.
2. Sensayng i phyēnci lul ssuko iss.ess.ey yo. Kulenun cwung ey cēnhwa ['phone call'] ka wass.ey yo.
3. An(h)ay ka cēnhwa lul kēlko iss.ess.ey yo. Kulenun cwung ey ayki ka mun ul yēlko, pang ey se na kass.ey yo.
4. Nay ka eceyq pam sinmun ul poko iss.ess.ey yo. Kulenun cwung ey khun soli lul tul.ess.ey yo.
5. Wuli ka ku yenghwa lul kwūkyeng hako iss.ey yo. Kulenun cwung ey ay ka cass.ey yo.
6. Ai tul i kāy wa kath.i nol.ass.ey yo. Kulenun cwung ey, kāy ka cic.ki sīcak hayss.ey yo.

VIII

Each of the following items contains two sentences. Combine these into a single sentence, in each of two ways: (1) Use -ci anh.ko so that it means 'didn't do this— did that instead'; (2) Use -nun tāysin ey to make it mean 'instead of doing this, [he] did that.' For example, the first will be:

(1) Na nun kongpu haci anh.ko, sānqpo lul kass.ey yo. 'I didn't study—I went for a walk.'

(2) Na nun kongpu hanun tāysin ey, sānqpo lul kass.ey yo. 'Instead of studying, I went for a walk.'

1. Na nun kongpu haci anh.ess.ey yo. Sānqpo lul kass.ey yo.
2. Kāy nun mul ul masici anh.e yo. Cic.ki man hay yo.
3. Na nun Kim sensayng ul mannaci anh.keyss.ey yo. Ku puin ul mannakeyss.ey yo. [Not necessary to use future gerund.]
4. Wuli atul i pakk ey na kaci anh.e yo. Cip ey se chayk man ilk.e yo.
5. Wuli ka yeki se sālci anh.e yo. 'Yeypay-tang(q) yeph ey iss.nun cip ey se sal.e yo.
6. Haksayng tul i cēncha lul thaci anh.keyss.ey yo. Kel.e wa to cōh.keyss.ey yo.

CONVERSATION

Plan a dinner party with a friend. Discuss the guest list and the time you will begin, and what sort of things might happen during the event. Make your conversation as real and lively as possible, and use a number of expressions like these:

I hope . . .
Let's decide to . . .
[It or they] really . . .
[He, she, they] do(es) nothing but . . .
[I or someone else] want(s) or like(s) or dislike(s) to . . .
We'll be busy . . .-ing.

VOCABULARY DRILL

I

Each word in the left-hand column has a matching word in the right-hand column of somewhat OPPOSITE MEANING. Call off the pairs one at a time, and translate them. Notice that a single word can sometimes have more than one opposite; that is why swiwe yo appears in both columns.

cīnan pom	cwuk.e yo
elyewe yo	kath.ey yo
īl hay yo	keli
keyulle yo	nac.e yo
(ayki ka) na yo	naa yo
noph.a yo	nol.a yo
pissa yo	onun pom
pyēng i na yo	pucilen hay yo
sikol	puncwu hay yo
swiwe yo	ssa yo
talle yo	swiwe yo
yēyki lul hay yo	tul.e yo

II

Here are some sentences with blank places. Say each one aloud in Korean three times, using a different expression— listed below for repetition.

1. I hope ___.
   it won't rain
   the lesson is easy
   he isn't lazy
2. I've decided to ___.
   eat a hot breakfast every morning
   study with all my might and main
   try to make a good record
3. The students are both ___.
   hard-working and lazy
   tall and short
   good and bad
4. I like to ___.
   finish my homework before class
   buy new watches
   understand the books I read
5. I'm going to try to ___.
   hand in my homework
   do nothing but sleep
   stop fooling around
6. He hates to ___.
   read books with hard words in them
   think
   go to school these days
7. I'm beginning to ___.
   do my homework
   eat my breakfast
   see the clouds
8. Do you want to ___?
   meet a nice-looking girl?
   go out for sports?
   go to a teashop with me?
9. Before I ___, I'll have to study hard.
   take the test
   graduate
   get my diploma
10. All he ever does is ___.
    give tests
    sing and dance
    look out the window

COMPREHENSION

Ask your Korean teacher to tell you about his school days. You want to know as much as he can tell you about the people in his class and their attitudes as well as his own; different schools he has attended; what he hoped for scholastically at the beginning, what he now looks forward to— anything he cares to tell you.

Listen carefully; then, among yourselves, discuss what he has said while he checks the completeness and accuracy of your comprehension.

LESSON 14. TENNIS, ANYONE?

BASIC SENTENCES

Korean	English	Amplification
1. Na nun cikum na hako kath.i wūntong halq sālam ul chac.nun cwung iey yo.	I'm looking for someone who will play (some game) with me now.	wūntong hay yo 'exercises; engages in athletics; plays (a game or sport)' wūntong halq salam 'a person who will exercise, play, etc.'
2. Yeki na hako theynisu halq sālam i iss.ey yo?	Is there anyone here who will play tennis with me?	theynisu, cengkwu 'tennis' theynisu/cengkwu (lul) hay yo 'plays tennis' theynisu halq sālam 'a person who will play tennis'
3. Wūntong-cang ey kal ttay, na l' pulusey yo.	When you go to the gym, call me.	wūntong-cang 'gymnasium' or 'playing field' ttay 'time, occasion' kal ttay 'when [you] go' (at the time you [will] go) na l' = na lul
4. Na n' elyess.ul ttay, wuli hyeng hako nul cengkwu lul hayss.ey yo.	When I was little, I played tennis with my older brother all the time.	na n' = na nun elyess.ul ttay 'when [someone] was quite young'
5. Ku ke l' cōh.a hayss.ey yo?	Did you enjoy that?	ku ke l' = ku ke lul = ku kes ul
6. Nēy. Ku ke n' caymi iss.nun wūntong ici yo.	Yes; it's (a sport that's) fun, you know.	ku ke n' = ku ke nun = ku kes un
7. Wuli hyeng i cengkwu sēnswu yess.ul ttay, na n' cengkwu sīhap ey mānh.i tanyess.ey yo.	When my brother was a tennis champion, I went to tennis matches a lot.	sēnswu 'champion' cengkwu senswu 'tennis champion' . . .iess.ul/yess.ul ttay 'when [one] was' sīhap 'game, match'
8. Cikum cengkwu-cang ey kalq ka yo??	Let's go to the tennis court now, shall we?	cengkwu-cang 'tennis court' kalq ka yo?? 'shall we go?; let's go, shall we?; how about going?'
9. Cengkwu-cang i com mel.e yo. Cacen-ke l' thako kalq ka yo, kel.e kalq ka yo.	The tennis court is a long way—shall we ride our bikes, or walk?	cacen-ke 'bicycle' cacen-ke l' = cacen-ke lul thako kalq ka yo? 'shall we go by riding? let's ride!'

Korean	English	Amplification
		kel.e kalq ka yo? 'shall we walk there? let's walk!'
10. Wuli cikum cengkwu halq ka yo!!	Let's play tennis now, shall we?	cengkwu halq ka yo!! 'shall we play tennis? how about playing tennis?'
11. Cikum pappe se, cenyek hwū ey (cengkwu lul) halq ka hay yo.	I'm busy now, so I'm thinking of playing (tennis) after supper.	pappe yo [pappu-] 'is busy' halq ka (yo) 'shall I (or we) do it?' halq ka hay yo 'is thinking of doing'
12. Cenyek hwū ey cengkwu halq swu iss.ey yo?	Can you play tennis after supper?	halq swu iss.ey yo 'can do, is able to do' cengkwu halq swu iss.ey yo? 'can you play tennis?'
13. Wūntong-cang mun ul tat.e se, cengkwu-cang ul ssulq swu ēps.ey yo.	They close the gym door, so you can't use the tennis court.	ssulq swu iss.ey yo 'can use' ssulq swu ēps.ey yo 'can't use'
14. Nal i etwuwe se, kōng ul polq swu iss.ey yo?	Won't it (the day) be too dark to see the ball? [= The day is dark, so can we see the ball?]	kōng 'ball' polq swu iss.ey yo 'can see, is able to see'
15. Yeph pang ey iss.nun Kim sensayng i cikum swīnun mo.yang iey yo. Ku pun kwa kath.i ka se hasici yo.	Miss Kim, in the next room, seems to be resting. Suppose you go with her to play.	mo.yang 'appearance' swīnun mo.yang 'the appearance of resting' swīnun mo.yang iey yo 'it is the appearance of resting; seems to be resting'
16. Āmu tāytap i ēps.ey yo. Ama ku i ka canun mo.yang ici yo!!	There isn't any answer. It looks as if she may be sleeping.	āmu . . . '[not] any . . . ; (= āmu salam) anyone' canun mo.yang 'the appearance of sleeping' . . .i 'person' (= sālam) ku i (= ku sālam) 'that person; he/him, she/her' canun mo.yang iey yo 'seems to be sleeping'
17. Ku i nun onul achim ey chwuk.kwu lul han mo.yang iey yo.	She seems to have played soccer this morning.	chwuk.kwu 'football, soccer' chwuk.kwu lul hay yo 'plays soccer' chwuk.kwu lul han mo.yang 'the appearance of having played soccer' chwuk.kwu lul han mo.yang iey yo '[it is the appearance of having played soccer=] seems to have played soccer'

Korean	English	Amplification
18. Kulena, swukcey lul tā han mo.yang iey yo.	But it looks as if she's done all her homework.	swukcey 'homework' swukcey lul han mo.yang 'the appearance of having done homework' swukcey lul han mo.yang iey yo 'seems to have done homework'
19. Tangsin un na wa kath.i cengkwu haki silh.e se, phingkyey l' hanun kes iey yo.	You don't like to play tennis with me, so you're making excuses.	phingkyey 'excuse, pretext' phingkyey l' hay yo = phingkyey lul hay yo 'makes excuses' phingkyey l(ul) hanun kes iey yo '[it is a making-excuses thing=] (one) is making excuses'
20. Wūntong haki silh.umyen, kuleh.key palo māl halq kes ici yo.	If you don't like to play, you should come right out and say so.	palo māl hay yo 'says so right (out)' māl halq kes ici yo '[it is a to-say thing=] ought to say'
21. Wūntong ul hamyen, maum i sāngkhway hay cye se, kongpu ka te cal toylq key yo.	If you exercise, your mind will get refreshed so your studying will improve.	maum 'mind, spirit' sāngkhway hay yo 'is refreshing, exhilarating' sāngkhway hay cye yo 'becomes or gets refreshed' toylq ke(y) yo = toylq kes iey yo 'will probably become' te cal toylq ke(y) yo 'will probably become better (= improve)'
22. Kuleh.ci man, i swukcey nun ˡnayil achim ey kkok pachye ya halq key yo.	(Yes,) but I'm going to have to hand in this homework tomorrow for sure.	kkok 'without fail, for sure' pachye yo 'hand over, hand in' pachye ya hay yo 'has to hand in or over' pachye ya halq ke(y) yo 'will have to hand in or over'
23. Na to kongpu halq key mānh.e yo.	I have lots of studying to do too.	(ku) key = (ku) kes i '(that) thing [AS SUBJECT]' kongpu halq key = kongpu halq kes i 'things to be studied [AS SUBJECT]'
24. Kuleh.ci man pān sikan man kōng ul chiko ku taum ey kongpu	But wouldn't it be all right if we hit the ball (back and forth)	chie yo [chi-] 'hit, strike' kōng (ul) chie yo 'hits the ball; plays ball (= any

Korean	English	Amplification
hamyen toyci anh.e yo?	for half an hour and then studied?	ball-hitting game, including tennis)'
25. Cenyek cen ey hak.kyo ey ka se, sensayng nim ul mannalq ka hay yo.	Before supper I think I'll go to school to see the teacher.	mannalq ka hay yo 'is thinking of meeting or seeing (a person)'
26. Ku taum ey n', tose-kwan ey ka se, chayk ul pillilq ka hay yo.	After that I think I'll go to the library and take out ['borrow'] a book.	ku taum ey n' = ku taum ey nun tose-kwan 'library (building)' pillye yo [pilli-] 'borrow' pillilq ka hay yo 'is thinking of borrowing'
27. Kuleh.ci man, yeses si hwū ey n', tose-kwan ey kalq swu ēps.ey yo.	But you can't go to the library after six o'clock.	yeses si hwū ey n' = yeses si hwū ey nun kalq swu ēps.ey yo 'can't go'
28. Cenyek ey n' sonayki ka ol mo.yang iey yo.	It looks as if we're going to have a shower this evening.	sona(y)ki, sonak pi 'shower, light rain' cenyek ey n' = cenyek ey nun ol mo.yang iey yo '[it is the appearance of going-to-come=] looks as if it will come'
29. Palam to pūl mo.yang iey yo.	It looks as if it's going to be windy too.	pūl mo.yang iey yo '[it is the appearance of wind going-to-blow=] seems that it will blow'
30. Ecey n' halwu congil nal i cōh.ass.ey yo.	Yesterday the weather was nice all day long.	halwu 'one day' halwu congil 'all day long, the whole day through'

SUPPLEMENTARY VOCABULARY

tosi	a city	sī-nay(q mul)	a stream
. . .-si	the city of . . .	[< sīl 'thread']	
Taykwu-si	the city of Taegu, Taegu City	kang	a river
		tāyhoy	a match, a tournament
keli	city (streets), downtown; the city (as opposed to the country)	kyēngki	contest, competition
		ˡyuksang kyēngki	field and track events
sīnay	within the city; the city proper	pingsang kyēngki	ice events
		khochwi or khochi	(athletic) coach
keli/sīnay ey na ka yo	goes down town	emphaie	umpire
		sangtay phyen/pang	the other side, the opposing side
sikol	rural area, country (as opposed to city)	thīm	team

(s)sēpisu	service (tennis/ restaurant/etc.)	sēnswu	champion; athlete
		wusung, ikim	victory
neythu, mang	net	ikye yo [iki-]	wins
yākwu	baseball	cie yo [ci-],	loses, is defeated
paykwu	volleyball	phāy hay yo	
thak.kwu, phingphong	table tennis, pingpong	ūngwen	cheering, rooting
		ūngwen (ul) hay yo	cheers, roots

NOTES

14.1. Contractions.

The topic and object particles, in their post-vowel shapes (nun and lul respectively), often drop everything but the first consonant, so that nun becomes n' and lul becomes l':

kongpu l(ul) hay yo 'studies'
cenyek ey n(un) 'in the evening'

The post-consonant shape of the object particle—ul—may drop out entirely after words ending in l, so that the expected -l ul may be pronounced simply -l:

phul (ul) kkakk.e yo 'cuts the grass'

(To be sure, the subject and object particles are freely dropped after ANY noun in fast or sloppy speech and in certain common expressions even in slower speech.)

Other common contractions involve the pronunciation of kes 'thing.' This is often reduced to ke, dropping the final s, and when this reduced form appears as topic or object, the combined contractions of noun and particle result in these pronunciations:

i ke n' 'this thing' [as topic]
i ke l' 'this thing' [as object]

Kes (reduced to ke) followed by the i shape of the subject particle or by the copula (i)ey yo often results in these contractions:

i ke + i → i key 'this thing [as subject]'
i ke + iey yo (→ i ke 'ey yo →) → i ke(y) yo 'is this thing'

We would expect ke to be followed by the shape ka, rather than i, since it ends in a vowel, but i ke ka is seldom heard. In earlier times, Koreans used the i shape of the subject particle after vowels as well as consonants, and some speakers still do this in a few expressions such as hana i tōy yo for hana ka tōy yo 'becomes one, unites.'

14.2. Prospective modifiers.

1. wūntong halq sālam 'a person who will exercise'
2. theynisu halq salam 'a person who will play tennis'

Halq in these sentences is the PROSPECTIVE MODIFIER form of hay yo. This form has the meaning 'who or which is to [do so-and-so]' or who or which is to [be so-and-so]': wūntong halq sālam is literally 'a (who-is-going-) to-exercise person' and theynisu halq sālam is 'a who-will-play-tennis person.'

The two-shape prospective modifier ending ul/-l is pronounced -ul(q) after consonants and -l(q) after vowels:

CONSONANT BASES

'wear'	ip-	ip.ul
'want to'	siph-	siph.ul
'lack'	ēps-	ēps.ul
'close it'	tat-	tat.ul
'take off'	pes-	pes.ul
'look for'	chac-	chac.ul
'eat'	mek-	mek.ul
'polish'	takk-	takk.ul
'read'	ilk-	ilk.ul
'be young'	celm-	celm.ul
'plant'	sīm-	sim.ul
'wear (shoes)'	sin-	sin.ul
'sit down'	anc-	anc.ul
'walk'	kēl-	kel.ul
'be good'	cōh-	cōh.ul
'help'	tōw-	towul
'get better'	nā(s)-	naul

VOWEL BASES

'wait for'	kitali-	kitalil
'become'	toy-	toyl
'write'	ssu-	ssul
'do like that'	kule-	kulel
'buy'	sa-	sal
'give'	cwu-	cwul
'look at'	po-	pol
'live'	sā-l-	sāl
'be far'	mē-l-	mēl
'call'	pulu-	pulul
'be blue/green'	phulu-	phulul
'take exam'	chilu-	chilul

AMBIVALENT BASES

'be like that'	kuleh-/kule-	kulel

There is also a past prospective modifier, of more limited use, formed by adding the ending -ul/-l to the past base: elye yo 'is small' → elyess.ey yo 'was small' → elyess.ul ttay 'when [one] was small.' Past prospective modifier forms of adjectives, as you see, have special uses, discussed below (‖ 14.4).

When a word that begins with p, t, c, k, or s (but not ph, th, ch, kh!) directly follows the prospective modifier with no intervening pause, the initial consonant is reinforced, i.e. pronounced double (pp, tt, cc, kk, ss). This doubling is usually ignored in the Korean spelling, since you know where to expect it if you know which words are prospective modifiers, but we have noted it in our romanization by adding a final -q after the ending: phiwul 'to smoke' + tāmpay 'cigarettes' → phiwulq tāmpay 'cigarettes [that I'm going] to smoke,' sal 'to buy' + kes 'things' → salq kes 'things [that I'm going] to buy,' kyēysil 'to be (here)' + sensayng 'teacher' → kyēysilq sensayng 'the teacher [who is going] to be here,' pūl 'to blow + palam 'wind' → pūlq palam 'the wind [which is going] to blow,' phal 'to sell' + cip 'house' → phalq cip 'the house [that we are going] to sell.'

‖ 14.3. Prospective modifier clauses.

Prospective modifier clauses—clauses ending with a prospective form—modify nouns in the same way as other modifier clauses, with one of these meaning relationships:

1. hal A 'an A which is to do something' or else 'an A which is to be done something to':
   kaluchilq sālam 'a person who is going to teach' OR 'a person whom someone is going to teach = who is going to be taught'
   mannalq sensayng 'a teacher who is going to meet [someone]' OR 'a teacher whom [someone] is going to meet'
2. A i/ka hal B 'a B which A is to do' (A is the subject of the modifying verb):
   nay ka sim.ul kkoch 'the flowers that I'm going to plant'
   Kim sensayng i halq kongpu 'the studying which Mr. Kim is to do'
3. B ul/lul hal A 'an A which is to do something to B' (B is the object of the modifying verb):
   kkoch ul sim.ulq sālam 'the person who is to plant the flowers'
4. A i/ka B ul/lul hal C 'a C where (when, etc.) A is to do B'
   nay ka kongpu lul hal hak.kyo 'the school I'm going to study at'
   col.ep hal nal 'the day we'll graduate'

More examples:

1. I īl ul halq sālam i iss.ey yo?	Is there anyone here who'll do this work?
2. Mannasilq sensayng i Hankwuk sālam iey yo?	Is the teacher you're going to see Korean?
3. Mek.ulq kes i ēps.ey yo.	We haven't got anything to eat.
4. Path ey kkoch namu lul sim.ulq sālam ul āsikeyss.ey yo?	Do you know the person who's to plant the flower trees in the garden?
5. ˡNayil achim ey Sewul lo kalq sālam i iss.ey yo?	Is there anyone here who's going to Seoul tomorrow morning?
6. I kyōsil an ey se kaluchilq sensayng uy ilum un mues iey yo.	What's the name of the teacher who is to teach in this classroom?
7. Nay ka onulq pam ey kkok hay ya halq kongpu lul tā machici mōs hayss.ey yo.	I wasn't able to finish all the studying I was supposed to do this evening.

‖ 14.4. Prospective modifier clauses with ttay 'time (when).'

The noun ttay means 'time,' and with a prospective modifier form before it, it sometimes means 'when . . . ,' as you have seen in Basic Sentence 3:

kal ttay 'when you go (or went)'

The modifier is always in the prospective form in this construction—regardless of the time meaning of the corresponding English verb.

Another meaning of this construction is 'time to do something':

Sīcak hal ttay ka wass.ey yo (or tōyss.ey yo). 'It's time to begin.'

Past prospective modifiers of descriptive verbs and the copula are used before ttay to indicate specifically past conditions that are now over, as in Basic Sentence 4 and 7:

elyess.ul ttay 'when [someone] was young'
sēnswu yess.ul ttay 'when [he] was champion'

1. Pap ul mek.ko iss.ul ttay nwu' ka wass.ey yo?	Who came when I was eating?
2. Pi ka ol ttay wūsan i iss.e ya hay yo.	You should carry an umbrella when it rains.
3. Sīnay ey na kal ttay mata, pi ka wa yo.	Every time I go downtown, it rains.
4. Ku sālam i kal ttay nun, na to kakeyss.ey yo.	When he goes, I'm going too.
5. Pak sensayng i hak.kyo ey kasil ttay, na to kath.i ka to kwaynchanh.e yo?	When you go to school, Mr. Pak, may I go with you?
6. Hānkwuk ey sāsil ttay, Hānkwuk mal ul hay ya hay yo.	When you live in Korea, you have to speak Korean.
7. Poktong-i ka ayki yess.ul ttay ku apeci ka Mikwuk ey ka se acik tol.a oci anh.ess.ci yo.	When Poktong-i was a baby, you see, his father went to America and has never come back.
8. Tōn i ēps.ess.ul ttay ilen cōh.un ūmsik ul mek.ulq swu ēps.ess.ci yo.	When I had little money I couldn't eat such fine dishes, you know.
9. Kongwen ey sānqpo kako siph.ul ttay mata pi ka onun mo.yang ici yo.	You know, every time I want to go to the park for a walk it seems to rain.

‖ 14.5. Prospective modifier clauses with the post-modifier ka.

8. kalq ka yo? 'shall we go? How about going?'
9. thako kalq ka yo? 'shall we go (riding) on . . . ?'
   kel.e kalq ka yo? 'how about walking (there)?'
10. cengkwu halq ka yo? 'how about playing tennis?'

The little word ka is a "post-modifier"—a noun that always has a modifier in front of it—with the meaning '[it's a] question [of . . .]' Prospective modifiers followed by ka yo (→ -ulq ka yo) make future questions like the future ending -keyss.ey yo? But the questions are usually directed to oneself 'shall I . . .' or 'shall we . . .' and often they are rhetorical (not expecting an answer). Sometimes they make a future suggestion—'shall we do so-and-so?' or 'how about doing so-and-so?'—which means about the same thing as suggesting 'let's do so-and-so.'

Another construction involving ka is -ulq ka hay yo, which means 'is thinking of [do]ing so-and-so,' as in Basic Sentences 11, 25, and 26:

cengkwu lul halq ka hay yo. 'I'm thinking of playing tennis.'
sensayng nim ul mannalq ka hay yo. 'I'm thinking of seeing the teacher.'
chayk ul pillilq ka hay yo. 'I'm thinking of taking out some books.'

If some esteemed person is contemplating an action you do well to use honorifics for both verbs: kasilq ka hasey yo 'he's thinking of going.'

We see that the verb hay yo besides meaning 'does' and sometimes (as an auxiliary) 'is,' also means 'thinks'; later you will find one other meaning 'says.'

You may occasionally run across the post-modifier ka after other modifiers: hanun ka yo, han ka yo. This is just another way to make questions; as compared with hay yo?, the questions made with modifier + ka yo are often rhetorical (not really expecting an answer) or addressed to oneself ('I wonder if/whether/what/who . . .').

NOTE: Some Koreans spell -ulq ka as -ulkka.

Here are some more examples:

1. Na nun nēy si ka toymyen cenyek ul mek.ulq ka hay yo.	I'm thinking of eating supper at four o'clock
2. Sim-sim hay se chinkwu lul cēnhwa lo pulle polq ka haci yo.	I'm bored, so I think I'll call a friend on the phone.
3. Hal-apeci nun noph.un namu ka phuluko museng han ku san ey kalq ka hasyess.ey yo.	Grandfather was thinking of going to that mountain, where the tall trees are green and thick.
4. Phul ul kkakk.un taum ey com swīlq ka hayss.ci man, sensayng nim i cengkwu-cang ey kasilq ka hasimyen, na to kath.i ka se kōng ul chikeyss.ey yo.	I had been thinking I'd rest a bit after mowing the lawn but if you are thinking of going to the tennis court, I wonder if I should go along with you and play some tennis?
5. Acik nuc.ci anh.ess.ci man, ˡnayil halq īl i mānh.e se incey calq ka hay yo.	It ('hasn't got' =) isn't very late yet, but I've got a lot of things to do tomorrow so I think I'll turn in (= go to bed) now.

Sometimes the reference is to someone else's actions, and the translation called for is 'I wonder whether' or 'I think that surely' or the like: Ku i ka swii olq ka hako kitalyess.ey yo 'I waited thinking he would come soon.'

‖ 14.6. Prospective modifier clauses with the post-modifier swu.

The post-modifier swu means 'case, circumstance' and swu (ka) iss.ey yo means literally 'the case exists.' But following the prospective modifier the meaning is rather 'possibility, ability.'

Expressions meaning 'can' and 'can't' are made in Korean by using one of these phrases with -ulq swu (iss.ey/ēps.ey yo). You have learned such expressions in the Basic Sentences:

12. cengkwu halq swu iss.ey yo? 'can [you] play tennis?'
13. ssulq swu ēps.ey yo 'can't use'
14. polq swu iss.ey yo? 'can [we] see?'
27. kalq swu ēps.ey yo 'can't go'

Expressions with swu (ka) ēps.ey yo correspond to one of the meanings of negative forms with mōs: kalq swu ēps.ey yo = mōs ka yo or kaci mōs hay yo 'can't go.'

Here are some more examples of this construction:

1. Onulq pam ey wuli cip ey osilq swu iss.ey yo?	Can you come to our house this evening?
2. Sensayng ul mannalq swu iss.keyss.ey yo?	Will we be able to see the teacher?
3. Hānkwuk mal ul ssulq swu ēps.ey yo.	I don't know to [= can't] write Korean.
4. Sikan i ēps.e se, kongpu halq swu ēps.ess.ey yo.	I couldn't study—I didn't have time.

5. Onul un pi ka wa se, kongwen ey se sānqpo lul halq swu ēps.ess.ey yo.
   It was raining today, so we couldn't take a walk in the park.
6. Yuli chang ey se kongwen ul polq swu ka iss.ey yo?
   Can you see the park from the windows?
7. I ^{1}yuseng-ki nun soli ka nappe se tut.ki ka elyepci yo. Talun kes ulo pakkwulq swu ka iss.umyen cōh.keyss.ey yo.
   This phonograph has such poor sound it is hard to listen to. I hope if we can trade it for a different one.

NOTE: Some Koreans spell -ulq swu as "-ulsswu."

‖ 14.7. Prospective modifier clauses with kes iey yo [→ ke(y) yo].

A prospective modifier + kes iey yo [usually shortened to ke(y) yo; cf. ‖ 14.1 above] has a PROBABLE FUTURE meaning:

21. te cal toylq ke(y) yo 'it will probably improve'
22. pachye ya halq ke(y) yo 'I'll probably have to hand it in'

This differs from future forms in -keyss.ey yo in that -keyss.ey yo expresses a DEFINITE future, or a probable PRESENT:

cōh.kessey yo 'it will be nice' or 'it's probably nice'
ūmsik-cem ey iss.keyssey yo 'he will be at the restaurant' or 'he must be [= probably is] at the restaurant'

But sometimes, especially with the copula, -ulq ke(y) yo is the equivalent of -keyss.ey yo as a probable present: Swunnam-i ape' nim un kwun.in i ani 'myen swunkyeng ilq key yo 'If Swunnan-i's father isn't a serviceman he must be a policeman.' Ku kes i Kim haksayng uy cip ani 'lq key yo 'That surely wouldn't be student Kim's house.'

Here are more examples of the probable future.

1. ^{1}Nayil un pi ka olq key yo.
   It will probably rain tomorrow.
2. Ku sālam un i pen sihem ul cal chiluci anh.umyen an toylq key yo.
   He surely ought to pass this (next) test.
3. Col.ep ul ppalli hay ya halq key yo.
   He will probably have to graduate soon.
4. Pam i toymyen chwuwulq key yo.
   I will probably be cold when night comes.
5. Pak sensayng sik.kwu nun sikol (ey) se sālko iss.ulq key yo.
   Mr. Pak's family probably will be (or are) living in the country.
6. Ama ku hal-'meni nun acik sal.e kyēysici anh.ulq key yo.
   His grandmother likely won't be alive any more.
7. Tangsin eykey nun ku sonq swuken ul pillye cwuko siph.e haci anh.ulq key yo.
   He probably won't want to lend you his handkerchief.
8. Ku sālam un ku uy emeni ka tol.a kasye se cikum āmu to manna poko siph.e haci anh.ulq key yo.
   His mother has died, so he probably won't want to see anyone just now.
9. Han sikan ccum un ku ^{n}yeca lul kitalye cwuess.e ya hayss.ulq key yo.
   We will probably have ['had to wait' =] waited for her an hour. (Or We must have waited for her an hour.)

10. Hānkwuk ūmsik ul capswu(sy)e posyess.ulq key yo. — You must have tried Korean food, sir.

As the last two examples shows, you can use the past prospective modifier with . . .key yo to make a probable future perfect ('likely will have done') or— equivalent to -ess.keyss.ey yo—a probable past ('must have done').

‖ 14.8. Modifiers with kes iey yo [→ ke(y) yo].

Any modifier can be followed by kes iey yo [usually shortened to ke(y) yo literally 'it is a thing'] to mean 'it is a fact that someone does or is . . . ':

phingkyey l' hanun kes iey yo '[it is a fact that] you're making excuses'

The prospective modifier in this construction has in addition the meaning described just above (‖ 14.7); it can also have a meaning much like that of the construction an hamyen an tōy yo: 'one ought to do,' as in Basic Sentence 20:

kuleh.key palo māl halq kes iey yo '[= to say so is the thing one does or the thing to do=] you should come right out and say so'

A processive modifier (-nun) + kes usually means 'the act of doing so-and-so' or 'the fact that one does so-and-so':

pi ka onun kes 'the fact that it's raining'
sinmun ul ilk.nun kes 'the fact that he's reading the newspaper'

[But sometimes -nun kes can have the meaning 'ought to do'; see Sentence 5 below.]

The plain modifier (-un) + kes similarly means 'the fact that one did PROCESSIVE or that it is DESCRIPTIVE':

pi ka on kes 'the fact that it rained'
tōn i mānh.un kes 'the fact that one has lots of money'

And the prospective modifier (-ul) can have similar meaning:

pi ka olq kes 'the fact that it will rain'
tōn i mānh.ulq kes 'the fact that one will have lots of money'

These expressions are used in sentences just like other noun expressions. In particular, you will find them as the object of pwa yo 'sees (that)' al.e yo 'knows that,' tul.e yo 'hears/understands that,' and similar verbs.

As the subject of swiwe yo, elyewe yo, cōh.a yo, silh.e yo and the like, modifier + kes is sometimes the equivalent of the nominative -ki (‖ 13):

Phiano chinun kes i cōh.a yo 'I like to play the piano.'
Māl hanun kes i swiwe yo. 'It is easy to talk.'

And, in addition to the various special meanings shown in this section, kes can have its usual meaning 'one, thing' after modifiers, so that ponun kes has not only the meanings 'fact of seeing, fact that one sees' and 'ought to see' and 'probably sees,' etc., but also 'the one who sees' and 'the thing [one] sees,' etc. In all its meanings, kes can always be abbreviated to ke.

Here are some examples:

1. Kim sensayng i kongwen ey se sinmun ul ilk.nun kes ul pwass.ey yo. — I saw Mr. Kim reading a newspaper in the park.
2. Pi ka onun kes ul pwa yo. — He's watching it rain.

3. Sensayng nim i Kim sensayng hako Hānkwuk mal lo yēyki hanun kes ul tul.ess.ey yo.	I heard you talking to Mr. Kim in Korean.
4. [1]Yu'-welq tal i toymyen pi ka olq kes iey yo.	When it gets to be June, it's sure to rain.
5. Yeki se tāmpay lul an phi(wu)nun kes iey yo.	You're not supposed to smoke here.
6. Ayki ka canun kes ul al.ess.ci yo.	I guess I realized that the child was sleeping.
7. Ku tāysa ka i uyca ey anc.ulq kes ici yo?	Should we have the ambassador sit here?
8. Na nun ku um.ak-ka ka toksin in kes to al.ess.ci yo.	I found out that musician is a bachelor, you see.
9. I yangsan ul cep.nun kes un mōlla to yēnun kes un al.e yo.	I don't know the way this parasol folds up, but I know how it opens.
10. I chayk kaps un emeni ka moca lul hana sanun kes uy pān pakk-ey an tōy yo.	The price of this book is no more than half what it costs mother to buy a hat.
11. [1]Nayil chwuwulq kes imyen cāngkap ul kkikeyss.ey yo.	I'll wear my gloves if it's going to be cold tomorrow.
12. Ku yēyki ka caymi iss.nun kes ie se cōh.a yo.	That story is fun; I like it.
13. Ku cip ey se wuli ay nōnun kes i silh.e yo.	I don't like my children playing at that house.
14. I ōythwu nun chwuwul ttay ip.nun kes iki ttaymun ey cikum ip.e yo.	This overcoat is for wearing when it's cold, so I am wearing it now.
15. Cōh.un kes iki ttaymun ey sass.ci yo.	It was good (<u>or</u> a good one) so I bought it, you see.
16. Thak.kwu nun caymi iss.nun kes iki ttaymun ey nul thak.kwu lul haci yo.	I always play pingpong because it's such fun, you see.
17. Ape' nim un wuli ka wūntong hanun kes ul posyess.ey yo.	Father saw us playing (at our sports).

‖ 14.9. Modifiers with <u>mo.yang</u>.

These expressions appeared in the Basic Sentences:

15. swīnun mo.yang iey yo 'seems to be resting'
16. canun mo.yang iey yo 'seems to be sleeping'
17. chwuk.kwu lul han mo.yang iey yo 'seems to have played soccer'
18. swukcey lul han mo.yang iey yo 'seems to have done [her] homework'
28. sonayki ka ol mo.yang iey yo 'looks as if it will shower'
29. pūl mo.yang iey yo 'looks as if it will blow'
30. pūl mo.yang iess.ey yo 'looked as if it would blow'

The noun <u>mo.yang</u> 'appearance' is used in expressing meaning 'seem, appear' with a modifier before it and the copula after it.

In this construction, both the modifier form and the copula can shift tense to make specific time meanings, as follows:

PRESENT COPULA

-nun: [pi ka o]nun mo.yang iey yo 'it seems to be [rain]ing'
-un/-n: [pi ka o]n mo.yang iey yo 'it seems to have [rain]ed'
[cōh.]un mo.yang iey yo 'it seems (to be) [good]'
-ul/-l: [pi ka o]l mo.yang iey yo 'it seems to be going to [rain]'
[nal i cōh.]ul mo.yang iey yo 'it seems as if the [weather] will be [good]'

PAST COPULA

-nun: [pi ka o]nun mo.yang iess.ey yo 'it seemed to be [rain]ing'
-un/-n: [pi ka o]n mo.yang iess.ey yo 'it seemed to have [rain]ed'
[cōh.]un mo.yang iess.ey yo 'it seemed (to be) [good]'
-ul/-l: [pi ka o]l mo.yang iess.ey yo 'it seemed as if it would [rain]'
[nal i cōh.]ul mo.yang iess.ey yo 'it seemed as if [the weather] would be [good]'

FUTURE COPULA

-nun: [pi ka o]nun mo.yang ikeyss.ey yo 'it will seem to be [rain]ing' or 'it must seem to be [rain]ing'
-un/-n: [pi ka o]n mo.yang ikeyss.ey yo 'it will seem to have [rain]ed' or 'it must seem to have [rain]ed'
[cōh.]un mo.yangikeyss.ey yo 'it will seem (to be) [good]' or 'it must seem (to be) [good]'
-ul/-l: [pi ka o]l mo.yang ikeyss.ey yo 'it will seem to be going to [rain]' or 'it must seem to be going to [rain]'
[cōh.]ul mo.yang ikeyss.ey yo 'it will seem to be going to be [good]' or 'it must seem to be going to be [good].'

More examples:

1. Eceyq pam nwūn i on mo.yang iey yo.	It looks as if it snowed last night.
2. Hay ka na onun mo.yang iey yo.	The sun seems to be coming out.
3. Pi ka tto ol mo.yang iey yo?	Does it look as though it's going to rain some more?
4. Mikwuk salam i iss.nun mo.yang ici yo!!	It looks as if there are some Americans here, doesn't it?
5. Onul un pappun mo.yang iey yo.	He seems to be busy today.
6. Pak sensayng puin un ^{1}nayil osil mo.yang iey yo?	Does it look as if Mrs. Pak will get here tomorrow?
7. Kim sensayng isin mo.yang iess.ey yo.	It looked like Mr. Kim. [It seemed to be Mr. Kim.]
8. Ku kāy ka koki ka mek.ko siph.un mo.yang imyen cwusey yo.	If the dog seems to want (to eat) some meat, give it to him.
9. Ku ^{n}yeca nun nai ka acik mānh.ci anh.un mo.yang imyen se (to) elin ay tul i mānh.e yo.	While she still seems not very old, she has a lot of children.
10. Tōn i ēps.nun mo.yang ie se tōn ul pillici mos hayss.ey yo.	He seemed to have no money so we couldn't borrow any from him.

11. Acwumeni nun ku kum panci lul sasye ya hal mo.yang ikeyss.ci yo?	Do you think it will seem as though Auntie has to buy the gold ring?
12. Sangtay phyen i ikil mo.yang ici man te ũngwen hakeyss.ey yo.	The other side seems to be going to win, but we will root some more (for our side).
13. Ape' nim kkey tulimyen cōh.a hasil mo.yang iki to haci man emeni eykey tulikeyss.ey yo.	It really looks as though Father would like for us to give it to him, but let's give it to Mother.
14. Hay ka nal mo.yang ie ya keli ey na kakeyss.ey yo.	I won't go to town unless it seems as though the sun will be out.
15. Son nim i ilccik tol.a kasici anh.ul mo.yang iki ttaymun ey, mence cass.ey yo.	I took a nap first, because it seems the guests will not go home early.
16. Pelsse enni nun sīnay ey na kan mo.yang ici yo?	Does it seem as though my older brother has already gone to town, do you suppose?
17. Nwū' nim un acik kyelhon hako siph.ci anh.un mo.yang ie se cikum to īl hako kyēysici yo.	My older sister is now working, apparently not wanting to get married yet, you see.
18. Kapang i mukewul mo.yang ıey yo?	Does the briefcase (or bag) seem heavy?
19. I kes ul ku kes ulo pakkwuci mōs hal mo.yang ici yo.	It looks as though we won't be able to trade this for that.
20. Sōk ey tun kes i kapyepci anh.un mo.yang iess.ey yo.	It seemed that what was inside was not light (in weight).
21. Elyewun mūncey 'n mo.yang iey yo.	It seems to be a difficult problem.

EXERCISES

I

Each of the following items contains two sentences. Combine the sentences with a prospective modifier; then translate the combined sentence. For example, the first will be: <u>Wuli ka sālq cip un sikol ey iss.ey yo</u>. 'The house where we're going to live is in the country.'

1. Wuli ka ku cip ey se sālkeyss.ey yo. Ku cip un sikol ey iss.ey yo.
2. Nay ka phyēnci lul ssukeyss.ey yo. Ku phyēnci ka mānh.e yo.
3. Kim sensayng i [1]naynyen hak.kyo ey se kaluchikeyss.ey yo. Ku hak.kyo lul āsikeyss.ey yo?
4. Onulq cenyek ey wuli ka ūmsik ul mek.keyss.ey yo. Ku ūmsik un Hānkwuk ūmsik ikeyss.ci yo!!
5. Wuli atul i chinkwu hanthey cēnhwa lul kēlkeyss.ey yo. Ku chinkwu nun Pak moksa atul ici yo.
6. Ku āy ka [1]nayil say kwutwu lul sin.keyss.ey yo. Ku kwutwu nun Mikwuk se on kes iey yo.
7. Ku sālam i [1]nayil achim Cang sensayng ul mannakeyss.ey yo. Ku sālam un Mikwuk se on senkyo-sa 'ci yo?
8. Onulq pam ey ku yūmyeng han sengak-ka ka nolay lul pulukeyss.ey yo. Ku nolay nun musun nolay 'lq ka? [nolay 'lq = nolay ilq]

9. ^{1}Nayil son nim i okeyss.ey yo. Ku son nim un hal-apeci chinkwu 'keyss.ci yo.
10. Nay ka ku tose-kwan ey se ku chayk ul pillikeyss.ey yo. Ku tose-kwan un wuli cip ey se cham kakkapci yo.

II

Each of the following items contains two sentences, the second of which begins with Ku ttay 'at that time.' Link the two sentences with -ul ttay so that the meaning of the combined sentence is 'When . . . .' Then translate. For example, the first will be: Wuli ka nolay lul pulul ttay, kāy to pulless.ey yo. 'When we sang, the dog sang too.' Remember to use past prospective modifiers for descriptive verbs, when appropriate. Otherwise use the simple prospective modifier -ul/-l. But don't forget to add the -(q) where appropriate; in other words, in pronouncing the combined sentence, don't forget to double any p, t, c, k, or s that follows the prospective modifier.

1. Wuli ka nolay lul pulless.ey yo. Ku ttay kāy to pulless.ey yo.
2. Tangsin tul i ^{1}yuseng-ki um.ak ul tut.keyss.ey yo. Ku ttay, wuli lul pulle cwusey yo.
3. Wuli ka Mikwuk se sal.ess.ey yo. Ku ttay Hānkwuk ūmsik ul mek.ulq swu ēps.ess.ey yo.
4. Ku yenghwa ka wuli tosi ey okeyss.ci yo. Ku ttay wuli ka kwūkyeng kalq ka yo??
5. Nay ka Kim sensayng ul chac.ess.ey yo. Ku ttay Kim sensayng i cip ey an kyēysyess.ey yo.
6. Sensayng i ku māl ul kaluchisyess.ey yo. Ku ttay tangsin i tut.ci anh.ess.ci yo??
7. Pumo ka celm.usyess.ey yo. Ku ttay um.ak-hoy ey cal kasyess.ey yo.
8. Kāy ka cic.e yo. Ku ttay ayki ka calq swu ēps.ey yo.
9. Wuli ka tōn i mānh.ess.ey yo. Ku ttay, āmu īl to an hayss.ey yo.
10. ^{1}Naynyen tōn i cēk.keyss.ey yo. Ku ttay nun, achim mata ilcciki il.e na se īl ul ka ya hakeyss.ey yo.
11. Wuli ka ku Hānkwuk nolay lul pulless.ey yo. Ku ttay, ai tul i cham cōh.a hayss.ey yo.

III

Each of the following sentences means 'someone will do (or did) something.' Change the sentence so that it means 'someone is (or was) thinking of doing something.' Then translate. For example, the first will be: Nay ka ku mun ul tat.ulq ka hay yo. 'I'm thinking of closing that door.'

1. Nay ka ku mun ul tat.keyss.ey yo.
2. Nay ka i kwutwu lul takk.keyss.ey yo.
3. Ku ai ka ku ippun moca lul ssukeyss.ey yo.
4. Nay ka ce uyca ey anc.keyss.ey yo.
5. Sensayng nim i ku chinkwu lul kitalisikeyss.ey yo? [Better to make hay yo honorific also!]
6. Nay ka com swīkeyss.ey yo.
7. Nay ka tāmpay lul phi(w)ess.ey yo.
8. Wuli ka ilkop si pān ey cass.ey yo.
9. Nay ka cip ey se na kass.ey yo.

10. Kim sensayng i ku sōsel chayk ul pwass.ey yo.
11. Nay ka chang ul yēlkeyss.ey yo.

IV

Each of the following sentences means either 'someone does (or did) something' or 'someone doesn't (or didn't) do something.' Change each so that it means either 'someone can (or could) do something' or 'someone can't (or couldn't) do something.' Then translate the sentence. For example, the first will be: Ku āy ka yenphil ul kkakk.ulq swu ēps.ess.ey yo. 'The child wasn't able to sharpen the pencil.'

1. Ku āy ka yenphil ul kkakk.ci mōs hayss.ey yo.
2. Hānkwuk ey se to Mikwuk ūmsik ul mek.e yo?
3. Wuli sensayng i Yenge lul kaluchye yo?
4. Hānkwuk mal ul Mikwuk yenphil lo to sse yo.
5. Nay ka Hānkwuk ey se sal ttay, tōn ul mānh.i mōs ssess.ey yo.
6. Hak.kyo ey nun cēncha lul thako kaci anh.e yo.
7. Nay ka ayki hanthey ūmsik ul cwuci mōs hayss.ey yo.
8. Ai tul i ce kongwen ey se nōlkeyss.ci yo.
9. Wuli ka sensayng ul cēnhwa lo pulle yo.
10. Ecey nun nay ka hak.kyo ey oci anh.ess.ey yo.
11. Wuli ka apeci hanthey cēnhwa lul kēlci mōs hayss.ey yo.

V

Each of the following sentences means 'something does (is), did (was), or will do (will be) something.' Change each so that it means 'It seems . . . .' Then translate the sentence. For example, the first will be: Pi ka ol mo.yang iey yo. 'It seems that (or looks as if) it's going to rain.'

1. Pi ka okeyss.ey yo.
2. Wuli ka canun sai ey totwuk nom i tul.e wass.ey yo.
3. Cikum pakk ey nwūn i wa yo.
4. Ku sālam un tōn i mānh.e yo.
5. Kim sensayng cip i cāk.ci anh.e yo.
6. Ku yenghwa-kwan i mel.e yo.
7. Yeyil tāyhak i cham khuci yo??
8. Hal-ape' nim i pelsse cip ey se na kasyess.ey yo.
9. [1]Nayil Yun sensayng i kaluchikeyss.ci yo.
10. Ecey chac.e on sālam i ku pyengceng iey yo.
11. Payk sensayng i say cacen-ke lul kacyess.ey yo.

CONVERSATION

1. Pair off and practice conversing in Korean about making an arrangement to play tennis together. Settle on a day and hour (this might require several questions-and-answers, false starts, since both of you are busy people who have many other things to do); then arrange where you will meet, how you will get there, how long you will play, and what you will do afterward.

2. Change pairs, and discuss X when you are sure he can't overhear you. Talk about his tennis playing as compared with his ability at other sports; whether

he is a good team man; whether he is ever likely to become a champion at anything; what you saw him doing at the gym the other day and what you overheard him saying to Y; whether he is neglecting his studies for sports; and so on. Since it is all in fun, feel free to exaggerate your opinions.

3. Tell your fellow students, in a monologue, what you are thinking of doing next year. Plan the monologue out in advance and go into detail so that your exposition will consume 3 to 5 minutes of reasonably steady talking; you might make notes in English (or Korean) to help you remember what you want to say, but don't write the Korean sentences out.

VOCABULARY DRILL

Say each of the following sentences in Korean three times, filling in the blanks each time with a different item from among those listed.

1. It looks as if ___.
   Mr. Kim has gone to play volleyball
   that student plays soccer very well
   there will be a tennis tournament in Seoul next year
2. It doesn't matter whether ___.
   we win or lose
   we cheer for this team or that team
   we play baseball or pingpong
3. That person over there is the one who's going to ___.
   do homework all day long
   play volleyball with our team
   be(come) our baseball coach
4. He looks as if he can't ___.
   hit the ball
   ride a bicycle very well
   play soccer with us
5. I went to the gym a lot ___.
   when I was in school
   when I was young
   when I lived in Seoul
6. Can you ___ tomorrow?
   watch the pingpong tournament with me
   take out some books from the library
   hand in your homework

COMPREHENSION

Listen while your Korean teacher talks to you about sports. He may tell you about sports he has engaged in himself; or the athletic program at his university; or sports on the national scene in Korea; or anything else he chooses. The chances are he will occasionally use words and expressions you don't know yet, but see how much of his talk you can grasp. After he has finished, he will discuss what he has said with you in Korean, asking you questions to see how well you are following him.

LESSON 15. REVIEW

I. VOCABULARY REVIEW

Here are 20 groups of words and phrases. Either individually, or as a group in class, make up 20 Korean sentences, each of which uses all the words of one of the groups (the first, for example, will use tul.e yo, ^{l}yuseng-ki, and tose-kwan). Put the verbs into any form you like, and make the sentences as long as you like, putting in any additional words you may need. When you have finished you will have made up 400 different sentences.

1. tul.e yo
^{l}yuseng-ki
tose-kwan
2. kum
un
kaps
3. ttus
al.e yo
mōlla yo
4. keyulle yo
kacang cōh.a yo
ca yo
5. phiano pancwu
sengak-ka
tokchang
6. machye yo
hwū ey
sōsel chayk
7. pyēng
pala yo
naa yo
8. yelqsim ulo
swukcey
pachye yo
9. sikyey
pissa yo
totwuk nom
10. namu
phulule yo
noph.a yo
11. talk
swii
al
12. sihem
swiwe yo
elyewe yo
13. tong-an
caymi iss.ey yo
yēyki
14. wūntong-cang
cengkwu-cang
cen ey
15. cali
kukcang
kyohyang-ak
16. sēnswu
āy lul sse yo
yūmyeng hay yo
17. san
sikol
pōy yo
18. kath.ey yo
tosi
talle yo
19. ^{l}yoli-cem
ssa yo
tāysin ey
20. pucilen hay yo
tanye yo
cemqswu

II. VERB REVIEW

Say the following sentences aloud in Korean three times, completing them in each of the ways indicated.

1. Mr. Kim took ___ to the violin recital.
   his mother
   his son
   a book

2. Mr. Pak is ___.
   a good man
   the man who's drinking tea
   the one we saw at the tennis match yesterday

3. Have you ever ___?
   worn a blue shirt
   heard Mrs. Kim sing
   listened to my record player

4. I'll play tennis with you ___.
   before I study
   after I go to the library
   when I've finished my homework

5. The chicken ___.
   got sick
   got well
   laid an egg

6. Will you bring ___ to the gym?
   the children
   the balls
   the teacher

7. ___ learn to play tennis well.
   I hope to
   I can't
   I've decided to

8. Shall we ___?
   dance
   go there on our bicycles
   have some tea at this tea-shop

9. How about chatting a little ___?
   before we eat
   while we walk to the soccer match
   after we finish our homework

10. I can't ___ very well.
    write with a pen
    ride a bicycle
    play pingpong

11. It looks as if ___.
    she's asleep
    he can't find it
    our team is going to lose

12. I never ___.
    go to the movies
    ride in taxis
    drink tea

13. He does nothing but ___.
    make excuses
    borrow pencils
    play tennis all day

14. Here comes the man who ___.
    is going to be the umpire
    will finish this job
    is going to wear that coat

15. I read that novel ___.
    when I lived in Korea
    when I was young
    while I was riding on the train

16. I'm busy ___.
    doing my homework
    learning to write Korean
    shaving

17. This book seems to be ___.
    the same as that one
    very interesting
    expensive

18. Can you ___?
    see the bank from here
    play tennis with me before dinner
    go to the store with me after breakfast

19. I saw Mr. Kim ___.
    going to school
    writing words in his notebook
    looking out the window

20. I've decided to wear my new ___.
    shoes
    hat
    suit

21. Where should we hang ___?
    this picture
    our overcoats
    our hats

22. This textbook really is ___.
    interesting
    heavy
    hard to read

23. I hope ___.
    the briefcase is light
    there are lots of stars
    we can trade our old car for a new one

III. KOREAN-ENGLISH SENTENCE REVIEW

Translate the following Korean sentences into English. After you finish each one, make up another Korean sentence on the same pattern.

1. Eceyq pam wuli wa kath.i cenyek pap ul capswusin pun i apeci 'ey yo.
2. Pissan sikyey to ssan sikyey to cōh.a yo.
3. Pi ka on kkatalk ulo say kwutwu lul sin.ulq swu ēps.ess.ci yo.
4. Pānghak ie se [1]nayil cip ey kalq key yo.
5. Nay yeph ey anc.ulq sālam i wa yo. ['Here comes . . .']
6. Tangsin i sinmun ul ilk.nun tong-an (ey), na nun swukcey lul machikeyss.ey yo.
7. Tangsin i māl han kes ul tut.ci mōs hayss.ey yo.
8. Ūmsik-cem ey se mek.nun tāysin ey, onul un cip ey se mek.keyss.ey yo.
9. Kim sensayng taum ey anc.un sālam i yūmyeng han umak-ka 'ci yo.
10. Sinmun ey se ilk.ki ey nun, cōh.un nal-ssi ka toylq key yo.
11. Wuli path ey kkoch ul sim.un sālam i tto Kim sensayng uy path ey to sim.ess.ey yo.
12. Yuli chang ey se nun noph.un cip to polq swu iss.ko, nac.un cip to polq swu iss.ey yo.
13. Tapang ey kath.i ka se, cha com masilq ka yo?
14. Pam ey nwūn i on mo.yang iey yo.
15. Ileh.key noph.un san ul posin īl i iss.ey yo?
16. Latio lul com tut.ci yo. Tut.ki nun tut.ci man tut.ki sil.he yo.
17. Wūntong-cang ey iss.ess.ul ttay, haksayng tul i wūntong ul hanun kes ul pwass.ey yo.
18. Na nun i īl ul ppalli machiko siph.e yo. Tte nasiki cen ey, towa cwusilq swu iss.usey yo?
19. Phyēnci lul māyil wuphyen-kwuk ey kaciko kanun sālam i iss.ey yo.
20. Ecey cenyek ul mek.ko iss.ul ttay son nim i osyess.ey yo.
21. Nemu chwuwun nal ie se cip ey iss.keyss.ci yo.
22. [1]Naynyen ey tāyhak ul col.ep haki ey āy sse pokeyss.ey yo.
23. Ilpon mal un cal ilk.ulq swu ēps.ci man, Cwungkwuk mal un com ilk.ulq swu iss.ey yo.
24. Ku ai ka mek.ulq swu to (ēps.umyen se) calq swu to ēps.ey yo.
25. Wuli ka cengkwu lul chinun tong-an ey pi ka oki sīcak hass.ey yo.
26. Wuli thīm i [1]nayil chwuk.kwu sīhap ey ikiki lul pala yo.
27. Achim cwung nemu pappess.ki ttaymun ey, unhayng ey kalq sikan i ēps.ess.ey yo.
28. Um.ak-hoy ey kel.e kanun tāysin ey catong-cha lul pululq ka yo?
29. Ku sangcem ey pissan os to iss.ko, ssan os to iss.ey yo.
30. Tangsin uy sayngkak ey nun, i twūl i kath.ci yo? Ani yo?? Talle yo.
31. Wuli eykey Yenge lul kaluchye cwusinun pun i Kim sensayng (eykey) to kaluchye tulye yo.

32. Unhayng ey mence ka ya mulken ul salq swu iss.ci anh.e yo?
33. Ku sālam un kyeyuluci nun anh.ci man, pucilen haci to anh.e yo.
34. Achim ul mek.ul ttay 'n mo.yang iey yo.
35. Pak haksayng uy [l]yuseng-ki lul tul.usilq swu iss.ey yo?
36. Ku [n]yeca nun nolay puluki lul cōh.a haci to anh.ko, phiano chiki to cōh.a haci anh.e yo.
37. Eceyq pam ey, Kim sensayng i cacen-ke lul thanun kes ul pwass.ey yo.
38. Pap ul mek.un hwū ey kanun tāysin ey cikum yenghwa kwūkyeng ul kalq ka yo?
39. Eceyq pam pon yenghwa nun cōh.ci anhess.ey yo.
40. Cham caymi iss.nun yēyki yess.ci yo?
41. Ileh.key caymi iss.nun yēyki lul tul.usin il i iss.ey yo?
42. Eceyq pam ey latio lo tul.un nolay lul han sālam i yūmyeng han sengak-ka 'ey'yo.
43. Phingkyey man hasinun mo.yang iey yo.
44. Palam pūnun kes ul tul.ulq swu iss.ey yo?
45. Ce sensayng nim twī ey anc.un sālam i nwukwu 'ey yo.
46. Eceyq pam [l]yoli-cem ey se cenyek ul mek.nun tong-an Kim sensayng ul pwass.ey yo.
47. Nay ka sako siph.un yangpok un tāytan hi pissa yo.
48. [l]Nayil kkaci kitalinun tāysin ey, way cikum swukcey lul haci anh.e yo.
49. Yengkwuk ey ka pon īl un ēps.ci man Mikwuk ey ka pon īl i iss.ey yo.
50. Na nun Mikwuk se nass.ci man elyess.ul ttay Hānkwuk ey wass.ey yo.

IV. ENGLISH-KOREAN SENTENCE REVIEW

Express the following sentences aloud in Korean. Your tutor will help you improve on your wording whenever it seems to need it.

1. I suppose the books in this store are pretty expensive?
2. Do you know Mr. Kim's aunt who lives in Pusan?
3. I've never been this sick before.
4. Can you see the tall green trees on that far-off mountain?
5. He told me a story, but I didn't understand it.
6. How about playing tennis with me?
7. I've decided not to go out this evening.
8. The food we had last night was delicious.
9. You do nothing but eat!
10. People who live in Korea eat a lot of rice.
11. He plays baseball well, and also plays the piano well.
12. The house in back of ours is blue.
13. You like music, don't you?—Of course!
14. Before we go play soccer, let's rest a little.
15. Did you see the man who went into that low building over there?
16. I don't like to study, but I have to if I want to get good marks.
17. It's exam time, so I can't fool around these days.
18. I don't like days when it's raining.
19. What are you planning to do after you graduate from high school?
20. I'm sorry you got sick and couldn't go to the concert last night.
21. Did the burglar who stole your watch get away by the gate?
22. Who's that man standing in front of the bank?
23. It looks as if it's beginning to snow.

24. How about talking to me while you eat?
25. What kind of weather do you like?—I like sunny days and I also like cloudy days.
26. Whose textbook is that on the chair?
27. Do you like to take walks in the rain (= while it's raining)?
28. This bookshop is nice and big, isn't it?
29. In my opinion, this is a very cheap dress.
30. It looks as if we won't have time to finish our game before it gets dark.
31. They hit tennis balls back and forth while I was doing my homework.
32. If you'd like, you may bring a friend to the soccer game with you.
33. I hope our team will win the soccer game!
34. See that man? He's a famous novel writer.
35. The movie theater is so far from here that I think we'd better take a taxi.
36. My brother plays tennis well and studies hard too.
37. We'd better take a taxi so we can get home before it rains.
38. I hope to learn to play tennis next year.
39. I'm doing my best to finish reading this book before it's time to go to bed.
40. I can read English, but I can't read Russian.
41. You're going to the tennis court? You do nothing but go to the tennis court all the time!
42. My mother promised to bring me a new blue dress.
43. Do you ever have breakfast in bed?
44. It looked like rain, so I decided not to go downtown.
45. According to what I read in the papers, the famous singer is sick and can't come to our school tomorrow.
46. Why don't you read this book?—I DID read it, but I didn't understand it.
47. Instead of getting sunny, it turned cloudy.
48. That student has a fine attitude, but he seems to be lazy.
49. You must hate having to get up so early in the morning, don't you?
50. It snowed while we were asleep.

V. TEST

Your Korean tutor will read the following passage aloud to you, while you listen attentively with your book closed. After he has read the passage once, he will pause and then read it again. Now he will ask you some questions about it to see whether you have followed.

Nōlki man han nal

Onul un, palam un com pūlci man, nal-ssi ka cōh.ass.ki ey sik.kwu ka tā kath.i sikol ey ka se nol.ass.ey yo. Wuli nun sik.kwu ka mānh.ki ttaymun ey apeci catong-cha lo man kalq swu ka ēps.e se, acessi uy khun cha lul pillye se kass.ey yo. Catong-cha lul thako kanun tong-an ey wuli nun nolay to hako yēyki to hay se caymi iss.ess.ey yo. Wuli ka kan kos ey nun khuko cōh.un namu ka mānh.ki nun hayss.ci man sālam tul i mānh.ess.ey yo. Kulay se, wuli nun swuph sōk ulo tul.e ka se phul to sī'-nayq mul to iss.nun kos ey se nōlki lo hayss.ey yo.

Emeni wa apeci ka ūmsik ul mayntusinun tong-an ey, na nun hyeng nim kwa tongsayng tul kwa kath.i kōng ul chiko nol.ass.ey yo. Nwū' nim un wūntong hanun kes ul cōh.a haci anh.nun mo.yang ulo ayki tongsayng kwa nōlko iss.ess.ey yo. Com nōnun tong-an ey Pok.nam-i ka poici anh.e se chac.e pwass.ey yo. Ku āy nun swuph sōk ey se sāy ka nah.un al ul kaciko na wa se wuli nun tā kippe hayss.ey yo.

Pap ul mek.un hwū ey wuli nun twū phyen ulo nanwe chwuk.kwu lul hayss.ey yo. Na nun wuli phyen i ikiki lul palass.ci man sangtay phyen uy hyeng nim i nemu cal hasinun kkatalk ulo wuli ka ciess.ey yo. Kulay to apeci nun māl-ssum hasiki lul "Hyeng to cal hayss.ci man tongsayng to cal hayss.ci" hasyess.ey yo. Wuli ka nōnun tong-an ey ayki nun cam man cass.ey yo.

Nēy si pān i tōy se, cip ey tol.a kal ttay ka tōyss.ey yo. Tol.a onun kil ey, apeci wa nwūna wa ayki pakk-ey nun tā tāytan hi phikon hayss.ey yo. Ayki wa nwūna nun wūntong haci anh.e se phikon haci anh.un mo.yang iey yo. Nwūna nun yēyki halq sālam i ēp.se se sim-sim hayss.ulq key yo.

Cip ey tol.a wa se, mok.yok ul hako cenyek ul cokum mek.ko latio lul tul.ess.ey yo. [1]Nayil un pi ka ol mo.yang iey yo. Kulena, chang ulo nun pyēl man poici yo. Onul pi ka oci anh.un kes i cōh.ass.ci yo. Tongsayng tul un tā pelsse caci yo. Na to calq ka yo?? Caki cen ey [1]nayil sensayng nim kkey tulilq swukcey lul machiko siph.ess.ci man, nemu cako siph.e se [1]nayil tulici anh.ki lo hayss.ey yo. Cikum kongpu an hanun tāysin ey [1]nayil yelqsim ulo kongpu hakeyss.ey yo.

Cen ey chinkwu tul kwa sikol ey ka se nol.a pon īl un mānh.ess.ci man, onul i kacang caymi iss.ess.ey yo.

If there is time, your tutor will prepare and read you other, similar passages, and ask you questions about them. This will test your ability to follow a Korean when he tells a story.

LESSON 16. AROUND THE HOUSE

BASIC SENTENCES

Korean	English	Amplification
1. Pap hal ttay, nay ka tōpci yo.	Let me help you when you get the meal.	pap (ul) hay yo 'prepares a meal'
2. Cang pole kal ttay, na hako kath.i ka yo.	When you go shopping, go with me.	cang (ul) pwa yo 'does the marketing' [cf. īl ul pwa yo 'takes care of the work'] pole '(goes/comes) for the purpose of looking (<u>or</u> taking care of, doing)' cang pole ka yo 'goes marketing'
3. Cang ey kata ka wuphyen-kwuk ey tullilq ka yo??	When we go to the market, shall we stop in at the post office?	kata ka 'while going . . .' [action broken into by another action] tullye yo [tulli-] <u>or</u> tulle yo [tullu-] 'stops in, drops by'
4. Cang ey kass.ta ka wuphyen-kwuk ey tullilq ka yo??	Shall we go to the market and then drop by the post office?	kass.ta ka 'after going; go, and then . . .'
5. Cang ey kass.ta wuphyen-kwuk ey kass.ta hay se, cenyek i nuc.e cimyen etteh.key hay yo.	What will we do if dinner gets late because of our going to the market and to the post office and so on?	. . . ey kass.ta (ka) . . . ey kass.ta (ka) hay yo 'keeps going to [do] . . . and to [do] . . .' etteh.key 'how; how come, why' etteh.key hay yo '[does how=] does what'
6. Cham kuleh.kwun yo.	Why, that's true.	kuleh.kwun 'it's so! it's like that (I suddenly realize)!'
7. Wuphyen-kwuk ey nun, onul kaci mālci yo.	Suppose we don't go to the post office today.	
8. Cenyek hal ttay ka tōyss.ey yo?	Is it time to get dinner?	. . .-ulq ttay ka tōyss.ey yo? 'has it become time to . . . ?'
9. Cenyek hal ttay ka acik an tōyss.ey yo.	It's not time to get dinner yet.	

Korean	English	Amplification
10. Kulen tey, onul achim ey eti kass.ta osyess.ey yo.	By the way, where have you been this morning?	kass.ta osyess.ey yo? '[have you gone and then come back?=] have you been (there)?'
11. I ka aphe se, chiq-kwa ey kass.ta, sangcem ey tullyess.ta, chinkwu uy cip ey kass.ta wass.ey yo.	I had a toothache, so I went to the dentist's; and I dropped in at the store; and I went to a friend's house.	i, iq-pal 'tooth' aphe yo [aphu-] 'is painful, hur chiq-kwa 'dentistry; (= ~ uywen) dentist's office' kass.ta (ka) . . . 'went, and then . . .' tullyess.ta (ka) . . . 'dropped in, and then . . .' kass.ta (ka) wass.ey yo 'went, and then came [home]'
12. I hana ka nul aphess.ta kwaynchanh.ess.ta hay yo.	One of my teeth keeps aching off and on.	aphess.ta (ka) kwaynchanh.ess.ta (ka) 'alternatively hurts and is all right'
13. Ku uysa nun i lul ppop.ul mo.yang iess.ta, an ppop.ul mo.yang iess.ta hay se, na nun etteh.key halq cwul (ul) molukeyss.ey yo.	The doctor keeps acting as if he were going to pull the tooth and then acting as if he weren't going to pull it, so I don't know what to do.	ppop.a yo 'pulls, draws' ppop.ul mo.yang iess.ta (ka) an ppop.ul mo.yang iess.ta (ka) hay yo 'by turns seems as if he will pull and seems as if he will not pull' halq cwul 'way of doing; how (what) to do' etteh.key halq cwul '[how=] what to do'
14. Ku uysa nun etten ttay nun chincel hayss.ta (ka), etten ttay nun pul-chincel hayss.ta (ka) hay yo.	The doctor is sometimes kind and sometimes unkind.	etten ttay 'certain times, sometimes' chincel hay yo 'is kind, considerate' chincel hayss.ta (ka) 'is kind, and then (after that) . . .' pul-chincel hay yo 'is unkind, inconsiderate' pul-chincel hayss.ta (ka) 'is unkind, and then (after that) . . .' chincel hayss.ta (ka) pul-chincel hayss.ta (ka) hay yo 'changes off being kind and unkind'
15. Pap hata (ka), mues ul hasey yo.	What do you do while you're getting a meal?	pap hata (ka) 'while (in the mid dle of) getting a meal . . . [another action takes place]'

Korean	English	Amplification
16. Pap hata chayk ilk.umyen pap i cal an tōy yo.	If you read while you're getting a meal, the meal doesn't turn out well.	pap hata chayk ilk.e yo 'reads a book while (interrupting the action of) getting a meal'
17. Na nun han pen pap hata chayk ul ilkess.ta ka, pap i tha se mōs mek.ess.ey yo.	I once read a book while I was getting a meal, and the food burned so we couldn't eat it.	chayk ilk.ess.ta (ka) 'while (in the middle of) reading a book [something interrupted]' tha yo 'it burns, gets burned'
18. Tayk ey se nun nwu' ka pap ul hay yo.	Who gets the meals at your house?	
19. Emeni kkey se hay cwusey yo.	Mother does it for us.	
20. Ku tāysin, panu' cil un nay ka hay ('ta) tulye yo.	Instead of that [getting meals], I do the sewing for her.	panul 'needle' panu' cil 'sewing, needlework' panu' cil hay yo 'sews, does sewing' panu' cil hay tulye yo <u>or</u> panu' cil hay 'ta (ka) tulye yo 'does sewing for someone (somewhere else)'
21. Sang ul com pwa cwusey yo.	Please set the table (for me).	sang ul pwa yo 'sets the table; looks after the table, waits on the table'
22. Nēy. Sang pwa tulici yo.	Yes, let me set the table (for you).	
23. I kulus tul to ssis.e tulilq ka yo??	Shall I wash these dishes for you too?	kulus 'dish' ssis.e yo 'washes'
24. Ani yo?? Ku kes un nay ttal i ssis.e cwue yo.	No, my daughter will do those for me.	
25. Tta' nim i pelsse selkeci lul halq cwul al.e yo?	Does your daughter already know how to do dishes?	selkeci 'dishwashing; cleaning up after a meal' selkeci (lul) hay yo 'washes dishes, does dishwashing' selkeci (lul) halq cwul 'way of washing dishes, how to wash dishes'
26. Ālko mālko yo. Ūmsik to halq cwul al.e yo.	Of course she knows. She even knows how to prepare food.	. . .-ko mālko yo <u>or</u> . . .-kwu mālkwu yo 'of course . . .!' ūmsik (ul) hay yo 'prepares food'

Korean	English	Amplification
		ūmsik halq cwul 'how to prepare food'
27. Sōcey to halq cwul ālko, ppallay to halq cwul al.e yo.	She also knows how to clean the house, and how to do the laundry, too.	sōcey 'housecleaning' sōcey (lul) hay yo 'cleans house, does housecleaning' ppallay 'laundry' [to be washed]; laundering' ppallay (lul) hay yo 'launders, does laundry, washes clothes'
28a. Cham sinthong hay yo.	Why, that's wonderful!	sinthong hay yo 'is marvelous, wonderful'
28b. Wuli ttal un acik āmu kes to halq cwul mōlla yo.	My daughter doesn't know how to do a thing.	āmu kes to mōlla yo 'doesn't know anything at all' āmu kes to halq cwul 'the way to do anything (at all)'
28c. Malwu to ssulq cwul moluko, kulus to ssis.ulq cwul moluci yo.	She doesn't know how to sweep the floor, nor to wash the dishes, either.	patak 'ground, bottom' (malwuq) patak, malwu 'floor' patak ul <u>or</u> malwu lul ssul.e y [ssu-l-] 'sweeps the floor' pang ul ssul.e yo 'sweeps the room'
29. I kes i kimchi 'n ka yo? Kulay yo.	Is this kimchi? Yes.	kimchi 'pickled vegetables, Korean pickles'
30. I namul ul et'ta (ka) noh.usey yo.	Where shall I put this salad?	eti (ey) 'ta (ka), et'ta (ka) '(over) to where' namul 'salad, dressed greens' noh.a yo 'puts, sets, places'
31. Kimchi yeph ey ('ta) noh.usey yo.	Put it beside the kimchi.	yeph ey ('ta) '(over) to the side' noh.usey yo 'please put'
32. I kwuk un kac'ta (ka) pap ol(h.)un phyen ey noh.a cwusey yo.	Take this soup and put it to the right of the rice.	kwuk 'soup' kacye 'ta (ka), kac'ta (ka) 'takes, and then . . .'
33. I cak.un swuce nun nwukwu uy kes in ka yo.	Whose are these little spoon and chopsticks?	swuce 'set (= place setting) of spoon and chopsticks' nwukwu uy kes in ka yo = nwukwu uy kes iey yo 'whose (thing) is it'

Korean	English	Amplification
34. I swuce nun ileh.key cak.e se mues ey ('ta) sse yo.	These spoon and chopsticks are so small, what are they used for?	mues ey ('ta) '[toward=] for what'
35. Ku kes un wuli aykiq kes ici yo.	They're the baby's.	ayki uy kes, aykiq kes 'the baby's things; baby things'
36. Onulq cenyek ey son nim i meych pun osina yo.	How many guests are coming this evening?	osina yo = osey yo? 'are they coming?'
37. Son nim i osimyen, elma 'na olay kyēysina yo.	When the guests come, how long will they stay?	olay yo [olay-] 'is long (in duration)' kil.e yo [kī-l-] 'is long (in space or time)' olay, olayq tong-an 'for a long time' kyēysina yo = kyēysey yo 'do they stay'
38. I chang pakk ul nāy 'ta posey yo.	Look out the window.	nāy ('ta) pwa yo 'looks out'
39a. Hanul ul chye 'ta poci mālko, hayng-kil ul naylye 'ta posey yo.	Don't look up at the sky, look down at the street.	hanul 'sky, heaven' chye 'ta pwa yo 'looks at, looks up at' hayng-kil = han-kil '[big road=] the street' naylye yo [nayli-] 'descend, go down' naylye ('ta) pwa yo 'looks down'
39b. Son nim tul i pelsse osey yo.	The guests are already coming.	
40. Son nim tul i yeph cip tam ul cakkwu nemkye 'ta pwa yo.	The guests keep looking across the wall of the next house.	tam 'wall' (exterior) cakkwu 'continuously, repeatedly; keep [do]ing' nemkye yo [nemki-] 'put [something] over <u>or</u> across nemkye ('ta) pwa yo 'looks over <u>or</u> across'
41. Cikum un tāymun ul tul.ye 'ta pwa yo.	Now they're peeking in the front gate.	tāymun 'entrance gate, front gate' tul.ye yo [tul.i-] 'lets it in' tul.ye ('ta) pwa yo 'looks in, peeks in'
42. O o! Ku cip ttul uy kkoch ul ponun kwun yo.	Oh! Why, they're looking at the flowers in the garden at that house!	ttul 'garden' ponun kwun yo '[I realize] they're looking!'

SUPPLEMENTARY VOCABULARY

swuq-kalak, swuq-kal, swu'l [but usually spelled swut-kal(ak)]	spoon
ceq-kal(ak), ce'l, ce	chopsticks
ceq-kalak cil	using chopsticks
achim(q pap) or copan	breakfast
cemsim(q pap)	lunch
cenyek (pap)	dinner, supper
ppang	bread
(p)pethe or (p)pathe or ppata or (p)patha	butter
wuyu or milkhu	(cow's) milk
khulīm	cream
selthang	sugar
(khulīm/selthang ul) chie yo [chi-]	puts in, adds (cream/sugar)
neh.e yo	puts in(side), inserts
tul.e yo [tu-l-]	lifts it up; holds, has; partakes, drinks, eats [also enters; costs—see Lesson 8]
khephi	coffee
hong-cha	black tea
um.lyo-swu	drinking water
kkulh.in mul	boiled water
kkulh.ye yo [kkulh.i-]	boils it
kkulh.e yo [kkulh-]	it boils
kkul.e yo [kku-l-]	drags it, pulls it
kwuk (mul)	(Korean) soup, broth
kwukswu	noodles
mantwu	meat-stuffed bun
kan-cang	soy sauce
pap; cīnci [HONORIFIC]	cooked rice, food
ssal	grain, hulled (but uncooked) rice
pye	rice plants, unhulled rice
ttek	rice cake
pipimq pap	rice hash (cooked rice with other things in it)
panchan	dishes served to go with the rice, side dishes
kwuwun koki	sliced beef broiled with seasoning in oil and soy sauce
sān-cek	egg-dipped shish kebab
so	ox, cow, cattle
so koki, so (u)y koki	beef
twāyci or to.yaci	pig, hog
twāyci koki	pork
talk [pronounced /tak/]	chicken
talk koki [pronounced /takkoki/]	chicken (meat)
kamca	potatoes
hō-pak	squash
... cēn	fried
hō-pak cēn	fried squash
pul	fire; light
pul ul khie yo [khi- (often spelled khye-)]	turns on the lights
pul ul kke yo [kku-]	turns off the lights
kawi	scissors
sīl	thread, yarn
caypong-thul	sewing machine
kkun, no-kkun	string
kwutwu kkun	shoe string(s), laces
kkunh.e yo	breaks it, snaps it (in two)
kkunh.e cye yo	it breaks, snaps in two
kkay-ttulye yo	breaks (smashes, shatters) it
kkāy-cye yo	it breaks (smashes, shatters)
pus(w)e yo [pus(w)u-], pus(w)e ttulye yo	breaks (crumbles, demolishes) it
pus(w)e cye yo	it breaks (crumbles, is demolished)
ttel.e ttulye yo	drops it
ttel.e cye yo	it drops
kayksil	guest room
chīmsil	bed room
menci	dust

NOTES

16.1. Ways to say 'when.'

There are a number of Korean expressions that translate English 'when, while' in various shades of meaning. You have learned these:

-umyen [conditional] 'when, whenever, if':
pi ka omyen . . . 'when(ever) it rains . . .'
-umyen se 'when or while . . .' [simultaneously, by the same subject]:
pap ul mek.umyen se . . . 'while I eat, I . . .'
-ul ttay 'when, at the time that . . .':
ku sālam i ol ttay . . . 'when he gets here . . .'
celm.ess.ul ttay 'when I was young . . .'

-nun { sai / cwung / tong-an } ey 'when or while (in the midst of) . . .'

chayk ul ilk.nun sai [etc.] ey . . . 'while (in the middle of) reading a book . . .'

Compare also gerunds, and infinitives with se, which sometimes have 'when'-like meanings:

hay se . . . 'does, and then . . .' or 'does, so . . .'
hako . . . 'does, and (also) . . .'

Still another 'when, while' expression is described in the following section.

16.2. Verbs: transferentive form: -ta (ka)

3. Cang ey kata ka wuphyen-kwuk ey tullilq ka yo?? 'When we go to the market, shall we stop in at the post office?'
4. Cang ey kass.ta ka, wuphyen-kwuk ey tullilq ka yo? 'Shall we go to the market and then drop by the post office?'
5. Cang ey kass.ta wuphyen-kwuk ey kass.ta hay se, cenyek i nuc.e cimyen etteh.key hay yo? 'What will we do if dinner gets late because of our going to the market and (going) to the post office and so on?'
10. . . .eti kass.ta osyess.ey yo. '. . . where have you been?'
11. . . .chiq-kwa ey kass.ta, sangcem ey tullyess.ta, chinkwu uy cip ey kass.ta wass.ey yo. '. . . I went to the dentist's and I dropped in at the store, and I went to a friend's house (and came home).'
12. I hana ka nul aphess.ta kwaynchanh.ess.ta hay yo. 'One of my teeth keeps aching off and on.'
13. Ku uysa nun i lul ppop.ul mo.yang iess.ta, an ppop.ul mo.yang iess.ta hay se . . . 'The doctor keeps acting as if he were going to pull the tooth and then acting as if he weren't, so . . .'
14. . . .etten ttay nun chincel hayss.ta (ka), etten ttay nun pul-chincel hayss.ta (ka) hay yo. '. . .is sometimes kind and (is) sometimes unkind.'
15. Pap hata (ka) mues ul hasey yo. 'What do you do while you're getting a meal?'
16. Pap hata chayk ilk.umyen, . . . 'If you read while you're getting a meal . . .'
17. Na nun han pen pap hata chayk ilkess.ta (ka), pap i tha se . . . 'I once read a book while I was getting a meal, and the food burned . . .'

Transferentive verb forms, with the ending -ta (optionally followed by ka), indicate a shift in action: either of the verb action itself, or of its direction, or of the recipient of its benefit.

Attached to a verb base, the ending makes the form mean 'WHEN so-and-so happens . . .'; this is followed by another action which interrupts or shifts the trend of the first, so that it is discontinued in favor of the second. (It is not clear from the construction alone whether the interruption is later resumed.) This kind of meaning is illustrated in Basic Sentences 3, 15, 16 and 17 (hata).

Attached to a past base, to make a past transferentive form -ess.ta (ka), the ending conveys the meaning 'when so-and-so has happened . . . ' and the following verb tells of something contradictory or unanticipated that happened right after the action of the past transferentive form. This meaning is illustrated in Basic Sentence 4, 10, 11, and 17 (ilk.ess.ta ka).

Another construction involving transferentive forms employs two such forms, of opposite or contrasting meaning— either present or, more commonly, past— rounded off by a form of hay yo. This construction means that the two actions keep interrupting each other.

For example:

Sālam i wass.ta kass.ta hay yo. 'People keep coming and going.'

Tal un han tal mata khe {cita ka / cyess.ta ka} cak.e {cita ka / cyess.ta ka} hay yo.

'The moon waxes and wanes each month'— 'The moon gets big and gets small each month.'

This construction appears in Basic Sentences 5, 12, 13, and 14.

It is important not to confuse the past-tense transferentive form kass.ta (ka) 'went, and then . . .' with the abbreviation kac'ta (ka) < kacye 'ta (ka) 'carry and then (shift)' as seen in Basic Sentence 32:

I kwuk un kac'ta ka pap ol(h.)un phyen ey noh.a cwusey yo. 'Take this soup and put it to the right of the rice.'

This verb form conveys the meaning 'take and shift (the position of). Kac'ta cwusipsio means 'Please bring it to me,' a useful expression when ordering food in a restaurant.

The transferentive form iss.ta (ka) 'stays and then' has the additional meaning 'in a little while' or 'later on'; in this meaning it is often spelled itta (ka).

Here are more examples of transferentive forms.

1. Pakk ey com na kass.ta osey yo.	Go outside a while (and then come back).
2. Wuphyen-kwuk ey ota ka ku sālam ul mannass.ey yo.	I met him on my way [= while coming] to the post office.
3. Sangcem ey kass.ta wass.ey yo.	I've been to the store. (I went to the store and then came back.)
4. Wuli ayki nun eceyq pam ey cenyek ul mekta ka cass.ey yo.	The baby fell asleep while he was eating his dinner last night.
5. Kass.ta ka palo osey yo.	Come right back!
6. Kel.e kata ka, phikon hay se, cēncha lul thass.ey yo.	While I was walking, I got tired and got on a streetcar.
7. Sālam i tul.e wass.ta na kass.ta hay yo.	People keep coming in and going out.
8. Ssan kes ul sass.ta ka, pissan kes ulo pakkwess.ey yo.	I bought a cheap one but I exchanged it for an expensive one.
9. Com iss.ta ka cenyek ul mek.keyss.ey yo.	I'll eat supper in a little while. (I'll wait a while and then eat supper.)
10. Ku swuce lul tul.ess.ta noh.ass.ta haci mal.e yo.	Stop picking up and putting down your spoon and chopsticks.
11. Pi ka ota mālta hay yo.	It rains off and on. (It keeps raining and then stopping.)

The last example shows that you use the auxiliary mā-l- 'desist' (put after suspective -ci to make negative commands and suggestions) when you want to use a negative instead of some completely different second verb. An example with the present transferentive: Pi ka ota (ka) mal.ess.ey yo 'It started to rain and then stopped.'

‖ 16.3. The copula transferentive: special uses.

20. Ku tāysin, panu' cil un nay ka hay ('ta) tulye yo. 'Instead, I do the sewing for her.'
34. . . . mues ey ('ta) sse yo. '. . . what are they used for?'
38. I chang pakk ul nāy 'ta posey yo. 'Look out the window.'
39. Hanul ul chye 'ta poci mālko . . . 'Don't look up at the sky . . .'
40. Son nim tul i yeph cip tam ul cakkwu nemkye 'ta pwa yo. 'The guests keep looking across the wall of the next house.'
41. Cikum un tāymun ulo tul.ye 'ta pwa yo. 'Now they're peeking in the front gate.'

There is a special use of the transferentive copula ita (always pronounced 'ta here because it follows infinitives, which end in vowels). It is inserted into verb phrases, between the infinitive and its following verb, where the last verb is cwue yo (tulye yo) 'does for someone,' noh.a yo 'puts somewhere; does in advance, does for later,' pwa yo 'looks (in some direction),' or the like. Note the special use of -e noh.a yo to mean 'does for later (use or benefit), does now (so that the result will be ready),' in which noh.a yo 'puts' is used as an auxiliary. The 'ta (which can be followed by ka) shows that there is a shift in the direction of the action (as looking toward something), or in the recipient of the benefit (as in favors). In phrases with cwue yo or tulye yo 'does for someone' the 'ta (ka) indicates that the favor is done either in a different place from where the recipient is, or else after the elapse of a considerable length of time: there is thus a shift in either space, or time, often both. These are typical 'ta phrases:

chayk ul sa 'ta cwue/tulye yo 'buys a book for someone'
kacye 'ta cwue yo > kac'ta cwue yo 'brings it to someone' (= kacye wa yo)
kyouy lul kkul.e 'ta noh.a yo 'pulls up a chair (to sit on)'
pap ul hay 'ta noh.a yo 'gets dinner ready (so we can eat)'
phyo lul sa 'ta noh.keyss.ey yo 'will buy the tickets in advance'
tul.ye 'ta pwa yo 'looks in'
nāy 'ta pwa yo 'looks out'

The copula transferentive is also used after the particle ey to show a shift of location or purpose:

sang wi (ey) 'ta noh.a yo 'puts it on the table'
congi wi ey 'ta sse yo 'writes on the paper'
Mues ey 'ta sse yo. 'What do you use it for?'

A special contraction is eti (ey)'ta > et'ta 'where to?' The particle ey, as you have seen, often drops after front vowels (i, ey, ay).

You have seen these forms in Basic Sentences 30 and 31:

30. I namul ul eti 'ta (ka) noh.ulq ka yo. or I namul ul et'ta (ka) noh.ulq ka yo. 'Where shall I put this salad?'

31. Kimchi yeph ey ('ta) noh.usey yo. 'Put it beside the kimchi.'

In all these uses the copula transferentive is optional; that is, you can freely leave the 'ta out, and the meaning will be much the same but without the emphasis on SHIFT.

‖ 16.4. Apperceptive sentences.

6. Cham kuleh.kwun yo. 'Why, that's true!'
42. O o! Ku cip ttul uy kkoch ul ponun kwun yo. 'Oh! Why, they're looking at the flowers in the garden at that house!'

The apperceptive marker kwun yo (or kwumen yo) is attached as an ending to the bases of descriptive verbs (adjectives) [and of iss-, ēps-] as well as to all past and future bases:

iss.kwun yo (iss.kwumen yo) 'Why, there's . . . !'
ēps.kwu(me)n yo 'Well—there isn't . . . !'
hayss.kwu(me)n yo 'Why, he did . . . !'
hakeyss.kwu(me)n yo 'Well! He's going to . . .'

With processive verb bases, the marker is used not as an ending; rather, it comes after the processive modifier form as a post-modifier.

Tal ul ponun kwu(me)n yo! 'What do you know! They're looking at the moon!'

This marker adds a surprised note to the sentences where it occurs; typical English equivalents are 'Well, I'll be . . . !' or 'Well, what do you know . . . ', or simply 'Why!' (as an exclamation). It shows a sudden realization: 'Oh, I see!,' 'Now I realize . . . .'

Here are some more examples:

1. Onulq pam pyēl i cham manh.kwun yo.	My, what a lot of stars are out tonight.
2. I yuli chang i kkāy-cyess.kwun yo.	I see this window's broken.
3. O! Swuq-kalak ul ttel.e ttulyess. kwun yo.	Oh, I've dropped my spoon.
4. Ppang i pus(w)e cinun kwun yo.	The bread crumbles, I see.
5. Sīl ul kkunh.usikeyss.kwun yo.	I see you're going to snap the thread.
6. Sāy cip i namu ey se ttel.e cyess.kwun yo.	The bird house has fallen from the tree, I see.
7. Os i elin ay hanthey cak.e cyess.kwun yo.	I see the child has outgrown his clothes!
8. Ku kwutwu ka Poktong-i hanthey nemu khukwun yo.	Why, those shoes are too big for you, Poktong-i!

‖ 16.5. Prospective modifiers with cwul.

13. . . . etteh.key halq cwul (ul) molukeyss.ey yo. 'I don't know what to do.'
25. . . . selkeci lul halq cwul al.e yo? 'Does she know how to wash dishes?'
26. . . . Ūmsik to halq cwul al.e yo. 'She knows how to cook, too.'
27. . . . ppallay to halq cwul al.e yo. 'She also knows how to do laundry.'
28. . . . āmu kes to halq cwul mōlla yo. 'She doesn't know how to do anything.'

The noun cwul means 'assumed fact; presumption.' When it has a prospective modifier in front of it and al.e yo (mōlla yo) after it, the expressions means 'knows (doesn't know) how to . . .' Here are some more examples:

Pusan ey honca kalq cwul ul mōlla yo. 'He doesn't know how to get to Pusan by himself.'

Hānkwuk mal ul ilk.ulq cwul āsey yo? 'Do you know how to read Korean?'

Ceq-kalak ulo mek.ulq cwul mōlla yo. 'We don't know how to eat with chopsticks.'

Yenphil lo ssulq cwul mōlla yo? 'Don't you know how to write with a pencil?'

Notice that this construction is often translated by English 'can' (or 'can't): I can eat with chopsticks, I can't speak Japanese, etc. This means that English 'can(not)' has three separate equivalents in Korean:

1. can = it is possible:
   ūmsik ul halq swu iss.ey yo (ēps.ey yo) 'can (can't) cook'
2. can = knows how to:
   Hānkwuk mal ilk.ulq cwul al.e yo (mōlla yo) 'can (can't) read Korean'
3. can = has permission to:
   yenghwa ey ka to cōh.a yo (cōh.ci anh.e yo) 'can (can't) go to the movies'

‖ 16.6. Polite style questions: complex type 1 (. . .ka yo).

29. I kes i kimchi 'n ka yo? 'Is this kimchi?'
33. . . . nwukwu uy kes in ka yo. 'Whose are they?'

A special way of asking questions in the polite style—with the same meaning as the simple way—is to use ka preceded by a modifier, instead of the regular form used at the end of sentences. This is more commonly done with descriptive verbs and the copula:

Cōh.un ka yo? 'Is it nice?'
Mēn ka yo? 'Is it far?'
Chayk in ka yo? 'Is it a book?'

However, you will occasionally hear a processive verb used the same way:

Kongpu hanun ka yo? 'Is he studying?'

For future, you can use -ulq ka yo: Kongpu halq ka yo? 'Is he going to study?' But that more commonly has the meaning 'shall we . . . ?' or 'how about?,'— 'Shall we study?' This use appears also in Basic Sentences 3, 4, and 23 of this lesson.

There are special FUTURE PROCESSIVE and PAST PROCESSIVE modifiers -keyss.nun and -ess.nun that are limited to positions before certain postmodifiers only: ka, ya (‖ 19.3), ci (‖ 21.1), tey (‖ 21.5), and ke l' (‖ 22.9).

To say 'Have you eaten?' you can say Mek.un ka yo?, but Mek.ess.nun ka yo? is more common, and still more common is Mek.ess.na yo? (explained in the next section). Similarly, to say 'Will you eat?' you can say Mek.ulq ka yo?, but Mek.keyss.nun ka yo? is more common (for that meaning), and still more common is Mek.keyss.na yo? The expression -ulq ka yo often suggests PROBABLE present or future, especially with descriptive verbs (or with iss.ey yo, ēps.ey yo): Chwuwulq ka yo? 'Is it (likely to be) cold?' NOTE: There is some question whether anyone actually uses such forms as (?) Mek.un ka yo? so the student would do well to avoid them. Some speakers apparently will not use . . . ka yo? for questions about the second person ('you'), preferring sentences with . . . -na yo? instead.

1. Sensayng i eti kass.ta osyess.nun ka yo.	Where has the teacher been?
2. Pak sensayng ul manna polq swu ka iss.ulq ka yo?	Shall I be able to see Mr. Park?
3. Cikum kongpu hanun ka yo?	Are they studying now?

4. Ku catong-cha ka ppalun ka yo?	Is that car fast?
5. Ku cengkwu-cang ey neythu ka iss.nun ka yo?	Is there a net in that tennis court?
6. Cang i kakkawulq ka yo?	Is the market (probably) near?
7. Cenyek ey mek.ulq so koki ka mānh.un ka yo?	Is there plenty of beef for supper?
8. Seki ka acik sāmu-sil ey iss.ulq ka yo?	Would the secretary still be in the office?
9. Pānghak tong-an ey nun hak.kyo ey haksayng i ēps.nun ka yo?	Aren't there any students in the school during the vacation?
10. Chāyso path ey hō-pak i ēps.ulq ka yo?	Isn't there any squash in the vegetable garden?
11. Khulīm ul chie tulilq ka yo?	Would you like cream (in your coffee/tea)?
12. Mues ul com tusilq ka yo?	Will you have something (to eat/drink)?
13. Wuyu lul han can tu(si)lq ka yo?	Let's have a glass of milk.

16.7. Polite style questions: complex type 2 (-na yo).

36. Onulq cenyek ey son nim i meych pun osina yo. 'How many guests are coming tonight?'

37. Son nim i osimyen, elma 'na olay kyēysina yo. 'When the guests come, how long will they stay?'

Polite questions of a second complex type are more common with processive than with descriptive verbs. This second type uses the ending -na (followed by yo to end the sentence), which is attached to bases of processive verbs and of iss- '(there) is' and ēps- '(there) isn't' as well as to past and future bases of all verbs. A convenient rule to follow with complex questions is to use the ka type questions described in the preceding section with present descriptive verbs only (except, of course, when you want to use a processive verb in the construction 'shall we . . . ?') and the -na type described here with processive verbs and with past and future bases of both descriptive and processive verbs. Actually, in Seoul, the simple type of polite question is used more commonly than any of these; the form is the same as for statements: -e yo, etc.

Here are some more examples of complex questions with -na yo:

1. Ku sālam un māyilq pam ona yo?	Does he come here (= Is he here) every night?
2. ^{1}Nayil swukcey lul pachikeyss.na yo?	Are you going to turn in your homework tomorrow?
3. Nay ka sensayng nim cali ey anc.e iss.na yo?	Am I sitting in your seat?
4. Ku tosi ey nun kotung hak.kyo ka ēps.na yo?	Isn't there any high school in that city?
5. Ku um.ak-ka ka yēncwu hanun kes ul myech pen ina pwass.na yo.	How many times have you seen that musician play?
6. Yetel(p)q si pan imyen nuc.ci anh.keyss.na yo?	Won't 8:30 be (too) late?
7. Nwu' ka i kulus ul ssis.keyss.na yo.	Who will wash these dishes?
8. Ku ^{n}yeca ka phulun os ul ip.ess.na yo?	Did she wear a blue dress?

9. Ka ya halq kos un unhayng iess.na yo?	Was the place you had to go the bank?
10. Ku ttay Poktong-i ka acik elyess.na yo?	Was Poktong-i still quite young at that time?
11. Ecey yākwu lul hasye se, phal i aphusina yo?	Is your arm hurting because you played baseball yesterday?
12. I pang i māl-ssum hasin secay 'na yo?	Is this the study you have spoken about?
13. Sensayng nim (uy) ape' nim un chwunchwu ka meych isina yo.	How old is your father?

As the last three examples show, you MAY run into -na yo with descriptive verbs and the copula in the present, despite our rule of thumb.

‖ 16.8. Uses of pwa yo.

The ordinary meaning of pwa yo is 'looks at'; it can also mean 'sees': Poko iss.ess.ey yo—Pwass.ey yo 'I was looking at it—I saw it' (compare Chac.ko iss.ess.ey yo—Chac.ess.ey yo 'I was looking for it—I found it'). But when you say sālam ul pwa yo it means either 'looks AT a person' or 'looks AFTER a person' (so that ayki ponun i 'the one who looks after the baby' is, of course, a baby-sitter); to say 'sees a person (to talk to etc.)' you use the expression sālam ul manna yo 'meets a person' or sālam ul manna pwa yo 'meets a person (to see him).' For sang ul pwa yo 'looks after the table' (in some contexts it could mean 'looks AT the table') the translation may be either 'sets the table' (at home) or 'waits on the table' (in a restaurant or the like). Cang pwa yo 'looks after the market(ing)' means 'does the marketing (grocery-shopping)'; īl ul (or sāmu lul) pwa yo 'looks after the work' means 'takes care of the work' or 'does one's work.' Caymi (lul) pwa yo means either 'has a good time' or (to a shopkeeper) 'has good (profitable) business.' When you leave a shop you often say Caymi posipsio! or Caymi posey yo! for your goodbye; and when someone is leaving for something enjoyable you say the same thing as a parting greeting: 'Have a good time!'

And don't forget that -e pwa yo (‖ 8.11.1) means 'does to see (how it will be) = tries doing': Mul.e posipsio 'Ask and see.' Ka popsita 'Let's go and try (or see) it.' Hānkwuk ūmsik ul mek.e pwass.ey yo? 'Did you try (eating) Korean food?' Ku kūlim ul yeki ('ta) kel.e polq ka yo? 'Let's try hanging the picture here.' Ce tam ul puswe ttulye pomyen etteh.keyss.ey yo 'How about trying to tear down that wall over there?'

EXERCISES

I

The connective expression kuleta (ka) means 'while doing that, in the meantime (something unanticipated interrupts).' In each of the following items there are two sentences, the second of which begins with Kuleta ka. Make the two sentences into one by using the ordinary transferentive form; then translate. For example, the first will be: Sensayng i kaluchita ka chang ul yel.e yo. 'The teacher is teaching and stops to open the window.' or 'While the teacher is teaching, he opens the window.'

1. Sensayng i kaluchye yo. Kuleta ka, chang ul yel.e yo.

2. Nay ka tanchwu han kay lul chac.ko iss.ess.ey yo. Kuleta ka, ttel.e cin tōn ul pwass.ey yo. [iss.ess.ey yo → iss.ta ka]
3. Na nun Ilpon mal ul paywess.ey yo. Kuleta ka, Hānkwuk mal ul paywuki sīcak hayss.ey yo.
4. Kim sensayng i hak.kyo ey wa yo. Kuleta ka, sinmun ul sass.ey yo.
5. Kim sensayng i kongpu hay yo. Kuleta ka, latio lul tul.e yo.
6. [1]Yu sensayng uy Hānkwuk yēyki lul tul.ess.ey yo. Kuleta ka, na nun kōhyang sayngkak ul hayss.ey yo.
7. Nay ka moca lul kel.ess.ey yo ['hung it up']. Kuleta ka, moca ey menci ka mānh.un kes ul pwass.ey yo.
8. Kwutwu lul sin.ess.ey yo. Kuleta ka, kwutwu kkun ul kkunh.ess.ey yo.
9. Na nun os ul pes.ess.ey yo. Kuleta ka, ānkyeng ul kkay-ttulyess.ey yo.
10. Kicha lul thass.ey yo. Kuleta ka, Kim sensayng ul mannass.ey yo.
11. Onul achim il.e nass.ey yo. Kuleta ka, Kim sensayng sayngkak ul hako, ku pun hanthey cēnhwa lul kel.ess.ey yo.
12. Ānkyeng ul takk.ess.ey yo. Kuleta ka, ttel.e ttulyess.ey yo.

II

The connective expression kulayss.ta (ka) means 'did that and then, after that; then (something contrary or unanticipated happens).' In each of the following items there are two sentences, the second of which begins with Kulayss.ta ka. Combine the two sentences by using the PAST TRANSFERENTIVE form (-ess.ta ka); then translate. For example, the first will be: Wuphyen-kwuk ey kass.ta ka, unhayng ey kass.ey yo. 'I went to the post office and then I went to the bank.'

1. Wuphyen-kwuk ey kass.ey yo. Kulayss.ta ka, unhayng ey kass.ey yo.
2. Na nun cāngkap ul kkiess.ey yo. Kulayss.ta ka, nal i tewe se ku kes ul pes.ess.ey yo.
3. Pissan moca lul sass.ey yo. Kulayss.ta ka, ssan moca lo pakkwess.ey yo.
4. Kim sensayng i wuli cip ey osyess.ey yo. Kulayss.ta ka, [1]Yu sensayng uy cip ey kasyess.ey yo.
5. Na nun ku chayk ul ilk.ess.ey yo. Kulayss.ta ka, nemu caymi ka iss.e se, pam ey an cass.ey yo.
6. Onul achim [1]yeypay-tang ey kass.ey yo. Kulayss.ta ka, ōhwu twū si ey tol.a wass.ey yo.
7. Na nun Cwungkwuk ūmsik ul mek.ess.ey yo. Kulayss.ta ka, ūmsik i cōh.ci anh.e se, mōs cass.ey yo.
8. Chinkwu lul chac.ess.ey yo. Kulayss.ta ka, chinkwu ka ēps.e se, honca tapang ey ka se cha lul masyess.ey yo.
9. Kayksil ey ku kūlim ul kel.ess.ey yo. Kulayss.ta ka, ku kes i nemu khe se, chīmsil ey kel.ess.ey yo.
10. Na nun ku ōythu lul ip.ess.ey yo. Kulayss.ta ka, ku ōythwu ka nemu mukewe se, pes.ess.ey yo.
11. Achim ey nal i chwuwess.ey yo. Kulayss.ta ka, ōhwu ey tewe cyess.ey yo.

III

The following sentences are simple questions in the polite style. Rephrase them in the more complex way of making polite-style questions; then translate.

1. Atu' nim i acik to elye yo?
2. Onul nal i chwuwe yo?

3. Ku i ka cikum ca yo?
4. Kulay, Kim sensayng i Pak sensayng ul mannass.ey yo?
5. Tayku ['Taegu'] ka yeki se mel.e yo?
6. Kim puin i ku ōythu lul sakeyss.ey yo?
7. Ku um.ak-hoy ka caymi iss.keyss.ey yo?
8. Ku ūmsik i nappess.ey yo?
9. Poktong-i ka cikum kongwen ey se nōlko iss.ey yo?
10. Tta' nim i [1]Ihwa Tāyhak ey kako siph.e hay yo?
11. Nay ka onulq cenyek ey yenghwa-kwan ey ka to cōh.a yo?

CONVERSATION

I

By pairs, assume the role of a couple of Korean housewives who are chatting while they ought to be working. Compare notes on when you go shopping and do errands; what time you start dinner; what your husband does if dinner is late, or burned; what you are going to have tonight, and whether or not you have prepared it; any particular rewards or punishments you might feel are a part of the housewife's lot. Toss in a little gossip about the neighbors: whose daughters do things to help around the house and which ones do nothing.

II

Prepare a brief monolog describing one of your busy days—one that involved a lot of running around seeing people, doing errands at various places of business, keeping appointments with doctors or dentists, and so on. Make it sound so harried that your listeners can hardly wait for their turn to tell what a busy day THEY had.

III

Describe an imaginary visit to the dentist. Tell how you put off going by first doing this and that (shopping, going to the post office, buying a newspaper and then dropping in at a tea-shop to have a cup of tea while reading it, dropping in at a friend's, etc.), and then finally went. Tell how many people you saw waiting when you peeked in the door, and how long you had to sit and wait for the dentist ('doctor'). What did you do while waiting? (Read magazines? Look out the window? Play with someone's baby?) When the dentist saw you, what did you tell him? Did he show uncertainty about pulling your tooth or not? Was he alternately gentle and rough? Did he make an unpleasant noise? How long did you have to stay? Did he tell you to come back? When? What did you do after you left the dentist's? Were you glad it was over? Would you like to pull people's teeth? How often do you go to the dentist? Do people who brush their teeth all the time have good teeth? Do people who drink milk have good teeth?

VOCABULARY DRILL

Say the following sentences aloud in Korean, completing them in each of the ways indicated.

1. This evening we're going to have ___ for dinner.
   salad
   meat dumplings
   noodles
   beef
   rice

2. Yesterday while I was ___ (-ta ka) I got sick.
   doing some sewing
   washing the dishes
   doing the laundry
   getting dinner
   cleaning the house

3. Will you put the ___ on the table?
   spoons
   soy sauce
   squash
   rice cakes
   chopsticks

4. That man keeps ___.
   looking up(ward) and down(ward)
   eating rice and drinking tea (alternately)
   going out and coming in (again)
   reading and (then) writing in his notebook
   looking out the door and looking out the window

5. Did you have ___ or ___ for lunch?
   chicken—pork
   soup—tea
   bread—rice
   pickles—squash
   rice hash—broiled beef

COMPREHENSION

Let your Korean teacher describe typical daily activities of various kinds of people, while you listen attentively. He may begin with something like: Na nun han sālam ul al.e yo; ku sālam un . . . He may tell about what a housewife does, or a teacher, or a student, or a clerk in an office, or something else. Each time he describes the activities of a person, be prepared to tell him when he finishes what sort of person he has been describing. Then be prepared to converse with him about what he has said: he may ask you why you came to the conclusion you did, what other things such a person might do, specific questions about what he has told you.

LESSON 17. A VISIT FROM A MISSIONARY

BASIC SENTENCES

Korean	English	Amplification
1. Annyeng hasip.nikka? Pok.nam-i emeni 'sip.nikka?	Good morning. Are you Pok.nam-i's mother?	Pok.nam [a boy's name] + -i [suffix added to children's names ending in consonants] = 'little Pok.nam, Pok.nam-i' (i)sip.nikka 'is [someone esteemed] . . . ?' [FORMAL]
2. Nēy. Kuleh.sup.nita. Nwukwu 'sip.nikka.	Yes, I am. Who are you?	kuleh.sup.nita 'that is so, it is like that' [FORMAL] (-h.s- → /-ss-/)
3. Ce nun i tōngney Kam.li-kyo 'yeypay-tang moksa 'p.nita.	I'm the pastor of the Methodist Church in this community.	ce 'I' tōngney, tōng.li 'village' Kam.li-kyo 'Methodism' (i)p.nita 'is' [FORMAL]
4. Kuleh.sup.nikka? Pok.nam-i hanthey se kakkum māl-ssum (ul) tul.ess.ˢup.nita. Musun īl lo osyess.ˢup.nikka.	Oh? I've heard (of you) now and then from Pok.nam-i. What matter have you come about?	māl-ssum 'word(s), talk [to or by an esteemed person]' kakkum 'sometimes, now and then, from time to time' tul.ess.ˢup.nita 'heard, listened to' [FORMAL] musun īl lo 'by (or on account of) what matter?' osyess.ˢup.nikka 'did (someone esteemed) come?' [FORMAL]
5. Cāmqkan sīmpang wass.ˢup.nita. Pok.nam-i ka kwiyewe se, ku pumo nim ul han pen pōypko siph.ess.ˢup.nita.	I've just come for a short call. Pok.nam-i is so sweet, I wanted to see his parents (once).	cāmqkan 'a while' [also spelled camkkan] sīmpang or pāngmun 'a call, a visit' sīmpang/pāngmun hay yo 'visits, calls at, calls on' wass.ˢup.nita 'came [FORMAL] kwiyewe yo 'is cute, dear, sweet, precious' pōywe yo 'sees or meets (an esteemed person)'

Korean	English	Amplification
		pōypko siph.ess.^{s}up.nita 'wanted to see (someone esteemed)' [FORMAL]
6. Komapsup.nita. Pok.nam-i nun onul hak.kyo ey kako ēps.^{s}up.nita.	Thank you. Pok.nam-i [went to=] is at school, he isn't (here).	ēps.^{s}up.nita '(there) isn't; isn't (in a place)' [FORMAL]
7. Kuleh.sup.nikka? Pok.nam-i apeci kkey se nun an kyēysip.nikka?	Oh? (And) isn't Pok.nam-i's father here?	kyēysip.nikka 'is (someone esteemed) (here)?' [FORMAL]
8. Pok.nam-i apeci nun cikum path ey se īl hasip.nita. Cenyek ey cip ey osip.nita. Musun hasil māl-ssum i iss.^{s}up.nikka?	Pok.nam-i's father is working in the field(s) now. He comes home in the evening. Is there something you would like to say (to him <u>or</u> us)?	hasip.nita '(someone esteemed) does' [FORMAL] osip.nita '(someone esteemed) comes' [FORMAL] hasil māl-ssum 'words (someone esteemed) will say' iss.^{s}up.nikka? 'is (there)? is (something somewhere)?' [FORMAL]
9. Ani yo?? Pyel lo ēps.^{s}up.nita. Ce . . . tayk ey se Yeyswu lul mit.usip.nikka?	No, there's nothing special. Uh . . . does your family believe in Christ?	pyel 'special, particular' pyel lo '(not) specially, (nothing) in particular' ce . . . 'uh . . ., ah . . .' Yeyswu 'Jesus' mit.e yo [mit-] 'believes (in), trusts, has faith (in)' mit.usip.nikka 'does (someone esteemed) believe?' [FORMAL]
10. Ani yo?? Ce-huy cip un Pulkyo lul mit.sup.nita.	No; our family believes in Buddhism.	ce-huy 'we' [FORMAL= wuli] Pulkyo 'Buddhism' mit.sup.nita 'believes (in), trusts, has faith (in)' [FORMAL]
11. Kuleh.sup.nikka? Kulen tey, etteh.key Pok.nam-i lul Cwuil hak.kyo ey nul ponaysip.nikka.	Really? Then, how is it that you're always sending Pok.nam-i to Sunday school?	Cwuil hak.kyo 'Sunday school' ponay yo [ponay-] 'sends' ponaysip.nikka 'does (someone esteemed) send?' [FORMAL]
12. Cheum ey nun cip ey se pāntay lul mānh.i hayss.^{s}up.nita.	At first, we put up a lot of opposition.	cheum ey 'at first' pāntay 'opposition' pāntay (lul) hay yo 'opposes' hayss.^{s}up.nita 'did' [FORMAL]

Korean	English	Amplification
13. Wuli nāy-oy ka Pok.nam-i hanthey Yeyswu lul mōs mit.key hayss.ˢup.nita.	My husband and I wouldn't let Pok.nam-i believe in Christ.	nāy-oy = pupu 'married couple, husband and wife' mit.key 'so that [one] believes' mit.key hay yo 'causes one to believe; makes/lets one believe' . . . hanthey mōs mit.key hay yo 'causes . . . not to believe at all'
14. Tekwuna, Pok.nam apeci nun Pok.nam-i lul kongil imyen pakk ey mōs na kakey hayss.ˢup.nita.	Moreover, Poknam-i's father wouldn't let him go out of the house on Sunday.	tekwuna, tekwuntana 'moreover, furthermore' kongil 'Sunday (= Il.yo-il), Sabbath' kongil imyen '[when it's Sunday=] on Sunday(s)' kakey 'so that [he] goes' mōs na kakey 'so that [he] can't go out' mōs na kakey hay yo 'makes it so that [he] can't go out, doesn't let [him] go out'
15. Kuleh.ci man, Pok.nam-i ka nemu kako siph.e hay se, nācwung ey n' ponayss.ci yo.	However, Pok.nam-i wanted to go so badly, we finally sent him.	nācwung (ey) 'in the end, at last, finally'
16. Pok.nam-i ka ama cincca Yeyswu cayngi ka toynun kes kath.sup.nita.	It looks as if Pok.nam-i were becoming a real "Christer."	ama 'perhaps, probably' cincca, cinqca 'genuine article' . . . cayngi 'person <u>or</u> thing characterized by . . .' Yeyswu cayngi 'a Christer' [vulgar term used by non-Christians] toynun kes 'fact of becoming' toynun kes kath.e yo '[is like the fact of becoming=] seems as if [he] is becoming'
17. Kuleh.sup.nikka? Kulay, Pok.nam-i ka Cwuil hak.kyo tanin hwū lo, etteh.sup.nikka.	Oh? And how has it been since Pok.nam-i's been attending Sunday school?	tanye yo [tani-] 'goes regularly' (also tannye yo [tanni-], tayngkye yo [tayngki-]) tanin hwū lo 'since [he] has been going (regularly)' etteh.sup.nikka 'how is it?' [FORMAL]

Korean	English	Amplification
18. Moluci yo. Ha.ye-kan, Cwuil hak.kyo ey se nappun kes un an kaluchilq cwul āp.nita.	I don't know. Anyway, I assume they wouldn't teach anything bad in Sunday school.	ha.ye-kan 'anyway, in any event' kaluchilq cwul 'the assumed fact that [one] will teach' an kaluchilq cwul al.e yo 'presumes that [one] won't teach' āp.nita 'knows' [FORMAL]
19. Pok.nam-i ka ku cen ey tanin cel ey se to nappun īl un an kaluchyess.ulq cwul lo āp.nita.	I feel sure that they didn't teach any bad things at the Buddhist temple where Pok.nam-i went before.	ku cen ey '[before that =] before, earlier' cel 'Buddhist temple' kaluchyess.ulq cwul 'the presumption that [one] taught' an kaluchyess.ulq cwul lo āp.nita 'presumes [one] did not teach' [FORMAL]
20. Mullon kuleh.keyss.ci yo. Cwuil hak.kyo ey se to cōh.un īl ul kaluchip.nita.	Of course that's so. At Sunday school too, good things are taught.	kaluchip.nita 'teaches' [FORMAL]
21. I pen Cwuil ey Pok.nam-i ape' nim kwa kachi wuli ^{1}yeypay-tang ey osikeyss.^{s}up.nikka?	This Sunday, would you like to come to our church with Pok.nam-i's father?	osikeyss.^{s}up.nikka? 'will [someone esteemed] come? [FORMAL]
22. Kulssey yo. Congkyo nun tā machan-kaci ka ani 'p.nikka? Pulkyo nun congkyo ka ani 'p.nikka?	Well, I don't know . . Aren't all religions alike? Isn't Buddhism a religion?	kulssey yo 'well, let me think, well . . .' [showing reservations] congkyo 'religion; a religion' machan-kaci 'the same thing, an identical thing' [< machi han kaci as if one kind]
23. Mullon, Pulkyo to cōh.un congkyo 'p.nita. Kuleh.ci man, Yeyswu-kyo ka te cōh.sup.nita.	Of course Buddhism is a good religion too. But Christianity is better.	Yeyswu-kyo, Kitok-kyo 'Christianity' cōh.sup.nita 'is good' [FORMAL] te cōh.sup.nita 'is [more good =] better'
24. Etteh.key te cōh.sup.nikka.	How is it better?	cōh.sup.nikka 'is it good?' [FORMAL]
25a. Cikum yeki se ccalp.key selmyeng haki elyepsup.nita.	It's hard to explain briefly here, right now.	ccalp.e yo 'is short, brief' ccalp.key 'briefly [pronounced /ccalkkey/] selmyeng 'explanation' selmyeng (ul) hay yo 'explains'

Korean	English	Amplification
		elyepsup.nita 'is hard, difficult' [FORMAL]
25b. 'Yeypay-tang ey osimyen cha-cha āsikey toyp.nita.	If you come to church, you will gradually (come to) understand.	cha-cha 'gradually, bit by bit' āsikey 'so that [someone esteemed] knows' āsikey toyp.nita 'becomes knowing, get so that one knows' [FORMAL]
25c. Ha.ye-kan Yeyswu-kyo ka cham congkyo 'p.nita.	In any event, Christianity is the true religion.	cham 'truth, genuineness, real-ness' [<u>also</u> 'very; oh!']
26. Ca, i chayk ey ilen mal i iss.^{s}up.nita.	Now, in this book there are such words as these.	ca 'now! well!' iss.^{s}up.nita '(there) is/are' [FORMAL]
27. "Hana' nim i sēysang ul i chelem salang hasa, toksayng-ca lul cwusyess.uni, nwukwu 'tun ci Ce lul mit.umyen, myelmang haci anh.ko, yēngsayng ul et.ulila."	"(For) God so loved the world, that He gave His only begotten son, that whosoever believeth in Him shall not perish but shall have everlasting life."	Hana' nim 'God' (Christian pronunciation of Hanu' nim [< hanul]) sēysang 'world' i chelem 'like this' salang 'love' salang (ul) hay yo 'loves' hasa [LITERARY] = hay se toksayng-ca 'only son' cwusyess.uni . . . '[someone esteemed] gave and so' nwukwu 'tun ci 'whoever (it might be)' ce = ce i 'that person, he/him' myelmang hay yo 'perishes' yēngsayng 'eternal life' et.ulila = et.keyss.ta 'will obtain' [PLAIN STYLE]
28. Al.e tut.keyss.^{s}up.nikka?	Do you understand it?	al.e tul.e yo [tul-] 'understands (what one hears)' tut.keyss.^{s}up.nikka? 'will you hear <u>or</u> listen?' [FORMAL]
29. Ani yo?? Cal mōs al.e tut.keyss.^{s}up.nita.	No, I don't understand it (very) well.	tut.keyss.^{s}up.nita 'will hear, listen' [FORMAL]
30. Swīpkey māl hamyen, ileh.sup.nita.	To [= If I] put it more simply, it's like this.	swīpkey 'simply' [swīw- 'be easy, simple'] ileh.sup.nita 'it's this way, it's like this' [FORMAL]

Korean	English	Amplification
31. Hana' nim kkey se wuli sālam tul ul salang hasiki ttaymun ey ku uy oy atul Yeyswu lul wuli eykey cwusyess.^{s}up.nita.	Because God loved us people, He gave His only son Jesus to us.	wuli sālam tul 'we people' ku (i) uy 'of that (one) = his' oy . . . 'single, lone, only' oy atul Yeyswu 'only son Jesus' cwusyess.^{s}up.nita '[someone esteemed] gave' [FORMAL]
32. Kulay se, nwukwu 'tun ci Yeyswu lul mit.umyen, cwukci anh.ko, yēngwen hi salq swu iss.^{s}up.nita.	And so, whoever (it is, if he) believes in Jesus can live eternally, and not die.	cwuk.e yo [cwuk-] 'dies' yēngwen hi 'forever, eternally'
33. Wuli sālam tul ul salang hasiki ttaymun iey yo?	It's because He loves us people?	
34. Nēy. Kuleh.sup.nita.	Yes, that's right.	
35a. Ha.ye-kan, i chayk ul twuko kap.nita.	Anyway, I'll leave this book.	twue yo [twu-] 'puts it (somewhere), leaves it' twuko kap.nita '[puts it and goes =] leaves it (behind)'
35b. Sikan (i) iss.usimyen, ilk.e posipsio.	If you have time, try reading it.	posipsio 'look (at it)!' [FORMAL] ilk.e posipsio 'read! try reading! read and see (what it is like)!' [FORMAL]
35c. Kuliko, taum Cwuil ey ^{l}yeypay-tang ey na osipsio.	And, next Sunday come (out) to church.	osipsio 'come' [FORMAL]
36. I chayk i musun chayk ip.nikka.	What book is this?	. . . ip.nikka 'is it . . . ?' [FORMAL]
37. Sēngkyeng ip.nita. Yeyswu kkey se hasin īl kwa māl-ssum ip.nita.	It's the Bible. It is the things Jesus said and did.	Sēngkyeng 'Bible'

SUPPLEMENTARY VOCABULARY (for Missionaries)

pha	group branch, sect	^{l}Noma-kyo	the Roman (Catholic) faith
kyōpha	denomination		
Cang.lo-kyo	Presbyterian faith	sinca	believer, Christian
chim.lyey	baptism by immersion	pulqsin-ca	unbeliever, heathen
Chim.lyey-kyo	Baptist faith	hanu' nim	god
Sinkyo	Protestant(ism)	Hana' nim	God (Protestant)
Chencwu-kyo, Khathollik(-kyo), Kwūkyo	Catholic(ism)	Chencwu	the Lord (usually Catholic)
		Cang.lo	an Elder

chōng.li(-sa) or kamtok	bishop
cwukyo	Catholic bishop
kam.li-sa	district superintendent
sinpu	priest, Father (person or title)
cwung	Buddhist priest
su'-nim	Buddhist priest (person or title)
cento-sa	lay (unordained) pastor
cento(q) puin	Bible woman, woman evangelist
swunye	nun, Sister (person or title)
Selkyo	sermon
^{l}yeypay	(Protestant) service, worship
misa	(Catholic) Mass
^{l}yeypay (lul) hay/pwa yo	worships, holds (Protestant) services
misa lul pwa yo	says (reads) mass
kito	prayer
kito-hoy	prayer meeting
pok	blessing
pil.e yo [pī-l-]	prays for, asks
pok ul pil.e yo	asks a blessing
chwukpok kito or cwukto	benediction
kāmsa	gratitude, thankfulness
kāmsa (lul) hay yo	gives thanks, expresses gratitude
chān.yang-tay or sēngka-tay	choir
chānsong-ka	hymn(s)
sēngka	Catholic hymn(s)
hēnkum; yēnpo; swucen	offering
Kwū-yak	Old Testament
Sin-yak	New Testament
Cwu kito-mun or Cwu uy kito-mun	(text of) the Lord's prayer
Chencwu-kyeng	the Lord's prayer (Catholic term)
mit.um or sīn.ang	faith
kwuwen	salvation, redemption
cōy	sin
cie yo [cī(s)-]	builds, makes
cōy lul pēm hay yo or cōy (lul) cie yo	sins, commits sin
hōykay	repentance
hōykay (lul) hay yo	repents
capok (= capayk), kōpayk	confession
kōhay	Catholic confession
sēylyey; [Catholic] ^{l}yengsey	baptism
sēylyey (lul) cwue yo; [Catholic] ^{l}yengsey (lul) hay yo	baptizes
sēylyey (lul) pat.e yo; [Catholic] ^{l}yengsey (lul) pat.e yo	gets baptized
sēng-manchan(q) sik	Communion service
chentang = hanul	heaven
chenkwuk or hanul nala	heavenly kingdom
ciok	hell
. . . cel	festival of . . .
Sēngthan (cel)	Holy Birth = Christmas
Pūhwal(q cel)	Resurrection = Easter
Kāmsa (cel)	Gratitude = Thanksgiving
^{n}yenhoy	annual conference
īm.wen or cik.wen	officers
īnto	leadership, guidance
īnto (lul) hay yo	leads, guides
swūnse	program, order of events
uynon, uy^{l}non	discussion
chayk.im	duties, responsibilities
Kitok Chengnyen Hoy	YMCA (the organization)
Kitok Chengnyen Hoy-kwan	YMCA (building)
^{n}Yeca Chengnyen Hoy	YWCA (the organization)
^{n}Yeca Chengnyen Hoy-kwan	YWCA (building)

NOTES

17.1. Formal Style.

Many of the sentence-final verbs in the Basic Sentences of this lesson are in the FORMAL STYLE. This style is used under conditions where formality is called for: in business situations where the relationships between the speakers is official and impersonal; in social situations where the speakers are newly acquainted and the ice is not yet broken; or in any case where reserve seems indicated or desirable. It is also often used in greetings and other conventional expressions (see the Basic Sentences of Lesson 1). This style usually gives way gradually as the formality of the situation ebbs—as when two speakers have progressed beyond the initial overtures of getting acquainted and feel more at ease—so that formal and polite style are often mixed together.

Notice that the keynote to the style that speakers are employing (aside from certain vocabulary items like ce for na 'I'), rests entirely in the verbs AT THE END OF SENTENCES. Gerunds, conditionals, infinitives, and all other non-final verb forms are neutral in this respect.

FORMAL STATEMENTS are made by attaching to the verb at the end of the sentence, an ending which has the shape -sup.nita (pronounced /-sumnita/) after consonants and -p.nita (pronounced /-mnita/) after vowels; if the base is an L-extending vowel base, the ending is added to the UNEXTENDED base (without the -l-).

South Koreans often spell -up.nita for -sup.nita after the bases iss- and ēps- and after all past and future bases (-ess- and -keyss-): this is a hold-over from an older usage which maintains -up.nita everywhere in place of -sup.nita. (You will still sometimes hear people say mek.up.nita instead of the expected meksup.nita.) In order to show both versions for iss-, ēps-, -ess-, and -keyss-, we write the s above the line: iss.ˢup.nita, ēps.ˢup.nita, -ess.ˢup.nita, -keyss.ˢup.nita.

FORMAL QUESTIONS are made by replacing the final ta of the formal statement with kka, in other words by adding an ending that has the shape -sup.nikka (pronounced /-sumnikka/) after consonants and the shape -p.nikka (pronounced /-mnikka/) after vowels. And we write iss.ˢup.nikka, ēps.ˢup.nikka, -ess.ˢup.nikka, -keyss.ˢup.nikka with the s above the line, just as for the statement form.

Here are some examples with typical verb bases:

VOWEL BASES

MEANING	BASE	FORMAL STATEMENT	PRONOUNCED
go	ka-	kap.nita	/kamnita/
tie, wear tie	māy-	māyp.nita	/māymnita/
see, look at	po-	pop.nita	/pomnita/
give	cwu-	cwup.nita	/cwumnita/
write	ssu-	ssup.nita	/ssumnita/
become	toy-	toyp.nita	/toymnita/
wait	kitali-	kitalip.nita	/kitalimnita/
(honorific)	-(u)si-	-(u)sip.nita	/-(u)simnita/
know	ā-l-	āp.nita	/āmnita/
hang it	kē-l-	kēp.nita	/kēmnita/
enter; cost; lift	tu-l-	tup.nita	/tumnita/
play	nō-l-	nōp.nita	/nōmnita/
be long	kī-l-	kīp.nita	/kīmnita/
not know	molu-	molup.nita	/molumnita/

be different	talu-	talup.nita	/talumnita/	
be early	ilu-	ilup.nita	/ilumnita/	
call	pulu-	pulup.nita	/pulumnita/	
be blue/green	phulu-	phulup.nita	/phulumnita/	

CONSONANT BASES

MEANING	BASE	FORMAL STATEMENT	PRONOUNCED	PRONUNCIATION RULE(S)
wear	ip-	ip.sup.nita	/ipssumnita/	ps→/pss/
want to	siph-	siph.sup.nita	/sipssumnita/	ph.s→ps→/pss/
receive	pat-	pat.sup.nita	/passumnita/	t.s→/ss/
take off (clothes)	pes-	pes.sup.nita	/pessumnita/	s.s→t.s→/ss/
look for, find	chac-	chac.sup.nita	/chassumnita/	c.s→t.s→/ss/
eat	mek-	meksup.nita	/mekssumnita/	ks→/kss/
polish	takk-	takk.sup.nita	/takssumnita/	kk.s→ks→/kss/
read	ilk-	ilk.sup.nita	/ikssumnita/	lk.s→ks→/kss/
plant	sīm-	sīm.sup.nita	/sīmssumnita/	m.s→/mss/
be young	celm-	celm.sup.nita	/cemssumnita/	lm.s→m.s→/mss/
wear (shoes)	sin-	sin.sup.nita	/sinssumnita/	n.s→/nss/
sit down	anc-	anc.sup.nita	/anssumnita/	nc.s→n.s→/nss/
help	tōw-	tōp.sup.nita	/tōpssumnita/	[w/p; ps→/pss/]
listen, hear	tul-	tut.sup.nita	/tussumnita/	[l/t; t.s→/ss/]
put	noh-	noh.sup.nita	/nossumnita/	h.s→t.s→/ss/
be much/many	mānh-	mānh.sup.nita	/mānssumnita/	nh.s→n.s→/nss/
be disliked	silh-	silh.sup.nita	/silssumnita/	lh.s→l.s→/lss/
be; stay; have	iss-	iss.^{s}up.nita	/issumnita/	}
(past)	-ess-	-ess.^{s}up.nita	/-essumnita/	} ss.s→t.s→/ss/
(future)	-keyss-	-keyss.^{s}up.nita	/-keyssumnita/	}
lack	ēps-	ēps.^{s}up.nita	/ēpssumnita/	ps.s→ps→/pss/

FORMAL COMMANDS are made by adding -usio to bases that end in consonants and -sio to bases that end in vowels; -sio is added to the UNEXTENDED shape of L-extending vowel bases (that is, to the shape without the -l-). This ending is often spelled -(u)siyo; that spelling also represents a variant of the ending -(u)sey yo (honorific polite—often used for commands).

Here are some examples of formal commands:

CONSONANT BASES	VOWEL BASES
ip.usio 'wear it!'	posio 'look!'
pat.usio 'receive it!'	kasio 'go!'
pes.usio 'take it off!'	cwusio 'give it (to me)!'
chac.usio 'look for it!'	ssusio 'write it!'
takk.usio 'polish it!'	kitalisio 'wait!'
ilk.usio 'read it!'	kēsio 'hang it!'
sim.usio 'plant it!'	tusio 'lift it!'
sin.usio 'put on (the shoes)!'	nōsio 'play!'
anc.usio 'sit down!'	pulusio 'call!'
towusio 'help!'	māysio 'tie it!'
tul.usio 'listen!'	pēysio 'cut it!'
noh.usio 'put it (there)!'	
iss.usio 'stay!'	

But honorific formal commands are made by adding -psio (often spelled -psiyo) after the honorific marker -(u)si-:

ip.usipsio 'wear it!'	kasipsio 'go!'
pat.usipsio 'receive it!'	posipsio 'look!'
etc.	etc.

You are familiar with this ending from the basic sentences of Lesson 1: Annyeng hi kyēysipsio!—Annyeng hi kasipsio! Honorific verbs which include -si- in their shape also add -psio: kyēysipsio 'stay!,' cwumusipsio 'sleep!,' capswusipsio 'eat!' The last verb also appears without -si-: capswu- from which we get capswusio 'eat!' Before endings that begin with a consonant, capswusi- is sometimes shortened so that you may hear capswus.ko for capswusiko 'someone esteemed eats and . . . .' See ‖ 18.6.

FORMAL SUGGESTIONS ('let's do it') are made by adding the ending -upsita (occasionally said as -supsita) to consonant bases and -psita to vowel bases (including the UNEXTENDED shape of L-extending vowel bases):

ip.upsita 'let's wear it!'	kapsita 'let's go!'
pat.upsita 'let's receive it!'	popsita 'let's see it!'
anc.upsita 'let's sit down!'	nōpsita 'let's play!'

You can, of course, make your formal suggestion on the honorific base, since the suggestion usually includes the person you are speaking to: kasipsita 'let's go!' Sometimes, however, the person you are speaking to is excluded and the meaning is more like 'let me (do it)! I think I'll do it.'

Since the endings -p.nita, -p.nikka, -sio and -psita are added to the UNEXTENDED shape of L-extending vowel bases, the resulting forms look as if they might be ordinary vowel bases, so that from the spelling you can't tell whether sāp.nita means sal.e yo (from sā-l-) 'lives' or sa yo (from sa-) 'buys.' The context will help you tell. Most of the L-extending bases have basically long vowels (not shown in the usual spelling) and this is also a help in telling them from ordinary vowel bases, many of which have basically short vowels.

‖ 17.2. Polite, casual polite, and formal styles: summary of endings.

You have learned a number of sentence-final endings—the endings which show what style you are speaking in. Here is a list, showing each in its relationship to the others.

	POLITE	CASUAL POLITE	FORMAL
		STATEMENTS	
Present	-e yo	-ci yo	-sup.nita / -p.nita
[HON.]	-(u)sey yo	-(u)sici yo	-(u)sip.nita
Past	-ess.ey yo	-ess.ci yo	-ess.sup.nita
[HON.]	-(u)syess.ey yo	-(u)syess.ci yo	-(u)syess.sup.nita
Future	-keyss.ey yo	-keyss.ci yo	-keyss.sup.nita
[HON.]	-(u)sikeyss.ey yo	-(u)sikeyss.ci yo	-(u)sikeyss.^{s}up.nita

QUESTIONS

Present	-e yo? -un ka yo? -na yo?	-ci yo?(?)	-sup.nikka? / -p.nikka?
[HON.]	-(u)sey yo? -(u)sin ka yo? -(u)sina yo?	-(u)sici yo?(?)	-(u)sip.nikka?
Past	-ess.ey yo? -ess.na yo?	-ess.ci yo?(?)	-ess.^{s}up.nikka?
[HON.]	-(u)syessey yo? -(u)syess.na yo?	-(u)syess.ci yo?(?)	-(u)syess.^{s}up.nikka?
Future	-keyss.ey yo? -(u)lq ka yo? -keyss.na yo?	-keyss.ci yo?(?)	-keyss.^{s}up.nikka?
[HON.]	-(u)sikeyss.ey yo? -(u)silq ka yo? -(u)sikeyss.na yo?	-(u)sikeyss.ci yo?(?)	-(u)sikeyss.^{s}up.nikka?

COMMANDS

	-e yo!	-ci yo!	-(u)sio!
[HON.]	-(u)sey yo!	-(u)sici yo!	-(u)sipsio!

SUGGESTIONS

	-e yo!	-ci yo!	-(u)psita!
[HON.]	-(u)sey yo!	-(u)sici yo!	-(u)sipsita!

APPERCEPTIONS

Present	-kwu(me)n yo -nun kwu(me)n yo
[HON.]	-(u)sikwu(me)n yo -(u)sinun kwu(me)n yo
Past	-ess.kwu(me)n yo
[HON.]	-(u)syess.kwu(men) yo
Future	-keyss.kwu(me)n yo -(u)sikeyss.kwu(me)n yo

17.3. Verbs: adverbative form -key.

11. . . . etteh.key Pok.nam-i lul Cwuil hak.kyo ey nul ponaysip.nikka. 'How is it that you're always sending Pok.nam-i to Sunday school?'
13. . . . Yeyswu lul mōs mit.key hayss.^{s}up.nita. '. . . wouldn't let him believe in Jesus.'
14. . . . pakk ey mōs na kakey hayss.^{s}up.nita. '. . . wouldn't let him go out.'
24. Etteh.key te cōh.sup.nikka. 'How is it better?'
30. Swīpkey māl hamyen, ileh.sup.nita. 'To put it simply (easily), it's like this.'

Verbs have an ADVERBATIVE FORM made by attaching the ending -key to the base. (This means that the -key form is pronounced just like the future -keyss.ey yo forms without the final -ss.ey yo.) The adverbative ending is used only with simple bases, plain or honorific—and not with past or future bases.

The -key forms may tell HOW something is done, or HOW the subject of the action is:

Nuc.key wass.ey yo. 'He came late.'
Etteh.key hap.nikka.—Ileh.key hap.nita. 'How do you do it?—You do it like this.'

Or it may tell HOW something CHANGES "so that it is (something new)"—referring either to the subject of an intransitive verb, or to the object of a transitive verb:

Ai ka khukey tōyss.ey yo. 'The child grew up [= got big].' (The child got so he was big.)
Cip ul khukey hayss.ey yo. 'They made the house big(ger).' (They made the house so it was big.)

Here are some more examples:

1. Com te khukey māl-ssum hay cwusipsio.	Please speak a little louder.
2. Ku sangcem ey se mulken ul ssakey phal.e yo?	Do they sell things cheap(ly) at that store?
3. I chayk ul caymi iss.key ilk.usipsio.	[Read this book with pleasure =] Have a good time reading this book.
4. I kes ul talukey hapsita.	Let's make this one different.
5. Cīnan pam ey chwupkey cwumusyess.ci yo?	Did you get cold [= sleep cold] in the night?

Both processive and descriptive verbs make adverbatives, but there is no form for the copula. Where you might expect such a form (*ikey 'so that it is') you find instead the adverbative form of the processive verb tōy yo 'becomes': toykey 'so that it becomes.'

17.4. Adverbative forms with hay yo.

Adverbative forms in -key combine into phrases with hay yo to mean 'causes [him/it] to do something' or 'causes [him/it] to be some way.' For example:

mek.key hay yo 'causes [someone] to eat'
chwupkey hay yo 'causes [something] to be cold'

If the -key form is a processive verb, it might be translated by 'make' or 'let' or 'have':

mek.key hay yo 'makes [someone] eat' or 'lets [someone] eat' or 'has [someone] eat'

The Korean expresses simple causation, emphasizing neither coercion (like 'make') nor permission (like 'let'). With descriptive verbs, the translation 'make' is more common.

Notice the particles used in this construction. Assume that B performs an action—either one that takes a direct object (TRANSITIVE: e.g. reads a book) or one that does not (INTRANSITIVE: e.g. goes to bed).

Transitive Pattern: B ka C lul hay yo
Example: Āy ka chayk ul ilk.e yo. 'The child reads the book.'
Intransitive Pattern: B ka hay yo.
Example: Āy ka iss.ey yo. 'The child stays.'

When these patterns are transformed into the -key hay yo construction, the following patterns result:

Transitive Pattern: A ka B eykey (or hanthey) C lul hakey hay yo.
Example: Emeni ka āy eykey (or hanthey) chayk ul ilk.key hay yo. 'The mother makes/has/lets the child read the book.'
Intransitive Pattern: A ka B lul hakey hay yo.
Example: Emeni ka āy ul iss.key hay yo. 'The mother makes/has/lets the child stay.

Here are more examples of this construction:

1. Ku chayk ul sakey hayss.ey yo. — I let him buy that book.
2. Āy tul ul kil ey se mōs nōlkey hay ya hay yo. — You have to see to it that children don't play in the streets. [=You have to make children not play . . .]
3. Cip ey iss.key hakeyss.ey yo. — I'll make/have/let him stay home.
4. Kuleh.key olay kitalisikey hayss.ey yo. — I kept you waiting so long.
5. Āy tul ul ilcciki cakey hayss.^{s}up.nita. — I made the children go to bed early.
6. Sensayng nim i haksayng tul eykey swukcey lul hakey hasyess.^{s}up.nita. — The teacher made the students do their homework.
7. Na nun tongsayng hanthey pap ul mek.key hayss.ey yo. — I made/had/let my little brother eat his food.
8. Latio lul com cāk.key hasey yo! — Turn the radio down a little.

In addition to this sort of periphrastic (or round-about) causative, some verbs have special derived causative forms; these are discussed in ‖ 26.1. Verbal nouns are often made causative by using sikhye yo [sikhi-] in place of hakey hanta (see ‖ 22.10).

‖ 17.5. Adverbative forms with tōy yo.

25. . . . ^{l}Yeypay-tang ey osimyen cha-cha āsikey toyp.nita. 'If you come to church, you will gradually come to understand . . .'

A -key form followed by tōy yo 'becomes, is' means 'gets to be so that . . . ,' expressing the gradual inception of an externally controlled condition.

This construction is similar in meaning to two others: the infinitive of a descriptive verb, followed by cye yo 'becomes, begins to be,' and the construction -ki (lul) sīcak hay yo 'begins to [do]' with verbs:

Tewe cye yo. 'It's getting hot.'
Pi ka oki (lul) sīcak hay yo. 'It's starting to rain.'

Here are some more examples of the construction -key tōy yo.

1. Caymi iss.key tōyss.^{s}up.nita. — It turned out to be interesting.
2. Ku taum ey nun etteh.key tōyss.ey yo? — What happened after that?
3. Mōs kakey tōyss.^{s}up.nita. — It's turned out that I can't go.
4. ^{l}Nayil puthe tose-kwan ey se īl hakey tōyss.ey yo. — (It has developed that) I'm to begin working at the library tomorrow.
5. Cenyek un mek.key tōyss.^{s}up.nita. — Dinner is ready to eat.

6. Nemu sim-sim hay se kongwen ey sānqpo wass.ta ka tangsin ul mannakey tōyss.ci yo. — I was so lonely I came to the park for a walk, and then I happened to run into you.

As the last example shows, sometimes the best translation is 'happens to, gets to, manages to, has the good fortune to.'

‖ 17.6. Derived adverbs and nouns: -i.

There is a suffix -i which is attached to some descriptive bases and makes them into adverbs. Here is a list of such words you have learned:

kath.i 'together' < kath- 'be similar to, be the same'
mānh.i 'many, much' < mānh- 'be many, much'
ppalli 'fast' < ppalu- 'be fast'

Others, made from bases you know, are:

ēps.i 'without' < ēps- 'be nonexistent'
kakkai 'near' < kakkaw- 'be near'
kiph.i 'depth; deeply' < kiph- 'be deep'
mēlli 'far' < mē-l- 'be far, distant' [note irregular -ll-]
olh.i 'rightly, correctly' [NOW RARE] < olh- 'be right, correct'
pappi 'busily' < pappu- 'be busy'

The form derived from the descriptive auxiliary ha- 'be' is hi. You have come across it in these expressions:

annyeng hi 'peacefully; well [HONORIFIC of cal]'
chēn-chen hi 'slowly'
tāytan hi 'very'

There are certain common expressions in which the derived adverb + iss.ey yo means about the same thing as the underlying descriptive verb by itself; the longer expressions are somewhat more common:

mānh.i iss.ey yo 'there are many, there is much' = mānh.e yo
kakkai iss.ey yo 'it's near(by)' = kakkawe yo
mēlli iss.ey yo 'it's far (off), it's a long way' = mel.e yo

Although many adjectives can be turned into adverbs in this way, not all of them freely add the -i ending. But you can always make an adverbative form with -key, and these are sometimes used in the same way as the derived adverbs; thus ppalukey means 'fast,' like ppalli, as well as 'so that it is or will be fast.' There are a few adverbs in -i which are not derived directly from adjectives; ilcciki comes from the adverb ilccik 'early,' derived from ilu- 'be early' + a suffix -cik 'a bit, somewhat.' There are a number of adverbs derived by repeating a short noun and adding -i: cipcip-i 'in every house,' kos.kos-i 'in every place,' chōnchon-i 'in every village,' na'nal-i 'every day' (= nal mata), ta'tal-i 'every month' (= tal mata).

The suffix -i is also used to derive nouns from a number of adjectives and verbs:

khi 'height (= stature), size' < khu- 'be large'
kil.i 'length' < kī-l- 'be long'
nelp.i 'width' < nelp- 'be wide'

nol.i 'game, amusement' < nō-l- 'play'
tewi 'heat, hot spell' < tēw- 'be hot, warm'
chwuwi 'cold, cold spell' < chwuw- 'be cold'

Occasionally, the resulting word can be either noun or adverb: kiph.i 'depth' or (= kiph.key) 'deeply,' noph.i 'height' or (= noph.key) 'highly.'

‖ 17.7. Modifiers with kes kath.e yo.

16. Pok.nam-i ka ama cincca Yeyswu cayngi ka toynun kes kath.sup.nita. 'Pok.nam-i seems to be becoming a real "Christer."'

In ‖ 14.9 you learned to say 'seems' or 'looks as if' with the construction modifier + mo.yang iey yo. Another expression meaning 'seems' or 'looks as if' is made by combining a modifier with the phrase kes kath.e yo, which means literally 'is the same thing as . . .' or 'is like the act of . . .' The modifier may be processive, to show an action now in progress; or it may be past or future. With descriptive verbs, the plain modifier is used for non-past meanings.

Here are more examples:

1. Ku chayk un tāytan hi caymi iss.nun kes kath.ey yo. — That book looks very interesting.
2. Kicha ka onun kes kath.sup.nita. — The train seems to be coming.
3. Phikon hay cinun kes kath.e yo. — He seems to be getting tired.
4. Ku sālam i puncwu han kes kath.e se, na nun tul.e kaci anh.ess.ey yo. — He looked busy, so I didn't go in.
5. Kōng i ttel.e cilq kes kath.ey yo. — The ball seems about to drop.

The same phrase, kes kath.ey yo, has a more literal meaning when not preceded by modifiers: Nay kes kath.ey yo (= Nay kes kwa kath.ey yo) 'It is like mine (my thing).' This meaning can be present with modifiers, too, so that Apeci ka pon kes kath.ey yo is ambiguous: it can mean either 'Father seems to have seen it' (= Apeci ka pon mo.yang iey yo) or 'It's like the one that Father saw' (= Apeci ka pon kes kwa kath.ey yo). Kath.e(y) yo is pronounced with or without the y.

‖ 17.8. Modifiers with cwul al.e yo.

18. . . . nappun kes un an kaluchilq cwul āp.nita. 'I assume they wouldn't teach anything bad.'
19. . . . nappun īl an kaluchyess.ulq cwul lo āp.nita. 'I feel sure that they didn't teach any bad things . . .'

The noun cwul means 'assumed fact' or 'presumption.' This is the same word you learned in the preceding lesson in the construction [ha]lq cwul al.e yo 'knows how to [do],' using a prospective modifier.

With a modifier of any appropriate tense before it, cwul al.e yo (or cwul lo al.e yo or cwul ul al.e yo) means 'assumes, presumes, thinks, or feels that [so-and-so is the case].' Often the best translation is 'realizes' or 'knows.'

Here are some more examples:

1. Kim sensayng i kan cwul ul āsip.nikka? — Are you aware that Mr. Kim has gone?
2. Ku sālam i on cwul mōllass.^s up.nita. — I didn't know he was here [= had come].
3. [1]Nayil olq cwul lo sayngkak hay yo. — I think he'll be [= come] back tomorrow.

4. Cikum cip ey ēps.nun cwul lo al.e yo.	I know he's not at home now.
5. Ku cip ey ay tul i iss.nun cwul mōllass.^{s}up.nikka?	Didn't you know they had children in that family?
6. Pok.nam i Hānkwuk kan cwul āsip.nikka?	Are you aware that Pok.nam has gone to Korea?

This means about the same thing as a similar construction with <u>kes ul al.e yo</u> (as in <u>cwun kes ul al.e yo</u> 'knows that he gave it.' Compare also these two constructions:

[modifier] <u>kes ul pwa yo</u>:
hanun kes ul pwa yo 'sees that [someone] is doing' or 'sees [someone] doing'
han kes ul pwa yo 'sees that [someone] has done
[modifier] <u>kes ul tul.e yo</u>:
hanun kes ul tul.e yo 'hears [someone] doing' NOT 'hears that someone is doing' which requires a more complicated construction involving quotations ‖ 19.1.

EXERCISES

I

Turn back to Exercise III of Lesson 16 and say all the polite-style sentences in the formal style.

II

Each of the following items contains two sentences, the second of which means something like 'I assume(d) that it is so.' Put the two sentences together so that the combined sentence has this same meaning, substituting the first sentence for the <u>kule-</u> portion of the second. For example, the first will be: <u>Na nun puin to osinun cwul al.ess.ey yo.</u> 'I thought your wife was coming too.'

1. Puin to osey yo. Na nun kulenun cwul al.ess.ey yo.
2. Tangsin i onul Sewul ey ka yo. Na nun kulenun cwul al.ess.ey yo.
3. Poktong-i ka cikum hak.kyo ey iss.keyss.ey yo. Kulelq cwul al.e yo.
4. Mikwuk ey se to ssal ul mek.e yo. Kulenun cwul al.e yo.
5. ["Kim sensayng i an osey yo?"] Nēy, ku pun i pappe se an osikeyss.ey yo. Kulelq cwul al.e yo.
6. ["Yo say Kim sensayng ul polq swu ka ēps.ey yo."] Kim sensayng i pelsse Hānkwuk ulo kass.keyss.ey yo. Kulayss.ulq cwul al.e yo.
7. ["Ecey Cwungkwuk ūmsik ul mek.ko, cal mōs cass.ey yo."] Ney, ku ūmsik i nappess.ey yo. Nay ka ku ttay kulen cwul al.ess.ey yo.
8. Kim sensayng i osyess.ey yo. Kulelq cwul al.ess.ey yo.
9. Pi ka okeyss.ey yo. San wi e kwulum ul poko, kulelq cwul al.ess.ey yo. ["Kuleh.ci man pi ka an wass.ey yo."]
10. I kkoch i cal calass.ey yo ['grow']. Kulelq cwul al.ess.ey yo.
11. Nay an(h)ay ka cip ey tol.a wass.ey yo. Mun soli ka nass.ki ttaymun ey, na nun kulen cwul al.ess.ey yo. [soli ka na yo 'a sound is produced (made, heard), occurs']

III

Each of the following items contains two sentences, the second of which means 'I know (knew) that something is so.' Put the two together into one sentence, then translate. For example, the first will be: Nay ka Pak Pok.nam-i ka cōh.un haksayng in kes ul al.e yo. 'I know that Pok.nam-i Pak is a good student.' (The nay ka could of course come right before al.e yo; but unless the rest of the sentence is very long, it is better at the beginning.)

1. Pak Pok.nam-i ka cōh.un haysayng iey yo. Nay ka kulen kes ul al.e yo.
2. Pak puin i New York ey kass.ey yo. Nay ka kulen kes ul al.e yo.
3. Ku atul i ^{l}naynyen ey Yeyil Tāyhak ey kalq key yo. Wuli ka kulelq kes ul al.e yo.
4. Ku ay ka cikum tose-kwan ey se kongpu hay yo. Emeni ka kulenun kes ul al.e yo.
5. Mikwuk kwa Hānkwuk i cōh.un chinkwu 'ey yo. Wuli ka kulen kes ul al.ess.ey yo.
6. Ku āy ka cikum tose-sil ey se sinmun ul ilk.ko iss.ey yo. Kulenun kes ul al.e yo.
7. Kim sensayng i sinmun ey nass.ey yo ['appeared']. Ku ay ka kulen kes ul al.ess.ey yo.
8. Son nim i wass.ey yo. Emeni ka mun soli lul tut.ko, kulen kes ul al.ess.ey yo.
9. Ku um.ak i cōh.a yo. Nay ka kulen kes ul al.ess.ey yo.
10. Ku sangcem ey se mulken i pissakeyss.ey yo. Wuli ka kulelq kes ul pelsse puthe al.ess.ey yo.
11. Ku sālam i īl ul cal hakeyss.ey yo. Nay ka ku sālam ul cheum pwass.ul ttay, kulelq kes ul al.ess.ey yo.

IV

Now, return to Exercises II and III just above. Take the FIRST sentence from each item (11 in each exercise) and restate it in the formal style, rather than the polite style in which it now appears. Keep the meaning the same in each case.

VOCABULARY DRILL

I

(for Missionaries)

Missionaries should drill in the vocabulary of this lesson by making use of the list of Supplementary Vocabulary to practice conversing about church matters. They might also try conducting a service in Korean, with the help of a Korean minister.

II

Express the following sentences in Korean, IN THE FORMAL STYLE, completing them in each of the ways indicated.

1. I know that you are a ___.
   Methodist
   Buddhist
   Catholic

2. I heard him singing hymns in the ___.
   temple
   YMCA building
   church

3. I like to listen to ___.
   a woman evangelist
   a church service
   good discussions

4. Your son Pok.nam ___.
   attends Sunday school regularly
   is cute
   lives in this neighborhood

5. I want to ___.
   meet you [showing esteem]
   pay a call on the minister
   believe in God

6. There are many people in the word who believe in ___.
   Christianity
   the Bible
   the Baptist faith

7. I make (or let) him ___.
   read the New Testament
   leave this town
   listen to my sermon

8. He seems to ___.
   go to the prayer meeting
   believe in God
   lead us to Heaven

9. We got ___.
   to see an interesting movie
   so we were out of money
   so we couldn't sleep

10. They made the food ___.
   so it was easy to eat
   so that everyone wanted to eat it right away
   so that you could eat it with chopsticks

COMPREHENSION

Here is a conversation between an officer of the American Air Force (Mi-Kongkwun) stationed in Korea and a Korean mother. Your tutor will read it to you while you listen with your book closed. Then he will ask you questions about what was said. After he has tested your immediate comprehension in this way, study through the conversation to see what passages caused you trouble.

A. Annyeng hasip.nikka? Pok.nam-i emeni 'sip.nikka?

B. Nēy, kuleh.sup.nita.

A. Ce nun i tōngney wa taum tōngney sai ey se īl hako iss.nun Mi-Kongkwun cāngkyo 'p.nita. Pam ey i tōngney hak.kyo ey wa se ai tul hanthey Yenge lul kaluchinun sālam ip.nita.

B. Kuleh.sup.nikka? Ese tul.e osipsio. Pok.nam-i hanthey se māl-ssum mānh.i tul.ess.[s]up.nita.

A. Pok.nam-i ka yo say hak.kyo ey oci anh.nun kes ul pwa se, cāmqkan tullyess.[s]up.nita. Pok.nam-i ka cal iss.[s]up.nikka?

B. Nēy, cal iss.[s]up.nita. Sikol hal-'meni kkey se pyēng i nasye se, sikol kass.[s]up.nita. [l]Nayil ccum tol.a olq kes ip.nita. Pam mata Yenge kaluchisiki ey elma 'na swūko hasip.nikka!

A. Ai tul i tā ttok-ttok hay se, kaluchiki ey caymi iss.[s]up.nita.

B. Pok.nam-i nun Yenge paywuki sīcak han hwū puthe nun, pakk ey na ka se nōlci to anh.ko, cip ey se nul Yenge kongpu man hap.nita.

A. Cham kwiyewun atu' nim ip.nita.

B. Komapsup.nita. Apeci to ēps.ko hyengcey to ēps.e se, ku ai lul cal kiluki ey āy lul ssuko iss.[s]up.nita. Kulen tey, nac ey nun kongkwun ey se īl ul posiko, pam ey nun Yenge lul kaluchisye se, phikon hasikeyss.[s]up.nita.

A. Halq īl i ēps.umyen cip sayngkak i nemu mānh.i na se, pappun kes i nās.sup.nita ['is better']. Ai tul i cōh.ki ttaymun ey, ku kongpu lul com tōpko siph.e cyess.ci man, i tōngney celm.un hak.kyo sensayng ul cīnan kaul ey mannakey tōy se pam ey Yenge lul kaluchikey tōyss.[s]up.nita.

B. Sik.kwu tul i mānh.sup.nikka? Mikwuk eti kyēysip.nikka.

A. Nyu-Yok si ey iss.[s]up.nita. Pumo nim hako nwui tongsayng tul ip.nita.
B. Kulen kos ey se sal.e pwass.umyen cōh.keyss.[s]up.nita.
A. Pok.nam-i ka khumyen kath.i osipsio.
B. Pok.nam-i nun pelsse puthe Mikwuk tāyhak ey ka se kongpu halq sayngkak ul hap.nita. Kuleh.ci man, ce nun kulen kos ey ka se māl to moluko, chinkwu to ēps.e se etteh.key sālq swu iss.keyss.[s]up.nikka.
A. Kulssey yo. Kulen kes tul un mūncey ka an toylq kes ip.nita. Ha.ye-kan, sayngkak hay posipsio. Kulem, ce nun polq īl i mānh.e se, ka pwa ya hakeyss.[s]up.nita. Cham, i chayk un Mikwuk se wass.[s]up.nita. Ilk.ki swiwun chayk iki ttaymun ey, atu' nim hanthey ilk.key hako siph.[s]up.nita. Pok.nam-i omyen cwusipsio.
B. Kāmsa hap.nita. Kulem, tto osipsio. Annyeng hi kasipsio.
A. Annyeng hi kyēysipsio.

CONVERSATION

After you have studied the comprehension exercise, carry on a conversation with your Korean tutor (or with another student) along similar lines. Assume that Pok.nam-i and his mother did indeed come to America and that you are a teacher speaking to the mother about her son's work at the university. Frame your questions so as to find out what you can about the background of the family and their adjustment to life in a new country.

LESSON 18. ATTENDING A DINNER PARTY

BASIC SENTENCES

[Han and Pak are two Americans living in Korea. They have adopted Korean names. H = Han, P = Pak, K = Kim, M = Mrs. Kim, D = Driver.]

	Korean	English	Amplification
P. 1.	Sikan i nuc.ess.uni. wuli catong-cha thako kapsita.	As it's late, let's go in a cab.	sikan i nuc.e yo 'the time gets late' nuc.ess.uni 'as it's become late, since <u>or</u> because it's grown late'
2.	Na nun cikum pappuni-kka n', tangsin i catong-cha lul pulusio.	Since I'm busy now, you call the cab.	pappuni-kka n' <u>or</u> pappuni-kl nun 'as <u>or</u> since [I'm] busy
H. 3a.	Ca, catong-cha lul ellun thapsita.	Well, let's get right in the taxi.	ca 'well, come on!' [urging, inviting] ellun 'right away, immedi- ately'
3b.	Ye' po, wūncen-swu, Samcheng Tong Sip-chil Penci lo kapsita.	Say, driver, let's go to Number 17, Samcheng Tong.	wūncen (ul) hay yo 'drives <u>or</u> operates (a vehicle)' wūncen-swu 'driver, op- erator (of a vehicle)'
P. 4.	Sip-o pun an ey kalq swu iss.key, wūncen ul ppalli hasio.	Drive fast so that we can get there within fifteen minutes.	ppalli 'fast' iss.key 'so that there is' halq swu iss.key 'so that one can'
D. 5a.	Nēy. ^{n}Yēm.lye māsipsio.	Yes, don't worry.	^{n}yēm.lye <u>or</u> kekceng 'worry, concern' ^{n}yēm.lye (lul) hay yo <u>or</u> kekceng (ul) hay yo 'wor- ries, is concerned' ^{n}yēm.lye (haci) māsipsio 'don't worry!'
5b.	Kil i com nappuna, catong-cha ka cōh. uni-kka, ppalli kalq swu iss.^{s}up.nita.	The road is rather bad, but since it's a good car, we can go fast.	nappuna . . . 'is bad, but . . . cōh. uni-kka 'it is good, so . . . ; since <u>or</u> as it is good . . .'
6.	Samcheng Tong Sip-chil Penci 'p.nita Naylisipsio.	[This] is Number 17 Samcheng Tong. Please step out.	naylye yo [nayli-] 'descends; gets off <u>or</u> out of [a ve- hicle]'

	Korean	English	Amplification
H. 7.	Kim sensayng, kyēysip.nikka?	Mr. Kim, are you in?	
K. 8.	Nēy. Nwukwu 'sip.nikka. A, Pak sensayng, Han sensayng isip.nikka? Ese tul.e osipsio.	Yes. Who is it? Oh, is it Mr. Pak and Mr. Han? Come right in.	
P. 9a.	Ileh.key nuc.e se mian hap.nita.	I'm sorry we're so late.	
9b.	Mōtwu tul annyeng hasip.nikka?	How is everyone?	mōtwu 'all, everyone'
9c.	Puin un eti kyēysip.nikka.	Where's your wife?	
K. 10a.	Puekh ey iss.ˢup.nita.	She's in the kitchen.	puekh 'kitchen'
10b.	Incey kot, na okeyss.ci yo.	She'll be right out any minute now.	incey 'now; before long' kot 'immediately, right away' away'
10c.	Ye' po! Keki se mues ul hay yo.	Hey, what are you doing (in) there?	
10d.	Son nim tul i osyess.ey yo.	The guests have arrived.	
M. 11a.	Nēy? Kulay yo? Pak sensayng nim Han sensayng nim osyess.ey yo?	Oh? Have they? Are Mr. Pak and Mr. Han here?	Pak sensayng nim (hako) Han sensayng nim 'Mr. Pak and Mr. Han'
11b.	Mēlli osye se komapsup.nita.	Thank you for coming such a distance.	
11c.	Cip ina swīpkey chac.usyess.ey yo?	Did you find the house [easily=] with no trouble?	cip ina 'the house (and all)'
H. 12a.	Nēy. Kot chac.ess.ˢup.nita.	Yes, we found it right away.	
12b.	Cip i khuko kkaykkus hako cōh.sup.nita.	Your house is nice and big and neat.	kkaykkus hay yo 'is clean, neat'
K. 13.	Chen-man uy māl-ssum ip.nita. Ce-huy cip un nul tēlepsup.nita.	Not at all. Our house is always a mess.	tēlewe yo [tēlew-] 'is untidy, messy, dirty'
M. 14a.	Cenyek capswus.ki cen ey mues com tusilq ka yo??	Before eating dinner, won't you have a little something to drink?	tul.e yo 'lifts; has=eats <u>or</u> drinks'

	Korean	English	Amplification
			tusilq ka yo?? 'will you drink or eat [partake of]?'
14b.	Tewun cha lul tulilq ka yo, khephi lul tulilq ka yo.	Shall I bring you hot tea, or coffee?	khephi 'coffee'
P.15.	Wuli cha lul masipsita. Cha lul cwusipsio.	Let's drink tea. Please give us some tea.	
K.16.	Cham. Ye' po. Sang ey samci-chang kac'ta noh.ass.ey yo?	Uh, dear, did you put the forks on the table?	samci-chang 'fork' kac'ta [= kacye 'ta (ka)] noh.a yo 'takes and puts'
M.17.	Nēy. Kac'ta noh.ass.ey yo.	Yes, I put them there.	
K.18.	Cenyek i tā cwūnpi toyn mo.yang ini, yele pun ese siktang ulo kasipsita.	As the dinner seems to be all ready, let's go right along to the dining room.	cwūnpi (lul) hay yo 'prepares, makes ready' cwūnpi (ka) tōy yo 'is prepared, is ready' yele pun 'you all; ladies and gentlemen; ladies; gentlemen' cwūnpi toyn mo.yang ini 'as or since it seems to be ready . . .' siktang 'dining room'
19.	Ca. Pak sensayng un yeki anc.usiko Han sensayng un mac.un phyen ey anc.usici yo.	Now, Mr. Pak, please sit here, and Mr. Han, please sit on the opposite [facing] side.	
P.20.	Musun ūmsik ul ileh.key mānh.i ma(y)ntu-syess.[s]up.nikka.	My, what a lot of dishes you've prepared! [= What dishes did you prepare in such quantity!]	ma(y)ntul.e yo [ma(y)ntu-l-] 'makes, prepares'
M.21a.	Pyel kes un ēps.una-ma, cengseng kkes ma(y)ntul.ess.uni, mānh.i capswusipsio.	There isn't anything special, but since I put my heart into making it, please eat lots.	ēps.una '(there) isn't, but ...' ēps.una-ma '(there) isn't, but anyway ....' . . . kkes 'to the full extent of, to the utmost of ...' cengseng 'sincerity' cengseng kkes 'with one's whole heart' ma(y)ntul.ess.uni 'since or as [someone] made ...'

	Korean	English	Amplification
21b.	Sa.yang māsiko ese tusipsio.	Please help yourself.	sa.yang hay yo 'declines politely, shows social reticence' Sa.yang (haci) māsey yo 'Please don't be reticent'
22.	Hānkwuk ūmsik, mānh.i capswe posyess.sup.nikka?	Have you tried eating Korean food much?	
H.23a.	Nēy. Pelsse yele pen mek.ess.^{s}up.nita.	Yes, we've eaten it a number of times now.	yeles 'a goodly number; several' yele . . . 'a number of . . . ; several, various, many'
23b.	Kulena, ileh.key mas i 'ss.nun ūmsik un cheum ip.nita.	But, it's the first time for such delicious food.	kulena '(it is so) but . . .' mas 'taste, flavor' mas i (i)ss.ey yo 'it has taste, it is delicious' cheum 'the first time' cheum iey yo 'it is the first time' cheum ulo 'for the first time'
P.24.	I kes un musun ūmsik ip.nikka. Mas i cōh.sup.nita!	What dish is this? It tastes wonderful.	
M.25.	Ku kes un capchay 'p.nita. So ('y) koki hako Tang myen hako yele kaci chāyso lo ma(y)ntul.ess.^{s}up.nita.	That's capchay. It's made with beef and 'nylon' noodles and all kinds of vegetables.	Tang myen '"nylon" (= thin transparent) noodles' kaci 'kind, variety' yele kaci 'all kinds (of things); all kinds of . . .'
P.26.	Mas i māl halq swu ēps.i cōh.sup.nita!	It's indescribably delicious.	māl halq swu ēps.i '[without being able to say =] indescribably, beyond words'
M.27.	Swuq-kalak ulo capswusici mālko, ceq-kalak ulo capswusipsio.	Don't eat with a spoon—eat with chopsticks.	
P.28.	Ceq-kalak cil ul hamyen, sikan i nemu (olay) kellye se, pay ka kopha yo.	If I use chopsticks, it takes so much (so long a) time, I get hungry.	sikan i kellye yo [kelli-] 'time is required = takes time' pay 'stomach' pay ka kopha yo [kophu-] 'is <u>or</u> gets hungry'
M.29.	Kulemyen, ku yeph ey iss.nun samci-chang ulo capswusici yo!	Then eat with the fork beside them.	

	Korean	English	Amplification
P. 30.	Komapsup.nita. Ce nun samci-chang ulo mek.keyss.^{s}up.nita.	Thank you. I'll eat with the fork.	
M. 31.	Kulen tey way Han sensayng un an capswusip.nikka.	Well, now, why aren't you eating, Mr. Han?	
H. 32a.	Meychil cen ey alh.ko na se, ip mas ul ilh.e pelyess.^{s}up.nita.	I've just got over being sick a few days ago, and I lost my appetite.	. . . cen ey '. . . ago, earlier' [<u>also</u> 'before'] alh.e yo 'is <u>or</u> gets sick <u>or</u> ill; ails in (a part of the body)' ip mas /immas/ '[mouth taste =] appetite' ilh.e yo 'loses' pelye yo [peli-] 'discards, throws away' -e (p)pelye yo 'finishes, completes, does completely or exhaustively' ilh.e (p)pelye yo 'loses completely'
32b.	Kuleh.ci man, onulq cenyek ey nun ūmsik i mas i 'sse se, mānh.i meksup.nita.	But the food this evening is so good I'm eating lots.	
M. 33.	Eti lul alh.ko nasyess.^{s}up.nikka.	What was wrong with you? [= Where were you ailing?]	
H. 34.	Pay thāl i nass.ess.ey yo.	I had a stomach upset.	thāl 'something wrong, something amiss, a hitch; (= pyēng) an illness' thāl i na yo 'gets out of order; falls ill' pay thāl 'a stomach upset'
H. 35.	I kes i kimchi 'p.nikka? Kimchi nun etteh.key ma(y)ntup.nikka.	Is this kimchi? How do you make kimchi?	
M. 36a.	Mence muwu wa pāychwu lul calkey ssēp.nita.	First you cut the white radishes and cabbage up (so that they are) fine.	mence 'first (of all), to begin with' muwu, mū '(giant white) radish' paychwu '(Chinese) cabbage'

Korean	English	Amplification
		cal.e yo 'is fine, small' calkey '(cut) in short pieces, (chopped) fine' ssel.e yo [ssē-l-] 'slices, cuts up'
36b. Kuliko, ku wi ey sokum ul ppulye twup.nita.	Then, you sprinkle salt over them (and get that out of the way).	sokum 'salt' ppulye yo [ppuli-] 'sprinkles <u>or</u> shakes (onto)' twue yo [twu-] 'puts it away, leaves it (somewhere)' . . .-e tw(u)e yo 'does it and gets it over with' ppulye tw(u)e yo 'sprinkles (and gets it out of the way), finishes up sprinkling'
37. Elma hwū ey sokum mul ul peliko, ccalp.kcy ssēn pha, manul, kochwu wa sekk.e se, hangali ey tām.sup.nita.	Somewhat later you throw away the brine, mix it with finely chopped scallions, garlic, and pepper, and stuff it in a pot.	elma hwū 'sometime later on, somewhat later' sokum mul 'salt(y) water, brine' pha 'scallion, onion' manul 'garlic' kochwu 'red pepper' hwuchwu 'black pepper' sekk.e yo 'mixes it (together), combines it' hangali 'pot, crock' tam.e yo [tām-] 'puts it (into), stuffs <u>or</u> crams it (into)'
38. Ttwukkeng ul teph.e (se) han sahul twuess.ta ka meksup.nita.	You cover it with a lid and let it stand [= leave it there] for about three days, and then eat it.	ttwukkeng 'lid, cover' teph.e yo [teph-] 'puts (a lid on), uses (a cover) to cover something' twuess.ta ka . . . 'leaves [it], and then . . .'
39a. Kimchi com capswe posipsio.	Have some kimchi.	
39b. Kuleh.ci man, maywun kes ul silh.e hasimyen, capswus.ci māsipsio.	But if you don't like highly seasoned things, don't eat it.	maywe yo [mayw-] 'is hot(ly seasoned), spicy, highly seasoned'
H.40. Kimchi yēyki lul ha to mānhi tul.e se amman maywe to mek.e poko ya mālkeyss.^{s}up.nita.	I've heard ever so much about kimchi, so no matter how hot it may be, I'll simply have to try eating it anyway.	ha 'much, greatly' ha to 'much indeed' amman [<āmu man] = āmuli 'however (much)'

	Korean	English	Amplification
			amman . . . -e to 'however (much) . . . is/does' amman maywe to 'however hot it is, no matter how hot it is' . . .-ko ya mal.e yo 'simply has to . . . , must . . .'
41.	Kimchi lul mek.ko nani-kka n', ip an i ēl-el hap.nita.	I've just eaten some kimchi and (now) the inside of my mouth is burning.	mek.ko nani-kka n' . . . 'has just eaten, and now . . .' ēl-el hay yo 'is burning, tingling, smarting'
M.42.	Cīnci com te capswusipsio.	Have a little more rice.	
H.43.	Ani 'p.nita. Ku man mek.keyss.ˢup.nita. Cham mānh.i mek.ess.ˢup.nita.	No, that's fine, thanks; I've eaten really a lot.	ku man mek.keyss.ˢup.nita 'I'll eat only that' (= I can't eat any more)
M.44.	Kulemyen, i kwāil com capswusici yo. Hwūsik ip.nita.	Then have some of this fruit. It's (for) dessert.	kwāil 'fruit' hwūsik 'dessert'
P.45.	Sakwa mas i cōh.sup.nita!	The apple tastes good.	sakwa 'apple'
H.46.	Incey nun nuc.e se, ka pwa ya hakeyss.ˢup.nita.	It's late now, so we'll have to [see=] think about leaving.	
M.47.	Pelsse kasey yo!! Com te nōsita kasici yo.	Leaving already?! Stay a little longer.	nōsita kasici yo 'visits or plays a while and then goes'
P.48.	Ani 'p.nita. Cham cal mek.ko, cal nōlta (ka) kap.nita. Annyeng hi kyēysipsio.	We mustn't. We've had such a good meal and such an enjoyable visit. Goodbye!	[= No. After eating well and amusing ourselves well, we go.]
K.49.	Kulem, tto osipsio. Annyeng hi kasipsio.	Well—come again! Goodbye.	

SUPPLEMENTARY VOCABULARY

phāthi	party	siksa	meal; eating
yēnhoy	dinner party, banquet	siksa lul hay yo	has a meal; eats
chotay(q cang)	a (written) invitation	cha(y)lim phyo	menu
cheng hay yo	invites	cēngsik	the fixed (table-d'hote) dinner

swul	wine
(mulq) koki or (as food) sayngsen	fish
sikthak	dinner table
sangq po	tablecloth
yuli can	glass, tumbler
chaq can	teacup
swulq can	winecup
cepsi	plate
kulus	food container, dish(es)
sapal	porcelain rice-bowl
cwupal	metal rice-bowl
cwupin	guest of honor
paypin	other guests
ceptay (lul) hay yo or tāycep (ul) hay yo	entertains (a person)
pay ka pulle yo [pulu-]	is full, replete
ūngcep-sil	living room
secay	study, den
chīm-pang	bedroom
kwāng	storeroom
il-chung	first floor
alay chung [often spelled alayq chung]	downstairs
wu chung, wi chung [often spelled wiq chung]	upstairs
ī-chung	second floor

tali	bridge [also leg]
chungchung-tali or chungchung-tay or kyeytan	stairs, staircase
sa(tak)-tali	ladder
sungkang-ki	elevator
kakwu	furniture
cwūthayk	residence
pyelqcang	summer cottage
sēyq cip	rented house
sēyq pang	rented room(s)
sēy	rent
cip sey	house rent
pangq sey	room rent
talq sey	monthly rent
censey	rent deposit (refunded on leaving)
pocung-kum	security, guarantee fund
kwucen	commission
poktek-pang	house broker's office, rental agent
ic.e yo [ic-]	forgets
insa	greetings, courtesies
insa (lul) hay yo	greets, says hello (or good-bye) to
mūn.an	regards (to someone)

NOTE: A list of foods will be found in the supplementary vocabulary of Lesson 16.

NOTES

‖ 18.1. Verbs: the sequential form -(u)ni.

Verbs have a SEQUENTIAL FORM, which is made by attaching the ending -(u)ni to them: -uni after consonants, -ni after vowels. The ending may also be attached to past bases to make past-tense forms (-ess.uni), and to future bases to make future-tense forms (-keyss.uni):

hani 'as [he] does . . .'
hayss.uni 'as [he] did . . .'
hakeyss.uni 'as [he] is going to do . . .'
mek.uni 'as [he] eats . . .'
mek.ess.uni 'as [he] ate . . .'
mek.keyss.uni 'as [he] will eat . . .'

This ending means 'as' or 'since' or 'because' or 'in view of the fact that,' and it occurs in the following Basic Sentences of this lesson:

1. Sikan i nuc.ess.uni . . . 'It has become late, so . . .'
18. Cenyek i tā cwūnpi toyn mo.yang ini . . . 'Since dinner seems to be ready . . .'
21. . . . cengseng kkes ma(y)ntul.ess.uni . . . 'since I put my heart into making it . . .'

The EXTENDED sequential form is pronounced -(u)ni-kka or -(u)ni-kka n' (with an abbreviation of the particle un/nun) and has about the same meaning as -(u)ni. Both, but particularly the extended sequential, also have the meaning 'when in the past [something happened], then . . . ,' indicating a close sequence of actions. Examples of the extended sequential appear in the following Basic Sentences:

2. Na nun cikum pappuni-kka n'. . . 'In view of the fact that I'm busy now . . .'
5. . . . catong-cha ka cōh.uni-kka . . . 'since this is a good car . . .'

Here are more examples of the sequential form.

1. Nemu cek.uni, pelipsita.	It's too small—let's throw it away.
2. Onul un com pappuni, ku īl un ^{l}nayil hakeyss.^{s}up.nita.	I'm rather busy today, so I'll take care of that matter tomorrow.
3. Onul cenyek un Pak sensayng tayk ey se Hānkwuk ūmsik ul mek.key toykeyss.uni, mānh.i capswus.ci māsiyo.	We're going to have Korean food at Mr. Pak's house tonight, so don't eat much [now].
4. Cēnhwa lul hani-kka, āmu to pat.ci anh.ess.ey yo.	When I telephoned, nobody [received it =] answered.
5. Nay ka kani-kka ku sālam i sinmun ul poko iss.ess.ey yo.	When I went [to see him], he was reading the newspaper.
6. Mēlli se poni-kka n' sān salam kwa kath.sup.nita.	When you look at it from a distance, it's like a live person. [Sān is the modifier from sā-l- 'live.']
7. Onul achim cēncha ey sālam i mānh.uni, kel.e kapsita.	There are so many people on the streetcar this morning, let's walk.
8. Halq īl i ēps.uni, sānqpo 'na halq ka yo?	Since we have nothing to do, shall we take a walk?
9. Cikum nay ka kongpu lul hani, kath.i hapsita.	I'm studying now—let's do it together.
10. Pam i okeyss.uni, ppalli īl hapsita.	Night is coming, so let's work fast.
11. Mas i iss.nun ūmsik ul cwūnpi hayss.uni, com capswusipsio.	I've prepared some good food, so have some.
12. Nyū-Yok ey ^{l}nayil kakeyss.uni kitalisio.	I'm going to New York tomorrow, so wait for me.
13. Cēki sungkang-ki ka naylye oni, ellun ka se thapsita.	There's an elevator coming down over there, so let's hurry and take it.
14. Hānkwuk mal ul cal moluni chēn-chen hi māl-ssum hay cwusipsio.	I don't know Korean very well, so please speak slowly.

18.2. The auxiliary verb mal.e yo.

The auxiliary verb mal.e yo [mā-l-] is used at the end of verb phrases, either after the gerund -ko or after the suspective -ci.

After a gerund, this auxiliary means 'finishes' or 'completes,' so that phrases ending -ko mal.e yo mean 'finishes [do]ing' or '[does] completely' or 'ends up [do]ing.' When the particle ya 'only if' intervenes, the translation sometimes comes out 'simply has to (must),' as in Basic Sentence 40:

. . . mek.e poko ya mālkeyss.^{s}up.nita. 'I'll simply have to try eating it.'

This meaning could be more literally rendered as something like 'only if it's by trying to eat it will I end the matter.' It is somewhat stronger than . . . mek.e pwa ya hakeyss.^{s}up.nita 'I will have to try eating . . . .'

Here are some examples of gerunds with mal.e yo after them:

1. Ppalli siksa lul kkuth nāyko mal.ess.ess.ci yo.	I finished up my meal in a hurry.
2. Na nun sayngsen ul mek.umyen ēncey 'na pay thāl i nako ya mal.e yo.	I end up getting a stomach-ache every time I eat fish.
3. Ip mas ul ilh.e peliko mal.ess.ey yo.	I have completely lost my appetite.
4. Cham, ^{l}nayil imyen nay ka mahun sal ina tōy peliko māl.keyss.kwun yo.	What do you know, I will be forty years old tomorrow!
5. Ku ^{n}yeca ka cenyek ey chotay han kes ul ic.e peliko mal.ess.uni etteh.key haci yo.	What shall I do?! I had completely forgotten about her dinner invitation.
6. Ku pupu nun ecey pelsse pyelqcang ulo tte nako mal.ess.ci yo.	The couple had already left for their summer cottage yesterday, you see.
7. I swukcey lul ^{l}nayil ccum un pachiko ya mālkeyss.ey yo.	I'll simply have to hand this homework in by tomorrow.

Another kind of expression involves two consecutive gerunds, the first from any verb and the second always mālko, with the meaning 'of course . . .' as in Basic Sentence 16 of Lesson 16:

Ālko mālko yo. 'Of course she knows!'

The sentence ends in yo because you are talking polite style; if you drop the yo it is still the same sentence, but now in the INTIMATE style—essentially the polite style minus the particle yo, as you will see in ‖ 22.4. In Seoul, the ending -ko is commonly pronounced -kwu; since the expressions with -ko mālko are so colloquial, you are likely to hear them more often as -kwu mālkwu: Ālkwu mālkwu yo!

Here are some more examples:

1. Mek.ko mālko yo.	Of course I'm eating!
2. Onul hak.kyo ey kap.nikka?—Kakwu mālkwu yo.	Are you going to school today?—Of course I'm going.
3. Onulq cenyek ey cwumusikeyss.^{s}up.nikka?—Cako mālko yo.	Are you going to go to bed tonight?—Of course I am!
4. Khuko cōh.sup.nikka?—Khuko cōh.ko mālko yo.	Is it nice and big?—Of course it's nice and big.
5. Nappun kes ul kaluchici anh.ko mālko yo.	Of course they don't teach bad things.

You have already learned that the suspective -ci followed by mal.e yo is a way to make negative commands (‖ 7.4) with a more literal translation of 'avoid/refrain/desist from doing.' These expressions are largely limited to commands and suggestions as in some of the early Basic Sentences, as well as some in this lesson:

Chayk ul posici māsipsio. 'Please don't look at your book(s).'
Yenge lo haci māsipsio. 'Please don't say it in English.'
40. . . . capswus.ci māsipsio. 'Don't eat it.'

With verbal nouns and other expressions involving the auxiliary hay yo you get the expected form . . . haci mā-l- but the haci can be freely dropped, as you see in Basic Sentence 5 where you find "Yēm.lye māsipsio 'Don't worry' instead of the equally acceptable "Yēm.lye haci māsipsio. An example that does not involve a verbal noun is Elyewe (haci) māsey yo 'Don't feel embarrassed,' with the emotional meaning of the adjective elyewe yo 'it is difficult; I am embarrassed' (as in Elyepci man . . . 'It is embarrassing [= I am sorry to trouble you] but . . .') turned into a processive verbal phrase by using the infinitive -e + hay yo (‖ 8.10).

Here are some more examples of negative commands and suggestions made with -ci mā-l-:

1. [1]Nayil pi ka omyen, sangcem ey kaci māpsita.	If it rains tomorrow, let's not go to the store.
2. [1]Nayil ilcciki il.e naci māpsita.	Let's not get up early tomorrow.
3. Onulq cenyek ey nun kongpu māpsita.	Let's not study this evening.
4. Ku chayk i nemu pissamyen, saci māsipsio.	If that book is too expensive, don't buy it.
5. Sikan i nemu nuc.ess.uni, unhayng ey kaci māsipsio.	It's too late, so don't go to the bank.
6. I cip i poki cōh.ci anh.uni, yeki se sālci māsey yo.	This house isn't pretty—don't live in it.
7. Onulq cenyek ey ūmsik cip ey se mekci mal.e yo.	Don't eat at a restaurant tonight.

Within sentences containing a pair of opposite commands or suggestions, the first may be expressed by -ci mālko ('instead of —ing, without —ing'), as in Basic Sentence 27:

Swuq-kalak ulo capswusici mālko, ceq-kalak ulo capswusipsio. 'Don't eat with a spoon—eat with chopsticks.'

Here are more examples:

1. Ūmsik cip ey se mannaci mālko, [1]yekwan ey se mannapsita.	Let's not meet at the restaurant, let's meet at the hotel.
2. Cēncha lo kaci mālko, catong-cha lo kapsita.	Let's not take a streetcar, let's take a cab.
3. Kicha lo kaci mālko, pihayng-ki lo kasio.	Don't go on the train—take a plane!

From this use comes the handy phrase Ic.ci mālko . . . [+ affirmative command] 'Don't forget to . . .' as in these sentences:

1. Ic.ci mālko son ul ssis.usey yo.	Don't forget to wash your hands.

2. Ic.ci mālko phyēnci lul ssusipsio.	Don't forget to write the letter.
3. Ic.ci mālko emeni hanthey ku yēyki lul hay tulisey yo.	Don't forget to tell that to Mother.
4. Ic.ci mālko na hanthey tōn ul cwusey yo.	Don't forget to give me the money.
5. Ic.ci mālko kwutwu lul takk.usey yo.	Don't forget to shine your shoes.

You recall that in STATEMENTS and QUESTIONS, 'instead of or without —ing' is expressed by -ci anh.ko:

1. Ūmsik cip ey se mannaci anh.ko, [l]yekwan ey se mannass.ey yo.	We didn't meet at the restaurant, we met at the hotel.
2. Pak sensayng i sinmun ul ilk.ci anh.ko, kongpu lul hap.nita.	Mr. Pak isn't reading the newspaper, he's studying.
3. Wuli ayki nun cenyek ul mekci anh.ko cass.ey yo.	Our baby went to sleep without eating supper.
4. Kicha lo kaci anh.ko, pihayng-ki lo kalq ka yo??	Shall we take a plane instead of a train?

You will sometimes find mālko used in the middle of a sentence directly after a noun or a noun + particle with the meaning 'not being . . .'; in this use we can say that the gerund is functioning as a PSEUDO-PARTICLE, and it does not call for a command or suggestion at the end of the sentence:

1. I kes (un) mālko ce kes ul sasipsio.	Buy this one and not that one.
2. Wuli atul mālko talun ai lul chac.ko iss.ey yo.	They are looking for some other boy, not our son.
3. I kes mālko com khun kapang i ēps.[s]up.nikka?	Don't you have any suitcases bigger than this?

18.3. Verbs: the adversative form -(u)na.

5. . . . Kil i com nappuna, cōh.un catong-cha 'ni-kka, ppalli kalq swu iss.[s]up.nita. 'The road is rather bad, but since it's a good car, we can go fast.'

23. . . . Kulena, ileh.key mas i 'ss.nun ūmsik un cheum ip.nita. '[It is so] but it's the first time for such delicious food.'

Verbs are put into the ADVERSATIVE FORM by attaching the ending -(u)na to them: -una after consonants, -na after vowels. The ending is added to the base of processive or descriptive verbs (including the copula), or to the honorific base; for past tense, it is attached to the past base or the honorific past base; and for future forms, it is added to the future or future honorific base. Here are some examples:

kana 'goes, but . . .'	kasina '[someone esteemed] goes, but . . .'
cōh.una 'is good, but . . .'	cōh.usina '[someone esteemed] is good, but . . .'
nōna 'plays, but . . .'	nōsina . . . '[someone esteemed] plays, but . . .'

puluna 'calls, but . . .'	pulusina '[someone esteemed] calls, but . . .'
kass.una 'went, but . . .'	kasyess.una '[someone esteemed] went, but . . .'
cōh.ass.una 'was good, but . . .'	cōh.usyess.una '[someone esteemed] was good, but . . .'
nol.ass.una 'played, but . . .'	nōsyess.una '[someone esteemed] played, but . . .'
pulless.una 'called, but . . .'	pulusyess.una '[someone esteemed] called, but . . .'
kakeyss.una 'will go, but . . .'	kasikeyss.una '[someone esteemed] will go, but . . .'
cōh.keyss.una 'will be good, but . . .'	cōh.usikeyss.una '[someone esteemed] will be good, but . . .'
nōlkeyss.una 'will play, but . . .'	nōsikeyss.una '[someone esteemed] will play, but . . .'
pulukeyss.una 'will call, but . . .'	pulusikeyss.una '[someone esteemed] will call, but . . .'

The adversative ending -<u>(u)na</u> means 'does, but . . .' or 'does, but yet . . . .' Basic Sentence 21 contains an example of the EXTENDED ADVERSATIVE: the regular ending -<u>(u)na</u> with -<u>ma</u> after it. This -<u>ma</u> element adds the meaning '. . . but anyway' to the form:

Pyel kes un ēps.una-ma, . . . 'There isn't anything special, but anyway . . .'

Here are more examples of sentences with adversative forms.

1. Nac un tewuna, cenyek un senul hay yo.	The days are hot, but the nights are cool.
2. Khi nun khuna, him un cēksup.nita.	He's tall, but [his strength is small =] he's weak.
3. Kako siph.una, sikan i ēps.^{s}up.nita.	I'd like to come, but I haven't got time.
4. Ku nun yel.uy nun iss.una caycwu ka ēps.^{s}up.nita.	He has enthusiasm but not talent.
5. Achim ey nun pi ka wass.una, ōhwu ey nun hay ka na wass.^{s}up.nita.	It rained in the morning, but the sun came out in the afternoon.
6. Hānkwuk mal ul mānh.i kongpu hayss.una, cal mōlla yo.	I studied my Korean a lot, but I don't know it very well.
7. Nay an(h)ay nun onulq cenyek ey cip ey iss.keyss.una, na nun ēps.keyss.^{s}up.nita.	My wife will be at home tonight, but I won't.
8. Na nun kongpu lul hakeyss.una, Kim sensayng un mōs halq kes iey yo.	I'm going to study, but Mr. Kim won't be able to.
9. Mas un cōh.ci mōs hana-ma, hana capswusio.	They're not very good, but have one anyway.
10. Cip un cak.una-ma, cali ka cōh.ci yo??	The house is small, but anyway it's in a nice location, isn't it??

Adversative forms have the same general meaning as the -ci man construction (kongpu haci man . . . 'studies, but . . . ; although [he] studies . . . '). The adversative, however, is somewhat weaker: it conveys some reservation, or doubt, about the action or condition. The quasi-particle ina/'na that you learned about in Lesson 6 (see ‖ 6.3) is related to the adversative form, both in pronunciation and in meaning: it conveys doubt or reservation, or vagueness, about the noun expression it follows, or about the sentence as a whole. Compare also ina in Basic Sentence 11 of this lesson:

. . . Cip ina swipkey chac.usyess.ey yo? 'Did you find the house all right?'—'Did you have any difficulty about finding the house?'

Here are some more examples:

Swul ina masipsita.	Let's drink some wine or something.
Talun kes un ku man twuko kongpu 'na cal hasio.	Put other things aside and just study hard.
Pap ina capswusipsio.	Have something to eat.

When two ina-phrases are together the translation is usually '(either . . .) or' or '(both . . .) and' or 'and/or': yenphil ina kong-chayk ina 'pencils and/or notebooks'; I cip ina ce cip ina tā kath.ey yo 'This house and that one [regardless which you look at] are both alike.' (The second ina can be omitted, often in favor of a particle like i/ka or ul/lul, to specify the relationship of the larger phrase to the rest of the sentence.) Sometimes ina means '(regardless) whether it is' and with question words '-ever it may be':

I kes ina ce kes ina mues ina tā cōh.a yo.	Whether it's this or that or whatever it is, it's all right.
Nwukwu 'na tā al.e yo.	Anyone and everyone knows.
Enu phyen ina sikan i kellye yo.	Either way will take time.

The extended adversative of the copula ina-ma 'it is but anyway; although it is' is also used as a quasi-particle with the translation 'anyway, at least; even':

Mas ēps.nun kes ina-ma mānh.i capswusio.	Please help yourself, though it isn't a tasty dinner.
Tēlewun os ina-ma, (halq swu ēps.i) ip.e ya hakeyss.ey yo.	I'll just have to wear my dirty clothes.

‖ 18.4. More verb phrases with specialized meanings.

32. . . . ip mas ul ilh.e pelyess.^{s}up.nita. 'I lost my appetite completely.'
36. . . . ku wi ey sokom ul ppulye twup.nita. 'You sprinkle salt over them (and get that out of the way).'

Certain Korean verbs mean one thing when they are used by themselves, but combine into phrases with infinitives to mean something different. You have learned these:

pwa yo 'sees'	hay pwa yo 'tries (out) doing'
cwue yo 'gives'	hay cw(u)e yo 'does for [someone]'
tulye yo 'gives [to someone esteemed]'	hay tulye yo 'does for [someone esteemed]'

Three more such combinations are made by putting together an infinitve with another verb, all meaning various shades of 'finish doing' or 'do completely':

noh.a yo 'puts' [often pronounced nwa yo]	hay noha yo 'gets it done, does it now (in anticipation of a later need), does it for later'
pelye yo 'throws away, discards'	hay (p)pelye yo 'does it completely or exhaustively' [The form with pp is livelier.]
twue yo 'puts or leaves (somewhere)'	hay tw(u)e yo 'does something and gets it out of the way, does it and gets it over with; finishes up doing something'

You have seen each of these verbs used by itself in Basic Sentences of this lesson:

16\. . . . Sang ey samci-chang kac'ta noh.ass.ey yo? 'Did you put the forks on the table?'

37\. Elma hwū ey sokom mul ul peliko . . . 'Somewhat later you throw away the brine . . .'

38\. . . . han sahul twuess.ta ka meksup.nita. '. . . you leave it for about three days and then eat it.'

Here are some more examples of their use in phrases with infinitives.

1. Wuli ka chāyso lul sa noh.umyen, Kim sensayng puin i kimchi lul ma(y)ntulkeyss.ci yo.	If we buy vegetables [in advance, ahead of time], Mrs. Kim will make the kimchi, you see.
2. Kongpu lul cal hay noh.a ya toykeyss.ey yo.	I have to do my studying well [in preparation for something].
3. Ūmsik ul cal cwūnpi hay noh.ass.ey yo.	We've prepared the food well [ahead of time].
4. Ku ūmsik i nemu mas i iss.e se, tā mek.e pelyess.ˢup.nita.	That food tasted so good that I ate it all up.
5. Ce nun ic.e peliko, chayk ul mōs kaciko wass.ey yo.	I completely [forgot and didn't bring =] forgot to bring the book.
6. Kim sensayng i sangcem ey se tōn ul ilh.e pelyess.ey yo.	Mr. Kim lost his money at the store.
7. Cenyek hwū ey palo cip ulo ka pelipsita.	Let's go home right after dinner.
8. Ic.e pelici mālko, Kim sensayng eykey i chayk ul tulisio.	Don't forget to give this book to Mr. Kim.
9. Celm.ess.ul ttay kongpu lul hay twue ya hay yo.	Study while you are still young.
10. Cikum tā mek.e twue yo.	You'd better eat all of it now.
11. Hānkwuk salam un kimchi lul kaul ey ma(y)ntul.e twuess.ta ka kyewul tong-an nul mek.e yo.	Koreans make kimchi in the fall, and have it throughout the winter.

Other phrases are similar but use gerunds instead of infinitives. Two examples are -ko mal.e yo (from mal.e yo 'finishes, does completely') and -ko na yo (from na yo 'happens, occurs'). Here are some examples:

1. Cenyek ul mek.ko mal.ess.ˢup.nita.	I've finished eating my dinner.
2. I chayk ul ilk.ko mal.ess.ˢup.nikka?	Have you finished reading this book?

3. Tōn ul tā ssuko mal.ess.ey yo.	I've spent all my money.
4. Kim sensayng i pelsse na kako mān mo.yang iey yo.	Mr. Kim seems to have already gone out.
5. Pap ul mek.ko nass.ey yo.	I've just finished dinner.
6. Kongpu lul hako na se yenghwa kwūkyeng ul kalq ka yo??	Shall we go see a movie after we have finished our studying?
7. I chayk ul cēmsim kkaci ey nun tā ilk.ko nakeyss.ey yo.	I will have finished reading this book by lunch.
8. [1]Nayil kkaci kitaliko na se phyēnci ssukeyss.ey yo.	I will wait till tomorrow to write the letter.

Notice, however, the special expression [ha]ko ya mal.e yo, which means much the same thing as [ha]ko ya hay yo, namely 'must [do], has to [do]':

40. . . . mek.e poko ya mālkeyss.[s]up.nita. 'I'll have to try eating it.'

Here, for your reference, is a summary of the verb phrases presented in this lesson, with a key to their central meanings.

1. -e tw(u)e yo 'does and gets out of the way; gets something done and over with; finishes up doing' [completive]
2. -e noh.a yo (nwa yo) 'does for later' [anticipatory]
3. -e (p)pelye yo 'does completely' [exhaustive]
4. -ko mal.e(ss.ey) yo 'finish(es/ed) doing' [terminative]
5. -ko na yo 'just did, has just done' [transitional]

‖ 18.5. Some more dropped particles.

It often happens that Korean nouns in a list that would normally be joined in the English equivalent by 'and' are simply strung together with no connecting particle (such as the expected hako or kwa/wa):

8. A, Pak sensayng Han sensayng isip.nikka? 'Oh, is it Mr. Pak and Mr. Han?
11. . . . Pak sensayng nim Han sensayng nim osyess.ey yo? 'Are Mr. Pak and Mr. Han here?'

A similar example occurred in Sentence 7 of Lesson 6:

. . . Pelsse ttal hana atul hana ka iss.ey yo 'They now have a daughter and a son.'

In some conventional phrases consisting of noun and verb, too, the particle indicating the grammatical function is dropped. One such phrase is mas i iss.ey yo 'it has flavor, it tastes (good),' which is sometimes reduced to mas iss.ey yo /matisseyyo/, though more commonly the particle stays and the initial vowel of iss.ey yo drops: mas i 'ss.ey yo /masisseyyo/; the negative is either mas i ēps.ey yo, or (with dropped particle) mas ēps.ey yo /matēpsseyyo/. A similar situation is seen in the case of many processive verbal nouns: kongpu hay yo (for kongpu lul hay yo), sānqpo hay yo (for sānqpo lul hay yo), and so on. In everyday speech many particles drop freely—or, rather, never get put in to begin with—especially the subject and object particles.

‖ 18.6. The base of capswe yo.

The honorific verb capswe yo '[someone esteemed] eats' has a couple of peculiarities. For one thing, it is sometimes pronounced capse yo; in sloppy speech w drops readily after a consonant, especially a labial like p. For another, its honorific base form capswusi- often drops the final i when a consonant comes right after it (that is, when a one-shape ending is attached to it). Here is a list of some of the forms.

	BASE	HONORIFIC BASE
	capswu-	capswusi-
TWO-SHAPE ENDINGS:		
Formal Statement	capswup.nita	capswusip.nita
Formal Question	capswup.nikka	capswusip.nikka
Formal Command	capswusio	capswusipsio
Formal Suggestion	capswupsita	capswusipsita
Conditional	capswumyen	capswusimyen
Sequential	capswuni	capswusini
Adversative	capswuna	capswusina
ONE-SHAPE ENDINGS:		
Gerund -ko	capswuko	capswusiko or capswus.ko
Suspective -ci	capswuci	capswusici or capswus.ci
Future base -keyss-	capswukeyss-	capswusikeyss- or capswus.keyss-
Adverbative -key	capswukey	capswusikey or capswus.key
Processive modifier -nun	capswunun	capswusinun or capswus.nun
Transferentive -ta (ka)	capswuta (ka)	capswusita (ka) or capswus.ta (ka)

Observe, incidentally, the use of the two words for 'eat' (capswu- and mek-) in the Basic Sentences of this lesson. When the host and hostess urge their guests to eat, or otherwise refer to the guests' ingestion, they use the honorific word; in their replies, however, Mr. Pak and Mr. Han of course use mek- (NOT the honorific word!) to refer to their own action of eating. For example:

29. [Puin] Kulemyen, ku yeph ey iss.nun samci-chang ulo capswusipsio. 'Then eat with the fork beside them.'
30. [Pak sensayng.] Komapsup.nita. Ce nun samcichang ulo mek.keyss.ˢup.nita. 'Thank you. I'll eat with the fork.'
31. [Puin.] . . . way Han sensayng un an capswusip.nikka. 'Why aren't you eating, Mr. Han?'
32. [Han sensayng.] . . . mānh.i meksup.nita. 'I'm eating lots.'

Also, when the hostess is telling how to make kimchi, she uses mek- (not capswu-) to talk about eating it when it is finished; this is a general or impersonal meaning 'eat' and does not refer to the actions of anyone in particular to whom she might wish to show esteem:

38. . . . han sahul twuess.ta ka meksup.nita. 'You [or We] let it stand for about three days, and then eat it.'

18.7. The post-noun kkes.

The post-noun kkes means 'to the full extent of, to the utmost of (capability or capacity).' It occurs after a few nouns to produce a phrase meaning 'wholeheartedly' or the like: him kkes īl hay yo 'works to the utmost of one's strength (him), works as hard as one can'; cengseng kkes ma(y)ntul.e yo 'pours one's heart into making, makes with great devotion'; maum kkes wul.e yo 'cries one's heart out.' The meaning of kkes is somewhat like that of kkaci '(all the way) up to,' and the two words may be related. A synonym is . . . ul tā hay se 'exhausting one's . . . , using one's . . . to the limit': him ul tā hay se īl hay yo 'exerts all one's strength to do the job.' This comes from tā hay yo which means 'pours all (into), exhausts, runs through (everything)' and also 'it comes to an end, it runs out, it gets exhausted.'

EXERCISES

I

Each of the following sentences is a simple statement in the polite style. Change each one so that it is four different things in the FORMAL style: (1) a simple command; (2) an honorific command; (3) a simple suggestion; and (4) an honorific suggestion. For example, the first will be:

1. Yeki anc.usio.
2. Yeki anc.usipsio.
3. Yeki anc.upsita.
4. Yeki anc.usipsita.

Remember that anh.e yo is replaced by mal.e yo in commands and suggestions. In the formal style, when the reference includes someone other than the speaker, mek.e yo is usually replaced by capswe yo, ca yo by cwumus.ey yo, and iss.ey yo 'stays' by kyēysey yo.

1. Yeki anc.e yo.
2. Cal tul.e yo.
3. Tut.ki man hay yo.
4. Nuc.key oci anh.e yo.
5. Keki iss.ey yo.
6. Com kitalye yo.
7. Sip-pun swie yo.
8. Ayki hanthey ūmsik ul cwuci anh.e yo.
9. Hak.kyo ey kaci anh.ko, cip ey iss.ey yo.
10. Ku sālam hanthey cēnhwa lul kel.e yo.
11. Yenge lo ssuci anh.e yo.

II

Each of the following items contains two sentences, the second of which begins with kuleni(-kka n') 'as this is the case . . . or . . . so.' Connect the two sentences with the appropriate sequential form and translate the sentence. For example, the first will be: Onul ōhwu ey kongpu lul cal hayss.uni(-kka n'), cenyek ey nun yenghwa kwūkyeng ul ka to cōh.a yo. 'Since you studied hard this afternoon, you may go to the movies this evening.'

1. Onul ōhwu ey kongpu lul cal hayss.ey yo. Kuleni(-kka n'), cenyek ey nun yenghwa kwūkyeng ul ka to cōh.a yo.

2. [1]Nayil son nim i osey yo. Kuleni(-kka n'), wuli ka sōcey lul hay ya hay yo.
3. Nay ka selkeci lul halq cwul al.e yo. Kuleni(-kka n'), towa tulilq ka yo??
4. Kako siph.un kos i yeki se mel.e yo. Kuleni(-kka n'), kel.e kalq swu ēps.e yo.
5. Nay ka ku sinmun ul mōs pwass.ey yo. Kuleni(-kka n'), ku kes ul mōllass.ey yo.
6. Kim sensayng i khun soli lo catong-cha lul pulle yo. Kuleni(-kka n'), catong-cha han tay ka ppalli wass.ey yo.
7. Na nun neykthai lul māyci anh.ess.ey yo. Kuleni(-kka n'), kulen kos ey tul.e kako siph.ci anh.ess.ey yo.
8. Onul ōhwu ey palam i pūlko, pi ka ol mo.yang iey yo. Kuleni(-kka n') sānqpo lul kaci mālko, cip ey iss.upsita.
9. Nay ka chinkwu lul pulle to āmu tāytap i ēps.ess.ey yo. Kuleni(-kka n'), honca ka ya hakeyss.ci yo.
10. Nay ka sangcem ey kata ka wuphyen-kwuk ey tullikeyss.ey yo. Kuleni(-kka n'), enni ka eceyq pam ssun phyēnci lul puchilq ka yo??
11. I congi nun mōs sse yo. Kuleni(-kka n'), pelye to cōh.a yo.

III

Each of the following items contains two sentences, the second of which begins with kulena '. . . but.' Connect the two sentences with the appropriate adversative form and translate the combined sentence. For example, the first will be: Nay ka sang ul pwass.una, son nim i onun kes ul mōllass.ey yo. 'I set the table, but I didn't know a guest was coming.'

1. Nay ka sang ul pwass.ey yo. Kulena, son nim i onun kes ul mōllass.ey yo.
2. Wuli ka senkyo-sa hanthey to ceq-kalak ul cwuess.ey yo. Kulena, senkyo-sa ka ceq-kalak ul ssulq cwul mōllass.ey yo.
3. I kes i kimchi 'ey yo. Kulena, cham kimchi ka ani 'ey yo.
4. Nay ka ku yenghwa lul kwūkyeng hako siph.ess.ey yo. Kulena, yenghwa-kwan i cip ey se mel.e se kaci mōs hayss.ey yo.
5. Onulq cenyek ey Kim sensayng ul pāngmun halq ka hayss.ey yo. Kulena, nal i chwuwe cyess.uni-kka n', Kim sensayng cip ey kaci anh.ko, cip ey iss.keyss.ey yo.
6. Congkyo nun tā cōh.sup.nita. Kulena, tā kath.ci anh.sup.nita.
7. Yeyswu-kyo lul swīpkey selmyeng haki ka elyepsup.nita. Kulena, i chayk ul com ilk.usimyen, cha-cha āsikey toyp.nita.
8. Wuli kāy ka nappun ūmsik ul mek.ko cwuk.ess.ey yo. Kulena, wuli ka āy tul hanthey kāy ka cwuk.un kes ul māl haci anh.ess.ey yo.
9. Cīnan Cwuil ey [1]yeypay-tang ey na on sālam i cek.ess.[s]up.nita. Kulena, moksa nim kkey se hasin selkyo ka caymi iss.ess.[s]up.nita.
10. Wuli sensayng i pappuki to hasey yo. Kulena, sikan i nemu kellici anh.umyen, wuli haksayng tul hanthey i yēyki lul selmyeng hay cwusilq key yo.
11. Wuli ttal i capchay lul ma(y)ntulko siph.e hayss.ey yo. Kulena, Tang myen i ēps.e se etteh.key halq cwul mōllass.ey yo.

IV

Tell your friend 'Don't forget to ___':

1. bring your little brother when you come to dinner.
2. give the dog something to eat if he barks.
3. brush your teeth before going to bed.

4. comb your hair after washing up.
5. slice the radishes and cabbage up fine.
6. put a lid on the pot that you have stuffed the kimchi in (and leave it).
7. stop and buy some fruit on your way home.
8. say hello to each person who comes in.
9. set the table.
10. have your meal before you go to the concert.
11. mail my letter on your way to school.
12. go to the bank and THEN do the marketing.

CONVERSATION

I

When you are a guest in a Korean home, it is polite to speak favorably of everything—the home, the food, the view, the children, etc. On the other hand, Korean hosts and hostesses customarily talk down their possessions and belittle their efforts to prepare nice food (while at the same time urging more and more upon a guest). You should be equipped to handle both these situations conversationally. Accordingly while Student A assumes the role of a guest, Student B should welcome him to his home and offer him an abundance of hospitality. Converse appropriately. Then, Student B becomes a guest in the home of Student C, and so on until A has had his turn to be host.

II

Prepare a short talk in Korean describing the layout of your home—what rooms are on each floor, and what is outside as well as inside. Then describe the (real or imaginary) place where you or your spouse (real or imaginary) goes to work every day, including its setting among the other buildings nearby.

III

Think of three or four simple American meals or dishes you know how to fix; prepare to tell how to make each dish. Go into as much detail as necessary; but try to stick to vocabulary you know. If necessary, prepare a list of additional words you need and ask you tutor for them a day or two BEFORE you are to be called upon. Be prepared to answer the questions your tutor (and/or the other students) will ask you.

VOCABULARY DRILL

Say each of the following sentences aloud in Korean, completing it in each of the ways indicated. (Repeat the whole sentence each time.)

1. I've ___ (and got it over with).
   made the kimchi
   chopped the scallions and garlic
   covered the crock with a lid

2. That house is ___.
   a long way off
   neat
   messy

3. Let's ___ (in advance).
   prepare the food
   make the capchay
   cut up the radishes and cabbage

4. I like food that ___.
   is not too highly spiced
   tastes good
   you can eat with chopsticks

5. Have you forgotten to ___ ?
set the table
invite the guest of honor
clean the living room

6. Please put the ___ on the table.
plates
teacups
tablecloth

7. Please don't ___ [= finish doing].
lose this money
drink all the wine up
forget to telephone me

8. Who is that man who's ___ ?
so busy
driving the car fast
getting off the streetcar

9. Mr. Pak is in the ___.
dining room
kitchen
bedroom

10. Let's drink our ___.
tea
coffee
wine

11. Do you like to eat with ___ ?
a fork
chopsticks
a spoon

12. We haven't got much furniture ___.
upstairs
in our summer cottage
in the study downstairs

COMPREHENSION

As a class, pretend that you are all at a dinner party together, just finishing up the dessert. Chat for a few minutes about the meal you have just eaten. Then have the host (or hostess) introduce the guest of honor and ask him to make a speech; this is your Korean teacher. He will then speak, while you listen intently. He may talk for five or ten minutes. He may decide to talk about food; he may compare eating habits (and manners) in different countries he knows about. He may discuss the ways in which food is prepared. He may talk about his personal preferences. Perhaps he will tell you what sort of thing he would eat in the course of a typical day in Korea (or Japan or China) and compare it with a day in America. If he has to use new words that you do not know, jot the words down; when he has finished and asks for questions, tell him you do not understand certain words. Have him explain them in Korean; if you still do not understand, he may be able to write an English translation on the board for you. (But remember that many food terms are very hard to translate.) DON'T make him speak English to you in explaining the words!

When the questions are finished, discuss among yourselves the things he has said. Say what you thought about the particular parts of his speech. Ask other people what they thought about this or that, mentioned by the speaker.

Finally, the Korean teacher may ask various people about things he said that have not been covered in the discussion.

LESSON 19. A SICK CALL

BASIC SENTENCES

Korean	English	Amplification
1. Kim sensayng i pyēngwen ey kanta ko māl hayss.ey yo.	Mr. Kim said he's going to the hospital.	pyēngwen 'hospital' kanta 'goes' [plain style] . . . ko '(saying) that . . .' kanta ko māl hay yo 'says that [one] goes'
2. Ku uy puin i alh.nunta ko hayss.ey yo.	He said his wife is sick.	alh.nunta /allunta/ [alh-] 'is sick' [plain style] alh.nunta ko hay yo 'says [someone] is sick'
3. Ku uy puin i yel i noph.ta ko kulayss.ey yo.	He said that his wife has a high fever.	yel 'fever, temperature' noph.ta /noptta/ [noph-] 'is high' [plain style] noph.ta ko kulay yo 'says that [it] is high'
4. Kulay se, ecey pyēngwen ey ip.wen hayss.ta ko hayss.ey yo.	So yesterday she entered the hospital, he said.	ip.wen 'entrance <u>or</u> admission to hospital as a patient' ip.wen hay yo 'enters <u>or</u> is admitted to a hospital' ip.wen hayss.ta 'entered <u>or</u> was admitted' [plain style] ip.wen hayss.ta ko hayss.ey yo 'said that [one] was admitted <u>or</u> entered'
5. Kim sensayng un onul ōcen ey hak.kyo ey se kaluchiko, ōhwu ey n' puin ul pāngmun hanta ko kulayss.ey yo.	Mr. Kim said that today he's going to teach at school in the morning and in the afternoon he's going to visit his wife.	pāngmun 'a visit, a call' pāngmun (ul) hay yo 'makes a call, pays a visit, visits' pāngmun (ul) hanta 'visits' [plain style] pāngmun hanta ko kulayss.ey yo 'said [he] visits'
6. Catong-cha lo kaci anh.ko, cēncha lo kanta ko kulayss.ey yo.	He said that he's not going in a car, he's going on the streetcar.	kanta ko kulayss.ey yo 'said that [one] goes'

Korean	English	Amplification
7. Kil i mikkulewe se catong-cha lul wūncen haki (ka) elyepta ko hayss.ey yo.	He said the streets are slippery, so it's hard to drive a car.	kil 'road, street' mikkulewe yo [mikkulew-] 'is slippery' elyepta [elyew-] 'is hard, difficult' [plain style] elyepta ko hayss.ey yo 'said that [it] is difficult'
8. Kim sensayng un pappuko phikon hay se, pyēngwen ey ka se olay iss.ci mōs hakeyss.ta ko kulayss.ey yo.	Mr. Kim said he is busy and tired, so when he goes to the hospital he won't (be able to) stay long.	hakeyss.ta 'will do' [plain style] mōs hakeyss.ta ko kulayss.ey yo 'said that [he] won't be able to do'
9. Pyēngwen ey kal ttay na wa kath.i kaca ko hayss.ey yo.	He suggested I go along when he goes to the hospital.	kaca 'let's go' [plain style] kaca ko hayss.ey yo 'said let's go; suggested going, suggested that we go'
10. Pyēngwen ey kaki cen ey mence kkoch cip ey tullye se kkoch ul sa kaciko kaca ko kulayss.ey yo.	He suggested stopping by a flower shop first, before going to the hospital, to buy some flowers to take along.	sa kaciko kaca ko kulayss.ey yo 'suggested that we buy and carry and go'
11. Kim sensayng un caki ka kaluchinun tong-an na tele honca ka se kkoch ul sala ko hayss.ey yo.	Mr. Kim told me to go buy the flowers by myself while he (himself) was teaching.	caki 'oneself' caki ka kaluchinun tong-an 'while he himself is teaching' na tele 'to me' [in a command] sala 'buy!' [plain style] sala ko hayss.ey yo '[said, "buy!"=] told [one] to buy'
12. Kim sensayng un (māl haki lul) sīcheng yeph ey iss.nun hoysayk tōlq cip i ku puin i ip.wen hako iss.nun pyēngwen ila ko kulayss.ey yo.	Mr. Kim said the gray stone building next to the city hall is the hospital his wife is in.	māl haki lul 'what [one] said' sīcheng 'city hall' hoysayk 'gray' tōl 'stone' hoysayk tōlq cip 'gray stone house <u>or</u> building' pyēngwen ila ko kulay yo 'says it is a hospital'
13. Ku pyēngwen ilum i Cēycwung-wen ila ko hayss.ey yo.	He said the name of the hospital is Cēycwung-wen.	cēycwung 'salvation of the people' Cēycwung-wen ila ko hay yo 'says it is Cēycwung-wen'

Korean	English	Amplification
14. Pak ila 'nun uyhak paksa ka ku pyēngwen wēncang ici yo.	A doctor of medicine called Pak is the director of that hospital, you know.	uyhak 'medicine [as a branch of learning]' paksa 'doctor, holder of a degree' uyhak paksa 'doctor of medicine' Pak ila 'nun uyhak paksa 'a doctor of medicine called Pak' wēncang 'head (of an institution), director, chief'
15. Kim sensayng puin uy tam.im uysa nun O Namswu 'la 'nun yūmyeng han nāyq-kwa uysa 'ci yo.	The doctor in charge of Mrs. Kim is a famous physician called O Namswu.	tam.im 'charge, responsibility; person in charge' [often mispronounced /tanim/] tam.im (ul) hay yo 'has or takes charge, is in charge' Kim puin uy tam.im uysa 'the doctor in charge of Mrs. Kim' O Namswu 'la 'nun . . . uysa 'a doctor named O Namswu' nāy . . . 'internal, inside, interior' nāyq-kwa 'internal medicine; a specialist in internal medicine' nāyq-kwa uysa 'doctor of internal medicine, physician'
16. O uysa nun Mikwuk Cconsu Hopkhinsu 'la 'nun tāyhak ey se uyq-kwa lul kongpu hayss.ci yo.	Dr. O studied medicine at Johns Hopkins University in America, you know.	Cconsu Hopkhinsu 'Johns Hopkins' Cconsu Hopkhinsu 'la 'nun tāyhak 'a university called Johns Hopkins' uyq-kwa 'medical specialty, medical course'
17. Ku uy puchin in O Hanchang ssi nun yūmyeng han hakca lo, Sewul Tāyhak munq-kwa kwacang iey yo.	His father Mr. O Hanchang is a famous scholar and the head of the literature department at Seoul University.	. . . ssi 'Mr; Mrs; Madam' [IMPERSONAL] puchin 'father' [IMPERSONAL] ku uy puchin in O Hanchang ssi 'Mr. O Hanchang who is his father' hakca 'scholar' hakca lo = hakca (i)ko 'is a scholar, and . . .'

Korean	English	Amplification
		mun = munhak 'literature' kwa 'course; subject(s); department' munq-kwa 'course <u>or</u> department of literature' kwacang 'department head'
18. Ku uy mōchin in ^{l}Yu ssi nun tongyang-hwa hwāka 'ey yo.	His mother Madame ^{l}Yu is an artist of the Oriental school.	mōchin 'mother' ku uy mōchin in ^{l}Yu ssi 'his mother, who is Madame ^{l}Yu' tongyang 'the East, the Orient' (opposite of se.yang 'the West, the Occident') tongyang-hwa 'Oriental art' hwāka 'artist, painter'
19. O uysa uy puin i toyn sayksi nun Sewul sīcang uy ttal lo koyngcang han miin ici yo.	The girl who is Dr. O's wife is the daughter of the mayor of Seoul and a magnificent beauty.	sayksi 'girl' sayksi ka puin i tōyss.ey yo 'the girl became a wife' puin i toyn sayksi 'girl who [has become =] is a wife' sīcang 'mayor (of a city)' ttal lo . . . = ttal iko 'is the daughter, and . . .' koyngcang hay yo 'is wonderful, marvelous, magnificent' miin 'beautiful woman'
20. Kim sensayng kwa na nun kanho-pu eykey Kim sensayng puin i enu pyēngsil ey iss.nun ya ko mul.ess.ey yo.	Mr. Kim and I asked the nurse what room Mrs. Kim was [is] in.	kanho-pu 'nurse' enu . . . 'which . . . , what . . .' pyēngsil 'hospital room' enu pyēngsil ey iss.nun ya 'what room is [one] in?' [plain style] mul.e yo 'ask, inquire' enu pyēngsil ey iss.nun ya ko mul.ess.ey yo 'asked what room she [is=] was in'
21. Kanho-pu nun māl haki lul "Hwānca ka canun cwung ini han sam-sip pun kitalilq swu iss.keyss.^{s}up.nikka?" hako māl hayss.ey yo.	The nurse said, 'Could you wait about 30 minutes, as the patient is (in the midst of) sleeping?'	māl haki lul ". . ." hako (māl) hay yo 'says ". . ."' [DIRECT QUOTATION]

Korean	English	Amplification
22. Kanho-pu nun wuli hanthey eti se wass.nun ya ko mul.ess.ci yo.	The nurse asked where we had come from.	wuli hanthey ". . ." ko mul.ess.ey 'asked us . . .' eti se wass.nun ya 'where did [one] come from?' [plain style] eti se wass.nun ya ko mul.ess.ey yo 'asked where [one] came from'
23. Wuli nun kanho-pu eykey ecey uysa uy cīntan i ette hayss.nun ya ko mul.e pwass.ci yo.	We asked the nurse what [= how] the doctor's diagnosis was yesterday.	mul.e pwa yo 'asks (to find out), tries asking (to see what the answer will be)' cīntan 'diagnosis' ette hay yo = ettay yo 'how is it?' ette hayss.nun ya ko mul.e pwass.ey yo 'asked how it was'
24. Pyēngmyeng un mues iko, pyēng i cwūng han ya ko mul.ess.ci yo.	We asked what the name of the disease was, and whether it was serious.	pyēngmyeng 'the name of a disease' cwūng hay yo 'is serious, important' cwūng han ya 'is it serious?' [plain style] cwūng han ya ko mul.ess.ey yo 'asked whether it was serious' [= asked, is it serious?]
25. Ēncey thōywen halq swu iss.keyss.nun ya ko mul.ess.ci yo.	We asked when she would be able to leave the hospital.	thōywen 'discharge (from a hospital)' thōywen (ul) hay yo 'leaves <u>or</u> is discharged from a hospital (as a patient)' thōywen halq swu iss.keyss.nun ya 'will [one] be able to leave (the hospital)?' [plain style]
26. Kanho-pu nun (tāytap haki lul) caki nun cal moluni, tam.im uysa in O uysa lul manna pola ko kulayss.ey yo.	In reply, the nurse told us that she herself didn't know, so we should try seeing Dr. O, who is in charge.	tāytap haki lul 'the answer [one] made; in reply' tam.im uysa in O uysa 'Dr. O who is the doctor in charge' manna pola 'try seeing him!' [plain style] manna pola ko kulayss.ey yo 'tell [one] to try seeing [him]'

Korean	English	Amplification
27. O uysa nun Kim sensayng puin uy pyēng i kwā hi cwūng haci anh.ta ko kulayss.ey yo.	Dr. O told us Mrs. Kim's illness is not too serious.	kwā hay yo 'is excessive' kwā hi 'excessively, overly, too' [with negative] cwūng haci anh.ta 'it isn't serious' [plain style] cwūng haci anh.ta ko kulayss.ey yo 'said that it isn't serious'
28. Ku pyēng un puin tul eykey hun hi iss.nun pyēng ulo, olay kaci anh.nunta ko hayss.ey yo.	He said the illness was a common one for women (to have), and wouldn't last long.	hun hay yo or hunh.e yo 'is common, plentiful' hun hi 'common(ly)' hun hi iss.nun pyēng 'a commonly had disease' pyēng ulo = pyēng iko 'it is a disease, and . . .' (sikan i) ka yo '(time) passes, goes by; lasts, persists' olay ka yo 'lasts long' kaci anh.nunta 'doesn't go/last' [plain style] olay kaci anh.nunta ko hayss.ey yo 'said that it doesn't last long'

SUPPLEMENTARY VOCABULARY

uy-hak.kyo	medical school
uyq-kwa tāyhak	medical college
uyhak-sayng or uyq-kwa tāyhak-sayng	medical student
silqsup-sayng	intern, apprentice
uywen	clinic; doctor's office
sōaq-kwa	pediatrics
puinq-kwa	gynecology
sānq-kwa	obstetrics
i-pi-inhwuq kwa	otorhinolaryngology, ear-nose-throat specialty
ānq-kwa	ophthalmology, eye specialty
chiq-kwa	dentistry; dentist's office (=∼ uywen)
chiq-kwa uysa	dentist
hwānca or pyēngca	patient
phyēy [N. Korean spelling phey]	lungs
phyēyq-pyeng	lung trouble, tuberculosis

phyēyyem [pronounced /phēylyem/]	pneumonia
sohwa	digestion
sohwaq pyeng	dyspepsia, indigestion
hongyek	measles
son nim or māma	smallpox
thiphusu or cilpusa	typhus
cang-thiphusu or cang-cilpusa	typhoid fever
kāmki	a cold
kāmki (ka) tul.e yo [tu-l-] kāmki (ey) tullye yo [tulli-] kāmki ey kellye yo [kelli-]	catches a cold
kēmsa	inspection, examination, checkup
kēmsa (lul) hay yo	gives a checkup
kēmsa (lul) pat.e yo	has or undergoes a checkup

sinchey or mom	body
sinchey kēmsa	physical examination
swuswul	(surgical) operation
swuswul (ul) hay yo	has or performs an operation
hwānca lul swuswul hay yo	operates on a patient
swuswulq-sil	operation room
cīnchal	medical examination
cīnchal (ul) hay yo	gives a medical examination, examines
cīnchal ul pat.e yo	has a medical examination
cīnchalq-sil	examining room
Eyksu-kwangsen	X-ray
cwūsa	injection, shot
cwūsa lul noh.a yo	gives an injection
cwūsa lul mac.e yo	gets/takes an injection
yēypang cwūsa	vaccination
wutwu	smallpox vaccination
wutwu lul mac.e yo	gets vaccinated for smallpox
wutwu lul noh.a yo	vaccinates for smallpox
yak	drug, medicine
yak ul mek.e yo	takes drugs/medicines
yakcey-sa, cēyyak-sa	pharmacist
chilyo	(medical) treatment
chilyo lul hay yo	gives/administers treatment
chilyo lul pat.e yo	has/receives treatment
ūngkup chilyo	first aid, emergency treatment
cen.yem (ul) hay yo	is contagious
cen.yemq pyeng	contagious disease
cheyon	(body) temperature
cheyon kēmsa	temperature check
cheyon-kyey	(clinical) thermometer
han.lan-kyey [N. Korean han.nan-kyey]	(weather) thermometer
hyel.ayk or phi	blood

hyel.ayk kēmsa or phi kēmsa	blood test
sōpyen or ocwum	urine; urinating
sōpyen ul pwa yo [po-] or nwue yo [nwu-] or ssa yo ocwum ul nwue yo or ssa yo	urinates
sōpyen kēmsa	urine test
sōpyen-ki	urinal
pyenki [sometimes mispronounced phyenki]	chamberpot, bed-pan
tāypyen or ttong or twī or pyen	feces; defecating, a bowel movement
tāypyen ul pwa yo [po-] or nwue yo [nwu-] twī lul pwa yo ttong ul nwue yo or ssa yo [ssa-]	defecates, has a bowel movement
kichim	a cough
kichim (ul) hay yo	coughs
caychayki	a sneeze
caychayki (lul) hay yo	sneezes
kalyewe yo [kalyew-]	is itchy, itches
kulk.e yo [kulk-] or kalk.e yo [kalk-]	scratches
pyēng i na yo [na-]	gets sick, falls ill
naa yo [nā(s)-]	1. is better, is preferable [DESCRIPTIVE]; 2. gets better [PROCESSIVE]
pyēng i naa yo	illness gets better, improves
pyēng mūn.an	a sick call (visit)
cosep, coli	taking care of one's health
cōsim	(pre)caution, being careful
mom cōsim	taking care of oneself

Cosep ul (cal) hasipsio!	Take good care of your health!	Cōsim (ul) hasipsio! Mom cōsim cal hasipsio!	Be careful! Take good care of yourself!

NOTES

19.1. Quotations: direct and indirect.

There are two ways to report what someone has said or asked or commanded or suggested: a direct quotation, which gives the exact words spoken, and an indirect quotation, which gives only the gist. Both kinds of quotations are used in Korean, as in English, but Korean uses the direct quotation less frequently.

In the direct quotation, often introduced by mā̄l haki lul . . . 'what is said is . . .' or mūt.ki lul . . . 'what is asked is,' the references such as 'me' and 'you' and the endings of the verbs (polite, formal, honorific, and so forth) can be left as originally spoken. The quotation is followed by hako 'quote' (the gerund of hay yo which means 'says' as well as 'does/is'—it also sometimes means 'thinks'), usually added right on as a particle, and it ends up with a quoting verb—such as hay yo or māl hay yo 'says,' kulay yo 'says (like that),' mul.e yo 'asks,' mul.e pwa yo 'inquires,' etc. (If you introduce a question with mūt.ki lul . . . , you usually end with just hay yo rather than with mul.e yo.)

Indirect quotations are less frequently introduced by māl haki lul . . . or mūt.ki lul . . . . In indirect quotations, you have to change references to persons (so that 'he said "I will see you and him" may become 'he said that he would see me and you'); you must be careful not to retain honorifics that would not be appropriate to the "changed" persons; and you must put the verb form into a neutral or PLAIN style that is used mainly in quotations. The plain style is explained in the following section. After the quotation you add a quotation particle ko '(saying) that . . . ,' but—like English 'that'—ko can freely drop. When the particle is present (as in kanta ko hay yo 'says that he will go') we call it an EXPANDED QUOTATION; when the particle drops (as in kanta hay yo 'says he will go') we call it a SIMPLE QUOTATION. And the simple quotation is sometimes abbreviated further, by dropping the base ha- of the verb 'say' altogether, leaving forms like kanta 'y yo 'says he'll go.' (The -ta 'y is pronounced, of course, as a single syllable /tay/.) These we call CONTRACTED QUOTATIONS.

Notice the following quotations, given in several forms:

1. STATEMENT
   What was said: Kap.nita. 'I'm going.'
   Direct quote: (Māl haki lul) "Kap.nita" hako hayss.ey yo. 'He said, "I am going."'
   Indirect quote, expanded: Kanta ko hayss.ey yo. 'He said that he was going.'
   Indirect quote, simple: Kanta hayss.ey yo. 'He said he was going.'
   Indirect quote, contracted: Kanta 'yss.ey yo. 'He said he was going.'

2. QUESTION
   What was said: Kasip.nikka? 'Are you going?'
   Direct quote: (Mūt.ki lul) "Kasip.nikka?" hako hayss.ey yo. 'He asked, "Are you going?"'
   Indirect quote, expanded: Kanun ya ko mul.ess.ey yo. 'He asked whether I was going.'
   Indirect quote, simple: Kanun ya mul.ess.ey yo. 'He asked if I was going.'
   Indirect quote, contracted: NONE.

3. COMMAND
What was said: Kasipsio! 'Go!'
Direct quote: (Māl haki lul) "Kasipsio" hako hayss.ey yo. 'He said, "Go!"'
Indirect quote, expanded: Kala ko hayss.ey yo. 'He told me to go.'
Indirect quote, simple: Kala hayss.ey yo. 'He told me to go.'
Indirect quote, contracted: Kala 'yss.ey yo. 'He told me to go.'

4. SUGGESTION
What was said: Kapsita! 'Let's go!'
Direct quote: (Māl haki lul) "Kapsita" hako hayss.ey yo. 'He said, "Let's go!"'
Indirect quote, expanded: Kaca ko hayss.ey yo. 'He suggested that we go.'
Indirect quote, simple: Kaca hayss.ey yo. 'He suggested we go.'
Indirect quote, contracted: Kaca 'yss.ey yo. 'He suggested we go.'

If you want to mention the person who did the saying, the usual place is at the beginning (Kim sensayng i kaca ko māl hayss.ey yo 'Mr. Kim suggested that we go') unless the quotation is very long; in that case you may want to put the subject next to the final quoting verb (Onul i nal i cōh.a se sānqpo 'na kaca ko Kim sensayng i māl hayss.ey yo 'Mr. Kim suggested we go for walk or something since the weather's so nice today'). Of course, if you start with māl haki lul . . . , you will want to put the subject in front of that (Kim sensayng i māl haki lul . . .).

Reflexive requests—asking someone to do something for you as with hay cwusipsio—are quoted in a special way (hay tālla ko . . .); you will find out about this in Lesson 29.

‖ 19.2. Plain style: statements.

Statements in the plain style end with plain-style verb forms. These forms, unlike statement forms in the other styles, have different endings depending on whether the verb is processive or descriptive. And the copula has a special form for use in quotation (‖ 19.6).

‖ 19.2.1. Descriptive and processive verbs.

Descriptive verbs form plain-style statements by attaching the ending -ta to the base; for L-extending vowel verbs the ending is attached to the EXTENDED base. If the base ends in a consonant, there are the usual sound changes to make:

MEANING	BASE	STATEMENT	PRONOUNCED	PRONUNCIATION RULE(S)
be high, tall	noph-	noph.ta	/noptta/	ph.t → pt → /ptt/
be easy	swīw-	swīpta	/swīptta/	w → p; pt → /ptt/
be better	nā(s)	nās.ta	/nātta/	s.t → t.t → /tt/
be late	nuc-	nuc.ta	/nutta/	c.t → t.t → /tt/
be small	cāk-	cākta	/cāktta/	kt → /ktt/
be young	celm-	cem.ta	/cemtta/	lm.t → m.t → /mtt/
be good	cōh-	cōh.ta	/cōtha/	h.t → /th/
be disliked	silh-	silh.ta	/siltha/	lh.t → /lth/
be much/many	mānh-	mānh.ta	/māntha/	nh.t → /nth/
be cheap	ssa-	ssata		
be cloudy	huli-	hulita		
be bad	nappu-	napputa		
be blue/green	phulu-	phuluta		
be far	mē-l-	mēlta		
be long	kī-l-	kīlta		

Processive verbs are made into plain-style statements by an ending which has the shape -nta when attached to vowel bases (including the UNEXTENDED shape of L-extending bases) and -nunta when attached to consonant bases. If the base ends in a consonant, there are the usual sound changes to make:

MEANING	BASE	STATEMENT	PRONOUNCED	PRONUNCIATION RULE(S)
wear	ip-	ip.nunta	/imnunta/	p.n → /mn/
help	tōw-	tōp.nunta	/tōmnunta/	w → p; p.n → /mn/
plant	sīm-	sīmnunta		
close it	tat-	tat.nunta	/tannunta/	t.n → /nn/
comb	pis-	pis.nunta	/pinnunta/	s.n → t.n → /nn/
get better	nā(s)-	nās.nunta	/nānnunta/	
look for; find	chac-	chac.nunta	/channunta/	c.n → t.n → /nn/
follow	coch-	coch.nunta	/connunta/	ch.n → t.n → /nn/
put	noh-	noh.nunta	/nonnunta/	h.n → t.n → /nn/
wear (shoes)	sin-	sinnunta		
sit down	anc-	anc.nunta	/annunta/	nc.n → /nn/
not do (...-ci)	anh-	anh.nunta	/annunta/	nh.n → /nn/
listen; hear	tul-	tut.nunta	/tunnunta/	l → t; t.n → /nn/
lose	ilh-	ilh.nunta	/illunta/	lh.n → l.n → /ll/
eat	mek-	mek.nunta	/mengnunta/	k.n → /ngn/
polish	takk-	takk.nunta	/tangnunta/	kk.n → k.n → /ngn/
read	ilk-	ilk.nunta	/ingnunta/	lk.n → k.n → /ngn/
wait	kitali-	kitalinta		
tie	māy-	māynta		
look; see	po-	ponta		
give	cwu-	cwunta		
write	ssu-	ssunta		
call	pulu-	pulunta		
not know	molu-	moluntа		
become	toy-	toynta		
buy	sa-	santa		
live	sā-l-	sānta		
hang it	kē-l-	kēnta		
enter; cost	tu-l-	tunta		
play	nō-l-	nōnta		

Honorific bases, of course, are treated like other bases that end in i: celm.usita '[someone esteemed] is young,' tul.usinta '[someone esteemed] listens,' nōsinta '[someone esteemed] plays.' Choice of -ta or -nta depends on whether the underlying base is descriptive or processive.

‖ 19.2.2. Ambivalent bases.

There are some verbs that straddle the fence and belong in both the processive and the descriptive categories. Hay yo, for example, has the adjective ending -ta with descriptive verbal nouns and the verb ending -nta with processive verbal nouns:

Processive	Descriptive
ip.wen hanta 'enter [hospital]'	cwūng hata 'is serious'
pāngmun hanta 'visits'	hun hata 'is common'
thōywen hanta 'is discharged'	kkaykkus hata 'is clean'

wūncen hanta 'drives'	chincel hata 'is kind'
^{n}yēm.lye hanta 'worries'	pul-chincel hata 'is unkind'
cwūnpi hanta 'prepares'	phikon hata 'is tired'

Similar is the negative auxiliary anh.e yo, which takes either -ta or -nunta, depending on what kind of verb it is making negative:

Negative Processive Verb	Negative Descriptive Verb
anc.ci anh.nunta 'doesn't sit'	cōh.ci anh.ta 'isn't good'
mekci anh.nunta 'doesn't eat'	kakkapci anh.ta 'isn't near'
nwupci anh.nunta 'doesn't lie down'	mēlci anh.ta 'isn't far'
sālci anh.nunta 'doesn't live'	nappuci anh.ta 'isn't bad'
cwūnpi haci anh.nunta 'doesn't prepare'	kkaykkus haci anh.ta 'isn't clean'
kongpu haci anh.nunta 'doesn't study'	phikon haci anh.ta 'isn't tired'

Notice what happens with ile hay yo 'does/is this way,' kule hay yo 'does/is that way,' and cele hay yo 'does/is that way over there' and their abbreviations:

Processive					Descriptive	
ile hanta ilenta	'does this way'	←	ile hay yo ilay yo	→	ile hata ileh.ta	'is this way'
kule hanta kulenta	'does that way'	←	kule hay yo kulay yo	→	kule hata kuleh.ta	'is that way'
cele hanta celenta	'does that way'	←	cele hay yo celay yo	→	cele hata celeh.ta	'is that way'

Some other bases you have had that can be either processive or descriptive are these:

Processive				Descriptive
nās.nunta 'gets better'	←	naa yo	→	nās.ta 'is better'
khunta 'gets big(ger)'	←	khe yo	→	khuta 'is big'
nuc.nunta 'gets late'	←	nuc.e yo	→	nuc.ta 'is late'

19.2.3. The bases iss-, ēps-, and kyēysi-.

The base iss- is particularly tricky; it has three meanings 'stays,' 'is,' and 'has' (with the object possessed taking the subject particle i/ka). Now let us see how each of these behaves:

Processive				Descriptive
		iss.ey yo 'stays; is; has'	→	iss.ta
an iss.nunta	←	an iss.ey yo 'doesn't stay'	→	an iss.ta
iss.ci anh.nunta	←	iss.ci anh.e yo 'doesn't stay	→	iss.ci anh.ta
		an iss.ey yo 'is not'	→	an iss.ta ēps.ta
		iss.ci anh.e yo 'is not'	→	iss.ci anh.ta

		ēps.ey yo 'has not'	→	ēps.ta
mōs iss.nunta	←	mōs iss.ey yo 'can't stay'		
iss.ci mōs hanta	←	iss.ci mōs hay yo 'can't stay'		
		iss.ci mōs hay yo 'isn't at all'	→	iss.ci mōs hata
		iss.ci mōs hay yo 'doesn't have at all	→	iss.ci mōs hata
kyēysinta	←	kyēysey yo 'stays; is' [HONORIFIC]	→	kyēysita
an kyēysinta	←	an kyēysey yo 'does not stay; is not'	→	an kyēysita
kyēysici anh.nunta	←	kyēysici anh.e yo 'does not stay; is not'	→	kyēysici anh.ta
		iss.usey yo 'has' [HONORIFIC]	→	iss.usita
		ēps.usey yo 'has not' [HONORIFIC]	→	ēps.usita

As you can see, there are two ways to treat some of the categories ('doesn't stay'; HONORIFIC 'stays,' 'is,' 'does not stay,' 'is not'); for these categories, you are free to treat the bases as either processive or descriptive. But for the other categories, you are forced to make a choice: You must treat as descriptive the plain 'stays; is, has' 'is not,' 'has not,' 'is not at all,' 'doesn't have at all'; the honorific 'has' and 'has not.' You must treat as processive 'can't stay.'

The auxiliary iss- (in -ko iss-, -e iss-) behaves like 'stays' except that there are no an/mōs . . . iss.nunta forms:

		thako iss.ey yo 'is riding'	→	thako iss.ta
		an thako iss.ey yo 'isn't riding'	→	an thako iss.ta
thako iss.ci anh.nunta	←	thako iss.ci anh.e yo 'isn't riding'	→	thako iss.ci anh.ta
		mōs thako iss.ey yo 'can't be riding'	→	mōs thako iss.ta
thako iss.ci mōs hanta	←	thako iss.ci mōs hay yo 'can't be riding'		
		anc.e iss.ey yo 'is seated'	→	anc.e iss.ta
		an anc.e iss.ey yo 'is not seated'	→	an anc.e iss.ta

anc.e iss.ci anh.nunta ← anc.e iss.ci anh.e yo → anc.e iss.ci anh.ta
'is not seated'

mōs anc.e iss.ey yo → mōs anc.e iss.ta
'can't be seated'

anc.e iss.ci mōs hanta ← anc.e iss.ci mōs hay yo
'can't be seated'

‖ 19.2.4. Past and future forms.

Past and future forms of ALL verbs (whether descriptive or processive) attach -ta: -ess.ta /-etta/ and -keyss.ta /keytta/. Here are some examples:

PROCESSIVE VERBS

anc- 'sit'	anc.ess.ta 'sat'
	anc.keyss.ta 'will sit'
mek- 'eat'	mek.ess.ta 'ate'
	mek.keyss.ta 'will eat'
sā-l- 'live'	sal.ess.ta 'lived'
	sālkeyss.ta 'will live'
pulu- 'call'	pulless.ta 'called'
	pulukeyss.ta 'will call'
kongpu ha- 'study'	kongpu hayss.ta 'studied'
	kongpu hakeyss.ta 'will study'

DESCRIPTIVE VERBS

pissa- 'be expensive'	pissass.ta 'was expensive'
	pissakeyss.ta 'will be expensive'
cōh- 'be good'	cōh.ass.ta 'was good'
	cōh.keyss.ta 'will be good'
mē-l- 'be far'	mel.ess.ta 'was far'
	mēlkeyss.ta 'will be far'
ppalu- 'be fast'	ppalless.ta 'was fast'
	ppalukeyss.ta 'will be fast'
phikon ha- 'be tired'	phikon hayss.ta 'was tired'
	phikon hakeyss.ta 'will be tired'

Here are more examples of plain-style verbs used in quotations.

1. Tōn i ēps.ta ko hay yo.	He says he has no money.
2. ^{l}Nayil sangcem ey ka cwukeyss.ta ko hayss.ey yo.	He said he'd go to the store for me tomorrow.
3. Ilcciki ca ya (ha)nta 'y yo.	He says he has to go to bed early.
4. Kongwen ey se sānqpo hako siph.ta ko hayss.ey yo.	He said he'd like to take a walk in the park.
5. Īl ul hakeyss.ta 'yss.ey yo.	He said he'd do the job.
6. ^{l}Yekwan ey phyēnci ka wass.ta ko hayss.ey yo.	He told me a letter had come for me at the hotel.
7. Cip ul sass.ta ko hayss.ey yo.	He said he had bought a house.
8. Cēnhwa hasikeyss.ta ko kulayss.^{s}up.nikka?	Did you say you were going to make a telephone call?
9. Ape' nim un onulq cenyek ey cip ey kyēysikeyss.ta ko hasyess.^{s}up.nita.	Father said he would stay home this evening.

10. Hānkwuk mal kongpu lul cal hanta ko yēyki lul tul.ess.ey yo.	I hear he's studying Korean hard.
11. Cham pwuncwu hata ko hay yo.	He says he's very busy.

‖ 19.3. Plain style: questions, Type 1.

QUESTIONS in the PLAIN STYLE consist of modifier forms plus the post-modifier ya (outside quotations sometimes pronounced i). Processive verbs along with iss- and ēps-, have their processive modifier form:

ka- 'go'	kanun ya (kanun i) 'does [he] go?'
mek- 'eat'	mek.nun ya (mek.nun i) 'does [he] eat?'
sā-l- 'live'	sānun ya (sānun i) 'does [he] live?'
pulu- 'call'	pulunun ya (pulunun i) 'does [he] call?'
iss 'stay, be, have'	iss.nun ya (iss.nun i) 'does [he] stay? is [he]? does [he] have?'
ēps- 'lack'	ēps.nun ya (ēps.nun i) 'does [he] lack?'

Descriptive verbs (which of course lack processive modifier forms) use the simple modifier form -(u)n:

pissa- 'be expensive'	pissan ya (pissan i) 'is [it] expensive?'
cōh- 'be good'	cōh.un ya (cōh.un i) 'is [it] good?'
mē-l- 'be far'	mēn ya (mēn i) 'is [it] far?'
ppalu- 'be fast'	ppalun ya (ppalun i) 'is [it] fast?'

For past and future, the processive modifier ending -nun is attached to the past and future bases of ALL verbs:

kass.nun ya 'did he go?'	kakeyss.nun ya 'will he go?'
mek.ess.nun ya 'did he eat?'	mek.keyss.nun ya 'will he eat?'
sal.ess.nun ya 'did he live?'	sālkeyss.nun ya 'will he live?'
pulless.nun ya 'did he call?'	pulukeyss.nun ya 'will he call?'
pissass.nun ya 'was it expensive?'	pissakeyss.nun ya 'will it be expensive?'
cōh.ass.nun ya 'was it good?'	cōh.keyss.nun ya 'will it be good?'

This kind of past and future processive modifier form is RESTRICTED. The forms -ess.nun and -keyss.nun are used ONLY before ya or i (or ka ‖16.6) in plain-style questions and in three other constructions (before ci, before tey, and before ke l') which you will learn later.

Questions, like statements, appear as EXPANDED QUOTATIONS (-nun ya ko hay yo), SIMPLE QUOTATIONS (-nun ya hay yo), and sometimes CONTRACTED QUOTATIONS (-nun ya 'y yo). The processive -nun ya is sometimes slurred -n' ya (iss.n' ya = iss nun ya, mek.n' ya = mek.nun ya); after vowels (kan' ya = kanun ya) this sounds like the descriptive -(u)n ya (pissan ya, mēn ya).

Here are more examples of quoted questions.

1. Mues ul hanun ya ko mul.e pwass.ey yo.	I asked them what they were doing.
2. Eti kanun ya 'yss.ey yo.	I asked him where he was going.
3. Pap ul mek.nun ya ko mul.ess.ey yo.	I asked if they were eating.
4. Nay chayk ul eti 'ta twuess.nun ya ko mul.e pwass.ey yo.	I asked her where she had put my book.

5. Eti lul kakeyss.nun ya ko mul.e posipsio.	Please ask him where he's going to go.
6. Apeci ka na hanthey tōn i ēps.nun ya mul.ess.ey yo.	Father asked me if I was out of money.
7. Sensayng eykey sikan i iss.nun ya ko mul.e popsita.	Let's find out if the teacher has some time.
8. Pusan i mēn ya ko mul.e posey yo.	Ask if Pusan is far.
9. Na nun ku āy hanthey etteh.key kwutwu kkun ul kkunh.ess.nun ya ko mul.ess.ey yo.	I asked her how (come) she had broken the shoe lace.
10. Uysa hanthey pyēng i olay kakeyss.nun ya ko mul.e posipsio.	Ask the doctor if the illness will last long.

Negative questions are usually made on the long negative:

1. Kaci anh.nun ya ko mul.ess.ey yo.	I asked if he was not going.
2. Mekci anh.ess.nun ya ko mul.ess.ey yo.	I asked if he had not eaten.
3. Com swīkeyss.nun ya ko mul.ess.ey yo.	I asked if we were going to take a rest-break.
4. Keki ka chwupci anh.keyss.nun ya ko mul.e posey yo.	Find out if it wouldn't be cold there.
5. Kil i nappuci anh.un ya ko mul.e popsita.	Let's ask if the roads aren't bad.
6. Sensayng i na hanthey way com ilcciki kaci mōs hayss.nun ya māl hayss.ey yo.	The teacher asked me why I couldn't get there a little earlier.

19.4. Plain style: suggestions.

9. Pyēngwen ey kal ttay na wa kath.i kaca ko hayss.ey yo. 'He suggested I go along when he goes to the hospital.'

10. . . . kkoch ul sa kaciko kaca ko kulayss.ey yo. 'He suggested . . . buying some flowers to take along.'

Corresponding to the formal-style ending -(u)psita 'let's . . .' is the PLAIN-STYLE SUGGESTION ending -ca, used in quotations:

sa- 'buy'	saca 'let's buy it'
mek- 'eat'	mekca 'let's eat'
sā-l- 'live'	sālca 'let's live'
pulu- 'call'	puluca 'let's call'

Only processive verbs occur in suggestions. The ending -ca attaches to bases just like the suspective -ci, with the usual sound changes required for bases ending in consonants. Although both endings are supposed to be attached to the EXTENDED shape of L-extending verbs (hence nōlci, nōlca), a common variant drops the l (nō'ci, nō'ca), especially with the ending -ca. That is why the plain suggestion form of mal.e yo 'desists, refrains' is often heard as mā'ca instead of mālca. When you quote someone as making a negative suggestion (Kaci māpsita 'Let's not go!) you use this form: Kaci mā(l)ca ko hayss.ey yo 'He suggested we not go.'

Suggestions, like statements, appear as EXPANDED QUOTATIONS (-ca ko hay yo), SIMPLE QUOTATIONS (-ca hay yo), and sometimes CONTRACTED QUOTATIONS (-ca 'y yo).

Here are more examples of quoted suggestions.

1. Onulq cenyek kath.i kongpu haca ko hapsita.	Let's suggest studying together this evening.
2. Pak sensayng un 'nayil Pusan kaca ko hayss.una, īl i nemu mānh.e se, mōs kakeyss.ey yo.	Mr. Pak suggested that we go to Pusan tomorrow but I have so much work I can't go.
3. Pak sensayng puin eykey onulq cenyek wuli cip ey osye se cīnçi capswus.ca ko hayss.ey yo.	We asked Mrs. Pak if she'd like to come to our house to eat tonight.
4. Onul ōhwu ey pi ka omyen sangcem ey kaci mālca ko hakeyss.ey yo.	If it rains this afternoon, I'm going to suggest that we don't go to the store.
5. Pokswun-i ka pakk ey ka se nōlca 'yss.ey yo.	Pokswun-i suggested we go outside and play.
6. Nay chinkwu ka yeki iss.ci mālca hayss.ey yo.	My friend suggested we not stay here.
7. Sensayng i Yenge lul haci mālca ko hayss.^{s}up.nita.	The teacher suggested we not talk English.
8. Yenge lul haci mālko, Hānkwuk mal ul haca hayss.^{s}up.nita.	He suggested that we talk Korean instead of English.
9. Wūncen hanun sālam i cēki se naylica ko hayss.ci yo.	The (one driving =) driver suggested we get out there, you see.
10. Ku kes i poko siph.umyen keki kakkawun kos ey iss.ca ko hayss.ci man, sikan i com nuc.ess.uni-kka n', poci anh.ko tol.a oki lo hayss.ci yo.	He suggested we stay nearby if we wanted to see it, but as it was late we decided to come back without seeing it.

‖ 19.5. Plain style: commands, Type 1; the particle tele.

11. Kim sensayng un . . . na tele honca ka se kkoch ul sala ko hayss.ey yo. 'Mr. Kim told me to buy the flowers by myself.'

PLAIN-STYLE COMMANDS have the ending -ula (attached to consonant bases) or -la (attached to vowel bases) to make forms which correspond in meaning to the formal-style ending -(u)psio, -(u)sipsio. The ending -la is added to the extended form of L-extending bases (kēlla 'hang it!'; cf. kēlmyen 'if [he] hangs it').

For example:

ka- 'go'	kala '[says] go!'
mek- 'eat'	mek.ula '[says] eat!'
sā-l- 'live'	sālla '[says] live!'
pulu- 'call'	pulula '[says] call!'

Only processive verbs have command forms. The negatives are made with mālla: kaci mālla '[says] don't go,' mekci mālla '[says] don't eat,' etc. But the word mālla is often pronounced mā'la.

Commands, like statements, appear as EXPANDED QUOTATIONS (-ula ko hay yo), SIMPLE QUOTATIONS (-ula hay yo), and sometimes CONTRACTED QUOTATIONS (-ula 'y yo).

In commands, the particle hanthey (or eykey) is often replaced by the particle tele, meaning 'to' with the person TO whom the command is directed, provided the person is not of higher status. This particle is not translated in English when the command verb is 'tell' but appears instead as an indirect object: He told [ ] the child to come home early.

Here are some more examples of quoted commands.

1. Nay ka ku sālam hanthey ola ko hayss.ey yo. — I told him to come.
2. Kongpu hala ko kulelq ka yo?? — Shall I tell them to study?
3. Atul tele phyēnci lul ilk.ci mālla hayss.ey yo. — I told my son not to read the letter.
4. Kaci mālla ko hayss.una-ma kass.ey yo. — He told me not to go, but I went anyway.
5. Emeni ka na tele onul achim ilcciki il.e nala 'yss.ey yo. — Mother told me to get up early this morning.
6. Sensayng i ku haksayng tele iss.ci mālla (ha)syess.ey yo. — The teacher told that student not to stay.
7. Apeci ka na tele kulen yēyki lul tut.ci mālla 'yss.ey yo. — Father told me not to listen to such stories.
8. Sensayng i wuli tele Yenge lul haci mālla hayss.^{s}up.nita. — The teacher told us not to talk English.
9. Yenge lul haci mālko, Hānkwuk mal ul hala 'yss.^{s}up.nita. — He told us to talk Korean instead of English.
10. Emeni ka na tele cip ey iss.ula ko māl hayss.ey yo. — Mother told me to stay at home.

19.6. The plain-style copula.

The plain-style statement form of the copula is ita (base i- plus descriptive verb ending -ta). But this form is NOT used in quotations; instead, it is replaced by the special form ila. [The form ita is used in children's speech, described in Lesson 22.]

Other statement forms of the copula behave just like those of descriptive verbs. The past form is iess.ta and the future ikeyss.ta. Questions are also like descriptive-verb questions: in ya or (outside quotations) sometimes in i. (The copula, again like descriptive verbs, lacks suggestions and command forms.) The only negative possible for the copula is ani '-, since there is no long form; the plain form is ani 'ta, in quotations ani 'la.

Here are some examples of the copula in quotations:

1. Nwukwu 'n ya ko mul.e posey yo. — Find out who it is.
2. Kim sensayng isin ya ko hasey yo. — Ask if it's Mr. Kim.
3. Kim sensayng i ani 'sin ya ko hayss.ey yo. — I asked if it wasn't Mr. Kim.
4. Wuli atul iess.ta 'y yo. — He says it was my son.

5. Um.ak-hoy ka Tho-yoil ey 'keyss.ta ko yēyki lul tul.ess.ey yo. — I heard the concert would be on Saturday.
6. Caymi iss.nun chayk i ani 'ess.nun ya ko mūt.keyss.ey yo. — I'll ask if it was not an interesting book.
7. Sāy ka ttel.e cil mo.yang ila ko kulayss.ci yo. — You see, he said the bird was going to fall.
8. Poktong-i hanthey ku key nay kes ila ko [or nay ke 'la ko] hasey yo. — You tell Poktong-i that is mine.
9. Poktong-i (uy) kes i ani 'la ko hasey yo. — Tell Poktong-i it isn't his.
10. Say sīcheng i ani 'keyss.nun ya ko mul.ess.ey yo. — I asked whether it wouldn't be the new city hall.

‖ 19.7. Special uses of the quoted copula.

When the copula is quoted in present statement form, it is pronounced ila. Translation of the quoted copula sometimes involves unexpected expressions like 'says it to be = calls it.'

Here are a few more examples of quoted copular statements.

1. I kes un mues ila ko hay yo? — What do you call this thing?
   (or : I ke n' mwe 'la ko hay yo.
   I ke n' mwe 'la hay yo.
   I ke n' mwe 'la 'y yo.)
2. ¹Yuseng-ki 'la ko hay yo. — It's called a record player.
3. I kes un Hānkwuk mal lo mues ila hay yo. — How do you say this in Korean?
4. Nwukwu 'la ko kulayss.ey yo. — Who did you say it was?
5. Eti 'la 'yss.ey yo. — Where did you (or they) say it was?

A special quoting construction involving this form of the copula translates the English phrase 'an A called X.' The expanded form of this construction is:

X ila ko hanun A

As you can see, this is simply the regular quoting pattern (X ila ko hay yo) made into a modifier for another noun expression. The simple, unexpanded form is:

X ila hanun A

But ordinarily the abbreviated form is used:

X ila 'nun A

And often you will hear it further reduced to:

X ila 'n' A

When you hear this reduced form it sounds just like X ila 'n A, the reduction of X ila (ko) han A 'an A which has been called X,' and the meaning is so close that it often wouldn't matter which way you interpreted what you hear. Compare this meaning of 'an A called X' with the use of simple modifiers in equational constructions:

X in A 'an A which is [=] X'

X i toyn A 'an A which is [has become] X'
sensayng in nay hyeng nim or sensayng i toyn nay hyeng nim 'my older brother who is [has become] a teacher'
uysa in Kim Pok.nam or uysa ka toyn Kim Pok.nam 'Poknam Kim, who is [has become] a doctor'

Here are more examples of the modifying quoted copula.

1. Latio 'la 'nun māl un Yenge 'ey yo, Hānkwuk mal iey yo.	Is the word latio English or Korean?
2. Pusan ila 'nun tosi nun eti iss.ey yo.	Where is the city [called=] of Pusan?
3. Sinchey ila 'n' māl un mues iey yo.	What does the word sinchey mean?
4. Nyū-Yok ila 'n' kos un elma 'na khe yo.	How large is [the place called] New York?
5. Ecey Kim Pok.nam ila 'nun sālam i chac.e wass.ey yo.	Somebody named Pok.nam Kim came to visit yesterday.

In Basic Sentence 16 of Lesson 27 you will run across . . . ila 'nun [treated as an abbreviation of . . . ila (ko) hanun kes un 'the thing said to be'] used as a synonym for the topic particle un/nun 'as for . . . (guess what?) . . . For still another use for the word ila see ‖ 24.3.

‖ 19.8. The particle ulo: more meanings.

Basic Sentences 17, 19, and 28 show the particle ulo in a new meaning, as a stylistic variant of the copula gerund iko, meaning 'is [such-and-such a noun], and . . .'

17\. . . . yūmyeng han hakca lo, . . . 'He's a famous scholar, and . . .'
19\. . . . Sewul sīcang uy ttal lo koyngcang han miin iey yo. 'She's the daughter of the mayor of Seoul and is a magnificent beauty.'
28\. . . . puin eykey hun hi iss.nun pyēng ulo . . . 'It's a common illness for women, and . . .'

This meaning of (u)lo blends in with another translation which is often useful for it: 'as' or 'for (=in the capacity of),' as follows:

1. I pang ul kyōsil lo sse yo.	They use this room as (for) a classroom.
2. Sensayng ulo kuleh.key hamyen an tōy yo.	As a teacher, you ought not to do that sort of thing.
3. Tāyhak kyōswu lo kyēysey yo.	He teaches at the university. [=He is at the university as a teacher.]
4. Ilponq salam ulo nun, Yenge lul cal haci yo??	He speaks English well for a Japanese, doesn't he?
5. Cwungkwuk salam ul pomyen, Cwungkwuk salam ulo ālkeyss.ey yo?	If you see a Chinese person, can you tell that he's Chinese [=do you recognize him as a Chinese person]?

In these meanings, the particle (u)lo is sometimes followed by the particle se to strengthen its meaning: kyōsil lo se, sensayng ulo se, tāyhak kyōswu lo se, Ilponq salam ulo se nun, etc.

Other meanings you will find for this particle are:

1. manner: Yelqsim ulo kongpu hay yo. 'He studies with zeal.'
2. exchange: Pissan kes ul ssan kes ulo pakkwe yo. 'He exchanges an expensive one for a cheap one.'

   Chen wen ulo sa yo (phal.e yo). 'He buys (sells) it for a thousand wen.'
3. direction: Ōyn phyen ulo kasey yo. 'Go to the left.'

   I kil lo kamyen Uycwu lo kako, ce kil lo kamyen Wensan ulo kap.nita. 'This road will take you to Uycwu, and that one to Wensan.'

   Na hanthey lo osey yo. 'Come to me.'
4. time: Aph ulo tto mannapsita. 'See you again in the days ahead.'
5. change of state: Khun hakca lo tōyss.ey yo (=Khun hakca ka tōyss.ey yo). 'He turned into [became] a great scholar.'
6. means: Yenphil lo ssusey yo. 'Write in [with a] pencil.'

   Pihayng-ki lo kapsita. 'Let's go by plane.'
7. material: Namu lo (Tōl lo) ciun cip iey yo. 'It's a house made of wood (of stone).'
8. cause, reason, purpose: Phyēyq-pyeng ulo cwuk.ess.ey yo. 'He died of [from, with] TB.'

In the last three examples, the meaning of the particle can be strengthened by adding the word sse (infinitive from ssu- 'use') after it: Pihayng-ki lo sse kapsita. Namu lo sse ciun cip iey yo. Phyēyq-pyeng ulo sse cwuk.ess.ey yo.

EXERCISES

I

Make each of the following statements mean 'Mr. Kim said that . . .' and then translate. Use kulayss.ey yo for 'said.' For example, the first will be: Kim sensayng i ku puin to onta ko kulayss.ey yo. 'Mr. Kim said that [his wife =] Mrs. Kim is coming too.'

1. Ku puin to wa yo.
2. Ku uy chinkwu ka tōn i mānh.e yo.
3. (Kim sensayng i) kāy ka cic.nun kes ul tul.ess.ey yo.
4. Ku uy atul i wuli catong-cha to ssis.ko takk.keyss.ey yo.
5. Ku uy ttal i acik to elye yo.
6. (Kim sensayng i) nal mata tāmpay lul yelq-twū kay ssik phi(w)e yo.
7. Payk sensayng i wuli apeci hanthey cēnhwa lul kēlkeyss.ey yo.
8. Sensayng nim kkey se ku i hanthey caymi iss.nun phyēnci lul ssusyess.ey yo.
9. Ku uy ai tul i taninun hak.kyo ka cip ey se mēlci anh.e yo.
10. Onul un Cang sensayng i kaluchici anh.e yo.
11. Ku kwāyngi ka cham ippe yo.
12. (Kim sensayng) puin i pyēngwen ey ip.wen hako iss.ey yo.
13. (Kim sensayng i) Poktong-i lul pulless.ci man, tāytap i ēps.ess.ey yo.
14. Ilcciki cako siph.e haci anh.e yo.
15. Ku puin i pap hal ttay, caki to towa yo.
16. Ku cāngmo ka yūmyeng han hwāka 'ey yo.

II

Make each of the following questions mean 'Mr. Kim asked . . .' and then translate. For example, the first will be: Kim sensayng i wuli apeci ka pyēng i nass.nun ya ko mul.ess.ey yo. 'Mr. Kim asked if my father was ill.'

1. Wuli apeci ka pyēng i nass.ey yo?
2. Ku wuphyen-kwuk un kakkawe yo?

3. Haksayng tul i eti se mek.na yo.
4. Ku uy puin i yel i noph.a yo?
5. Eti anc.umyen cōh.keyss.ey yo.
6. Ku hakca ka chayk i mānh.un ka yo?
7. Wuli ka eti se sal.e yo.
8. Nay ka nwukwu lul pulless.ey yo.
9. Pakk i chwupci anh.e yo?
10. Nay ka mues ul hako siph.e yo.
11. Nwu' ka wuli hak.kyo ey ku capci tul ul cwuess.na yo.
12. Mikwuk yāyki lul hanun sālam i nwukwu 'ey yo.
13. Nay ka kaciko iss.nun mānnyen-phil i Mikwuk se on kes iey yo?
14. Nay ka meli ka aph.e yo?
15. Ku haksayng i meli lul alh.e yo?
16. Ai tul i pelsse os ul pes.ess.ey yo?

III

Make each of the following suggestions mean 'Mr. Kim suggested that we . . .' For example, the first will be: Kim sensayng i ilcciki il.e na se sānqpo haca ko kulayss.ey yo. 'Mr. Kim suggested we get up early and take a walk.'

1. Ilcciki il.e na se sānqpo kapsita.
2. Hānkwuk ūmsik ul capswusipsita.
3. Emeni lul tōpci yo!
4. Com swīlq ka yo??
5. Cang pole kass.ta on sālam ul mannamyen, onul mulken kaps tul i etten ya mul.e popsita.
6. Say cip ul chac.ulq ka yo??
7. Kath.i phul ul kkakk.upsita.
8. Ōyn phyen ey anc.upsita.
9. Kkoch ul sa kaciko olq ka yo??
10. Mun ul com yēlci yo.
11. Hōysa ey cēnhwa lul kēpsita.

IV

Make each of the following commands mean 'Mr. Kim told (asked) someone to . . .' The person told is given in parentheses. Use tele for an inferior, hanthey otherwise. In some cases ('Mr. Kim to his wife,' for example) either is all right. The first will be: Kim sensayng i na tele yeki anc.ula ko kulayss.ey yo. 'Mr. Kim told me to sit here.'

1. Yeki anc.usipsio. [Na]
2. Ku chayk ul hak.kyo ey kaciko osey yo. [Wuli an(h)ay]
3. Say kwutwu lul sin.e yo! [Ku atul]
4. Os ul pes.usipsio. [Hwānca]
5. Cip ey kyēysey yo. [Ku puin]
6. Ku chayk ul ilk.usey yo. [Haksayng tul]
7. Onulq pam ey neykthai lul māysipsio. [Ku chinkwu]
8. Uysa hanthey cēnhwa lul kēsey yo. [Ku ttal]
9. Tōn ul mānh.i ssuci mal.e yo! [Ku atul]
*10. Yenge lul haci māsio. [Haksayng tul]
*11. Kuleh.key khun soli lo puluci māsey yo. [Puin]

*NOTE: Drop the honorific in quoting māsi-. The honorific element is often omitted in quoting any command, even when the commanded person merits esteem from the quoter as well as the commander.

CONVERSATION

I

Persuade your Korean teacher to turn doctor (or nurse) temporarily and try diagnosing each of your aches and pains, in turn. Answer his questions about what's wrong with you (using imaginary symptoms—unless you've got some good ones that are real), and volunteer any further information you feel is important. Do as the doctor says. If he recommends going to the hospital for an operation, or for a good rest, don't fight it. If he feels you need a shot, bear up bravely. If he doesn't think there's anything serious the matter with you, take his word for it.

II

Now is your chance to talk about your operation in Korean. Prepare a brief talk about such an experience (real or imaginary), or an illness suffered by someone in your family. Go into detail about the preparations, entering the hospital, the doctor, the nurses. Tell how long the operation took and how long it took you to get better. Tell about the visitors who called upon you before you were discharged; what they brought you, what they had to say about their own hospital experiences. Don't forget to mention what the weather was like, what you were allowed to eat, how long it was before you could play tennis, and other comments to practice vocabulary from earlier lessons as well as this one.

VOCABULARY DRILL

Translate the following sentences into Korean, in each of the ways indicated.

1. Mrs. Kim says her husband ___.
   has a cold
   has a headache
   had a checkup last week

2. Mr. Pak said his son ___.
   graduated from medical school last year
   is an interne at the hospital
   is studying pediatrics

3. The doctor told me to ___.
   be vaccinated for smallpox
   take care of myself
   see my dentist twice a year

4. My friend suggested that we ___.
   pay a sick visit to Mr. Pak
   take flowers to the teacher
   drive, even though the streets are slippery

5. I asked Pok.nam Kim whether ___.
   he is all well now
   his fever was still high
   it's hard for him to take medicine

6. I just saw the nurse ___.
   come out of the operating room
   go into the examining room
   give the patient a shot

7. Shall I tell you about ___?
   my operation
   the first-aid treatment I had
   my blood test

8. I asked the child if he ___.
   had a contagious disease
   had ever had measles
   was studying literature in school

9. When I entered the hospital, I was examined by ___.
   a medical student
   an interne
   an ear-nose-throat specialist

10. He suggested that we ___ after I get out of the hospital.
    go see the people who live in that gray stone house
    speak to the doctor in charge of the hospital
    visit the mayor's daughter, who is so beautiful

COMPREHENSION

Your tutor will read you the following passage in Korean while you listen with your book closed. Afterward he will ask you questions to see how well you have understood. Then he will read through the passage with you, sentence by sentence, while you look at your book to see what parts were causing you trouble. After you are satisfied that you know what each sentence means separately, close your book and let your tutor read the passage to you again. Now you should be able to understand everything you hear.

Pak sensayng ayki ka sohwa ka nappe cin mo.yang ulo eceyq cenyek to mekci anh.ko pam ey cam to cal caci anh.ess.ta ko kulayss.ey yo. Kulay se way soaq-kwa ey kaci anh.nun ya ko mul.ess.ci man, ku uysa nun uyhak paksa imyen se to chincel haci anh.ta ko kulay yo. Kulay to, ayki pyēng i te cwūng hay ciki cen ey ka pola hayss.ci yo. Pak sensayng puin un na wa kath.i kaca 'yss.una sikan i ēps.e se Pok.nam-i emeni tele kath.i kala ko hayss.ey yo. Cenyek hwū ey ayki ka com etten ya ko cēnhwa lo mul.ess.uni, incey nun mānh.i naass.ta ko haci yo. Kulemyen se, Kim paksa ka kuleh.key nappun sālam i ani 'n mo.yang ila ko kkaci haci anh.e yo?? Ku uysa uy cīntan ulo n' ayki ka sohwaq-pyeng i ani 'ko yel i noph.ko kichim ul hanun kes i kāmki ka tun kkatalk iess.ta 'y yo. Yak ul sa wass.nun ya ko mul.e poni, kyewul nal i nemu chwuwe se catong-cha ka mōs kakey tōyss.uni-kka n' yak-pang ey kaci mōs hayss.ta ko haci yo. Kulemyen wuli cha lo tanye ola ko hayss.ey yo. Cikum Kim sensayng puin i yak-pang ey kass.ta wa se komapta ko hanun kwun yo. [1]Nayil tangsin to sikan i iss.umyen ayki pyēng mūn.an ul ka posey yo.

LESSON 20. REVIEW

I. VOCABULARY REVIEW

Here are 20 groups of five Korean expressions. Read each group aloud. If all the expressions in the group have meanings relating to the same general subject, name or describe the subject in Korean and go to the next. If the majority are about the same subject but one or two do not belong, name the subject matter and then pick out the misfit or misfits. For example, in the first group all but aphe yo 'hurts' name household tasks, so you might answer Emeni ka hanun īl iey yo 'They are things the mother does.' Use your ingenuity to describe what the words have in common.

1. aphe yo
   cang pole ka yo
   panu' cil hay yo
   pap hay yo
   socey hay yo
2. namul
   kwukswu
   hanul
   panchan
   hong-cha
3. anq-kwa
   chiq-kwa
   munq-kwa
   nāyq-kwa
   soaq-kwa
4. capok
   kito
   selkyo
   sēng-manchan sik
   sēylyey
5. achimq pap
   cakkwu
   cēmsim
   cenyek
   copan
6. pāntay hay yo
   ppallay hay yo
   sang ul pwa yo
   selkeci lul hay yo
   sinthong hay yo
7. ip.wen
   pyēngwen
   tam.im uysa
   thōywen
   ttwukkeng
8. kan-cang
   kimchi
   kwuk
   mantwu
   ttek
9. so
   talam-cwi
   talk
   tōngney
   twāyci
10. cwung
    hakca
    hwāka
    hyel.ayk
    kanho-pu
11. congkyo
    Cang.lo-kyo
    Kam.li-kyo
    Pulkyo
    Yeyswu-kyo
12. hongyek
    kāmki ka tul.ess.ey yo
    māma
    olay
    yel i noph.a yo

13. swuce
    kulus
    sapal
    samci-chang
    yuli can

14. cel
    hoysayk
    pyēngwen
    sīcheng
    ^{n}Yeca Chengnyen Hōykwan

15. ceptay hay yo
    chotay
    cwūpin
    sēysang
    paypin

16. chānsong-ka
    chentang
    Hana' nim
    selmyeng
    Sēngkyeng

17. cha-cha
    tam
    tāymun
    ttul
    ^{n}yēm.lye

18. chāyso
    hayng-kil
    manul
    muwu
    Tang myen

19. chīm-pang
    puekh
    pyēngsil
    siktang
    ūngcep-sil

20. chilyo lul pat.e yo
    cwūsa lul mac.e yo
    kēmsa lul hay yo
    wutwu lul mac.e yo
    yak ul mek.e yo

II. REVIEW OF FORMAL STYLE

Each of the following items is a statement or question in the polite style. Change them to formal style. (Remember that the formal equivalent of na 'I' is ce, of tangsin 'you' is sensayng nim, and of wuli 'we' is ce-huy or ce-huy tul.) Translate each sentence.

1. Tangsin i Yengkwuk salam in ka yo?
2. Na nun Yengkwuk salam i ani 'ey yo.
3. Kulem, eti se osyess.na yo.
4. Mikwuk se wass.ey yo.
5. Mikwuk un Hānkwuk se kakkawe yo?
6. Kakkapci anh.e yo. Tāytan hi mel.e yo.
7. Mikwuk ey se nun musun īl ul hasyess.na yo.
8. Hak.kyo ey se kaluchyess.ey yo.
9. Cikum wuli hak.kyo lul com kwūkyeng hasikeyss.ey yo?
10. Nēy. Haksayng tul ul mannako siph.e yo.
11. Wuli hak.kyo nun cākci man, haksayng un mānh.e yo.
12. Tāmpay lul hana phisikeyss.ey yo?
13. Komapsup.nita. Na nun tāmpay lul nemu cōh.a hay se, nul phi(w)e yo.
14. Haksayng tul i eti se mek.na yo.
15. Haksayng tul un tā kakkawun cip ey se sal.e yo. Kulay se, cip ey ka se mek.e yo.
16. Sensayng tul un ettay yo.
17. Wuli nun hak.kyo yeph ey iss.nun hōykwan ey ka se, um.ak ul tul.umyen se pap ul mek.ko cha lul masye yo.
18. Yeki ka wuli secay 'ey yo.
19. Cham khun secay 'ey yo.
20. Khuki nun khuci man, chayk i mānh.ci anh.e yo.
21. Wuli hak.kyo nun tōn i ēps.e yo. Kulay se, chayk ul mānh.i mōs sass.ey yo.

22. Kuleh.ci man, wuli haksayng pumo tul i chayk ul meych kwen cwuess.ey yo.
23. Cikum meych si 'n ka yo. Twū si pān iey yo? Na nun kicha lul tha ya hay yo.
24. Cengke-cang un yeki se etteh.key kana yo.
25. Palun phyen ulo kamyen, keki sip-pun an ey kel.e kalq swu iss.ey yo.

III. GRAMMAR REVIEW

A

Change the verb in each of the following to the sequential form (-[u]ni or -[u]ni-kka; see ‖ 18.1)—any tense you like. Then finish the sentence by making up another clause to go with it. Translate the completed sentence.

1. Ip mas i ēps.ey yo.
2. Ecey phyēnci lul ssess.ey yo.
3. Wuli uysa ka chincel hay yo.
4. I pang i tēlewe yo.
5. Yeyswu-kyo lul mit.e yo.
6. Ppalli wūncen hayss.ey yo.
7. I chayk ul cheum ulo ilk.ko iss.ey yo.
8. Kulus ul ssis.ci anh.ess.ey yo.
9. I pyēng i hun hay yo.
10. Kimchi lul mek.ess.ey yo.

B

Each of the following sentences asks a question. Quote each of them, by making it mean 'The teacher asked whether . . .' Translate the completed sentence.

1. Kongpu lul cal hayss.ey yo?
2. Yak-pang ey tullikeyss.ˢup.nikka?
3. Pay ka kopha yo?
4. Nal mata wuphyen-kwuk ey kaci anh.e to kwaynchanh.e yo?
5. Kongpu hay pelisyess.ey yo?
6. Chayk ul ilh.ess.ey yo?
7. Tali ka aphe yo?
8. Ūmsik i nemu maypsup.nikka?
9. I uysa ka i lul ppopci anh.keyss.ˢup.nikka?
10. Kil i mikkulepsup.nikka?

C

Change each of the following sentences to make it mean 'I make (let, have) someone do so-and-so.' For example, the first will be: Nay ka atul eykey [or hanthey] phul ul kkakk.key hayss.ey yo. 'I had my son mow the lawn.' [The person caused to act has the particle eykey, or hanthey, PROVIDED the verb already has an object; if the verb has no object in the non-causative sentence, the person caused to act has the particle ul/lul.] Translate the completed sentence.

1. Atul i phul ul kkakk.ess.ey yo.
2. Chinkwu ka nuc.key cass.ey yo.
3. Ku haksayng i chang ul yēlkeyss.ey yo.
4. Kim sensayng i mun ul tat.ulq ka hay yo.
5. Ttal i kulus ul ssis.e yo.

6. Pap hal ttay, ku sālam i towa yo.
7. Kim sensayng atul i wuli cip ey tullikeyss.ey yo.
8. Senkyo-sa ka Hānkwuk ūmsik ul mek.ess.ey yo.
9. Kāy ka cic.ci anh.keyss.ey yo. [Make it mean: 'I'll get the dog not to bark.']
10. Poktong-i ka apeci eykey phyēnci lul ssukeyss.ey yo.

D

Change the verb in each of the following to the transferentive form (-ta [ka]—see ‖ 16.2); then complete the sentence, and translate.

1. Ppallay lul hayss.ey yo.
2. Ku haksayng ul towa yo.
3. Poktong-i ka emeni hanthey cēnhwa lul kel.ess.ey yo.
4. Nolay lul hayss.ey yo.
5. Copan ul mek.ess.^{s}up.nita.
6. Onul achim hak.kyo ey wass.ey yo.
7. Congkyo lul uynon hayss.ey yo.
8. Pap ul cwūnpi hayss.ey yo.
9. Tāyhak ul tanyess.^{s}up.nita.
10. Pyēngwen ey kass.^{s}up.nita.

E

Each of the following sentences makes a suggestion. Quote each, by putting it in a sentence meaning 'My wife/husband suggested that we . . .' Translate.

1. Onul ōhwu ey wuphyen-kwuk ey se mannapsita.
2. I ūmsik cip ey se mekci māpsita.
3. Yeki anc.upsita.
4. Os ul ip.upsita.
5. Cikum phyēnci lul ssuci māpsita.
6. Say cip ul ciupsita.
7. Ilcciki sīcak hapsita.
8. I chayk ul kath.i ilk.upsita.
9. Sik.kwu tul uy sin ul takk.upsita.
10. Kim sensayng hanthey cēnhwa lul kēpsita.

F

Change each of the following sentences so that it means 'comes or gets to do something' or 'turns out that someone does something.' For example, the first will be: Wuli ka ku yenghwa lul kwūkyeng hakey tōyssey yo. 'We got to see that movie.'

1. Wuli ka ku yenghwa lul kwūkyeng hayss.ey yo.
2. Nay ka Kim sensayng ul mannass.ey yo.
3. Wuli cip i Yeyswu-kyo lul mit.keyss.^{s}up.nita.
4. Wuli atul ul Cwuil hak.kyo ey ponayss.^{s}up.nita.
5. Apeci to ^{l}yeypay-tang ey kakeyss.^{s}up.nita.
6. Nay ka Hānkwuk ey kako siph.ess.ey yo.
7. Ku kwāyngi ka nappe se, Kim sensayng un ku kwāyngi lul silh.e hayss.ey yo.
8. Ku sālam i nal mata cip ey iss.ess.ey yo.
9. Ēncey puthe tāmpay lul phi(wu)syess.ey yo.
10. Sikan i nuc.ess.ey yo.

G

Change each of the following sentences so that it means '[someone] knows (or knew) how to . . .' Then translate.

1. Ayki ka pap ul mek.e yo.
2. Ayki ka honca sin ul pes.sup.nita.
3. Ku ai ka honca kass.[s]up.nikka?
4. Tto honca anc.sup.nikka?
5. Kimchi lul mayntup.nita.
6. Ku mun ul yēp.nikka?
7. Kkoch ul sīm.sup.nita.
8. Ai ka honca yenghwa kwūkyeng ka yo.
9. Ilpon mal ul ilk.e yo.
10. Ceq-kalak ulo meksup.nita.

IV. MORE GRAMMAR REVIEW

A

The following sentences say that someone (A) is something (X). Make each mean 'X who is called A'; then put the phrase into a Korean sentence, and translate.

1. Kim puin i kanho-pu 'ey yo. [→ A nurse called Mrs. Kim . . .]
2. Kim Poktong i haksayng iey yo.
3. Hānkwuk i mēn kos iey yo.
4. Pak Yengswun i sayksi 'ey yo.
5. Cang Pok.nam i senkyo-sa 'ey yo.

B

Change each of the following sentences so that it means 'I saw [so-and-so happen].' For example, the sentence Ayki ka wuyu lul mek.e yo 'the baby drinks its milk' would become Ayki ka wuyu lul mek.nun kes ul pwass.ey yo 'I saw the baby drinking its milk.'

1. Ku haksayng i cal kongpu hay yo.
2. Ai tul i Kim sensayng cip twī ttul ey se nol.a yo.
3. Kim sensayng puin i cip ey iss.ey yo.
4. Poktong-i ka tōn i ēps.ey yo.
5. Ku tose-kwan uy chayk i mānh.e yo.
6. Wuli chinkwu ka cha lul masye yo.
7. Ku ai ka meli lul pis.e yo.
8. Ku ai ka moca lul pes.e yo.
9. Atul i i lul takk.e yo.
10. Ku hak.kyo ka kakkawe yo.

C

Put each of the following statements into a sentence meaning 'The minister [or priest] said (that) . . .'; then translate.

1. [1]Yeypay-tang i mēp.nita.
2. [1]Yeypay-tang i kakkapsup.nita.
3. Ūmsik i tha to kwaynchanh.e yo.
4. Pok.nam-i ka kwiyewe yo.

5. Tam ul nemkye pwass.ey yo.
6. Kim sensayng puin i cikum alh.ci anh.e yo.
7. Kāy ka cwuk.ess.ey yo.
8. Puin i yel i noph.a yo.
9. I kes ul mōlla yo.
10. Tam.im uysa ka chincel hay yo.

D

Put the verb in each of the following into the adversative form (-[u]na; see ‖ 18.3)—any tense you like. Then complete the sentence, and translate.

1. Onul achim ey nun cham tewess.ey yo.
2. Nwūn i oci anh.sup.nita.
3. Kyewul ey nun chwupsup.nita.
4. Pihayng-ki lo ponaymyen, ppaluta ko hay yo.
5. Nay ka kalq cwūnpi tā tōyss.ey yo.
6. Wuli cip i nemu khuci anh.e yo.
7. Ūmsik i ēps.ey yo.
8. Ku ayki ka cham elye yo.
9. Kim sensayng un mōlla yo.
10. Sangcem ey kaci anh.keyss.ey yo.

E

Change each of the following sentences to make it mean 'I heard . . .' (For example, The neighbor's dog was barking would become I heard the neighbor's dog barking . . . cic.nun kes ul tul.ess.ey yo.) Translate the completed sentence.

1. Ku senkyo-sa ka Mikwuk yēyki lul hay yo.
2. Kim sensayng i khun soli lo catong-cha lul pulle yo.
3. Palam i pul.e yo.
4. Wuli cip ey se kakkawun hak.kyo uy haksayng tul i nal mata nolay hay yo.
5. Mā sensayng i ku yēyki lul Hānkwuk mal lo ilk.e yo.
6. Cang sensayng i taumq pang ey se kaluchye yo.
7. Ai tul i cip twī ttul ey se nōlko iss.ey yo.
8. Emeni ka Kim sensayng puin hanthey cēnhwa lul kel.e yo.
9. Ku yūmyeng han sengak-ka ka tokchang hay yo.
10. Poktong-i ka cip ey tul.e wass.ey yo.

F

Quote each of the following commands by making it mean '[someone] told him to . . .' Specify who did the commanding and who was commanded. Translate the completed sentence.

1. I chayk ul sensayng nim eykey tulisipsio.
2. Cikum kongpu lul hasipsio.
3. Hangali ey nun ttwukkeng ul teph.usipsio.
4. Hwānca lul kēmsa hasipsio.
5. Ceq-kalak ul sang ey 'ta kac'ta noh.usio.
6. I ūmsik cip ey se mekci māsipsio.
7. Nemu pissamyen ku os ul saci māsipsio.
8. Onulq cenyek ey nun Poktong-i ka kulus ul ssis.usio.
9. I uyca ey anc.usipsio.
10. Emeni hanthey cēnhwa lul kēsipsio.

G

Each of the following sentences is a quotation. Read each aloud; then say what the original words probably were, before the sentence was quoted. (Assume it was spoken in the formal style.) For example, if the quoting sentence were Kongpu hanta ko kulay yo 'He says he's studying,' the original would be Kongpu hap.nita 'I'm studying.' Translate the completed sentences.

1. Wuli hyeng-nim un cal nōlko iss.ta ko kulay yo.
2. Kicha lo kamyen ppaluta ko hay yo.
3. Ilcciki ca ya hanta ko hap.nita.
4. Wuli wa kath.i kaca ko hayss.ey yo.
5. Kim sensayng un tōn i mānh.ta ko kulayss.ey yo.
6. Cēnhwa hasikeyss.ta ko kulayss.^{s}up.nikka?
7. I chaýk ul ilk.ci mālla ko hayss.ey yo.
8. Kim sensayng i pyēnho-sa 'la ko kulayss.ey yo.
9. Ce sālam un tōn ul kaciko wass.ta ko hay yo.
10. Yeki se anc.ci mālko yuli chang kakkai anc.ca ko hayss.ey yo.
11. Nwūn i omyen, kongwen ey se sānqpo haci mālca ko hakeyss.ey yo.
12. Cip ul sakeyss.ta ko kulayss.ey yo.
13. Tose-kwan ey ka ya hakeyss.ta ko hayss.ey yo.
14. Kim sensayng puin eykey wuli cip ey osila ko yele pen māl hayss.ey yo.
15. I kes ul Hānkwuk mal lo kimchi 'la ko hayss.ey yo.
16. Onul un cham chwupta ko hayss.ey yo.
17. Cēmsim ul ōcen yel han si ey mek.ess.uni, cikum un cham pay ka kophuta ko hayss.ey yo.
18. Ku phyēnci lul ponayla ko hayss.ey yo.
19. Catong-cha lo kamyen twū sikan ina kellinta ko kulayss.ey yo.
20. Onul un hak.kyo ey an onta ko hayss.^{s}up.nita.

V. TEST

Translate the following sentences into Korean. Please read the sentences carefully and be sure your Korean version carries the same meaning. Parentheses enclose elements needed in Korean but awkward in English. Brackets enclose elements not needed or said differently in Korean, but useful for a smooth English translation.

1. I want to get some exercise.
2. My son knows how to wash the car.
3. I have to write a letter to Mr. Kim.
4. I'm glad I saw the missionary.
5. I wish I had some new shoes.
6. The man who came yesterday is my friend.
7. Does your father want to mow the grass?
8. Mr. Kim wants to go to Korea before he writes [his] book.
9. May we listen to the radio this evening?
10. I hope the weather will be nice tomorrow.
11. I'd like you to sharpen this pencil for me.
12. If the weather is bad tomorrow, I don't want to visit Mr. Kim.
13. She says the children are in the midst of (eating) their dinner.
14. My father said he had never heard such fine music.
15. She studies while she's walking to school.
16. When we lived in America, we weren't able to eat Korean food.
17. Now our mother lets us eat Korean food all the time.

18. They asked us if we had ever been to Japan.
19. On my way to school I'm thinking of dropping in at the library to borrow a book.
20. He said he would go to the library and THEN go to school.
21. He suggested that since we don't have to go to bed early, we go for a walk.
22. He told me to wait for him outside the library.
23. I ought to read the newspaper every day.
24. It really snowed last night!
25. You shouldn't just [do nothing but] drink tea [all the time].
26. I told the child not to talk while he was eating.
27. I was looking for a pencil, but I couldn't find [one].
28. I got the missionary to try eating kimchi, but he (the missionary) said it was too spicy so he didn't like it.
29. He said Father seems to have gone out.
30. Mr. Kim must have called (= probably called) a taxi.
31. I asked Mr. Kim if he had called a taxi.
32. The baby seems not to be eating. [= The baby doesn't seem to be eating.]
33. Poktong-i probably hasn't any money.
34. I told Poktong-i not to buy anything expensive.
35. The school that Poktong-i will go to [regularly] seems not to be far [away]. [= . . . doesn't seem far away]
36. This food is very hot(ly seasoned) but I'm eating it anyway.
37. She suggested that we not set the table now but prepare the food instead. [= instead of setting . . .]
38. He says he isn't very hungry now since he ate so much [for] lunch.
39. I'll call my friend on the phone after the concert is over.
40. I can't go to the movies because I haven't any money.
41. The people who come to our church are many because the pastor is famous. [= Many people come to our church because we have a famous pastor.]
42. Our house isn't large, it's quite small.
43. Poktong-i DOES go to school [all right], but he doesn't study much.
44. Mother told me not to eat up all the salad.
45. That minister says he'd like to go to Korea as a missionary.
46. I saw that the children had already [got] dressed.
47. I knew that it was Sunday.
48. I thought that it was going to snow, but instead of snowing it rained.
49. The day is so dark, it would (= will) probably be hard to see the ball.
50. Shall we have a cup of tea?

VI. CONVERSATION

Carry on conversations in Korean along the following outlines. Include as many of the grammatical constructions from Lessons 16–19 as you can; try to use them over and over.

A

A mother is teaching her daughter how to make kimchi. After the lesson, the two of them prepare the evening meal: the mother asks the daughter to do certain tasks (making the salad, setting the table) and the child asks whether she should put the chopsticks here or there, where to place the rice bowl, etc.

B

Along similar lines, a father and his son are planning out the work around the yard: planting flowers, mowing the lawn, washing the car, etc. The father tells the son that after they finish the jobs, he'll teach him how to play tennis, baseball, etc., and does so.

C

[For missionaries] A missionary calls on a Korean family (assign roles to each member) and explains about the Christian church he represents, tells them of Christianity itself and why he wishes they would become converted to it, and describes the services of his church.

[For air-force officers] An air-force officer visits the mayor of a small Korean city to discuss possibilities of organizing the young people of the town, and making available recreation facilities for them. He offers to get fellow servicemen to teach the young Koreans English and sports. They discuss the places that might be used for such purposes: schools, parks, streets not much used by cars, etc.

[General] An American calls on a Korean family and introduces himself as a newcomer who lives near them. He asks about the people around town, the public buildings, the churches, places to buy various things, etc. He explains who he is and why he has come to Korea (a doctor? nurse? teacher?), and ends up by urging them to call on him soon at his home.

D

Describe (in a monologue) to a friend a dinner you recently had at the home of some Korean friends. Or, describe the sort of dinner you might have if you visited a Korean home.

E

Your husband, wife, sister, or brother has just returned from a visit to an old family friend in the hospital. You are naturally anxious for a report: ask everything you can think of, about the patient's condition, exactly what is wrong, when he entered and when he expects to leave the hospital, what the doctor said about his condition and what the nurse reported about his behavior; whether the patient needs anything, or would like some flowers, magazines, fruits, etc. Ask about the advisability of you yourself visiting the patient soon.

LESSON 21. PLANNING A PICNIC

BASIC SENTENCES

(Mrs. Min is talking to Mrs. Sōng.)

Korean	English	Amplification
M. 1. I pen puin-hoy wēn.yu-hoy lul eti lo kanun ci mul.e pwass.ey yo?	(Mrs. Sōng,) did you find out where we're going for the women's club picnic this year?	i pen . . . wen.yu-hoy 'this [time's =] year's picnic' hōy 'group, company, club' puin-hoy 'women's club' wēn.yu-hoy 'picnic (in a park); garden party' yā.yu-hoy 'picnic' kanun ci 'the (uncertain) fact of going' kanun ci mul.e pwa yo 'finds out whether [one] is going' eti lo kanun ci mul.e pwa yo 'find out where [one] is going'
S. 2. Nēy. Puin-hoy hōycang hanthey mul.e pwass.ey yo. I pen Tho-yoil ey Wui Tong ulo kanta ko hay yo.	Yes, I asked the president of the women's club. She says we're going to Wui Tong this Saturday.	hōycang 'president of a club or company' Wui Tong 'Ox-ear Village' [name of popular picnic area near Seoul]
M. 3. Kulay yo?? Na nun tōngmul-wen ulo kanun cwul al.ess.ey yo!	Oh? I thought we were going to the zoo.	tōngmul 'animal' tōngmul-wen 'zoo'
S. 4. Na nun cīnan pen hōy ey se tōngmul-wen ulo cēng hayss.nun ci, Wui Tong ulo cēng hayss.nun ci, ic.e pelyess.ey yo.	I've forgotten whether at the last meeting we decided on the zoo or (whether we decided on) Wui Tong.	hōy 'meeting' [also 'club'] cīnan pen hōy '[last-time meeting =] the last meeting' . . . ulo cēng hay yo 'decides on . . .' cēng hayss.nun ci 'whether [one] decided' ic.e yo 'forgets' ic.e pelye yo 'forgets (completely)'

Korean	English	Amplification
M. 5. Kuleh.ci man, i pen Tho-yoil ey pi ka omyen ama nalq-ca lul pyēnkyeng hal.nun ci to mōlla yo.	However, if it rains this Saturday, they may change the date.	i pen Tho-yoil 'this Saturday' nalq-ca '(agreed-on) date' [also spelled nalcca] pyēnkyeng 'a change, a shift' pyēnkyeng (ul) hay yo 'changes, shifts' pyēnkyeng hal.nun ci 'whether [one] will change it' . . . -nun ci to mōlla yo '[not even know whether . . .=] perhaps . . .'
S. 6. Celqtay lo pi nun an olq key 'p.nita.	It's surely not going to rain.	celqtay lo 'absolutely positively' an olq key 'p.nita 'it probably won't come'
M. 7. Meych sālam ina kanun ci āsey yo?	Do you know how many people are going?	kanun ci āsey yo 'knows whether [one] is going'
S. 8. Mōlla yo. Wui Tong i com mel.e to, keki pec kkoch i yūmyeng hani-kka n', sālam tul i mānh.i kalq cwul al.e yo.	I don't know. Since, even though Wui Tong is a bit far, the cherry blossoms there are famous, I assume a lot of people will go.	pec namu 'cherry tree' pec kkoch 'cherry blossoms'
M. 9. Cham. Cāy-cak.nyen wēn.yu-hoy nun eti se hayss.nun ci kiek hasey yo?	Uh, (Mrs. Sōng,) do you recall where we held the picnic year before last?	cak.nyen, cīnan hay 'last year' cāy-cak.nyen, ci-cinan hay, kulekkey 'year before last' hayss.nun ci 'whether [someone] did' eti se hayss.nun ci 'where [someone] did' kiek hay yo 'remembers, recalls' eti se hayss.nun ci kiek hay yo 'remembers where [one] did'
S.10. Kiek hako mālko yo. Acha, ku man sayngkak i an nap.nita.	Of course I recall. Oh— I just don't recollect.	acha 'oh! gee! gosh!' ku man 'just, only, with that' sayngkak i an na yo '[the thought doesn't come out =] doesn't remember'

Korean	English	Amplification
M.11. Wuli cip salang ey se haci anh.ess.ey yo? Ku nal pi ka wa se Changkyeng-wen ey mōs kako . . .	Didn't we have it in the guest room at my house? It rained that day so we couldn't go to the Changkyeng gardens (, and) . . .	salang 'guest room' [= room for entertaining groups of guests] Changkyeng-wen [name of an old palace garden in Seoul]
S. 12. Incey ya sayngkak i nap.nita. Tayk i cēy-il khuko cōh.a se keki se hayss.ci yo.	NOW I remember! Your house was the nicest and biggest, so we had it there.	incey ya '(only) now' cēy-il 'number one; (= kacang) most, -est' cēy-il khe yo = kacang khe yo 'it's the biggest'
13. Ku nal kkoch kwūkyeng un mōs hayss.e to, phek caymi iss.ess.ey yo.	That day even though we didn't get to see the flowers, we had a lot of fun.	phek 'very'
14. I pen ey nun cēypal nal i cōh.umyen cōh.keyss.ey yo.	This time I certainly hope the weather's nice.	cēypal 'certainly, strongly (hopes); hopefully, I hope; please'
15. Na nun Wui Tong pec kkoch ul mōs pon ci ka pelsse sā-nyen i tōy yo.	It's been four years now since I've been able to see the cherry blossoms in Wui Tong.	pon ci 'the time since one has seen' mōs pon ci 'the time since one got unable to see'
M.16. Na nun ku pota hwelssin te olay tōy yo. Wui Tong ey ka pon ci ka cham olay yo.	It's been much longer than that for me. It's a very long time since I've been to see Wui Tong.	. . .pota '(more) than' ku pota '(more) than that' ku pota te olay yo 'is longer than that' hwelssin 'much, way, (by) far' ka pon ci ka 'the time since going to see' [as subject]
S. 17. Tekswu emeni to i pen wēn.yu-hoy ey mullon osici yo??	Mrs. Min, you're coming to this picnic, of course, aren't you?	Tekswu emeni 'Tekswu's mother' = Mrs. Min
M.18. Kulssey yo . . . Kako nun siph.ci man . . .	W-e-l-l . . . I WANT to go, but . . .	kulssey yo 'well . . .' [showing reservations]
S. 19. Ku key musun māl-ssum iey yo. Tekswu emma ka an osimyen nwu' ka wa yo.	What kind of talk is that? If you don't come, Mrs. Min, who WILL come?	emma 'mama, mom(my)'
M.20. Han tases si ccum tol.a olq swu iss.ulq ka yo? Yeses si cha lo sikol com ka ya hakeyss.nun tey . . .	Will you be able to come back around five? I have to take a little trip out to the country by the six o'clock train, so . . .	ka ya hakeyss.nun tey . . . 'will have to go, so . . .' cha 'vehicle; (= catong-cha) car, automobile; (= thayksi) taxi, cab; (= kicha, cēncha) train'

	Korean	English	Amplification
S. 21.	^{n}Yēm.lye māsey yo! Ōhwu nēy si ccum tol.a onun catong-cha han tay ka iss.nun kes ul nay ka al.e yo. Ku cha lo osici yo.	Don't worry! I know that there's a car returning about 4 p.m. (Suppose) you come in that car.	
22.	Ce nun ku nal say chinkwu twū pun ul mōsiko ka yo.	That day I'm taking a couple of new friends with me.	
M. 23.	Kulay yo? Nwukwu 'ey yo.	Oh? Who are they?	
S. 24.	Twū pun tā Cwungkwuk se yo say osyess.ey yo. Han pun un Wang sensayng puin iko, tto han pun un Ho sensayng puin iey yo.	Both recently came from China. One is Mrs. Wang, the other is Mrs. Ho.	hana . . . tto hana 'one . . . (and) the other'
25.	Wuli Hānkwuk ^{n}yeseng tul ul mannako siph.e hanun tey . . . Tekswu emma ka kkok osye ya hay yo.	They want to meet some of us Korean women, so . . . Mrs. Min, you must come for sure.	^{n}yeseng 'women, womankind, a woman (as an example of womankind)' -ko siph.e hanun tey . . . 'want to do it, so . . .' kkok 'for sure, without fail'
26.	Wang sensayng puin un Cwu-Han Cwungkwuk Tāysa uy nwui-tongsayng ulo sēykyey ^{l}yehayng ul hanun tocwung ey wuli Hānkwuk ey tullyess.ey yo.	Mrs. Wang is the younger sister of the Chinese Ambassador to Korea, and has stopped by Korea on her way around the world.	cwu- 'stationed in (a place)' cāy- 'resident in (a place)' cwu-Han 'stationed in Korea' cāy-Han 'resident in Korea' sēykyey 'world' ^{l}yehayng (ul) hay yo 'takes a trip, makes a journey' tocwung 'in the midst of' sēykyey ^{l}yehayng ul hanun tocwung ey '[while in the midst of world-traveling =] on the way around the world'
27.	Ho sensayng puin un Cwungkwuk Tāysa-kwan seki-kwan uy puin ulo han tal cen ey Hānkwuk ey osyess.ey yo.	Mrs. Ho is the wife of the secretary of the Chinese embassy and came to Korea a month ago. [OR: . . . came to Korea a month ago as the wife of . . .]	Tāysa-kwan 'embassy' seki(-kwan) '(official) secretary' -kwan 'building' (as in tāysa-kwan 'embassy') -kwan 'official (as in ōymu-kwan 'diplomat')

	Korean	English	Amplification
M.28.	Caymi iss.nun pun tul kath.un tey yo. Na to manna pomyen cōh.keyss.nun tey . . . Ku pun tul i Hānkwuk mal ul halq cwul al.e yo?	They sound like very interesting people! I'd like to meet them too[, but] . . . Do they know how to speak Korean?	. . . kath.un tey yo. 'how . . . [they] seem!' cōh.keyss.nun tey . . . 'how nice it would be . . .'
S. 29.	Cwungkwuk salam ie se mōs hay yo. Ho sensayng puin uy namphyen un ōykyo-kwan ie se com haci yo.	They're Chinese, so they don't. Mrs. Ho's husband is a diplomat, so he knows some (Korean), you see.	ōykyo-kwan 'diplomat'
30.	Cey ka Cwungkwuk mal ul thongyek halq swu iss.ci yo. Kuleh.ci man Cwungkwuk mal ul hay pon ci ka pelsse sip-nyen i tōyss.ey yo.	I can interpret Chinese, you know. But it's been ten years now since I've tried talking Chinese.	thongyek (ul) hay yo 'interprets'
31.	Cōh.un say chinkwu tul to sakwilq kyem, (kkoch kwūkyeng to halq kyem,) kkok osey yo.	With the chance to get acquainted with nice new friends as well (as seeing the flowers and all), do come for sure.	sakwie yo 'is <u>or</u> gets acquainted' [often pronounced sakoy yo] sakwilq kyem '(combining) getting acquainted (with doing something else)' kwūkyeng halq kyem '(doing) flower-viewing (along with other things)'

SUPPLEMENTARY VOCABULARY

hōy lul yel.e yo <u>or</u> hay yo	has (holds) a meeting, meets	pū-hoycang	vice-chairman, vice-president
hwan.yeng	welcoming	hōykyey	treasurer
hwan.yeng (ul) hay yo	welcomes [someone]	hōywen	member
		hōypi	dues, membership fees
hwan.yeng-hoy	welcoming party, welcoming meeting	wiwen	committee member(s), committee
		wiwen-hoy	committee, commissions; committee meeting
sōngpyel	farewell, send-off		
sōngpyel (ul) hay yo	says farewell to, sends [someone] off	chwulqsek (ul) hay yo	is present (for a meeting)
sōngpyel-hoy	farewell party, farewell meeting	kyelqsek (ul) hay yo	is absent (from a meeting)
cheng hay yo	asks for; invites	sahoy (lul) hay yo	presides
īm.wen	staff, officers		

hōylok or hōyuy-lok	minutes
hōy(uy-)lok ^{1}nāngtok	the reading of the minutes
hōy(uy-)lok ^{1}nāngtok (ul) hay yo	reads the minutes
cepswu (lul) hay yo	accepts (minutes, reports)
cemmyeng or homyeng or (military) cemho	roll, roll call
chwulqsek (ul) pulle yo [pulu-], homyeng (ul) hay yo	calls the roll
pōko	report
thōuy	discussion
thōuy sāhang	items for discussion, agenda
tōnguy	(parliamentary) motion
tōnguy (lul) hay yo	makes a motion, moves
cāycheng	second (to a motion)
cāycheng (ul) hay yo	seconds a motion
kā-pu	pros and cons
kākyel (ul) hay yo	decides in favor of
pūkyel (ul) hay yo	decides against
kēswu (kākyel)	(affirmative, decision by) raising hands
thwuphyo (kākyel)	(affirmative decision by) ballot
sēnke	election
pu	a government ministry (department)
cāngkwan	a cabinet minister
Ōymu Pu	Ministry of Foreign Affairs (of the Republic of Korea)
Ōymu Cāngkwan	Minister of Foreign Affairs
kongsa	minister (to a foreign country)
kongsa-kwan	legation
^{1}yengsa	consul
^{1}yengsa-kwan	consulate
kyengchi	scenery
phie yo [phi-]	blooms, blossoms
pen.yek (ul) hay yo	translates
yaksok	promise; engagement, date
yaksok ul hay yo	makes a promise or engagement, promises
ūykyen	opinion, view; advice
ūykyen ul tul.e yo [tul-]	gets (listens to, takes) advice

NOTES

‖ 21.1. The post-modifier ci.

Constructions consisting of a modifier form followed by the post-modifier ci have two uses in Korean.

One of these, in expressions followed by an information verb, is for asking oblique questions; this is discussed below in ‖ 21.2.

With a past modifier, ci is used for expressions meaning 'since' (that is, time SINCE something happened and not SINCE meaning 'in view of the fact that' or 'so'), as in Basic Sentences 15,16, and 30:

> Na nun Wui Tong pec kkoch ul mōs pon ci ka pelsse sā-nyen i tōy yo. 'It's been four years now since I've been able to see the cherry blossoms in Wui Tong.'
>
> Wui Tong ey ka pon ci ka cham olay yo. 'It's a very long time since I've been to see Wui Tong.'
>
> . . . Cwungkwuk mal ul hay pon ci ka pelsse sip-nyen i tōyss.ey yo. 'It's been ten years now since I've tried talking Chinese.'

The pattern for these expressions is:

As subject:		As predicate:
PAST MODIFIER + ci (ka)	TIME WORD + a form of	iey yo [copula] 'it is' / tōy yo 'becomes'
	olay yo 'is long'	
	olay tōy yo 'becomes long'	

Kan ci (ka) 'Time since I've gone'	olayp.nita. 'is long'	'It's a long time since I've gone there.'
Ilk.un ci (ka) 'Time since I've read'	sēk tal i tōyss.ey yo. 'is three months.'	'It's been three months since I read it.'

Here are some more examples of this construction.

1. Sensayng nim ul poywun ci ka olayp.nita (or olay toyp.nita/tōyss.[s]up.nita). — It's been a long time since we've seen you.
2. Phyēnci lul pat.un ci (ka) sēy cwuil i tōyss.ey yo. — It's been three weeks since I got a letter.
3. Yeki on ci ō-nyen i tōyss.ey yo. — I haven't been here for five years. (= It's been five years since I came here.)
4. Kim sensayng ul mannan ci elma 'na toyp. nikka. — How long is it since you've seen Mr. Kim?
5. Ku kes i kuleh.key toyn ci elma 'na olayp.nikka. — How long is it since that happened?
6. Say os ul san ci ka ī-nyen tōyss.ey yo. — I haven't bought any new clothes for two years.

Notice that a negative modifier clause in this construction actually refers to the same situation as if the clause were affirmative; the situation is just viewed differently:

Kim sensayng ul mannan ci ka sēk tal i tōy yo. 'It's been three months since I saw Mr. Kim.' [= I haven't seen Mr. Kim for three months.]
Kim sensayng ul mōs mannan ci ka sēk tal i toy yo. 'It's been three months that I haven't seen Mr. Kim.' [= I haven't seen Mr. Kim for three months.]
Hānkwuk ūmsik ul mek.un ci ka olay yo. 'It's a long time since I've eaten Korean food.' [= I haven't eaten Korean food for a long time.]
Hānkwuk ūmsik ul mōs mek.un ci ka olay yo. 'It's a long time that I haven't been able to eat Korean food.' [= I haven't been able to eat Korean food for a long time.]

It is more common to use the strong negative expression (mōs hayss.ey yo 'couldn't do; didn't do at all') rather than the simple negative (an hayss.ey yo 'didn't do').

This expression implies that the time involved seems long, so you would not ordinarily use it for such things as 'three hours,' 'a few days,' 'a week and a half,' or the like.

‖ 21.2. Oblique questions.

An oblique question is used as part of a larger sentence that contains an INFORMATION VERB:

al.e yo	knows, realizes
mōlla yo	doesn't know

ic.e yo forgets
kiek hay yo remembers
sayngkak na yo remembers, recalls
kaluchye yo tells [= teaches]

In English, the actual question is a relative clause introduced by a question word: whether, where, who, which, etc. In Korean, the actual question is stated as a modifier plus ci. Here are some examples:

nwukwu 'n ci who he is
pi ka onun ci whether it's raining
eti kass.nun ci where he went
kongpu hal.nun ci whether he'll study
ēncey wass.nun ci when he came
etten kes i iss.nun ci which things there is

Oblique questions combine these two expressions. The chief difference is that in English the question part comes AFTER the information verb; in Korean, it comes BEFORE.

Here are some examples:

Kongpu hanun CI āp.nikka?
Do you know WHETHER he's studying?

Kongpu hayss.nun CI āp.nikka?
Do you know WHETHER he studied?

Kongpu hakeyss.nun CI āp.nikka?
Do you know WHETHER he's going to study?

For processive verbs, as well as iss- and ēps-, the processive modifier form is used. For descriptive verbs, which have no processive modifier forms, the -(u)n modifier is used:

Descriptive

Chwuwun ci al.e yo? 'Do you know whether it's cold?'
Mēn ci al.e yo? 'Do you know whether it's far?'
Pissan ci al.e yo? 'Do you know whether it's expensive?'
Phikon han ci al.e yo? 'Do you know whether he's tired?'

Processive

Ilk.nun ci al.e yo? 'Do you know whether he's reading?'
Iss.nun ci al.e yo? 'Do you know whether it's (here)?'
Kongpu hanun ci al.e yo? 'Do you know whether he's studying?'
Ssunun ci al.e yo? 'Do you know whether he's writing?'

Oblique questions in the past and future require the use of restricted modifiers of ALL verbs (see ‖ 19.3 above). These are made by adding -nun to the past or future base:

Descriptive

Chwuwess.nun ci al.e yo? 'Do you know whether it was cold?'
Chwupkeyss.nun ci al.e yo? 'Do you know whether it will be cold?'
Mel.ess.nun ci al.e yo? 'Do you know whether it was far?'
Mēlkeyss.nun ci al.e yo? 'Do you know whether it will be far?'
Pissass.nun ci al.e yo? 'Do you know whether it was expensive?'
Pissakeyss.nun ci al.e yo? 'Do you know whether it will be expensive?'

Phikon hayss.nun ci al.e yo? 'Do you know whether he was tired?'
Phikon hakeyss.nun ci al.e yo? 'Do you know whether he's going to be tired?'

Processive

Ilk.ess.nun ci al.e yo? 'Do you know whether he read it?'
Ilk.keyss.nun ci al.e yo? 'Do you know whether he's going to read it?'
Iss.ess.nun ci al.e yo? 'Do you know whether there was any?'
Iss.keyss.nun ci al.e yo? 'Do you know whether there will be any?'
Kongpu hayss.nun ci al.e yo? 'Do you know whether he studied?'
Kongpu hakeyss.nun ci al.e yo? 'Do you know whether he's going to study?'
Ssess.nun ci al.e yo? 'Do you know whether he wrote it?'
Ssukeyss.nun ci al.e yo? 'Do you know whether he's going to write it?'

The futures may optionally have a specially restricted modifier form before ci, a form made by adding -nun to the prospective modifier form to produce -ul.nun (ci):

Kal.nun ci al.e yo? 'Do you know whether he'll go?'
Mek.ul.nun ci al.e yo? 'Do you know whether he'll eat?'

Or, less often, a simple prospective modifier form may be used instead:

Kalq ci al.e yo? 'Do you know whether he'll go?'
Mek.ulq ci al.e yo? 'Do you know whether he'll eat?'

When an oblique question is given with the information verb mul.e yo 'asks,' the sentence means the same thing as a plain-style question quoted (above, ‖ 19.3):

Pap ul mek.nun ya ko mul.ess.ey yo. OR
Pap ul mek.nun ci mul.ess.ey yo.
'I asked whether he was eating.'
Ēncey kongpu hanun ya ko mul.upsita. OR
Ēncey kongpu hanun ci mul.upsita.
'Let's ask him when he does his studying.'

If a Korean oblique question contains a question word, it is the translation of this word that introduces the corresponding relative clause in English:

ETI lul kanun ci al.e yo? 'Do you know WHERE he's going?'
ĒNCEY mek.keyss.nun ci al.e yo? 'Do you know WHEN he's going to eat?'
MUES ul hayss.nun ci al.e yo? 'Do you know WHAT he did?'

If there is no question word in Korean, English supplies 'whether' or 'if' to introduce the clause:

Kanun ci al.e yo? 'Do you know WHETHER (IF) he's going?'
Mek.keyss.nun ci al.e yo? 'Do you know WHETHER (IF) he's going to eat?'
Hayss.nun ci al.e? 'Do you know WHETHER (IF) he did it?'

It is this question word that distinguishes oblique questions from other, similar expressions containing information verbs, which in English introduce the relative clause with THAT, corresponding to Korean cwul or kes:

Descriptive:

Phikon han cwul (lo) al.e yo. 'I assume that he's tired.'
Chwuwun cwul (lo) al.e yo. 'I assume that it's cold.'
Mēn kes ul al.e yo. 'I know it's a long way [far].'
Pissan kes ul al.e yo? 'Do you know that it's expensive?'

Processive

Kongpu hanun cwul (lo) al.e yo. 'I take it that he's studying.'

Cikum pap ul mek.nun kes ul al.e yo? 'Do you know that he's eating now?'

I phyēnci lul ssun cwul (lo) al.e yo. 'I figure (= assume) that he wrote this letter.'

Eceyq pam ey pi ka on kes ul al.e yo? 'Do you know that it rained last night?'

Chayk ul kaciko kalq cwul (lo) al.e yo. 'I assume he's going to bring his book.'

Cey ka ^{l}naynyen Hānkwuk ey kalq kes ul al.e yo? 'Do you realize that I'm going to Korea next year?'

Here are more examples of oblique questions.

1. Eti iss.nun ci mōlla yo.	I don't know where he is.
2. Mues in ci al.e yo.	He knows what it is.
3. Nwukwu 'n ci āsip.nikka?	Do you know who he is?
4. Ēncey wass.nun ci mōlla yo.	I don't know when he came.
5. Way wass.nun ci mōlla yo.	I don't know why he came.
6. Eti kass.nun ci mul.e posipsio.	Please ask him where they went.
7. Meych si 'n ci molukeyss.ey yo.	I don't know what time it is.
8. Eti se mek.ess.nun ci māl hasio.	Tell me where you ate.
9. Sewul i eti 'n ci āsey yo?	Do you know where Seoul is?
10. Kim sensayng i ceq-kalak ulo mek.ulq cwul ānun ci āsey yo?	Do you know whether Mr. Kim knows how to eat with chopsticks?
11. Yeki se wuphyen-kwuk i elma 'na mēn ci āsey yo?	Do you know how far it is from here to the post office?
12. Son ey mues i iss.nun ci na hanthey pōy cwusio.	Show me (= Let me see) what you have in your hand.
13. I chayk ul ilk.e ya halq ci ce chayk ul ilk.e ya halq ci molukeyss.ey yo.	I don't know whether I've got to read this book or that book.
14. Cengke-cang i eti 'n ci mul.ess.ey yo.	I asked him where the station was.
15. Kil i etwuwe se eti ka eti 'n ci molukeyss.ey yo.	The road is so dark I can't tell [what place is what place=] where things are.
16. Sālam i nemu mānh.e se nwu' ka nwukwu 'n ci ālq swu ēps.ey yo.	There are so many people you can't tell who is who.
17. Sensayng nim i māl-ssum ul nemu ppalli hasye se mwe ka mwe 'n ci molukeyss.^{s}up.nita.	You are talking too fast for me to [tell what is what=] follow.

Consecutive oblique questions of opposite or contrasting meaning are sometimes translated directly and sometimes, more conveniently, by 'whether . . . or not . . .':

18. Congi ka iss.nun ci ēps.nun ci molukeyss.ey yo.	I don't know whether or not there's any paper.
19. Kim sensayng i olq ci an olq ci [or ol.nun ci an ol.nun ci or okeyss.nun ci an okeyss.nun ci] mōlla yo.	I don't know whether Mr. Kim will be coming or not.
20. Pi ka onun ci an onun ci āsikeyss.ci yo?	Do you know whether or not it's raining?

21. Cōh.un ci an cōh.un ci āsici yo? — Do you know whether it's any good or not?
22. Pakk i tewun ci chwuwun ci moluci yo? — Don't you know whether it's hot or cold outside?
23. Ku sālam i pelsse kass.nun ci iss.nun ci āsikeyss.ey yo? — Do you know whether he's left or whether he's (still) here?

Oblique questions are sometimes used as a complete sentence, followed by the polite particle yo, with the meaning 'I wonder . . .'; Nwukwu 'n ci yo 'I wonder who it is.' Tā wass.nun ci yo 'I wonder if everyone is here.' Pi ka okeyss.nun ci yo 'I wonder if it will rain.' Sometimes the best translation is that of the next section (-nun ci to mōlla yo) 'maybe': Tōn ul mōs pat.ess.nun ci yo 'Maybe he didn't get the money.'

‖ 21.3. Oblique questions with to mōlla yo 'perhaps.'

5. . . . nalq-ca lul pyēnkyeng hal.nun ci to mōlla yo. 'Perhaps they'll change the date.' or 'They may change the date.' [= I don't even know whether they will change the date.]

A roundabout equivalent of 'perhaps, maybe'—emphasizing the uncertainty—is made by reinforcing the emphasis of an indirect question with the particle to 'even' and then quoting it with mōlla yo 'doesn't know.' The uncertainty may be reinforced by introducing the sentence with ama 'perhaps, maybe' as in Basic Sentence 5. (In translating this construction, notice that English 'may' used as an auxiliary verb and spoken with strong accent has the same force as 'maybe' or 'perhaps' used as an adverb.)

As with other indirect questions, it is the restricted processive modifiers that are used here. And as usual the -(u)n modifier of descriptive verbs is used, since these verbs lack processive forms. Because of the nature of the meaning, prospective modifier forms (-ul or -ul.nun) are more common.

Descriptive

pissalq ci to mōlla yo
(pissan ci to mōlla yo) — 'maybe it's expensive'

chwuwess.ulq ci to mōlla yo
(chwuwess.nun ci to mōlla yo) — 'it may have been cold'

coh.ulq ci to mōlla yo
coh.ul.nun ci to mōlla yo
(coh.keyss.nun ci to mōlla yo) — 'maybe it'll be good'

Processive

os ul ip.nun ci (ipko iss.nun ci) to mōlla yo — 'maybe he's getting dressed'

yenphil ul chac.ess.ulq ci to mōlla yo
(yenphil ul chac.ess.nun ci to mōlla yo) — 'he may have found his pencil'

pap ul mek.ul.nun ci to mōlla yo
pap ul mek.ulq ci to mōlla yo
(pap ul mek.keyss.nun ci to mōlla yo) — 'perhaps he's going to eat'

More examples:

1. Kim sensayng puin i alh.nun ci to mōlla yo.	Maybe Mrs. Kim is sick.
2. Pok.nam-i ka eti iss.ey yo?—Taum pang ey se sinmun ul ilk.ko iss.nun ci to mōlla yo.	Where's Pok.nam?—Maybe he's reading the paper in the next room.
3. I os ul saci māpsita. Nemu pissan ci to mōlla yo.	Let's not (or I guess I won't) buy this dress. It may be too expensive.
4. Ku cip i mues in ci āsikeyss.ey yo?—Hak.kyo 'lq ci to mōlla yo.	Do you know what that building is?—Maybe it's a school.
5. Wuli tōngney sālam tul i ku Mikwuk tāysa lul hwan.yeng hakeyss.nun ci to moluci yo.	Maybe the people of our village will greet the American ambassador, you see.
6. Hōycang i alh.e se kyelqsek hayss.uni, pū-hoycang i hōylok ^{l}nāngtok (ul) hakeyss.nun ci to mōlla yo.	The chairman is out sick so perhaps the vice-chairman will read the minutes.
7. Īm.wen sēnke nun thwuphyo lo haci anh.ko, kēswu lo hayss.nun ci to mōlla yo.	They may have elected the officers by hand vote rather than ballot.
8. Wasingthon si uy yūmyeng han pec namu ka cikum ccum un tā phiess.nun ci to mōlla yo.	The famous cherry blossoms in (the city of) Washington may have bloomed by now.
9. Wui Tong kanun kes i tōngmul-wen kanun kes pota cōh.un ci to mōlla yo.	Going to Wui Tong may be better than going to the zoo.
10. Cīnan pen wiwen-hoy ey se cemmyeng han sālam i Yūn paksa iess.nun ci to mōlla yo.	It may have been Dr. Yun who took the roll at the last committee meeting.

21.4. The topic particle un/nun with gerunds.

18. . . . kako nun siph.ci man . . . 'I WANT to go, but . . .'

In gerund constructions—for example, gerund plus siph.e yo 'wants to do'—use of the topic particle un/nun after the -ko form has the effect of setting it off to emphasize the following words. Basic Sentence 18 is, literally: 'As for going—I WANT to, all right, but . . .'

Here are some more examples:

1. Ku sālam ul mannako nun siph.ci man nemu pappe yo.	I want to meet him, but I am too busy.
2. Ku sōsel-chayk i sako nun siph.ess.ci man tōn i ēps.ess.^{s}up.nita.	I wanted to buy that novel, but I didn't have the money.
3. Nyū-Yok ey se sālko siph.ci nun anh.ci man han pen ka poko siph.e yo.	I don't want to live in New York, but I would like to visit there.
4. Kimchi lul han pen mek.e poko nun siph.ci man nemu maypci anh.ulq ka yo?	I'd like to try kimchi [once=] sometime but I wonder if it wouldn't be too spicy [for me]?

5. Te mek.ko nun siph.ci man nemu pay ka pull.e yo.	I want to eat some more, but I'm too full.
6. Say os ul ipko nun iss.ci man, na lul polq sālam i ēps.ci yo.	I am wearing my new clothes, but there's no one to look at me.
7. Sensayng nim māl-ssum ul tut.ko nun iss.ci man mwe ka mwe 'n ci molukeyss.[s]up.nita.	I'm listening to what you have to say, but I'm not following you.
8. Chayk ul kaciko nun wass.ci man, nay chayk i ani 'n kwun yo.	I brought a book, but I see it isn't my book.

The meaning is fairly close to that of -ki nun haci man (etc.), ‖ 13.4. And in ‖ 24.12 you will learn the use of -ko nun hay yo for habitual actions.

‖ 21.5. Modifiers with tey: circumstantial constructions.

20. . . . Yeses si cha lo sikol com ka ya hakeyss.nun tey . . . 'I have to take a little trip out to the country by the six o'clock train, so . . .'

25. Wuli Hānkwuk [n]yeseng tul ul mannako siph.e hanun tey . . . 'They want to meet some of us Korean women, so . . .'

28. . . . Na to manna pomyen cōh.keyss.nun tey . . . 'I'd like to meet them too, but . . .'

In addition to their uses with the post-modifier ci, restricted modifiers form constructions with the post-modifier tey.

As usual, descriptive verbs use the -(u)n modifier form and processive verbs (together with all pasts and futures) use the -nun modifier:

Descriptive	Processive
[pissa]n tey	[ka]nun tey
[pissa]ss.nun tey	[ka]ss.nun tey
[pissa]keyss.nun tey	[ka]keyss.nun tey

One meaning of such constructions is circumstantial: 'given the circumstance that . . .' or 'in view of the circumstance that . . .' The most practical translation for the construction is usually the catch-all word 'so' (Sentence 20, 'in view of the circumstance that I'm to take a trip . . .' and Sentence 25, 'given the circumstance that they want to meet . . .'). An occasional use of -nun tey corresponds more closely to English 'but,' as in Sentence 28.

A special suspensive intonation, here marked by three dots (. . .), often accompanies this construction; the voice hesitates, with a slight dip.

Here are more examples.

1. Nal i ileh.key chwuwun tey . . . eti lul kasey yo.	Where are you going on such a cold day?
2. I kongkwa nun swiwun tey . . . elyepta ko hamyen an tōy yo.	This lesson is easy; you mustn't say it's hard.
3. Onul un palam i pūlko, pi ka olq kes kath.un tey . . . ilcciki cip ey tol.a kapsita.	The wind is blowing and it looks like rain today; (in view of this) let's go home early.
4. Onul un tāytan hi pappun tey, [1]nayil manna to kwaynchanh.e yo?	I'm very busy today; would it be all right to get together tomorrow?

5. Yenge lul cal ānun tey, way ku phyēnci lul Yenge lo an sse yo.	You know English—why don't you write that letter in English?
6. I pen pom ey Hānkwuk ulo kakeyss.nun tey, musun mulken ul kaciko kamyen cōh.keyss.ey yo.	I'll be going to Korea this spring, so what things should I take along?
7. Onul catong-cha lo mēn kil ul ka ya hakeyss.nun tey, achim ul mānh.i mek.upsita.	(In view of the circumstance that) we have a long way to go in the car today, let's eat a big breakfast.
8. Ssepisu ka cōh.ta ko hanun ku ^{l}yoli-cem ey kass.umyen cōh.keyss.nun tey, eti ey iss.nun ci yo.	It would be nice to go to that restaurant where they say the service is so good; I wonder where it is.
9. Ai tul i nēy-keli ey se nōlmyen an toynun tey, way yeki se nōlko iss.ci yo.	The children shouldn't play at crossroads; why are they playing here?
10. Wēn.yu-hoy nal ul onun Tho-yoil lo cēng hayss.nun tey, cēypal tto pyēnkyeng haci māsipsio.	Having decided on the coming Saturday for our picnic, please don't change it again.
11. I sakwa lul ho-cwumeni(q) sōk ey neh.e kako siph.un tey, ho-cwumeni ka nemu cāk.ci yo??	I'd like to put this apple in my pocket, but I bet the pocket is too small.
12. Hōykyey ka sēykyey ^{l}yehayng ul tte naki ttaymun ey, sōngpyel-hoy lul hay cwue ya hakeyss.nun tey hōywen tul i hōypi lul te nāylq ka yo?	Since the treasurer of our group is going on a trip around the world, we'll have to give him a farewell party; I wonder if the members will have to pay more dues.
13. Say hōycang to cōh.un pun ie ya hakeyss.nun tey, nwukwu l' sēnke hasikeyss.^{s}up.nikka.	Our new president must be a good person, too, so whom shall we elect?

You will sometimes find the circumstantial construction followed by the particle to meaning 'but' or 'even though': Pi ka onun tey to chac.e wa cwusye se komapsup.nita 'Thank you for coming to see me in spite of the rain.' This usage can be taken as an abbreviation of . . . tey to pulkwu hako 'disregarding the circumstance that . . .': Chwuwun tey to (pulkwu hako) na ka nōlko siph.e yo? 'You want to go out and play in spite of the cold?'

‖ 21.6. Modifiers with tey: exclamatory constructions.

28. Caymi iss.nun pun tul kath.un tey yo.	'They sound like such interesting people!'

When a modifier + tey appears at the end of a sentence, with yo in polite style and without yo in the intimate style (‖ 22.4), it often has an exclamatory meaning: 'how . . . ! what a . . . ! my, such a . . . !'

Here are some more examples:

1. Kulen tey yo.	Isn't that true, though!
2. Pi ka mānh.i wass.nun tey (yo)!	My what a lot it rained!
3. Onul un nal i cham tewun tey yo.	What a hot day it is!

4. I pang un nemu cak.un tey yo. — This room is too small!
5. I hwānca nun swuswul ul kot hay ya hakeyss.nun tey yo! — We must operate on this patient at once!
6. I tongyang-hwa ka hwullyung han tey yo. — How splendid this oriental picture is!
7. Kulen cōh.un kakuk ul tul.e pon īl i ēps.nun tey yo! — I've never heard such a fine opera!
8. Pelsse kaul in tey (yo)! — Why it's autumn already!
9. Sensayng nim kkey mul.e ponun ke l' ice pelyess.nun tey! — I forgot to ask the teacher!
10. Kyengchi ka cōh.un tey yo! — What fine scenery!

Compare these exclamatory sentences with APPERCEPTIVE sentences that end in (-)kwun yo (‖ 16.4). The meaning is very similar, but the apperceptive sentences emphasize sudden realization rather than intense reaction. Both exclamatory and apperceptive sentences are limited to the two styles polite and intimate, as are casual sentences (-ci yo). The intimate style (‖ 22.4) is simply the polite style without the particle yo.

‖ 21.7. Other uses of tey.

In addition to the circumstantial and exclamatory uses, tey occurs as a quasi-free noun (that is, a noun that cannot begin a sentence, but must always be modified by something in front of it) with the meaning 'place, spot' or sometimes 'circumstance, occasion'—from which the other uses are derived. When the meaning is 'place' the noun kos can often be used instead. Here are some examples: chwuwun tey 'a cold spot,' kyengchi ka cōh.un tey 'a place where the scenery is nice = a scenic spot,' talun tey (yaksok i iss.ey yo) '(has an engagement) somewhere else,' ney ka os ul san tey 'the place you bought the clothes,' sālq tey 'a place to live,' ssulq tey ēps.e yo 'lacks a place to use it = is useless, is worthless,' āmu tey 'any place.' You will notice that the usual modifiers are used, not the restricted modifiers: sālq tey means only 'a place to live' and sālkeyss.nun tey means only '(given the circumstance that) one will live, (so) . . .'; pon tey means only 'the place I saw (or saw it)' and pwass.nun tey means only '(given the circumstance that) [one] saw it (so) . . .' But chwuwun tey is ambiguously (1) 'cold spot' and (2) '(given the circumstance that) it is cold, (so) . . .' since the restricted processive modifiers are limited to use with processive verbs or with pasts and futures.

Some of the phrases with the quasi-free noun tey come to have specialized meanings: phyo phanun tey 'the place where they sell tickets = the ticket seller's, the ticket window,' os ul pes.nun tey 'the place where one undresses = the (un)dressing room.'

‖ 21.8. The particle pota.

16. Na nun ku pota . . te olay tōy yo. 'It's been longer than that for me.'

The particle pota means 'more than' or (‖ 27.5) 'rather than.' Most often, pota is not translated next to the noun it follows, but instead shows up as the modifier of an adjective elsewhere in the sentence—either the suffix -er, or the word 'more':

I kes un ku kes POTA khe yo. 'This is bigGER than that.' [= This thing, MORE THAN that thing, is big.]

Yelum i kyewul POTA cōh.a yo. 'Summer is nicER than winter.' [= Summer, MORE or RATHER THAN winter, is nice.]

Onul un ecey POTA sikan i mānh.i iss.ey yo. 'I have MORE time today THAN yesterday.' [= Today, MORE THAN yesterday, I have lots of time.]

Mikwuk ey nun Yengkwuk POTA catong-cha ka mānh.e yo. 'There are MORE cars in America THAN in England.' [= MORE THAN in England, there are many cars in America.]

I sangcem ey se nun ce sangcem pota kaps i ssa yo. 'Things are LESS expensive in this store THAN in that one.' [= In this store MORE THAN that one, prices are low.]

Onul un ecey POTA palam i pūlko, chwuwe yo. 'It's coldER and windiER today than it was yesterday.' [= Today MORE THAN yesterday is cold and windy.]

Sometimes pota is followed by the particle to for emphasis: Hong-cha pota to khephi ka mek.ko siph.e yo 'I'd rather have coffee (even more) than tea.' San pota to noph.ko paṭa pota to kiph.e yo 'It is taller than the mountains and deeper than the sea.'

And somtimes pota is followed by the particle un/nun for deemphasis or contrast: Tangsin pota nun nay ka pappuci yo 'I'm certainly busier than you.'

‖ 21.9. The post-modifier kyem.

31. Cōh.un say chinkwu tul to sakwilq kyem, kkoch kwūkyeng to halq kyem, kkok osey yo. 'With the chance to get acquainted with nice new friends as well as seeing the flowers and all, do come for sure.'

A prospective modifier plus the postmodifier kyem is a construction used in lists of verbs, to mean 'combining (the activity with) . . .' or 'doing (the activity) along with (another activity).' Here are the common patterns in which kyem appears with verbs.

[ha]lq kyem, . . . [ha]ko, . . . MAIN VERB.
[ha]ko, . . . [ha]lq kyem . . . MAIN VERB.
[ha]lq kyem, . . . [ha]lq kyem, . . . MAIN VERB.

Here are some more examples:

Sewulq kwūkyeng to {halq kyem / hako} hōy ey to {kako / kalq kyem} taum cwuil ey nun Sewul ey kakeyss.ey yo. 'I'm going to Seoul next week to combine sightseeing and attending a meeting.'

Cha to masiko, cōh.un um.ak to tul.ulq kyem, Kumkang Tapang ey kasipsita. 'Let's go to the Kumkang ["Diamond"] Tea Shop and (combine) drink(ing) tea and listen(ing) to some good music.'

Kongpu to hako, kwūkyeng to halq kyem, na nun Sewul ey se hak.kyo ey tanikeyss.ey yo. 'I'm going to go to school in Seoul and combine studying with sightseeing.'

Tōn to cheng hako, mūn.an to hako, ūykyen to tul.ulq kyem, na nun kīn phyēnci lul ssess.ey yo. 'I've written a long letter to ask for money, send greetings, and [listen to =] get some advice.'

The word kyem is also used after nouns in series, on this pattern: NOUN kyem, NOUN kyem, NOUN + PARTICLE.

For example:

Na nun nay pang ul chīm-pang kyem, secey kyem, kayksil lo sse yo. OR Chīm-pang kyem, secey kyem, kayksil lo, na nun pang hana lul sse yo. 'I use my (one) room as a bedroom, library, and living room.'

EXERCISES

I

Make each of the following sentences mean 'Do you know whether (who, where, etc.) . . .' For example, the first will be: Ku haksayng i eti se sānun ci āsikeyss.ey yo? 'Do you know where that student lives?' You might vary your questions by making some of them casual (. . . āsikeyss.ci yo?) and some of them formal (. . . āsikeyss.^{s}up.nikka?).

1. Ku haksayng i eti se sal.e yo.
2. Kim sensayng i nwukwu lul teyliko wass.^{s}up.nikka.
3. Ku ōykyo-kwan i ^{1}naynyen sēykyey ^{1}yehayng ul hakeyss.ey yo?
4. Twū nalq-ca ka kkok kath.ey yo?
5. Onulq pam ey osin son nim i Kim sensayng puin iey yo?
6. Wuli ka ku seki-kwan kwa sakwilq swu iss.ey yo?
7. Apeci ka ēncey na kass.ey yo.
8. Ai tul i eti se nōna yo.
9. Kāy ka way kuleh.key cic.e yo.
10. Nwu' ka catong-cha lul ssis.ko takk.keyss.ey yo.
11. Wuli hak.kyo ka kakkawe yo?

II

Make each of the following sentences mean 'I've forgotten whether (who, where, etc.) . . .' For example, the first will be: Nay ka Poktong-i hanthey tōn ul elma 'na cwuess.nun ci ic.e pelyessey yo. 'I've forgotten how much money I gave Poktong-i.' Vary your sentences by making some of them casual (. . . ic.e pelyess.ci yo) and some of them formal (. . . ic.e pelyess.^{s}up.nita).

1. Nay ka Poktong-i hanthey tōn ul elma 'na cwuess.ey yo.
2. Kim sensayng i onulq pam ey ona yo, ^{1}nayilq pam ey ona yo.
3. Ku ūmsik i pissa yo?
4. Ku tose-kwan ey chayk i mānh.un ka yo, cek.un ka yo.
5. Nay ka acik to nwukwu hanthey cēnhwa lul kēlci anh.ess.ey yo.
6. Wuli ka eti anc.ess.ey yo.
7. Sensayng i swul ul masip.nikka?
8. Sensayng i cōh.a hasin sacin i i sacin ip.nikka?
9. Mikwuk Tāysa-kwan i sensayng(q) tayk ey se mel.e yo?
10. Poktong-i hal-apeci ka Pulkyo lul mit.e yo?
11. Cey ka eti se sensayng nim ul cheum poywess.^{s}up.nikka.

III

Make each of the following sentences mean 'I don't recall . . .' or 'It doesn't come to mind whether (who, where, etc.) . . .' For example, the first will be: Wuli ka Kim sensayng ul pāngmun hayss.nun ci sayngkak naci anh.e yo. 'I don't recall whether we visited Mr. Kim (or not).' Vary your sentences by making some of them casual (. . . sayngkak naci anh.ci yo) and some of them formal (. . . sayngkak naci anh.sup.nita).

1. Wuli ka Kim sensayng ul pāngmun hayss.ey yo?
2. Nay ka ku phyēnci lul eti noh.ass.^{s}up.nikka.
3. Nay ka ēncey meli lul kam.ess.ey yo.
4. Nwu' ka i os ul ppalless.ey yo.

5. Nal mata swukcey lul nuc.key pachinun haksayng i Poktong ip.nikka?
6. Ku ttay palam i pūlko iss.ess.^{s}up.nikka?
7. Nay ka nwukwu hanthey se ku chayk ul pillyess.ey yo.
8. Nay ka ku swukcey lul machyess.ey yo?
9. Emeni ka ku yenghwa lul silh.e hayss.ey yo?
10. Totwuk nom i kum sikyey lul hwumchyess.ey yo, un sikyey lul hwumchyess.ey yo.
11. Hwānca ka yel i noph.sup.nikka?

IV

Make each of the following sentences mean 'Do you remember whether (who, where, etc.) . . . ?' For example, the first will be: Nwu'ka catong-cha lul wūncen hayss.nun ci kiek hasey yo? 'Do you remember who drove (the car)?' Vary your sentences, as before, with . . . kiek hasici yo? and . . . kiek hasip.nikka?

1. Nwu' ka catong-cha lul wūncen hayss.^{s}up.nikka.
2. Sip-o pun an ey kalq swu iss.ess.ey yo?
3. Kil i nappess.^{s}up.nikka?
4. Wuli ka Sewul eti se naylip.nikka.
5. Hal-'meni ka mues ul capswusyess.^{s}up.nikka.
6. Apeci emeni ka cwūnpi lul tā hasyess.ey yo?
7. Ku kongwen ey kamyen meych sikan ina kellip.nikka.
8. Wuli ka mence muwu wa pāychwu lul ccalp.key ssel.ess.ey yo?
9. Kim puin i mayntun kimchi ka nemu maywess.^{s}up.nikka?
10. Nwu' ka ecey kaluchyess.ey yo.
11. Ecey achim meych si ey il.e nass.ey yo.

NOTE: Items 4 and 7 involve not the memory of a single incident, but a constant fact. For such sentences, it is somewhat more common to say (-nun/-un) kes in ci '(whether) it is a fact that (it does/is).'

V

Make each of the following statements mean 'perhaps . . . .' For example, the first will be: Yenghwa ka pelsse kkuth nass.nun ci (or nass.ulq ci) to mōlla yo. 'Perhaps the movie is already over.' If the verb is timeless, it is more common to say -ULQ ci to mōlla yo than -NUN ci to mōlla yo. If the verb is past, it is more common to say -ESS.ULQ ci to mōlla yo than -ESS.NUN ci to mōlla yo.

1. Yenghwa ka pelsse kkuth nass.ey yo.
2. Kim sensayng i totwuk ul mac.ess.^{s}up.nita.
3. Ku cip i mel.e yo.
4. Ku kūlim ul i pyek ey ('ta) kēlmyen cōh.keyss.ey yo.
5. Wuli ka nal mata sinmun ul ilk.ci anh.umyen an toykeyss.ey yo.
6. Ku pumo nim i celm.e yo.
7. Mikwuk salam i tā tōn i mānh.keyss.^{s}up.nita.
8. Namphyen i tā tāmpay lul cal phi(wu)nun kes iey yo.
9. Han sensayng i Pusan ey ka pon īl i ēps.ey yo.
10. Kim sensayng catong-cha ka nemu khe yo.
11. Ku cip i cāksup.nita.

VI

Make each of the following statements mean 'It's been a long time since . . .' For example, the first will be: Nay ka kukcang ey ka pon ci ka olay tōy(ss.ey) yo. 'It's (been) a long time since I've been to the theater.'

1. Nay ka kukcang ey ka pwass.ey yo.
2. Wuli ka catong-cha lul ssis.ess.ey yo.
3. Poktong-i ka phul ul kkakk.ess.ey yo.
4. Ku mun ul yel.ess.ey yo.
5. Wuli ka Sewul ey se sal.ess.ey yo.
6. Ileh.key ippun neykthai lul māyss.ey yo.
7. Ileh.key koyngcang han miin ul mannass.ey yo.
8. O uysa ka uyhak ul kongpu hayss.[s]up.nita.
9. Nay ka Hānkwuk mal ul hay pwass.ey yo.
10. Nay ka say moca lul sass.[s]up.nita.
11. Ileh.key mas i 'ss.nun ūmsik ul mek.e pwass.[s]up.nita.

VII

Make each of the following sentences mean 'My, but it's . . . !' or 'How . . . it is!' For example, the first will be: Pakk i chwuwun tey yo! 'My, but it's cold outside!'

1. Pakk i chwuwe yo.
2. Ku sayksi ka ippe yo.
3. Hānkwuk kyengchi ka cōh.a yo.
4. Wuli ka pole kanun cang i mel.e yo.
5. I kil i nappe yo.
6. I sōsel i caymi iss.ey yo.
7. Tose-kwan i kakkawe yo.
8. Kim sensayng(q) tayk i khe yo.
9. San ey namu ka museng hay yo.
10. Wuli chinkwu ka cwuk.un hwū lo, sim-sim hay yo.
11. I māl ul cal ssuki ka elyewe yo.

CONVERSATION

I

Pretend that you have just been chosen to conduct a meeting of some group (women's club, teachers' meeting, missionary group, or whatever you choose) and don't know exactly what order you should do things in. Explain the problem to your neighbor and ask him how to go about conducting the meeting. Listen carefully to his answers, and then as a summation repeat the things he has told you to do, in the proper order.

II

Now, pretend that you are the same person but that the meeting is over. Describe what it was like.

III

With a friend, plan an outing in detail. Decide on where to go, just what activities to include, who is to bring what, who else will be asked to come along, transportation arrangements, when you will leave and when return, etc. etc.

VOCABULARY DRILL

I

Here are some words naming people or things. Read each word aloud and translate it; then give the Korean word for one or two logical PLACES where you might find this person or thing. For example, if the word was sensayng 'teacher,' you might say hak.kyo 'school' or tāyhak 'college.'

1. hōy
2. hōycang
3. kēswu
4. kongsa
5. ōykyo-kwan
6. Ōymu Pu
7. pec namu
8. salang
9. sayngkak
10. sēnke
11. Tāysa
12. wēn.yu-hoy
13. wiwen-hoy
14. ^{1}yehayng
15. ^{1}yengsa-kwan

II

Now, here is another list of things. Proceeding as above, give a verb or two in Korean telling what you might logically DO TO the thing named. Use your imagination!

1. catong-cha
2. cemmyeng
3. hōypi
4. māl
5. nalq-ca
6. pec kkoch
7. pōko
8. puin-hoy
9. say chinkwu
10. seki
11. sēykyey
12. thōuy sāhang
13. tōngmul
14. tōngmul-wen
15. tōnguy

III

Still proceeding in the same way, tell in Korean WHAT SORT OF PERSON might logically be expected to do the following things. It may, but need not, be a single word; for some a long descriptive phrase will be more appropriate.

1. cāycheng ul hay yo
2. cepswu lul hay yo
3. chwulqsek ul hay yo
4. hōykyey ka tōy yo
5. hōylok ^{1}nāngtok ul hay yo
6. hwan.yeng ul hay yo
7. kiek hay yo
8. kyelqsek ul hay yo
9. pyēnkyeng hay yo
10. sāhoy lul hay yo
11. sakwie yo
12. sōngpyel ul hay yo
13. thongyek ul hay yo
14. tōnguy lul hay yo
15. ^{1}yehayng ul hay yo

COMPREHENSION

Ask your Korean teacher to talk to you about some special event he has been to recently (real or imaginary). Listen carefully while he gives you a detailed account about it: who went with him, where they went, how long it took, what they did when they got there, how long they stayed, what they had to eat and where they ate it, when they got back. After he has finished, he will ask you questions about what he has said, for you to answer in Korean.

LESSON 22. LET'S MAKE A SNOW MAN!

BASIC SENTENCES

Korean	English	Amplification
T. 1. Hongsik a! Na wa nol.a!	Hey Hongsik! Come out and play!	Hongsik [a boy's name] . . . a [after consonant], ... ya [after vowel] 'hey. . . , oh. . .' [vocative particle] nol.a! 'play!' [INTIMATE style]
H. 2. Nwukwu 'n ya! Ung, Tekswu 'n ya? Wuli musun cangnan halq ka!	Who is it? Mmh, is it (you), Tekswu? What shall we play?	ung 'mmh; yeah' Tekswu [a boy's name] cangnan 'game, sport, amusement'
T. 3. Nwūn i mānh.i wass.uni, wuli nwūnq salam ma(y)ntulca.	Since it's snowed a lot, let's make a snow man.	nwūn 'snow' nwūnq salam 'snow man'
H. 4. Kulay. Kuleh.ci man, na n' son i silye se etteh.key ma(y)ntuni.	OK. But my hands are cold so how can I make (one)?	silye yo [sili-] 'is cold (of the body or parts of the body)' ma(y)ntuni 'does [one] make?' [PLAIN style]
5. Meychil cen ey cāngkap ul ilh.e pelyess.ta!	I lost my gloves a few days ago.	meychil 'a few days' [also 'how many days?']
T. 6. Wuli cip ey cāngkap (i) tto han khyelley iss.ta.	We've got another pair of gloves at our house.	khyelley 'pair'
7. Nay ka ka se kacye olq key. Ne n' yeki se kitalye la.	I'll go bring them. You wait here.	olq key 'I'll come' [INTIMATE style] ne 'you' [to a child] kitalye la 'wait!' [PLAIN style]
8. Ca, ese nwūnq salam ma(y)ntulca. Hongsik a. Ese nwūn ul kwūllye la.	Now let's get our snow man made. Hongsik, get some snow rolled up.	ese 'now, quickly' kwūllye yo [kwūlli-] 'rolls it up' kwūllye la 'roll it up!' [PLAIN style]
H. 9. Tekswu. Way nay nwūnq tengeli nun khe cici anh.ni!!	Tekswu, why doesn't my ball of snow get bigger?	tengeli, te(y)ngi 'lump, mass, ball' nwūnq tengeli 'snowball'

Korean	English	Amplification
		khe cici anh.ni? 'doesn't it become big' [PLAIN style]
T.10. Mence nwūn ul son ulo ttan-ttan hakey mungchye se nwūn wi ey cakkwu kwullye p(w)a.	First pack the snow tight with your hands, and then keep rolling it up on top of the snow and see.	son 'hand' ttan-ttan hay yo 'is firm, tight' mungchye yo [mungchi-] 'packs, lumps together' cakkwu 'continuously; keep —ing'
11. Eti poca. Nay nwūnq tengeli ka khuni, nay kes ulo mom-ttwungi lul ma(y)ntulko, ney kes ulo nun meli lul ma(y)ntulca.	Let's see now. Since my ball of snow is big(ger), let's make the body out of mine, and with yours let's make the head.	eti poca 'let's see, let me see' [PLAIN style] mom-ttwungi 'body' (= mom) meli 'head; hair'
H.12. I swuch tengi tul un mues hani.	What do we do with [= make out of] these pieces of charcoal? [What are these pieces of charcoal for?]	swuch 'charcoal' hani 'does [one] do?' [PLAIN style]
T.13. Nwun, kho, ip, kwi lul ma(y)ntunta.	We make eyes, nose, mouth, and ears.	nwun 'eye' ip 'mouth' kwi 'ear'
14. Hongsik a. Ne nwun ulo mues ul hanun ci āni?	Hongsik, do you know what we do with nwun?	āni 'does [one] know?' [PLAIN style]
H.15. Musun NWUN māl in ya. Wuli elkwul uy NWUN māl in ya . . . (i nwūnq salam ma(y)ntunun NWŪN māl in ya.)	What nwun do you mean? Do you mean the nwun in our faces, or . . . (do you mean the nwūn we're making our snowman with)?	. . . māl in ya '[is it the word . . . ? =] does [one] mean?' [PLAIN style] elkwul 'face'
T.16. Elkwul uy NWUN māl ita.	I mean the nwun on our faces.	. . . māl ita 'I mean' [PLAIN style]
H.17. Hung. Ku-kkacis kes ul mōlla!! Poci . . . tto wūlci, wūs.ci . . .	Hmph. Don't I know such a (little) thing?! We see . . . and we cry, and laugh, and . . .	hung 'hmph!' ku-kkacis . . . 'such a (little, trivial) . . .' mōlla!! 'don't I know?!' [INTIMATE style] poci 'sees' [INTIMATE style, casual] wūlci [wū-l-] 'cries, weeps' [INTIMATE style, casual] wūs.ci 'laughs' [INTIMATE style, casual]

Korean	English	Amplification
T.18. Acwu ssek cal ānun tey?? Ca. Ese nwūnq salam ma(y)ntulca.	You really know quite well indeed! Well, let's get our snow man made.	acwu 'very, indeed' ssek 'greatly, exceedingly, quite' ānun tey 'you know indeed!' [INTIMATE style, exclamatory]
H.19. Nal i etteh.key chwuwun ci, nwun ey se nwun mul i na onta!	[The weather=] It is so cold that [tears are coming out of my eyes=] my eyes are watering.	nwun mul '[eye water=] tear(s)'
T.20. Kuleh.key chwuwun ya? Com cham.e la.	[Is it that cold?=] It's not so cold! Just put up with it.	cham.e yo [chām-] 'is patient with . . . , puts up with . . . , bears' cham.e la 'be patient! put up with [it]!' [PLAIN style]
21. Mence i twungkule'n swuch ulo nwun ul puth.ica.	First let's stick on the eyes with these round pieces of charcoal.	twungkul.e yo [twungku-l-] or twungkulewe yo [twungkulew-] 'is round' twungkule'n [abbreviation< twungkulewun] or twungkun . . . ' . which is round' twungkule'n swuch 'round (pieces of) charcoal' puth.e yo 'it sticks, adheres' puth.ye yo /puche.yo/ [puth.i- /puchi-/] 'sticks it on, makes it adhere, puts it on to (it)' puth.ica 'let's stick it (on)' [PLAIN style]
22. Kho nun i twū nwun sāy ey 'ta puth.iko, ip un kho palo mith ey 'ta puth.ica.	Let's put the nose between these two eyes, and the mouth right below the nose.	sāy = sai 'between'
23. Kwi nun elkwul 'yāng phyen ey 'ta puth.ica.	Let's stick the ears on either side of the face.	[1]yāng phyen '(on) both sides, (on) either side'
H.24. Phal hako tali nun an ma(y)ntuni?	Don't we make any arms or legs?	phal 'arm' tali 'leg'
T.25. Ung. Ku kes tul un ēps.e to cōh.ta. Elyewe se mōs ma(y)ntunta.	[Yeah=] No, we don't have to make them. It's (too) hard, so we won't (or can't) make them.	

Korean	English	Amplification
26. Ya! Mēlli se poni-kka n', chen.yen sān sālam kath.ta.	Hey! When you look at it from a distance, it's like a real live person.	ya or yāy 'hey!' chen.yen 'nature, natural' sālam (kwa) kath.ta 'it's like a person' [PLAIN style]
27. Kkoma ey, ttwungttwung-po ey . . . Hongsik a. Kkok, ne-huy apeci kath.ta!	A runt and a fatso and . . . Hey Hongsik, he's just like your father!	kkoma 'short fellow, runt' kkoma ey . . . 'a short fellow, and . . .' ttwungttwung-po 'fat fellow, fatso' ttwungttwung-po ey . . . 'a fat fellow and . . .' ne-huy [pronounced /nei/] 'you (all)' apeci (wa) kath.ta 'like or the same as a father'
H.28. Nwun-ttakpuli ey, kho-cwupu ey, na n' kkok ne-huy apeci kath.ta.	Goggle-Eyes and Big-Nose and just like YOUR father, to me!	nwun-ttakpuli ey . . . 'Goggle-Eyes and . . .' kho-cwupu ey . . . 'Big-Nose and . . .'
T.29. Way wuli apeci ka nwun-ttakpuli ya, kho-cwupu ya.	Why is my father Goggle-Eyes and Big-Nose?	nwun-ttakpuli ya (= ia) 'is Goggle-Eyes' [INTIMATE style] kho-cwupu ya (= ia) 'is Big-Nose' [INTIMATE style]
H.30. Kulem, ne n', way wuli apeci tele ttwungttwung-po, kkoma 'la ko hayss.ni!!	Well, why did YOU call MY father fatso and runt!?	hayss.ni 'did [one] do or say?' [INTIMATE style]
31. Wuli apeci hanthey ilulq ke l'!	But I'm going to tell Father (on you), so there!	ille yo [ilu-] 'tells; admonishes, informs' ilulq ke l', ilulq kes ul 'but I'll tell, so there!'
T.32. Khi ka cāk.ko, ttwung-ttwung hani-kka n' kulayss.ci.	I said it because he's short and fat.	khi 'height, stature' khi ka khe yo 'is tall' khi ka cak.e yo 'is short' ttwung-ttwung hay yo 'is fat' kulayss.ci 'said so' [INTIMATE style, casual]
H.33. Ne-huy apeci nun kho ka khuni-kka n' kho-cwupu 'ci. Nwun i khuni-kka n' nwun-ttakpuli 'ci.	Your father is Big Nose because he has a large nose. He's Goggle-Eyes because he has large eyes.	'ci [= ici] 'is' [copula INTIMATE style, casual]

Korean	English	Amplification
34. Kuleh.ci man, ney ka mence kulen māl ul sīcak hayss.ta!	Anyway, you started that sort of talk first.	ney ka 'you' [as subject]
T.35. Kulay, nay ka calmos hayss.ta. Yongse hay la.	Then I was in the wrong. Excuse me.	calmos 'a mistake' calmos (ul) hay yo 'makes a mistake, does wrongly, misdoes' [Compare cal mōs hay yo 'can't do well'] yongse hay la 'excuse me!' [PLAIN style]
36. Hongsik a. Wuli tongmu tul ul pulle oca. Wuli nwūnq salam ul kwūkyeng sikhica.	Hongsik, let's call our friends over. Let's show them our snow man.	pulle wa yo 'calls [to someone to] come' pulle oca 'let's call [them to] come' [PLAIN style] sikhye yo [sikhi-] 'has or allows [someone] to . . . ; orders (food, a meal); orders someone to do something' kwūkyeng sikhica 'let's let or have [them] look at it'

SUPPLEMENTARY VOCABULARY

ima	forehead	sonq-patak	palm (of hand)
ppyam or pol	cheek	tung or cantung(i)	back
thek	chin	sonq-tung	back of hand
i or iq-pal [S.Korean spelling i-ppal]	tooth	kasum	chest, breast
		heli	waist; loin
ip-swul	lip	heli kkun	a belt
hye	tongue	heli tti	a sash, a waistband
nwunq-sep [S.Korean spelling nwun-ssep]	eyebrow		
		pay	stomach
sōk nwunq-sep	eyelash	muluph	knee
tōngca [LITERARY] (= sōnyen)	child, boy	sal	flesh
		phipu	(human) skin
nwunq-tongca	pupil (of eye)	salq kyel	(texture of) skin, complexion
kwumeng	hole		
khoq-kwumeng	nostril	ppye	bone
thel	hair, fur	cāng nim or sōkyeng	blind person
meli-thel or meli-khal(ak)	hair (on head)	pengeli	mute person
		kwi-mekeli	deaf person
sonq-kalak (in Seoul also -kwulak)	finger	kwi (ka) mek.e yo [mek-mek.nunta]	goes deaf, loses one's hearing
palq-kalak (in Seoul also -kwulak)	toe		
		nwun i mel.e yo [mē-l-, mēnta]	goes blind, loses one's eyesight
son-thop	fingernail		
patak	bottom; surface; ground, floor	yuchi-wen	kindergarten

kanul.e yo [kanu-l-]	is thin, slender, small around
kwulk.e yo [kwulk-]	is thick, burly, big around
yalp.e yo [yalp-]	is thin (and flat)
twukkewe yo [twukkew-, twukkepta]	is thick (through)
sēy yo [sēy-] or kang hay yo or him (i) iss.ey yo	is strong
wusuwe yo [wusuw-, wusupta]	is funny, comical
olh.a yo	is right, correct
olh.ci!	that's right! OK!

accwu!	indeed! and how! (from acwu 'quite')
ku'h.ci (abbreviated from kuleh.ci)	that's right!
way kulay	how come? why? [INTIMATE style]
mwe or me (abbreviated from mues)	what; something
ani?? [= ani yo??]	no [INTIMATE style]
ani 'ta	no [PLAIN style]
emma	Mommy, Mom, Mama
appa	Daddy, Dad, Papa
cangnanq kām or wānkwu	toy
yāy (ya)!	(hey) you!

NOTES

‖ 22.1. Children's speech.

The way children speak to each other is different from the way they speak to adults, and the way adults speak to children is different from the way they speak to other adults. The Basic Sentences of this lesson comprise a conversation between two children. In general, when either a child or an adult addresses a child, the plain style is used; sentences in the INTIMATE STYLE (the POLITE style minus yo) are mixed freely. And, occasionally, sentences in the FAMILIAR style (‖ 28.1) may be used.

For statements, verbs appear in the plain style (described above ‖ 19.2), with the processive ending -nta or -nunta and the descriptive ending -ta. The copula (though quoted as ila) has the shape ita.

Suggestions are also in the plain style (above, ‖ 19.4), with the ending -ca.

Commands and questions for children's speech are discussed in the following sections.

‖ 22.2. Plain-style commands (Type 2); irregular infinitives.

Plain-style commands as used in children's speech differ slightly from those used in quotations (above ‖ 19.5) in that they are made by using the PARTICLE la after the infinitive, rather than attaching the ENDING -(u)la to the base.

In the case of most vowel-base verbs ending in -a, -ēy, and -āy, the bases and infinitives are the same; the two imperatives are therefore pronounced alike:

Base	Quoted Imperative	Children's Imperative
sa- 'buys'	sala '[tells him] to buy'	sa la 'buy!'
māy- 'ties'	māyla '[tells him] to tie'	māy la 'tie!'
pēy- 'cuts	pēyla '[tells someone] to cut'	pēy la 'cut!'

Vowel-base verbs that end in -ōy usually make their infinitives the same, but some people pronounced the infinitive as -wāy and spell it as either -way or -oye:

pōy- 'show'	pōyla '[tells someone to] show'	pōy la (or pwāy la, poye la) 'show!'

In Seoul speech, there are no regular vowel verbs that end in -e, but a few verbs that end in -u or -i are often spelled as if they ended in -e or -ye. For example, su- 'stand' is usually spelled se-; since the infinitive of su- is se, in speech there is a distinction between sula '[tells him] to stand' and se la 'stand!,' but sula is often written "sela." Some people use the irregular form suke la ("seke la").

A few common verbs have an irregular infinitive form before the imperative particle la (though some people use the regular infinitive—for some or all of the verbs):

Base	Imperative made with irregular infinitives	Imperative made with regular infinitives
ka- 'go'	kake la 'go!'	ka la
ca- 'sleep'	cake la 'go to sleep!'	ca la
toy- 'become'	toyke la 'become!'	tōy la (or twāy la, toye la)
iss- 'be, stay'	iss.ke la 'stay!'	iss.e la
anc- 'sit'	anc.ke la 'sit!'	anc.e la
tul- 'listen'	tut.ke la 'listen!'	tul.e la
cwuk- 'die'	cwuk.ke la 'die!'	cwuk.e la
o- 'come'	one la 'come!'	wa la

For all except the last (o- → one la), the irregular infinitive ends in -ke.

Negative commands (i.e. PROHIBITIONS) are regularly made by following the -ci form of the verb with mal.e la, but this is often abbreviated to mā' la:

Poci mal.e la! or Poci mā' la! 'Don't look!'

‖ 22.3. Plain-style questions (Type 2); with -ni.

When you quote, you use the Type 1 plain-style questions discussed in ‖ 19.3 above: ya following the ending -nun except for the tenseless form of descriptive verbs, which have -(u)n.

When children speak among themselves, they are most likely to use plain-style questions of Type 2: these are made by attaching the ending -ni to bases of processive verbs, and to the past and future bases of all verbs. For the tenseless form of descriptive verbs, Type 1 questions with -(u)n ya [or -(u)n ka—usually rhetorical, ‖ 14.5] are more common, except for the negative base anh-, which is usually anh.ni when combined with either a processive or a descriptive verb: see Basic Sentence 9. But you will also hear -ni attached to descriptive bases: cōh.ni? /cōnni/ = cōh.un ya 'is it nice?'

The plain-style question ending -ni differs from the sequential ending -(u)ni, described in ‖ 18.1 in that it is a ONE-SHAPE ending: it is always pronounced -ni; the sequential ending is pronounced -ni only after vowels, and -uni after consonants. As a result, the sequential form and the Type 2 plain-style question forms are pronounced alike for vowel verbs (including the L-extending ones, which appear unextended) but differently for all consonant bases—including ANY past or future base.

Some examples:

Base	Type 2 Questions	Sequential
ka- 'go'	kani 'does [he] go?'	kani 'goes, so . . .'
ā-l- 'know'	āni 'does [he] know?'	āni 'knows, so . . .'
molu- 'know not'	moluni 'doesn't [he] know?'	moluni 'doesn't know, so . . .'
mek- 'eat'	mek.ni 'does [he] eat?'	mek.uni 'eats, so . . .'
hayss- 'did'	hayss.ni 'did [he] do?'	hayss.uni 'did, so . . .'
hakeyss- 'will do'	hakeyss.ni 'will [he] do?'	hakeyss.uni 'will do, so . . .'

This kind of -ni question is most apt to be used by children talking with other children. When adults speak to children, they may also use this form; or, they may use the Type 1 questions used in quotations ‖ 19.3). A third alternative is to put the question in the intimate style (-e?) or the familiar style (-na?, ‖ 22.5). When children speak to adults, the appropriate style is the polite or the formal.

In greeting a child, instead of using the expression Annyeng hasip.nikka? (or Annyeng hasey yo?) 'Are you well?,' you may say Cal iss.ni? (plain style), Cal iss.e? (intimate style), or Cal iss.na? (familiar style). For good-bye, instead of Annyeng hi kasipsio! and Annyeng hi kyēysipsio! (or Annyeng hi kasey yo! and Annyeng hi kyēysey yo!), you say Cal kake la! and Cal iss.ke la!, or Cal ka! and Cal iss.e!

‖ 22.4. Intimate style.

The INTIMATE STYLE is the polite style minus the ending yo. Here are the intimate-style Basic Sentences from this lesson:

2. . . . Wuli musun cangnan halq ka. 'What shall we play?'
7. Nay ka ka se kacye olq key . . . 'I'll go bring them . . .'
17. . . . Ku-kkacis kes ul mōlla? 'Don't I know such a (little) thing?'
18. Acwu ssek cal ānun tey! . . . 'You really know quite well indeed!'
29. Way wuli apeci ka nwun-ttakpuli ya, kho-cwupu ya. 'Why is my father Goggle-Eyes and Big-Nose?'
32. . . . **kho ka khuni-kka n' kho-cwupu 'ci. Nwun i khuni-kka n'** nwun-ttakpuli 'ci. 'Your father is Big Nose because he has a large nose. He's Goggle-Eyes because he has large eyes.'

A few special points about the intimate style should be mentioned.

1. Infinitives which end in -ey before yo usually drop the y in the intimate style:

POLITE STYLE	INTIMATE STYLE
iss.ey yo '(there) is'	iss.e '(there) is'
-(e)ss.ey yo [past]	-(e)ss.e [past]
e.g. wass.ey yo 'came'	e.g. wass.e 'came'
-keyss.ey yo [future]	-keyss.e [future]
e.g. pokeyss.ey yo 'will look at'	e.g. pokeyss.e 'will look at'

An exception is the verb kath.ey yo 'is (a)like, is the same,' which in the intimate style is often kath.ey rather than kath.e. [Some people, you will notice, say iss.e yo (and the like), without the y, especially in deliberate speech.]

2. The copula is usually pronounced ia after consonants (corresponding to polite-style iey yo) and ya after vowels (corresponding to 'ey yo):

Chayk iey yo [polite style] = Chayk ia [intimate style] 'It's a book.'
Hong-cha 'ey yo [polite style] = Hong-cha ya [intimate style] 'It's tea.'

But when NOT sentence-final, the copula is usually ie (after consonants), ye (after vowels):

chayk ie to 'though it's a book . . .'
chayk ie se 'it's a book, so . . .'
hong-cha ye to 'though it's tea . . .'
hong-cha ye se 'it's tea, so . . .'

Koreans often spell ia and ie as "iya" and "iye," just as they often spell the formal command endings -(u)sio and -(u)sipsio as "-(u)siyo" and "-(u)sipsiyo."

3. The copula is sometimes dropped altogether in the intimate style. At other times it may be reduced to y and pronounced as part of the preceding vowel. Compare these probable-future forms all meaning 'will probably come':

POLITE STYLE	INTIMATE STYLE
olq kes iey yo	olq kes ia
olq ke 'ey yo	olq ke ya
olq key yo	olq key

4. Negative commands (i.e. PROHIBITIONS) are regularly made by following the -ci form of a verb with mal.e, but this is often abbreviated to mā':

Poci mal.e! or Poci mā'! 'Don't look!'

‖ 22.5. Familiar-style questions.

In addition to the plain style and the intimate style, you will sometimes hear children use the FAMILIAR style, with its characteristic endings -ney for statements, -na for questions. This style is not explained to you until Lesson 28. But you might like to know about the question forms now, since the -na ending underlies one way of making questions in the polite style (-na yo, ‖ 16.7).

You will recall that the -na yo ending is more common after processive verb bases (in addition to iss-, ēps-, and the past and future of ANY bases); simple descriptive bases prefer to take -(u)n ka yo, though you may occasionally hear -na yo with these adjectives too. When you remove the yo you have a question in the FAMILIAR style. The question ending -na differs from the adversative ending -(u)na 'but' in the same way that the question ending -ni differs from the sequential ending -(u)ni (‖ 22.3 just above): it is a ONE-SHAPE ending, always pronounced -na regardless of what kind of sound precedes it. Notice these examples:

	-na	-(u)na
ka-	kana? 'does he go?'	kana 'he goes but'
kass-	kass.na? 'did he go?'	kass.una 'he went but'
mek-	mek.na? 'does he eat?'	mek.una 'he eats but'
mek.ess-	mek.ess.na? 'did he eat?'	mek.ess.una 'he ate but'
mek.keyss-	mek.keyss.na? 'will he eat?'	mek.keyss.una 'he will eat but'
kaci anh-	kaci anh.na? 'doesn't he go?'	kaci anh.una 'doesn't go but'
pissa-	pissana? = pissan ya? 'is it expensive?'	pissana 'it is expensive but'
pissass-	pissass.na? 'was it expensive?'	pissass.una 'it was expensive but'
pissaci anh-	pissaci anh.na? = pissaci anh.un ya? 'isn't it expensive?'	pissaci anh.una 'it isn't expensive but'

Here are some sentences:

Tōn i iss.na?	Do you have any money?
Eti kana?	Where are you going?
Cal hayss.na?	Did you do well?
Caymi pwass.na?	Did you have fun?
Meych si ey tol.a okeyss.na?	What time will you return?

Nal i chwup.na = Nal i chwuwun ya? Is it cold?
Ku os i ippuna? = Ku os i ippun ya? Is the dress pretty?

There is a special use for this type of question put into sentences which are not restricted to the familiar style: that is for wondering to oneself.

With a form of hay yo after it, this type of question enters into a construction similar to that in ‖ 14.5 (-ulq ka hay yo). Since this is a way of reporting "talking to oneself" (and you usually talk to yourself in plain or intimate styles), it is more often heard as the preamble to some action on one's part:

Pang an ey nwu' ka iss.na hako tul.ye 'ta pwass.ey yo. 'I looked in wondering if there was anyone in the room.'

Ku sensayng i pelsse cip ey tol.a kass.na hako tul.ye 'ta pwass.ey yo. 'I looked in to see if he had already gone home.'

The verb hay yo in addition to meaning 'does,' 'is,' and 'says' (= māl hay yo), also has the meaning 'thinks' (= sayngkak hay yo).

In ‖ 24.11 you will find the familiar question form -na used as a variant of plain modifier + ka with the auxiliary adjective pwa yo 'it looks as though':

Nwu' ka wass.na pwa yo (= Nwu' ka wass.nun ka pwa yo). 'I think someone's here.'

We say that pwa yo is an ADJECTIVE here because the plain form is pota (Nwu' ka wass.na pota); -na is also used with the processive verb pwa yo (plain form ponta) in the meaning 'looks at, sees':

Etteh.key tōyss.na lul popsita = Etteh.key tōyss.nun ka lul popsita. 'Let's see how it turned out.'

‖ 22.6. 'So [much] that . . .'

19. Nal i etteh.key chwuwun ci, nwun ey se nwun mul i na onta. 'It's so cold that my eyes are watering.'

One way of saying 'so [adjective] that . . .' is to use etteh.key (or etteh.key to) 'how' followed by the adjective in its modifier form and the post-modifier ci. (Another way is to use nemu 'too' followed by the infinitive and se). Some examples:

Etteh.key phikon han ci [or Nemu phikon hay se] īl ul mōs hayss.ey yo. 'I was so tired I couldn't do any work.' [= I was too tired to (do any) work.]

Etteh.key to tewun ci [or Nemu tewe se] kongpu lul mōs hay yo. 'It's so hot I can't study.' [= It's too hot to study.]

I os i etteh.key ssan ci [or I os i nemu ssa se] sass.ey yo. 'This dress was so inexpensive, I bought it.'

Etteh.key puncwu han ci [or Nemu puncwu hay se] sēyswu to mōs hayss.ey yo. 'I was so busy I didn't get to wash up.'

Yēyki ka etteh.key wusuwun ci wūs.ci anh.ulq swu ēps.ess.ci yo. 'The story was so funny, I couldn't help laughing.'

‖ 22.7. The particle ey: enumerative use.

In addition to its other meanings, involving time and direction and benefit, the particle ey has an enumerative usage, as illustrated in Basic Sentences 27 and 28:

Kkoma ey, ttwungttwung-po ey . . . 'A runt and a fatso . . .'

Nwun-ttakpuli ey, kho-cwupu ey, ne-huy apeci kath.ta. 'Goggle-Eyes and Big-Nose and just like your father.'

In linking a series of coordinate nouns in this way, ey is the same as the particle hako (above, ‖ 3.4); it is often used in reciting a list. Here are some more examples:

1. Tōn ey, cōh.un cip ey, ippun puin ey, cham ku sālam un cōh.keyss.e.	Money, a fine house, a pretty wife, why he really has it nice!
2. Pap ey, kimchi ey, capchay ey, namul ey, mānh.i to mek.ess.ci.	Rice and kimchi and capchay and namul — we've eaten a lot, you know.
3. Cang ey ka se, pāychwu ey, muwu ey, pha ey, Tang myen ey hō-pak ul sa wa.	Go to the market and buy cabbage and radishes and onions and "nylon" noodles and squash.
4. Poktong-i ey, Swunnam-i ey, Hongsik-i ey, tā nwūnq salam kwūkyeng wass.ci.	Poktong-i and Swunnam-i and Hongsik-i and Tekswu all came to see the snow man.

‖ 22.8. The vocative-exclamatory particle a/ya.

When the children in the Basic Sentences of this lesson call each other by name, they add a particle which is pronounced a after consonants, ya after vowels. This particle combines a vocative function (as when calling to someone— 'hey!,' 'say!,' 'oh!') with an exclamatory one (speaking to the person interestedly, or to call their attention to something).

This particle is also heard after the intimate apperceptive forms that end in (-)kwun: Chwupkwun a = Chwupkwun (yo) 'It's cold, I see!' Pi ka onun kwun a = Pi ka onun kwun (yo) 'Oh, it's raining!' The effect is to make the intimate form (which is the polite form with the particle yo removed) somewhat more friendly or relaxed. [As in many other cases, the usual Korean spelling practice is to leave ending + particle unanalyzed, so that in the script you will find -kwun a and -kwun yo usually spelled -kwuna, -kwunyo.]

‖ 22.9. The direct object particle ul/lul: antithetical use.

31. Wuli apeci hanthey ilulq ke l'. 'But I'm going to tell my father, so there!'

The particle ul/lul has, in addition to its other meanings, an antithetical use: 'but; although, even though.' Here is a list of constructions which illustrate this meaning.

1. After ke or kes in the middle of a sentence. Here, ul/lul (often reduced to l') means 'but; although, in spite of the fact that . . . .' It is commonly used in such contexts as 'When A did so-and-so, B countered with something else' or 'When A happened, the B (of an opposite or contrary nature) resulted.' Some examples:

Silh.ta ko hanun kes ul pumo ka kyelhon hakey hayss.ci yo.	You see, his parents made him get married in spite of his objections.
Eceyq pam ey cip ey se kongpu halq ke l' kukcang ey ka se onul ku sihem ul cal mōs pwass.e.	I was going to study at home last night but (instead) I went to the theater so I didn't do very well in that test today.

2. At the end of a sentence, . . . ke l(ul) or . . . kes ul may mean 'but' or 'after all' or 'but . . . so there!' as in Basic Sentence 31. Here are some more examples:

Keki n'cham pissalq ke l'.	But that place would be very expensive.
Ku yenghwa nun wuli Inchen ey to olq ke l'.	That movie will come to us in Inchen after all.
Kim sensayng uy yēyki nun cheum tut.nun ke l'.	Why this is the first time I've ever heard Mr. Kim say anything!
Ku sālam i him i sēyn kes ul.	But he is (so) strong!
Ku tōn un tā sse pelin ke l'.	(I'm sorry) but I have spent all the money.
Swul i ēps.e cin ke l'.	But we've run out of liquor, so there!
Ku moca nun na hanthey com khulq ke l'.	I guess that hat is a bit too big for me, after all.

In this meaning only, the ke l' can be preceded by the restricted modifiers -ess.nun and -keyss.nun (optionally used instead of -un and -ul):

Son nim i pelsse wass.nun ke l'.	But the guests are already here!
Sayngkak ul calmos hayss.nun ke l'.	But you've got the wrong idea.
Incey ka ya hakeyss.nun ke l'.	But I'll have to leave now.

3. Another sentence-final meaning of . . . ke l(ul) or . . . kes ul is '(I wish I had done it) but . . .' to show regret at lost opportunities. The modifier is often prospective or past prospective:

Ecey um.ak-hoy ka(ss.u)lq ke l'.	If only I had gone to the concert yesterday.
Yuli can ul ttel.e ttulici anh.(ess.)ulq kes ul.	If only I hadn't dropped the glass!
Tōn ul com te pillye cwulq (cwuess.ulq) ke l'.	I wish he would lend me (would have lent me) a little more money, but . . .
Māl ul halq (hayss.ulq) ke l'.	If only I had spoken up!

4. A similar kind of sentence not only shows regret at the lost opportunity, but includes the reason for the regret: 'If A had happened then B would have happened, but [it didn't so . . .].' The 'if it had happened' part is typically expressed by the retrospective conditional forms (‖ 24.1) -(ess.)tumyen or -(ess.)tula 'myen:

Sīcheng i ileh.key mēn cwul al.ess.tumyen cēncha lul thass.ulq ke l'.	If I'd known the City Hall was this far, I'd have taken a streetcar.
I sihem i ileh.key elyewun cwul al.ess.tumyen, ecey nōlci mālko kongpu hayss.ulq ke l'.	Had I known the test would be this hard, I would have studied yesterday instead of fooling around.
Hayss.tula 'myen cōh.ass.ulq ke l'.	I wish he'd done it anyway (but he didn't).
Pi ka olq cwul al.ess.tumyen wūsan ul kaciko onun ke l' (kulayss.ta).	If I'd known it was going to rain I'd have brought my umbrella (but I didn't).

5. With a question intonation at the end of a sentence . . . ke l(ul) or . . . kes ul means 'but (I wonder if . . .)' or 'but (do you think . . .).' The modifier is usually prospective:

Kel.e naylye kanun kes i ppalulq ke l'?	But I wonder if it would be (still) faster to go down on foot?
Ku "yeca ka acik to cēki se sālko iss.ulq ke l'?	But do you suppose she is still living there?

In the sentence-final use, you can always add the polite particle yo to make the sentence polite: Ama molusilq ke l' yo 'But you probably wouldn't know.' Before yo the construction ALWAYS appears in its abbreviated form . . . ke l' (yo).

‖ 22.10. Causative formations with verbal nouns: sikhye yo.

36. . . . Wuli nwūnq salam ul kwūkyeng sikhica. '. . . Let's show them our snow man.'

In ‖ 17.4 you learned to make causative sentences by changing the sentence-final verb to the adverbative form (-key) and then adding the auxiliary hay yo: Ai ka wuyu lul masye yo 'The child drinks his milk' → Emeni ka ai hanthey (or eykey) wuyu lul masikey hay yo 'The mother makes/lets/has the child drink his milk.' As a new subject (emeni ka) is introduced the subject of the underlying sentence becomes the indirect object of the causative sentence (ai ka → ai hanthey); if the original verb does not take a direct object (that is, if it is an intransitive verb like anc.e yo 'sits' or any of the descriptive verbs like pappe yo 'is busy'), the subject of the underlying sentence is often turned into the direct object of the causative sentence: Ai ka yeki ey anc.ess.ey yo 'The child sat here' → Emeni ka ai lul yeki ey anc.key hayss.ey yo 'The mother made/let/had the child sit here.' For some verbs there are also special derived causative bases, often with specialized meanings: anc.hye yo [anc.hi-] 'seats,' mek.ye yo [mek.i-] 'feeds' etc. These are discussed in ‖ 26.1.

In general, verbal nouns + hay yo behave like other verb expressions, with the appropriate switches made on the auxiliary base ha- 'do/be.' But alongside the expected causative formation we find an optional substitution of the verb sikhye yo [sikhi-] 'orders, causes' in place of hakey hay yo:

Tongmu tul i nwūnq salam ul kwūkyeng hanta 'Our friends look at the snow man'
→ Wuli ka tongmu tul hanthey nwūnq salam ul kwūkyeng hakey hanta OR
→ Wuli ka tongmu tul hanthey nwūnq salam ul kwūkyeng sikhinta
'We make/let/have our friends look at the snow man.'

Once you have the new (causative) sentence, of course, you are free to turn it into any of the many expression types you have learned, such as the suggestion form found in Basic Sentence 36: . . . kwūkyeng sikhinta. → kwūkyeng sikhica.

EXERCISES

I

Here are some STATEMENTS that might be made by one child to another, or by an adult to a child. Change each to the appropriate question; then translate the question. For example the first will be Ne nun sēyswu haci anh.ess.ni? 'Didn't you wash your hands and face?'

1. Ne nun sēyswu haci anh.ess.ta.
2. Ney say os i phuluta.
3. I key ney kes ita.
4. Emma ka pakk ey na ka nōlla ko hayss.ta.
5. Nay kōng i keki iss.keyss.ta.
6. Latio soli ka nemu khuta.
7. Appa ka ilen ke l' cōh.a hasici anh.nunta.
8. Ne to i sāy lul poko siph.ta (or siph.e hanta).
9. Ānkyeng ul ttel.e ttulye (se) kkay-ttulyess.ta.
10. Ne to nolay lul pulukeyss.ta.

11. Tōn ul tā sse pelyess.ta.
12. Caki cen ey pul ul kkuci anh.e to kwaynchanh.ta.

II

Here are some suggestions ('Let's do it!') in the plain style. For each suggestion, think up some protest against the idea and express it in a sentence that ends with . . . ke l' 'But . . . !' Make your protest interesting and relevant. For example, to the first sentence Yenghwa kwūkyeng kaca! 'Let's go see a movie!' you might protest Yenghwa-kwan i mēn ke l'! 'But the theater is so far away!' or Kongpu lul hay ya hanun ke l'! 'But I have to study!' or Emma ka cip ey iss.ula ko hayss.nun ke l'! 'But Mamma told me to stay at home!' etc., etc.

1. Yenghwa kwūkyeng kaca!
2. Kimchi lul ma(y)ntulca!
3. Sakwa lul sa (se) mekca!
4. Cip ey tol.a ka se caca!
5. San ulo ka se nōlca!
6. Wuphyen-kwuk ey ka se i phyēnci lul puchica!
7. Al ul nah.ca!
8. Tōn ul nāyci mālca!
9. Emma uy cāngkap ul kkica!
10. Chwupci man com chām.ca!
11. Pul ul khica!

III

Here are some commands in the plain style. For each of these, think up some protest and express it with . . . ke l' 'But . . . !' For example, to the first command I congi ey 'ta ilum ul sse la 'Write your name on this (piece of) paper' you might protest Ssulq cwul molunun ke l'! 'But I don't know how to write (it)!' or Ingkhu ka ēps.e cyess.nun ke l'! 'But I'm out of ink!' or Yenphil to mānnyen-phil to ēps.nun ke l'! 'But I don't have either a pencil or a pen!'

1. I congi ey 'ta ilum ul sse la.
2. Kwaynchanh.umyen, onulq cenyek ilcciki tol.a one la!
3. Chinkwu uy cip ey kaci mālko cip ey iss.ke la (or iss.e la)!
4. Nay māl ul cal tut.ke la (or tul.e la)!
5. Say kwutwu lul sin.e la!
6. Hēn os ul ip.e la!
7. Say cip ul cie la!
8. Kulen yēyki lul tul.umyen wus.e la!
9. I chīm-pang ey se cake la (or ca la)!
10. Latio lul com cāk.key hay la!
11. Kkoch ul kaciko pyēngwen ey kake la (or ka la)!

IV

Here are some sentences containing verbal nouns, meaning someone does something. Change each one so that it means 'They make or let or have [someone] do it.' First use the hakey hay yo form (‖ 17.4), then use the sikhye yo form (‖ 22.10). For example, the first will be Nal mata ai tul ul sānqpo hakey hay yo, . . . sānqpo sikhye yo 'Everyday they [or we etc.] have the children take a walk.' Keep your resulting sentence in whatever style of speech the original is in. Remember that the subject of the original (. . . i/ka) will change to the indirect object (. . . hanthey or . . . eykey) of the new sentence, but may optionally appear as the direct object (. . . ul/lul) if the underlying verbal noun is intransitive.

1. Nal mata ai tul i sānqpo hay yo.
2. Ku haksayng i mues ul kongpu hayss.^{s}up.nikka.
3. Wuli cip ey on son nim tul i atul i ma(y)ntun nwūnq salam ul kwūkyeng hayss.ci yo.
4. Ku twū sālam i kyelhon hakeyss.ey yo.
5. Ku sālam tul i yeses si pān ey īl ul sīcak hayss.e yo.
6. Wuli ttal i pom ey col.ep halq ke yo.
7. Nay ka ku nal īl ul sayngkak hayss.ci yo.
8. Elin ay ka emeni ka mūt.nun kes ul tāytap hayss.ey yo.
9. Kim sensayng i catong-cha lul wūncen hapsita!
10. Poktong-i ka son nim kkey insa lul hayss.ta.
11. Alh.nun puin i pyēngwen ey ip.wen hayss.ci yo.
12. Sensayng i nwukwu lul pāngmun hasikeyss.ey yo.
13. Ku hwānca ka thōywen haci anh.ess.^{s}up.nita.
14. Hōycang i wēn.yu-hoy nalq-ca lul pyēnkyeng hakeyss.ci yo.
15. Na nun elyess.ul ttay lul sayngkak hayss.^{s}up.nita.
16. Ku ōykyo-kwan i sēykyey lul ^{l}yehayng hayss.ey yo.
17. Chinkwu ka na hako kath.i kyengchi lul kwūkyeng halq kes ul yaksok hayss.ta.
18. Yenge lul cal ānun sālam i ku chayk ul pen.yek hayss.ulq ke 'ci yo.

V

Each of the following sentences is in the polite style or the formal style. Restate each sentence as one child might say it to another, or as an adult might say it to a child. Then translate the sentence. (Remember that while children might often use honorifics—hasinta etc.—of other people, such as teachers and older relatives, they will not use them in reference to each other.)

1. Āsikeyss.^{s}up.nikka?
2. Kwaynchanh.e yo.
3. Komapsup.nita.
4. Mian hap.nita.
5. Cey ilum un Kim Pok.nam iey yo.
6. Cikum mues ul hasey yo.
7. Pokswun-i, tangsin cham ilcciki na wass.ey yo.
8. Kulay yo. Onul un mues hako nōlq ka yo.
9. Tangsin capci lul mānh.i kaciko na wass.ey yo?
10. Kongwen ey ka se nōpsita.
11. Ama ku sacin i cōh.ulq ke(y) 'p.nita.
12. Ape' nim un nul cēki anc.usey yo?
13. Kulus ul ssis.upsita.
14. Nēy. Kuleh.key hapsita.
15. Pumo nim i acik to celm.usey yo.
16. Onul ōhwu ey kongwen ey se mannapsita.
17. I uyca ey anc.usio.
18. Onulq cenyek ey nun Poktong-i ka kulus ul ssis.usio.
19. Pap com te cwusipsio.
20. Ilkop si pān ey il.e nako, pam yel han si ey ca yo.
21. Yeki se kongpu hako siph.e yo, kyōsil ey se kongpu hako siph.e yo.
22. Cey tongsayng un acik to mek.ko iss.ey yo.
23. Tangsin uy os i chīm-pang an ey ēps.ey yo?

24. Namu mith ey se chayk ul ilk.keyss.ey yo.
25. Yuli chang ey se san i pōy yo?
26. Onulq cenyek ey wuli kath.i kongpu hapsita.
27. Onul i musun nal ip.nikka.
28. Eme' nim i kitaliko kyēysip.nita.
29. Cwungkwuk mal ul molup.nikka?
30. Eme' nim i tangsin ul pulup.nita.
31. Pom mata yele kaci chāyso lul sīm.sup.nita.
32. Mānnyen-phil hana sa se sensayng nim kkey tulipsita.
33. Kil i com mel.e to, wuli kel.e kapsita.
34. Kil i com mēni, wuli kel.e kaci māpsita.
35. Hak.kyo ey nun pi ka wa to ka ya hako, an wa to ka ya hay yo.
36. Ku phyēnci lul ilk.e tulyess.ey yo.
37. Ku phyēnci lul ilk.e cwuess.ey yo.
38. Ku sangcem ey se chāyso man sako, koki nun saci māsio.
39. Cey ka wuphyen-kwuk aph ey se catong-cha yeses tay lul pop.nita.
40. Cēki ce hak.kyo ey Poktong-i to tanyess.ko, ce to tanyess.^{s}up.nita.
41. Nemu chwuwe se sangcem ey kaci mōs hay yo.
42. Nal i chwuwumyen cang pole kalq swu ēps.^{s}up.nikka?
43. Pi ka omyen, cip ey iss.keyss.^{s}up.nita.
44. Phikon hamyen, com swīsipsio.
45. Yo say nun mulken i tā pissa cip.nita.
46. Kongpu cwūnpi ka tā tōyss.^{s}up.nikka?
47. Pay ka kophuci man, com te cham.usipsio.
48. I chayk i pissaci man, sapsita.
49. Eme' nim i cal kyēysinta ko cēnhwa lul hasyess.ey yo.
50. Cip ul sakeyss.ta ko hayss.^{s}up.nikka?
51. Cwuil nal achim ey ilkop si ey il.e naci māpsita.
52. I pap un tewuna, ce pap un tēpci anh.e yo.
53. Hulin nal un hay ka naci anh.sup.nita.
54. Ecey ku sangcem ey se pon cāngkap i cey ka sako siph.un cāngkap iey yo.
55. Kicha lo kaci mālko, catong-cha lo kapsita.
56. Unhayng ey se chac.un tōn i pelsse tā ēps.e cyess.ey yo.
57. I chayk i cīnan cwuilq tong-an ey cey ka ilk.un chayk ip.nita.
58. I chayk i cīnan cwuilq tong-an ey tangsin i ilk.usin chayk ip.nikka?
59. Tōn ul kaciko oci anh.un sālam ul tul.e okey (haci) māsio.
60. Yeki se cacen-ke thalq cwul ānun pun i meych ina toykeyss.^{s}up.nikka.

CONVERSATION

I

Take the part of an American newly arrived in Korea. As you wander around the streets of Seoul (or Pusan, or any city), you stop a child and ask him some questions. (Your Korean teacher will play the role of the child.) You tell the child who you are and what you are doing in Korea; ask him what his name is, where he lives, how many brothers and sisters he has, where he goes to school and whether he likes it, etc., etc. Then tell him you'd like to look around the city a bit and ask him what would be most interesting to see, and where various things are. When you finish, be sure to express your appreciation to the child.

II

Your teacher will play the part of a Korean child who is lost. Taking turns, each member of the class will ask the child questions: what his name is, how old he is, where he has been and what he has been doing, when he last saw his mother, where she usually goes and what she usually does each day, whether he goes to school (and where), and so on. Try to comfort the child as you quiz him (or her). Let one member of the class play the part of the missing mother (or father), who eventually shows up, asks the child what has happened (and perhaps scolds him or her for wandering off), and thanks the other members of the class for their kindness.

VOCABULARY DRILL

I

Say the Korean words for _____

1. Five facial features;
2. Five other parts of the body;
3. One of two articles of clothing for each part named in 2.;
4. Five emotions (a verb or verb phrase);
5. Five kinds of physical handicap or defect.

II

Everyone take a pencil and a sheet of paper, held so that no one else can see your work. One student acting as leader draws a picture of a human head on his paper, telling the others what features he is drawing; they should draw the same ones. The face should be peculiar in some ways (lacking one of the eyebrows or ears, having big teeth, etc.). Then the leader checks the drawings of the others against his own to see how well they followed directions.

Take turns being leader.

COMPREHENSION

Here is a conversation between a mother and her child. Listen while your tutor reads through it, taking the two parts. Then take turns around the class going through the conversation, so that each member of the class gets a chance to be first mother then child.

Pokswun. Emma, na ka nol.a to kwaynchanh.e yo?

Emeni. Yāy ya, pakk i tāytan hi chwuwuni na kamyen kāmki tullikeyss.ta. Cip an ey se nol.a la. Ung??

P. Cip ey se n' sim-sim han ke l' yo. Kulem emma ka caymi iss.nun yēyki hay cwe ya haci!

E. Caymi iss.nun yēyki ka kuleh.key swii sayngkak naci anh.ulq ke l'. Yēyki tāysin nay ka mul.e pomyen ne nun tāytap hay la. Kho lo mues hanun ci āni?

P. Ku kes to mōlla yo?? Caychayki lul hay yo.

E. Ha ha, kuleh.kwun. Kulem kwi nun?

P. Ayki wūnun soli lul tut.ci yo.

E. Olh.a! Wuli Pokswun-i nun ttok-ttok to haci! Kulem i pen ey n' ney ka mul.e la. Nay ka tāytap hay polq key.

P. Emma, way kwi nun twūl iey yo?

E. E . . . , ku kes un, ku kes un . . . , kwi ka twūl iss.e ya ānkyeng ul ssuci.

P. Ha ha ha, emma nun wusupki to hay yo.

E. Yāy ya, nay ka ciess.kwun a. Ku man haca.

LESSON 23. GETTING A WATCH REPAIRED

BASIC SENTENCES

[A = Mrs. Kim, B = the watch repairman, C = Mr. Kim, S = Kim Sen-il.]

Korean	English	Amplification
A. 1. Tayk ey se sikyey swusen hasey yo?	Do you do watch repairing here [= at your place]?	swusen 'repairs, restoration' swusen (ul) hay yo 'repairs, does repairing'
B. 2. Nēy. Hap.nita. Swusen halq sikyey lul kaciko osyess.^{s}up.nikka?	Yes, we do. Did you bring a watch to be repaired?	
A. 3. Nēy. I hoycwung sikyey nun wuli namphyen uy kes iko, i phal-mok sikyey nun nay kes iey yo.	Yes. This pocket watch is my husband's, and this wrist watch is mine.	ho-cwumeni 'pocket' hoycwung 'inside one's pocket' phal-mok '[arm neck=] wrist'
4. I phal-mok sikyey nun halwu pōthong ō-pun ssik ttukey ka yo.	This wrist watch usually runs five minutes a day slow [= late].	halwu 'one day' pōthong 'usual(ly), ordinar(il)y' tte yo [ttu-] 'is slow, sluggish' ttukey ka yo '[a timepiece] goes late, runs slow'
5. I hoycwung sikyey nun halwu ey to meych pen ssik kata ka nun se yo.	This pocket watch (goes and then) stops several times a day.	meych pen ssik 'several times (each, apiece)' se yo [su-] '[stands=] stops (moving)'
B. 6. A a, ālkeyss.^{s}up.nita. I phal-mok sikyey nun sōcey man hamyen toykeyss.^{s}up.nita.	Ah, yes, I see. All we have to do is clean this wrist watch.	a 'ah!' 'oh!' sikyey lul sōcey hay yo 'cleans a watch' [. . . This wrist watch, if we only clean (it), it will be(come) all right).]
7. Kulen tey, i hoycwung sikyey nun mūncey ka com khun tey yo??	But, this pocket watch presents a little bigger problem!	mūncey 'problem, question'
8. Tasi māl hamyen, meych kaci pusok-phum ul kal.e ya 'keyss.^{s}up.nita.	In other words, we'll have to replace a few parts.	tasi 'again' tasi māl hamyen '[if I say it again=] in other words' pusok-phum '(mechanical) parts'

Korean	English	Amplification
		han kaci 'one kind; one item; one piece' kal.e yo [ka-l-] 'changes, exchanges (for), replaces (with)'
A. 9. Kulem, twuko kap.nita. Cal swusen hay cwusipsio.	Then I'll leave them. Please fix them properly.	twuko ka yo 'leaves it (and goes)'
10. Ēncey tōy yo. Ēncey chac.ule olq ka yo.	When will they be done? When shall I come for them?	chac.ule . . . '(comes/goes) to seek' chac.ule wa yo 'comes to get'
B.11. ^{1}Naycwu Swu-yoil ey han pen tullye posipsio.	Try stopping in around next Wednesday.	^{1}naycwu 'next week' ^{1}naycwu Swu-yoil 'next Wednesday [= Wednesday of next week]'
A.12. Cham. Swusenq-^{1}yo nun elma 'p.nikka.	Oh, how much is the charge for repairing them?	. . .-^{1}yo = ^{1}yōkum 'charge, fee, cost' swusenq-^{1}yo /swusennyo/ 'repair charge'
B.13. Han pen sōcey hanun tey kaps i ō-wen ipnita.	The price for a [one-time] cleaning is five wen.	kaps 'price'
14. I hoycwung sikyey nun swusen hay pwa ya ālkeyss.^{s}up.nita. ^{1}Yōkum un ku ttay ey allye tulici yo.	As for this pocket watch, we won't know till we repair it and see. I'll let you know the charge then.	allye yo [alli-] 'let know, inform, tell'
15. I sikyey ka Sēseq-cey ci yo??	This watch is a Swiss make, isn't it?	Sēse 'Switzerland' . . .q-cey 'made in . . .' Sēseq-cey 'Switzerland-made, Swiss make' etiq-cey 'what (country's) make?'
C.16. Ye' po! Sikyey chac.e wass.ey yo?	Say, did you go get the watches?	chac.e wa yo '[seeks and returns=] goes and gets' [also: 'comes visiting, comes on a visit' 4.SV]
A.17. Nay kes man chac.e oko, tangsin(q) kes un mōs chac.e wass.ey yo.	I just (went and) got mine—I couldn't get yours.	
C.18. Way. Ku sikyey-cem sīn.yong i tomuci ēps.kwun!	How come? Why, what a totally undependable watch shop!	sikyey-cem 'watch shop' tomuci '(not) at all; altogether, totally'

Korean	English	Amplification
		sīn.yong 'faith, trust, dependability' sīn.yong (i) iss.ey yo 'is trustworthy, dependable' sīn.yong (i) ēps.kwun 'is undependable, I see!'
A.19. Tangsin(q) kes un han han tal te kellinta ko haptita!	They said yours will take about another month.	han han tal te 'about [han 1] one [han 2] month [tal] more [te]' kellinta [kelli-] 'takes, requires' haptita 'I observed that [they] said; I recall [their] saying'
20. Kikyey pusok-phum ul wuli nala ey se nun kwu halq swu ēps.e se, Mikwuk ulo cwūmun hayss.ta ko haptita.	They said they can't obtain parts for the works in ['our' =] this country, so they ordered them ['to' =] from America.	kikyey 'works, mechanism' kwu hay yo 'obtains, gets; buys; seeks' cwūmun 'an order [for something]' cwūmun (ul) hay yo 'orders [something]'
C.21. Cēykil! Ōykwuk-cey sikyey nun cōh.ki nun haci man, kōcang i namyen pulphyen hata 'n māl ia.	Damn! A foreign watch is nice, all right, but if something happens to it, it's a nuisance, I tell you.	cēykil [a strong expletive] ōykwuk 'foreign country' ōykwuk-cey 'foreign-made' kōcang 'trouble, disorder' kōcang (i) na yo 'trouble occurs, disorder happens' phyen.li hay yo 'is convenient' pulphyen hay yo 'is inconvenient; is uncomfortable, unwell' . . . (han) māl ita 'it means . . .' . . . ia [INTIMATE style copula] = ita
22. Sikyey ēps.i etteh.key han tal ul cīnana.	How can I get along for a month without a watch?	ēps.i 'without' cīna yo 'passes, goes by' han tal ul cīna yo 'passes a month, goes through a month'
23. Cham. Ku cen ey ssutun nay hēn sikyey acik to iss.e yo?	Oh, is the old watch I used to use still around?	ku cen ey 'before [that=] this; used to . . .' ssutun sikyey 'watch that [one] has been using' hel.e yo [hē-l-] 'gets worn out, suffers from age'

Korean	English	Amplification
		hēn . . . 'old (not new) . . .' (= nalk.un) nay hēn sikyey 'my old watch'
A.24. Ku sikyey nun nemu hel.e se mōs ssukeyss.[s]uptita.	(I've observed that) that watch is too worn out to be any good.	ssukeyss.[s]uptita 'it has been observed that [one] will use [it]' mōs sse yo [ssu-] '[we] can't use it = it is useless, no good'
C.25. Kulem, tangpun-kan kaps ssan sikyey hana lul sa se cha ya hakeyss.kwun.	Well, I see I'll have to buy a cheap watch and carry that for the time being.	tangpun-kan 'for the present' kaps (i) ssan sikyey 'watch whose price is cheap' cha yo [cha-] 'carries (on one's person); wears (what is pinned, tied, or strapped on)' hakeyss.kwun 'I see [one] does'
A.26. Yeph cip Hongsik emma ka kulenun tey, meychil cen ey cēntang-pho ey se sikyey hana lul sass.nun tey, kkway cōh.tula ko yo.	(Hongsik's mommy=) Mrs. Kim next door says she bought a watch a few days ago from a pawnshop and it's been quite good.	kulenun tey . . . ko (hay) yo 'talks . . . and says' cēntang-pho 'pawnshop' kkway 'quite, very; fairly' coh.tula ko/kwu yo 'says it has been [observed to be] good'
27. Yo say saynghwal-nan ulo sālam tul i kwīcwung-phum ul mānh.i cap.hitula ko yo.	I hear people (have been observed to be=) are pawning lots of their precious things because of the hardships of living these days.	saynghwal 'life, living' saynghwal-nan ulo 'because of economic hardship (trouble earning a living)' kwīcwung-phum 'precious belongings; valuables' cap.hye yo [cap.hi-] 'has it taken; pawns it' [often pronounced /cayphi-/] cap.hitula ko yo 'hears that they have been pawning'
28. Hongsik emma ka san sikyey nun kwuksan-phum ici man, sip-chil sek ey kkway say kes iko, kakyek un siqka uy sam-pun uy il ila ko haptita.	The watch Mrs. Kim bought is a Korean make, but it is 17 jewels and quite a new one, and she told me the price was a third of current prices.	kwuksan-phum 'native product' pōsek 'jewel' sip-chil (pō)sek ey . . . 'is 17 jewels, and . . .' kakyek 'price, cost' siqka 'current price' sīqka 'market price' sam pun uy il 'one-third'

Korean	English	Amplification
C.29. Kulay, ku sikyey ka cal kanta ko haptikka?	And did she tell you the watch runs well?	haptikka? 'has it been observed that [one] said?'
A.30. Acwu cēnghwak haci nun mōs hako, halwu ey pōthong ilq-ī pun ppaluta ko yo.	She says it's not quite precise; it's usually one or two minutes fast each day.	acwu 'very; indeed' cēnghwak hay yo 'is precise, is exactly accurate' ilq-ī /illī/ 'one or two'
31. Nay cang ey kanun kil ey ku cēntang-pho ey tullye se kaps ssako cōh.un kes i iss.umyen sa olq ka yo??	On my way to the market, shall I stop in at that pawnshop and if they have a good cheap one, buy it?	nay = nay ka . . . kanun kil ey 'on the way [going TO a place]' sa wa yo 'buys and comes (back)' sa olq ka yo?? 'shall I buy (and come back)? shall I buy (and bring home)?'
32. Ca. I sikyey com posey yo. Cang ey kass.tun kil ey sa wass.ey yo.	Now, have a look at this watch. I went and bought it after I had been to the market.	. . . kass.tun kil ey 'on the way back [after HAVING GONE to a place]' sa wass.ey '[bought and came=] went and bought'
C.33. Ke. Sangtang hi cōh.un tey??	My, it's quite nice!	ke 'my! oh! why!' sangtang hi 'considerably, rather, quite, very'
34. Sen.il a. Wa se emeni ka sa on sikyey pwa la. Ney sayngkak ey nun etten ya. Ney maum ey tun ya?	Sen-il, come look at the watch Mother went and bought. What do you think of it? Do you like it?	maum 'mind, spirit, feeling(s)' (. . . uy) maum ey tul.e yo '[enters the mind/spirit (of . . .)=] pleases, appeals to'
S. 35. Cham cōh.un tey yo, apeci. Ce to ilen sikyey hana iss.umyen cōh.keyss.ey yo.	It's very nice, Father. I wish I had a watch like this too.	
36. Cey tongmu tul cwung ey se, sikyey ēps.nun ay nun ce pakk-ey ēps.ey yo.	I'm the only boy among my friends who doesn't have a watch.	ce pakk-ey ēps.ey yo '[outside of me, there are none=] I'm the only one' = ce man iss.ey yo
C.37. Ye' po. I sikyey kath.un kes tto iss.^{s}uptikka?	Dear, did you notice, do they have any more watches like this?	iss.^{s}uptikka 'did [you] observe, are there?'
38. Ani 'ta. Kongyen hi tto salq kes ēps.e.	No, there isn't any point in buying another for no reason.	kongyen hi 'pointlessly, unreasonably' [often pron. /koyn(h)i/ or /kwayn(h)i/] salq kes ēps.ta 'there's no reason to buy it'

Korean	English	Amplification
39. Nay ka i sikyey lul han tal man ssuko ne cwum a.	I'll use this watch for (just) a month and give it to you.	ne cwum a [= ne hanthey cwum a] 'I'll give to you'
40. Cham. Nay ka tangsin hanthey i sikyeyq kaps ul cwuess.tun ka yo?	Oh, did I give you the money for the watch (did you notice)?	sikyeyq kaps 'the price of the watch; what the watch cost = the money for the watch' cwuess.tun ka yo? 'has it been observed that [one] gave?'
A.41. An cwuess.ey yo. Ic.ki cen ey ese cwusey yo.	No, you didn't. Give it to me right away before you forget.	

SUPPLEMENTARY VOCABULARY

pōsek-sang	jewelry shop	panul	needle; hand (of time-piece)
swusen-so	repair shop		
swusen-kong	repairman	chochim	second hand
yangphum	imported goods (from America and Europe)	punchim	minute hand
		cangchim	['long'=] hour hand
catong sikyey	automatic clock	tānchim	['short'=] minute hand
cēnki sikyey	electric clock	sikan phyo	timetable, schedule
kwāycong	wall clock	kicha(q) sikan phyo	train schedule
cwācong	table clock		
kyēngcong *or* camyeng-cong *or* (bowl[-shaped]) sapal sikyey	alarm clock	chīmtay	berth, bed
		chīmtay-cha	sleeper, Pullman car
		chīmtay ˡyōkum	berth charge
yākwang sikyey	clock with illuminated dial	siktang-cha	diner, dining car
		kup.hayng-cha	an express (train)
yuli al	(watch) crystal	kesulumq tōn	change (returned when paying for a purchase)

NOTES

‖ 23.1. Retrospective aspect.

Korean has a set of RETROSPECTIVE verb endings; those that occur at the end of statements may be translated 'it has been observed that [so-and-so happens]' rather than simply '[so-and-so happens]' like other statement endings. Retrospective questions mean 'has it been observed *or* has [someone] noticed, did [so-and-so happen], was [so-and-so happening]?' rather than simply 'does *or* did [so-and-so happen]?' Past and future forms also have retrospective aspects.

This is a difficult aspect for English speakers to grasp, since it does not directly translate anything we say; it involves a dimension of meaning which English lacks. The translation is sometimes 'I saw . . .' or 'I noticed . . .,' sometimes 'I heard . . .' or 'I understand . . . , sometimes just 'did' or 'was' or 'was doing [when someone was observing].'

Here are the retrospective endings for the various styles.

	STATEMENT	QUESTION
FORMAL STYLE	-suptita [after consonant] /-ptita [after vowel]	-suptikka [after consonant] /-ptikka [after vowel]
Past:	-ess.^{s}uptita [etc.]	-ess.^{s}uptikka [etc.]
Future:	-keyss.^{s}uptita	-keyss.^{s}uptikka
POLITE STYLE	[NONE]	-tun ka yo
Past:		-ess.tun ka yo
Future:		-keyss.tun ka yo
PLAIN STYLE	-tula	-tun ya, -tun ka, -ti
Past:	-ess.tula	-ess.tun ya/ka, -ess.ti
Future	-keyss.tula	-keyss.tun ya/ka, -keyss.ti
INTIMATE STYLE	[NONE]	[NONE]

There is also a retrospective statement ending for the FAMILIAR style which you will learn in Lesson 28: -tey (but the copula is iley).

As you can see from the table, there are no retrospective forms in the intimate style and no statement forms in the polite style. What, then, does the Korean do when he wants to say something "retrospectively" in those styles? The easiest thing is just to shift into one of the other styles. Another way is to rephrase the sentence to take advantage of the restrospective modifier -tun (‖ 23.2) and say something like 'it's a fact that it has been observed that it happened': -tun kes iey yo or -tun ke(y) yo [POLITE], -tun kes ia or -tun ke(y) ya [INTIMATE].

Here are some more sentences ending with retrospective forms. They are all in the formal style; practice putting them into the other styles.

1. Kongpu haptita.	He's studying [and I know this because I saw him doing it].
2. Capci lul poptita.	He's reading a magazine [or was when I just saw him, anyway].
3. Pok.nam-i ka hak.kyo ey kass.^{s}uptita.	Pok.nam has gone to school [—I saw him leave].
4. Kim sensayng i eti iss.^{s}up.nikka. —Tose-kwan ey kaptita.	Where's Mr. Kim?—He was going to the library [I understand].
5. Ku sālam i han sikan cen ey chayk ul ilk.ko iss.^{s}uptita.	I saw him reading a book about an hour ago.
6. Ēncey kakeyss.ta ko haptikka?	Did you hear him say when he's going?
7. Kulen sālam i mānh.i iss.nun mo.yang iptita.	I've been given to understand that there seem to be many such people.
8. Emeni ka koki lul sa wass.^{s}uptikka?	[Do you know] did Mother go buy the meat?
9. Ecey nun phek chwupsuptita.	It was quite cold yesterday [I found].
10. Kumkang san ul ka poni-kka cham hwullyung han san iptita.	I went to see the Diamond Mountains and my what splendid mountains they turned out to be!
11. Elma 'na khuptikka.	How big was it?
12. Mues iptikka.	What was it? What did it turn out to be?
13. Ku hwānca ka kkok cwuk.keyss.^{s}uptita.	[From what I observed of his condition] that patient is going to die for sure.
14. Etteh.key mas i 'ss.nun ci yelq kay to te mek.keyss.^{s}uptita.	They were so tasty I could have eaten ten more of them.

15. Sahul man iss.umyen kkoch i phikeyss.[s]uptita. — In three days the flowers will be in bloom [from what I have seen of them].
16. Kulay ku āy ka ku īl ul cal hakeyss.[s]uptikka. — So, do you think he will handle the job all right?

‖ 23.2. Retrospective modifiers.

Retrospective modifiers are made by attaching the one-shape ending -tun to simple bases and to the past (-ess-) and future (-keyss-) markers.

In some contexts verbs with this ending have a modifier meaning corresponding to the sentence-final retrospective meanings discussed just above, namely '. . . which had been observed to [do so-and-so].' In other contexts, the retrospective modifier means '. . . which has been [doing so-and-so],' or, in the past, '. . . which has been [doing so-and-so].'

Basic Sentence 32 contains a special phrase with this modifier: kass.tun kil ey, which means 'on the way back (from having gone somewhere).' This contrasts with a processive modifier phrase, kanun kil ey, which means 'on the way (going to a place).'

Here are some more examples of retrospective modifiers.

1. Ecey wass.tun sālam i tto wass.[s]up.nita.	That person I saw come yesterday is here again.
2. Olayq tong-an mannako siph.tun sālam i onul wass.ey yo.	Someone I've been wanting to see for a long time is here today.
3. Ku sālam i māl-ssum hasitun sālam iey yo?	Is he the person I've heard you talking about?
4. Kim sensayng i wuli kyōsil ey se Hānkwuk mal ul kaluchitun pun iey yo.	Mr. Kim is the one who has been teaching Korean in our classroom.
5. Elyess.ul ttay tongmu tul hako kath.i nōltun ttay ka cikum to sayngkak na yo.	I can still remember the time I used to play with my chums when I was little.
6. Eceyq pam ey pūltun palam i onul achim ey to pul.e yo.	The wind (that I heard) blowing last night is still blowing this morning.
7. Han sikan cen ey i kongwen ey se nōltun ai tul i acik to nol.a yo.	The children (that I saw) playing in this park an hour ago are still playing [there].
8. Ecey hatun īl ul acik kkaci machici mōs hayss.ey yo.	I still haven't been able to finish the work I was doing yesterday.
9. Alh.tun i lul ppopkey hayss.ey yo.	I had the tooth pulled that had been hurting me.
10. Ecey kiph.tun mul i onul un yath.kwun yo.	I see that the water which was deep yesterday is shallow today.

You will notice that some Koreans spell "-ten" for -tun; this is explained in a note at the end of ‖ 24.5.

‖ 23.3. Apperceptive retrospective sentences.

As you have learned (in ‖ 16.4), apperceptive sentences, with such meanings as 'why . . . !' 'what do you know . . . !' '. . . I see!' are made for processive verbs by following the processive modifier form -nun with the POST-MODIFIER kwun or kwumen; descriptive verbs, as well as all past and future bases, attach the ENDING -kwun or -kwumen.

If the apperceptive is followed by yo, it is in the polite style; without yo, it is in the intimate style. Followed by the particle a, (-)kwun is especially intimate or friendly.

The retrospective form of these apperceptive sentences is made in either of two ways.

1. The retrospective modifier form, with ending -tun (‖ 23.3) is followed by kwun or kwumen; OR
2. A one-shape ending -tukwun or -tukwumen is attached to the base.

The latter can be thought of as an abbreviation of the former: -tu' kwu(me)n.

Turn back to the list of examples in ‖ 23.1 and turn them all into apperceptive statements. (Some may seem a bit strange, but you can probably think of a situation in which the 'oh, I see . . . !' meaning is appropriate.)

‖ 23.4. The topic particle un/nun used for emphasis.

5. . . . meych pen ssik kata ka nun se yo. 'It stops several times a day.'
[= It goes AND THEN STOPS . . .]

21. . . . cōh.ki nun haci man . . . 'it's nice, but . . .'

One function of the topic particle is to set apart the expression before it, in order to emphasize the following words.

In the phrase kata ka nun (Basic Sentence 5), the particle nun emphasizes the interruption.

The nun after cōh.ki in Basic Sentence 21 emphasizes the contrast: cōh.ki nun haci man . . . 'it IS nice—BUT . . .'

‖ 23.5. Negative 'only' expressions.

In Lesson 8 (‖ 8.1), we discussed the quasi-particle pakk-ey + a negative verb with the meaning 'outside of X (there is)n't = 'only X.' Another example appears in the lesson:

36. . . . ce pakk-ey ēps.ey yo. 'I'm the only one . . .'

The literal meaning is more like 'outside of me there isn't anyone.' In English it amounts to the same thing as using 'only' with an affirmative; in Korean, too, an affirmative verb following a phrase marked by the particle man adds up to the same thing as a negative verb following a phrase marked by pakk-ey: Na man iss.ey yo 'There's only me.'

A less colloquial synonym of pakk-ey is ōy-ey. (Ōy is a literary equivalent of pakk 'outside.')

‖ 23.6. Making promises with -um a/sey.

39. . . . ne cwum a. 'I'll give it to you.'

Cwum a is the verb base cwu- 'give' in its SUBSTANTIVE form made by attaching the ending -(u)m (‖ 26.3), followed by the post-substantive a to give a special meaning 'let me just [do so-and-so]' or 'I'll just [do it] for you.' The expression shows a willingness to do something, especially something helpful; often a PROMISE is implied, sometimes that of assuming another's burden.

Instead of a, the post-substantive may be sey; the promises with a are usually made to people you address in the intimate or plain style (such as children). Those with sey are made to people you address in the FAMILIAR style which will be introduced in Lesson 28.

Here are some more examples of promises made with -um a:

1. Kulay, palo cenyek ul cwūnpi ham a. — All right, I'll prepare supper right away.
2. Ney ka ol ttay kkaci pōsek-sang ey se kitaliko iss.um a. — I'll be waiting at the jeweler's till you come.
3. Ku sikyey-cem ey tullimyen ney sikyey yuli al to say kes ulo pakkwum a. — When I drop by the watch shop, I'll have your watch crystal replaced with a new one too.
4. Sensayng nim eykey ney ka hayss.ta 'nun ke l' iluci anh.um a. — I won't tell the teacher that you did it.
5. ˡNayil kam a. — I'll [go (to you)=] come tomorrow.
6. I os i na 'ykey cak.e cimyen ne 'ykey cwum a. — When these clothes get too small for me I'll give them to you.

And here are a couple of examples of the familiar style -um sey:

7. Nay (ka) twī lo kam sey. — I'll be along later.
8. Ku chayk un nay ka ilk.um sey. — I'll be glad to read the book.

These two sentences could be said in the plain style, of course, and the earlier sentences could be said in the familiar style, though in that style references to 'you' would replace ne with caney.

Koreans usually spelled these forms as simple, unanalyzed verb endings: -(u)ma and -(u)msey. A "post-substantive," by the way, is a kind of post-noun that occurs only after substantives.

‖ 23.7. Dropped particles again.

31. Nay (ka) cang ey kanun kil ey . . . 'On my way to the market . . .'
29. . . . ne (hanthey) cwum a. 'I'll give it to you.'

As we have observed from time to time, relaxed speech permits the omission of various particles, especially those marking subject and object. The Basic Sentences of this lesson give us a couple of examples, as quoted above. In Sentence 31 you will notice that na 'I' appears in the shape you would expect if the particle ka were not dropped (nay ka); if we were to use the more formal 'I' (ce) or the plain 'you' (ne), they too would appear in the special shapes you expect before the particle ka: cey cang ey kanun kil ey . . . , ney cang ey kanun kil ey . . . . Be careful not to confuse these shapes nay, cey, and ney in this use with the same shapes in another use, as abbreviations of na (ce, ne) + uy:

1. nay ka / cey ka / ney ka } [subject, with particle ka]

2. nay / cey / ney } [subject, with particle ka omitted]

3. nay . . (= na uy . . .) / cey . . (= ce uy . . .) / ney . . (= ne uy . . .) } [abbreviation]

From the grammar alone you might interpret Sentence 31 as saying '. . . to MY market' (nay cang ey = na uy cang ey), but of course that wasn't what the speaker meant to say.

In both relaxed and more formal kinds of speech, the particle kwa/wa is usually omitted in the expression X kwa kath- 'be like X': Apeci kath.ey yo 'It's like Father.' Apeci kath.ess.ey yo 'It was like Father.' (But in writing, the particle often appears.) The form X kwa kath.i /kachi/ can mean either 'like X' or (= X kwa hamkkey) 'together with X,' but it is customary in speech to insert the particle ONLY in the latter meaning: apeci wa kath.i (or apeci hako kath.i) 'with Father' (= apeci wa hamkkey) but apeci kath.i 'like Father.'

‖ 23.8. Hearsay reporting.

26. . . . kkway cōh.tula ko yo. '. . . and it's been quite good [she says].'

27. . . . sālam tul i kwīcwung-phum ul mānh.i cap.hitula ko yo. 'People have been pawning their precious things [I hear].'

30. . . . ilq-ī pun ppaluta ko yo. 'It's a minute or two fast [she tells me].'

Hearsay can be reported several ways in Korean. You can, of course, give a direct or (more commonly) indirect quotation of what was said, ending up with some such forms as . . . ko hayss.ey yo or . . . ko kulayss.ey yo 'said that . . .'; in Korean you need not mention WHO said whatever was said, so such sentences (without a subject for the verb of saying) can sometimes be translated 'As I hear tell, ...' Another way to report hearsay is to avoid not only any reference to the person who did the saying but even the verb of saying itself; this leaves us with the quotation particle ko (often pronounced kwu) and the sentence-final polite particle yo, as in the Basic Sentence quoted above. Here are some more examples of hearsay reporting.

1. Tekswu ka nwūnq salam ul mantultula ko yo.	Tekswu is/was making a snow man, I am told.
2. Kako siph.ci anh.e to, ka ya hanta kwu yo.	He says he has to go, even though he doesn't want to.
3. Cēntang-pho se mulken ul ssakey salq swu iss.tula ko yo.	I've heard it said you can get things cheap(er) at a pawnshop.
4. Eceyq pam ey mōs cako pappukey cīnass.ta kwu yo.	She said she didn't get any sleep at all last night, she was so busy.
5. Tāysa-kwan ey kanun kil ila kwu yo.	He says he's on his way to the Embassy.

Do not confuse this usage with the use of a sentence-final gerund (usually followed by yo) to express afterthoughts, ‖ 24.16.

NOTE: Recently the "hearsay" forms in . . . ko (yo) have become a popular way to put sentences whether they are hearsay or not; this usage, not illustrated here, is said to have come in from the North where the "quotational" form is used to avoid making a commitment of speech style.

‖ 23.9. Errand reporting.

16. Ye' po! Sikyey chac.e wass.ey yo? 'Say, did you go get the watches?'

Errands involve three things: you GO, you DO something, and you COME back. In English we report an errand by mentioning the first two of these operations: 'He went and bought me a newspaper,' etc. We seldom mention the final "coming back." (If the errand is reported from the other end, of course, the "going" and "coming" are reversed: you COME, you DO something, and you GO back.)

In Korean you sometimes mention only the last two operations when you report an errand; you say such things as 'He bought me a newspaper and came,' etc. (If the "going" and "coming" are reversed, you get such sentences as the Korean 'He got the watch and went' = English 'He came and got the watch.') This sort of sentence in Korean is usually limited to situations where as a result of the errand, the object is taken away (or brought), so you can't use it with all verbs that you might consider errands.

Here are some examples:

1. Poktong-i ka sakwa lul phal.e wass.ey yo.	Poktong-i went (out) and sold his apples.
2. Swul ul twū pyeng te sa omyen komapkeyss.ey yo.	I'd like you to go and buy a couple more bottles of wine.
3. Ku kwutwu ka nemu cak.umyen khun kes ulo pakkwe kasey yo.	If the shoes are too small come (to our store) and exchange them for larger ones.
4. Chinkwu ka cacen-ke lul swusen hay kass.ey yo.	My friend came and fixed his bicycle (at my place).
5. Say moca lul sa osey yo.	Go buy a new hat.
6. Ecey sinmun ul chac.e wa cwusey yo.	Go get me yesterday's newspaper.

As you can see from the last example (and from Basic Sentence 16) the verb chac.e yo 'seeks (out), looks for; finds' is often translated 'gets.' Another meaning you have learned is 'visits': Wuli cip ul chac.e osipsio 'Please come visit us.'

Not every case of -e wa yo or -e ka yo is an errand, as you can see from such expressions as kacye wa yo 'brings' and kacye ka yo 'takes,' kel.e ka yo 'walks (away)' and kel.e wa yo 'walks (here),' etc. Chac.e wa yo can have two different meanings, depending on whether it is taken as an errand 'goes and gets' or as a compound verb 'comes on a visit.'

Although ka yo usually translates English 'goes' and wa yo is usually equivalent to English 'comes,' there are some situations in which the two are reversed from the English pattern. In Korean the reference is always to where the SPEAKER is located when speaking. On the telephone from "our" house you might promise a little friend Nay ka ney cip ey kam a 'I'll [go=] come over to your house' rather than Nay ka ney cip ey om a 'I'll come over (here) to your house' since that would imply you were already at "his" house when talking. In other words, wa yo means 'comes HERE' and ka yo means 'goes or comes THERE.'

Another way to talk about errands, more widely useful since it is not limited to situations where the object is taken away or brought, is to use the infinitive of the movement verb usually followed by the particle se: ka/wa se . . . 'goes/comes and . . . [does].' You have had this expression in sentences like Sangcem ey ka se mulken ul sapsita 'Let's go to the store and buy things.'

EXERCISES

I

The following sentences say 'Someone does so-and-so' or ask 'Does someone do so-and-so?' Change each to make it mean 'Someone has been observed (or Has someone been observed?) to do so-and-so,' using a formal-style retrospective verb form; then translate the sentence into normal English.

1. Kim sensayng i hatun īl ul ppalli machiko kass.ey yo.

2. Wuphyen-kwuk ey honca kalq cwul ul mōlla yo.
3. Tali ka aphe se anc.ess.ey yo.
4. Pok.nam-i ka ku sang wi ey iss.nun sakwa han kay lul mek.ess.ey yo.
5. Ku sālam i Kim sensayng hanthey Hānkwuk mal lo yēyki hayss.ey yo.
6. Ilcciki ca ya hanta ko hay yo.
7. Ku sālam un chayk ul kaciko kakeyss.ta ko hayss.ey yo.
8. Wi chung ulo olla kass.ey yo.
9. Cengke-cang ulo ka se chinkwu lul mannass.ey yo.
10. Ku catong-cha wa kicha nun kkok kath.un sikan ey wass.ey yo.

II

Each of the following sentences makes a statement. Change each into an apperceptive retrospective sentence (‖ 23.3) and translate it into natural English.

1. Ku sālam i kuleh.key halq swu ēps.ey yo.
2. Ku sin ul sin.ulq swu ēps.ey yo.
3. Kuleh.key elyewun chayk ul ilk.ulq swu iss.ey yo.
4. Say cip ey se san i pōy yo.
5. Ai tul i nōnun kes kwūkyeng haki ka cham caymi iss.ey yo.
6. Nay tongsayng i pakk ey com na kass.ta wass.ey yo.
7. Yo say nun koki ka acwu pissa yo.
8. Ku pang i cham khuko cōh.a yo.
9. Ku ūmsik cip ey sālam i cham mānh.e yo.
10. Pokswun a, ne cham ilcciki na wass.ey yo.

III

Each of the following items contains two sentences. Make the first into a retrospective modifier, and combine the sentence; then translate. For example, the first will be: <u>Ecey wass.tun sālam i tto wass.ey yo.</u> 'The person who was here yesterday has come again.'

1. Ecey sālam i wass.ey yo. Ku sālam i tto wass.ey yo.
2. Eceyq cenyek ey pap ul mek.ess.ey yo. Ku pap ul onul to mek.key tōy yo.
3. Han sikan cen ey sālam i kongwen ey se sinmun ul ilk.ko iss.ess.ey yo. Ku sālam i acik to ilk.ko iss.ey yo.
4. Ecey īl ul hayss.ey yo. Ku īl ul acik kkaci machici mōs hayss.ey yo.
5. Kyewul ey palam i chwuwe yo. Yelum ey nun ku palam i tewe cici yo.
6. Nal mata sālam i wuli cip aph ulo cīna ka yo. Ku sālam i onul un an cīna ka yo.
7. Cīnan cwuil ey sensayng i i kyōsil ey se kaluchyess.ey yo. Ku sensayng i onul to tto kaluchye yo.
8. Chinkwu ka olayq tong-an poko siph.ess.ey yo. Onul un ku chinkwu ka wass.ey yo.
9. Uysa ka tangsin uy namphyen ul pwass.ey yo. Ku uysa ka cikum cey namphyen ul pwa yo.
10. Mulken ul sako siph.ess.ey yo. Sangcem mata tā tanye pwass.una, ku mulken un saci mōs hayss.ey yo.
11. Ku talk i al ul nah.ass.ey yo. I al i ku al ici yo.

CONVERSATION

Act out the following conversations in Korean.

I Is your best clock running all right? Pretend it isn't, and explain to your neighbor exactly what is wrong with it, and ask what he recommends

II You are planning to buy a watch, but you want to look before you leap. Ask someone who has a wrist watch whether he recommends that, or thinks a pocket watch would be better. Ask someone who owns a Swiss watch whether it's worth the extra money. Decide for yourself whether you want a gold watch (kum sikyey) or a silver watch (un sikyey), and tell why.

III Assume the role of a jewelry shop owner who is beset with troubles. Customer A storms in and says you gave him back the wrong watch: he describes his wife's watch that he brought in for repairs, and tells what kind of watch he got back instead. Straighten this out. Customer B complains about the delay—you promised him his watch last week and it still isn't ready; appease him. Customer C, who has a very cheap watch, wants to know why it's always breaking down; try to sell him an expensive one and justify the reasoning behind the suggestion. Finally, along comes Customer D, who is satisfied with everything and just dropped in to tell you how much he appreciates the good job you did repairing his watch, and how well it is working now.

When the customers have left, close shop and walk home with the owner of a bicycle repair shop that is across the street. On the way home, tell him about each customer, what he said and did and what you said and did in reply. Let the bicycle repairman tell you about his day and the complaints of HIS customers. Remember to use hearsay sentences when appropriate. When you get home, tell both stories to your young son, using plain or intimate style.

Each member of the class can take turns in the various roles, including that of the young son, who can interrupt his father every now and then (using the polite style) to make sure he is getting all the details.

VOCABULARY DRILL

Pick out those expressions below each sentence which make sense when inserted in the blanks. Translate each completed sentence; then make up a sentence using each discarded expression.

1. Cēntang-pho ey se ___.
   sikyey lul salq swu iss.ey yo
   sikyey swusen hay yo
   pusok-phum ul kal.e yo
   sikyey lul cap.hilq swu iss.ey yo
   kwīcwung-phum i mānh.i iss.ey yo.

2. ___ sālam i pōthong ulo namca 'ey yo.
   phal-mok sikyey lul ssunun
   sikyey swusen hanun
   namphyen i toyn
   hoycwung sikyey lul chanun
   hēn os ul ip.nun

3. Sikyey ka kata ka sumyen, ___.
   pōsek-sang ey twuko ka yo hay yo
   mūncey ka khe yo
   meych kaci pusok-phum ul kal.e
   ya hay yo
   chac.ule wa ya hay yo
   sōcey hal.nun ci to molla yo

4. Cey ___ halwu ey sip-il pun ssik ttukey ka yo.
   catong sikyey nun
   cēnki sikyey nun
   kyēngcong un
   yuli al un
   yākwang sikyey nun

5. Nay kwāycong un ___ i iss.ey yo.
   - meli thel
   - punchim
   - pōsek
   - cangchim
   - kōcang

6. Chinkwu uy cip ey se ___ (l)ul chac.e wass.ey yo.
   - sikan phyo
   - ^{l}yōkum
   - sangtang hi
   - kikyey
   - kakyek

7. Wuli hal-ape' nim uy sikyey ka ___.
   - kwuksan-phum iey yo
   - cēnghwak hay yo
   - hel.e yo
   - sīn.yong i ēps.ey yo
   - ōykwuk-cey 'ey yo

8. Sikyey swusen-kong i kikyey pusok-phum ul ___.
   - cwūmun hay yo
   - kwu hay yo
   - phyen.li hay yo
   - kongyen hay yo
   - pulphyen hay yo

COMPREHENSION

Listen while your tutor reads each of the following questions aloud; then answer it in Korean. Put enough into your answer so there is no doubt you have understood everything in the question. Don't look at the printed form of the question until afterward.

1. Cīnan pen sikyey swusen hal ttay, elmaq tong-an ina pōsek-sang ey twue ya hayss.^{s}uptikka.
2. Phal-mok sikyey pota hoycwung sikyey ka cōh.usey yo?
3. Tangsin kyēngcong i cal ka yo? Ppalli katun īl i iss.ey yo? Ttukey katun īl i iss.ey yo?
4. Tangsin sayngkak ey nun i tosi ey se enu sikyey swusen-so ka cēy-il cōh.suptikka.
5. Cīnan pen catong-cha lul swusen hay wass.ul ttay, pusok-phum i swusenq-^{l}yo pota te pissatun ka yo?
6. Cēntang-pho ey kwīcwung-phum ul cap.hye pon īl i iss.usey yo?
7. Sikyey sōcey ^{l}yōkum un pōthong elma 'ci yo?
8. Tayk ey se wuphyen-kwuk kkaci kanun tey elma 'na kelliko, cengke-cang kkaci nun elma 'na kelliptikka.
9. Cangchim i "ō" ey iss.ko tānchim i "il" ey iss.ta 'myen, meych si 'keyss.ci yo.
10. Tangsin sikyey nun Sēseq-cey 'ci yo? Kuleh.ci anh.umyen eti se on ke yo.
11. Cēntang-pho ey se mues ul hana sa posin il i iss.usey yo? Etten kes itun ka yo.
12. Onul Hānkwuk mal sikan ey tangsin pakk-ey nuc.key an wass.ey yo?
13. Kichaq sikan phyo ka nul cēnghwak hay yo?
14. Punchim i "chil" ey iss.ko tānchim i "sip" kwa "sip-il" sai ey iss.ta 'myen meych si 'keyss.^{s}up.nikka.
15. Tangsin i hak.kyo ey kass.ulq ttay pi ka otun ka yo?

LESSON 24. AFTERTHOUGHTS

BASIC SENTENCES

Korean	English	Amplification
1. Kihoy ka iss.ess.ul ttay Hānkwuk mal ul com te yelqsim hi paywess.tula 'myen cōh.ass.ess.keyss.ey yo.	I wish I had put more into my study of Korean when I had the chance.	kihoy 'opportunity, chance' yelqsim hi [= yelqsim ulo] 'earnestly, enthusiastically' paywess.tula 'myen 'if I had studied' cōh.ass.ess.keyss.ey yo 'it would have been good'
2. Halwu ey tā-man pān sikan ssik ila to māyil kyēysok hay se kongpu hayss.ess.tumyen, cikum un ^{l}yuchang hakey māl hakey tōyss.ulq ke 'ey yo.	If only I had just kept studying for even half an hour each day, (by) now I would have got so I talked fluently.	tā-man 'only, just' pān sikan ssik ila to 'even though it's half an hour apiece' kyēysok 'continuation' kyēysok (ul) hay yo 'continues' kongpu hayss.ess.tumyen 'if [I] had studied' ^{l}yuchang hay yo 'is fluent' tōyss.ulq ke 'ey yo 'would have (be)come'
3. Ku ttay nun way kuleh.key Hānkwuk mal paywuki ka silh.ess.(ess.)tun ci mōlla yo.	I don't know why I hated to study Korean so at that time.	way silh.ess.(ess.)tun ci mōlla yo '[I] don't know why I disliked'
4. Way kulayss.(ess.)tun ci, tangsin un āsikeyss.ey yo?	Would you know why it was like that?	way kulayss.(ess.)tun ci 'knows why [it] was like that'
5. Hānkwuk malq sikan man toymyen way kuleh.key haphum i nako cam i wass.tun ci mōlla yo.	I don't know why I would get to yawning and nodding so whenever it got to be Korean (class) time.	Hānkwuk malq sikan man toymyen 'if it only became Korean time' haphum '(a) yawn' haphum i na yo '[a yawn appears=] yawns' cam 'sleep(iness)' cam i wa yo 'sleep comes; gets sleepy' way cam i wass.tun ci mōlla yo 'doesn't know why [he] got sleepy'

Korean	English	Amplification
6. Tangsin to kulen kyenghem i iss.ey yo?	Do you have [or Have you had] that (kind of) experience too?	kyenghem 'experience'
7. Cōnun na lul poko sensayng i mian hay halq ka pwa (se), nwun ul puth.ici anh.ulye ko, āy lul ssuko nun hayss.ci man, na to molunun sāy ey cam i oko nun hayss.ey yo.	Looking at drowsy me, the teacher would seem uneasy, so I used to try to keep my eyes from closing, but I would fall asleep before I knew what was happening.	col.a yo [cō-l-] 'drowses; dozes' cōnun na 'dozing me' mian hay hay yo 'feels uneasy' halq ka pwa yo 'seems to do, looks as if [one] does' mian hay halq ka pwa yo 'looks uneasy, seems to be uneasy' nwun ul puth.ye /puche/ yo [puth.i- /puchi-/] 'closes one's eyes = dozes off' puth.ici anh.ulye ko 'trying not to close, intending not to shut tight' molunun sāy (ey) 'during the interval [one] doesn't know; unbeknownst' cam i oko nun hayss.ey yo 'sleep used to come'
8. Wuli pan ey se na ōy-ey tto nwu' ka na mankhum nul col.ass.nun ci āsey yo?	In addition to me, do you know (whether there was) anyone else in our class who was as sleepy all the time as I was?	na ōy-ey 'outside of me, in addition to me' nwukwu 'someone; who' tto nwu' ka 'someone else (= additional) [as subject]' . . . mankhum 'to the same extent, as much as . . .' na mankhum 'as much as me' col.ass.nun ci 'whether [one] got sleepy'
9. Ālkwu malkwu yo. Pyen Caychil ila 'nun chōngkak iess.ci yo!	Of course! There was that bachelor, Caychil Pyen!	ālkwu malkwu [= ālko malko; cf. ‖ 18.2] Pyen [a surname] chōngkak 'bachelor, unmarried man'
10. Ku chōngkak un pam imyen, capci wenko ssunula ko, pam nuc.key ca se col.ass.ci man, na nun way col.ass.tun ci āsey yo?	That fellow was sleepy because he [went to bed late=] at night (what with) writing magazine articles every night but do you know why I was sleepy?	pam imyen 'if it is night = nights, of a night, every night' wenko 'manuscript' ssunula (ko) 'what with writing (and all); with the idea (intention) to write'

Korean	English	Amplification
		way col.ass.tun ci al.e yo 'knows why [one] was sleepy'
11. Na nun musun īl itun ci, caymi ka ēps.umyen, pantusi col.a yo.	Whatever (thing) it may be, if it's not interesting, I inevitably get sleepy.	musun īl itun ci 'whatever (thing) it is' pantusi 'inevitably, unfailingly, without exception'
12. Incey nai ka tul.e se ya, mues itun ci kihoy iss.ul ttay yelqsim hi hay ya hanta 'nun kes ul kkaytal.ess.ey yo.	Only now that I've grown older have I realized that whatever it is, if I have the opportunity, I must do it enthusiastically.	nai ka tul.e yo '[age enters=] grows old(er)' mues itun ci 'whatever it may be, no matter what it is' kkaytal.e yo [kkaytal-, kkaytat.nunta] 'becomes or is aware, realizes'
13. Kuleh.ci man, nwukwu 'tun ci, kulen kihoy lul hepi haki ka swiwe yo.	But it's easy for anybody to waste such opportunities.	nwukwu 'tun ci 'anybody (at all), whoever it is, no matter who' hepi 'waste, wasting' hepi (lul) hay yo 'wastes'
14. Kulen īl i ēps.tolok wuli tul un ēncey 'tun ci caki lul kyēngkyey hay ya hay yo.	We have to guard ourselves at all times so that such a thing will not happen.	ēps.tolok 'to the point where there are not; so that there aren't' ēncey 'tun ci 'whenever, all the time, no matter when it is' kyēngkyey 'guarding, watching' kyēngkyey (lul) hay yo 'guards, watches'
15. Musun īl itun ci, cengseng ul tā hay hamyen, pōthongq salam imyen sengkong halq cwul al.e yo.	Whatever the task, if he does it with his whole heart and soul, the ordinary person will succeed, I feel.	cengseng 'soul, heart and soul' tā hay yo 'exhausts, uses up, pushes to the limit' pōthongq salam 'ordinary person, average person' pōthongq salam imyen 'if it's the average person' sengkong 'success' sengkong (ul) hay yo 'succeeds'
16. Ku ttay, Hānkwuk mal paywul ttay, pyel lo kongpu haci anh.ko hak.kyo ey man kass.tuni, pyel hyōqkwa ka ēps.ess.ey yo.	At that time, when I was studying Korean, I would just go to school without working at all, and (so) I've nothing special to show for it.	pyel lo [+ negative] '[not] especially'

Korean	English	Amplification
		kass.tuni 'when or since [one] went; as it has been observed that [one] went' hyōqkwa 'effect, effective results'
17. Kuleh.ci man, nay an(h)ay lul posey yo. Ku nun na wa pāntay lo yelqsim ulo Hānkwuk mal ul paywutuni, cikum un na wa ku sai ey khun chai ka iss.ci anh.e yo?	But look at my wife. I've seen her studying Korean with enthusiasm, the opposite of me, and now isn't there a big difference between her and me?	ku = ku sālam, ku i 'he/him, she/her' pāntay '(being) opposite, contrary' pāntay lo 'opposite(ly)' na wa pāntay lo 'the opposite [with=] of or from me' paywutuni 'it has been observed that [one] studies, so . . .' chai 'difference'
18. Nay an(h)ay nun sallim ina kongpu 'na tā cal haci yo.	My wife is good both at housekeeping and at studying, you see.	sallim 'housekeeping; household; livelihood'
19. Sāsil māl hamyen, nay an(h)ay nun musun īl īna, caki eykey takchimyen, cal kamtang haci yo.	To tell the truth, my wife can handle nicely any task she comes up against.	sāsil 'truth, fact' musun il ina 'whatever job it is, any job at all' takchye yo [takchi-] 'it impends, it draws near, it faces one' kamtang 'ability to handle or cope' kamtang (ul) hay yo 'can handle, is capable of coping with'
20. Nay an(h)ay nun wen.lay caycwu to iss.keni wa, mues ina caki ka math.un īl imyen, cengseng ul tul.ye se hay yo.	In addition to my wife's having talent to begin with, she puts her soul into anything she takes up.	wen.lay 'originally, from the start' caycwu 'talent, ability' iss.keni wa 'together with the fact that [someone] has; not only has, but . . .' math.e yo [math-] 'undertakes, assumes (a responsibility, a task)' math.un īl 'a task undertaken' mues ina math.un īl imyen 'whatever task it is, any job that has been taken on'

Korean	English	Amplification
21. Kule han an(h)ay lul kacin na nun hāyngpok han sanay 'ci yo??	Don't you think I'm a lucky man having such a wife?	kule han an(h)ay lul kacin na 'I, who have that kind of wife' hāyngpok 'happiness, good fortune' hāyngpok hay yo 'is happy, is fortunate, lucky' sanay 'man, male (= namca); married man (= namphyen)'
22. Ku wa pāntay lo, na kath.un namphyen ul kacin ⁿyeca nun pulhayng hako yo.	And on the contrary, a woman having a husband like me is unfortunate.	na kath.un namphyen 'a husband like me' pulhayng 'unhappiness, misfortune' pulhayng hay yo 'is unhappy, is unfortunate, unlucky'
23. Amman sayngkak hay to, na nun caycwu ka ēps.nun kes kath.ey yo.	However hard I think, (I find) I seem to have no talents.	amman . . . -e to 'however . . . [one] may do, no matter how . . . [one] does'
24. Ku pānmyen ey, nay an(h)ay nun caycwu ka mānh.un kes kath.ey yo.	On the other hand, my wife seems to have lots of talents.	pānmyen 'the other side, the opposite, the reverse'
25. Mān-il, nay an(h)ay kkaci caycwu ka ēps.ess.tumyen, etteh.key halq pen hayss.ess.keyss.ey yo.	If, by any chance, even my wife hadn't had any abilities (either), what would we have done?	mān-il 'ten thousand (to) one = if by any chance' nay an(h)ay kkaci 'even my wife' ēps.ess.tumyen 'if there had not been' etteh.key halq pen hayss.ess.keyss.ey yo 'what would we have nearly done? what might well almost have happened?' halq pen hayss.ey yo 'nearly did, almost did; barely escaped doing'
26. Wuli ai tul un tāychey lo emma lul talm.e se caycwu ka iss.ulq kes kath.ey yo.	Our children take after their mother in general, so it seems as if they will be capable.	tāychey lo 'in general, generally speaking' talm.e yo [talm-] 'resembles, takes after'
27. Thukpyel hi ku ōy-copu ka haksik i mānh.ess.ko, caycwu ka mānh.ess.tun kes kath.ey yo.	Their maternal grandfather, in particular, was very learned and had a great deal of ability, it seems.	thukpyel (hay yo) '(is) special, particular' thukpyel hi 'especially, particularly, in particular' ōy-copu 'mother's father' haksik 'learning, schooling'

Korean	English	Amplification
28. Tasi pon yēyki lo tol.a ka se, yēyki haci yo.	Let's get back to what I was saying before.	pon . . 'original. . . , main . . .' pon yēyki/iyaki 'the original talk (= subject); the main story' tol.a ka se yēyki haci yo 'let's turn back and talk'
29. Hānkwuk mal paywul ttay na nun nōlki man cōh.a hako, sensayng hako [1]nōngtam man hayss.tuni, cikum to [1]nōngtam man un cal na wa yo.	When I studied Korean I just liked to play, and all I did was joke with the teacher, and now (too) [only jokes come out easily=] jokes are all I have to show for it.	[1]nōngtam 'joke, kidding' [1]nōngtam (ul) hay yo 'jokes, kids around' hayss.tuni 'when [one] did; it has been observed that [one] did, so . . .'
30. Nay an(h)ay nun hak.kyo lul na on hwū ey to, yeksi kyēysok hay se munqpep hako tokpon ul toksup hatuni, cikum un māl hanun tey, ssunun tey, elyewum i ēps.nun kes kath.ey yo.	After my wife left school, she went right on studying the grammar and reader by herself, and now when it comes to talking or (when it comes to) writing, she seems to have no difficulties.	yeksi 'also, too, as well' kyēysok hay se 'continuing, continued and . . . , continued to . . . , kept on [do]ing' munqpep 'grammar' tokpon 'reader' toksup hay yo 'studies alone (without a teacher); teaches oneself' toksup hatuni 'as it has been seen that she studies alone . . . ; when she studied alone . . . ; she studied alone so . . .' elyewum 'difficulty'
31. Na nun Hānkwuk mal lo yēnsel un khenyeng, kantan han il.yong hōyhwa to mōs haci man, nay an(h)ay nun kongsek ey se [1]imsi yēnsel kkaci Hānkwuk mal lo [1]yuchang hakey hay yo.	Me, far from making a speech in Korean, I can't even carry on a simple everyday conversation in Korean, but my wife speaks Korean fluently to the point of (giving) impromptu speeches in public.	yēnsel 'speech' yēnsel un khenyeng 'far from a speech; much less a speech; let alone a speech' kāntan hay yo 'is simple, plain' il.yong 'everyday, mundane' hōyhwa 'conversation' kongsek '(the presence of) the public' [1]imsi 'impromptu, improvised; temporary, emergency' [1]imsi yēnsel kkaci 'even impromptu speeches'

SUPPLEMENTARY VOCABULARY

hwūhoy	regret(s), remorse
hwūhoy (lul) hay yo	regrets, feels remorse
cāng.lye	encouragement
cāng.lye (lul) hay yo	encourages
silphay	failure
silphay (lul) hay yo	fails
kyelkwa	result
ceymok	theme, subject, title
sangkwan	concern, involvement; relevance
sankgwan (i) ēps.ey yo	it doesn't matter, it makes no difference, it is of no concern
cam i tul.e yo [tu-l- 'enter']	falls asleep
cōllye yo [cōlli-]	gets sleepy (drowsy)
(hayq) pyeth	sunshine
kēnmul	a building

sēng (i) na yo or sēng (ul) nāy yo hwā (ka) na yo or hwā (lul) nāy yo kol (i) na yo or kol (ul) nāy yo pūn (i) na yo or pūn (ul) nāy yo	gets angry (mad), loses one's temper
cangsa	trade, peddling, selling
cangsa lul hay yo	engages in trade (business)
cangsaq-kwun, cangswu	trader, tradesman, merchant, seller, dealer, peddler, hawker
nam (ccok)	south
puk (ccok)	north
tong (ccok)	east
se (ccok)	west
nolyek	effort, endeavor
nolyek (ul) hay yo	tries, makes an effort

NOTES

‖ 24.1. Verbs: retrospective conditional.

1. . . . com te yelqsim hi paywess.tula 'myen . . . 'If I had studied a little harder . . .'
2. . . . kyēysok hay se kongpu hayss.ess.tumyen . . . 'If I had kept at it and studied . . .'

25. Mān-il . . . caycwu ka ēps.ess.tumyen . . . 'If she hadn't had any talents . . .'

RETROSPECTIVE CONDITIONAL forms are made by attaching the retrospective marker -tu- to the past base of the verb, then putting on the conditional ending -myen:

hayss.tumyen 'if [one] had done'

Another way to say the same thing is to add 'myen (an abbreviation of hamyen 'if we say') to the plain past retrospective -ess.tula:

hayss.tula 'myen 'if [one] had done'

These expressions have a past conditional meaning: 'if so-and-so had happened.' Although there is a separate past conditional form, made by attaching -umyen to past bases (-ess.umyen; see Lesson 28), the retrospective conditional—which has the same meaning—is the one most commonly used.

‖ 24.2. Verbs: past-past, past-future, and past-past future.

1. . . . cōh.ass.ess.keyss.ey yo. 'It would have been good.'
2. . . . kongpu hayss.ess.tumyen, cikum un [1]yuchang hakey tōyss.ess.keyss.ey yo. 'If I had studied, by now I would have got so that I could speak fluently.'
3. . . . way . . . silh.ess.(ess.)tun ci mōlla yo. 'I don't know why I hated it.'
4. . . . way kulayss.(ess.)tun ci . . . āsikeyss.ey yo? 'Would you know why that was so?'

25. . . . etteh.key halq pen hayss.ess.keyss.ey yo. '. . . what would we have done?'

Each of the verb forms quoted above contains at least two tense markers: past + past giving us the "past-past," past + future giving us the "past-future," and "past-past" + future giving us the "past-past future." These formations were discussed in ‖ 9.2. As you will recall, the past-past is used when the event is more remote, often with some later reversal or change implied: wass.ey yo means 'came = is here,' wass.ess.ey yo means 'came (and left) = was here.'

The future marker has two meanings, as you have seen. Sometimes it refers to a definite event in some future time: 'will do/be' or 'would do/be.' But other times it refers to a likely or probable PRESENT event: 'probably does/is = evidently must do/be.' You can have both these meanings when the future marker is attached to the past marker (-ess.keyss-), but you have to add the meaning of the past to your translation:

1. 'will have done/been' or 'would have done/been'
2. 'probably has done/been = evidently must have done/been'

In the second (probable) meaning you often find -ess.ulq ke(y) yo. See how this works with the examples of the past-past given above:

kass.ess.keyss.ey yo
1. 'will/would have gone (and returned) = will/would be back from going'
2. 'probably went (and returned) = evidently must be back from going' [= kass.ess.ulq ke(y) yo]

wass.ess.keyss.ey yo
1. 'will/would have come = will have been here'
2. 'probably came (and left) = evidently must have been here' [= wass.ess.ulq ke(y) yo]

In the first meaning, definite future, choice of 'will' or 'would' in the English translation depends on the tense of the other verbs in the English sentence.

Here are some more examples. Notice that the first part of the sentence often ends with a retrospective conditional -(ess.)tu(la ')myen:

1. Sikan i iss.ess.tumyen, kel.e kass.keyss.ey yo [= kass.ulq ke(y) yo].	If we had had time, we would have walked (there).
2. Catong-cha lul thako wass.tumyen, sikan i com te iss.ess.keyss.ey yo [= iss.ess.ulq ke(y) yo].	If we had taken a cab (here), we would have had a little more time.
3. Onul achim ey nal i cōh.ci anh.ess.tula 'myen, kongwen ey kaci mōs hayss.ess.keyss.ey yo [= hayss.ess.ulq ke(y) yo].	If it hadn't been nice out this morning, we wouldn't have been able to go to the park.

4. Nay chayk ul cip ey kaciko kass.tumyen, kongpu lul halq swu iss.ess.keyss.ey yo [= iss.ess.ulq ke(y) yo].	If I had taken my book home, I would have been able to do my studying.
5. Pak sensayng i onul wass.tumyen, Sewul kwūkyeng ul kass.keyss.ey yo [= kass.ulq ke(y) yo].	If Mr. Pak had come today, we would have gone [= be out] sightseeing (around) Seoul.
6. Onul ōhwu ey pi ka wass.tumyen, kongwen ey kaci mālla ko hayss.ess.keyss.ey yo [= hayss.ess.ulq ke(y) yo].	If it had rained this afternoon, I would have told them not to go to the park.

‖ 24.3. Some uses of ila.

2. Halwu ey . . . pān sikan ssik ila to . . . kongpu hayss.ess.tumyen . . . 'If only I had studied for even (though it's) half an hour a day . . .'

Ila to 'even though it is' (as in Basic Sentence 2) means about the same thing as the particle to 'even' by itself; sometimes 'at least' is a good translation. Ila is a rather literary variant form of the copula infinitive (alternating with the regular form ie). For example:

Onul i Il-yoil ila kicha ey ileh.key sālam i manh.e yo. 'The train is crowded because it is Sunday.'

Another use of ila, you will recall, is as the equivalent of ita (the plain copula) in quotations, ‖ 19.7. We have three kinds of quotations: simple (. . . ila hanta), expanded (. . . ila ko hanta), and contracted (. . . ila 'nta). Notice some of the contracted forms:

. . . ila (ko) hamyen → ila 'myen
ila (ko) haca → ila 'ca
ila (ko) hal → ila 'l
ila (ko) hanun → ila 'nun
ila (ko) han → ila 'n
ila (ko) ham a → ila 'm a
ila (ko) hako → ila 'ko
ila (ko) haci → ila 'ci
ila (ko) hay → ila 'y
ila (ko) hakey → ila 'key

Many of the cases where these constructions are used are quotations in form only. Sometimes there is a discernible meaning like 'call(ed)' or 'so-called,' but in other cases the quoting meaning is obscure, as you can see from the following examples:

1. Ku san ey kkoch ila 'nun kes un hana to ēps.ey yo.	There isn't a single (thing called a) flower on that mountain.
2. Ku sālam un hakca 'la 'lq su ēps.ey yo.	He can't be called a scholar.
3. Talun kes i ēps.umyen, i kes ila to cōh.a yo.	This one will be all right, if you haven't got any others.
4. Ce nun mōs kakeyss.uni, tangsin ila to kass.ta osio.	As I won't be able to go, at least you go (without me).

5. I kes ul Hānkwuk mal lo mues ila 'p.nikka. — What do you call this in Korean?
6. Onul achim ey Kim sensayng ila 'nun pun i chac.e wass.ess.ey yo. — A man named Mr. Kim was here to see you this morning.
7. Wensan ila 'n' kos un elma 'na khe yo. — How large a place is Wensan?

‖ 24.4. Retrospective modifiers + ci with information verbs.

3. . . . way . . . silh.ess.(ess.)tun ci mōlla yo. 'I don't know why I hated it.'
4. Way kulayss.(ess.)tun ci, tangsin un āsikeyss.ey yo? 'Would you know why it was like that?'
5. . . . way . . . cam i wass.tun ci mōlla yo. 'I don't know why I got sleepy.'
10. . . . na nun way col.ass.tun ci āsey yo? 'Do you know why I was sleepy?'

Retrospective modifiers—either in the past form or in the past-past form, the alternatives shown in Sentences 3 and 4—are used in oblique questions just as other types of modifiers are (above, ‖ 21.2). Retrospective modifiers mean 'which has been observed to [do or be so-and-so]' but in many cases there is not much practical difference between a retrospective modifier and a past modifier in this construction. (Cf. Basic Sentence 8 of this lesson: . . . nwu' ka na mankhum nul col.ass.nun ci āsey yo? 'Do you know anyone who was always as sleepy as me?')
Here are more examples:

1. Kaps i elma 'na tōyss.tun ci kiek i an na yo. — I don't remember how much it was.
2. Ku kes i mues iess.tun ci sayngkak i an na yo. — I can't recall what it was.
3. Ku kes i khutun ci cāktun ci āsey yo? — Do you know whether it was large or small?
4. Elma 'na mānh.ess.tun ci kiek i an toyp.nita. — I don't remember how many of them there were.
5. Ku sālam i nwukwu yess.tun ci ic.e pelyess.ey yo. — I have forgotten who he was.
6. Cip ey iss.ess.tun ci ēps.ess.tun ci mul.e posio. — Find out whether he was at home or not.
7. Hānkwuk ey se kaluchyess.tun ci to mōlla yo. — He may have been teaching in Korea (for all I know).

‖ 24.5. Retrospective modifiers + ci in generalized expressions.

11. Na nun musun īl itun ci, caymi ka ēps.umyen, pantusi col.a yo. 'Whatever (thing) it may be, if it's not interesting, I invariably get sleepy.'
12. . . . mues itun ci . . . yelqsim hi hay ya hanta . . . 'Whatever it is . . . I must do it enthusiastically.'
13. . . . nwukwu 'tun ci, kulen kihoy lul hepi haki ka swiwe yo. 'It's easy for anybody (at all) to waste such opportunities.'
15. Musun īl itun ci, . . . sengkong halq cwul al.e yo. 'In any task whatever . . . I feel [he] can succeed.'

INTERROGATIVE words (mues 'what?,' nwukwu 'who?,' ēncey 'when?,' eti 'where?,' meych 'how many?,' elma 'how much?,' musun . . . or enu . . . or etten . . . 'which . . . ? what (kind of] . . ?') also have INDEFINITE meanings:

mues 'something, anything'
nwukwu 'somebody, anybody'
ēncey 'some time, any time'
eti 'somewhere, anywhere'
meych (. . .) 'some [number of] (. . .s), several (. . .s), any (. . .s)'
elma (. . .) 'some [amount of] (. . .)'
musun . . . , enu . . . , etten . . . 'some . . . , any . . . , a certain . . . , certain . . .s.

The words have these indefinite meanings when they are used (1)in statements, rather than in questions, or (2)in yes-or-no questions rather than specific questions that ask for particular information:

Meych chayk i iss.ey yo. 'There are several books (here).'
Nwu' ka wass.ey yo. 'Someone came.'
Ēncey kapsita. 'Let's go some time.'
Eti kapsita. 'Let's go somewhere.'
Mues ul hasikeyss.ey yo? 'Are you going to do something?'
Yenphil i meych kay iss.ey yo? 'Have you got several pencils?'
Elmaq tong-an kongpu hayss.ey yo? 'Did you study for some (amount of) time?'
Etten salam i tose-kwan ey nul ka yo? 'Do some people go to the library all the time?'

Negatives for these words have āmu before the corresponding noun and to after; the resulting phrase is used with a negative verb:

Āmu kes to haci anh.keyss.ey yo. 'I'm not going to do anything.'
Āmu (sālam) to ēps.ey yo. 'There's nobody (here).'
Āmu kos ey to kaci māsio. 'Don't go anywhere!'
Āmu chayk to ilk.ci māsio. 'Don't read any books!'
Koki nun āmu sangcem ey to ēps.ess.ey yo. 'There was no meat at any store.'

As the second example shows, you can abbreviate āmu sālam to to āmu to.

When words of this interrogative-indefinite category are followed by -tun ci (a retrospective modifier + the post-modifier ci), they have a generalized or all-inclusive meaning. The -tun ci adds the meaning '-ever' or 'at all':

mues itun ci 'whatever (it is), no matter what (it is), anything (at all), everything'
nwukwu 'tun ci 'whoever (it is), anybody (at all), everybody'
ēncey otun ci 'whenever [he] comes, any time [he] comes, every time [he] comes'
eti katun ci 'wherever [you] go, anywhere or everywhere [you] go'
musun chayk ul ilk.tun ci 'any book [you] read, whatever book [you] read, no matter what book [you] read'
meych yenphil i iss.tun ci 'no matter how many pencils you have, however many pencils you have'
elmaq tong-an kongpu hatun ci 'no matter how long [= how much time] you study, however much time you study'

Similar expressions are made with words other than interrogative-indefinite words, by using amman at the beginning and infinitive + to at the end, as in Basic Sentence 23:

Amman saynggkak hay to, na nun caycwu ka ēps.nun kes kath.ey yo. 'However hard I think, I seem to have no talents.'

Instead of itun ci (the copula in its retrospective modifier form + ci), the quasi-particle ina can also be used in these constructions, with the same meaning, as in Basic Sentence 19 and 20:

. . . nay an(h)ay nun musun īl ina . . . cal kamtang hay yo. 'My wife handles any task at all . . .'

. . . mues ina . . . cengseng ul tul.ye se hay yo. 'She puts her heart and soul into everything.'

Consecutive itun ci (or ina) phrases of opposite or contrasting meaning are used to mean 'either [x] or [y]':

I kes itun ci, ku kes itun ci, hana capswusio. or
I kes ina, ku kes ina, hana capswusio.
'Have [= Eat] either this one or that one.'

Instead of the copula, other verb forms of opposite meaning can be used:

Sālam i mānh.tun ci cēktun ci sangkwan i ēps.ey yo. or
Sālam i mānh.una cek.una sangkwan i ēps.ey yo.
'It's all right whether there are lots of people or few people.'

But many people prefer to insert the tentative element -ke- to make the TENTATIVE ADVERSATIVE form -kena in these cases of opposite pairs: . . . mānh.kena . . . cēk.kena. (Compare the tentative sequential form -keni, ‖ 24.7.) Follow your teacher's preference.

Here are more examples of these constructions:

1.	Ecey tangsin i mues ul hayss.tun ci, onul un īl ul hay ya hay yo.	No matter what you did yesterday, today you have to work.
2.	Ku sālam i eti lul katun ci kkok ce 'ykey phyēnci lul hay yo.	Wherever he goes, he writes to me without fail.
3.	Elma 'na kellitun ci, na nun sakeyss.ey yo.	I'm going to buy it—regardless of how much it costs.
4.	Ku chayk ul ilk.ko siph.tun ci (ilk.ko siph.ci) anh.tun ci ilk.e ya hay yo.	I have to read that book whether I want to or not.
5.	Kaps i elma 'tun ci sangkwan ēps.ey yo.	It doesn't matter how much it costs.
6.	Tangsin i eti lul katun ci, na to kath.i kakeyss.ey yo.	Wherever you go, I'll go with you.
7.	Ku sālam i wass.tun ci an wass.tun ci sangkwan i ēps.ey yo.	It makes no difference whether he was here [= had come and left] or not.
8.	Āmu kes ina cōh.a yo.	Anything at all will do.
9.	Āmu ttay 'tun ci osio.	Come any time.
10.	Mues itun ci tangsin i kacin kes un tā cōh.a yo.	Whatever you have is all right.
11.	Nwukwu 'na tā osipsio.	Everybody come!
12.	Yenphil lo 'na mānnyen-phil lo 'na, etten kes ulo 'tun ci ssulq swu ka iss.ey yo.	Whether it's (with) a pencil or (with) a pen—no matter what it is (with), I can write with it.

13. Pi ka otun ci an otun ci sangcem ey kakeyss.ey yo. — I'm going to the store, whether it rains or not.
14. Hak.kyo ey kako siph.una an kako siph.una, ka ya hay yo. — I have to go to school, whether I want to or not.
15. Mikwuk ūmsik itun ci Hānkwuk ūmsik itun ci tā cōh.a hay yo. — I like American food, Korean food, any kind of food at all.

You will sometimes find -tun ci in this meaning abbreviated to just -tun: Mikwuk ūmsik itun Hānkwuk ūmsik itun . . Many Korean grammarians prefer to spell "-ten" for any case of -tun other than that of -tun (ci) WITH THE MEANINGS GIVEN IN THIS SECTION. They will write, for instance "ilk.ten sālam" instead of ilk.tun sālam 'the man who was reading,' "Way cam i wass.ten ci mōlla yo" instead of Way cam i wass.tun ci mōlla yo 'I don't know why I got sleepy.'

‖ 24.6. Verbs: retrospective sequential -tuni.

16. . . . hak.kyo ey man kass.tuni, pyel hyōqkwa ka ēps.ey yo. 'just went to school, and now I have nothing special [to show for it].'
17. . . . Ku nun . . . yelqsim ulo Hānkwuk mal ul paywutuni, cikum un . . . khun chai ka iss.ci anh.e yo? 'She studied hard, and now isn't there a big difference?'
29. . . . [1]nōngtam man hayss.tuni, cikum to [1]nōngtam man un cal na wa yo. 'I just made jokes, and now jokes are all that come out.'
30. . . . yeksi . . . toksup hatuni, cikum un . . . elyewum i ēps.nun kes kath.ey yo. 'She kept studying alone, and now she seems to have no difficulties.'

Verbs have a RETROSPECTIVE SEQUENTIAL form, made by attaching the sequential ending -(u)ni (‖ 18.1) to the retrospective base (the base or past base of a verb with the one-shape retrospective marker -tu- attached to it):

	Present Retrospective Seq.	Past Retrospective Seq.
ha- 'do'	hatuni	hayss.tuni
o- 'come'	otuni	wass.tuni
mek- 'eat'	mektuni	mek.ess.tuni

Retrospective sequential forms mean 'does (did), and NOW as an aftermath . . .' Sometimes 'but' is a closer translation than 'and.' (If the final verb of the sentence is past, the retrospective sequential form means 'does (did), and THEN as an aftermath . . .)

Here are more sentences using this form:

1. Pi ka otuni nal i ttattus hay cyess.ey yo. — It's been raining, and now it's turned warm.
2. Ecey nun chwuptuni, onul un tewe yo. — It was cold yesterday, but today it's warm.
3. Kongpu lul hayss.tuni meli ka aph.e yo. — I've been studying and now I've got a headache.
4. Onulq cenyek ey kāngyen i iss.ta ko hay se wass.tuni, [1]nayilq cenyek ey iss.ta ko hay yo. — I heard there was to be a lecture tonight, so I came, and now they tell me it's tomorrow.
5. Cōh.keyss.ta ko sayngkak hayss.tuni, cōh.ass.ey yo. — I thought it would be good, and it was.

6. Cōh.keyss.ta ko sayngkak hayss.tuni, cōh.ci anh.ess.ey yo.	I thought it would be good, but it wasn't.
7. Nwūn i okeyss.ta ko sayngkak hayss.tuni, nwūn i wass.ey yo.	I thought it would snow, and it did.
8. Nwūn i okeyss.ta ko sayngkak hayss.tuni nwūn i an wass.ey yo.	I thought it would snow, but it didn't.
9. Kim sensayng un cikum īl ul hatuni, eti kass.nun ci molukeyss.ey yo.	Mr. Kim was doing some work just now, but I don't know where he's gone.
10. Sangcem ey kass.tuni sakwa ka ēps.e, kyul man sa kaciko wass.ey yo.	When I went to the store they were out of apples so I just bought some oranges.

‖ 24.7. Verbs: tentative sequential -keni.

20. Nay an(h)ay nun wen.lay caycwu to iss.keni wa, mues ina . . . cengseng ul tul.ye se hay yo. 'In addition to my wife's having talents, she puts her soul into everything she does.'

Verbs have a TENTATIVE SEQUENTIAL form, made by attaching the sequential ending -ni to the tentative base: the base plus the one-shape tentative marker -ke-.

This form is often accompanied by the particle wa 'with.' Its meaning is 'together with [the fact that someone] does . . .' or 'for the (probable) reason that so-and-so happens].' It can often be translated 'and' but with the feeling that this means 'in addition to . . .'

Here are more examples:

1. Masikeni mek.keni hay se, tōn ul tā sse pelyess.ey yo.	What with drinking and eating he has spent all his money.
2. Ku haksayng un wūntong to cal hakeni wa, kongpu to cal hay yo.	That student is a fine student as well as being a good athlete.
3. Ku sālam un Pusan ey hyeng i iss.e se kakeni wa, tangsin un way kap.nikka.	He's going because he has a brother in Pusan, but why are you going?
4. Pi to okeni wa phikon hay se, onul ōhwu ey na kaci mōs hakeyss.ey yo.	It's raining, and in addition I'm tired, so I won't go out this afternoon.
5. Ku āy nun caycwu ka mānh.e se nōlmyen se to ku īl ul ppalli machilq swu iss.keni wa, ne nun (kongpu haki ey to him tun tey) ku īl ul ēncey machikeyss.ni.	He has lots of ability and even though he fools around he will be able to get that work done fast, but you (when it's hard even for you to study) when will you get it done?!
6. Ku sālam un tōn to iss.keni wa caycwu to mānh.e yo.	He not only has money, but he has a lot of ability too.

‖ 24.8. Verbs: the projective form -tolok.

14. Kulen īl i ēps.tolok . . . caki lul kyēngkyey hay ya hay yo. 'We have to watch ourselves . . . so that that kind of thing won't happen.'

The one-shape ending -tolok means 'until . . .' or 'to the point that . . .' Combined with a verb expression meaning 'try,' it means 'try TO DO [so-and-so].' Often the adverbative -key 'so that' can be used with much the same meaning.

Here are some more examples:

1. Katolok hay posio.	Try to go.
2. Eceyq pam ey nun nwun i aphutolok kongpu lul hayss.ey yo.	Last night I studied till my eyes ached.
3. Kongpu hako siph.ess.una, cal āltolok kongpu haci mōs hayss.ey yo.	I wanted to study it, but until I understood it thoroughly, I couldn't study it.
4. Yelq si ey copan ul mektolok hay cwusio.	Please prepare my breakfast so that I can eat it at ten o'clock.
5. Nwun mul i na otolok wus.ess.ey yo.	I laughed till the tears ran down my face. (I laughed to the point of tears.)

With the verb tōy yo 'is; becomes,' the projective form has a special meaning: toytolok or toytolok imyen 'as . . . as possible; if possible'

6. [1]Nayil un toytolok ilccik il.e nakcyss.ey yo.	I'm going to get up as early as possible tomorrow morning.
7. Toytolok imyen ilccik osipsio.	Come early if you can.

You may hear some people use an extended form of the projective, for emphasis: -tolok-i. A similar extended form exists for the adverbative: -key-sili. But many people do not use these forms.

The projective, like the adverbative, can be attached to either processive or descriptive verb bases. (An example with a descriptive base is aphutolok in sentence 2 above.) But the copula does not occur with either the projective or the adverbative, i.e. there is no form *itolok 'to the point of its being,' nor is there a form *ikey 'so that it is.' Where you might want to use such forms you substitute the processive verb tōy yo 'becomes,' saying toytolok 'to the point of its becoming' and toykey 'so that it becomes.'

‖ 24.9. Verbs: intentive form -(u)lye and purposive form -(u)le.

7. . . . nwun ul puth.ici anh.ulye ko . . . 'trying to keep my eyes from closing . . .'

The INTENTIVE verb ending -(u)lye is a two-shape ending pronounced -ulye after consonants, -lye after vowels and the extended base of L-extending verbs:

mek- 'eats'	mek.ulye 'intending or desiring to eat'
anc- 'sits'	anc.ulye 'with the intention or desire to sit, ready (willing) to sit'
ka- 'goes'	kalye 'intending or desiring or ready or willing to go'
sā-l- 'lives'	sāllye 'with the intention or desire or willingness to live'

The form is used in sentences followed by the quotation particle ko with some form of ha- 'do/think' after it, to mean such things as: 'intends to [do]; plans or wants to [do]; is going or intending to [do]; is ready or willing to [do]; tries to [do], sets about [do]ing.'

The expression -(u)lye ko ha- is a kind of EXPANDED QUOTATION in form; the simple quotation is -(u)lye ha-, and there is a contracted form -(u)lye '-:

EXPANDED		SIMPLE		CONTRACTED
kalye ko hanta	←	kalye hanta	→	kalye 'nta
		'intends to go'		

Instead of ha-, you may find just -(u)lye (ko) ending a phrase, with the main verb later in the sentence.

There is also a PURPOSIVE form -(u)le, which looks like an abbreviation of -(u)lye; it is used only in phrases that involve GOING or COMING "for the purpose of . . ." You have already met this in cang pole ka yo 'goes to do the marketing' and chac.ule wass.ey yo 'came looking for (you).' Chac.ule wa yo is also used with the same meaning as chac.e wa yo 'comes visiting'; chac.ule ka yo can mean the same thing as chac.e ka yo 'goes visiting.'

1. Han sēk tal te iss.ulye ko hay yo.	I intend [or am prepared] to stay another three months.
2. Kūlim ul pōy tulilye ko hay yo.	I'm going to show you some pictures.
3. [1]Nayil ku chayk ul salye ko hay yo.	I intend to buy that book tomorrow.
4. Cenyek ul mek.ulye ko hayss.ci man, sikan i ēps.e se, mōs mek.ess.ey yo.	I was about to eat my dinner but I couldn't because there was no time.
5. Ne nun hak.kyo ey kkok mues ul paywulye man kanun cwul āni?!	Do you think we're going to school [only with the intention of learning something=] just to learn things?!
6. [1]Nayil achim unhayng ey kalye ko sayngkak hay yo.	I think I'll go to the bank tomorrow morning.
7. Olye ko kulayss.ey yo.	I intended to come.
8. Chayk ul kaciko kalye 'p.nikka?	Are you going to take along a book?
9. Yeses si ey il.e nalye ko hayss.tuni, phikon hay se, yetelq si kkaci cass.ey yo.	I had intended to get up at six o'clock, but I was so tired that I slept till eight.
10. Nay ka palo ku yēyki lul halye 'tun kil iey yo.	I was just going to talk about that.
11. Ce nun Hānkwuk ey kalye ko, cikum Hānkwuk mal ul kongpu hay yo.	I'm learning Korean, with the intention of going to Korea.
12. Kim sensayng ul com mannalye ko wass.ey yo.	I've come to see Mr. Kim.
13. Phyēnci lul ssule wi chung ulo olla kass.ey yo.	He's gone upstairs to write a letter.
14. Cengke-cang ulo chinkwu lul mannale ka ya hay yo.	I have to go to the station to meet a friend.
15. Onul achim Kim sensayng ul chac.e kass.tuni, i chayk ul cwuess.ey yo.	I went to visit Mr. Kim this morning and he gave me this book.

You will often hear these forms as -(u)llye and -(u)lle; they are a common dialect variants. You may also hear -(u)lye (ko) hay to 'even though [one] intends to do' abbreviated to -(u)llay: Kath.i kallay kwaynchanh.e yo? 'I want to go too, if that's all right with you.'

Another way to say 'go to do something,' you will recall, is to use the infinitive followed by the particle se: Sangcem ey ka se mulken ul sa yo 'goes to the store and buys things = goes to the store to buy things.' Compare Mulken ul sale sangcem ey ka yo 'goes to the store (with the purpose) to buy things'; the latter expression does not tell you whether the mission was actually accomplished. The expression ka se sa yo emphasizes the BUYING, the expression sale ka yo emphasizes the GOING. Intentive and purposive forms are made only on PROCESSIVE verb bases; there are no -ulye or -ule forms for descriptive verbs, nor for the copula.

‖ 24.10. Verbs: adjunctive forms -nula and -(u)lla.

Processive verbs have ADJUNCTIVE forms: a processive adjunctive made with the one-shape ending -nula and a prospective adjunctive made with the two-shape ending -(u)lla, which appears as -ulla attached to a consonant base and as -lla attached to a vowel base (including the UNEXTENDED shape of L-extending bases).

BASE	PROCESSIVE ADJUNCTIVE	PROSPECTIVE ADJUNCTIVE
ha- 'do'	hanula	halla
kitali- 'wait'	kitalinula	kitalilla
nō-l- 'play'	nōnula	nōlla
kē-l- 'hang'	kēnula	kēlla
kēl- 'walk'	ket.nula /kēnnula/	kel.ulla
pat- 'receive'	pat.nula /pannula/	pat.ulla
pis- 'comb'	pis.nula /pinnula/	pis.ulla
chac- 'look for'	chac.nula /channula/	chac.ulla
iss- 'stay'	iss.nula /innula/	iss.ulla
cī(s)- 'make'	cīs.nula /cīnnula/	ciulla
noh- 'put'	noh.nula /nonnula/	noh.ulla
tōw- 'help'	tōp.nula /tōmnula/	towulla
ip- 'wear'	ip.nula /imnula/	ip.ulla

Both processive and prospective modifiers typically have the meaning 'what with . . .ing' or 'as a result of . . .ing':

Kongpu hanula, phyēnci lul ssunula, cham puncwu hay yo. or Kongpu halla, phyēnci lul ssulla, cham puncwu hay yo. 'What with studying and writing letters, I'm very busy.'

Adjunctives are often followed by ko, with no change in meaning:

. . . capci wenko ssunula ko, pam nuc.key ca se . . . 'What with writing magazine articles (and all), he stayed up late at night . . .'

Cēmsim mek.nula (ko) nuc.ess.ey yo. 'What with eating lunch and all I was late' = 'Lunch made me late.'

Prospective adjunctives are also used in warnings, to mean 'lest . . .' or 'for fear that [it will happen]':

Pi ka olla wūsan kaciko kake la! 'It may rain—take your umbrella!'

Pyēng nalla ku man mek.e la! 'Stop eating before you get sick!'

Processive adjunctives are sometimes used like intentive forms in -(u)lye:

Phyēnci ssunula ko (= ssulye ko) pam nuc.key cass.ey yo. 'I stayed up late trying to get a letter written.'

Catong-cha lul kochinula ko (= kochilye ko, kochiki ey) āy lul sse yo. 'I'm making an effort to repair the automobile.' = 'I'm trying to get the car fixed.'

‖ 24.11. Modifier + ka pota.

7. . . . mian hay halq ka pwa se . . . 'seemed to be uneasy. . .'

There is an auxiliary descriptive verb pwa yo: it is descriptive because the plain form is pota, not ponta (which is the processive verb 'sees') and it is an auxiliary because it always follows either the familiar question form -na (‖ 22.5) or a modifier + the post-modifier ka 'question.' The meaning of the expression is 'it looks as if' or the like; it is very similar to the expressions made up of modifier + kes kath.ey yo 'it seems, it looks as if' (‖ 17.7) and modifier + mo.yang iey yo 'it appears' (‖ 14.9):

Pi ka {onun ka / ona} pwa yo. Pi ka onun kes kath.ey yo. Pi ka onun mo.yang iey yo.	'It seems to be raining.'
Pi ka otun ka pwa yo. Pi ka otun kes kath.ey yo. Pi ka otun mo.yang iey yo.	'It seems to have been raining.'
Pi ka {wass.nun ka / wass.na} pwa yo. Pi ka on kes kath.ey yo. Pi ka on mo.yang iey yo.	'It seems to have rained.'
Pi ka {olq ka / okeyss.nun ka / okeyss.na} pwa yo. Pi ka olq kes kath.ey yo. Pi ka ol mo.yang iey yo.	'It looks as if it would rain.'
Nal i {cōh.ulq ka / cōh.un ka / cōh.na} pwa yo. Nal i cōh.un kes kath.ey yo. Nal i cōh.un mo.yang iey yo.	'The weather seems to be nice.'

You will recall that the expression -ulq ka hay yo = -ulq ka hanta means 'is thinking of doing,' ‖ 14.5.

Here are some more examples of ka pota:

1. I kes i ku kes pota khulq ka pota.	This one looks (as if it would be) bigger than that one.
2. Kim sensayng in ka pwa yo.	It seems to be Mr. Kim.
3. Talun sālam tul i kani, na to ka polq ka pop.nita.	Since the others are going, I might as well go, too.
4. Nwu' ka wass.na pota.	I think someone's here.
5. Ku cip i i kongwenq yeph ey iss.ess.na pota.	That house seems to have been next to this park.
6. Pakk i chwuwun ka pota.	It seems to be cold out.
7. Appa ka sēng nass.na pota.	Daddy seems to have lost his temper.

You may notice that people often drop the "w" in pwa: p'a /pa/. The sound "w" drops freely after consonants, especially labials (p, pp, ph, m).

‖ 24.12. Prospective modifier + pen hata.

The word pen (often spelled "ppen") is closely tied to the words on either side of it: On the one hand it is a post-modifier that appears only after the prospective modifier -ul(q), on the other hand it is a descriptive verbal noun always followed by the auxiliary descriptive verb hata 'is.' The expression -ulq pen hay yo means 'almost (very nearly) does, barely escapes doing, is on the verge of,' and most often it occurs in the past, with the implication that the thing that 'almost' did or did not happen was avoided at the last minute:

Na nun cwuk.ulq pen hayss.ey yo. 'I thought I'd die.'
Hwā lul nāylq pen hayss.ci yo. 'You see, I almost lost my temper.'
Kalq pen hayss.ey yo. 'He came very near to going.' or 'It's a wonder that he didn't go.'
Mōs kalq pen hayss.ey yo. 'He very nearly didn't go.' or 'The wonder is that he went at all.'

A word with grammar much like that of pen is man 'worth (doing)'; it too is tied to a preceding prospective modifier -ul and at the same time it is a descriptive verbal noun tied to the following hata. An example is pol man hay yo 'is worth seeing'; more examples will be found in ‖ 27.7. You will find the grammar of (l)ak hata (‖ 28.4) similar, too.

‖ 24.13. Habitual actions: -ko nun hanta.

7. . . . āy lul ssuko nun hayss.ci man . . . cam i oko nun hayss.ey yo. '. . . I used to try . . . but I would fall asleep.'

To talk about actions that are habitual or regularly performed you use an expression that consists of the gerund -ko + the particle nun (often abbreviated to n') followed by the auxiliary processive verb hanta 'does.' What you get is a sentence that can be translated into English by such expressions as '[does] from time to time' or 'sometimes [does]' or 'makes a habit or practice of [doing]' or 'keeps (repeatedly) doing.' In the past tense 'used to [do]' or 'would [do] (as a regular thing)' are the normal translations.

Here are some more examples:

1. Sānqpo kako nun hay yo.	I sometimes go for walks.
2. Kongwen ey ka se nōlko n' hayss.ey yo.	We used to go to the park and play.
3. Sensayng hako ˡnōngtam ul hako nun hayss.ey yo.	We would joke with the teacher (on occasion).
4. Molunun sālam poko insa hako nun haci anh.ci yo.	I don't make a practice of greeting people I don't know, you see.
5. Molunun sālam poko insa haci anh.ko nun haci yo.	I make a practice of never greeting people I don't know, you see.
6. Wuli ka ilcciki cako n' hayss.ey yo.	We used to go to bed early. (or We would go to bed early.)
7. Wuli ka ilcciki caci anh.ko n' hayss.ey yo.	We never used to go to bed early. (or We would never go to bed early. or We made it a practice not to go to bed early.)
8. Wuli ka ilcciki cako n' haci anh.ess.ey yo.	We didn't use to go to bed early. (or We wouldn't go to bed early. or We didn't make it a practice to go to bed early.)

9. Sikol ey ka se sālmyen ilccik-i cako n' hakeyss.ci yo.	When you go to the country to live I guess you'll make it a practice to go to bed early.
10. Sikol ey se sālko iss.ess.tula 'myen ilcciki cako n' hayss.ulq ke 'ci yo.	If we'd been living in the country I guess we'd have made a practice of going to bed early.

‖ 24.14. The particle khenyeng.

31. Na nun Hānkwuk mal lo yēnsel un khenyeng . . . 'Me, far from speeches in Korean . . .'

The particle khenyeng, following nouns, means 'far from [being or doing the noun]' or 'let alone [that noun].' When you want to use a verb in such an expression, you first have to turn it into a noun by using the nominative (-ki) form. The particle is optionally preceded by un/nun, the topic particle, with no change in meaning.

More examples:

1. Na nun cip khenyeng, calq pang to ēps.ey yo.	Far from a house, I haven't got a room to sleep in.
2. Chayk i mānh.ki (nun) khenyeng, twū kwen pakk-ey ēps.ey yo.	Far from having lots of books, I've only got two.
3. Ttek (un) khenyeng pap to ēps.ess.ey yo.	Cake? We didn't even have rice. [= Far from cake, there wasn't even rice.]
4. Sip-wen khenyeng (to) sip-cen to mōs pat.keyss.ey yo.	Ten wen?! Why, we won't even get ten cen.
5. Sip-wen khenyeng payk-wen ila to pat.keyss.ey yo.	Ten wen?! Why, we'll get all of a hundred wen!

‖ 24.15. The particle mankhum.

8. . . . nwu' ka na mankhum nul col.ass.nun ci āsey yo. 'Do you know anyone who was as sleepy as I was?'

The particle mankhum after a noun means 'as much as [that noun]' or 'equal to [that noun].'

Here are some more examples:

1. Onul to ecey mankhum sikan i iss.ey yo.	I have as much time today as I had yesterday. [= Today also, as much as yesterday, there is time.]
2. Onul un ecey mankhum sikan i ēps.ey yo.	I haven't got as much time today as I had yesterday. [= Today, as much as yesterday, there isn't time.]
3. Ne to ku sālam mankhum halq swu iss.ta.	You can do as well as he can. [= You too, as much as that person, are capable.]
4. I kes to ku kes mankhum cōh.a yo.	This one is as good as that one.
5. Na nun ce sālam mankhum mōs ca yo.	I don't sleep as much as he does.
6. Kaul nal un pom nal mankhum an ttattus hay yo.	Fall days aren't as warm as spring days.

You may run across a variant form of this particle with the shape manchi.

‖ 24.16. Expressing afterthoughts.

22. . . . na kath.un namphyen ul kacin "yeca nun pulhayng hako yo. 'And . . . a woman having a husband like me is unfortunate.'

Koreans, like other people, don't always think ahead and organize what they are going to say. Most of the sentences in this book are well organized with the parts where a Korean would feel they ought to go if he stopped to think about it; the verb, for example, always comes at the end. But in unguarded speech, people will often blurt out the verb (or some larger part of the sentence), and then—as an AFTERTHOUGHT—add one or more of the phrases that they should have put in earlier: Pelsse wass.na yo?—son nim tul i. 'Are they already here—the guests?' Kāy ka mekess.ta 'na yo?—ku koki lul. 'You say the dog ate it—that meat?'

As you have learned, a sentence whose final verb is turned into a gerund -ko 'and . . .' is normally put BEFORE some other sentence it joins to make a compound sentence. But as an afterthought you can add the gerund-ending sentence after you have said the other sentence. The afterthought sentence will have the normal intonation (statement, question, command, etc.) you would expect of it if it were an ordinary sentence, and if you are talking polite style you will add the particle yo.

Here are some more examples of these "afterthought sentences":

1. Phyo nun eti se sa yo.—Tto kaps un elma 'ko yo.	Where do we buy the tickets?—And how much are they?
2. Pipimq pap un ili cwusey yo.—[l]Nayngmyen un celi tulisiko yo.	The mixed rice here, please, waiter—and the cold noodles there, please.
3. Ka (se) cwumusey yo. Na ttaymun ey caci anh.ko kitalici māsiko yo.	Go to bed; don't wait up for me.
4. I kes un tangsin uy moca 'ko, ce kes un tangsin uy chayk iko yo.	This is your hat, and that is your book.
5. I pun un nwukwu 'ko, ce pun un nwukwu 'ko yo.	Who is this person and who is that one over there?

The last two examples are somewhat different from the others in that neither part of the sentence is given in the expected "final" form.

Do not confuse this use of sentence-final gerund -ko (+ yo) to express afterthoughts with the sentence-final particle ko (+ yo) to report hearsay, ‖ 23.8.

EXERCISES

I

The following items are retrospective conditional clauses: unfinished 'if' sentences. Make up a reasonable completion for each; say the whole sentence aloud, then translate.

1. Say cip ul ciess.tumyen . . .
2. Cip aph path ey nun kkoch ul sim.ess.tumyen . . .
3. Ecey ku sangcem ey kass.tumyen . . .
4. Ecey cenyek ey nun ilcciki cass.tula 'myen . . .
5. Onul achim hak.kyo ey nuc.key oci anh.ess.tumyen . . .
6. Īl haki cen ey com swiess.tumyen . . .

7. Ecey nal i ttattus hayss.tula 'myen . . .
8. Nemu pissaci anh.un mulken ul sass.tumyen . . .
9. Cey kwutwu lul takk.e cwusyess.tula 'myen . . .
10. I moca lul saki cen ey sse pwass.tumyen . . .
11. Kim puin i onul ōhwu ey sangcem ey kaci mālca ko hayss.tumyen . . .
12. Cākci anh.ko, khess.tumyen . . .

II

This exercise is the reverse of the preceding one. The completions for retrospective conditional sentences are given; you are to supply the condition, and translate. For example, if the given portion were . . . te cōh.ass.keyss.ey yo, you might supply the clause Kongpu hayss.tumyen . . . or Kongpu hayss.tula 'myen . . . 'I wish I had studied' [= If I had studied, it would have been better].

1. . . . hēn catong-cha lul phal.usyess.keyss.ey yo.
2. . . . cenyek ul ilcciki mek.ess.keyss.ey yo.
3. . . . sangkwan ēps.ess.keyss.ci yo.
4. . . . cēncha lul thako wass.keyss.ey yo.
5. . . . kwūkyeng ul kass.keyss.ey yo.
6. . . . com te ttattus hayss.keyss.ey yo.
7. . . . cikum un Hānkwuk mal cal halq cwul al.ess.keyss.ci yo.
8. . . . emeni hanthey chayk ul sa kaciko wass.keyss.ey yo.
9. . . . sikol ey sal.ess.keyss.ci yo.
10. . . . kongwen ey se sānqpo lul hayss.keyss.ey yo.
11. . . . sensayng i kol ul nāyci anh.ess.keyss.ci yo.

III

Translate the following sentences into Korean.

1. He may not have slept at all last night, for all I know.
2. Is the concert tonight just for students?—No; anybody can go.
3. Yesterday I walked till [= to the point that] my feet got sore.
4. I brought along pencils and paper with the intention of writing an article.
5. I've got to find my watch, wherever it is.
6. What with taking my watch to be repaired and buying things for the picnic, I've had a lot to do this morning.
7. Do you remember whether or not you have been vaccinated for smallpox?
8. Drive as fast as possible, so we'll get to the hospital before the doctor leaves.
9. We intended to go to Wui Tong while the cherry trees are in bloom.
10. It looks as if Pok.nam and Tekswu are making a snow man.
11. It isn't even cold outside—much less snowing.
12. It isn't as cold today as it was yesterday.
13. Did you notice, is Hongsik as tall as his older sister?
14. When I was a child, we often used to have picnics at the zoo.
15. Just give a little speech: it doesn't matter what you say.
16. It was so cold I nearly died!
17. Send this letter to Mr. Pak. And this one to Mr. Kim.
18. What with visiting my friend, going to look at the new pictures in the art gallery, and going shopping in the stores, I was so busy I almost missed my bus.

19. We have to have a person who knows English in addition to knowing Japanese well.
20. I don't care whether I graduate this year or next year.
21. Mine is as big as yours, I bet.
22. You ought to make it a practice to do your homework before you eat your dinner.
23. Mrs. Yun never used to come to our meetings; I wonder how come she attends regularly now.
24. We used to have a good time, what with making snow men, building snow houses, and making ice cream out of the snow.
25. We always try to keep the radio low when the children are studying.

CONVERSATION

I

Carry on a conversation in Korean with A taking the role of a student and B acting as his conscience. B asks A whether he is satisfied with the work he has done this year in school; A is not. B probes: he asks why A didn't work harder; why he was always sleepy in class; how he did on his tests, and whether he knows how he might have done better; whether it annoyed him to be in the same class with that smart lady who studied so hard; whether he would do better if he had a second chance. Student A should answer all the questions fully, and add some comments at the end if he cares to.

II

Make up a monologue (five or ten minutes long) to present in class, all about the frustrations of your school days. If you had no frustrations, make some up, or borrow some from your friends. It doesn't matter whether it was grade school, high school, or college; tell about your shortcomings and compare yourself with more industrious (and more virtuous) friends or relatives. Prepare your talk carefully, and practice saying the things you want to include; but DON'T WRITE ANY KOREAN SENTENCES DOWN. Instead, jot down notes in English to outline your speech for you and remind you of what you want to say. Prepare your Korean sentences orally. If you have to look up a word, jot it down, but try to memorize it before you give your talk.

VOCABULARY DRILL

Make up a single Korean sentence which uses all three expressions of each of the following groups (not necessarily in the order given). For example, if the given words in one group were cal, cikum, and kongpu, you might make up a sentence Kongpu lul yelqsim hi hayss.uni, cikum un yēnsel ul Hānkwuk mal lo halq swu iss.ey yo. 'He studied hard, and now he can give speeches in Korean.' Use the verbs in any form you like—gerund, modifier, intentive, etc. etc.

1. amman
   chōngkak
   kyelhon
2. cam
   haphum
   pantusi
3. cāng.lye
   kamtang
   wen.lay
4. caycwu
   pāntay lo
   sallim

5. caymi ēps.ta
   kyenghem
   nwun ul put.hye yo

6. cengseng
   kkaytal.e yo
   wenko

7. chai
   munqpep
   tāychey

8. col.a yo
   hepi
   mankhum

9. elyewum
   sangkwan
   toksup

10. hāyngpok
    pulhayng
    sanay

11. hyōqkwa
    sāsil
    tā-man

12. kāngyen
    kyēysok
    kihoy

13. kyēngkyey
    nolyek
    silphay

14. [1]nōngtam
    nol.a yo
    sēng (i) na yo

15. hwā (lul) nāy yo
    nuc.e yo
    tol.a wa yo

COMPREHENSION

Let your Korean teacher talk to you about a student he knows (or once knew). Listen attentively while he tells you what sort of habits this student had and how he changed (or should have changed, or shouldn't have changed) during the course of a few years; and what has become of him now.

Afterwards, your teacher will ask you a series of questions about his story. Write each of your answers down and be prepared to read them aloud and discuss or enlarge on them orally, when called upon to do so.

LESSON 25. REVIEW

I. VOCABULARY REVIEW

Each of the following sentences contains a blank, and has a list of words below it. Choose all the words from the list which make sense inserted into the blank; read the sentence aloud for each completion, and translate. Give the meaning of each word you discard.

1. Onul un hak.kyo ey ___ iss.uni, kkok osipsio.
   cangnan
   panul
   phal-mok
   wēn.yu-hoy
   yēnsel

2. ___ ey katolok hay posipsio.
   salang
   swuch
   swusen-so
   tokpon
   yuchi-wen

3. Yo say nun ___ eti se 'tun ci salq swu ka iss.ey yo.
   cāngkap
   cēy pal
   kwuksan-phum
   kyēngcong
   sēykyey

4. Ku sālam un pam itun ci nac itun ci sangkwan ēps.ko, pam-nac ___.
   col.a yo
   kyēysok hay yo
   nolyek hay yo
   sakwie yo
   wul.e yo

5. [1]Nayil achim ___ ey kallye ko sayngkak hay yo.
   cēntang-pho
   ōykwuk
   tōngmul-wen
   [1]yehayng
   [1]yengsa-kwan

6. Kim sensayng i ___ cwul ul āp.nikka?
   cal kamtang halq
   cemmyeng halq
   maum ey tulq
   sengkong halq
   thongyek halq

7. Ku cēnki sikyey ka ___ ka pwa yo.
   cēnghwak halq
   hēn
   olh.ulq
   sililq
   twungkule'n

II. GRAMMAR REVIEW

Build an imaginative and interesting Korean sentence around each of the following words or phrases. Use each phrase precisely as it is given. Let the student next to you translate it, and correct him if he is wrong. Take turns going around the class.

1. pyēnkyeng han ci
2. pū-hoycang pota
3. phyen.li han ci al.e yo?

4. sangkwan i ēps.ess.keyss.ey yo.
5. kanun kil ey
6. kyēysok hayss.nun tey
7. olq key yo
8. sōngpyel-hoy lul hayss.^{s}uptikka?
9. hayss.nun ci āp.nikka?
10. cīnan pen sēnke
11. sako siph.tun sikyey
12. pole kass.tun cang
13. tōngmul mankhum
14. kiek han ci
15. pulhayng haki nun haci man
16. tokpon ōy-ey
17. ic.e pelyess.ey yo
18. ^{l}yehayng ul hayss.tumyen
19. kōcang i nal.nun ci
20. cakkwu kwūllyess.tun ci
21. sa olq ci to mōlla yo
22. mues ina
23. kongsa 'la 'p.nita
24. hanun ci āp.nikka?
25. kako siph.ci anh.tula ko yo
26. silin tey yo
27. i pen kāngyen-hoy
28. toksup hanun tey
29. etteh.key cōnun ci
30. tōnguy lul han ci ka
31. kyelqsek hayss.tun ka yo?
32. sengkong hayss.nun ci silphay hayss.nun ci
33. olh.ki nun haci man
34. cēy-il hēn kes ila ko
35. Il-yoil ila to
36. sikhilye ko hani
37. ēncey 'na
38. chakeyss.nun tey
39. nwukwu lul mannass.tun ci
40. kalq kyem
41. iss.nun ci ēps.nun ci
42. elmaq tong-an ina
43. kaps ssan sikyey pota
44. kass.tun kil ey
45. talun kes pota com khess.tuni
46. ēps.keni wa
47. nwukwu 'tun ci
48. ma(y)ntullye ko
49. hakeyss.nun ci āp.nikka?
50. hōycang un khenyeng
51. halq pen hayss.ey yo
52. iss.nun ci al.e yo?
53. hako siph.ci anh.un ci
54. hayss.tun ci moluci yo
55. hatolok
56. cēy-il
57. tol.a kaci anh.ess.tumyen
58. nwun ul puth.ici anh.ess.tun haksayng
59. kalq key yo
60. ma(y)ntulq kyem
61. ^{n}yeca lul silh.e hatun chōngkak
62. ssess.tun kwumen yo
63. anh.tolok
64. cham.ess.tun kes kath.ey yo
65. sa kaciko wass.tumyen
66. tanilye ko
67. hakeni wa
68. pulphyen han tey yo
69. mek.ko siph.tun ci anh.tun ci
70. hayss.tun ci kiek hap.nikka?
71. eti 'tun ci
72. seykyey ^{l}yehayng ul hayss.keyss.ey yo
73. pec kkoch pakk-ey
74. chwulqsek hayss.^{s}uptikka?
75. kwūkyeng sikhikeyss.nun tey

III. SENTENCE REVIEW

Here is a lesson-by-lesson reprise of what you have learned in Lesson 21–24. Express the following items in Korean (not necessarily verbatim), as directed.

Lesson 21

1. Tell Mrs. Kim that
   a. the president of the women's club said next year's picnic would be at the zoo.
   b. the secretary forgot to change the date of this year's picnic.
   c. it positively will not rain on the day you are going to see the famous cherry blossoms.

2. Ask Mrs. Kim whether
   a. she remembers about how large your guest room is.
   b. how long it has been since she was a committee member.
   c. whether she has done any interpreting lately.
3. Suggest to Mrs. Kim
   a. that you and she take a trip around the world together.
   b. how nice it would be to get acquainted with some new friends.
   c. that the two of you visit the wife of the American consul.

Lesson 22

4. Ask Tekswu
   a. whether his hands aren't cold without any gloves.
   b. whether he ought to laugh or cry if someone calls his father Goggle-Eyes or Fatso.
   c. if he'll let you borrow his hat, since your head is so cold.
5. Tell Hongsik
   a. to wait here while you go get a few pieces of charcoal to make the snow man some eyes and nose and mouth.
   b. to call Pok.nam over to help you make your snow man.
   c. if his eyes are watering from the cold, just to put up with it.
6. Suggest to Pok.nam
   a. that he roll up two balls of snow, a big one for the body and a smaller one for the head.
   b. that he stick the ears on the snow man's head.
   c. that you and he make a snow man that looks just like a human being.

Lesson 23

7. Ask your wife (husband)
   a. whether (s)he was able to find you a good watch at the pawn shop.
   b. how come so many people are pawning their valuables these days.
   c. what to do when your watch keeps stopping all the time.
8. Tell a friend of yours
   a. that your new watch is a 17-jewel Swiss watch, whereas your old one was just a cheap native product.
   b. that you don't care whether you have a pocket watch or a wrist watch, just so it runs all right—not fast or slow.
   c. that you took your watch to a repair shop last Tuesday and are supposed to pick it up this afternoon.
9. Suggest to a prospective watch buyer
   a. that if he gets a foreign-make watch, he may have a lot of problems getting parts for it.
   b. that since his son is the only one among his friends who has no watch, he should buy this old one of yours.
   c. that perhaps it would be better if he bought an electric clock instead.

Lesson 24

10. Tell your students
   a. that if they don't settle down and study, they'll never become fluent in Korean.

b. that if they keep on yawning and falling asleep in class, they're going to fail.
c. that whatever they do, they should do it with enthusiasm when they have the chance.

11. Ask your students
a. why they don't study harder, like that talented student over there.
b. if they don't think they should guard themselves against joking all the time in class.
c. to put their whole heart and soul into every task that is assigned to them.

12. Assure your teacher
a. that you feel very fortunate to have such a fine teacher.
b. that you would feel very unlucky if you had a teacher who knew as little as you know.
c. that your maternal grandfather was quite a scholar and that you intend to follow in his footsteps.

IV. TEST

Translate the following 25 Korean sentences into English. Make the English as natural as possible; but if it differs radically from the Korean, you should enclose in parentheses after the translation a more literal rendition which reveals the structure of the Korean sentence.

1. Cōh.un kes ul cōh.a hako, nappun kes ul silh.e hanun kes un nwukwu 'na tā kath.ey yo.
2. Onul achim Kim sensayng ul mannass.ul ttay nun pelsse talun pun kwa yēyki hako kyēysiptita.
3. Nay ka Pak puin polye kal ttay mata, Kim puin to iss.ko nun hay yo.
4. Ku sālam i wuli hako kath.i ˡnayil tōngmul-wen ey kana mul.e posio.
5. Cenyek cikum sikhilq swu iss.ulq ka yo?
6. Sewul ey se on ci ka han sahul pakk-ey an tōyss.ey yo.
7. Phyēnci wass.na com ka posio.
8. Cak.nyen ey nun elyewun īl to hayss.tuni kumnyen un halq swu ka ēps.ey yo.
9. Mikwuk ūmsik itun ci Hānkwuk ūmsik itun ci etten ūmsik itun ci na nun tā cōh.a hay yo.
10. Ecey ilkess.tun capci wenko lul acik kkaci machici mōs hayss.ey yo.
11. Eceyq pam ey wuli cip ey se cwumusyess.tumyen cōh.ass.keyss.ey yo.
12. Kwutwu lul takk.e cwuess.tun ci kiek i an toyp.nita.
13. Ku sālam i onta ko hatuni, an wass.ci yo.
14. Onulq cenyek yūmyeng han hakca ka yēnsel ul hanta ko hay se, wass.tuni, ˡnayilq cenyek ila ko hay yo.
15. Kim sensayng ul il-chen kwu-payk sā-sip nyen ey mannatun ci il-chen kwu-payk sā-sip il-nyen ey mannatun ci ic.e pelyess.ey yo.
16. Ku pōsek-sang ey se nun etten sikyey swusen ina tā halq swu iss.tula ko yo.
17. Aphuta ko hasituni, hak.kyo ey wass.ˢuptita.
18. Ku kongsa nun caycwu iss.keni wa, tōn to mānh.e yo.
19. Na nun kongwen ey nun khenyeng, cang ey to kalq sikan ēps.keyss.ey yo.
20. Ceki ce haphum hanun sālam mankhum na nun cōl.ci anh.e yo.
21. Yenphil lo 'na mānnyen-phil lo 'na, etten kes ulo 'tun ci ssulq swu ka iss.ey yo.
22. Ku tōn ulo catong-cha lul sakeyss.ta ko sayngkak hayss.tuni, pelsse tōn ul tā hepi hayss.ey yo.

23. Sangcem ey kanula, tāyhak ey se kaluchinula, cham phikon hay yo.
24. Kyēngcong i khuna cak.una sangkwan ēps.ey yo.
25. Eti katun ci ai tul i nōnun kes kwūkyeng haki ka caymi iss.ci yo.

V. SPEAKING PRACTICE

A

A is your Korean teacher pretending for the moment (as usual, we hope!) that he knows no English. B is an American, newly arrived in Korea, pretending that he knows no Korean. C takes the role of interpreter between the two. B tells why he is here and how long ago he came, and amenities follow, with the Korean speaker asking about the journey, where B is staying, etc. Then B wants to find out something about the city, and asks questions for C to interpret; C must also interpret the replies. A, the Korean teacher, should step out of his role only to correct C.

After a while, switch the B and C roles around. B should keep C on his toes and cover a wide variety of subjects. If C is unable to handle some subjects, switch to others.

B

In a monologue, explain in detail to a child how to make a snow man.

C

Deliver a monologue about the virtues of your husband or wife (or what you will expect of this person when the time comes).

D

A, a parent, asks B, a child, what he did all day; the child says he played in the snow, ard made a snow man. A asks with whom, then asks specific questions about how they made the various parts of the snow man, whether they got cold while they were playing, etc., etc.

Reverse the roles, so that you each have a chance to practice the speech of an adult to a child.

E

Your group is holding a meeting to decide on the details of the spring party. Select a chairman, and someone to keep minutes. Decide what sort of party to have, and where and when to have it; who is to bring what; transportation; entertainment; when to disband—all the details. Conduct the meeting in a businesslike way.

This need not be a fictitious party, of course; if it is actually to come about, you will be able to judge whether there is any need to reiterate the plans in English.

LESSON 26. A VISIT TO SONGTO

BASIC SENTENCES

[A is showing B around Songto]

	Korean	English	Amplification
A. 1.	Yeki se Sencwuk-kyo ka pōy yo.	From here Sencwuk Bridge can be seen.	pōy yo [pōy-] or po.ye yo [poi-] 'is visible, can be seen; shows it'
2.	Ce cak.un cip aph ey pōynun tali ka Sencwuk-kyo 'ey yo. Pōy yo?	The bridge which is (to be seen) in front of that little building over there is Sencwuk Bridge. Can you see it?	tali 'bridge' -kyo '. . . bridge' Sencwuk-kyo 'Sencwuk Bridge'
B. 3.	Cenyek ānkay ey ssāy se cal an poinun kwun yo. Ānkyeng ul ssuko pwa ya hakeyss.kwun yo.	It's enveloped in the evening fog so that I can't see it well, I find. I'll have to look [using or wearing=] with my glasses.	ānkay 'fog, mist' ssa yo 'wraps up, envelops' ssāy yo [ssāy-] or ssa.ye yo [ssai-] 'gets wrapped, enveloped'
4.	A! Cēki pōynun kwun yo. Kēli ka mel.e se kulen ci (—) yeki se poni-kka n', ku tali ka phek cāk.key pōyp.nita.	Ah—there I see it! Maybe it's that it's such a distance, but seen from here the bridge looks quite small.	kēli 'distance, farness' mel.e se kulen ci (to mōlla yo) 'maybe it's that way because it is distant' phek 'very, quite'
5.	Silmul to kwā.yen kuleh.key cak.un ka yo?	Is the real thing actually that small?	silmul 'real thing, actual object' kwā.yen 'sure enough, actually, in reality'
A. 6.	Nēy. Kuleh.ci man, Sencwuk-kyo lul kinyem hanun ^{l}īyu nun olay cen ey i tali wi ey se il.e nan ^{l}yeksa-cek sāsil ey iss.ey yo.	Yes. However, the reason for remembering Sencwuk Bridge lies ['is'] in historical facts that happened on this bridge a long time ago.	kinyem hay yo 'commemorates, remembers, celebrates' [often mispronounced /kilyem/] ^{l}īyu 'reason, cause' il.e na yo 'happens, occurs' [also 'gets up'] ^{l}yeksa 'history' ^{l}yeksa-cek 'historic(al)' sāsil 'fact'
7.	Cikum ulo puthe han il-chen nyen cen ey, Hānkwuk un Kolye 'la ko pulless.ey yo.	About a thousand years ago (from now), Korea was called Kolye. Songto was the capital	Kolye [old name of Korea] Songto [a city in old Korea, near modern Kayseng] swuto 'capital (city)'

Korean	English	Amplification
Songto ka palo ku ttay swuto yess.ci yo.	right at that time, you see.	
8. Kolye mal uy chwungsin Ceng Mongcwu sensayng i ku tali wi ey se chamsal ul tang hayss.ci yo.	Mr. Ceng Mongcwu, a faithful subject of the last days of Kolye, was murdered on this bridge.	mal = kkuth 'end' Kolye mal 'final days (end) of Kolye' chwungsin 'faithful subject' chamsal 'murder, assassination' chamsal ul tang hay yo 'get murdered, undergoes murder'
9. Ku ttay ka cikum puthe han 'yuk-payk nyen cen ip.nita.	That (time) was about 600 years ago (from now).	
B.10. Ceng Mongcwu sensayng ila 'ni Phoun māl-ssum ici yo?	By Ceng Mongcwu, I wonder if you mean Phoun?	C.M. ila 'ni = C.M. ila (ko) hani 'when you say C.M.' . . . māl(-ssum) iey yo '[one] means . . .'
A.11. Nēy. Phoun un ku uy ho 'ci yo.	Yes, you see Phoun is his pen name.	ho 'pseudonym, pen name'
B.12. Ku tali ka ama tōl tali 'n ka pwa yo.	The bridge looks as though it were (probably) a stone bridge.	tōl 'stone' tali (i)n ka pwa yo 'looks as if it is a bridge'
A.13. Kuleh.ci yo. Ce māycem ey se kūlimq yepse to phanun kwun yo.	Yes, it is. Oh, they've got picture postcards (among other things) for sale at that shop over there.	māycem 'store, shop' yepse 'post card' kūlimq yepse 'picture postcard'
14. Keki Sencwuk-kyo kūlim i iss.ulq kes kath.sup.nita.	[It seems that they would have=] They ought to have a picture of Sencwuk Bridge there.	
15. Kūlimq yepse uy Sencwuk-kyo lul pōy tulici yo.	Suppose I show you Sencwuk Bridge on a picture postcard.	pōy tulye yo 'shows [to someone esteemed]'
16. Yeki Sencwuk-kyo kūlim i iss.kwun yo. Somun ey pi hay se silmul un cham mal lo pin.yak haci yo??	Here's a picture of Sencwuk Bridge! Compared with what you've heard, the real thing is really insignificant, isn't it.	somun 'rumored thing, hearsay' pi hay yo 'compares' . . . ey pi hay se 'compared with <u>or</u> to . . .' cham mal 'true word, real word' cham mal lo 'in truth, actually, in reality'

Korean	English	Amplification
	right at that time, you see.	pin.yak hay yo 'is meager, insignificant'
B.17. Kōcek tul un keuy tā kuleh.ci anh.sup.nikka?	Aren't almost all historic spots like that?	kōcek 'historic remains, (= kōcek-ci) historic(al) spot' keuy /kei/ 'almost, nearly'
18. Kulen tey, i tali wi ey pulk.un cem un mwe 'p.nikka.	By the way, what is that red spot on the bridge?	pulk.e yo [pulk-] 'is red' cem 'spot, dot, point' m(w)e 'p.nikka = mues ip.nikka
A.19. Cēnsel ey uy hamyen ku kes i Ceng Mongcwu sensayng uy phi 'ci yo.	Why, according to tradition, that's the blood of Ceng Mongcwu.	cēnsel 'tradition' . . . ey uy hamyen '(if we rely on=) according to'
20. Chwunguy uy phi 'la ēps.e cici anh.ko ēncey 'na ku cali ey nam.e iss.ta ko haci yo.	They say since it is (called) the blood of loyalty, it remains in that place forever without disappearing.	chwunguy /chwungi/ 'loyalty' ēps.e cye yo 'disappears, becomes nonexistent' cali 'place, spot' nam.e yo [nam-] 'remains, stays, is left (over)'
B.21. Way i tali wi ey se cwuk.ess.na yo.	Why did he die on this bridge?	cwuk.e yo [cwuk-] 'dies'
A.22. Āmsal iey yo. Ī Thayco ka Kolye uy wang ul ēps.ayko caki ka wang i toylye ko, kac.un kkoy lul ssutun ttay Phoun i cangay ka toym ulo sālam ul sikhye se āmsal ul hayss.ci yo.	It was an assassination. At the time when Lee Thayco was applying his wiles with the idea of eliminating the king and becoming king himself, Phoun got in the way, so he [Lee Thayco] had someone assassinate him.	āmsal 'assassination' āmsal (ul) hay yo 'assassinates' Ī Thayco [founder of the Lee (or Yi) Dynasty] wang 'king' ēps.ay yo [ēps.ay-] 'makes nonexistent, eliminates, exterminates, gets rid of' kkoy 'wiles, craft' kac.un (<u>or</u> kacin) . . . 'all sorts of . . . , complete . . . , perfect . . .' kac.un kkoy lul (tā) sse yo [ssu-] '[uses all sorts of wiles=] strains one's wits, taxes one's ingenuity' cangay 'obstacle' cangay ka tōy yo '(becomes=) is an obstacle, gets in the way'

Korean	English	Amplification
		cangay ka toym ulo 'because of the fact that it gets in the way'
23. Phoun i chwul.ip hal ttay 'myen, i tali wi lul cīnako n' hayss.ta ko hay yo.	When Phoun came and went, he used to pass over this bridge, they say.	chwul.ip hay yo 'goes back and forth, comes and goes, enters and leaves' cīna yo 'passes' cīnako n(un) hay yo 'customarily passes'
24. Ku uy cip i i tali kūnche ey iss.ess.na pwa yo.	His house seems to have been in the vicinity of this bridge.	kūnche 'vicinity, neighborhood' iss.ess.na pwa yo 'looks as if it was, seems to have been'
25. Ku nal to pam nuc.key cip ey tol.a otun kil ey i tali mith cy oc sālam i na wa se cwuk.ess.ta ko hay yo.	On that very day, when he was returning home late at night, a man came out from under the bridge and killed him, they say.	cwuk.ye yo [cwuk.i-] 'kills'
B.26. Kulen tey, Sencwuk-kyo 'la 'ni, musun ttus ip.nikka. Tay namu lo ma(y)ntun tali nun ani 'ci yo??	Well, what do they mean calling it Sencwuk Bridge? It's not a bridge made of bamboo, is it?	sencwuk 'fine (good, noble) bamboo' ttus 'meaning, significance' musun ttus iey yo 'what does it mean?' tay 'bamboo' tay namu 'bamboo tree; bamboo wood'
A.27. Ilq-sel ey uy hamyen, Phoun i cwukca mā'ca ku cali ey tay han cwu ka nass.ta ko hay se, Sencwuk-kyo 'la ko hanta ko hay yo.	According to one version, (it is said that) no sooner had Phoun died than a bamboo appeared on the spot, so they call it Sencwuk Bridge.	sel 'version, story; (= haksel) theory' cwukca mā'ca 'as soon as [one] dies' cwu '(root=) counter for rooted plants' tay han cwu 'one bamboo'
28. Sencwuk-kyo uy "Sen"q ca nun chak hata, cōh.ta 'nun ttus iko, "Cwuk" ca nun tay namu 'la 'nun ttus iey yo.	The (written) character 'Sen' in Sencwuk Bridge means 'is noble' and the character 'Cwuk' means 'bamboo tree.'	ca '(written) character' chak hay yo 'is good, virtuous, noble' cōh.ta 'nun ttus iey yo [= cōh.ta (ko) hanun ttus iey yo] 'means <u>cōh.ta</u>'
29. Ama chak han tay namu ka nan tali 'la 'nun ttus in ka pwa yo.	It seems to mean 'a bridge where a noble bamboo tree arose.'	. . . ttus in ka pwa yo 'it seems to mean . . .'

Korean	English	Amplification
30. Hānkwuk ey nun caylay lo chwunguy wa tay namu wa kiph.un kwankyey ka iss.ci yo.	In Korea there has always been a deep relationship between loyalty and the bamboo tree, you see.	caylay uy . . . 'conventional, usual' caylay lo 'conventionally = always' chwunguy 'loyalty, faithfulness' kwankyey 'relation(ship)'
31. Kwup.hici anh.nun chwunguy uy cengsin ul kkos-kkos han tay namu lo sangcing hana pwa yo.	It seems we symbolize the spirit of unswerving loyalty by means of the unbending bamboo tree.	kwup.e yo 'is bent' kwup.hye yo [kwup.hi-] 'bends it' kwup.hici anh.nun chwunguy 'loyalty which does not yield to bending' = 'unswerving loyalty' cengsin 'spirit, feeling' kot.a yo 'is straight, unbent, direct' kkos-kkos hay yo 'is perfectly straight <u>or</u> stiff, unbending' sangcing 'symbol' sangcing hay yo 'symbolizes' sangcing hana pwa yo 'seems to symbolize'
B.32. Pappusin tey caymi iss.nun yēyki mānh.i hay cwusye se komapsup.nita.	Thank you for telling me so many interesting things when you are (so) busy.	pappusin tey '(on) an occasion when [someone esteemed] is busy' <u>or</u> '[someone esteemed] is busy and/but'
33. I pakk-ey to, Songto ey nun kōcek tul i mānh.keyss.ci yo?	Aside from this, are there many historic spots in Songto?	
A.34. Nēy. Yēys nal cel tul, tāykwel tul, tto ca.yen ulo nun Pak.yen Phokpho tūng i iss.ci yo.	Yes, there are the ancient temples, the palaces, and then for natural beauty, there are the Pak.yen Falls, and so on.	yēys (nal) 'ancient (days), olden times, (of) yore' cel 'temple' tāykwel = kwungkwel 'palace' ca.yen 'nature, natural feature' Pak.yen [a name] phokpho 'falls, waterfall' . . . tūng 'and so on, etc.' . . . tūng-tung 'etc., etc.'

SUPPLEMENTARY VOCABULARY

[1]yeksa-hak	(the study of) history
[1]yeksa-ka	historian
kōcek-ci	historical spot, ruins, place where there are remains
myengsung-ci or myengso	famous places
[1]yeksa-cek inmul	historical characters
sāhwa	historical stories
silhwa	actual stories, true accounts
sillok	annals, chronicles, historical records
sinhwa	myths
tōnghwa	children's stories (of ancient times), fables
kwāke	the past
hyencay	the present
mīlay	the future
[n]yentay	era (name)
sāngko	archaic times
cwungko	ancient times
cwungsey	middle ages
kūnsey	recent times, the modern age
cin hay yo	(color) is dark; (liquid) is thick, rich, strong
cith.e yo [cith-]	(color) is dark; (fog, forest, hair) is thick, dense
yēn hay yo	(color) is light; is soft, tender
yath.e yo [yath-] or yeth.e yo [yeth-]	(color) is light; is shallow
pich or pich-kal [sometimes spelled pich-kkal] or sayk(-kal)	color

huye yo [huy-] (pronounced /hie/ or /hyē/ [hi-])	is white
kem.e yo [kēm-], kemceng iey yo	is black
hoysayk iey yo, cayq pich iey yo	is gray
nwūlule yo [nwūlu-] or nwūlay yo [nwūle(h)-]	is yellow
nōlule yo [nōlu-] or nōlay yo [nōla(h)-]	is golden yellow
cholok sayk iey yo	is green
phulule yo [phulu-] or phelay yo [phele(h)-]	is blue (or green)
phalay yo [phala(h)-]	is bright blue
cec.e yo [cec-]	gets wet
mall.e yo [malu-]	gets dry
nal.e yo [na-l-]	flies
nalle yo [nalu-]	carries, loads
kkāy yo [kkāy-]	wakes up; sobers up
kkaywe yo [kkaywu-]	wakes/sobers [someone] up
mul.e yo [mu-l-]	bites
mul.e yo [mūl-]	asks
cap.e yo	catches
pālp.e yo	steps on
kwulm.e yo	starves, is starving
kam.e yo [kām-]	bathes, washes, shampoos
nelp.e yo	is wide, broad
cop.a yo	is narrow
el.e yo [ē-l-]	it freezes
el.um	ice
(kkwum ul) kkwue yo [kkwu-]	dreams (a dream)
ānkay ka kkie yo [kkī-]	fog gathers, it fogs up
kwulum i kkie yo [kkī-)	clouds gather, it clouds up

NOTES

‖ 26.1. Verbs: causative and passive derivations.

The Basic Sentences of this lesson contain these verb forms:

pōy yo (or pwāy yo) [pōy-] or po.ye yo [poi-] 'is seen, is visible; shows, causes to see'

cwuk.ye yo [cwuk.i-] 'kills, causes to die'

These are derived, respectively, from po- 'looks at, sees' and cwuk- 'dies.' Through this derivation pōy yo acquires a CAUSATIVE MEANING ('shows') as well as a PASSIVE MEANING ('can be seen, is visible') while cwuk.ye yo acquires only the causative meaning ('kills, makes die').

A number of other verbs (though by no means all of them) are also subject to this type of derivation. The derivation process changes the meaning of the original verb from intransitive (not able to have an object—e.g. kkuth na yo 'it stops, comes to an end') to transitive (e.g. kkuth nāy yo 'makes it stop, stops it, brings it to an end'); or else a transitive verb is changed into a causative or a passive one, or, in some cases, both (like the verb derived from po-).

Causative verbs are sometimes translated 'has someone do it,' sometimes 'makes someone do it,' sometimes 'lets someone do it,' sometimes 'gets someone to do it'; the Korean form does not make it clear whether the "causative" is by coercion, persuasion, or permission. Passive verbs are often translated by 'it can be done': Pata ka pōynta usually means 'You (or I or anyone) can see the sea' rather than 'The sea gets looked at' (= Pata lul ponta with the subject unmentioned).

You will notice that the causative or passive is usually derived with some suffix such as -i-, -ki-, -hi-, -li-, -wu-, -chwu-, etc. When the suffix contains an -i-, in relaxed pronunciation the last vowel of the verb base may acquire a -y (that is, be fronted): /meykinta/ for mek.inta, /cayphinta/ for cap.hinta, etc. The shapes and meanings are largely unpredictable, so you do best just to learn each derived form as a separate, though related, verb.

Here is a list of some of the verbs you have learned, together with other verbs derived from them as passives or causatives. They are given in the plain present form.

BASIC VERB	DERIVED VERB
ānta [ā-l-] 'knows'	allinta 'lets [him] know, informs'
anc.nunta 'sits'	anc.hinta 'seats [him]'
cap.nunta 'catches'	cap.hinta 'gets caught; has [it] caught; has [him] catch'
cec.nunta 'gets wet'	ceksinta 'wets [it], makes [it] wet'
copta 'is narrow'	cop.hinta 'makes [it] narrow, narrows [it]'
cwuk.nunta 'dies'	cwuk.inta 'kills'
ēps.ta 'is lacking'	ēps.aynta 'eliminates; gets rid of'
ip.nunta 'gets dressed'	ip.hinta 'dresses [him]'
kām.nunta 'bathes, washes'	kamkinta 'has someone bathe or wash'
kēnta [kē-l-] 'hangs it'	kellinta 'it hangs, is hanging'
kēt.nunta [kēl-]	kellinta 'has [him] walk'
kkāynta '[he] wakes up'	kkaywunta 'wakes [him] up'
kkuth nanta 'it stops'	kkuth nāynta 'stops it, finishes it'
kwulm.nunta 'is starving'	kwulm.kinta /kwumkinta/ 'allows [him] to go hungry'
kwupta 'is bent'	kwup.hinta 'bends it'
mānta [mā-l-] 'avoids, doesn't do'	mallinta 'prevents [him] from doing; stops [his doing]; dissuades [him from doing]'
malunta 'gets dry'	mallinta 'dries it, makes it dry'
mek.nunta 'eats'	mek.inta 'feeds, lets [him] eat'
	mek.hinta 'gets eaten, gets swallowed up'
nanta 'exits, (goes/comes) out'	nāynta 'puts/takes out; pays; mails'

nanta [na-l-] 'it flies'	nallinta 'flies it; makes/lets it fly'
nāmnunta 'remains, is left'	namkinta 'leaves it [remaining behind]'
nelp.ta 'is wide, broad'	nelp.hinta 'widens, broadens'
noh.nunta /nonnunta/	noh.inta /no(h)inta/ or /nōynta/ 'gets put'
nōnta [nō-l-] 'plays; has a day off'	nollinta 'lets [him] play; gives [him] a day off'
noph.ta 'is high'	noph.inta 'raises (up), elevates'
nuc.ta 'is late; is loose'	nuc.chwunta 'postpones; loosens'
olunta 'rises, goes/comes up'	ollinta 'raises, lifts; presents, gives'
pālp.nunta 'steps on'	palp.hinta 'gets stepped on'
pis.nunta 'combs [one's hair]'	pis.kinta 'combs [someone's hair]'
pes.nunta 'gets undressed, takes off [one's clothes]'	pes.kinta 'undresses one, takes [some-one's clothes] off'
ponta 'sees, looks at'	pointa <u>or</u> pōynta 'is visible, can be seen; shows, lets [him] see'
pulunta 'calls'	pullinta 'has [him] call'
sānta [sā-l-] 'lives'	sallinta 'makes/lets live; saves, revives'
sunta [often spelled senta] 'stands'	seywunta 'stands it up, erects, builds'
sin.nunta 'wears [on own feet]'	sinkinta 'puts it on [someone's feet]
tat.nunta 'closes it'	tat.hinta /tachinta/ 'it closes'
tēpta [tē-w-] 'is hot, warm'	teywunta 'heats it, warms it up'
thanta 'it burns'	thay(wu)nta 'burns it; (= phiwunta) smokes'
tōnta [tō-l-] 'it turns'	tollinta 'turns it, makes/lets it go around; passes it around'
tut.nunta 'listens to, hears'	tullinta 'it sounds, is heard, is audible'
yēnta [yē-l-] 'opens it'	yellinta 'it opens'

Here are examples of some of these derived verbs in sentences:

1. Sāmu-wen ul nolliko siph.ci anh.e se halq īl i mānh.ta ko phingkyey lul hayss.ci yo.	You see, I didn't want to give the office help the day off, so I made the excuse that there was a lot of work to do.
2. Ayki lul honca kellye pwass.ci man acik cal mōs kel.e yo.	I tried having the baby walk by himself but he still isn't able to walk very well.
3. Ku ōyq-kwa uysa nun ku hwānca lul sallye cwuko siph.ess.ki ttaymun ey swuswul hayss.ta p.nita.	The surgeon said he operated because he wanted to save the patient.
4. I hēn tali lul ēps.ayci anh.umyen wihem hay yo.	If they don't get rid of this old bridge it will be dangerous.
5. Ānkay ey ssāy se pata ka cal an poinun tey yo.	It's so covered with fog you can't see the sea very well!
6. Kāy ka pay thāl i na se, kwulm.kye ya hakeyss.ey yo.	The dog has stomach trouble so we'll have to keep him off his food.
7. Ppallay lul mallici anh.umyen an toynun tey, pi ka oki sīcak hani etteh.key haci yo.	I ought to dry this laundry, but what can I do now that it's starting to rain?
8. Tāymun aph uy kil ul nelp.hikeyss.ta ko sīcheng ey se sālam i wass.ey yo.	A man came from City Hall to say they are going to widen the street in front of our gate.
9. Nwu'ka say cip ul seywess.una chang i hana to ēps.ey yo.	Someone built a new house, but without a single window.

10. Chwungsin tul ul cwuk.ica ˡĪ Tayco nun caki ka wang i tōy pelyess.ˢup.nita.	Upon killing the loyal subjects Lee Thayco himself became king.
11. Ūmsik ul namkici mālko tā mek.e la!	Clean your plate!
12. Kwuk ul teywe se mek.ulq ka yo?	Shall we heat the soup and eat it?
13. Ai tul ul cēki ey anc.hisimyen etteh.sup.nikka.	How about having the children sit over there?
14. Ai (uy) os ul pes.kye tulilq ka yo?	Shall I undress the child for you?
15. Pap ul com tollisey yo.	Pass the rice, please.
16. Chīm-pang ey se to latio ka tullinta 'nun māl-ssum iey yo?	You mean you can hear the radio all the way from your bedroom?
17. Hōycang hanthey allye ya toykeyss.ey yo.	We ought to tell the president of the society.
18. I chang i cal yellici anh.nun tey kochilq swu iss.keyss.ci yo?	This window doesn't open properly; I wonder if it can be fixed?
19. Māl ul com noph.isio.	Elevate your speech a bit. (= Speak more politely.)

You will recall that the usual way to make a causative construction out of any verb is to put the verb into its adverbative form -key and add some form of hanta 'does' (‖ 17.4), so that mek.key hanta 'makes/lets eat' means much the same thing as mek.inta 'feeds.' There is no simple way to use just any verb in a passive construction; the form -key toynta (‖ 17.5) usually means 'gets so that it does/is' or 'gets to do/be.' And the form [DESCRIPTIVE VERB]-e cinta (‖ 9.8) usually means 'gets so it is = becomes' as in Sentence 20 of this lesson: . . . ēps.e cici anh.ko 'not disappearing, not becoming nonexistent.' A somewhat stilted passive can be made, however, by putting the verb into its substantive form -(u)m (‖ 16.3) and using it as the direct object of the verbal noun expression tang hanta 'suffers, undergoes': mek.um ul tang hanta 'undergoes (suffers) eating.'

In the case of verbal nouns like chamsal hanta 'assassinates' you make the passive by using the verbal noun with hanta as the object of tang hanta; an example of this appears in Sentence 8: . . . chamsal ul tang hayss.ci yo 'suffered assassination.' To make a verbal noun expression causative, ordinarily you change hanta to sikhinta (where you would expect hakey hanta, see ‖ 22.10): haksayng hanthey kongpu sikhinta 'causes the student to study = makes/lets the student study.' But sometimes a more roundabout expression is used, as in Sentence 22: . . . sālam ul sikhye se āmsal ul hayss.ci 'ordered people to assassinate him = had him assassinated by people.' The verb sikhinta by itself means 'orders (people or food).'

‖ 26.2. Special constructions with po- and poi-.

You have learned several ways to say 'seems, appears' or the like: modifier + mo.yang ita (‖ 14.9), modifier + kes kath.ey yo (‖ 17.7), modifier + ka pota (‖ 24.11). Let us reconsider the latter construction along with a similar one based on the related verb pointa (or pōynta):

1. When pointa 'is seen = seems' follows a descriptive verb either in its infinitive form or with the adverbial ending -key, the meaning is 'seems to be . . . , looks as if [it]'s . . .':

4. . . . cāk.key pōyp.nita. 'It looks small.' [= cak.e pōyp.nita]

2. Another way to get the same meaning is to take the modifier form of a descriptive verb or of the copula, add the post-modifier ka, and then follow with some form of the auxiliary descriptive verb pota 'it seems' (‖ 24.11):

12. . . . tōl tali 'n ka pwa yo. 'It looks as if it's a stone bridge.' 'It looks like a stone bridge.'

29. Ama chak han tay namu ka nan tali 'la 'nun ttus in ka pwa yo. 'It seems to mean "bridge where a noble bamboo tree rose."'

3. Processive verbs, together with iss- and eps- as well as ALL past (-ess-) and future (-keyss-) bases, are put in the -na interrogative form before pota is added to make the construction:

24. . . . i tali kūnche ey iss.ess.na pwa yo. 'It seems to have been near this bridge.' 'It looks as if it was near this bridge.'

31. . . . sangcing hana pwa yo. 'It seems that we symbolize . . .'

Here are some more examples of these constructions.

1. Kim sensayng i onul tāytan hi kippukey pōy yo.	Mr. Kim seems to be very happy today.
2. Hanul i hulye pōy yo.	The sky looks cloudy.
3. Ku sālam i tōn i ēps.na pwa yo.	That man looks as if he has no money.
4. Eme' nim i onulq cenyek ey cip ey kyēysikeyss.na pwa yo.	It looks as if Mother is going to stay home this evening.
5. Pak puin uy ōythwu ka pissan ka pwa yo.	Mrs. Pak's overcoat looks expensive.
6. Ilcciki cass.na pwa yo.	It looks as if he's gone to bed early.
7. Nwūn i te oci anh.na pwa yo.	It doesn't seem to be snowing anymore.
8. I pap un kuleh.key tēpci anh.un ka pwa yo.	This rice doesn't seem to be so hot.
9. I hak.kyo ey se kongpu han īl i iss.na pwa yo.	It seems to me that he once studied at this school.
10. Mēlli se to ku san i noph.key poici anh.ni?	Doesn't that mountain look tall, though, even from a distance?!
11. Namphyen pota puin i phek celm.e pōyci yo.	You see, the wife looks much younger than the husband.

‖ 26.3. Verbs: the substantive form -(u)m.

16. [Lesson 9] . . . chwum ul chwue yo. 'He dances (a dance) . . .'

39. [Lesson 23] . . . ne cwum a. 'I'll give it to you.'

5. [Lesson 24] . . . way haphum i nako cam i wass.tun ci to mōlla yo. 'I don't know why yawns happened and sleep came.'

30. [Lesson 24] . . . elyewum i ēps.nun kes kath.ey yo. 'She seems to have no difficulties.'

14. [Lesson 26] Kūlimq yepse uy Sencwuk-kyo lul pōy tulici yo. 'Suppose I show you Sencwuk Bridge on a picture post card.'

The words in the sentences quoted here are all formed from verb bases by adding the two-shape ending -(u)m, pronounced -um after consonants, -m after vowels and after the l extension of such bases as ā-l- 'knows': in ālm 'knowledge' the l is pronounced only when the next sound is a vowel in ālm i 'knowledge [as subject]' but ālm man /āmman/ 'only knowledge.' We can call this form the SUBSTANTIVE and it can be made from any verb, including the copula. The substantive has a number of uses and in addition frequently serves as a noun of somewhat unpredictable meaning relating to the underlying verb, as kūlim 'picture' is related to kūli- 'draw.'

One use of the substantive was described in ‖ 23.6—followed by the post-substantive a or sey, a construction expressing a promise:

I os ul ne 'ykey cwum a. 'I'll give you these clothes.'
[1]Nayil kam sey. 'I'll go tomorrow.'
Ku īl un nay (ka) math.e pom a. 'I'll take care of that matter.'

The basic meaning of -(u)m substantives is 'the act or fact of doing/being so-and-so.' Here are some examples of these noun-like derivations:

Substantive	Verb Base from Which Derived
ālm 'knowledge'	ā-l- 'know'
cam 'sleep, a nap'	ca- 'sleep'
chwum '(a) dance'	chwu- 'dance'
elyewum 'difficulty'	elyew- 'is difficult'
kel.um 'walk, step, gait'	kēl- 'walks'
kippum 'happiness'	kippu- 'is happy'
kkwum 'a dream'	kkwu- 'dreams'
kūlim 'picture, drawing'	kūli- 'draws'
mit.um 'faith, belief'	mit- 'believes, trusts'
sallim 'livelihood; housekeeping'	salli- 'makes live'
sālm 'life'	sā-l- 'lives'

You will find a few irregular derived substantives alongside the regularly expected ones, usually with a difference of meaning: el.um 'ice' alongside ēlm 'freezing'; sālam 'human being' alongside sālm 'life, living'; cwukem 'corpse' alongside cwuk.um 'death, dying.' Only the regular forms enter into such freely productive uses as the "promise" forms of ‖ 23.6 (-um a/sey).

Substantives, like other nouns, show up as subject or object:

Māl hanun tey elyewum i ēps.ey yo. 'He has no difficulty in talking.'
Cam i wass.ey yo. 'Sleep came [to me] = I fell asleep.'
Kippum ul cwuess.ey yo. 'You have given me happiness = You have made me happy.'

There are a few substantives which act as complementary objects to the related verbs:

Chwum (ul) chwue yo. 'He dances (a dance).'
Cam (ul) ca yo. 'She sleeps (a sleep).'
Kkwum (ul) kkwue yo. 'I dream (a dream).'

In written Korean, and in somewhat old-fashioned or formal spoken Korean (as in citing proverbs), you find not only single substantives that behave like simple nouns but also even whole sentences which are nominalized by turning the verb into its substantive form:

Yelq pen tul.um i han pen pom man kath.ci mōs hay yo. 'One look is better than ten hearings. [Looking once is better than listening ten times.]'

In less formal spoken Korean, it is more common to nominalize a sentence by using the nominative -ki form (Lesson 13) rather than the substantive -(u)m form, and another way of nominalizing a sentence is to turn it into a modifier of kes 'thing, fact, act':

Yelq pen tut.nun kes i han pen ponun kes man kath.ci mōs hay yo. 'Listening ten times is in no way like just looking one time.'

In documentary style (the way notices are often written), the substantive nominalization is often used as a complete sentence all by itself. You may notice Korean cigarette stands sometimes carry the notice "Tāmpay ēps.um." which means '(We are) out of cigarettes.'

‖ 26.4. Substantives with the particle (u)lo.

A verb substantive -(u)m with the particle ulo (see ‖ 19.8) after it forms expressions meaning 'because of so-and-so happening (or being)' or 'with the doing (or being) so-and-so.' The substantives in such expressions may be past or future as well as present—that is, the ending -(u)m may be added to past and future bases as well as to simple bases:

ha- 'does; is'	hayss.um 'the act of having done; the state of having been'	hakeyss.um 'the act of intending to do; the state of going-to-be'

Here are some examples:

1. Kim sensayng i na kass.um ulo, poci mōs hayss.ey yo.	I couldn't see Mr. Kim because he had gone out.
2. Nal i ccalp.um ulo īl ul mānh.i halq swu ka ēps.ey yo.	I can't do much work because of the day being short.
3. Onulq cenyek cha ey nay chinkwu ka om ulo, yeses si ey mannakeyss.ey yo.	A friend of mine is coming in on the evening train, so I'm going to meet him at six o'clock.
4. Nemu chwuwess.um ulo mōs cass.ey yo.	It was so cold that I couldn't sleep.
5. Ku congi lul el.um wi ey noh.umyen cec.keyss.um ulo noh.ci mal.e yo.	If you put that paper on the ice, it'll get wet, so don't.
6. Cīnan pamq tong-an cha ey se cass.um ulo sikan kanun kes ul mōllass.ey yo.	I slept on the train last night, so I wasn't aware that the time was passing.
7. Nemu mānh.i īl ul hayss.um ulo phikon hay yo.	I'm tired from working so hard.
8. Khi ka cak.um ulo ku lul Kkoma 'la ko pulless.ey yo.	We called him Shorty because he is small.
9. Na lul cakkwu chye 'ta pom/pwass.um ulo musun īl in ya ko mul.e pwass.ta.	He kept looking up at me, so I asked him what was the matter.
10. Ku pun i pelsse māl-ssum tulyess.keyss.um ulo cey ka tasi māl-ssum tulici anh.keyss.^{s}up.nita.	Since he must have told you about it already, I won't tell you over again.
11. Hānkwuk salam im ulo ku hanthey Hānkwuk mal lo sse to cōh.sup.nita.	Since he is a Korean, you can write him in Korean.

This expression (-um ulo) is more commonly written than spoken. The more colloquial ways to say 'since . . . ,' 'because . . .' are these:

-e se (‖ 8.9)
-ki ttaymun ey (‖ 13.9)
-nun (etc.) kkatalk ey/ulo (‖ 12.8)
-(u)ni, -(u)ni-kka (n') (‖ 18.1)
-nun tey (‖ 21.5)

Less colloquial ways to say 'since . . . ,' 'because . . .,' etc. in addition to -um ulo are -ki ey (‖ 13.8) and -um ey (‖ 26.5).

‖ 26.5. Substantives with the particle ey.

An expression somewhat similar in meaning to the one described just above is an -(u)m substantive with the particle ey. Hayss.um ey, for example, like hayss.ki ey can mean 'since or because [it] did or was' or 'in view of the fact that so-and-so happened.'

Here are some examples:

1. Pom ey pissa pōy yo.	From its appearance it looks expensive.
2. Pi ka om ey mōtwu kippe hayss.ey yo.	Everyone was happy that it rained.
3. Ku sēnmul pat.um ey kippess.ey yo.	I was happy to receive the gift.
4. Kim sensayng i ku chayk ul ilk.um ey na nun twīq nal ilk.ki lo hayss.ey yo.	Since Mr. Kim is reading the book, I've decided to read it [a later day =] some other day.

Sometimes the translation is better 'upon doing' or '(just) when'; in such cases, Korean grammarians prefer to treat -um ey as a separate ending which they spell "-(u)may": Nay ka māl ul ham ey Kim sensayng i tol.a 'ta pwass.ˢup.nita. 'When I spoke, Mr. Kim looked around.'

All sentence-derived expressions involving the substantive -(u)m are a bit old-fashioned; since there are other ways to say the same thing, you would do well to avoid using the -(u)m forms very much in your own speech. See the note at the end of ‖ 26.4.

‖ 26.6. Another meaning for plain suggestion forms in -ca.

27. . . . Phoun i cwukca mā'ca . . . 'no sooner had Phoun died . . .'

Plain suggestion forms are made by attaching the one-shape ending -ca to verb bases; at the end of a sentence they mean 'Let's do it' (and are limited to PROCESSIVE verbs). They are also used in the middle of sentences, to mean 'as soon as . . .' and need not be limited to processive verbs. The expressions are often intensified by the -ca form of the negative auxiliary mā-l- combined into a phrase with the first -ca form:

oca or oca mā(l)ca 'as soon as [someone] comes'

In these expressions you usually do not hear the l of mā(l)ca, so we spell it mā'ca. This is true for any L-extending verb: moca lul kē'ca (mā'ca) 'as soon as I hang up my hat,' mulken ul pha'ca mā'ca 'as soon as I sell the goods.'

Here are some more examples:

1. Nay ka cengke-câng ey oca mā'ca, kicha ka tte nass.ey yo.	The train left as soon as I got to the station.
2. Nal i ttattus haca pi ka wa yo.	As soon as the weather is warm, it starts raining.
3. Nwupca cam i tul.ess.ey yo.	I fell asleep as soon as I lay down.
4. Kongpu lul machica mā'ca, cip ey tol.a kass.ey yo.	He went home as soon as he finished his studying.
5. Pap ul mekca sālam i wass.ey yo.	I had no sooner eaten than someone came.
6. Kim sensayng i na osica sīcak hapsita.	Let's begin as soon as Mr. Kim comes out.
7. Pusan ey naylica mā'ca Kim sensayng ul mannass.ey yo.	I saw (<u>or</u> met) Mr. Kim as soon as I got off at Pusan.
8. Ku sangcem ey se mulken ul totwuk cil haca mā'ca cap.hyess.ta.	He had barely stolen the goods in the store when he was caught.
9. Yēypang cwūsa lul mac.ca mā'ca yel i nass.ey yo.	I came down with a fever as soon as I had the shot.
10. Talk un al ul nah.ca mā'ca wul.e yo.	A hen cackles as soon as she lays an egg.
11. Oppa ka than pihayng-ki ka tte naca mā'ca nwun mul i nass.ey yo.	Tears came to my eyes as soon as the plane took off with my big brother aboard it.
12. Ku nolay lul tut.ca yēys nal sayngkak i nass.ci yo.	Hearing that song reminded me of the days gone by.
13. Ku sōsel chayk ul ilk.ki sīcak haca mā'ca pul i kke cyess.ey yo.	No sooner had I started to read that novel than the lights went out.
14. Ku hwāka nun myengseng ul et.ca mā'ca tol.a kasyess.ey yo.	The artist had barely made his name when he died.
15. Ecey sikyey lul pōsek-sang ey se chac.e oca tto kōcang i nass.uni ku sangcem sīn.yong ēps.kwun.	I went and got my watch at the jeweler's yesterday and right away something got the matter with it again, so I see that store can't be relied on.

EXERCISES

I

Each of the following sentences makes a statement. Change each so that it means 'it seems <u>or</u> looks as if [what the statement says],' using one of the constructions described in ‖ 26.2. Then translate the sentence.

1. Ūmsik i tā cwūnpi tōyss.ey yo.
2. Ku ^{l}yehayng i yelhul kellye yo.
3. Mikwuk kyewul to Hānkwuk kyewul chelem chwuwe yo.
4. Nay sayngkak ey nun, i kūlim i Sencwuk-kyo kūlim i ani 'ey yo.
5. Yeki se puthe cip tul i huye yo. Huyn cip man iss.ey yo.
6. Ku tose-sil ey nun chayk i sam-chen kwen ina iss.ey yo.
7. I māycem ey se kūlimq yepse lul mānh.i sass.ey yo.
8. I tali nun tay namu lo ma(y)ntun tali 'ey yo.

9. Yo say nun koki wa kwāsil i acwu pissa yo.
10. Wuli ka ama han ō-payk wen kacye ya hay yo.

II

Choose any ten words from the right-hand column of the list in ‖ 26.1 above and make up a Korean sentence containing each one; then give the meaning of the sentence in English. Make your sentences interesting; don't hesitate to try out complicated expressions you have learned in earlier lessons.

III

Add to the beginning of each of the following sentences a clause ending with -(u)m ulo or -(u)m ey as an explanation of the given part. For example, given . . . saci mōs hayss.ey yo 'I couldn't buy it,' you might put before it Tōn i ēps.um ulo . . . 'Because (of the fact that) I have no money . . .' Say the entire sentence aloud, then give its English meaning. Afterward, say the sentence again, using the more colloquial -ki ttaymun ey for the 'because' of the first part.

1. Cip e oca mā'ca pap ul mek.keyss.ey yo.
2. Yetelq si kkaci cass.ey yo.
3. Halwu congil āmu kes to mōs hayss.ey yo.
4. Nwun i aphe yo.
5. I kongpu lul machica mā'ca cip ey kakeyss.ey yo.
6. Ūmsik i mānh.i nam.e yo.
7. Phoun i chamsal ul tang hayss.ey yo.
8. Yepse lul sako siph.ci anh.ess.ey yo.
9. Ku ^{l}yeypay-tang i phek cāk.key pōy yo.
10. Com te khukey māl hay ya hay yo.

IV

Say the following things in Korean:

As soon as ___

1. winter comes the roads get slippery.
2. I put on my glasses the lights went out.
3. Mr. Pak's father died Mr. Pak went to live in the country.
4. Phoun had passed over the bridge they assassinated him.
5. I saw the old man I knew something had happened.
6. something got the matter with my watch I took it to the jeweler's to be repaired.
7. Poktong-i came to believe in Christianity he seemed happy.
8. I heard the chicken cackle I started to look for the egg.
9. the student would doze the teacher would wake him up.
10. I fell asleep I started dreaming.
11. we ran out of money we decided to walk home.
12. my wife left school she began studying by herself.
13. I had pawned my one and only watch I began to regret it.
14. we got out of school we made a snow man.
15. Miss Han graduates she will go to work as a nurse in a hospital.
16. you get the postcard I sent you, let me know.
17. we arrive in Seoul, let's go see the art gallery.
18. the guests arrive, bring out the food.

19. your friend has left, come help me with my homework.
20. a tooth starts hurting you ought to get a dentist to pull it out.
21. something gets the matter with your car, take it to the repair shop.
22. I started to want to see that movie, sure enough it came to us in Inchen.
23. Father told me he would like to have me go to Kayseng with him, I packed my bag (= put my clothes in suitcase).
24. Poktong-i took off his clothes and lay down, he fell asleep and dreamed he was in some far-off country.
25. you finish reading the book I lent you, please return it, because Miss Kim wants to read it next.

CONVERSATION

Prepare a little talk in Korean about some spot of historic, scenic, or other interest which you have visited or know about. Plan to speak for about five or ten minutes. Then be prepared to answer the questions of your fellow students; make sure everybody asks you at least one question.

VOCABULARY DRILL

Make up a single Korean sentence using the words and phrases of each group below (one sentence using all 3 items in Group 1, one using the 3 items of Group 2, etc.).

1. keli
   tay namu
   tōl

2. pappe yo
   phek
   yepse

3. Kolye
   sāsil
   ^{l}yeksa

4. cēnsel
   ho
   swuto

5. chamsal
   kinyem hay yo
   yēys

6. keuy
   māycem
   pī hay yo

7. pulk.e yo
   uy hamyen
   yel.e yo

8. cec.e yo
   phokpho
   tali

9. cem
   ēps.e cye yo
   malla yo

10. silhwa
    ilq-sel
    ttus

11. cāylay lo
    sangcing
    kkos-kkos hay yo

12. cin hay yo
    cholok sayk
    phulule yo

COMPREHENSION

The story of Phoun, as related in the Basic Sentences of this lesson, has its roots in historic fact.

Persuade your Korean teacher to tell you another traditional Korean story—historical, or mythological, or perhaps a child's fairy tale. See how well you can follow the narrative; at its conclusion, your teacher will ask you questions, to clarify obscure points as well as to determine how well you understood.

The teacher may have to use words you don't know. Stop him and ask the meaning of words you don't remember hearing before. Whenever possible, he will explain them to you in Korean; if they can't be explained very well in Korean, he will write the English version of the words on the board.

LESSON 27. A JOB IN KOREA

BASIC SENTENCES

[Miss A. is talking to her friend Miss B.]

Korean	English	Amplification
A. 1. Swii Hānkwuk ulo tte-nanta 'nun somun tul.ess.ci. Kulay ēncey ccum tte-nal yēyceng ia.	I've heard rumors that you're leaving for Korea soon. So when do you plan to leave?	. . . ulo tte-nanta 'leaves for . . .' yēyceng 'intention' . . .ia = . . .ita [INTIMATE] tte-nal yēyceng ita '[it is the intention of going-to-leave=] intends to leave'
B. 2. I pen [1]Yu'-wel ey tte-nalq sayngkak ia.	I'm thinking of leaving this June.	tte-nalq sayngkak ita '[it is going-to-leave thought=] intends to leave, thinks of leaving'
A. 3. Kulen tey, Hānkwuk ey nun mues hale ka. [1]Yehayng man i yuil han mokcek i ani 'keyss.ci??	Well—what are you going to Korea for? Travel alone isn't your only aim, is it?	hale ka 'goes in order to do' [INTIMATE] Hānkwuk ey nun mues hale ka 'You are going to Korea in order to do what?' [1]yehayng man i 'just travel [as subject]' yuil han . . . 'unique . . .' mokcek 'purpose, aim, goal' mokcek ani 'keyss.ci?? 'it isn't the purpose, is it' [INTIMATE CASUAL]
B. 4. [1]Yehayng khenyeng īl hale ka.	Hardly travel—I'm going to work.	hale ka 'goes to do' [INTIMATE]
5. Sāsil un Hānkwuk nongchon ey ka se nongchon punye tul kwa īl halye ko hay.	In fact, I intend to go to a Korean farm village to work with farm village women.	nongchon 'farm village' punye 'woman' halye ko hay 'intends to do'[INTIMATE]
A. 6. Hānkwuk ey se nun Yenge lul an ssuci anh.e? Māl i thong haci anh.e se etteh.key īl ul hay.	Isn't it true that in Korea they don't use English? How will you do your work, not being understood?	thong hanta 'gets through, penetrates; gets understood' māl i thong haci anh.e se . . . 'your words don't get through, so . . .'

Korean	English	Amplification
B. 7. Kulay se, nay ka il-nyenq tong-an ina Hānkwuk mal ul paywuko iss.ci anh.e?	Well, haven't I been studying Korean for about a year?	
8. ˡYu'-wel kkaci han sene tal te iss.uni-kka, ku tong-an yelqsim ulo paywulq cakceng ia.	As there are about three more months before June, I've decided to study very hard during that time.	senes/sene . . . 'about three' sene tal 'about three months' cakceng 'intention, plan, decision' paywulq cakceng ita '[it is a going-to-study decision=] decides to study'
A. 9. Cikkum ccum un Hānkwuk mal lo il.yong hōyhwa nun ˡyuchang hakey halq swu iss.keyss.kwun.	Why, right now you can carry on an everyday conversation in Korean fluently, I see!	cikkum [LIVELY] = cikum il.yong 'for ordinary (everyday) use' hōyhwa 'conversation' iss.keyss.kwun [future = lively present, ‖ 11.2]
B.10. Kyewu ūysa ˡna phyo haci.	I can barely express my ideas.	kyewu 'barely' ūysa 'intention(s), what is on one's mind; one's will, desire, inclination' phyo hanta = natha-nāynta 'expresses, shows'
11. Hānkwuk mal man ul hanun sāhoy ey kamyen ce-cel lo cal hakey toylq cwul lo sayngkak hay.	I feel that when I get to a society where they talk just Korean I will get so I talk well spontaneously.	sāhoy 'society, group, community' (ce-)cel lo 'spontaneously, without effort'
12. Māl un hamyen, halq swulok nunun kes i ani ya?	Isn't it true that the more you speak a language, the better you get at it?	. . .-ulq swulok 'to the degree that . . .' mal un hamyen, halq swulok . . . '[if you speak, to the extent that you speak=] the more you speak . . .' nunta [nul.e yo, nu-l-] 'it lengthens, increases, spreads, grows, progresses' . . .kes i ani ya? 'isn't it a case of . . .' [INTIMATE]
A.13. Kulen tey, phungsok kwa supkwan i talun nala ey ka se etteh.key honca sal.e.	But how are you going to go live alone in a country where the customs and habits are different?	phungsok 'custom' supkwan 'habit' nala 'country, nation' sal.e 'lives' [INTIMATE]

Korean	English	Amplification
B.14. Pyelq soli tā hay. Hānkwuk punye tul kwa kath.i īl hamyen se sānun tey, way honca sal.e.	Don't be silly. I'll be living there working with Korean women; how will I be living alone?	pyelq soli tā hay '[you are making all special sounds=] you are unduly concerned' or 'don't mention it'
A.15. Musun tōngki lo Hānkwuk ul īl the lo thayk hayss.e.	With what motive did you choose Korea as a place to work?	tōngki 'motive, reason' the 'place, site (for something)' īl the 'work(ing) place, place to work' thayk hanta 'chooses, selects' thayk hayss.e 'chose, selected' [INTIMATE]
B.16. Tōngki nun, kāntan haci.	As far as motive is concerned, it's simple.	kāntan hata 'is simple, is uncomplicated' kāntan haci 'is simple, you see'[INTIMATE CASUAL]
17. Cenmun hak.kyo sitay ey Hānkwuk salam han myeng kwa kath.i kongpu lul hayss.e.	At the time I was in college, I studied with a Korean person.	cenmun hak.kyo 'college, professional school' sitay 'time, period, era'
18. Ku ttay, ku sālam kwa sakwiki sīcak hayss.nun tey, sakwimyen sakwilq swulok ku sālam eykey cōh.un cem i mānh.keyss.ci??	At that time, I began to get acquainted with him, and the more I got to know him, the more good points he had!	sakwinta [sakwi-] 'gets acquainted; associates (with)' sakwilq swulok 'to the extent that [we] became acquainted' sakwimyen sakwilq swulok '[when I got to know him, to the extent that I got to know him . . .=] the better acquainted we became, the more I got to know him' cem 'spot, dot, point'
19. Ku ttay puthe Hānkwuk ila 'n nala ey tāy hay se, kwansim ul kac'key toyko Hānkwuk ey kwan han chayk to ilk.ki sīcak hayss.ci.	From that time on I came to have an interest in the country of Korea and I began to read books about Korea too, you see.	. . .ey tāy hay yo 'concerns, is about' . . .ey tāy hay se 'about, concerning' kwansim 'interest, concern' kacinta 'has, possesses' kac'key = kacikey 'so as to have, so that one has' . . .ey kwan hay yo 'concerns, relates to, is about, has to do with'

Korean	English	Amplification
20. Kulen chayk ul ilk.umyen, ilk.ulq swulok Hānkwuk ul te [1]īhay hakey toyko, tto cōh.a hakey toytun kwun.	Why, the more I read books like that, the more I came to understand Korea, and also came to be fond of it.	ilk.umyen ilk.ulq swulok 'the more [I] read' [1]īhay hanta 'understands, comprehends'
21. Kulay se, nācwung ey nun na kath.un īlq-kwun i mānh.un Mikwuk ey se īl hanun kes pota nun, hyēncay īlq-kwun i pucok han Hānkwuk ey ka se īl hanun kes i te ttus i iss.nun kes kath.e se, Hānkwuk ulo ka se īl haki lo kyelqsim hayss.ci.	So, finally, rather than work in America where there are many workers like me, it seemed more sensible to go work in Korea where at present there is a shortage of workers, so I determined to go to Korea to work.	nācwung (ey) 'afterwards, in the end, at last, finally' īlq-kwun 'worker, person who works' hyēncay 'at present, now(adays)' pucok hata 'is scarce, is (in) short (supply)' ttus i iss.nun kes 'a meaningful thing, an act having meaning <u>or</u> sense' kyelqsim 'decision, determination' . . .-ki lo kyelqsim (ul) hanta 'decides (determines) to do'
A.22. Elyewun īl ul cakceng hayss.kwun.	I see you've decided on a hard job!	cakceng (ul) hanta 'decides (on)'
23. Cham. Hānkwuk ey nun [1]yeksa-sang ulo 'na cili-sang ulo pol man han kes i mānh.e?	Well, are there many things worth seeing in Korea from the standpoint of history or geography?	[1]yeksa-sang 'from the viewpoint of history, historywise' cili 'geography' cili-sang 'with respect to geography' pol man hata 'is worth seeing' pol man han kes 'a thing which is worth seeing'
B.24. Pol man han kes i mānh.ko mālko.	Of course—there are many things worth seeing.	
25. Na nun Hānkwuk kamyen toylq swu iss.nun tāy lo yehayng ul mānh.i halq sayngkak ia.	When I go to Korea I think I'll travel as much as possible.	. . . tāy lo 'in accordance with . . . , just (as)' toylq swu iss.nun tay lo 'as much as possible' halq sayngkak ita '[it is the going-to-do thought=] is thinking of doing'
A.26. Kulen tey, Hānkwuk kamyen etten īl ul	Well, what sort of work do you expect to do	hal they 'ta 'expects to do' kyēyhoyk 'plan, project'

Korean	English	Amplification
hal they ya. Kyēyhoyk i mānh.keyss.ci. Com kwuchey-cek ulo, casey hi yēyki hay cwue.	when you go to Korea? You must have lots of plans. Tell me about it concretely and in detail.	kwuchey = kwusang 'embodiment, concrete form' kwuchey-cek ulo 'concretely' casey hata 'is minute, detailed' casey hi 'in detail' hay cwue [INTIMATE] = hay cwue la 'do it for me!'
B.27. Na nun ches ccay lo thak.a-so 'na yuchi-wen kath.un kikwan ul seywul they ya.	First, I expect to set up a project like a nursery or kindergarten.	ches . . 'first' ches ccay 'first place, No. 1' ches ccay lo 'in the first place, firstly, to begin with' thak.a-so 'day nursery' kikwan 'organ, facility, project, institution' seywe yo [seywu-] 'sets up, constructs' seywul they 'ta 'intends to set up <u>or</u> establish'
28. Punye tul i path kwa non ey na ka se īl hanun tong-an na nun elin ai tul ul math.e se kiluko siph.e.	I want to take charge of (and raise) the little children while the women go to work in the fields and paddies.	non 'rice field, paddy' kilunta [kille yo, kilu-] 'raises, brings up, grows' kiluko siph.e 'wants to raise them' [INTIMATE]
29. Twūl ccay lo na nun nongchon punye lul sangtay lo, kāngsup-so lul hana kacilq sayngkak ia.	Secondly, I'm thinking of holding a school, with the farm village women for students.	twūl ccay lo 'in the second place, secondly, as no.2' sangtay 'opposite number, counterpart' punye lul sangtay lo 'with women as counterparts <u>or</u> opposite numbers' [here, students as the opposite numbers from the teacher] kāngsup 'lecture; training' kāngsup-so 'lecture room, training-place' kacilq sayngkak ita 'is thinking of having'
30. Kulay se punye tul eykey ches ccay, yuk.aq pep, twūl ccay, kaceng wisayngq	Then I expect to teach the women, first, child care (methods), second, household hygiene,	pep = pangpep 'method, way' yuk.a 'child care' yuk.aq pep 'child-care methods'

Korean	English	Amplification
pep, sēys ccay, kāntan han yang ^{l}yoliq pep, yang caypong tūng ul kaluchil they ya.	third, simple Western-style cooking, Western-style sewing, etc.	kaceng 'home, household, family' wisayng 'health, hygiene' sēys ccay 'third, no.3' yang 'Western-style, Occidental' ^{l}yoli 'cooking, cookery, cuisine' caypong 'sewing' kaluchil they 'ta 'intends to teach'
A.31. Kyēyhoyk hanun īl i mānh.kwun!	I see you're planning a lot!	
32. Mōtwu kachi iss.ko caymi iss.nun īl kath.ey.	They all seem to be worthwhile, interesting things.	motwu 'all' kachi 'value, worth' kachi (ka) iss.ey yo 'has value, is valuable <u>or</u> worthwhile'
33. Kamyen pūti mom kēnkang hi īl mānh.i haki lul pala.	When you go, I certainly hope you will accomplish many things in good health.	pūti 'without fail, for sure, certainly, be sure to . . .' kēnkang hata 'is healthy, sound' kēnkang hi 'in health, soundly' mom kēnkang hi 'with healthy body, in sound health' pala 'hopes for' [INTIMATE]

SUPPLEMENTARY VOCABULARY

(. . . pota) ohi.lye [often pronounced /oylye/ or /oyley/]	rather, preferably	chwuswu	harvest
nongcang	farm	kachwuk	domesticated animals
nongka	farmhouse	yāngkyey	chicken (poultry) raising
nongchon saynghwal	farm life	kyeylan <u>or</u> talkyal	(chicken) eggs
tohoy = tosi	city	mokcang	stock-farm, ranch
tohoy/tosi saynghwal	city life	(non ul) kānta [kal.e yo, kā-l-]	plows (the paddy field)
nongmin	farmers, peasants, the farm populace	cayngki	a plow
		pye	rice plants
hānnong-ki	the slack season for farmers	pye lul sīmnunta [sim.e yo, sīm-]	plants rice
cicwu	landowner	mo	rice seedlings
nongcak kikwu	farm machinery or equipment	mo lul nāynta [nāy yo, nāy-]	transplants (sets out) rice seedlings
kelum <u>or</u> pīlyo	fertilizer		

ketwunta [ketwe yo, ketwu-]	harvests, gathers up	pap	cooked rice (or other grain)
pye lul ketwunta	harvests the rice	huyn pap	plain ('white') rice
ppallay lul ketwunta	gathers up the laundry	poli	barley
		poli pap	cooked barley
		koksik	grain(s), cereals
ssal	uncooked hulled rice (or other grain)	mil	wheat
		milq kalwu	wheat flour
		kalwu	flour

NOTES

‖ 27.1. Intimate style: review.

The verb forms used to end the Basic Sentences of this lesson mark the tone of the conversation as friendly and intimate; the inference, from the use of these forms, is that the speakers are lively women who are close friends.

To refresh your memory about the specific verb forms used in sentence-final position in the intimate style, you may wish to reread ‖ 22.4. In general, you will recall, the intimate style is achieved by dropping the particle yo that marks the polite style.

‖ 27.2. Expressing intentions.

One way to express an intention in Korean is by using a future-tense verb: Hakeyss.ey yo 'I will do it.' But there are a number of other more specific ways to specify that you INTEND to do it. For instance, you can use the intentive form -ulye (ko hanta) which was discussed in ‖ 24.9; it appears again in Basic Sentence 5 of this lesson. Or, with verbs of going and coming, you can use the purposive form -ule (kanta/onta) which also was discussed in ‖ 24.9; it appears again in Basic Sentences 3 and 4. There are also the expressions with the nominative -ki lo hay yo 'decides or expects to (do),' -ki lo (cak)ceng hay yo 'decides or plans to (do)'; these were discussed in ‖ 13.10. Other ways of expressing intentions will be found among the Basic Sentences of this lesson; for instance:

1. Kulay ēncey ccum tte-nal yēyceng ia. 'So, when do you plan to leave?'
2. . . . tte-nalq sayngkak ia. 'I'm thinking of leaving . . .'
8. . . . yelqsim ulo paywulq cakceng ia. 'I plan to study very hard.'
25. . . . ^{l}yehayng ul mānh.i halq sayngkak ia. 'I think I'll travel a lot.'
26. . . . etten īl ul hal they ya. 'What sort of work do you expect to do?'
27. . . . kikwan ul seywul they ya. 'I expect to set up an institute.'
29. . . . kāngsup-so lul hana kacilq sayngkak ia. 'I'm thinking of holding a school . . .'
30. . . . yang caypong tūng ul kaluchil they ya. 'I expect to teach Western-style sewing, etc.'

These constructions involve the use of prospective modifiers followed by a noun-plus-copula phrase:

. . .-ul yēyceng ita '[it is the plan or intention=] plans, intends' (Basic Sentence 1)

. . .-ulq sayngkak ita '[it is the thought or idea=] is thinking of . . .ing' (Basic Sentence 2, 25, 29)

. . .-ulq cakceng ita '[it is the decision or project=] decides, plans' (Basic Sentence 8; cf. Basic Sentence 22, which uses cakceng hay yo 'decides (on), makes a decision (on)' with a noun object before it.)
. . .-ul they 'ta 'expects, (fully) intends; is supposed to' (Basic Sentences 26, 27, 30)

The expression -ulq they 'ta originally came from -ul the (i)ta 'it is (in) position [= basis for planning] to happen.' Nowadays -ul the 'ta 'it is the site for . . .ing' is limited to sentences like Cip ul ciul the 'ta 'It is the site where we will build the house.' Compare Cip ul ciul they 'ta 'We expect to build a house.' You will find that some Koreans write -ul they 'ta as -ul the ita.

Here are some more examples of -ul they 'ta:

1. Mek.ul they 'n ya an mek.ul they 'n ya.	Do you expect to eat or not?
2. Onulq cenyek ey eti kasil they ('ey) yo.	Where are you going to go tonight?
3. Onul kanun kes i cōh.ul they 'ci yo.	It will be better to go today, you know.
4. Kulen cip ey kwīcwung-phum to ēps.ul they 'n tey . . .	You wouldn't expect a house like that to have any valuables in it, but . . .
5. Ayki ka ani 'l they 'n tey!	You're not (supposed to be) a baby, after all!
6. Cikum ccum un ku i ka pyēngwen ey se na wass.ul they 'n tey . . .	He must have gotten out of the hospital by now, but (I haven't seen him).
7. Ku sālam to keki se mannakey toyl they 'ci yo.	I expect to get to see him there too.
8. 'Nayil achim swuswul hal they 'ni-kka onul halwu congil kwulm.ula 'yss.ci yo.	They told me to fast all day today as they will be operating on me tomorrow morning.
9. Um.ak-hoy ka ilkop si pān puthe sīcak hal they 'myen ppalli mek.ko ka ya 'keyss.ci yo.	If the concert is (supposed) to start at 7:30 we'll have to eat in a hurry (and go).
10. Cang pwass.ta ka sīcheng ey tullil they 'p.nikka?	Are you planning to do your shopping and then stop by the city hall?

‖ 27.3. Nouns with direct objects.

The particle ul/lul sometimes makes a noun into the direct object of another noun, rather than a verb as you would expect. You can think of such expressions as having at the end a "dropped" hako with the meaning 'treating (as) . . . , making (as) . . . , using (for) . . . . Some nouns commonly used in this way are:

cwungsim 'center of attention, focus of interest'
munqpep ul cwungsim ulo (hako) kongpu lul hay yo 'studies with chief emphasis on grammar, with grammar as the focus of attention'

sangtay 'opposite number, counterpart'
nongchon punye lul sangtay lo (hako) 'with farm women as opposite numbers'

kwūsil 'excuse'
pyēng ul kwūsil lo (hako) 'with (or using) his illness as an excuse'

‖ 27.4. 'The more . . . the more . . .'

12. Māl un hamyen, halq swulok nunun kes i ani ya? 'Isn't it true that the more you speak a language the better you get at it?'

18. . . . sakwimyen sakwilq swulok . . . cōh.un cem i mānh.keyss.ci?? 'The better I got to know [him], the more good points he had!'

20. Kulen chayk ul ilk.umyen, ilk.ulq swulok Hānkwuk ul te ^{l}ihay hakey toyko . . . 'The more I read books like that, the more I came to understand Korea . . .'

The pattern for Korean sentences meaning 'the more . . . the more . . .' is to repeat the initial verb—first using it in the conditional form (with -umyen), then as a prospective modifier (-ulq) with the post-modifier swulok. This takes care of both parts of the English expression; a regular statement (or question) will complete the sentence.

Here are more examples:

1. Khumyen khulq swulok cōh.a yo.	The bigger the better.
2. Cak.umyen cak.ulq swulok mas i iss.ey yo.	The smaller they are, the more flavor they have.
3. Ku yēyki nun tul.umyen tul.ulq swulok, caymi iss.ey yo.	The more you hear that story, the more interesting it is.
4. Tōn un, iss.umyen iss.ulq swulok ssunun kes iey yo.	The more money you have, the more you spend. [Money is a thing that the more you have the more you spend of it.]
5. Ku catong-cha nun pomyen polq swulok sako siph.e yo.	The more I look at that car, the more I want to buy it.

‖ 27.5. Another meaning of the particle pota.

21. . Mikwuk ey se īl hanun kes pota nun . . 'Rather than work in America . . .'

The use of the particle pota (sometimes pronounced potam by non-Seoul speakers) in comparisons was discussed in ‖ 21.7. Basic Sentence 21 of this lesson shows pota in the meaning 'rather than, in preference to.' The particle phrase may be followed by ohilye (often pronounced oylye or oyley) 'rather, preferably.'

The particle pota is also used to translate 'from' or 'than' in such expressions as 'different from' and (occasionally) 'differently than'; but some Koreans condemn this usage and prefer the particle kwa/wa or its synonym hako.

Here are more examples:

1. Nay os un Kim puin uy os pota (= os kwa) talle yo.	My dress is different from Mrs. Kim's.
2. Ce kicha pota ohilye i kicha ka ppalle yo.	This train is faster than that one.
3. Ku sālam un nay ka sayngkak hayss.tun kes pota khi ka khess.ey yo.	He was taller than I thought he would be.
4. Ku kes pota nun oylye i kes i cōh.a yo.	I would rather have this one than that one.
5. Payk pen tut.nun kes pota han pen ponun kes i cōh.a yo.	It's better to see a thing once (rather) than hear it a hundred times.

It may be helpful to remember that in origin pota is probably the transferentive of po- and means something like 'when you look at (e.g. A you find that B is big).'

‖ 27.6. Modifiers with tāy lo.

The post-modifier tāy is used with lo after it in two kinds of constructions.

1. With a processive modifier, it means 'as soon as [so-and-so] happens':

Kim sensayng i na osinun tāy lo kaluchye cwusio. 'Please let me know as soon as Mr. Kim comes out.'

You will recall there is another way to say 'as soon as': -ca (mā'ca), ‖ 26.6.

2. With modifiers of any appropriate tense, tāy lo means 'according to, in accordance with, as, with [something] still as it was.'

Here are some examples:

Halq tāy lo hasio. '[Do according to what you will do=] Do as you like.'
Olh.un tāy lo māl hay la. '[Speak according to what is true=] Tell the truth!'
Sensayng i māl hanun tāy lo hasio. 'Do as the teacher says.'

The expression halq swu iss.nun tāy lo and toylq swu iss.nun tāy lo means 'as much as possible' [= according to what is possible, in line with what can be done]:

Halq swu iss.nun tāy lo ppalli kasio. '[As much as possible, go quickly=] Go as quickly as possible.'

Another way of saying this is toytolok (‖ 24.8):

Toytolok ppalli kasio.

Tāy lo is also used after a few nouns, with similar meaning:

maum tāy lo '[following one's mind=] as [one] wants, wishes, likes'
ttus tāy lo '[in line with the intention or meaning=] as [one] expected'
ney māl tāy lo '[in accordance with your words=] as you say'

Here are more examples of tāy lo in sentences.

1. Sāsil tāy lo māl hasio.	[Speak according to=] Stick to the facts.
2. Na hanun tāy lo hay la.	Do as I do.
3. Emeni ka māl hasinun tāy lo tā cwūnpi hasio.	Prepare everything just as Mother says.
4. Kim sensayng i tul.e osinun tāy lo ce 'ykey cēnhwa hala ko hay cwusimyen komapkeyss.ˢup.nita.	Would you please ask Mr. Kim to call me as soon as he comes in?
5. Chayk ul noh.in tāy lo noh.a twuess.ey yo.	I left the book just as it was.
6. Halq swu iss.nun tāy lo ppalli tol.a ka ya hay yo.	I'll have to get back home just as soon as possible.
7. Sayngkak tāy lo hasio.	Do as you think best.
8. Ku tāy lo twusio.	Leave it as it is.
9. Kwutwu lul sin.un tāy lo pang ey tul.e kass.ey yo.	He went into the room with his shoes still on.
10. Kim sensayng i māl han tāy lo, Hānkwuk ey pol man han kes i mānh.e yo.	As Mr. Kim says, there are many things worth seeing in Korea.

‖ 27.7. The construction -ul man hata 'is worth doing.'

23. Hānkwuk ey nun . . . pol man han kes i mānh.e? 'Are there many things worth seeing in Korea?'
24. Pol man han kes i mānh.ko mālko. 'Of course—there are many things worth seeing.'

The descriptive verbal noun expression man hata is used as a postmodifier expression after the prospective modifier form (-ul) of a processive verb to give the meaning 'is worth . . .ing' or 'is good for . . .ing' etc.

Here are more examples:

1. Kim sensayng un mannal man han sālam iey yo.	Mr. Kim is a man worth meeting. or Mr. Kim is the man to see.
2. I kongwen i swīl man han kongwen iey yo.	This park is a good park to relax in.
3. Ku opheyla ka pol man to hako tul.ul man to hay yo.	That opera is worth both seeing and hearing.

Similar expressions are:

mit.ul man hata 'is trustworthy'
mek.ul man hata 'is catable, is worth eating'
ilk.ul man hata 'is readable, is worth reading'
kacil man hata 'is worth having or owning'
sal man hata 'is worth buying'
ip.ul man hata 'is (well) worth wearing, is (quite) wearable'

Make up some sentences using each of these expressions. Try using them in other places besides at the end of the sentence.

The descriptive verbal noun man (related perhaps to the particles man 'just, only' and mankhum 'as much as') is always tied in two directions: to the preceding prospective modifier (-ul) of -ulq and to the following descriptive verb hata. In that respect, it is like the pen of -ulq pen hata 'is on the verge of doing' (‖24.12).

‖ 27.8. Approximate numbers.

You have learned that you can put han . . . 'about' in front of a number to make it approximate or vague (‖ 6.3), with or without the word ina after the number. In addition (or instead), you can use some special APPROXIMATE NUMBER expressions. A list of these follows:

	WITH CHINESE NUMERALS	WITH KOREAN NUMERALS
'1–2'	ilq-ī	han(a)-twul / han-twu . . .
'about 1 or 2'		han-twues / han-twue . . .
'about 2'		twues / twue . . .
'2–3'	ī-sam	twu-seys / -sey . . . , -sek . . .
'about 2 or 3'		twu-senes / twu-sene . . .
'about 3'		senes / sene . . .
'3–4'	sam-sā	
'about 3 or 4'		sene-netes / sene-nete . . .
'about 4'		netes / nete . . .
'4–5'	sā-o	
'about 4 or 5'		ne(te)-tāys
'about 5'		tāys

'5–6'	ō-ˡyuk*	
'about 5 or 6'		tāy-yeses
'6–7'	ˡyuk-chil	
'about 6 or 7'		yey-nilkop
'7–8'	chil-phal	
'about 7 or 8'		il(ko)-yetelp
'8–9'	phal-kwu	
'about 8 or 9'		yet-ahop
'several; many'		yeles / yele . . .

Above ten, you find a few such expressions: 20–30 ī-sam sip, 30–40 sam-sā sip, etc. And you can add the suffix -ye to any Chinese numeral that would end with a zero in our way of noting them; the resulting numeral means '. . . odd': sip-ye 'ten odd, more than ten,' kwusip-ye 'ninety odd,' payk-ye 'over a hundred, etc. For '10 odd' to '90 odd' you also get expressions with the Korean numerals and the suffix -nam.un/-nam.u . . . (often spelled -namun/-namu): ye'-nam.un '10 odd,' sumu'-nam.un '20 odd,' selun-nam.un '30 odd,' mahun-nam.un '40 odd,' swīn-nam.un '50 odd,' yeyswun-nam.un '60,' ilhun-nam.un '70 odd,' yetun-nam.un '80 odd,' ahu'-nam.un '90 odd.' There are also such expressions as swū-sip 'several tens,' swū-payk 'several hundreds,' swū-chen 'several thousands,' swū-man 'tens of thousands,' swū-ek 'some hundreds of millions' (ek 'hundred million'). The word swū means 'number of . . .' when following a counter: kwēnq-swu 'number of (books)'; it means 'a number of, several' when preceding the counter: swū-kwen 'several (books).'

‖ 27.9. Ordinal numerals.

An ordinal numeral is one that tells you the 'how-manyeth' ('first, second, third . . .'). Chinese numerals are made ordinal by attaching a prefix cēy-; Korean numerals are made ordinal by adding the word . . . ccay '-th. But for 'first' there is a special form ches ccay, and the word ches . . . is often used alone to mean 'first' when followed directly by a noun. Here is a list of the ordinal numerals:

	Chinese	Korean
1st	cēy-il	ches ccay
2nd	cēy-i	twūl ccay [less commonly twū ccay]
3rd	cēy-sam	sēys ccay [also spelled sēy ccay]
4th	cēy-sa	nēys ccay [also spelled nēy ccay]
5th	cēy-o	tases ccay
6th	cēy-ˡyuk /ceyyuk/	yeses ccay
7th	cēy-chil	ilkop ccay
8th	cēy-phal	yetel(p) ccay
9th	cēy-kwu	ahop ccay
10th	cēy-sip	yel ccay
11th	cēy sip-il	yel-han ccay
12th	cēy sip-i	yelq-twul ccay
20th	cēy ī-sip	sumu ccay [less commonly sumul ccay]
100th	cēy-payk	payk ccay
133rd	cēy payk sam-sip sam	payk selun sēys ccay
'how many-eth?'		meych ccay

---

* Pronounced /o.yuk/ or /olyuk/ or /onyuk/.

You have run across the ordinals in the expression 'in the first (second, third) place = firstly (secondly, thirdly)': ches (twūl, sēys) ccay lo.

‖ 27.10. Some common derivational suffixes.

23. Hānkwuk ey nun ^{l}yeksa-sang ulo 'na cili-sang ulo pol man han kes i mānh.e? 'Are there many things worth seeing in Korea from the standpoint of history or (from the standpoint of) geography?'

^{l}Yeksa-sang 'from the standpoint of history' and cili-sang 'from the standpoint of geography' are examples of words derived from other words by adding a suffix. ^{l}Yeksa 'history' and cili 'geography' are the original words; -sang is a suffix, similar in meaning to the adverbial suffix '-wise' which has recently been gaining popularity in American English.

You have of course observed many such derivations. Others made from the noun ^{l}yeksa 'history' are:

^{l}yeksa-cek 'historical'
^{l}yeksa-hak '(study of) history, historical science'
^{l}yeksa-ka 'historian'

The suffix -hak means 'study' or 'science' or '-ology,' so that cili-hak means '[the study of] geography,' while -ka means 'person who engages in an activity professionally' so that a person who writes novels (sōsel) is called sōsel-ka 'novelist.'

Here are a few other deriving suffixes that combine with words you have learned.

-cang 'place where an activity is performed'
cengke-cang 'railroad station' [cengke 'stopping a vehicle']
cengkwu-cang 'tennis court' [cengkwu 'tennis']
wūntong-cang 'gymnasium' [wūntong 'sport, exercise']

-cey 'made in . . .'
ōykwuk-cey 'foreign make' [ōykwuk 'foreign country']
Sēseq-cey 'Swiss make' [Sēse 'Switzerland']
Ilponq-cey 'made in Japan' [Ilpon 'Japan']

-kwan 'building'
kongsa-kwan 'legation' [kongsa 'foreign minister']
^{l}yengsa-kwan 'consulate' [^{l}yengsa 'consul']
tāysa-kwan 'embassy' [tāysa 'ambassador']
tose-kwan 'library' [tose 'books']
yenghwa-kwan 'movie theater' [yenghwa 'movie']

-kwan 'government official'
seki-kwan '(official) secretary' [seki 'secretary']
kēm.yel-kwan 'censor' [kēm.yel 'censorship']
sihem-kwan 'official examiner' [sihem 'examination']

-phum 'goods, product'
kwīcwung-phum 'precious belonging' [kwīcwung hata 'is precious']
kwuksan-phum 'native product' [kwuksan 'domestic production']
pusok-phum '(mechanical) parts' [pusok 'attachment, addenda']

-pi 'fee, expense'
saynghwal-pi 'living expenses' [saynghwal 'living, life']
swusen-pi 'repair costs' [swusen 'repairing']
^{l}yehayng-pi 'traveling expenses' [^{l}yehayng 'travel, journey, trip']

-sa₁ 'scholar, person'
pyēnho-sa 'lawyer' [pyēnho 'pleading']
pihayng-sa 'aviator' [pihayng 'flying a plane']
kikwan-sa 'engineer' [kikwan 'engine']
-sa₂ 'person, master'
senkyo-sa 'missionary' [senkyo 'spreading the faith']
ˈīpal(q)-sa 'barber' [ˈīpal 'haircutting']
-sayng 'student'
tāyhak-sayng 'university student' [tāyhak 'university']
uyhak-sayng 'medical student' [uyhak 'medical science']
kāngsup-sayng 'short-course student' [kāngsup '(special) lectures']
-sil 'room'
cīnchalq-sil 'examining room' [cīnchal 'medical examination']
swuswulq-sil 'operating room' [swuswul 'surgical operation']
tose-sil 'library (room)' [tose 'books']
mok.yok-sil 'bath(ing) room' [mok.yok 'bathing']
-so 'place'
thak.a-so 'nursery' [thak.a 'taking care of children']
ˈīpal(q)-so 'barber shop' [ˈīpal 'haircutting']
sāmu-so 'office' [sāmu 'business affairs']
chilyo-so 'infirmary' [chilyo 'medical treatment']
kāngsup-so 'lecture room, special school' [kāngsup '(special) lectures']
-swu 'hand, person, operator'
wūncen-swu 'driver, operator' [wūncen 'operating, driving']
kikwan-swu 'locomotive engineer' [kikwan 'engine']
kyohwan-swu 'telephone operator' [kyohwan 'telephone exchange']
-wen₁ 'institution'
koa-wen 'orphanage' [koa 'orphan']
tāyhak-wen 'graduate school' [tāyhak 'university']
swuto-wen 'monastery' [swuto 'ascetic exercise']
micang-wen 'beauty parlor' [micang 'beauty culture']
-wen₂ 'garden, park, institute'
tōngmul-wen 'zoo' [tōngmul 'animal']
yuchi-wen 'kindergarten' [yuchi hata 'is infantile']
koa-wen 'orphanage' [koa 'orphan']
-yong 'for the use of'
haksayng-yong 'for students' [haksayng 'student']
kaceng-yong 'for household use' [kaceng 'household']
namca-yong 'for men' [namca 'male']
sāmu-yong 'for business (use)' [sāmu 'business affairs']

EXERCISES

I

Here are some statements in Korean. Change each one so that it expresses an intention, using one of the constructions described in ‖ 27.2 of this lesson; translate the result.

1. Kūlim ul pōy tulye yo.
2. Onulq cenyek ul eme' nim i mas i 'ss.key hasikeyss.ey yo.
3. Onul ōhwu ey yenghwa lul pokeyss.ey yo.

4. Wi chung ey ka se phyēnci lul ssukeyss.ey yo.
5. Kongpu machin hwū ey Hānkwuk ey ka se talun sālam tul ul towa cwukeyss.ey yo.
6. Chinkwu hanthey han cwuil ey phyēnci lul sēk cang ssik hakeyss.ey yo.
7. Kicha nun catong-cha pota ppaluki ttaymun ey, kicha lo kakeyss.ey yo.
8. Kaps i elma 'tun ci nay ka ku os ul sakeyss.ey yo.
9. Yelum nal ey īl haki nun ttukepko elyewe to, na nun yelqsim ulo īl hakeyss.ey yo.
10. Sānqpo hanun tāysin ey tose-kwan ey ka yo.

II

Here are some short statements in Korean. Supply a swulok expression (‖ 27.4) at the beginning of each, to make a sentence meaning 'the more . . . the more . . .'; then translate. For example, the first might be: Hānkwuk ūmsik ul mek.umyen mek.ulq swulok mas i iss.ci yo. 'The more Korean food I eat, the better it tastes.'

1. Hānkwuk ūmsik i mas i iss.ci yo.
2. Tewe cye yo.
3. Os ul mānh.i sa ya hay yo.
4. Tōn ul kaciko siph.e yo.
5. Phikon hay cyess.ey yo.
6. Chayk ul mānh.i ilk.ko siph.e yo.
7. Nunun kes iey yo.
8. Nay ka wus.ess.ey yo.
9. Ppalli kel.ess.ey yo.
10. Ūmsik kaps i pissa cye yo.

III

The following sentences say that one thing (X) is more so than another (Y). Say each aloud in Korean in such a way as to reverse the meaning— 'Y is more so than X.' Then give the English meaning of the reversed sentences.

1. Onul un ecey pota sikan i mānh.i iss.ey yo.
2. Kumnyen un cak.nyen pota pi ka te mānh.i wa yo.
3. I sangcem ey nun ce sangcem pota mulken to mānh.ko, kaps to ssa yo.
4. Hānkwuk pota Mikwuk ey nun catong-cha ka mānh.ci yo?
5. Cīnan Hwa-yoil pota onul un palam i pūlko chwuwe yo.
6. Kwi ka mek.nun kes pota nwun i mēnun kes i pulhayng hay yo.
7. Ca.yu ka ēps.nun kes pota cwuk.nun kes ul wēn hanta.
8. Palam i pūlci anh.ko hay ka nanun nal pota pi ka cokum ssik wa to palam i pūnun nal ey ppallay ka ppalli malle yo.
9. Tha pelin ūmsik pota maywun kes ul mek.keyss.ey yo.
10. Cwūsa lul mac.nun kes pota yak ul mek.nun kes i swiwe yo.

IV

Each of the following sentences is a statement. Expand it by putting at the beginning a pota expression meaning 'rather than,' on the pattern of Basic Sentence 21:

Mikwuk ey se īl hanun kes pota, Hankwuk ulo ka se īl haki lo kyelqsim hayss.ci. 'Rather than working in America, I've decided to go to Korea and work.'

1. Tāyhak ey se kaluchikeyss.ey yo.
2. Kongpu lul machica mā'ca cip ey kass.ey yo.
3. Pak sensayng puin i ^{l}nayil osil mo.yang iey yo.
4. Cang ey se kwāsil ul sako siph.e yo.
5. Pi ka wass.ta nwūn i wass.ta hay yo.
6. Yelq si ey cengke-cang ey se mannapsita.
7. Cey ka tōn ul tulil they 'ni, cang ul com pwa 'ta cwusio.
8. Cēncha lo kalq ka yo?
9. Halye ko sayngkak ul cēng hakey toykeyss.ey yo.
10. ^{n}Yeca Chengnyen Hōy-kwan ey um.ak ^{l}yēnsup i iss.e se, kaki lo kyelqsim hayss.ey yo.

CONVERSATION

I

Chat among yourselves about your plans for when you finish the Korean course you have undertaken. Be specific about your own plans, and listen with interest to what your fellow students are planning. Ask each other specific questions.

II

Pretend that you are an American farmer visiting a Korean farm village. The other members of the class will play the parts of Korean farmers. You are curious about their way of doing things; ask them questions. Find out what they plant and when. Ask about their houses and their families. Do their children go to school? Are the schools far away? Is there a bus? Are the school expenses high? Where do the farmers sell their crops? Are the prices higher this year than last year? What about the things the farmer has to buy in the city—are they more expensive than they used to be? Does the government help the farmer? How?

Now it's the turn of the Korean farmers to question you. How big are farms in America? Are most Americans farmers? If not, what do they do for a living? Do Americans eat much rice? Or do they prefer things made out of wheat flour? What part of America do they grow wheat in? What time of year is it harvested? Why does the price of wheat stay high even in years when so much of it is grown? Does America send wheat or wheat flour to other countries? Do the wheat farmers use plows like those the Korean farmers use? Do American farmers have large families? Do they send their children to school? Are the schools near the farms? Is there public transportation for the children? Do the children have to pay to go to school? To take the school bus? Do they serve the children food at school? What kind of food? What do you grow on your farm? Do you keep livestock? Does your wife have a flower garden? Do people come and buy the flowers? How about vegetables? How many rooms are there in your farmhouse? How many buildings are there on your farm? Do you have cows that give milk? Do you sell the milk? Do they raise tea in America? (If so, where? If not, where do they buy it from?) How about coffee?

Take turns being the American.

VOCABULARY DRILL

1. Say each of the following things three different ways in Korean:
   a. I'm planning to leave soon.
   b. I've decided to raise chickens.

c. I intend to establish a training course.

2. Say the following sentences aloud in Korean in each of the three ways indicated.

a. I'm going to teach ___.
sewing
cooking
geography

b. He explained ___ to the farm women.
the plan
his country's customs
how to plow the rice paddies

c. I want to be able to ___ rather than ___.
talk Korean automatically . . . having to translate
choose my own place of work . . . working in the same country where I was born
harvest the rice plants too . . . just transplanting the seedlings

d. Going to college ___.
is worthwhile
is usually not simple
makes you think about your purposes in life

e. The more ___ the more ___.
I read . . . enthusiastic I get
I see of farm life . . . I want to live in the country and grow rice
concretely he spoke . . . his ideas came through to me

f. Do you think ___ would be worth setting up?
a nursery
an institute for child care
a project for teaching American farming methods

3. Translate the following sentences into Korean.

a. You should pay for merchandise according to its value.
b. I hope some day to own my own farm and farm equipment.
c. According to many landowners, raising chickens is easier than raising other domesticated animals.
d. According to what I read in this magazine, Oriental farmers grow more rice than any other cereal grains.
e. Just as the farmer told me, there's something the matter with this plow; I wonder where we could get it fixed.

4. Say each of the following things twice, first with -ca (mā'ca) and then with -nun tāy lo.

a. Take this medicine as soon as the plane leaves, so you won't get sick.
b. As soon as I made myself understood they brought me what I wanted.
c. I thought I would go to Korea as soon as I got so I could express my ideas in Korean automatically.
d. As soon as my friend told me he intended to learn to play tennis I told him that the more you play tennis the better you get at it.
e. As soon as I asked him with what motive he had decided to go to college, his face turned red.
f. As soon as I came to get acquainted with my Korean friend I realized how many fine points Koreans have.

g. I find that as soon as I get an interest in a country like Korea I start wanting to go there (to see it).
h. Let's take Poktong-i there (to see how he gets along) as soon as they get the nursery set up.
i. As soon as we get to the farm village let's decide where to hold our school.
j. As soon as they have learned simple Western-style cooking we will teach them Western-style sewing.
k. It may rain; as soon as you are through with the dishes, you'd better gather up the laundry and bring it in, even if it hasn't all gotten dry.
l. We expect to let you know as soon as we decide on a place to build our house, so (don't worry).

COMPREHENSION

Listen while your Korean teacher tells you about a trip to the country he has made. He will tell you as much as he can remember about typical days on a farm, in various seasons. Follow his narrative closely and be prepared to answer his questions on the material afterwards. If he uses terms for farm implements and the like, ask him to explain what the implements look like and what they are used for; if necessary, get him to draw you a picture of things you don't understand. But be sure he uses no English in explaining the words to you. (For technical things like the parts of a Korean plow, there just aren't very good English equivalents, anyway.) After your tutor has told you everything he knows about farming, perhaps he will give you a similar sketch of Korean weaving (drawing a loom on the board and telling you about the parts and how they work), or Korean mining practices, or the way they go about building a Korean house—whatever he feels will be of interest to you. Be sure to ask questions about anything you don't understand, and write down the new words your tutor uses in his talk, even if you aren't exactly sure of their meanings.

LESSON 28. THE HENPECKED HUSBAND

BASIC SENTENCES

[Mr. Hong drops by Mr. Pak's house.]

Korean	English	Amplification
H. 1. Pak chemci. Ileh.key cōh.un nal caney cip sōk ey se mue l' hana.	Mr. Pak! What are you doing [cooped up] in the house on such a nice day?	. . . chemci 'Mr. . . .' [FAMILIAR] caney 'you' [FAMILIAR] mue l' hana 'what are you doing?' [FAMILIAR]
P. 2. Na cip poney. Ese tul.e okey.	I'm looking after the house. Come on in.	poney 'looks at <u>or</u> after' [FAMILIAR] okey 'come!' [FAMILIAR command]
H. 3. I sālam a! Ileh.key hwachang han nal cip ul pona? Wuli kang ulo nakk.si cil kasey. An ey se eti kass.na.	[Look at] you! Watching the house on such a glorious day? Let's go down to the river to fish. Where's your wife gone?	i sālam 'this person; you [INFORMAL]; I/me' hwachang hata 'is glorious, fine, splendid' pona 'are you looking at <u>or</u> after?' [FAMILIAR] kang 'river' nakk.si cil 'fishing, angling' nakk.si cil (ul) hanta 'fishes' nakk.si cil (ul) kanta 'goes fishing' an [FAMILIAR] = an(h)ay 'wife' an ey se 'wife [as oblique subject]' kass.na 'did [someone] go? has [someone] gone?' [FAMILIAR]
P. 4. Saypyek puthe na-tul.i kass.ta 'ney. Pam ey 'na onta 'ney.	She left the house at dawn, you see. (She says) she'll [come=] be back around evening.	saypyek 'dawn, sunrise' saypyek puthe 'since dawn, [from=] at dawn' na-tul.i 'going out of the house for a while (to be back later)=a woman's outing' [noun derived from na- 'emerge' + tu-l- 'enter'] na-tul.i (lul) hanta 'has her outing'

Korean	English	Amplification
		na-tul.i (lul) kanta 'goes on her outing' kass.ta 'ney = kass.ta ko haney '[one] says [someone] went' [FAMILIAR] = '(I tell you) she went' onta 'ney = onta ko haney '[one] says someone comes' = 'she says she'll come'
H. 5. Caney! Cip ul kkok pwa ya hana?	Look. Do you really have to look after the house?	caney 'you!' = 'look!'
6. Mun ul camke twumyen an toyna? Kanan han sallim ey kwī han mulken to ēps.ul they 'n tey . . .	Wouldn't it be OK to leave the door locked? Nobody would expect to find any valuable things in a poor (man's) household, so . . .	camkunta [camke yo, camku-] 'locks it' camke twue yo 'locks it, leaves it locked' an toyna? 'isn't it acceptable or all right?' [FAMILIAR] kanan hata 'is poor, poverty-stricken' kwī hata 'is valuable, precious'
P. 7. Nwu' ka āna. Wuli ^{n}yephyenney ka cip pi(wu)ci mālla ko holyeng hako kass.ney.	Who knows? My wife went off leaving me with strict orders not to leave the house empty.	āna 'does [one] know? [FAMILIAR]' ^{n}yephyenney 'wife' pīta [pie yo, pī-] 'is empty' pi(wu)nta [pi(w)e yo, pi(wu)-] 'makes/leaves it empty' pi(wu)ci mālla ko . . . '[saying] don't (allow it to be) empty!' holyeng 'a command, an order' holyeng (ul) hanta 'orders, commands' kass.ney /kanney/ 'went (away)' [FAMILIAR]
H. 8. Na kath.umyen, kulen ^{n}yephyenney kaman hi an twuney.	[If you were like me=] If I were you, I wouldn't put up with a wife like that.	kaman hi 'quietly' twunta [twue yo, twu-] 'puts (away); keeps, stores; maintains, has in one's house(hold)' ^{n}yephyenney lul twunta 'maintains (keeps, has) a wife' twuney 'puts (etc.)' [FAMILIAR]

Korean	English	Amplification
9. Ilen nal cip anq sōk ey iss.nun caney nun machi kam.ok ey kat.hye iss.nun cōyswu kath.ney.	You're just like a criminal shut up in jail, cooped up in the house on a day like this.	cip anq sōk ey 'inside (of the inside of) the house' cip anq sōk ey iss.nun caney 'you who are inside the house' machi 'just, as though, as if' kam.ok 'jail, prison' katwunta [katwe yo, katwu-] 'shuts in, confines' kat.hinta /kachinta/ [kat.hye /kache/ yo, kat.hi-] 'is shut in, confined, imprisoned' cōyswu 'convict, prisoner' kath.ney /kanney/ 'is the same, is like' [FAMILIAR]
10. Caney kath.un che-siha nun cheum poney.	I've never seen a henpecked husband like you before!	che-siha 'henpecked husband' cheum poney 'I see it for the first time' [FAMILIAR]
P.11. Māl mālkey. Kulay nwukwu hako nakk.si cil kana.	Don't talk about it. So who are you going fishing with?	māl (haci) mālkey 'don't talk!' [FAMILIAR]
H.12. Kēnneq maul Ko chemci hako, twīq maul An chemci hako kaki lo hayss.ney.	I've arranged to go with Mr. Ko from the village across the way and with Mr. An from the village back of here.	kēnnunta [kēnne yo, kēnnu-] 'crosses, goes across' kēnne(q) . . . 'the opposite . . . , the one across' maul 'village' kēnneq maul 'village across [from here]' twīq maul 'back village, village back [from here]'
13. Yo say kang ey mīl mul i tul.e wa se un.e ka cal cap.hinta ko hatey.	They say the tide has come in recently and (so) lots of sweetfish are caught.	mīl mul 'high tide' mīl mul i tul.e wa yo 'the tide comes in' un.e 'sweet smelt, sweetfish' cap.hinta [cap.hye yo, cap.hi-] 'gets caught' . . . ko hatey 'I recall hearing them say that . . . ; they've been saying' [FAMILIAR retrospective]
14. Un.e lul cap.e se nun kangq ka ey se kwuwe mek.ki lo hayss.ney.	When we catch the sweetfish, we've decided to broil them and eat them on the riverbank.	ka 'edge, border' kangq ka 'riverbank' kwup.nunta [kwuwe yo, kwuw-] 'broils'

Korean	English	Amplification
15. Kulay caney an olye 'na?	Well, you won't come?	olye (ko ha)na? 'does [one] intend to come?' [FAMILIAR]
P.16. Caney tul kkili kakey. Na n' mōs kaney.	You guys go on. I can't go.	. . . kkili 'the separate group of people (or of like-moving objects)' caney (tul) kkili 'you all' [FAMILIAR] mōs kaney 'can't go' [FAMILIAR]
17. Wuli mānwula māl an tul.umyen hon naney.	If I don't obey the old lady, I'll get scolded.	mānwula 'an old hag; one's wife [vulgar]' . . .(uy) māl (ul) tul.e yo '[listens to the words of . . .=] obeys' hon 'soul, spirit' hon (i) nanta 'has a hard time of it, is severely scolded (browbeaten); is startled, frightened' hon (ul) nāynta 'browbeats, bullies, scolds; startles, frightens'
H.18. Pak chemci. Nal i cemul.ess.nun tey way i kaycheng ka ey se wass.ta kass.ta hako iss.na?	Mr. Pak. It's got dark; why are you wandering back and forth on the bank of this creek?	cemunta [cemul.e yo, cemu-l-] 'gets dark, darkens' kaychen 'creek; ditch'
19. Mue l' ilh.e ppelyess.na?	Did you lose something?	-e ppelinta [LIVELY] = -e pelinta -e (p)pelyess.na 'did [one] do it completely?' [FAMILIAR]
20. I sālam a! Ku man olul ak naylil ak hako, kaman hi se se tāytap com hakey.	Look! Cut out that going up and down and stand still and answer me!	ku man . . . hanta '[does only that=] stops doing' olul ak naylil ak hanta 'goes up and down (by turns)' tāytap hakey 'answer!' [FAMILIAR]
P.21. Amman hay to sayngkak i an nanun tey??	However hard I try, I can't remember it!	amman . . . -e to 'no matter . . . however . . .' amman hay to 'no matter what I do, whatever I do'

Korean	English	Amplification
22. I kaychen ul kēnne ttwita (ka) kkampak ic.e ppelyess.ta 'n māl ia.	I mean, I forgot it all of a sudden when I jumped across this creek.	ttwinta [ttwie yo] 'jumps' kēnne ttwinta 'jumps across' kkampak 'suddenly, all of a sudden'
H.23. Ilh.e ppelici anh.ko, ic.e ppelyess.na?	You didn't lose something, you forgot something?	
24. Tāychey mues ul ic.e ppelyess.na.	Just what on earth did you forget?	tāychey 'substance, main points, (in) general; [+ QUESTION WORD] just (who, what, etc.), (who, what, etc.) in the world or on earth'
P.25. Nay māl com tul.e pokey, Hong chemci.	Listen to me, Mr. Hong.	tul.e pokey 'listen! try listening!' [FAMILIAR]
26. Onul wuli chekaq cip canchi ey kass.ta onun kil ilq sey.	I'm on my way back from a party at the house of my in-laws today.	cheka(q cip) 'a man's in-laws; the wife's family' sika(q cip) 'a woman's in-laws; the husband's family' canchi 'party' ilq sey 'it is' [= iney, FAMILIAR copula]
27. Wuli mānwula nun mom-sal lo mōs kako na tele ku canchi ūmsik cwung ey se, ku-cwung mas iss.nun kes ul al.e kaciko ola ko hatey.	My wife couldn't go because she wasn't feeling well and she told me to find out the best tasting things among the dishes at the party (and tell her).	mom-sal 'indisposition, slight illness; fatigue' ku-cwung 'number one, most' (= kacang) al. e kacinta 'finds out, obtains knowledge' ola ko hatey 'told [one] to come' [FAMILIAR retrospective]
H.28. Ha ha! Kulay ku ūmsik ilum ul ic.ess.ta 'n māl in ka?	Ha, ha! So you mean you forgot the name of that dish?	ha ha 'ha ha'
29. I sālam a! Kulay, i kaychen ul olul ak naylil ak hamyen sayngkak i nana?	Look—(you think) you'll remember it then if you keep going up and down this brook?	olul ak naylil ak hamyen 'if [one] goes up and down' sayngkak i nana 'does [one] recall?' [FAMILIAR]
P.30. Ku ttek ilum ul cal ōyko ota ka i kaychen ul kēnnunun palam ey ic.e ppeliko mal.ess.ney.	I (came having) memorized the name of that cake very well, and then, while I was crossing this creek, I completely forgot it.	ttek 'cake' ōynta [ōy yo ("way yo"), ōy-]= oywunta [oywe, oywu-] 'memorizes' . . .-nun palam ey 'under the influence of . . . , in the midst of . . .'

Korean	English	Amplification
		ic.e ppeliko mal.e yo [mā-l-] 'ends up completely forgetting'
H.31. Cham hansim han sālam ikwun.	What a sorry little man you are.	hansim hata 'is pitiful, sorry'
32. Ku-kkacis kes ic.e ppelyess.umyen, ic.e ppelyess.ci. Kep nana? Wūlci wul.e.	If you forget such a thing, why, you forgot it. Are you scared? Crybaby!	kep 'fear, fright' kep nanta /kemnanta/ '[fear occurs=] gets scared, is afraid, fears' kep nana 'is [one] afraid?' [FAMILIAR] wūlci wul.e 'go on and cry!'
P.33. Caney wuli mānwula sēngcil ālci!!	You know my wife's temper?	sēngcil 'temper, disposition'
34. Kkok chac.e kaciko ka ya hal they 'n tey . . .	I'm going to have to show up with it for sure, but . . .	chac.e kaciko 'with, having found' chac.e kaciko ka yo 'shows up with [it], goes having found [it]'
H.35. Mōs-nan soli ku man hakey.	Cut out (such) silly talk.	mōs-nata [-na yo, -na-] 'is ugly; is stupid' mōs-nan soli 'silly talk' ku man hakey 'stop [it]!' [FAMILIAR]
36. Kkwul mek.un pengeli kath.i mēng hani se iss.ci mālko ese ka pokey.	Don't just stand there with a blank face like a deaf-mute with his mouth full of honey—go on home!	kkwul 'honey' pengeli 'a mute person' mēng hani = mēng hakey 'blankly' mēng hata 'looks blank (vacant, expressionless)' ese ka pokey 'go right home (and see what happens)' [FAMILIAR]
P.37. Olh.ci! Chac.ess.ta! Chac.ess.e!	That's it! I've found it! I've got it!	olh.ci 'it is right' [INTIMATE casual]
38. Kkwul ttek ita, kkwul ttek ia!	It's honey cake, it's honey cake!	
39. Tto ic.e ppeliki cen ey ese ka pwa ya 'ci.	And before I forget it again, I've got to rush right home.	ese ka pwa ya 'ci [= ese ka pwa ya haci] 'I have to go right home (and see)'

SUPPLEMENTARY VOCABULARY

hoswu	lake	'yen-mos	(lily) pond
mos	pond	kaywul	small brook

hāypyen or pataq ka	seashore
nakk.siq tay	fishing pole
(nakk.si) kumul	(fishing) net
(nakk.si) mikki, nakk.siq pap	(fishing) bait
nakk.siq pay	a fisherman's boat
epu or koki cap.i	a fisherman
nakk.siq kwun	an angler, a fisher
nakk.nunta [nakk.e yo, nakk-]	fishes with a hook, angles for
nakk.si(q panul)	a fish-hook
nakk.siq cwul	a fishing line
kotung-e	mackerel
chenge, piwus	herring
myengthay	pollack
puk.e	dried pollack
mallin chenge	dried herring, kipper
coki	yellow corvenia
min.e	(sea) perch
tōm(i)	sea bream
nepchi, totali	flounder
kaca(y)mi	sole
songe	trout
cengeli	sardine
pinge	surf smelt
un.e	sweet smelt, sweetfish
talang-e	tuna
sange	shark
(paym) cang.e	eel
pāym	snake
saywu	shrimp
kēy	crab
cokay	clam
kwul	oyster
ocing-e	cuttlefish
nakci	squid
mun.e	octopus
hay ka tot.nunta [tot.a yo, tot-] or ttunta [tte yo, ttu-]	the sun rises
hay ka cinta [cie yo, ci-]	the sun sets
nal i palk.nunta [palk.e yo, palk-]	the day breaks
yēlq soy	key ['iron to open']
cam'ulq soy	(pad)lock ['iron to close']
yēlq /cam'ulq soy lo camkunta [camke yo, camku-]	locks
yelq /cam'ulq soy lo yēnta [yel.e yo, yē-l-]	unlocks
[1]yēngkam	an elderly gentleman; one's husband
. . . [1]yēngkam nim	(elderly) Mr. ...

NOTES

28.1. Familiar style.

Conversation between close friends is characterized by FAMILIAR-STYLE endings on the verbs at the end of their sentences:

-ney	STATEMENT (but iney or ilq sey for the copula)
-tey	RETROSPECTIVE STATEMENT (but iley for the copula)
-na	QUESTION
-key	COMMAND
-sey	SUGGESTION

The statement ending -ney, which corresponds to the plain-style -ta and -(nu)nta, to the intimate-style -e and the polite-style -e yo, and to the formal-style -(su)p.nita, appeared in the following basic sentences:

2. Na cip poney.	I'm looking after the house.
4. Saypyek puthe na-tul.i kass.ta [ko ha]ney. Pam ey 'na onta [ko ha]ney.	She left the house at dawn, you see. (She says) she'll be back around evening.

7. . . . cip pi(wu)ci mālla ko holyeng hako kass.ney.	She left with strict orders not to leave the house empty.
8. . . . kulen ^{n}yephyenney kaman hi an twuney.	I wouldn't put up with a wife like that.
9. . . . kat.hye iss.nun cōyswu kath.ney	You're like a confined criminal.
10. . . . cheum poney.	I'm seeing . . . for the first time.
11. . . . nwukwu hako . . . kana.	Who are you going with?
12. . . . An chemci hako kaki lo hayss.ney.	I've arranged to go with Mr. An.
14. . . . kwuwe mek.ki lo hayss.ney.	We've decided to broil and eat them.
16. . . . Na n' mōs kaney.	I can't go.
17. . . . hon naney.	I'll get scolded.
30. . . . ic.e ppeliko mal.ess.ney.	I ended up completely forgetting it.

The retrospective statement ending -tey, which corresponds to the plain-style -tula and the formal-style -(su)ptita, appeared in these basic sentences:

13. . . . un.e ka cal cap.hinta ko hatey.	They say a lot of trout are being caught.
27. . . . al.e kaciko ola ko hatey.	She told me to find out.

The question ending -na, which corresponds to the plain-style -nun/-un ya or -ni, to the intimate-style -e and the polite-style -e yo, and to the formal-style -(su)p.nikka, appears in these Basic Sentences:

1. . . . mue l' hana.	What are you doing?
3. . . . cip ul pona? . . . An ey se eti kass.na.	Are you looking after the house? Where's your wife gone?
5. Cip ul kkok pwa ya hana?	Do you really have to look after the house?
6. Mun ul camke twumyen an toyna?	Wouldn't it be OK to leave the door locked?
7. Nwu' ka āna.	Who knows?
15. Kulay caney an olye 'na?	Well, won't you come?
18. . . . way i kaycheng ka ey se wass.ta kass.ta hako iss.na?	Why are you wandering back and forth on the bank of this creek?
19. Mue l' ilh.e ppelyess.na?	Did you lose something?
23. Ilh.e ppelici anh.ko, ic.e ppelyess.na?	You didn't lose something, you forgot something?
24. Tāychey mues ul ic.e ppelyess.na.	Just what on earth did you forget?
29. . . . sayngkak i nana?	Do you remember it?

Suggestions in the familiar style have the suffix -sey, corresponding to formal -(u)psita and plain -ca, as in Basic Sentence 3:

. . . Wuli kang ulo nakk.si cil kasey . . . 'Let's go down to the river to fish.'

Commands have the suffix -key, which may be followed by the particle una/na (a kind of softener); the corresponding formal form is -(u)sio and -(u)sipsio, the corresponding plain forms are -(u)la and -e la. Familiar commands appeared in these Basic Sentences:

2. . . . Ese tul.e okey.	Come right in.
11. Māl [haci] mālkey . . .	Don't talk about it.
16. Caney tul kkili kakey . . .	You guys go on . . .

20. . . . tāytap com hakey.	Answer me!
25. Nay māl com tul.e pokey, Hong chemci.	(Try) listen(ing) to me, Mr. Hong.
35. Mōs-nan soli ku man hakey.	Stop talking so senselessly.
36. . . . ese ka pokey.	(Try) go(ing) on [home]!

The familiar-style retrospective statement ending -tey should not be confused with constructions which consist of modifier-plus-tey, examples of which appear in the following Basic Sentences (cf. also ‖ 21.5 and 21.6 above):

6. . . . Kanan han sallim ey kwī han mulken to ēps.ul they 'n tey . . .	Nobody would expect to find any valuable things in a poor man's household, so . . .
21. Amman hay to sayngkak i an nanun tey!	However hard I try, I can't remember it!
34. Kkok chac.e kaciko ka ya hal they 'n tey . . .	I'm going to have to show up with it for sure, but . . .

Intimate-style sentence endings (‖ 22.4) are often scattered through a familiar-style conversation: note Basic Sentences 22, 28, 33, 37, and 39. Plain-style forms may appear every now and then.

Another characteristic of the familiar style is that particles are frequently omitted entirely, or else reduced to their minimum form (n' for topics, l' for direct objects). Here are examples of this from the Basic Sentences:

1. . . . mue l' hana = mues ul hana.
2. Na cip poney. = Na nun cip ul poney.

Point out—in both the abbreviated and the full forms—similar examples in Basic Sentences 3, 7, 8, 12, 15, 16, 17, 19, 25, 26, 28, 30, 32, 33, 35, 36.

There are various other words of familiar-style reference: caney or i sālam for 'you'; chemci for sensayng 'Mr.'; etc.

As an exercise in using the familiar style, turn back to the Basic Sentences of Lesson 21 and, working two by two, restate them aloud as a conversation in the familiar style. Your tutor will correct you if you make any mistakes.

‖ 28.2. Contracted quotations used for emphasis.

You will recall that we have three kinds of quotations—simple (-ta hanta etc.), expanded (-ta ko hanta etc.), and contracted (-ta 'nta etc.). There is often a special meaning for statements that are "quoted" in the abbreviated form: 'I TELL you it is/does = it really is/does; mind you it is/does.' Sometimes the translation 'you see' or 'you know' or 'don't you know/see' is appropriate; sometimes irony is implied. This is more common with the plain (-ta 'nta) and formal styles (-ta 'p.nita), but it is also heard with the informal or authoritative style (-ta 'o ‖ 29.1) and the familiar style used in this lesson (-ta 'ney). An example is Basic Sentence 4: Saypyek puthe na-tul.i kass.ta 'ney 'She left the house at dawn, you see.' This sort of meaning is not ordinarily found in the intimate and polite styles, so that -ta 'y and -ta 'y yo mean only '[someone] says that . . .' or 'they say that . . . .'

‖ 28.3. Expressions meaning 'stop' and 'finish.'

The phrase ku man 'only that' is sometimes used with verbs to produce an expression meaning 'stops [the action of the verb]'—literally, 'does just that much.' This construction occurred in Basic Sentence 35:

Mōs-nan soli ku man hakey. 'Cut out such silly talk.' [= (Of) silly noise, do only that.]

Here are more examples:

1. Ku man mek.e la.	Stop eating.
2. Onul un ku man hay twuca.	That's all for today. [= Today, let's put it aside with just that much.]
3. Kulemyen ku man iey yo.	Well, that's all. = Let's stop here.
4. Kongpu lul ku man hapsita.	Let's stop studying.
5. Te yēyki haci mālki, ku man twusio.	Don't talk about it any more—let it go.
6. Chayk ku man ilk.ko cikum un na ka se nōsio.	Stop reading now and go out and play.

Another meaning for the construction ku man plus a verb is most easily translated by such colloquial phrases as 'up and does so-and-so' or 'does so-and-so, just like that.' A few examples may help:

1. Ku man kaca.	Let's just up and go.
2. Incey ku man cip ulo kake la.	Just go on home now!
3. Ku ai ka ku man cass.ey yo.	The child fell asleep, just like that.

Ku man twue yo means 'puts aside' or 'leaves alone, discontinues,' as in these examples:

īl ul ku man twunta 'lays aside one's work; "knocks off" for the day'
yēyki lul ku man twunta 'stops talking (about it); drops the subject'
swul ul ku man twunta 'gives up liquor; goes on the wagon'
hōysa lul ku man twunta 'leaves a company (i.e. resigns)'

You have observed the verb mā-l- in negative constructions [haci māsipsio 'don't do it!'; haci māpsita 'let's not do it'], as well as in constructions meaning 'of course . . . !' [hako mālko yo 'of course (I) do!']. You will find the verb used by itself after verbal nouns to mean 'stop' or 'avoid' or 'don't,' as an abbreviation of the construction haci mā-l-:

māl ul (haci) mal.e yo 'avoids talking, stops talking, drops the subject'
Īl ul (haci) mālko swie ya 'keyss.ey yo. 'I'll have to lay aside [give up] my work and take a rest.'
Kongpu (haci) mālko cangsa lul halye hay yo. 'I'm going to give up my studies and go into business.'

When you find a verb in the gerund -ko form followed by the auxiliary mā-l- it means 'finish doing [whatever action the gerund expresses]' or 'do [the action] completely or finally' or 'end up doing,' ‖ 18.2. This expression appears in Basic Sentence 30:

. . . ic.e ppeliko mal.ess.ney. 'I ended up completely forgetting it.'

Here are a few more examples:

1. Cēnhwa lul kēlko iss.nun tong-an ey sayngsen han mali lul ku man tā thaywe peliko mal.ess.kwun a.	I've ended up burning a fish up just like that while I was on the telephone.

2. Nakk.si cil kass.ta (ka) kaciko kan mikki man tā ilh.e peliko mal.ess.ney.
   I went fishing and ended up losing all the bait I had taken along.
3. Ku pōsek-sang ey tul.ess.tun totwuk nom i onul achim kyēngchal eykey cap.hiko mal.ess.ci.
   The thief that robbed the jewelry store finally got caught by the police this morning.
4. Olayq tong-an pi ka oci anh.e se pye ka tā malle peliko mal.ess.ney.
   The rice is all dried up from long lack of rain.
5. Sonayki lul manna se say os ul tā ceksiko mal.ess.ney.
   I ran into a shower and got my new dress all soaked.

‖ 28.4. Alternatives with ak hay yo.

18\. . . . way . . . wass.ta kass.ta hako iss.na? 'Why are you going back and forth?'

20\. . . . Ku man olul ak, naylil ak hako . . . 'Stop going up and down . . .'

29\. . . . i kaychen ul olul ak, naylil ak hamyen . . . 'if you keep going up and down this brook . . .'

A construction similar in meaning to the paired transferentive forms plus a form of ha- 'does' (‖ 16.2) that you see in Basic Sentence 18 of this lesson can be made by using two verbs of opposite or contrasting meaning, each in its prospective modifier form followed by the postmodifier ak, and finishing off with a form of the processive auxiliary hanta as illustrated in Basic Sentences 20 and 29. The post-modifier takes the shape lak after prospective modifiers from L-extending bases: mā-l- 'avoid [do]ing' → māl lak; nō-l- 'play' → nōl lak; etc.
Here are more examples:

1. Kwulum i ol ak kal ak hanta ko hay yo.
   He says that the clouds are going and coming.
2. Pi ka ol ak kal ak hanun kes kath.ey yo.
   It seems to be raining off and on.
3. Elkwul i pulk.ul ak phulul ak hayss.ey yo.
   His face got red and blue [with anger].
4. Ku sālam uy ilum i sayngkak nal ak māl lak hamyen se sayngkak naci anh.e yo.
   His name is on the tip of my tongue, but [= Even while I am between remembering and not remembering his name] I just can't think of it.
5. Onul un kwulum i mānh.e se hay ka nal ak māl lak hay yo.
   It's so cloudy today that the sun can't make up its mind whether to come out or not.
6. Māl ul hal ak māl lak hay yo.
   He is hesitating whether or not to speak.

You will notice that the second, contrasting condition, is often taken care of by māl lak and the translation is 'or not.' Korean grammarians consider this construction a separate ending and usually spell it -ullak/-lak (that is, -ullak after a consonant base, -lak after a vowel base and after the l-extension of L-extending vowel bases). Occasionally you may find the two -ul ak expressions followed by some other verb than hanta; in such cases we might consider that the gerund form of hanta (= hako) has dropped out.

‖ 28.5. Usage of mãl ia.

22. I kaychen ul kēnne ttwita (ka) kkampak ic.e ppelyess.ta 'n māl ia. 'I mean, I forgot it all of a sudden when I jumped across this creek.'

28. Ha ha! Kulay ku ūmsik ilum ul ic.ess.ta 'n māl in ka? 'Ha, ha! So you mean you forgot the name of that dish?'

The word māl (or its formal equivalent māl-ssum) usually means 'words, what is said' or the like, but sometimes it is better translated as 'meaning (of the words)'; you will recall Basic Sentence 10 of Lesson 26:

Ceng Mongcwu sensayng ila 'ni Phoun māl-ssum ici yo? 'By Ceng Mongcwu, I wonder if you mean Phoun?'

In Basic Sentence 22 and 28 of this lesson, you find māl preceded by a sentence that has been turned into a modifier, and the translation is 'I (You) mean . . .' This is a very common way to specify or amplify one's remarks in Korean.

Here are more examples:

1. Ku wa na wa kyelhon hanta 'n māl ici.	I mean, she and I are getting married, you see.
2. Tōn ul tā sse pelisyess.ta 'n māl-ssum ip.nikka?	You mean you spent all the money?
3. Sip-pun te kitalye ya 'nta 'n māl iey yo.	What I mean is we'll have to wait another ten minutes.

In addition to these perfectly acceptable expressions, there is another usage in which māl + copula (often in the familiar form ia or the abbreviation of that, ya) is interpolated as a kind of interjection after almost any part of the sentence, regardless of the form. This corresponds to such English expressions as 'I mean,' 'you-know' 'you-see' 'uh,' 'that is . . .' and the like. Overuse of this form (like overuse of the corresponding English fillers) sounds irritating to many people, so it should be used sparingly.

Here are a few examples:

1. Onul un pi ka oni-kka māl ia na kalq swu ēps.ta māl ita.	It's raining today, uh, so we can't go out, you see.
2. Cek.e to sam-nyen un kellilq kes ila māl iey yo.	It will take—well—at least three years.
3. Chac.e kani-kka māl ya cako iss.tula māl ia.	When I went, uh, to call on him, you know, he was asleep.
4. [1]Nayil māl ya wuli yenghwa kamyen ettelq ka.	How about us—uh—taking in a movie tomorrow?

‖ 28.6. Kaciko as a quasi particle.

27. . . . ku-cwung mas iss.nun kes ul al.e kaciko ola ko hatey. 'She told me to find out the best tasting thing among the dishes [= to come back with the knowledge of . . .].'

34. Kkok chac.e kaciko ka ya hal they 'n tey . . . 'I'm going to have to show up with it for sure, but . . . [= to go with—having found—it].'

Kaciko, the gerund form of kaci- 'have, hold, own take,' has particle-like uses in colloquial speech.

In the Basic Sentences quoted above, it means 'with'—that is, 'having, in possession of' applied to the action of a verb. With nouns, it can mean 'with, by means of':

kōng kaciko nōnta [= kōng ulo nōnta] 'plays with a ball'

In other constructions with nouns, kaciko is used in place of the direct object particle ul/lul:

Ku sālam kaciko nemu kuleci māsio. 'Don't [treat=] pick on that person so!'

It is sometimes difficult to distinguish the quasi-particle usage from the verb-gerund usage:

Chayk (ul) kaciko hak.kyo ey kass.ey yo. 'He took his books and went to school' or 'He went to school with [= holding or carrying] his books.'

28.7. Some common derivational prefixes.

In the last lesson you studied common suffixes that derive some words from other words. There are also a number of prefixes to derive words from other words. You will find a list of these below, with examples. Be prepared to run across new examples, but be wary of trying to make up new ones on your own; until you have heard a word with a prefix or suffix, you should not assume it exists.

cang-	'long' (opposite of tān-)	
	cang-keli 'long distance'	[kēli 'distance']
	cang-sikan 'long time'	[sikan 'time']
cenq-	'former, ex-'	
	cenq-puin 'ex-wife'	[puin 'wife']
	cen-namphyen 'former husband'	[namphyen 'husband']
	cenq-taysa 'former ambassador'	[tāysa 'ambassador']
	cenq-cwuso 'former address'	[cwūso 'address, residence']
cen-	'entire'	
	cen-seykyey 'the whole world'	[sēykyey 'world']
	cen-Hankwuk 'all Korea'	[Hānkwuk 'Korea']
	cen-hoysa 'the entire firm'	[hōysa 'firm, company']
cwung-	'middle'	
	cwung-hak.kyo 'middle school'	[hak.kyo 'school']
	cwung-kiep 'medium-sized enterprise'	[kīep 'enterprise']
cwūng-	'heavy' (opposite of kyeng-)	
	cwūng-kongep 'heavy industry'	[kong.ep 'industry']
	cwūng-ˡnotong 'heavy labor'	[ˡnotong 'labor']
hā-	'bottom, lower; 2d or 2 or 3' (opposite of sāng-)	
	hā-panki 'second term'	[pānki 'half-year term']
	hā-pansin 'lower half of body'	[pānsin 'half of body']
	hā-sakwan 'non-commissioned officer'	[sākwan 'officer']
hwū-	'later, after'	
	hwū-panki 'second term'	[pānki 'half-year term']
	hwū-hwunyen 'year after year after next = three years from now'	[hwūnyen (old-fashioned)= ˡnay-ˡnaynyen 'year after next']
kak-	'each, every'	
	kak-cipang 'every area (region)'	[cipang 'area, region, locality']
	kak-hak.kyo 'every school'	[hak.kyo 'school']
	kak-tapang 'every teashop'	[tapang 'teashop']

kwū-	'old' (opposite of sin-)	
	kwū-sahoy 'the old society'	[sāhoy 'society']
	kwū-ceyto 'the old system'	[cēyto 'system']
	kwū-seykyey 'the Old World'	[sēykyey 'world']
kyeng-	'light (in weight)' (opposite of cwūng-)	
	kyeng-kongep 'light industry'	[kongep 'industry']
	kyeng-kikwanchong 'light machine-gun'	[kikwan-chong 'machine-gun']
mān-	'fully, a full'	
	mān-onyen 'full five years'	[ō-nyen 'five years']
	mān-kihan 'full time limit'	[kihan 'time limit']
mī-	'not yet, un-, in-'	
	mī-kyelqceng 'indecision; undecided'	[kyelqceng 'decision']
	mī-kyoyuk '(being) uneducated'	[kyōyuk 'education']
	mī-wanseng '(being) incomplete'	[wānseng 'completion, perfection']
mu-	'lacking, without, -less	
	mu-uymi 'meaningless(ness)'	[ūymi 'meaning']
	mu-kwankyey 'irrelevance'	[kwankyey 'relevance']
nan-	'difficult'	
	nan-muncey 'hard problem'	[mūncey 'problem, question']
	nan-saep 'difficult undertaking'	[sāep 'undertaking, job, business']
^{1}nay-	'the coming'	
	^{1}nay-hak.ki 'the coming school term'	[hak.ki 'school term']
	^{1}nay-cwumal 'next weekend'	[cwumal 'weekend']
	^{1}nay-sengthancel 'the coming Christmas'	[sēngthan cel 'Christmas']
pān-	'anti-, counter'	
	pān-kwahakcek 'anti-scientific'	[kwahak-cek 'scientific']
	pān-hyek.myeng 'counter-revolution'	[hyek.myeng 'revolution']
	pān-cak.yong 'reaction'	[cak.yong 'effect, action']
	pān-Solyen 'anti-Soviet'	[Solyen 'Soviet Union']
pāy-	'anti-'	
	pay-Ilpon 'anti-Japan(ese)'	[īlpon 'Japan']
	pay-Mikwuk 'anti-America(n)'	[Mikwuk 'America']
	pay-cengpu 'anti-government(al)'	[cengpu 'government']
pi-	'not (being), un-'	
	pi-hoywen 'non-member'	[hōywen 'member']
	pi-kongsik 'informal(ity), (being) unofficial'	[kongsik '(being) official']
	pi-kwahakcek 'unscientific'	[kwahak-cek 'scientific']
pū-	'assistant; side, by-, subsidiary'	
	pū-hoycang 'assistant chairman'	[hōycang 'chairman']
	pū-kyocang 'vice principal'	[kyōcang 'school principal']
	pū-sanmul 'by-product'	[sānmul 'product']
	pū-cak.yong 'side effect'	[cak.yong 'effect, action']
pul- / pu-	(+ t-, c-) 'not, un-'	
	pul-chincel 'unkind(ness)'	[chincel 'kind(ness)']
	pul-phyengtung 'inequality'	[phyengtung 'equality']
	pu-ca.yen 'unnatural(ness)'	[ca.yen 'nature, natural']

pu-ca.yu 'discomfort' [ca.yu 'freedom']
pu-tonguy 'disagreement' [tonguy 'agreement']

sāng- 'upper, higher, top; first of 2 or 3; earlier' (opposite of hā-)
sāng-panki 'first term' [pānki 'half-year term']
sāng-pansin 'upper half of body' [pānsin 'half of body']
sāng-welkup 'top salary' [welkup 'monthly salary']

sō- 'small' (opposite of tāy-)
sō-hak.kyo 'primary school' [hak.kyo 'school']
sō-kwuk.ka 'small nation' [kwuk.ka 'nation']
sō-kyumo 'small scale' [kyumo 'scale']

sin- 'new' (opposite of kwū-)
sin-seykyey 'new world' [sēykyey 'world']
sin-kilok 'a new record' [kilok 'record (in sports etc.)']
sin-palmyeng 'new invention' [palmyeng 'invention']

ta- 'many, poly-, multi-'
ta-pangmyen 'many directions, multidirectional' [pangmyen 'direction']
ta-chwimi 'many hobbies' [chwīmi 'hobby']
ta-umcel 'polysyllable' [umcel 'syllable']

tān- 'short' (opposite of cang-)
tān-keli 'short distance' [keli 'distance']
tān-sikan 'short time' [sikan 'time']

tāy- 'great, big' (opposite of sō-)
tāy-hwal.yak 'great activity' [hwal.yak 'activity']
tāy-cengkecang 'major rail stations' [cengke-cang 'rail station']
tāy-centhwu 'a big battle' [cēnthwu 'battle']

EXERCISES

I

Translate each of the following into a Korean sentence that contains a ku man construction (above, ‖ 28.3).

1. Stop working now.
2. Stop walking in the street.
3. I'm going to put aside all my work now and go home.
4. Stop studying now and go to the movies.
5. Please drop the subject of henpecked husbands.
6. Last night I just fell asleep in the middle of reading the newspaper.
7. I wanted to talk with my friend at the station a little longer, but the train up and left on time.
8. Let's stop watching this opera now and leave.
9. On my way back from the market with the fruit I had bought, I got hungry and ate it all up, just like that.
10. Put aside that novel now—it's time to get at your homework.
11. Stop talking about leaving the door unlocked—nobody will steal your things.
12. Let's not talk about it any more; let's just go ahead and buy our train tickets.
13. Let's stop eating and hurry to school.
14. Why did you stop singing right in the middle of your song?
15. I'm going to stop studying grammar and see if I can carry on a conversation fluently.

II

Use each of the following verbs as the core of an ak . . . ak . . . alternative construction (‖ 28.4) and then build an interesting Korean sentence around it.

1. pōy yo 'is visible, can see'
2. pappe yo 'is busy'
3. yeth.e yo 'is light [of colors]'
4. se yo 'stands (up)'
5. khe yo 'is large'
6. tullye yo 'is audible, can hear'
7. huye yo 'is white'
8. cam'ulq soy lo yel.e yo 'unlocks'
9. swie yo 'rests'
10. caychayki lul hay yo 'sneezes'

III

1. Take each familiar-style sentence in the Basic Sentences and change it to intimate style (-e, -ci, ia, etc.).
2. Now take each sentence and quote it in the plain style: 'Mr. Pak says that . . .' or '. . . suggests that . . .' or '. . . tells me to . . . .'

CONVERSATION

I

What do you think of a wife who henpecks her husband? What do you think of a husband who allows himself to be henpecked? What should a husband do if his wife dominates him? Or consider the opposite case, the husband who dominates his wife—what is your opinion of that situation, and what should be done about it? As a group, discuss this topic in Korean. Give everybody an equal chance to talk.

To give the whole thing a friendly flavor, carry on your discussion in the FAMILIAR STYLE. By this time, you probably know each other well enough to use the familiar style occasionally without it seeming out of place.

II

By pairs, pretend you are two friends who do a lot of fishing. Discuss the best places to go fishing, and which fish you most enjoy going after. Talk about fish and sea food in general, how you like to eat it, or what your family thinks of it; who prefers which fish, and when; how they like it cooked. Discuss your fishing rods, your fish-hooks, and your lines. What kind of bait do you get the best results with? Do you like to go out fishing in a boat? When is the best time of day to go? Why? Does your wife keep complaining about how the price of fish keeps rising and falling in the market? Is she happy when you bring home the catch from your fishing trip? Do you ever take your son fishing, or is he too young? What age is a good age to start fishing? How old were you when you caught your first fish? How big was the fish?

VOCABULARY DRILL

The following exercises should be performed entirely in the familiar style.

Take turns assuming the A, B, C, and D roles. A asks the questions; B, C, and D must each give an answer. After each answer, A gives a comment—pertinent or impertinent—before going on to ask the next person the same question.

1. A asks B, C, and D what they are doing cooped up in the house on a beautiful day like this.
   B says he's looking after the children.
   C says he's getting ready to go fishing, but has to repair his fishing rod first.
   D says he's drawing a picture of a riverbank and bridge at dawn.

2. A asks what everybody's favorite kind of fish is.
   B says trout.
   C says oysters.
   D says shrimp.

3. A asks what's the best way to get across this river.
   B says he doesn't know—this is the first time he's ever been here.
   C says you have to wait till the tide goes out.
   D says that back at the little village there's a narrow place where you can jump across.

4. A asks what you fish with.
   B says a fishing pole.
   C says a fishing net.
   D says bait.

5. A asks what you should do when you leave your house.
   B says you should lock the front door.
   C says it's all right to leave the back door unlocked.
   D says he's poor and hasn't got anything valuable, so it doesn't matter.

6. A asks what everybody is going to do tomorrow.
   B says he has to go to a party at his in-laws'.
   C says he is going to stay home, like a criminal in jail, and make a honey cake.
   D says he doesn't know yet but that he'll find out when his wife tells him.

7. A asks where's the best place to fish.
   B says a stream.
   C says a creek.
   D says a fishing boat.

8. A asks what is the worst kind of wife to have.
   B says a wife who scolds her husband if he doesn't get home before dark.
   C says a wife who had a bad temper.
   D says a wife who cries all the time and is afraid of everything.

9. A asks everybody what his favorite time of day is.
   B says when the sun is just rising.
   C says just as the sun is setting.
   D says daybreak.

10. A asks where's the best place to spend your summer vacation.
    B says at a lake.
    C says at the seashore.
    D says where there's a brook to fish in.

COMPREHENSION

I

Ask your Korean teacher to tell you about the general subject of husband-wife relations in Korea, and specifically how—as he sees it—things are different in Korea and America, and in what ways they are the same. Encourage him to editorialize; ask him to tell you frankly what points about each setup are desirable and what things he would like to see changed, and how.

II

Is your Korean teacher an angler? Ask him to tell you about going fishing in Korea, and whether the same general procedures and attitudes prevail in Korea as in the United States, or in what aspects this sport differs in his country. Find out what he likes (or dislikes) about fishing as a way to spend time.

LESSON 29. A LAUNDRY PROBLEM

BASIC SENTENCES

[Mr. A., a hotel guest, talks to the clerk, C.]

Korean	English	Amplification
A. 1. Ye' po sāmu-wen! I 'yekwan ey se sēythak un etteh.key hao.	Say, clerk! How does one get one's laundry done in this hotel?	sāmu-wen 'clerk (in an office)' sēythak 'wash, laundry' sēythak (ul) hanta 'washes, launders; has laundry done hao 'does' [AUTHORITATIVE]
C. 2. Sēythak halq kes i iss.umyen, ēncey 'tun ci sāmu-sil lo ponaysipsio.	Any time you have something to be laundered, please send it around to the office.	sāmu-sil 'office' ponaynta [ponay-] 'sends'
3. Wuli tankol sēythak-so ka palo i kūnche ey iss.e se tāytan hi phyen.li hap.nita.	Our regular laundry is right in this vicinity, so it is quite convenient, sir.	tankol 'regular patronage; (= ~ cip) one's usual establishment/shop; (= ~ son nim) a regular customer/patron' sēythak-so 'laundry (establishment) tāytan hi 'very, quite'
A. 4. Ku sēythak-so ey se pōthong ppallay to hako, tulai-khullining to hao?	Do they do both regular laundry and dry cleaning at that laundry?	tulai-khullining 'dry cleaning' tulai-khullining (ul) hanta 'dry cleans; gets it dry cleaned'
C. 5. Nēy. Sēythak ey kwan han kes un mues ina tā haci yo.	Yes, they do anything in the way of laundry.	
6. Yēmsayk to hanta 'p.nita.	They do dyeing too, you know, sir.	yēmsayk 'dyeing' yēmsayk (ul) hanta 'dyes' hanta 'p.nita 'does, you see' (‖ 28.2)
7. Mues, ponaysilq key iss.^{s}up.nikka?	Do you have something to send, sir?	key = kes i mues ponaysilq kes 'something to be sent'
A. 8. Waisyassu to meych kay iss.ko, nāyuy to	I have several shirts and several pairs of under-	wais(y)assu 'Western-style shirt'

Korean	English	Amplification
meych pel iss.ko, tto tulai-khullining hal yangpok paci to hana iss.nun tey . . .	wear, and also there's a pair of suit trousers to be dry cleaned . . .	nāyuy or sōk os 'underwear' pel (counter for garments) yangpok 'Western-style suit' tulai-khullining hal yangpok 'suit to be dry cleaned' paci 'trousers'
9. Kulen tey, kiil un pōthong meychil ssik ina kellio.	By the way, as to the day when you get things back, about how many days does it usually take (each time)?	kiil 'appointed (designated) day' kellio '(time, money) is required' [AUTHORITATIVE]
C.10. Waisyassu 'na nāyuy kath.un kes un han sahul kelliko tulai-khullining un han ilq-cwuil kellip.nita.	Things like shirts or underwear take about three days, sir, and dry cleaning takes about a week.	
A.11. Talun kes tul un cey kihan ey chac.e to kwaynchanh.ci man, waisyassu hana nun kot tōyss.umyen cōh.keyss.nun tey . . . Kulelq swu iss.keyss.^{s}o?	I don't care when I get the other things, but [it would be good if I got=] I hope I can get a shirt done right away; would that be possible?	kihan 'term, time limit' cey kihan 'any time' kot 'right away, immediately' tōyss.umyen 'if [it] could become (ready)' iss.keyss.^{s}o? 'will there be?' [AUTHORITATIVE]
C.12. Kuleh.key halq swu iss.^{s}up.nita.	That can be done, sir.	
13. Thukpyel ^{l}yōkum man nāysimyen, kot ppal.e se, kot talye se han twue sikan an ey ip.usilq ke 'p.nita.	If you just pay a special rate, they will wash it right away, iron it right away, and within about two hours you'll be able to wear it.	^{l}yōkum 'fee, price, rate' ppanta [ppa-l-] 'launders, washes' talinta [tali-] 'irons [clothing]' twues/twue . . . 'about two, a couple'
A.14. Ke, cham. Phyen.li hakwun yo.	Uh . . . well, that is convenient.	ke (= ku ke) 'uh . . .'
15. Thukpyel ^{l}yōkum un elma 'na toyo.	How much does the special rate come to?	toyo 'it becomes' [AUTHORITATIVE]
C.16. Pōthong sēythakq-^{l}yo uy pāy 'p.nita.	It's double the usual laundry rate.	sēythakq-^{l}yo 'laundry rate' pāy '(a) double (amount), twice as much'
17. Waisyassu hana ey ō-sip cen ini-kka n', thukpyel ^{l}yōkum un il-wen ici yo.	As shirts are 50 cen apiece, the special rate is one wen.	hana ey '[the price] for one'

Korean	English	Amplification
A.18. Kulem, sēythak-mul ul kot kaciko okeyss.^{s}o.	Then I'll bring my laundry right away.	sēythak-mul 'laundry, things to be laundered'
19. Waisyassu hana nun onulq cenyek ey ip.ulq swu iss.key hay tālla ko hasio.	Ask them to do one shirt so that I can wear it tonight.	hay tālla ko hanta 'tells [one] to do it (for us)' hay tālla ko hasio 'tell [them] to do (for us)!' ip.ulq swu iss.key 'in such a way as to be able to wear'
20. Ha.ye-kan, toynun tāy lo kot kac'ta tālla ko hasio.	In any event, ask them to bring (the things) back as soon as possible.	ha.ye-kan 'anyhow, anyway, in any event, no matter what' toynun tāy lo 'as much as possible' toynun tāy lo kot '[as much as possible immediately=] as soon as possible' kac'ta [=kacye 'ta] tālla ko hasio 'tell [them] to carry <u>or</u> bring <u>or</u> take (for us)!'
C.21. Nēy. Kuleh.key hay tālla ko hakeyss.^{s}up.nita.	Yes, sir. I will ask them to do that.	hay tālla ko hakeyss.^{s}up.nita 'will tell [them] to do it (for us)'
22. Sēythak halq kes ul ese nāy noh.usipsio.	Please go ahead and put the things to be laundered out right away, sir.	ese 'without hesitation, right away; please' noh.nunta /nonnunta/ [noh-] 'puts, places' nāy noh.nunta 'puts out (for later)'

Korean	English	Amplification
23. Kot, sēythak-so lo ponayci yo.	I'll send them to the laundry at once.	

Korean	English	Amplification
C.24. Yeki sēythak-mul chac.e wass.^{s}up.nita.	Here, I've (gone and) got your laundry.	
25. I kes un tōn tālla 'nun chengkwu-se 'p.nita.	This is a bill asking for money [payment].	ton tālla (ko ha)nta '[tells someone to give one money=] asks for money' chengkwu-se 'bill, statement, request' tōn tālla(ko ha)nun chengkwu-se 'a bill that asks for money'
A.26. Eti popsita. Yo cenq pen waisyassu nun khalle ey phul ul	Let's see. Last time I found they had put too much starch in the	eti popsita [FORMAL], eti posey [FAMILIAR], eti poca [PLAIN] } 'let's see; let me see'

Korean	English	Amplification
nemu sēykey mek.yess.tukwun yo.	collars of my shirts.	yo cen 'not long ago, just recently, the other day' yo cenq pen '[the time before this=] last time' khalle 'collar' phul '(laundry) starch' sēyta [sēy-] 'is strong' sēykey 'strongly, so that it is strong' mek.inta '[makes (a shirt) eat (starch)=] starches a shirt'
27. E he! I kes, an tōyss.nun tey?? I syassu aph calak i nwūleh.key thass.nun tey . . . I kes, mōs ssukeyss.[s]o.	Oh-oh! This one's no good! The front ends of this shirt have been scorched . . . This won't do.	an tōyss.ta 'won't do, is no good' syassu = waisyassu (shirt) (os) calak 'end, bottom (of a garment)' thanta [tha-] 'it burns' nwūleh.ta [nwūle(h)-, nwūlay yo] 'is dark yellow' nwūleh.key tha yo 'gets yellow by burning; gets scorched' mōs ssukeyss.[s]o 'won't be any good (to use)' [AUTHORITATIVE]
28. Talun kes tul un kwaynchanh.so.	The other things are OK.	kwaynchanh.so 'is all right' [AUTHORITATIVE]
K.29. Kyohwan-swu: Meych pen iey yo.	Operator: Number please!	kyohwan-swu '(telephone) operator' meych pen iey yo 'what number is it?' [also 'how many times is it?']
C.30. Kwanghwa-mun il-chen sam-payk kwu-sip chil pen.	Kwanghwa-mun 1397 please.	
31. Kwangil Sēythak-so 'ey yo? Yeki n' Cosen [1]Yekwan ip.nita.	Is this the Kwangil Laundry? [Here=] This is the Cosen Hotel.	
32. Ce . . . Cokum cen ey nay ka sēythak-mul chac.e wass.ci yo!!	Uh . . . A little while ago, I went and got some laundry (from you), right?	cokum [= com] 'a little, a bit' cokum cen ey 'a little while ago'

Korean	English	Amplification
33. Kulen tey, waisyassu hana ka mopsi nwul.ess.ey yo.	Well, one shirt got terribly scorched.	mopsi 'very, extremely' nwūt.nunta [nwūl-, nwul.e yo] 'gets scorched'
34. Wuli son nim kkey se tāytan hi pulkhway hay hasip.nita.	Our guest is extremely displeased.	pulkhway hata 'it is unpleasant; I am displeased' pulkhway hay hanta 'is displeased at (it)' (‖ 8.10)
35. Mān-il cektang han sōnhay pāysang ul haci anh.nun kyengwu ey nun, kyēngchal ey kōso lul hakeyss.ta 'p.nita.	In the event you should not make appropriate compensation for the damage, (I want you to know) we will complain to the police!	cektang hata 'is appropriate <u>or</u> suitable' pu-cektang hata 'is inappropriate <u>or</u> unsuitable' sōnhay 'damage, injury, harm' pāysang 'recompense, compensation' kyengwu 'circumstance, event(uality)' kyēngchal 'the police' kōso '(legal) complaint' kōso (lul) hanta 'complains'
36. Etteh.key hay se kulen pu-cwuuy lul hayss.ey yo.	How could you have been guilty of such carelessness? [= How did you do that kind of careless thing?]	cwūuy /cwūi/ 'care(fulness)' cwūuy (lul) hanta 'exerts care, is careful' pu-cwuuy 'carelessness' pu-cwuuy (lul) hanta 'is careless, commits a careless act'
37. Kulem, kuleh.key son nim hanthey cen haci yo.	Well, I'll tell our guest that.	cen hanta 'conveys, reports, delivers, communicates, transmits, tells'
38. Ku sēythak-so cwuin i sākwa lul tulye tālla ko hap.nita.	The boss of that laundry asks me to offer their apologies.	cwuin 'boss, head, proprietor' sākwa 'apology' sākwa (lul) hanta 'apologizes' sākwa lul tulinta 'gives <u>or</u> offers an apology' sākwa lul tulye tālla ko hanta 'asks someone to give one's apology'
39. Kuliko, sōnhay pāysang ul hakeyss.ta 'p.nita.	And, he says they will compensate you for the damage.	hakeyss.ta 'p.nita 'says [one] will do'
40. Son nim tele ku sēythak-so lo osye se sōnhay pāysang chengkwu-se ey	He says to tell you [the guest] to come to the laundry and fill in a damage compensation	chengkwu-se 'request form; bill' kiip hanta 'fills in, makes out (a form)'

Korean	English	Amplification
cektang hi kiip hasila 'p.nita.	request (form) appropriately.	
41. Onul ōcen ey cēnki ka an tul.e wass.ta 'p.nita.	He says the electricity was off this morning.	cēnki 'electricity' an tul.e wa yo 'doesn't come on or in'
42. Kulay se, halq swu ēps.i swuch pul lo talim cil ul hay se kulen silqswu lul hayss.na pota 'p.nita.	So he says they were forced to do the ironing with a charcoal fire, and so that kind of blunder was made, it seems.	pul 'light; fire' swuch pul 'charcoal fire' talim(i) cil '(some) ironing, the ironing' halq swu ēps.i . . . talim cil ul hay se 'were forced to do the ironing' silqswu 'blunder, error, mistake' hayss.na pota 'p.nita 'he says it seems that [one] did'
A.43. Na nun cikum talun tey yaksok han sikan i iss.e mōs kakeyss.ˢo.	I have an engagement somewhere else now, so I won't be able to go.	. . . tey 'place that . . .' talun tey 'another place, somewhere else' yaksok 'promise, commitment, appointment' yaksok (ul) hay yo 'makes a promise, promises, agrees, commits oneself' yaksok han sikan 'appointment, engagement' kakeyss.ˢo 'will go' [AUTHORITATIVE]
44. Ku chengkwu-se lul ponay tālla ko hatun ci, kuleh.ci anh.umyen tangsin i nay tāysin ka cwutun ci, hay ya hakeyss.ˢo.	I'll have to ask them to send that request form, or else get you to go for me.	ponay tālla ko hay yo 'asks [one] to send (for one)' kuleh.ci anh.umyen 'if not; or else; otherwise' nay tāysin ka cwue yo 'goes for me (in my stead)' hakeyss.ˢo 'will do' [AUTHORITATIVE]
C.45. Kulem. Cey ka ka tulici yo.	All right, I'll go for you.	
A.46. Komapso. Ku syassu kakyek un sip-o wen ila ko ssusio.	Thanks. Write that the price of the shirt is 15 wen.	komapso 'thank you' [AUTHORITATIVE] kakyek 'price, value' ssu(si)o 'write' [AUTHORITATIVE]
47. Kulem tto pūthak hao.	(Thank you for taking care of it for me.)	pūthak 'a request (for a favor)'

Korean	English	Amplification
	I'll leave the matter in your hands [again].	pūthak (ul) hanta '(makes) a request; requests (a favor)'
48. Ilen īl i cōng-cong sayngkimyen wihem hay se, kwī han kes ul ponaylq swu iss.keyss.^{s}o?	If such cases arise time and again, it would be dangerous, so [how] can one send valuable things [to them]?	cōng-cong 'repeatedly, over and over, again and again, time after time' sayngkinta [sayngki-] 'happens, occurs, arises' wihem 'danger' wihem hata 'is dangerous' -ulq swu iss.keyss.^{s}o 'will [one] be able?' [AUTHORITATIVE]

SUPPLEMENTARY VOCABULARY

talimi	iron (for pressing)
intwu	small heart-shaped iron (with long handle); soldering iron
talimi phan	ironing board
talim(i) cil (ul) hanta	does the ironing
waisyassu lul talinta [tali-]	irons a shirt
ppallay lul pipinta [pipi-]	rubs the wash
ppallay lul ccanta [cca-]	wrings the wash
ppallay lul sālm.nunta [sālm-]	boils the wash
ppallay ka huyta [huy-]	the wash is [white=] clean
ppallay ka kkaykkus hata	the wash is clean
ppallay ka kēm.ta [kēm-]	the wash is (still) [black=] dirty
tēlepta [tēlew-]	is dirty
ppallay ka tēlepta	the wash is (still) dirty
os ul chwuk.inta [chwuk.i-]	dampens (wets) the clothes
cwul	rope, line, string
nēnta [nē-l-]	spreads out (to sun or air)
os ul cwul ey nēnta	puts clothes out on the line (to dry)
ppallay lul ketwunta [ketwu-]	takes the clothes in (off the line), gathers the wash up
ppallayq cwul	laundry line, clothesline
sēythak kikyey or sēythak-ki	washing machine
sēythak pinwu	laundry soap
mul	dye, coloring
tul.inta [tul.ye, tul.i-, causative < tu-l- 'enter']	puts it in
os ey mul ul tul.inta	[puts dye in clothes=] dyes clothes
os ey mul i tunta [tu-l-]	a garment is dyed
ppāynta [ppāy-]	removes, takes out
os ey mul ul ppāynta [ppāy-]	bleaches clothes
sōl	a brush
sōl cil (ul) hanta	brushes
com	moth
comq yak	mothballs
os ey com i mek.nunta	clothes get moth-eaten

ipul	coverlet
yo	(quilted) mattress
peykay	pillow
is	cover, sheet
ipulq is/ipullis/	a sheet to cover a coverlet
yoq is /yonnis/	a sheet to cover a mattress
peykayq is /peykaynnis/	a pillow slip (case, cover)
tāmq yo/tāmnyo/	a blanket
chīmkwu or ipu'-cali	bedding
pulphyeng	trouble, disturbance, dissatisfaction; indisposition, ailment
micikun hata	is lukewarm, tepid
nailon or nailong or naillong	nylon
"Nailon ey nun micikun han talimi ssulq kes."	"Nylon; use warm iron!"
"Syassu ey phul mek.ici mālq kes."	"No starch in shirts!"
"Tanchwu ēps.um."	"Button missing."
"Kkwēy cin tey kkwēy maylq kes."	"Mend torn spot!"
kkwēynta [kkwēy-]	pierces, thrusts
panul ey sīl ul kkwēynta	threads a needle
kkwēy cinta [ci-]	gets torn, ripped; bursts
kkwēy maynta [may-]	sews, stitches, patches, mends
wuphyo	postage stamp

NOTES

‖ 29.1. Authoritative style.

The Basic Sentences of this lesson present a conversation between a guest and the clerk at a Korean hotel. The guest speaks "authoritatively" to the clerk, and the clerk—using either the formal style or the polite style—speaks respectfully to the guest.

The AUTHORITATIVE (or INFORMAL) STYLE is used by a person taking command of a business-like situation that calls for an impersonal tone. Other cases of this type are a policeman speaking to a traffic offender; a customer to a laundryman or other service person; a passenger in a taxi; and so on.

You would never offend anyone, however, by using the polite style, and if you have any doubts about classifying a situation in which you find yourself, it is safer to speak too "high" than too "low."

The verb ending that characterizes the authoritative style for statements and questions (which differ from each other only in intonation) is -(s)o, pronounced -so after consonants and -o after vowels:

Vowel-base verbs:

ka-	'go'	kao
o-	'come'	oo
kitali-	'wait'	kitalio
ssu-	'write'	ssuo
sēy-	'be strong'	seyo
toy-	'become'	toyo
nāy-	'put out; pay; mail'	nayo
cwu-	'give'	cwuo
swī-	'rest'	swio
pulu-	'call'	puluo
phulu-	'be blue/green'	phuluo
kule-	'do like that'	kuleo

L-extending vowel-base verbs:

pha-l-	'sell'	phao
nō-l-	'play'	noo
kī-l-	'be long'	kio
mē-l-	'be far'	meo

Ambivalent verbs:

kule(h)-	'be like that'	kuleh.so /kulesso/

Consonant-base verbs:

ip-	'wear'	ipso /ipsso/
noph-	'be tall'	noph.so /nopsso/
tōw-	'help'	tōpso /tōpsso/
pat-	'receive'	pat.so /passo/
wūs-	'laugh'	wūs.so /wūsso/
cī(s)-	'build'	cīs.so /cīsso/
chac-	'look for, find'	chac.so /chasso/
coch-	'follow'	coch.so /cosso/
tul-	'listen, hear'	tut.so /tusso/
noh-	'put'	noh.so /nosso/
ilk-	'read'	ilk.so /iksso/
mek-	'eat'	mekso /meksso/
takk-	'polish'	takk.so /taksso/

As you can see, the ending attaches in just the same way as the formal ending -(su)p.nita. To iss-, ēps-, and all past (-ess-) and future (-keyss-) bases, you attach the ending as either -so or -o (since the sound changes come out the same way); in North Korea it is usually spelled -so and in South Korea more commonly -o, so we write it as -^{s}o just as we wrote -^{s}up.nita for the corresponding formal form. Here are some examples:

iss-	iss.^{s}o /isso/	iss.ess.^{s}o /issesso/	iss.keyss.^{s}o /ikkeysso/
ēps-	ēps.^{s}o /ēpsso/	ēps.ess.^{s}o /ēpssesso/	ēps.keyss.^{s}o /ēpkkeysso/
po-	poo	pwass.^{s}o /pwasso/	pokeyss.^{s}o /pokeysso/
ha-	hao	hayss.^{s}o /haysso/	hakeyss.^{s}o /hakeysso/
pat-	pat.so /passo/	pat.ess.^{s}o /patesso/	pat.keyss.^{s}o /pakkeysso/

Suggestions and commands in the authoritative style use the formal-style endings -(u)psita and -(u)sio WITHOUT the insertion of the honorific marker:

o-	'comes'	opsita	'let's come'	osio	'come!'
nāy-	'pays'	nāypsita	'let's pay'	nāysio	'pay!'
mek-	'eats'	mek.upsita	'let's eat'	mek.usio	'eat!'
kēl-	'walks'	kel.upsita	'let's walk'	kel.usio	'walk!'
kē-l-	'hangs it'	kēpsita	'let's hang it'	kēsio	'hang it!'

Here are some more examples:

1. Yeki se Cwungkwuk ūmsik ul mek.ulq swu iss.^{s}o?	Can I get [= eat] Chinese food here?
2. Pang i ēps.^{s}o?	Haven't you got any rooms?
3. Ppalli kasio.	Please go fast.
4. Tol.a kapsita.	Let's go home.
5. Cikum mek.ess.^{s}o.	I've just now eaten.
6. Ku chayk ul pelsse posyess.^{s}o?	Have you already seen (or read) this book?

‖ 29.2. Abbreviated forms of ha-.

6. Yēmsayk to hanta 'pnita. 'They do dyeing too, you know.
35. . . . kyēngchal ey kōso lul hakeyss.ta 'p.nita. 'We'll complain to the police.'
39. Kuliko, sōnhay pāysang ul hakeyss.ta 'p.nita. 'And he says they will compensate you for the damages.'
40. . . . kiip hasila 'p.nita. 'He says for you to fill in . . .'
41. Onul ōcen ey cēnki ka an tul.e wass.ta 'p.nita. 'He says the electricity was off this morning.'
42. . . . silqswu lul hayss.na pota 'p.nita. 'He says it seems a mistake was made.'

Each sentence portion quoted here involves a shortened form of the verb ha- with which the sentence ends.

The fullest form of these expressions are made by inserting ko ha- before the contracted form:

6. . . . hanta ko hap.nita.
35. . . . kōso lul hakeyss.ta ko hap.nita.
39. . . . pāysang ul hakeyss.ta ko hap.nita.
40. . . . kiip hasila ko hap.nita.
41. . . . an tul.e wass.ta ko hap.nita.
42. . . . silqswu lul hayss.na pota ko hap.nita.

Go back and read again the discussion of quotations and their uses in ‖ 19.1 and ‖ 28.2.

You will find that forms of ha- sometimes abbreviate in other expressions besides contractions. You may hear things like kāntan h'ta /tha/ for kāntan hata 'is simple,' kāntan h'ko /kho/ for kāntan hako, kāntan h'ci /chi/ for kāntan haci, etc. In these cases the h remains but changes places with the other consonant when the a between them drops. You have run across -e ya 'keyss.ta = -e ya hakeyss.ta 'will have to [do].' And you will recall that the "ambivalent" verbs (‖ 11.6) like kule(h)- are abbreviations of less colloquial versions like kule ha-.

‖ 29.3. Reflexive requests and favors (tālla, tao).

19. Waisyassu hana nun . . . hay tālla ko hasio. 'Ask them to do one shirt (for me).'
20. . . . kac'ta tālla ko hasio. 'Ask them to bring me . . .'
21. . . . kuleh.key hay tālla ko hakeyss.[s]up.nita. 'I will ask them to do that (for us).'
25. I kes un tōn tālla 'nun chengkwu-se 'p.nita. 'This is a statement asking for money.'
38. Ku sēythak-so cwuin i sākwa lul tulye tālla ko hap.nita. 'The boss of the laundry asks me to offer their apologies.'
44. Ku chengkwu-se lul ponay tālla ko hatun ci . . . 'I'll ask them to send the request form . . .'

Requests are ordinarily made with an honorific command form of the verb cwu- 'give' in one of the more polite styles: I kes com cwusipsio (cwusey yo) 'Please give this to me/him'; I kes com hay cwusipsio (cwusey yo) 'Please do this (for me/him).' But in PLAIN and AUTHORITATIVE styles there is a special device used to make a request REFLEXIVE so that it means '(I ask you) to give it to or do it for ME [rather than someone else]': instead of using cwue la or cwula 'give it!' you use tālla in the PLAIN style and tao (or tawu) in the AUTHORITATIVE style. (But in Seoul tālla is usually replaced by tao except in quotations.) These forms are made from a defective verb tā-l-.

Here are some examples:

Chayk ul tālla.	'Give me that book.'
Poktong-i hanthey chayk ul cwue la.	'Give Poktong-i the book.'
Ku kes kac'ta tao.	'Bring me that.'
Ku kes nay chinkwu hanthey kac'ta cwusio.	'Bring that to my friend.'

Requests are QUOTED in the expected fashion (changing cwusipsio to cwula) only if the request is for the benefit of someone other than the subject. To say 'he requests it for himself' (= 'he says "do it for me" or "give it to me"') you must change cwusipsio to tālla, rather than cwula.

The usual way of stating favors, as you know, is to use the infinitive -e followed by the auxiliary verb cwunta 'gives' (or tulinta 'gives to a superior [hence never "ME"]'): A ka B eykey X ul hay cwunta/tulinta 'A does X for B.' And favors can be requested: B eykey X ul hay cwusey yo (tulisey yo) 'Please do X for B.' So the requested favor can be quoted: C ka (A eykey nun) B eykey X ul hay cwula/tulila ko hanta 'C asks A to do X for B.' But if the favor requested is reflexive, cwula is replaced by tālla: C ka A eykey (nun) X ul hay tālla ko hanta 'C asks A to do X for him (C).'

As with other quotations there is a simple form (tālla hanta), an expanded form (tālla ko hanta), and an abbreviated form (tālla 'nta). Because of the latter form, some Korean dictionaries list a verb tallanta 'requests,' but this is misleading, since the fact that it is an abbreviation is clearly shown by the past tālla 'yss.ta (from tālla hayss.ta); if there were such a verb as "tallanta," the past would be *tallass.ta.

Here are some more examples of quoted requests.

1. Mikwuk ey ponay tālla ko hayss.ey yo.	He asked me to send him to America.
2. Nul tōn ul tālla 'p.nita.	He's always asking for money.
3. Kim sensayng kkey towa tālla ko hasio.	Ask Mr. Kim to help you.
4. Ku haksayng un īl halq kes ul tālla ko hay yo.	That student is asking for some work to do.
5. Nay chinkwu nun i mānnyen-phil ul sip-wen ey tālla ko hayss.ey yo.	A friend of mine asked me to give him this fountain pen for ten wen.
6. Ku son nim i i os ul sahul an ey hay tālla ko hana, kuleh.key haki tāytan hi elyepkeyss.^{s}up.nita.	That customer ['guest'] asked me to make (up) these clothes in(side of) three days, but that would be very difficult to do.
7. Mūn.an hay tālla ko hayss.^{s}up.nita.	He asked me to give his regards to you.

EXERCISES

I

For practice in using authoritative-style statements and questions, say each of the following verb bases aloud in the authoritative style; then give the appropriate past and future forms, and their translations. Make up a brief sentence using each form.

1.	anc-	'sit'	23.	mūl-	'ask'
2.	cap-	'catch'	24.	nām-	'remain'
3.	celm-	'be young'	25.	nelp-	'be wide'
4.	chwuw-	'be cold'	26.	nwūl-	'scorch'
5.	cīna-	'pass'	27.	olh-	'be right'
6.	cōh-	'be good'	28.	pappu-	'be busy'
7.	cwuk-	'die'	29.	pat-	'receive'
8.	ē-l-	'freeze'	30.	pes-	'get undressed'
9.	elyew-	'be difficult'	31.	pis-	'comb'
10.	ēps.ay-	'eliminate'	32.	ponay-	'send'
11.	haci anh-	'not do it'	33.	pulk-	'be red'
12.	huy-	'be white'	34.	su-	'stand'
13.	ip-	'wear'	35.	selmyeng ha-	'explain'
14.	kaci-	'have'	36.	seywu-	'stand it up'
15.	kē-l-	'hang it'	37.	sin-	'wear (shoes)'
16.	kēm-	'be black'	38.	swīw-	'be easy'
17.	kkwu-	'dream'	39.	tah-	'touch'
18.	kuleh-	'be so'	40.	takk-	'polish'
19.	kwūw-	'broil'	41.	tte-na-	'leave'
20.	malu-	'get dry'	42.	tul-	'listen'
21.	math-	'undertake'	43.	wū-l-	'cry'
22.	mit-	'believe'	44.	wūs-	'laugh'

II

Each of the following sentences is a request. Quote the request by reporting it to someone; then translate. For example, the first will be: Han pen te hay tālla ko hayss.ey yo. 'He asked me to say it once more.' Be careful to see which requests are NOT reflexive.

1. Han pen te hay cwusipsio.
2. Mul com cwusipsio.
3. ˈNayil sāmu-sil ey com ka cwusipsio.
4. Kim sensayng hanthey ku phyēnci lul ilk.e tulisio.
5. I chayk ul sensayng nim kkey tulisipsio.
6. Os ul i pang ey 'ta com kel.e cwusio.
7. Onulq cenyek wuli cip ey com wa cwusio.
8. Pap com te cwusipsio.
9. Wuphyo lul sa 'ta cwusio.
10. Os ul com ollye 'ta tulisipsio.
11. Yenphil ul com cwusipsio.
12. I koki lul kwuwe cwusio.
13. Talun yēyki lul com hay cwusipsio.
14. Ku mun ul com yel.e cwusipsio.
15. Kkoch kwa chāyso lul path ey 'ta sim.e tulisio.

III

Now, again relay each of the above requests by passing the buck: tell someone to ask someone to perform the requested action, and translate. For example, the first will be: Han pen te hay tālla ko hasio. 'Tell him to say it again.'

CONVERSATION

I

Ask your Korean teacher to act as a clerk in a laundry, while all of you line up with your bundles. One by one, explain to him in detail just what you want done to your things; in what way this is different from (or the same as) what you asked him to do the last time; and whether or not you are pleased with his work to date.

II

Now ask your Korean teacher to act as a policeman, directing traffic at a busy intersection. One by one you violate the regulations; take whatever medicine is dished out to you.

VOCABULARY DRILL

I

Translate each of the following sentences into Korean three times, once for each of the phrases below.

1. They do ___ in that building over there.
   laundry
   dry cleaning
   dyeing

2. Please tell the clerk to ___.
   get my laundry back in two days
   show concern about my laundry
   leave the shirts at the office

3. Where are the clothes that are to be ___?
   bleached
   dried
   taken off the line

4. I took ___ to the cleaners.
   two pairs of pants
   a lot of underwear
   all my shirts

5. If you want to get your laundry back right away, ___.
   you have to pay a special rate
   you have to pay double the usual rate
   you have to send it to them as soon as possible

6. I'm going to ask the boss of the laundry ___.
   not to scorch my shirts
   not to put in too much starch
   to iron the collars carefully

7. The hotel guest became very displeased and ___.
   complained to the clerk in the office
   telephoned the police
   demanded [= asked (them) to give him] recompense for the damage

8. He gave a(n) ___ reply to the apology.
   kind
   appropriate
   unsuitable

9. If ___, the police will help you.
   you ask the telephone operator
   you fill out a request form
   something dangerous happens

10. Mother is busy ___.
   wringing out the clothes
   hanging the clothes up to dry
   boiling the wash

II

Choose any of the words or phrases below each sentence that can appropriately fill the blank; read each completed sentence aloud, and translate. Give the English meaning of any words you discard. If a choice is difficult, discuss (in Korean) why you chose or rejected the word.

1. ___ ka tālla ko hayss.ey yo.
   - nay tāysin ey
   - ponay
   - talun tey

2. Nwukwu 'tun ci ___ sse ya hay yo.
   - cēnki lul
   - swuch pul ul
   - phul

3. Cokum cen ey Kim sensayng i ___ chac.e wass.ey yo.
   - sōnhay
   - chengkwu-se
   - cēnkiq ta(y)lim

4. Son nim i tāytan hi ___ hasey yo.
   - kyengwu
   - pulkhway hay
   - sayngkye

5. Eme' nim i ppallay lul ___ ey neh.e yo.
   - sēythak-ki
   - cwul
   - sēythak pinwu

6. I sēythak-so ey se ___ yo.
   - com i mek.e
   - mul ul ppāy
   - ppallay ka tēlewe

COMPREHENSION

Carrying on a telephone conversation can be an unnerving experience at the beginning of one's stay in a foreign country. To get pointers on how to do it in Korean, ask your Korean teacher to demonstrate by producing both ends of several conversations typical of those you might be called upon to conduct in Korean: between customer and electric (gas, etc.) company; ordering goods or supplies by telephone and completing delivery arrangements; asking the railroad clerk about rates to various cities; or whatever situations he can think of that would be practical and usual. After several demonstrations, you may want to participate yourself at one end of the wire.

A FURTHER NOTE ON THE AUTHORITATIVE STYLE

In Seoul a variant of the authoritative style is used within the family circle when speaking to seniors, including older servants. (To juniors, the plain or intimate forms are used.) Instead of -o and -so, the variant version uses the endings -wu and -swu. You will notice that wu often substitutes for o in Seoul speech, especially with common endings like -ko (→ -kwu) and particles like to (→ twu).

LESSON 30. REVIEW

I. VOCABULARY RECALL

Here is a list of 23 general subjects. Write down each subject as a column heading, and list below it as many Korean vocabulary items (together with their English meanings) as you can think of that relate to the subject: nouns, verbs, phrases. Each list should consist of at least a dozen items, and as many more as possible.

After your lists are complete, build them to maximum capacity by comparing notes with the other students and adding all the things they had that you omitted.

1. Anatomy
2. Buildings
3. Church Services
4. Dressing and Grooming
5. Eating Out
6. Family Life
7. Growing Things
8. Housekeeping
9. Inside the House
10. Jobs
11. Korean Food
12. Learning Things
13. Music
14. Neighbors
15. Outside the House
16. Pastimes
17. Repairs and Replacements
18. Sickness
19. Telling Time
20. Universities
21. Vacation Activities
22. Weather
23. Young People

II. VERB REVIEW

A. FORMS

Say aloud all of the verb bases in Column 1 below with EACH of the endings in Column 2 attached to it. (First make all of the bases into Plain Suggestion forms; then make all bases into Infinitive forms; and so on.) Translate as you go. Omit any which do not make sense. A few do not exist, e.g. processive modifier forms of adjective bases.

Column 1	Column 2
anc- 'sit'	-ca [Plain Suggestion]
celm- 'be young'	-e [Infinitive]
cīna- 'pass'	-(u)myen [Conditional]
cwuk- 'die'	-ki [Nominative]
ē-l- 'freeze'	-(u)l [Prospective Modifier]
(kongpu) haci anh- 'not (study)'	-(nu)nta/-ta [Plain Statement]
huy- 'be white'	-(u)n [Modifier]
ilk- 'read'	-ci [Suspective]
ip- 'wear'	-nun [Processive Modifier]
iss- 'exist'	-ta [Transferentive]
kuleh- 'be so'	-na [Plain Question]
mit- 'believe'	-(u)na [Adversative]
mūl- 'ask'	-ko [Gerund]

nelp- 'is wide'
olh- 'is right'
ponay- 'sends'
sīm- 'plants'
swīw- 'is easy'
wūs- 'laughs'

-tolok [Projective]
-(su)p.nita [Formal Statement]

B. CONSTRUCTIONS

You have learned a number of endings that make Korean verb forms, both alone and in longer constructions.

Here is an English-Korean catalog of these constructions. The section of the Notes in which each was discussed is given.

Make up two Korean sentences illustrating each Korean construction (not just one for each English meaning!). Vary the tenses and subject matter as much as possible.

'able to' SEE 'can'
'according to' SEE 'as'
'(action of) ___ing'
  -ki ‖ 13.2
  MODIFIER + kes ‖ 14.7, ‖ 14.8, ‖17.7
  -(u)m ‖ 26.3
'after ___ing'
  -(u)n hwū ey
  -(u)n twī ey } ‖ 12.5
  -(u)n taum ey
'agrees to ___' SEE 'decides to ___'
'almost (did)'
  -(u)lq pen hayss.ta ‖ 24.11
'along with ___ing'
  -(u)lq kyem ‖ 21.8
'alternatively ___ and ___' SEE 'keeps ___ing and ___ing'
'although' SEE 'but'
'and'
  [and also] -ko ‖ 8.4
  [= in order to, so as to] INFINITIVE + se ‖ 8.9
  [= in addition to] -keni ‖ 24.7
  -(u)lq kyem ‖ 21.8
'and (now)'
  -tuni ‖ 24.6
'___ and puts aside'
  -e twunta ‖ 18.4
'and (then)'
  -e se ‖ 8.9
  -ko ‖ 8.4
  -ta (ka) ‖ 16.2
'any . . . at all'
  -tun ci ‖ 24.5
'as, according to, in accordance with'
  -ki ey (nun) ‖ 13.8
  MODIFIER + tāy lo ‖27.6

'as if' SEE 'looks (as if), seems'
'as if (= almost did)'
  -(u)lq pen hayss.ta ‖ 24.11
'as soon as'
  -ca mā'ca ‖ 26.6
  -nun tāy lo ‖ 27.6
'asks [whether etc.]'
  -(u)n/-nun ya ko mūt.nunta ‖ 19.3
'asks [someone] to do for one'
  -e tālla ko hanta, -e tālla 'nta ‖ 29.3
'because' SEE 'so'
'because of ___'
  -nun kkatalk ey ‖ 12.8
  -ki ttaymun ey ‖ 13.9
'before ___ing'
  -ki cen ey ‖ 13.13
'begins (starts) to [be ___]'
  -e cinta ‖ 9.8
'begins (starts) to [do]'
  -ki (lul) sīcak hanta ‖ 13.5
'both . . . and . . .'
  -ki to hako, -ki to ha(n)ta ‖ 13.3
'but, although'
  -ci man ‖ 7.2
  -e to ‖ 8.13
  MODIFIER + tey ‖ 21.5
  -tuni ‖ 24.6
  -keni ‖ 24.7
'[. . . to be sure,] but'
  -ki nun . . .-ci man ‖ 13.4
'but anyway'
  -(u)na-ma ‖ 18.3
'called . . .'
  ila ‖ 19.7; ila (ko ha)n(un)
'can ___, is able to ___'
  -(u)lq swu (ka) iss.ta ‖ 14.6
'can ___, knows how to ___'
  -(u)lq cwul ānta (ā-l-) ‖ 16.5
'can't ___, isn't able to ___'
  mōs . . . ‖ 4.3
  -ci mōs hanta ‖ 7.3
  -(u)lq swu (ka) ēps.ta ‖ 14.6
'can't ___, doesn't know how to ___'
  -(u)lq cwul molunta ‖ 16.5
'certainly [does/is] ___.!'
  -ki to ha- ‖ 13.3
'completely ___'
  -ko mā-l- ‖ 18.2
  -e (p)peli- ‖ 18.4
'decides (agrees, promises) to ___'
  -ki lo ha- ‖ 13.10
  SEE ALSO 'plans to ___'

'dislikes to ___' SEE 'hates to ___'

'doesn't have to ___'

-ci anh.e to {cōh.ta / kwaynchanh.ta} ‖ 8.13

'don't ___!'

-ci mal.e la (mā' la, mālla, mā', mal.e, mālkey, mao, mālci, māsey yo, māsio/māsipsio) ‖ 7.4, ‖ 18.2, ‖ 22.2, ‖ 22.4

'even though ___'

-e to ‖ 8.13

-(u)myen se to ‖ 9.6

'ever (does/did)'

MODIFIER + īl i iss.ta ‖ 12.4

'. . .-ever'

-tun ci ‖ 24.5

'___ [does] for [someone]'

-e cwunta, -e tulinta ‖ 8.11

'___ [does] for [the speaker]'

-e tālla [PLAIN]
-e tao [AUTHORITATIVE]
-e cwu-, -e tuli- + COMMAND ENDING [OTHER STYLES]
} ‖ 29.3

'gets (= becomes) [+ ADJECTIVE]'

-e cinta ‖ 9.8

'gets so that ___'

-key toynta ‖ 17.5

'gets [someone] to do'

-key hanta ‖ 17.4

CAUSATIVE VERB ‖ 26.1

VERBAL NOUN + sikhinta ‖ 26.1

'gets [something done to one]'

-(u)m ul tang hanta ‖ 26.1

VERBAL NOUN ul tang hanta ‖ 26.1

PASSIVE VERB ‖ 26.1

'glad that ___'

-e se cōh.ta ‖ 8.9

'goes to [do] ___'

ka se . . . ‖ 8.9

-(u)le kanta ‖ 24.9, ‖ 27.2

'going to ___'

-keyss- ‖ 9.1

'good for ___ing' SEE 'worth ___ing'

'has to, ought to, must, should'

-e ya (+ hanta etc.) ‖ 8.12

-(u)myen cōh.keyss.ta ‖ 9.4

-ci anh.umyen an toynta ‖ 9.5

-ko ya mānta [mā-l-] ‖ 18.4

'hates (dislikes) to [do] ___'

-ki (ka) silh.ta, -ki (lul) silh.e hanta ‖ 13.7

'hears that ___'

-(nun)ta ko yo
-tula ko yo
} ‖ 23.8

'hopes (wishes) that ___'

-(u)myen cōh.keyss.ta ‖ 9.4

-ki (lul) palanta ‖ 13.12

'how about ___ing?' SEE 'shall we ___?'
'[knows] how to ___'
-(u)lq cwul (ul) ānta [ā-l-] ‖ 16.5
'if'
-(u)myen ‖ 9.4
'if . . . had [done/been]'
-ess.tu(la ')myen ‖ 24.1
'in ___ing'
-ki ey ‖ 13.8
'in a [certain] manner' SEE '-ly'
'___ing'
-ko iss.ta ‖ 8.5
'instead of ___ing'
-ci anh.ko . . . ‖ 8.4
-(u)n/-nun tāysin ey ‖ 12.7
'intends (plans, is going) to ___'
-keyss- ‖ 9.1
-ki lo hanta ‖ 13.10
-(u)lye ko hanta ‖ 24.9
-(u)le ‖ 24.9
-(u)l yēyceng ita ‖ 27.2
-(u)l they 'ta ‖ 27.2
-(u)lq cakceng ita ‖ 27.2
'keeps ___ing and ___ing; alternatively ___ and ___'
-ta (ka) . . .-ta (ka) hanta ‖ 16.2
-(u)l ak . . .-(u)l ak hanta ‖ 28.4
'let me just ___' SEE 'will just ___'
'lets/makes [someone] do'
-key hanta ‖ 17.4
CAUSATIVE VERB ‖ 26.1
VERBAL NOUN + sikhinta ‖ 26.1
'let's ___'
-(u)lq ka yo ‖ 14.5
'let's not ___'
-ci mālca (mal.e, māsey, māpsita/māsipsita) ‖ 18.2
'likes to ___'
-ki ka cōh.ta } ‖ 13.7
-ki lul cōh.a hanta }
'looks (as if), seems'
MODIFIER + mo.yang ita ‖ 14.9
MODIFIER + kes kath.ta ‖ 17.7
-(u)lq ka pota ‖ 24.11
-key poynta ‖ 26.2
-(u)n ka pota ‖ 26.2
-na pota ‖ 26.2
'-ly; in [a certain] manner'
-key ‖ 17.3
-i ‖ 17.6
'makes [someone] ___' SEE 'lets [someone] ___'
'may (perhaps)' SEE 'perhaps'
'may ___' [= has permission]
-e to cōh.ta ‖ 8.13

'may not' SEE 'must not'
'maybe' SEE 'perhaps'
'means'
  māl ita ‖ 28.5
'might as well ___'
  -(u)lq ka pota ‖ 24.11
'must ___' SEE 'has to ___'
'must [= probably] ___'
  -keyss- ‖ 9.1
'must have [done/been]'
  -ess.keyss- ‖ 9.2
'must (may) not ___' [= permission denied]
  -(u)myen an toynta ‖ 9.5
'never does/did'
  -nun/-un īl i ēps.ta ‖ 12.4
'not'
  an . . . ‖ 4.3
  -ci anh- ‖ 7.3
'not able to' SEE 'can't'
'not (at all)'
  mōs . . . ‖ 4.3
  -ci mōs ha- ‖ 7.3
'nothing but' SEE 'only'
'observes that ___'
  RETROSPECTIVE ASPECT ‖ 23.1
'of course!'
  -ko mālko ‖ 18.2
'(one) who ___' SEE '(that) which ___'
'only, nothing but . . .'
  . . . pakk-ey (or ōy-ey) + NEGATIVE ‖ 8.1; ‖ 23.5
  -ki man ha- ‖ 13.6
'ought to ___' SEE 'has to ___'
'perhaps, maybe'
  MODIFIER + ci to molunta ‖ 21.3
'plans to ___' SEE 'intends to ___'
'probably [does/is]'
  -keyss- ‖ 9.1
'probably [did/was]'
  -ess.keyss- ‖ 9.2
'probably will ___'
  -(u)lq kes ita ‖ 14.7
'promises to ___' SEE 'decides to ___'
'says "___"'
  (. . . i/ka) māl haki lul "___" hanta ‖ 13.14
'says that . . .'
  -(nun)ta ko hanta ‖ 19.1
'seems' SEE 'looks (as if)'
'shall [I, we] ___?' 'how about ___ing?'
  -(u)myen cōh.ta ‖ 9.4
  -(u)lq ka yo? ‖ 14.5
'should' SEE 'has to ___'

'since'
-(u)n ci + time expression ‖ 21.1
SEE ALSO 'after'
'so, because'
-e se ‖ 8.9
-ki ey ‖ 13.8
-ki ttaymun ey ‖ 13.9
-(u)ni, -(u)ni-kka (n') ‖ 18.1
MODIFIER + kkatalk ey/ulo/ita ‖ 12.8
MODIFIER + tey ‖ 21.5
-(u)m ulo ‖ 26.4
-(u)m ey ‖ 26.5
'so that'
-key ‖ 17.3
-tolok ‖ 24.8
'so . . . that'
nemu . . .-ki (ttaymun) ey ‖ 13.9
etteh.key (to) . . .-(u)n ci ‖ 22.6
nemu . . .-e se ‖ 22.6
nemu . . .-(u)m ulo ‖ 26.4
'sometimes ___'
-nun īl i iss.ta ‖ 12.4
'starts' SEE 'begins'
'stops ___ing'
ku man + VERB ‖ 28.3
'suggests that (we) . . .'
-ca ko hanta ‖ 19.4
'tells [someone] to do'
-(u)la ko hanta ‖ 19.5
-e tālla (ko hanta) ‖ 29.3
'[knows] that . . .'
MODIFIER + cwul (lo) ānta [ā-l-] ‖ 17.8
'(that) which ___, (one) who ___'
~ is/did -(u)n ‖ 12.1
~ does -nun ‖ 12.2
~ has been observed to do/be -tun ‖ 23.2
~ is to do/be (or be done) -(u)l(q) ‖ 14.3
~ will -(u)l(q) ‖ 14.3
'the more . . . the more . . .'
. . . -(u)myen . . . -(u)lq swulok ‖ 27.4
'thinks of ___ing'
-(u)lq ka hanta ‖ 14.5
-(u)lq sayngkak ita ‖ 27.2
SEE ALSO 'intends to'
'tries ___ing'
-e ponta ‖ 8.11
'tries to do'
āy/him sse + VERB ‖ 13.11
. . .-ki ey āy/him (ul) ssunta ‖ 13.11
'until'
-tolok ‖ 24.8

'up and ___'
  ku man + VERB ‖ 28.3
'usually'
  -ko n(un) ha- ‖ 24.12
'used to ___'
  -ko n(un) hayss.ta ‖ 24.12
'wants to ___'
  -ko siph.ta ‖ 8.6
  -keyss.ta ‖ 9.1
  -ki (lul) wēn hanta ‖ 13.7
'what (a) . . . !'
  -nun tey (yo)! ‖ 21.6
'what with ___ing'
  -nula (ko) ‖ 24.10
'what with ___ing and ___ing'
  -keni . . . -keni ha- ‖ 24.7
'when'
  -(u)l ttay ‖ 14.4
  -ta (ka) ‖ 16.2
  -uni(-kka) ‖ 18.1
  SEE ALSO 'while'
'when(ever)'
  -(u)myen ‖ 9.4
'[knows] whether (which, etc.) . . .'
  MODIFIER + ci + INFORMATION VERB ‖ 21.2
'[knows] whether (which, etc.) . . . did/was'
  -ess.tun ci + INFORMATION VERB ‖ 24.4
'while ___ing'
  -(u)myen se ‖ 9.6
  -nun {cwung / tong-an / sai} ey ‖ 12.6
'why . . . !'
  (-)kwu(me)n (yo)! ‖ 16.4
  -tun kwu(me)n (yo)! or -tu-kwu(me)n (yo)! ‖ 23.3
'will'
  -keyss- ‖ 9.1
'will just ___, let me just ___'
  -(u)m a ‖ 23.6
'will probably' SEE 'probably'
'wishes that . . .' SEE 'hopes that . . .'
'worth ___ing, good for ___ing'
  -(u)l man hata ‖ 27.7
'would ___'
  -keyss- ‖ 9.1
  -(u)lq kes ita ‖ 14.7
'would have [done/been]'
  -ess.keyss- ‖ 24.2
  -ess.ulq kes ita ‖ 14.7

III. COMPREHENSION TEST

Each of the following sentences contains a logical or factual error. Listen as your tutor reads the sentence aloud as it stands—or, if you are doing the exercise by yourself, read it aloud and then close your eyes. Now restate the sentence in Korean so that it makes better sense. Avoid translating into English. (For almost every one of the sentences there will be several sensible alternatives to the "absurdity" or "absurdities" in the sentence as it stands. Your tutor may want to quiz you on the particular alternative you choose; or, he may want to improve the grammar in the sentence as you say it.)

1. Sensayng tul un pōthong chayk kapangq sōk ey pitwulki lul neh.e kaciko tanye yo.
2. Wel-yoil puthe Kum-yoil kkaci nun ahuley 'ey yo.
3. Sengnyang to pinwu to Mikwuk ey se nun mantulci anh.e yo.
4. Tangsin kwa kyelhon han sālam ul tangsin uy yak.hon-ca 'la ko hap.nita.
5. Haksayng tul un nul pānghak tong-an ey hak.kyo ey kap.nita.
6. Elin ay tul un acik māl mōs hanun tong-an ey cal cic.e yo.
7. San i noph.umyen noph.ulq swulok oluki swiwe yo.
8. Namca 'tun ci ^{n}yeca 'tun ci nwukwu 'tun ci tā achim ey il.e naca mā'ca myēnto hay ya hap.nita.
9. Kyohyangak-tan un nolay hanun sālam tul hako chwum chwunun sālam tul lo tōyss.ey yo.
10. Hānkwuk ey se nun catong-cha lul ī-wen ō-sip cen ulo salq swu iss.ci man, Mikwuk se nun cha ka hwelssin te pissa yo.
11. Chang ulo nāy 'ta pwa to, hanul ul polq swu ēps.ci yo.
12. Emeni uy ^{n}yeca hyengcey lul hal-'meni 'la ko hap.nita.
13. Nongpu tul un pye lul Il-wel ey sīm.ko, Sip.i-wel ey ketwup.nita.
14. Sālam i kēt.ki ey nemu nulk.ess.umyen, cengkwu lul cal chilq key yo.
15. Kyewul ey ttattus 'i kyēysiko siph.usimyen, chang-mun ul tā yel.e twusye ya hap.nita.
16. Hwānca tul un ēncey 'na se se chayk ul ilk.ko phyēnci lul sse yo.
17. Sangcem ey se mulken ul phanun sālam ul cik.kong ila ko hay yo.
18. Sālam tul i sapal sikyey lul kaciko iss.nun kes un achim ey nuc.key kkaci calye ko haki ttaymun iey yo.
19. Tōngmul-wen ey iss.nun tōngmul tul eykey kimchi lul mek.il they 'p.nita.
20. Namu wa phul un kyewul ey phulule ciki sīcak hako pom ey cwuk.e yo.
21. Kacang cōh.un haksayng un swukcey lul kiil an ey nāynun īl i ēps.nun haksayng tul ip.nita.
22. Namca 'na ^{n}yeca nun tāmpay lul phiwuci man, ai tul man un swul ul masye yo.
23. Pi ka on hwū ey nun pōthong hanul i hulye ciki sīcak hap.nita.
24. Namca tul un khalle ey phul ul nemu sēykey mek.in kes ul cōh.a hay yo.
25. Yākwu sīhap ey se nun, emphaie nun mok.yok-sil ey anc.ci yo.
26. Sēykyey ^{l}yehayng hanun kes un pissaci anh.e yo.
27. Kwāyngi wa kāy nun selo tāytan hi cōh.a hay yo.
28. Yelq-twu sal toyn namca nun yel-ilkop sal toyn ^{n}yeca pota te nai ka mānh.e yo.
29. Cēncha nun mēlli iss.nun sālam hanthey yāyki hanun tey ssunun kes ip.nita.
30. Nwūn i ol mo.yang imyen ōythwu lul cip ey twuko ka ya haci yo.
31. ^{n}Yeca tul i cēy-il cōh.a hanun kes un selkeci 'na sōcey 'ci yo.
32. Mikkulewun kil ey se ppalli catong-cha lul wūncen hanun kes un wihem han īl i ani 'ci yo.

33. Tose-kwan ey se pillin chayk tul un chayk-cem ey se sanun chayk pota te caymi iss.ta.
34. Mikwuk salam tul un pōthong cip aph ey 'ta chāyso lul kille yo.
35. Ōcen yeses si sā-sip ō-pun puthe ōhwu yelq-twū si sip-o pun kkaci nun yeses sikan pān iey yo.
36. Mikwuk ^{n}yeca tul un cang pole kal ttay nul palq-kalak ey cāngkap ul kkip.nita.
37. Cip ey tul lak nal ak halye 'myen, mun ul camke twue ya haney.
38. Enu nala se 'tun ci sālam tul un tā siksa lul ceq-kalak ulo haci yo.
39. Ayki ka alh.umyen swul ul an cwumyen an tōy yo.
40. Āmu kongpu to haci anh.ko ēncey 'na nōlki man hamyen sihem ul tā swii chilulq swu iss.ey yo.
41. Kitok-kyo sīnca tul un Pulkyo sīnca wa kath.un congkyo lul mit.e yo.
42. Pyēngwen uy hwānca tul uy tam.im un pōthong yūmyeng han hwāka 'p.nita.
43. Sālam tul un pata lul kicha lo kēnne yo.
44. Namu nun calamyen calalq swulok te cak.e cici yo.
45. Sewul se Pusan i Inchen pota te kakkapsup.nita.
46. Hānkwuk salam un samci-chang ina swuq-kal lo mek.nun īl i ēps.ey yo.
47. Path ey pota swuph sōk ey hay ka te mānh.i na yo.
48. Sip-li kel.e kanun tey tas-say ccum kellici yo.
49. I hana ka aphumyen, chiq-kwa uysa eykey i lul tā ppāy pelikey haci anh.umyen an tōy yo.
50. So wa twāyci tul un Mikwuk uy khun tosi ey se sal.e yo.
51. Caki cip ey chotay hanun sālam un son nim iko, onun sālam un cwuin ip.nita.
52. Sālam tul i mānh.i kyohoy ey kanun nal un Mok-yoil ici yo.
53. Chayk-sa ey se nun kyōkwa-se nun phal.e to sōsel chayk un an phal.e yo.
54. Totwuk nom un kum sikyey pota nun ohilye swuch han teyngi lul hwumchilq kes iey yo.
55. Cāng nim tul un nal mata sinmun ul tā ilk.e yo.
56. Ōyn son ulo kul ul ssunun sālam tul un palun son ulo ssunun sālam tul pota mānh.e yo.
57. Īcwung-chang un twū sālam i hako, samcwung-chang un yelq-sēy sālam i hay yo.
58. Nwūn i omyen olq swulok tewe cip.nita.
59. Hōy ey se nwu' ka tōnguy lul hamyen, hōywen tul un ku kes ul thwuphyo hako, taum ey nun ku tōnguy ey nwu' ka cāycheng ul hanta.
60. Cēntang-pho ey se sanun mulken un ama say mulken mankhum ina pissaci yo.
61. Latio soli lul khukey hay noh.assul ttay cam i oki swiwe yo.
62. Chim.lyey-kyo wa Chencwu-kyo wa Cang.lo-kyo wa Kam.li-kyo nun mōtwu sinkyo 'p.nita.
63. Hānkwuk ūmsik un Mikwuk ūmsik kwa keuy kkok kath.sup.nita.
64. Pata ey nun talam-cwi ka mānh.e yo.
65. Achim ey nun sālam tul i sēyswu lul han hwū ey il.e na yo.
66. Kwutwu lul wūsan ulo takk.e to tōy yo.
67. Hānkwuk ey se Ilpon kkaci cēncha lo kalq swu iss.ey yo.
68. Etten tal ey nun yeses cwuil i iss.una Ī-welq tal ey nun sēk cwuil man iss.ey yo.
69. Oppa uy ai tul ul sawi 'la 'p.nita.
70. Caymi ēps.nun yāyki lul cōh.a haci anh.usimyen, nul ku kes ul tul.usici anh.umyen an tōy yo.
71. Mikwuk puin tul un tā kwuwun koki lul ^{l}yoli halq cwul al.e yo.
72. ^{l}Yeypay hal ttay, moksa nun kito tuliki cen ey selkyo lul hay yo.

73. Che-siha ka koki cap.i kakeyss.ta ko hamyen, ku uy an(h)ay nun ku lul kakey hap.nita.
74. Nwun un ip alay ey iss.ko kho nun meli uy ˡyāng phyen ey iss.ey yo.
75. Punchim i "il" ey iss.ko, chochim i "sip-il" ey iss.ul ttay nun han si ō-pun cen ip.nita.
76. Sōsel ey se nun sālam ul cwuk.in sālam i cap.hinun īl i ēps.ey yo.
77. Mulq koki nun namu wi ey se sālko, sāy nun namu mith ey se sal.e yo.
78. Sālam tul un tali ey tti lul māyko, meli ey swūken ul ssup.nita.
79. Ūmsik ul mantul ttay ūmsik i tha to mas i cōh.sup.nita.
80. Alh.nun sālam un kkwul ttek ul mek.umyen swii nās.keyss.ci yo.
81. Sikyey ka ppalli to nuc.key to kaci anh.key sikyey lul kochilq cwul ānun sālam un tose-kwan ey se īl ul hap.nita.
82. Elin i eykey nwūnq salam ul etteh.key mantunun ya ko mul.usimyen ama ku āy nun molunta ko māl halq kes ip.nita.
83. Khun tosi ey se sālki nun nongchon ey se sālki pota te him i tul.e yo.
84. Phyēnci lul ppalli ponaykey hako siph.umyen wuphyen-kwuk ey ka se puchici anh.ko kongcang ey ka se puchip.nita.
85. Kwi mek.un sālam tul un latio tut.ki lul cōh.a hay yo.
86. Nwuwe iss.nun tong-an ina sānqpo hanun tong-an ey sikyey swusen haki ka swīpsup.nita.
87. Sālam yeses kwa capci yel-yetel(p)q kwen i iss.umyen, sālam mata capci nēy kwen pān ssik kacilq swu iss.ey yo.
88. Hak.kyo ey se cōh.un sengcek ul et.ki ey him ul ssunun haksayng tul un pōthong col.ep hwū ey totwuk nom i tōy yo.
89. Elin ay eykey ku āy apeci ka nwun-ttakppuli 'ko ttwungttwung-po 'la ko māl hay cwumyen kippe hay yo.
90. Pōthong ulo tulai-khullining un sēythak pota ssa yo.
91. Mikwuk uy cengwen mata tay namu ka museng hap.nita.
92. Hōycang un hōypi lul ketwuko hōylok ˡnāngtok ul hap.nita.
93. Kan.ho-pu tul un cheyon kēmsa lul cal halq cwul mōlla yo.
94. Pulkyo sīnca tul i kanun cel ila 'n' kes un Kitok-kyo ˡyeypay-tang kwa taluci anh.key pōynta.
95. Na nun tali ka tāytan hi phikon hay se anc.ko siph.ci anh.e yo.
96. Cwungkwuk pota Mikwuk ey se cha lul te mānh.i kille yo.
97. Ilponq salam tul i mulq koki lul mek.ki lul silh.e hay yo.
98. Ai tul i hak.kyo ey taniko iss.nun ttay pota cip ey iss.nun ttay emeni tul un swīlq sikan i mānh.ci yo.
99. Pata lul chac.e kanun sālam un ama noph.un kos ulo kalq kes iey yo.
100. Cak.un sāy tul un kyewul imyen chwuwun kos ulo kako n' hanta.

IV. REVIEW OF STYLES

The various social styles were discussed in the following sections of the Notes:

Formal Style: ‖ 17.1, 17.2
Polite Style: ‖ 4.1, 11.1, 16.6, 16.7, 17.2
Intimate Style: ‖ 22.4, 22.5, 27.1
Plain Style: ‖ 19.2–6, 22.2–3
Familiar Style: ‖ 28.1
Authoritative Style: ‖ 29.1

Brush up on these by running through the following list of verb bases, saying each aloud as a statement, question, suggestion, and command in each style. Translate each form as you say it.

1. chac- 'finds, gets'
2. cōh- 'is good'
3. haci anh- 'doesn't; isn't'
4. ka- 'goes'
5. mek- 'eats'
6. pes- 'gets undressed'
7. pha-l- 'sells'
8. po- 'sees, looks (at)'
9. pulu- 'calls'
10. tul- 'hears, listens (to)'

Now, working alone or with another student, plan a short conversation that might be called for by each of the following situations. Try to include a couple of questions, statements, suggestions, and commands in each conversation. Make the conversations as natural and interesting as possible; each should include a dozen or so exchanges, in addition to greetings and other conventional expressions. Write no Korean down; if you need notes, prepare them roughly in English. Produce your Korean spontaneously.

1. A doctor calls on his patient.
2. A couple of housewives swap recipes.
3. A passenger directs a taxi driver to his destination.
4. A minister makes a welcoming call on a new member of his flock.
5. Two children plan a picnic.
6. A teacher shows a new member of the faculty around the school.
7. A customer tells the watch repair man what kind of second-hand watch he would like to acquire.
8. An American soldier takes a day off to go fishing with his Korean buddy.
9. The Korean neighbor of a new American resident in Korea tells of interesting things to see and do in Korea.
10. A Korean mother shows her daughter how to make kimchi.
11. An American resident in Seoul tells the laundry how he likes his things done.
12. A nurse who has worked in a hospital for a long time shows a new nurse around the hospital and explains to her who the people in charge are and what some of the specialists do.
13. An American visitor asks a Korean child what he did all day.
14. A teacher talks to a father about the son's school work.
15. A father has a talk with his son about school work.

V. TRANSLATION TEST

Prepare translations of the following sentences into Korean. First read the English sentence and try to say the same thing in Korean to yourself. Then look back at the English to see if you can improve upon your Korean version. Remember that there is more than one way to say anything!

1. My name is ___ and I've been studying Korean here for the past eight months.
2. A squirrel is an animal that lives in trees.

3. There are hundreds of novels, dictionaries, etc., in Mr. Kim's house, but no books at all in Mr. Pak's.
4. A person whose job is fishing has to use a net, but a man who just fishes during his vacation fishes with a pole.
5. If the train leaves a city at 10:13 a.m. and arrives at another city at 2:47 p.m., that means it takes four hours and 34 minutes to get there.
6. Both my uncle and my aunt like to go on picnics, but neither my sister nor I do.
7. If you go to a concert and leave your front door unlocked, a burglar may enter the house and steal things while you're away.
8. If only it hadn't been cloudy and rainy yesterday, we could have played tennis all day long.
9. Poktong, whether you want to or not, you have to finish your homework before you go outdoors and make a snow man with Pok.nam.
10. I'm going to start doing the laundry right now, instead of waiting, so that I can go on the picnic as soon as I finish.
11. The doctor told me to come to the hospital to be vaccinated, even though I had a vaccination for smallpox just last year.
12. Mrs. Kim says she hasn't decided yet whether or not she wants to go to Korea and start a kindergarten.
13. Some people believe that Buddhism is a better religion than Christianity, but it seems to me that they are basically similar and that one religion is as good as another.
14. I don't know how to speak Chinese as well as you do, Pok.nam, but I intend to study like mad until I get very fluent.
15. Mrs. Kim's child is only three years old, but she can already get dressed all by herself, except for tying her shoes.
16. When I was studying to be a singer back in my home town, I had hoped to become a famous opera tenor [soprano, bass].
17. After I ate that kimchi, I had to drink three or four glasses of ice-cold water, it made my mouth burn so.
18. I've never had any watch repairing done at that jewelry shop, but I hear that they're very competent.
19. When I asked the hotel clerk whether or not that laundry ever puts too much starch in the shirts, he said he didn't think so.
20. Since I've never done any sightseeing at all in Korea, my friend suggested that we go first to see the Pak.yen Falls and then after that look at some ancient temples.

VOCABULARIES

NOTE

The following vocabularies are intended to include all the words and endings that have been introduced in the lessons. But in general we have not included proper names and words introduced for pronunciation practice only. The English-Korean Vocabulary is a reminder list, but the Korean-English Vocabulary is also an index, for it tells you where the word is first introduced. The Korean entries are alphabetized according to the usual ABC order of the English alphabet; the following points, however, should be noted: (1) Parentheses, space, hyphen, and dot are all to be ignored except when their presence makes a minimal difference in two entries. Superscript letters, vowel length, and -q- are also to be disregarded, except when entries are otherwise identical. (For convenience, however, some entries with -q- are repeated where they would be expected if the -q- were not ignored in the alphabetizing.) This means that words beginning with ^{l}y and ^{n}y are put together with words that begin with just y. (2) When entries are otherwise identical, bound elements precede free elements, and more-bound elements precede less-bound elements. Suffixes precede particles, and these precede prefixes and (in turn) pre-nouns.

Abbreviations are used to show where the entry item is introduced in the lessons; the following are examples:

ABBREVIATION	TO BE READ
‖6.2	in Grammar Note ‖6.2
6.2	in Sentence 2 of Lesson 6
6.2A	in the Amplification of Sentence 2 of Lesson 6
6.SV	in the Supplementary Vocabulary of Lesson 6
6.C	in the Comprehension of Lesson 6

A swung dash (~) represents the entry word. Verbs are given in their polite forms (thus ka yo 'goes' will be found alphabetized after kayksil), with the base shown in brackets immediately after the entry.

KOREAN-ENGLISH VOCABULARY

...-a [infinitive when preceding syllable contains /o/ or, in written Korean, /a/] See ...-e

... a [vocative-exclamatory particle after consonant] ‖22.8 Cf. ... ya

a ah! oh! 23.6

accwu indeed! and how! 22.SV

acessi uncle 7.SV

acha oh! gee! gosh! 21.10

achim morning; (= achimq pap) breakfast 4.SV, 16.SV

acik (not) yet, still 4.5

acwu very, indeed 22.18; (not) quite 23.30

acwumeni aunt 7.SV

ahop nine (= kwu) 1.19, 6.SV

ahuley nine days 6.SV

ahun ninety (= kwu-sip) 6.SV

ahu'-nam.un,-nam.u ... ninety odd ‖27.8

ai child (= elin ai/ay/i) 3.SV Cf. āy

... ak hay yo ‖28.4

aki = ayki

al egg; (= talkyal, kyeylan) chicken egg 11.34

āl(q) ... prospective modifier < al.e yo

alay below, lower, down ‖3.5; (= alay chung) downstairs 18.SV; (nai ka~) younger ‖7.10

al.e yo [ā-l-] knows, understands 1.32

al.e kacye yo [kaci-] finds out, obtains knowledge 28.27

alh.e yo [alh-] is/gets sick, ill; ails in (a part of the body) 18.32, 19.2

allye yo [alli-] lets know, informs, tells 23.14

ālm knowledge 26.3

altho (= cēum) alto 12.SV

ama perhaps, maybe; probably 9.26

amman however much [< āmu man] 8.21, 18.40

āmsal assassination; ~(ul) hay yo assassinates 26.22

āmu ... (not) any ... 14.16; ~kes to anything at all 16.28

an ... (= ani) not, (is)n't, (does)n't 4.3

an the inside (of something rather empty), ... ~ey in(side) ... 3.4; [= an(h)ay] (one's own) wife 28.3

ān ... modifier < al.e yo

anay, anhay (one's own) wife 2.SV

anc.e yo [anc-] sits, sits down 4.19

anc.hye yo [anc.hi-] seats (someone) ‖26.1

anh.e yo [anh-] doesn't ...; isn't ... 7.5

ani no (intimate style) 22.SV; (= an ...) not

ani 'ey yo (it) is not, no (polite style) 2.7, ‖2.2

ani 'ta (it) is not, no (plain style) 22.SV

ani yo no (polite) 1.13

ānkay fog, mist 26.3; ~ka kkie yo [kkī-] fog gathers, it fogs up 26.SV

ānq-kwa ophthalmology, eye specialty 19.SV

ānkyeng (eye) glasses; ~ul sse yo puts on (or wears) glasses 8.SV

annyeng (hay yo, hi) being at peace, in good health 1.1, ‖4.6-7

Annyeng hasip.nikka? Annyeng hasey yo? How are you?

Annyeng hi kasipsio! Annyeng hi kasey yo! Goodbye! (to one leaving)

Annyeng hi kyēysipsio! Annyeng hi kyēysey yo! Goodbye! (to one staying)

ānq-kwa ophthalmology, eye specialty 19.SV

ānta = al.e yo knows 26.1

ānun processive modifier < al.e yo

apeci father 4.14

ape' nim esteemed father 4.14

aph the (place in) front; (= mīlay) the future; ... aph ey in front of ... 3.14

aphe yo [aphu-] is painful, sore; aches ‖4.4, 16.11

appa Daddy, Dad, Papa 22.SV

atul son 7.7

atu' nim esteemed son 7.SV

awu (childish term) younger sibling (= brother of boy, sister of girl) 7.SV

āy = ai (child)

āy the bowels (as the seat of one's feelings): pains, efforts; trouble, worry; one's reservoir of strength; ~(lul) sse yo [ssu-] tries, endeavors, takes pains, does one's best 13.7

ayki baby 3.SV

...-ca [plain-style suggestion] ‖19.4; ~ (mā'ca) ‖26.6

ca well! 6.C; come on! now! (urging, inviting) 12.3, 22.18, 23.32

ca (written) character 26.28

ca infinitive < ca yo
cacen-ke bicycle 14.9
cac.e yo [cac-] is frequent ‖4.6-7
cacwu often ‖4.6-7, 8.10
cakceng intention, plan, decision; ...-ulq ~ iey yo decides to ... 27.8
cak.e yo [cāk-] is little, small in size; is quiet, low (in sound) 4.SV
caki oneself 19.11
cakkwu continuously, repeatedly; ~ hay yo keeps doing 16.40
cak.nyen last year 6.23A
cak.yong effect, action ‖28.7
cal well 1.4; a lot, many, much 4.22
cal(q)... prospective modifier < ca yo
calak end, bottom (of a garment = os ~) 29.27
cala yo [cala-] it grows 9.3
cal.e yo [ca-l-] is fine, small 18.36
cali place, spot 26.20; seat (= cwāsek) 12.SV
calmos mistake; ~ hay yo does wrong, does badly; makes a mistake 22.35
cam sleep; ~ i tul.e yo [tu-l-] falls asleep 24.SV; ~ i wa yo [o-] gets sleepy 24.5, 26.3
camay sisters 7.SV
cāmqkan a short while 17.5
camke yo [camku-] locks 28.6; yēlq soy (or cam'ulq soy) lo ~ locks 28.SV; camke twue yo locks it up, leaves it locked
cam'ulq soy a (pad)lock 28.SV
can cup, cupful 6.SV, han ~ a cup(ful); swulq ~ wine cup, yuli ~ glass tumbler, drinking glass 18.SV
can... modifier < ca yo
canchi party 28.26
caney you (familiar style) 28.1
...-cang place 27.10
cang-... long ‖28.7
cang sheet, leaf (counter for flat objects, newspapers) 6.1
cang market (= sīcang); ~ (ul) pwa yo [po-] does the marketing 16.2
cāng a chest (for storage) 3.SV
cangay obstacle; ~ ka tōy yo is an obstacle, gets in the way 26.22
cangchim the hour hand 23.SV
cang-cilpusa = cang-thiphusu (typhoid fever) 19.SV
cange eel 28.SV
cāngin a man's father-in-law 7.SV
cāngkap glove(s) 8.6
cang-keli long distance ‖28.7
cāngkwan cabinet minister 21.SV
cāngkyo officer 2.SV
cang.lo an Elder 17.SV
Cang.lo-kyo Presbyterian faith 17.SV
cāng.lye encouragement; ~ (lul) hay yo encourages 24.SV
cāngmo a man's mother-in-law 7.SV
cangnan game, sport, amusement; ~ (ul) hay yo plays 22.2
cangnanq kām toy 22.SV
cāng nim blindman, blind person (= sōkyeng) 22.SV
cangsa trade, peddling, selling; ~ q-kwun a trader, merchant seller, peddler (= cangswu) 24.SV
cang-sikan long time ‖28.7
cangswu peddler, hawker, seller, trader 24.SV
cang-thiphusu typhoid fever 19.SV
cantung(i) back (= tung) 22.SV
canun processive modifier < ca yo
capayk confession 17.SV
capci magazine 2.8
cap.e yo [cap-] catches 26.SV
cap.hye yo [cap.hi-] gets caught ‖26.1; gets it taken, pawns it 23.27
capok (= capayk) confession 17.SV
capswe yo [capswu-] (someone esteemed) eats ‖18.6
casey hay yo is minute, detailed 27.26
casey hi in detail 27.26
catong-cha automobile, car; (= thayksi) taxi, cab 6.35
catong sikyey automatic clock 23.SV
cāy-... resident in ...; ~ Han resident in Korea 21.26A
cay ashes (<u>see</u> ~ q-ttel.i, ~ q pich)
cāy-cak.nyen year before last (= ci-cinan hay, kulekkey) 21.9
caychayki a sneeze; ~ (lul) hay yo sneezes 19.SV
cāycheng seconding (a motion); ~ (ul) hay yo seconds a motion 21.SV
caycwu talent, ability 12.5, 24.20
ca.yen nature 28.34
caykan = caycwu (talent) 12.5A
cāylay lo always, conventionally 26.30
cāylay uy ... conventional, usual 26.30
caymi interest, fun; ~ (ka) iss.ey yo is interesting, is fun 12.20
... cayngi person/thing characterized by ... 17.16
cayngki a plow 27.SV
ca yo [ca-] goes to bed, sleeps 1.5

caypong sewing 27.30; ~-thul sewing machine 16.SV
cayq pich gray (ash color) (= hoysayk) 26.SV
cay-ttel.i ash tray 2.SV
ca.yu freedom ‖28.7
ccalp.e yo [ccalp-] is short, brief 17.25
ccalp.key [pronounced ccalkkey] briefly 17.25
... ccay ...th (number) 27.27
cca yo [cca-] wrings; ppallay lul ~ wrings the wash 29.SV
ccok = phyen (direction) 3.20
... ccum about, approximately; by (a time) 1.54, ‖6.3
ce uh, ah 17.9
ce that (remote); (= ~kes) that thing, that (over there) 2.7
ce I, me (formal) 7.11 Cf. cey (ka)
ce = ceq-kal(ak) chopsticks 16.SV
(ce-)cel lo spontaneously, without effort 27.11
cec.e yo [cec-] gets wet ‖26.1
ce-huy we, us (humble) 17.10
... cek time that ... (= ttay); experience (= il) ‖12.4
ceq-kal(ak) chopsticks 16.SV
cek.e to even though it's small, even though (there are) few; at least 8.20
cek.e yo [cēk-] is small in quantity; are few in number 4.SV
cēki (that place) over there; (over) there 3.8
cekoli Korean jacket or blouse 8.SV
ceksye yo [ceksi-] wets it, makes it wet ‖26.1
cektang hay yo is appropriate, suitable 29.35
... cel festival of ... 17.SV
cel Buddhist temple 17.19, 26.34
ce'l = ceq-kal(ak) chopsticks 16.SV
celay yo [cele(h)-] is like that (over there); [cele-] does like that (over there) ‖11.5
cele hay yo does/is like that (over there) ‖11.6
celeh.key like that, in that way ‖11.6
cēli that way ‖11.5
cel lo = (ce-)cel lo
celm.e yo [celm-] (an adult) is young 7.27, ‖7.10
celqtay lo absolutely, positively 21.6
cem spot, dot, point 26.18
cemho (military) roll call 21.SV
cemmyeng roll, roll call; ~(ul) hay yo, calls the roll 21.SV, ‖21.3
cēmsim(q pap) lunch 16.SV
cemqswu mark(s), grade(s), score 13.33
cemul.e yo [cemu-l-] gets dark, darkens 28.18
cēm.wen (store) clerk 8.SV
cen-... entire ‖28.7
cen(q)-... former, ex- ‖28.7
... cēn fried ...; hō-pak ~ fried squash 16.SV
cen before 6.2; meychil ~ several days ago (back, earlier); ...-ki cen before ...-ing
cēn penny, cent, sen (small money unit) 6.SV
cēncayng war 12.SV
cēncha streetcar; electric train 8.SV
cēnchwuk electric record player, (radio-)phonograph 11.SV
cengeli sardine 28.SV
cēng hay yo decides (on) 21.4
cēnghwak hay yo is precise, is exactly accurate 23.30
... cēngkak exactly on the hour of ...; sēy si ~ three o'clock sharp, exactly three o'clock 6.9
cengke stopping a vehicle ‖27.10
cengke-cang railroad station 3.SV
cengkwu tennis (= theynisu) 14.4
cengkwu-cang tennis court 14.8
cengpu government ‖28.7
cengseng sincerity; ~ kkes with one's whole heart 18.21
cēngsik the set (table-d'hote) dinner 18.SV
cengsin spirit, feeling 26.31
Cengwel January 6.SV
cen hay yo conveys, reports, delivers, communicates, transmits, tells 29.37
cēnhwa telephone (call); ~ lul hay yo, ~ lul kel.e yo makes a phone call, telephones 8.23
cēnki electricity 29.41; ~ sikyey electric clock 23.SV; cēnkiq ta(y)limi electric iron 29.SV
cenmun hak.kyo college 27.17
cēnsel a legend, a tradition 26.19
censey rent deposit (refunded on leaving) 18.SV
cēntang-pho pawnshop 23.26
cēnthwu battle ‖28.7
centoq puin Bible woman, woman evangelist 17.SV
cento-sa lay (unordained) pastor 17.SV

cenyek evening 4.16; (= ~ pap) evening meal, dinner, supper 16.SV

cen.yem (ul) hay yo is contagious 19.SV

cen.yemq pyeng contagious disease 19.SV

cep.e yo [cep-] folds up, furls 8.SV

cepsi plate 18.SV

cepswu receipt; ~(lul) hay yo accepts (minutes, reports), receives 21.SV

ceptay reception, entertainment (= taycep); ~ (lul) hay yo entertains (a person) 18.SV

ceq-kal(ak) chopsticks 16.SV

cēum alto (= altho) 12.SV

cēy-... ...th (number) 27.9

... (q)-cey made in ... 23.15; ōykwuk ~ of foreign manufacture 27.10

cey see cey (ka)

cey-cel lo = (ce-)cel lo automatically, without effort 27.11

cēy-il (= ches ccay) first, number one; (= kacang) most, -est 21.12

cey (ka) I (as subject - formal) 17.3 (see ce)

cēykil damn [a strong expletive] 23.21

cey-kum = paio(l)lin violin 12.SV

ceymok theme, subject, title 24.SV

cēypal certainly, strongly (hopes): hopefully, I hope; please 21.14

cēyyak drug making; ~(ul) hay yo compounds medicine; fills a prescription 19.SV

cēyyak-sa pharmacist (= yakcey-sa) 19.SV

cha vehicle; (= catong-cha) automobile, car (= thayksi) taxi; (= kicha, cēncha) train 21.20

cha tea (usually green, cf. hong ~) 12.13

cha infinitive < cha yo

chaq can teacup 18.SV

chacang conductor (of bus, train, streetcar, etc.) 8.SV

chac.e yo [chac-] looks for (= chac.ko iss.e yo); finds (= chac.ess.e yo); looks up, visits 4.SV; chac.ule wa yo comes to get 23.10; chac.e wa yo comes on a visit, comes visiting 4.SV, fetches and returns, goes and gets 23.16, ‖23.9

cha-cha gradually, bit by bit 17.25

chaq cip = tapang (teashop) 12.10A

chai difference 24.17

chak hay yo is noble 26.28

chal(q) ... prospective modifier < cha yo

chalim-phyo see cha(y)lim-phyo

cham truth, genuineness, realness 17.25; very, real(ly) 4.11; uh, oh, why 16.6, 23.23, 29.14

cham substantive < cha yo

cham.e yo [chām-] is patient with ..., puts up with ..., bears endures, suffers 22.20

cham mal true (real) word, truth; ~ lo in truth, actually, in reality 26.16

chamsal murder, assassination; ~ (ul) tang hay yo gets assassinated 26.8

chan ... cold [modifier < cha yo]; ~ mul cold water 8.SV

chang window; yuli ~ glazed window 3.8

chansong-ka hymn 17.SV

chanun processive modifier < cha yo (fastens etc.)

chān.yang-tay choir 17.SV Cf. sēngka-tay

chaq pang pantry (in a house); (= tapang) teashop

chay (counter for buildings); cip han ~ one house 6.SV

chayk book 1.22

chayk-cāng bookcase 3.SV

chayk.im duties, responsibilities 17.SV

chayk-pang bookshop (= secem) 3.SV

chayk-sa bookshop (= secem) 3.SV

chayk-sang desk, table 3.24

cha(y)lim-phyo menu 18.SV

cha yo [cha-] is cold (to touch) 9.SV

cha yo [cha-] fastens it on, attaches it; carries it on one's person; wears (what is pinned, tied, or strapped on) 23.5

chāyso vegetable; ~ path vegetable garden 3.17

chaywe yo [chaywu-] fastens 8.SV

cheka(q cip) a man's inlaws, the wife's family 28.26

... chelem like (similar to) ... 4.22, ‖4.9; na ~ like me, similar to me; i ~ this much, like this 17.27

... chemci Mr. ... (familiar style) 28.1

chen thousand; 1000 (= il-chen) 6.SV

chenceng ceiling 3.35

chēn-chen hay yo is slow ‖4.6-7

chēn-chen hi slowly 1.36, ‖4.6-7

Chencwu the Lord (usually Catholic) 17.SV

Chencwu-kyeng the Lord's prayer (Catholic) 17.SV

Chencwu-kyo = Khathollik(-kyo) Catholic(ism) 17.SV

cheng hay yo invites 18.SV; requests, asks for 21.SV

chengcwung (listening) audience 12.SV
chenge herring; mallin ~ dried herring, kipper 28.SV
chengkwu-se request for payment, bill, statement 29.25
chenkwuk (= hanul nala) heavenly kingdom 17.SV
chen-man ten million; ~ uy māl-ssum, ~ ey (yo) not at all 1.15
chentang heaven (= hanul) 17.SV
chen.yen native, natural 22.26
ches ... the first, the beginning 1.24
ches ccay first (place), number one; ~ lo in the first place 27.27
che-siha henpecked husband 28.10
che 'ta = chye 'ta
cheum (for) the first time; ~ ey in the beginning, at first 17.12
chē yo = chyē yo = chie yo
cheyon (body) temperature; ~ kēmsa temperature check(up) 19.SV
chcyon kyey (clinical) thermometer 19.SV
chie yo [chi-] hits ‖8.7, strikes 14.24, pours in 16.SV; phiano (lul) ~ plays the piano 12.SV; kōng (ul) ~ hits the ball, plays ball 14.24; khulīm (ul) ~ pours cream in, takes cream 16.SV
chiq-kwa dentistry; (= ~ uywen) dentist's office; ~ uysa dentist 16.11
chil seven (= ilkop) 6.SV
chil(q) ... prospective modifier < chie yo
chile yo [chilu-] disburses, settles (a bill); takes or gets through (a test) 13.SV, 13.38
chil-phal seven or eight ‖27.8
chilphan blackboard 2.SV
chil-wel(q tal) July 6.SV
chilyo (medical) treatment; ~ (lul) hay yo gives (administers) treatment, treats; ~ lul pat.e yo has (receives) treatment 19.SV
chilyo-so infirmary ‖27.10
chim substantive < chie yo
chima skirt 8.SV
chīmkwu bedding (= ipu'-cali) 29.SV
chim.lyey baptism by immersion 17.SV
Chim.lyey-kyo Baptist faith 17.SV
chīm-pang bedroom 18.SV
chīm-sang bed 3.SV
chīmsil bedroom 16.SV
chīmtay berth, bed 23.SV
chīmtay-cha sleeping car, sleeper, pullman 23.SV
chīmtayq ^{l}yōkum a (pullman) berth charge 23.SV
chin ... modifier < chie yo
chincel kind(ness) ‖28.7; ~ hay yo is kind, considerate 16.14
chinkwu friend 2.31
chiq-kwa dentistry; (= ~ uywen) dentist's office; ~ uysa dentist 16.11
chinun processive modifier < chie yo
chi-sol toothbrush (= iq-sol) 8.SV
chiyak dentifrice 8.SV
chochim the second hand (of a timepiece) 23.SV
cholok sayk green 26.SV
chōnchon-i in every village ‖17.6
chōngkak bachelor, unmarried man 24.9
chōng.li(-sa) bishop (= kamtok) 17.SV
chotay invitation 18.SV
... chung floors, storeys (of a building): ...th floor 6.SV
chungchung-tali, chungchung-tay stairs, staircase (= kyeytan) 18.SV
chwīmi hobby ‖28.7
chwue yo [chwu-] dances (= chwum ul ~) 9.16
chwuk.kwu football, soccer; ~ lul hay yo plays soccer 14.16
chwukpok kito, chwukto benediction 17.SV
chwuk.um-ki phonograph, record player (= ^{l}yuseng-ki, leykhotu) 11.SV
chwuk.um-ki phan phonograph record (= ^{l}yuseng-ki phan, leykhotu phan) 11.SV
chwuk.ye yo [chwuk.i-] dampens it, wets it; os ul ~ dampens (wets) the clothes 29.SV
chwul(q) ... prospective modifier < chwue yo
chwul.ip hay yo goes back and forth, comes and goes, enters and leaves 26.23
chwulqsayng-ci birthplace 11.SV
chwulqsayng hay yo is born 11.SV
chwulqsek attendance, (seated) presence; ~ (ul) hay yo is present (for a meeting) 21.SV
chwum dance, dancing; ~ (ul) chwue yo dances 9.16, 26.3
chwun ... modifier < chwue yo
chwunchwu age [elegant] 11.SV Cf. nai
chwungsin faithful subject 26.8
chwunguy loyalty, faithfulness 26.20
chwunun processive modifier < chwue yo
chwuswu harvest 27.SV
chwuwe yo [chwuw-; chwupko, chwupta] is cold (weather) 9.5
chwuwi cold, cold spell ‖17.6
chye 'ta pwa yo looks up (at) 16.39
chyē yo = chie yo

...-ci [suspective] ‖7.1, ‖22.4, ‖27.1; ~ anh.e yo ‖7.3; ~anh.ko ‖12.7, ‖18.2; ~ mā' ‖22.4; ~ mā' la ‖22.2; ~ mālko ‖18.2; ~ man ‖7.2; ~ māsey yo ‖7.4; ~ yo ‖11.1
...ci [post-modifier] ‖21.1–3, ‖22.6, ‖24.4–5
cic.e yo [cic-] barks 4.20
ci-cinan hay year before last (= cāy-cak.nyen) 21.9A
cicwu landowner 27.SV
cie yo [ci-] loses, is defeated (= phāy hay yo) 14.SV, 28.SV
cie yo [ci-] sinks, drops; fades; hay ka ~ the sun sets; kkoch i ~ the flower fades 28.SV
cie yo [cī(s)-; cīs.ko, ciumyen] builds, makes; cōy lul ~ commits a sin, sins 17.SV
cihwi-ca conductor (of orchestra etc.) 12.SV
cik.kong factory worker 3.SV
cikkum [LIVELY] = cikum 27.9
cikum now 3.3
cik.wen officers, staff (= īm.wen) 17.SV, 21.SV
cil(q) ... prospective modifier < cie yo
... cil (hay yo) (engages in) the behavior of ... totwuk ~ thievery, theft 12.30
cili geography; ~ sang with respect to geography 27.23
cilmun question 1.44
cim substantive < cie yo
...-ci man (is/does) but; although; and (= but then on the other hand) 7.5
cin ... modifier < cie yo
cīnan ... last ...; ~ cwuil last week; ~ pom last spring 1.14, 6.5
cīna yo [cīna-] passes, goes by 11.14
cincca, (cinqca) genuine article 17.16
cīnchal medical examination ‖27.10
cīnchalq-sil examining room 19.SV
cīnci food (= pap); meals (for an esteemed person) 1.6
cin hay yo (color) is dark; (liquid) is thick, rich, strong 26.SV
cīntan diagnosis 19.23
cinun processive modifier < cie yo
ciok hell 17.SV
cip house 3.14; (= ~-an) family 7.SV
cipang area, region ‖28.7
cipcip-i in every house ‖17.6
cip sey rent (for house) 18.SV
cith.e yo [cith-] (color) is dark; (fog, forest, hair) is thick, dense 26.SV
cito map 4.C
...-ci yo see ...-ci

...-co = -cyo = -ci yo ‖11.1
co = ce (that) ‖3.5
coch.a yo [coch-] follows ‖8.3
cōh.a yo [cōh-] is good, right, satisfactory; likes 1.46, ‖7.9, ‖11.4
cokay clam 28.SV
cokha nephew; ~ ttal niece 7.SV
coki = ceki (over there) ‖3.5
coki yellow corvenia (fish) 28.SV
cokki vest, waistcoast 8.SV
cokum a little (bit) 4.SV, 8.11
cōl(q) ... prospective modifier < col.a yo
col.a yo [cō-l-] gets sleepy; dozes 24.7
cōllye yo [cōlli-] gets sleepy 24.SV
cole = cele (like that) ‖11.5
col.ep graduation; ~ (ul) hay yo graduates 13.SV
col.ep-cang diploma 13.SV
col.ep-sayng alumnus, graduate 13.SV
coli = cēli (that way) ‖11.5
coli taking care of one's health (= cosep) 19.SV
cōlm substantive < col.a yo
com a little (bit) (= cokum) 4.SV; just, only, please 11.9
com moth; os ey ~ i mek.e yo a garment gets moth-eaten 29.SV
como (nim) grandmother (= hal-'meni, hal-'me'nim) 7.30
comq yak mothballs 29.SV
cōn ... modifier < col.a yo
cōnun ... processive modifier < col.a yo
cōng-cong repeatedly, again and again, over and over, time after time 29.48
congi paper 2.SV
congil all day long, the whole day through 14.30
congkyo religion; a religion 17.22
copan breakfast (= achimq pap) 13.4
cop.a yo [cop-] is narrow 26.SV
cop.hye yo [cop.hi-] makes it narrow ‖26.1
copu (nim) grandfather (= hal-apeci, hal-ape' nim) 7.30
co-pumo (nim) grandparent(s) 7.SV
cosep taking care of one's health (= coli) 19.SV
cōsim caution, precaution; (mom ~) taking care of oneself 19.SV
cōy sin 17.SV; ~ (lul) pēm hay yo, ~ (lul) cie yo [cī(s)-] sins, commits sin 17.SV
cōysong hay yo = mian hay yo 1.SV
cōyswu convict, prisoner 28.9
cōy yo [cōy-] tightens it ‖22.2
cwācong table clock 23.SV
cwāsek seat (= cali) 12.SV

cwāwu (phyen) ey on left and right; on both sides 3.SV
cwi rat, mouse 3.11A
... cwu counter for rooted plants 26.27
cwu-... stationed in ...; ~Han stationed in Korea 21.26
cwue yo [cwu-] gives 1.35; ...-e ~ does ... as a favor, ...-e cwusipsio (cwusey yo) please do ... ‖8.11; wutwu lul ~ vaccinates 19.SV
cwuil week (= cwukan) 6.5
Cwuil (nal) Sunday, the Sabbath 4.SV
Cwuil hak.kyo Sunday school 17.11
cwuin boss, head, proprietor 29.38; (= namphyen) husband 7.SV
cwukan week; han ~ one week, a week 6.31
cwuk.e yo [cwuk-] dies 11.SV, 26.1
Cwūkito-mun = Cwū uy kito-mun (text of) the Lord's prayer 17.SV
cwuk.ye yo [cwuk.i-] kills 26.25
cwukyo Catholic bishop 17.SV
cwul rope, line, string 29.SV
cwul(q) ... prospective modifier < cwue yo
... cwul (assumed fact; presumption); halq ~ way of doing; how (what) to do 16.13; ~al.e yo ‖17.8
cwum substantive < cwue yo
cwumal weekend ‖28.7
cwumeni bag, purse; (= ho- ~) pocket 3.SV
cwūmun an order (for something); ~ (ul) hay yo places an order, orders 23.20
cwumusye yo [cwumusi-] (someone esteemed) goes to bed, sleeps 1.4
cwun ... modifier < cwue yo
cwūng-... heavy ‖28.7
cwung middle, midst; ...-nun ~(ey) (in) the midst of ...-ing, while ...-ing 12.13, ‖12.6, ‖16.1
cwūng Buddhist priest 17.SV
cwung-hak.kyo junior high school, middle school 28.7
cwūng hay yo is serious, important 19.24
cwungko ancient times 26.SV
Cwungkwuk China; ~mal Chinese (language); ~salam Chinese (person) 2.SV
cwungsey middle ages 26.SV
cwungsim center (of attention), focus (of interest); Sewul ul ~ulo with Seoul as the center ‖27.3
cwungwi 1st lieutenant; (hāykwun ~) lieutenant, junior grade 2.SV
cwūnpi preparation; ~(lul) hay yo prepares, makes ready 18.18
cwunun processive modifier < cwue yo
cwupal metal rice bowl (used in winter) 18.SV
cwupin guest of honor 18.SV
cwūsa injection, shot; ~lul cwue yo (or noh.a yo) gives an injection; ~lul mac.e yo gets (takes) an injection 19.SV
cwūso address, residence ‖28.7
cwūthayk residence 18.SV
cwūuy care(fulness); ~(lul) hay yo exercises care, is careful 29.36
cwuwi the place surrounding; ... cwuwi ey (in the place) around ... 3.18
... cye yo [ci-] gets to be ..., becomes ... ‖9.8
cye yo = cie yo
...-cyo = ...-ci yo ‖11.1
...-e [infinitive] ‖8.7-13, ‖22.4, ‖27.1; ~ se ‖16.1; ~ la ‖22.2; ~ 'ta ‖16.2-3 Cf. ...-a
eccay yo [ecce-] does it how/why [abbreviation of ecci hay yo] ‖11.6
ecci what way? how? why? ‖11.6
ecci hay yo does like what?; does how/why? ‖11.6
ecey yesterday 6.24
e he oh oh! 29.27
ek a hundred million ‖27.8
el(q) ... prospective modifier < el.e yo
ēl-el hay yo is burning, tingling, smarting 18.41
el.e yo [ē-l-] it freezes 26.SV
elin ai/ay/i child 3.SV, ‖7.10
elkwul face 13.19
ellun right away, immediately 18.3
ēlm substantive < el.e yo
elma how much? 6.22; elma 'na about how much; elmaq tong-an how long? how much time?; elma hwū sometime later on, somewhat later 18.37
el.um ice; ~mul ice water 8.SV, 26.SV
elye yo [eli-] (a child) is young ‖7.10
elyewe yo [elyew-] is hard, difficult 13.1; is embarrassing ‖18.2
elyewum difficulty ‖26.3
elye yo [eli-] (a child) is young 7.23
emeni mother ‖1.2
eme' nim esteemed mother 4.16
emma Mom(my), Mama, Mother 24.26
emphaie umpire 14.SV
ēn ... modifier < el.e yo
ēncey when?; sometime 6.1

enni older sibling (a male's older brother, a female's older sister) 7.4, 7.SV Cf. hyeng (nim)

enu ... which ...? 2.12, what ...? 19.20; ~kes which one? Cf. etten

ēnun ... processive modifier < el.e yo

ēps.ay yo [ēpsay-] makes nonexistent, eliminates, exterminates, gets rid of 26.22

ēps.e(y) yo [ēps-] is lacking, isn't; doesn't exist; doesn't stay; has not (got), lacks 3.11, ‖3.1–2, ‖19.2.3

... ēps.i without ... ‖17.6

epu fisherman (= koki cap.i) 28.SV

ese quickly, soon 9.33; without hesitation, right away, please 29.22; ~ tul.e osipsio come right in 17.C

...-ess- [past tense] did, was ‖6.5, ‖9.2, ‖19.2.4, ‖24.2

et.e yo [et-] receives, gets 13.33

eti where? 3.1; somewhere; etiq-cey what (country's) make 23.15A

et'ta = eti (ey) 'ta to what place?

ettay yo [ette(h)-] is like what? is how? ‖11.6

ette hay yo is like what? is how? ‖11.6

etteh.key how? in what way? how come? why? 4.30

etten ... what sort of ...? what ...?; ~kes what (sort of) thing? 2.12 (cf. enu)

etwuwe yo [etwuw-] is dark 9.SV

... ey in, at, on ... ‖3.4, ‖4.8; and ‖22.7; ...-ki ~‖13.8

... eykey = ... hanthey (to a person) ‖4.8

... eykey se = ... hanthey se (from a person) ‖4.8

Eyksu-kwangsen X-ray 19.SV

... ey l' = ... ey lul to (a place) ‖4.8

... ey se from ..., (happening) at ... 4.14, ‖4.8

... 'ey yo it is ... [copula after vowel] 2.7–9

hā-... bottom, lower; under; second of two or three ‖28.7

ha ha ha ha 28.28

...-hak study, science ‖27.10

hakca scholar 2.SV

hak.kyo school 3.2

... hako with; and 3.7, ‖3.4, ‖4.9

haksayng student 2.20

haksik learning, schooling 24.27

hal(q) ... prospective modifier < hay yo

hal-apeci grandfather 7.30

hal-ape' nim esteemed grandfather (= copu nim) 7.30

hal-'meni grandmother 7.30

hal-'me' nim esteemed grandmother (= como nim) 7.30

halwu one day, a day 6.11

ham substantive < hay yo

hamkkey together ‖4.7

han ... about, approximately 6.18, ‖6.3

han ... one ...; ~cwukan one week, a week 6.31

han ... [modifier < hay yo] ... which did; ... which is

hana one (= il) 1.19, 6.SV

Hana'nim God (Protestant) 17.27, 17.SV

Hān-e Korean (language) 24.3

hangali pot, crock 18.37

Hānkwuk Korea 1.28; ~mal Korean language 1.38

han.lan-kyey (weather) thermometer 19.SV

hānnong-ki slack season for farmers 27.SV

hansim hay yo is pitiful, sorry 28.31

... hanthey to/for (a person) 1.52; nwukwu ~ to whom 4.8; ~ se from whom

han-twues, han-twue ... about one or two ‖27.8

han(a)-twul, han-twu ... one or two ‖27.8

hanul sky, heaven 16.39

hanun ... processive modifier < hay yo

hapchang chorus 12.SV

haphum a yawn; ~i na yo yawns 24.5

hapsita let's do it 1.21

hapsung (thayksi) jitney (taxi) 6.SV

haptita I observed that (they) said 23.19

hasa [literary] = hay se 17.27

ha to much, greatly, much indeed 18.40

hay [infinitive of ha-] see hay yo

hay sun 9.6; ~ka na yo the sun shines; ~ka cie yo the sun sets; ~ka tot.a yo the sun rises 28.SV

hay year; han ~ one year 6.SV

ha.ye [literary infinitive of ha-] = hay

ha.ye-kan anyhow, anyway, in any event, no matter what 17.18, 29.20

hāykwun navy 2.SV

hayng-kil = han-kil street, thoroughfare 16.39

hāyngpok happiness, good fortune; ~hay yo is happy, fortunate, lucky 24.21

hāypyen seashore 28.SV

hayq pyeth sunshine 24.SV

hay yo [ha-] does; is 1.1, ‖4.6, ‖7.3, ‖8.12, ‖13.1, ‖13.4; ‖28.2, ‖29.2; ...-key ~‖17.4; ... ko n(un) ~‖24.13; ...-ulq ka ~‖14.5

hēl(q) ... prospective modifier < hel.e yo

hel.e yo [hē-l-] gets worn out, suffers from age 23.23
heli waist, loin; ~ kkun belt; ~ tti sash, waistband 22.SV
hēlm substantive < hel.e yo
hēn ... old (not new) ... [modifier < hel.e yo] ‖7.19, 23.23 (Cf. nalk.un)
hēnkum offering (= yēnpo, swucen) 17.SV
hēnun processive modifier < hel.e yo
hepi waste, wasting; ~ (lul) hay yo wastes 24.13
... hi [derived adverb from descriptive auxiliary ha-] ...-ly 1.16, 4.7, ‖17.6
him strength, power; ~ tul.e yo is difficult, hard, onerous 13.22; ~ (ul) sse yo, tries, makes an effort 13.32; ~ (i) iss.ey yo is strong 22.SV
ho pseudonym, pen name 26.11
ho-cwumeni pocket 3.SV
hōlyeng a command, an order; ~ (ul) hay yo orders, commands 28.7
homyeng roll call (= cemmyeng) 21.SV
hon soul, spirit; ~ (i) na yo gets scolded (browbeaten), gets startled or frightened; ~ (ul) nāy yo browbeats, bullies, scolds; startles, frightens 28.17
honca alone, by oneself 4.21
hong-cha black tea 16.SV
hongyek measles 19.SV
hō-pak squash; ~ cēn fried squash 16.SV
hoswu lake 28.SV
hōy meeting 7.18; association, society, club 21.3
hōycang president of a society or a company 21.2
hoycwung inside one's pocket; ~ sikyey pocket watch 23.3
hōyhwa conversation 24.31
hōykay repentance; ~ (lul) hay yo repents 17.SV
hōykyey treasurer 21.SV
hōylok minutes (of a meeting); ~ ˡnāngtok reading of the minutes 21.SV
hōypi dues, membership fee 21.SV
hōysa a company, a firm 8.23
hoysayk gray (= cayq pich) 19.12, 26.SV
hōywen member (of a group) 21.SV
hulye yo [huli-] is cloudy 9.10
hung hmph! 22.17
hun hay yo is common 19.28
hunh.e yo [hunh-] = hun hay yo
hun hi common(ly) 19.28
huye yo [huy-] is white 26.SV; ppallay ka ~ the wash is clean 29.SV
hwachang hay yo is glorious, fine, splendid 28.3
hwā anger; ~ (ka) na yo = ~ (lul) nāy yo gets angry 24.SV
hwāka artist, painter 19.18
hwal.yak active(ness) ‖28.7
hwānca patient (= pyēngca) 19.SV
hwan.yeng welcoming; ~ -hoy welcoming party; ~ (ul) hay yo welcomes (someone) 21.SV
Hwā-yoil Tuesday 4.SV
hwelssin much, way, (by) far 21.16
hwū after(ward), later; ...-un ~ (ey) after ...-ing 6.14, ‖12.5, ‖28.7
hwuchwu (black) pepper 18.37A
hwūhoy regret, remorse; ~ (lul) hay yo regrets, feels remorse 24.SV
hwū-hwunyen year after the year after next = three years from now ‖28.7
hwullyung hay yo is magnificent, is splendid ‖21.6
hwumchye yo [hwumchi-] wipes; swipes (= steals); ransacks 12.30
hwūnyen [old-fashioned] = ˡnay-ˡnaynyen (year after next) ‖28.7
hwūsik dessert 18.44
hye tongue 22.SV
hyek.myeng revolution ‖28.7
hyel.ayk blood (= phi); ~ kēmsa blood test 19.SV
hyēncay the present 26.SV; at present, now(adays) 27.21
hyeng (nim) a male's older brother; a female's older sister 7.SV
hyengcey brother(s) 7.SV
hyōqkwa effect, effective results 24.16
...-i [derives adverbs and nouns] ‖4.7, ‖17.6 Cf. ... hi
...'i = ... hi
... i [subject particle after a consonant] ‖2.1 Cf. ... ka
... i person (= sālam); ku ~ he/him, she/her; ku ~ tul they/them 14.16
i this; ~ kes this (thing) 1.48; <u>see also</u> ~ sālam
i tooth (= iq-pal) 8.SV, 16.11, 22.SV
ī two (= twūl) 6.SV; ī-nyen two years 6.35; ī-chung second floor 18.SV
ˡī Korean mile (li) 6.SV
ic.e yo [ic-] forgets 18.SV, ‖18.2-3, 21.4; ic.e (p)pelye yo forgets completely 28.30
... ici yo [casual polite style copula] 11.1

īcwung-chang (vocal) duet (= pyēngchang) 12.SV
īcwung-cwu (instrumental) duet 12.SV
... iey yo [i-] it is [after consonant ... 'ey yo] 1.15, 2.2
^{l}īhay hay yo understands, comprehends 27.20
ikye yo [iki-] wins 14.SV
...-il day(s) 6.SV
il one (= hana) 6.SV
īl work, task, job; ~(ul) hay yo works, 4.29; experience, (happening) ever/never/sometimes ‖12.4
... il(q) ... prospective modifier < iey yo
... ila [quoted copula after consonant] ... (that) it is ‖19.6–7, ‖24.3
ilay yo [ile(h)-] is like this; [ile-] does like this ‖11.6
il-chung first floor 18.SV
ilccik(i) early 4.SV
ile hay yo does/is like this ‖11.6
ileh.key like this, in this way ‖11.6
il.e na yo [il.e na-] gets up 4.SV; happens, occurs 26.6
... iley [familiar-style retrospective copula] ‖28.1
iley seven days 6.32
ilh.e yo loses 18.32; ilh.e pelye yo loses completely 18.32
ilhun seventy (= chilq-sip) 6.SV
ili this way ‖11.5
ilq-ī one or two; ~pun one or two minutes 23.30, ‖27.8
ilk.e yo [ilk-] reads 4.14
ilkop seven (= chil) 1.19, 6.SV
il(ko)-yetelp about seven or eight ‖27.8
ille yo [ilu-] is early 8.SV, ‖8.13.3
ille yo [ilu-] tells; admonishes, informs 22.31
īlq-kwun worker, workman 27.21
Ilpon Japan; ~mal Japanese (language) ~q salam Japanese (person)
... ilq sey = ... iney it is ... [familiar] ‖28.1
ilum name 11.SV
Il-wel(q tal) January (= Cengwel) 6.SV
Il-yoil Sunday 4.SV
il.yong everyday, mundane 24.31
... im substantive < ... iey yo
ima forehead 22.SV
^{l}imsi impromptu, off the cuff; ~yēnsel, impromptu speech 24.31
īm.wen (= cik.wen) officers, staff 17.SV, 21.SV

... in ... modifier < ... iey yo
... ina about, approximately; or the like [after vowel ... 'na]; meych sikan (ssik) ~about how many hours (each)? 6.11, ‖6.3, ‖7.6
incey now; starting now, from now on 11.9: before long 18.10; ~ya (only) now 21.12
ingkhu ink 2.SV
insa greetings, courtesies 18.SV
īnto leadership, guidance; ~(lul) hay yo leads, guides 17.SV
intwu small heart-shaped iron with long handle; soldering iron 29.SV
ip mouth 22.13
iq-pal tooth (= i) 8.SV, 16.11, 22.SV
^{l}īpal haircutting, hairdressing ‖27.10
^{l}īpal(q)-sa barber, hairdresser 2.SV
^{l}īpal(q)-so barber shop, hairdresser's ‖27.10
ī-payk two hundred 6.SV
ipcangq-kwen (admission) ticket 12.SV
ipcang-lyo admission price, fee 12.SV
ip.e yo [ip-] puts on, wears (clothing) 8.2
ip.hye yo [ip.hi-] dresses (someone) ‖26.1
i-pi-inhwuq kwa ear-nose-and-throat specialty, otorhinolaryngology 19.SV
ip mas appetite 18.32
ippal = iq-pal (tooth)
ipp.e yo [ippu-] is pretty, cute, lovable, precious ‖4.7
ip-swul lip 22.SV
ipu'-cali bedding (= chīmkwu) 29.SV
ipul coverlet 29.SV
ipulq is sheet to cover a coverlet 29.SV
ip.wen entrance (or admission) to hospital as a patient; ~(ul) hay yo enters (or is admitted to) a hospital 19.4
iq-pal tooth (= i) 8.SV, 16.11, 22.SV
iq-sol toothbrush (= chi-sol) 8.SV
is sheet, cover 29.SV
i sālam this person; you [informal]; I/me 28.3
ī-sam two or three ‖27.8
... isey yo [... isi-] (someone esteemed) is 2.22
iq-sol toothbrush (= chi-sol) 8.SV
iss.e(y) yo [iss-] exist(s), there is/are; is (in a place), stays 3.3, ‖3.1–2, ‖8.5, ‖8.11, ‖19.2.3 Cf. ēps.e(y) yo, kyēysey yo
iss.ta (ka) in a little while, later on ‖16.2

... ita [plain-style copula] it is ‖19.6, ‖22.1; [copula transferentive—used only as 'ta] ‖16.2–3

ithul two days 6.SV

itta (ka) = iss.ta (ka)

Ī-wel(q tal) February 6.SV

... iya [particle after consonant] only if (it be) Cf. ... ya

iyaki talk, conversation (= yāyki, yēyki); ~(lul) hay yo talks 1.42

... iyo [polite particle after a consonant] Cf. ... yo

ˡīyu reason, cause 26.6

...-ka professional, -ist, -er, person who engages in an activity; um.ak ~ musician; sōsel ~ novelist 12.2, ‖27.10

... ka [subject particle after a vowel] ‖2.1 Cf. ... i

... ka [question post-modifier] ‖14.5, ‖16.6; ~pota ‖24.11

ka infinitive < ka yo

kā edge, border, kangq ~ riverbank; pataq ~ seashore 28.14

kacang most (of all) 12.35

kaca(y)mi sole (fish) 28.SV

kaceng the home (as a center of domestic life) 7.16; home, household, family 27.30; ~ puin housewife 2.SV; ~-yong for household use ‖27.10

kache yo [kachi-] = kat.hye yo [kat.hi-]

kachi value, worth; ~(ka) iss.ey yo has value, is valuable, is worthwhile 27.32

kachi = kath.i (together; like)

kachwuk domesticated animal(s) 27.SV

kaci kind, variety; (counter for abstract things) 6.SV, ‖6.1

... kaciko with ..., by means of ... ‖28.6

kacin 1. (modifier < kacye yo); 2. = kac.un

kac'key = kacikey so that one has 27.19

kacok family 7.SV

kac'ta (= kacye 'ta) gets it and then (gives it); ~cwue yo brings ‖16.1

kac.un ... all sorts of ...; complete, perfect 26.23

kacye yo [kaci-] takes in hand, carries; has, owns, possesses; kacye/kaciko ka yo takes (= goes carrying); kacye/kaciko wa yo brings (= comes carrying) 12.29

kak-... each, every ‖28.7

kakkai near ‖17.6

kakkawe yo [kakkaw-] is near(by), close 8.SV

kakkum sometimes, now and then, from time to time 12.2, 17.4

kakuk opera (= opheyla) 12.SV

kakwu furniture 18.SV

kakyek price (level), cost 23.28; value 29.46

kākyel(ul) hay yo decides in favor (of) 21.SV

kal(q)... prospective modifier < ka yo, < kal.e yo (changes)

kāl(q)... prospective modifier < kal.e yo (plows)

kal.e yo [ka-l-] changes, exchanges (for), replaces (with) ‖19.8, 23.8

kal.e yo [kā-l-] plows; non ul ~ plows the paddy field 27.SV

kalk.e yo [kalk-] scratches 19.SV

kaluchye yo [kaluchi-] teaches 4.SV

kalwu flour, powder 27.SV

kalyewe yo [kalyew-] is itchy 19.SV

kalm substantive < kal.e yo (changes)

kālm substantive < kal.e yo (plows)

kam substantive < ka yo

kaman hi quietly 28.8

kamca potato 16.SV

kam.e yo [kām-] washes (body or hair), bathes, (meli lul ~) shampoos 8.SV, 26.SV

kāmki a cold; ~ka tul.ess.ey yo has (caught) a cold; ~(ey) tullye yo catches (suffers from) a cold 19.SV

kamkye yo [kamki-] bathes or washes (someone); has someone bathe or wash ‖26.1

Kam.li-kyo Methodism, Methodist 17.3

kam.li-sa district superintendent 17.SV

kam.ok jail, prison 28.9

kāmsa gratitude, thankfulness; ~(lul) hay yo gives thanks, expresses gratitude 17.SV

kāmsa(q cel) (Gratitude =) Thanksgiving 17.SV

kamtang ability to handle or cope; ~(ul) hay yo can handle, is capable of coping with 24.19

kamtok bishop 17.SV Cf. chōng.li(-sa)

kan ... modifier < ka yo, < kal.e yo (changes)

kān ... modifier < kal.e yo (plows)

kanan hay yo is poor, poverty-stricken 28.6

kan-cang soy sauce 16.SV

kang river 14.SV, 28.3

kang hay yo is strong 22.SV

kangq ka riverbank 28.14

kāngsup lecture; (special) training 27.29

kāngsup-sayng short-course student 27.10

kāngsup-so lecture room, training-place 27.29

kāngyen lecture 7.29, 24.SV

kanho-pu nurse 19.20

kāntan hay yo is simple, plain, uncomplicated 24.11, 27.16

kanul.e yo [kanu-l-] is thin, slender 22.SV

kanun modifier < kanul.e yo; processive modifier < ka yo, < kal.e yo (changes)

kānun processive modifier < kal.e yo (plows)

kapang bag, case, handbag, briefcase 3.5

kaps price, cost; ~i pissa yo is expensive 11.5

kapyewe yo [kapyew-] is light (in weight) 13.SV

kā-pu pro(s) and con(s) 21.SV

kasum chest, breast 22.SV

kaswu singer 12.3A

kath.e(y) yo [kath-] is the same (as), is like or similar ‖4.7, 12.23; ... kes ~ ‖17.7

kath.i together (= hamkkey); like, similar to (= chelem) 4.12, 4.18, ‖17.6

kat.hye yo [kat.hi-] is shut in, confined, imprisoned 28.9

katwe yo [katwu-] shuts in, confines 28.9

kaul autumn, fall 7.26, 9.SV

kawi scissors 16.SV

... kay item(s), unit(s), object(s) [general counter] 6.SV

kāy dog 3.15

kaychen creek; ditch 28.18

kayksil guest room 16.SV

... ka yo [questions] 14.8, ‖14.5, ‖16.6

ka yo [ka-] goes 1.16, ‖8.11; (time) passes, lasts 19.28

...-kaywel months 6.SV

kaywul small brook 28.SV

ke 1. = kes (thing) ‖14.1, ‖14.7-8; 2. = ku kes (that); 3. my! oh! why! 23.3, 29.14

kekceng = ˡyēm.lye (worry) 18.5A

keki that place; there (aforementioned) 3.9

ke l' = kes ul

kēl(q) ... prospective modifier < kel.e yo (hangs)

kel.e yo [kēl-; kēt.ko, kēt.nunta] walks 8.17

kel.e yo [kē-l-; kēlko, kēnta] hangs it up 13.SV; cēnhwa lul ~makes a phone call, calls (on phone) 8.23, 8.SV

kel.e ka yo goes (somewhere by) walking, goes on foot 8.17

keli downtown streets; downtown, the town 9.23; city streets, city (as opposed to country) 14.SV

kēli distance, farness 26.4

kellye yo [kelli-] 1. it takes, requires; sikan i ~it takes time 18.28, 23.19. 2. it hangs, is hanging ‖26.1; is caught (by), is infected, kāmki ey ~catches a cold 19.SV 3. makes/has someone walk ‖26.1

kēlm substantive < kel.e yo (hangs)

kel.ul(q) ... prospective modifier < kel.e yo (walks)

kelum fertilizer (= pīlyo) 27.SV

kel.um walk, step, gait ‖26.3 [substantive < kel.e yo (walks)]

kemceng black (color) 26.SV

kem.e yo [kēm-] is black 26.SV; ppallay ka ~the wash is (still) dirty 29.SV

kēmsa inspection, examination, checkup; ~(lul) hay yo gives a checkup; ~(lul) pat.e yo has (undergoes) a checkup 19.SV

kēm.yel censorship ‖27.10

kēm.yel-kwan censor ‖27.10

kēn ... modifier < kel.e yo (hangs)

kēnchwuk-ka architect 2.SV

...-keni [tentative sequential] ‖24.7

kēnkang hay yo is healthy, sound 27.33

kēnkang hi in health, soundly; mom ~ with healthy body, in sound health 27.33

kēnmul a building 24.SV

kēnne(q) ... the opposite ..., the one across 28.12

kēnne ttwie yo [ttwi-] jumps across 28.22

kēnne yo [kēnnu-] crosses, goes across 28.12

kēnun ... processive modifier < kel.e yo (hangs)

kep fear, fright; ~(i) na yo is afraid, fears 28.32

... kes thing, object; i ~this (thing); ku ~ that (thing) 2.1; ~iey yo ‖14.7-8; ~ kath.e yo ‖17.7; ~ul ‖22.9; ...-ulq ~ ēps.ey yo there's no reason to ... 23.38

kēswu raising one's hand 21.SV

kesulumq tōn change (returned when paying for a purchase) 23.SV

kēt.nun ... processive modifier < kel.e yo (walks)

ketwe yo [ketwu-] gathers up, takes in, collects, harvests 27.SV, 29.SV

keuy almost, nearly 26.17

...-key [adverbative] so that ...; such that ...; -ly ‖17.3-5; ~hay yo causes someone to (do/be ...) ‖17.4; ~tōy yo ‖17.5 See also ...-key (na)

... key = ... kes i 29.7; ~yo ‖14.7-8

kēy crab 28.SV

...-key (na) [familiar-style command] ‖28.1

...-keyss- [future] will do/be ‖9.1-2; does/is ‖11.2, ‖19.2.4, ‖24.2

keyulle yo [keyulu-] is lazy 13.20

khalle collar 29.26

Khathollik-kyo Catholic(ism) 17.SV

... khenyeng far from (being/doing)..., let alone ... ‖24.14

khephi coffee 16.SV, 18.14

khe yo [khu-] is large, big (in size) 4.SV, gets big(ger), grows ‖12.5

khi height, stature ‖17.6; ~ka cak.e yo is short; ~ka khe yo is tall 22.32

khie yo [khi-] lights, burns; saws; pul ul ~ turns on the lights 16.SV; paiollin ul ~ plays the violin 12.SV

kho nose 22.13

kho-cwupu Big-Nose 22.28

khoq-kwumeng nostril 22.SV

khōchi coach(ing); ~(lul) hay yo coaches 14.SV

khulīm cream 16.SV

khul(q) ... prospective modifier < khe yo

khum substantive < khe yo

khun ... modifier < khe yo

khunun ... processive modifier < khe yo (gets big)

khyelley pair 22.6

...-ki the act of ...-ing ‖13.2; ~cen ‖13.13; ~ey ‖13.8, ‖13.11; ~ka ‖13.7, ‖13.15; ~lo ‖13.10, ~lul ‖13.11-12, ‖13.14-15; ~man ‖13.5; ~nun ‖13.4; ~to ‖13.3; ~ttaymun ‖13.9

kicha (steam or diesel) train 8.SV Cf. cēncha

kichaq sikan phyo train schedule 23.SV

kichim a cough 19.SV

kiek hay yo remembers, recalls 21.9

kīep enterprise ‖28.7

kihan term, time limit; cey ~ any time 29.11

kihoy opportunity, chance 24.1

kiil appointed day 29.9

kiip hay yo fills in, makes out (a form) 29.40

kikwan organ, facility, project, institution 27.27; engine ‖27.10

kikwan-chong machine gun ‖28.7

kikwan-sa engineer ‖27.10

kikwan-swu locomotive engineer ‖27.10

kikyey machine(ry); works, mechanism 23.20

kil street, road 4.C, 16.39A

kīl(q) ... prospective modifier < kil.e yo

kil.e yo [kī-l-] is long (in space or time) 16.37A

kil.i length ‖17.6

kille yo [kilu-] raise, grows (animals or plants) 9.4

kilok record (in sports, etc.) ‖28.7

kīlm substantive < kil.e yo

kimchi pickled vegetables 16.29

kīn ... modifier < kil.e yo

kinyem commemoration; ~(ul) hay yo celebrates, commemorates, remembers 26.6

kiph.e yo [kiph-] is deep 12.SV

kiph.i depth; (= kiph.key) deeply ‖17.6

kippe yo [kippu-] is happy, glad; kippe hay yo rejoices 8.11

kippum happiness, joy ‖26.3

kitalye yo [kitali-] waits for 4.SV

kito prayer 17SV

kito-hoy prayer meeting 17.SV

Kitok Christ; ~-kyo Christianity 17.23A

Kitok Chengnyen Hoy(-Kwan) YMCA (building) 17.SV

... kkaci (up) to ..., until ..., till...; ēncey ~ till when? 6.10; ‖6.4

kkakk.e yo [kkakk-] cuts, trims, mows, peels, pares; sharpens (pencil) 4.15, 4.SV

kkampak suddenly, all of a sudden 28.22

kkatalk reason, cause; ku ~ ey/ulo by reason (because) of that 12.32, ‖12.8

kkāy-cye yo [-ci-] it smashes, shatters, breaks 16.SV

kkaykkus hay yo is neat, clean ‖4.6-7, 18.12; 29.SV

kkaykkus 'i neatly ‖4.6-7

kkaytal.e [kkaytal-] becomes (or is) aware, realizes 24.12

kkay-ttulye yo [-ttuli-] smashes, shatters, breaks it 16.SV

kkāy yo [kkāy-] wakes up, sobers up 26.SV

kkaywe yo [kkaywu-] wakes, sobers (someone) up 26.SV

... kkes to the full extent of, to the utmost of ... ‖18.7

kke yo [kku-] extinguishes; pul ul ~ turns off the lights 16.SV

... kkey to (an esteemed person) 7.20, ‖7.8

... kkey se from (an esteemed person); (= ...i/ka) (an esteemed person as subject) ‖7.8

kkichye yo [kkichi-] causes (trouble); swūko lul ~ is a bother 1.14
kkie yo [kkī-] puts on, wears (gloves, buttons, rings etc.) 8.6, 8.SV; (fog, cloud, etc.) gathers 26.SV
kkīl(q) ... prospective modifier < kkie yo
... kkili the separate group of people (or of like-moving objects); caney (tul) ~ you all, you guys 28.16
kkīm substantive < kkie yo
kkīn ... modifier < kkie yo
kkoc.a yo [kkoc-] sticks (or wedges) it in; phin ul ~ puts on (or wears) a pin 8.SV
kkoch flower 3.13
kkoch cip florist, flower shop 19.10
kkoch kwūkyeng flower viewing 7.30
kkoch namu flower(ing) tree or shrub 3.13
kkoch path flower garden 3.17
kkok exactly, just, for sure, without fail 12.35
kkoma short fellow, runt, midget 22.27
kkos-kkos hay yo is perfectly straight or stiff, unbending 26.31
kkoy wiles, craft, guile 26.22
kkul(q) ... prospective modifier < kke yo
kkūl(q) ... prospective modifier < kkul.e yo
kkul.e yo [kkū-l-] pulls, drags 16.SV
kkulh.e yo [kkulh-] it boils 16.SV
kkulh.ye yo [kkulh.i-] boils it 16.SV
kkūlm substantive < kkul.e yo
kkulh.in mul boiled water 16.SV
kkum substantive < kke yo
kkun string 16.SV
kkun ... modifier < kke yo
kkunh.e yo breaks it in two, snaps it 16.SV
kkunun ... processive modifier < kke yo
kkūnun ... processive modifier < kkul.e yo
kkuth end, termination 6.8
kkuth na yo [na-] ends, comes to an end, stops, is over 6.8, ‖26.1
kkuth-nay, kkuth.kkuth-nay to the very end 14.31
kkuth nāy yo [nāy-] stops it, finishes it ‖26.1
kkway quite, very; fairly 23.26
kkwēy yo [kkwēy-] pierces, thrusts; panul ey sīl ul ~ threads a needle 29.SV
kkwēy may yo [kkwēy may-] sews, stitches, patches, mends 29.SV
kkwēy cye yo [ci-] gets torn, ripped; bursts 29.SV
kkwul honey 28.36
kkwum a dream 26.3; ~ ul kkwue yo [kkwu-] dreams (a dream) 26.SV
kkyē yo = kkie yo
...-ko [gerund] and (also), ...-ing ‖4.5, ‖8.3-6, ‖16.1, ‖24.16; ~ iss.e(y) yo is ...-ing ‖8.5; ~ (ya) mal.e yo simply has to ..., must ... ‖18.2; ~ mālko (yo) of course ...! 16.26; ~ nun ‖21.4; ~ n(un) hanta makes a habit of ...-ing, keeps ...-ing ‖24.13; ~ siph.e yo wants to ... ‖8.6
... ko (saying) that ... 19.1, ‖23.8
kō ... the late ..., the deceased ... 11.SV
ko = ku (that) ‖3.5
koa orphan ‖27.10
koa-wen orphanage ‖27.10
kōcang trouble, disorder; ~ (i) na yo trouble occurs, gets out of order 23.21
kōcek historic remains, (= ~ -ci) historic(al) spot 26.17
kōcek-ci historical spot, ruins, place where there are remains 26.SV
kochwu (red) pepper 18.37
kōhay Catholic confession 17.SV
kōhyang home, home town 9.15
koki = keki (there) ‖3.5
koki meat (usually beef) 4.22; (= mulq~) fish (Cf. sayngsen) 18.2, 18.SV
koki cap.i fisher (= epu); fishing 28.SV
koksik grain(s), cereals 27.SV
kol anger; ~ (i) na yo = ~ (ul) nāy yo gets angry 24.SV
kole = kule (like that) ‖11.5
koli = kuli (that way) ‖11.5
Kolye [old name of Korea] 26.7
komawe yo [komaw-] is obliging; am thankful, grateful; ~ hay yo is grateful for 1.3, ‖8.10
kōng ball 14.14, ‖28.6
kongcang factory 3.SV
kong-chayk notebook 2.SV
kongep industry ‖28.7
kongil Sunday, Sabbath 17.14 Cf. Il-yoil
kongkwun air force 2.SV
kongpu study(ing), lesson, class; ~ (lul) hay yo studies, is studying 4.2
kongsa minister (to a foreign country) 21.SV
kongsa-kwan legation 21.SV
kongsek (the presence of) the public; ~ ey se in public 24.31
kongsik formal(ity), (being) official ‖28.7
kongwen public park 4.16

kongyen hi pointlessly, unreasonably [often pronounced koyni or kwayni] 23.38
kōpayk confession 17.SV
kopha yo [kophu-] (stomach) is/gets empty; pay ka ~ is/gets hungry 18.28
kos place 9.SV
kos.kos-i in every place ‖17.6
kōso (legal) complaint; ~ (lul) hay yo complains, files a complaint, sues 29.35
kot immediately, right away 18.10, 29.11
kot.a yo [kot-] is straight, unbent, direct 26.31
kotung-e mackerel 28.SV
kotung hak.kyo high school 13.SV
koum soprano (= sophulano) 12.SV
ko.yangi = kwāyngi (cat)
koyngcang hay yo is wonderful, marvelous, magnificent 19.19
koyni see kongyen hi
... ko yo ‖23.8
ku that (nearby or aforementioned); (= ku i) he/him, she/her; ~ taum after that, and then, next 1.54
kucekkey day before yesterday 9.28
ku-cwung among them; (= kacang) most (of all) 12.35, 28.27
ku'h.ci that's right [abbreviated from kuleh.ci] 22.SV
kukcang theater 12.SV
ku i he/him, she/her; ~ tul they/them 14.16
ku-kkacis kes such a trivial thing 28.32
ku-kkacis ... such a (little, trivial)... 22.17
kul sentence; composition; writing, script, letters, characters; learning, scholarship 1.41
kulay so, yes 11.25; and 23.29; ~ yo [kule(h)-] is like that, [kule-] does like that ‖11.6
kulay se and so ..., and then ... 1.SV
kulay to even so, nevertheless 1.SV
kule hay yo does/is like that (nearby or aforementioned) ‖11.6
kuleh.ci man but ..., however ... 1.SV
kuleh.key like that (nearby or aforementioned), in that way, so ‖11.6
kuleh.kwun it's so! it's like that (I suddenly realize)! 16.6
kulekkey year before last (= cāy-cak.nyen) 21.9A
kulem well ..., now ..., then ...; yes 1.SV
kulemyen then ..., in that case ... 1.SV
kulena but ..., still ..., yet ... 1.SV
kulen tey but ..., and then ..., by the way ... 1.SV
kuli that way ‖11.5
kuliko and ..., moreover ... 1.SV
kūlim picture, drawing 3.28, ‖26.3
kūlimq yepse postcard 26.13
kulk.e yo [kulk-] scratches 19.SV
kulssey yo well, let me think, well ... [showing reservations] 17.22
kulus dish, food container 16.23, 18.SV
kūlye yo [kūli-] draws (a picture) ‖26.3
kum gold 12.30
ku man just, only that, with that 21.10; ~ twue yo puts aside, leaves alone, discontinues; ~ hay yo (1) stops doing it, (2) up and does it or does it just like that, (3) does only that 28.20
kumkang diamond
kum.nyen this year 6.23A
Kum-yoil Friday 4.23
kumul net; nakk.si ~ fishing net 28.SV
kum-unq pang jewelry shop 12.SV
kūnche vicinity, neighborhood 26.24
kūnsey recent times, the modern age 26.SV
kunul shade 9.SV
kup.hayng-cha express 23.SV
... kwa [after consonant] with, and ‖4.9 Cf. ... wa
kwa lesson; course; subject(s); department 3.SV, 19.17
kwacang department head 19.17
kwahak science; ~ cek scientific ‖28.7
kwā hay yo is excessive 19.27
kwā hi excessively, overly, too 19.27
kwāil fruit 18.44
kwāke the past 26.SV
...-kwan government official 21.27 ‖27.10
...-kwan building 21.27, ‖27.10
kwancwung (viewing) audience, spectators 12.SV
kwāng storeroom 18.SV
(... ey) kwan hay yo relates (to), concerns, is about 27.19
kwankyey relation(ship) 26.30; relevance ‖28.7; ~ hay yo concerns, has something to do with 29.5
kwansim interest, concern 27.19
kwāycong wall clock 23.SV
kwā.yen sure enough, actually, in reality 26.5
kwaynchanh.e yo [kwaynchanh-] it does not matter, it is all right (OK), it

makes no difference 1.13, 8.13
kwāyngi cat 3.15
kwayni see kongyen hi
... kwen [counter for bound volumes] chayk han ~ a book, one book 6.SV
kwi ear 22.13; ~ (ka) mek.e yo [mek-] goes deaf, loses one's hearing 22.SV
kwīcwung hay yo is precious ‖27.10
kwīcwung-phum precious belongings/ goods, valuables 23.27, ‖27.10
kwī hay yo is valuable, precious 28.6
kwi-mekeli deaf person 22.SV
kwīyewe yo [kwīyew-] is cute, dear, sweet, precious 17.5
kwū-... old ‖28.7
kwu nine (= ahop) 6.SV
kwucen commission(s) 18.SV
kwuchey (= kwusang) embodiment, concrete form 27.26
kwuchey-cek (ulo) concrete(ly) 27.26
kwu hay yo obtains, gets; buys; seeks 23.20
kwuk soup 16.32
kwuk.ka nation 28.7
kwuk.min hak.kyo elementary school (= pōthong hak.kyo) 13.SV
kwuksan domestic production ‖27.10
kwuksan-phum native product 23.28
kwukswu noodles 16.SV
kwūkyeng viewing, watching, looking at; a show; ~ hay yo watches, views, sees 4.23
Kwūkyo Catholic(ism) 8.SV
kwul oyster 28.SV
kwūllye yo [kwūlli-] rolls it up 22.8
kwulm.e yo [kwulm-] starves, is starving ‖26.1, 26.SV
kwulm.kye yo [kwulm.ki-] lets someone go hungry ‖26.1
kwulum cloud 9.SV; ~ i kkie yo [kkī-] clouds gather, it clouds up 26.SV
...(-)kwumen [apperceptive] ‖16.4
kwumeng hole 22.SV
...(-)kwun [apperceptive] ‖16.4
kwungkwel palace (= tāykwel) 26.34
kwun.in serviceman 2.32
kwu-payk nine hundred 6.SV
kwup.e yo [kwup-] is bent 26.31
kwup.hye yo [kwup.hi-] bends it 26.31
kwusang see kwuchey
kwūsil excuse ‖27.3
kwutwu shoe(s) 8.5; ~ kkun shoe-string(s) 16.SV
kwuwe yo [kwūw-] broils 28.14
Kwu-wel(q tal) September 6.SV
kwūwen salvation, redemption 17.SV
kwuwun koki sliced meat broiled with seasoning in oil and soy sauce 16.SV
Kwū-yak Old Testament 17.SV
kyelqceng decision ‖28.7
kyelhon marriage; ~ hay yo marries, gets married 7.6
kyelkwa result 24.SV
kyelqsek absence; ~ (ul) hay yo is absent (from a meeting) 21.SV
kyelqsim decision, determination; (...-ki lo) ~ hay yo decides/determines (to do) 27.21
... kyem combining ... 21.31, ‖21.9
kyeng-... light, not heavy ‖28.7
kyēngchal police 29.35
kyēngchal-kwan = kyēngkwan (policeman) 3.SV
kyengchi scenery 21.SV
kyēngcong alarm clock (= camyeng-cong, sapal sikyey) 23.SV
kyenghem experience 24.6
kyēngki contest, competition 14.SV
kyēngkwan policeman 3.SV
kyēngkyey guard(ing), watch(ing); ~ (lul) hay yo guards, watches 24.14
kyengwu circumstance, situation, event(uality) 29.35
kyewu barely 27.10
kyewul winter 9.SV
kyēyhoyk plan, project 27.26
kyeylan chicken egg (= talkyal) 11.34
kyēysan calculation; ~ (ul) hay yo counts, calculates 17
kyēysok continuation; ~ (ul) hay yo continues 24.2
kyēysey yo [kyēysi-] (someone esteemed) is, exists, stays 1.17, 4.SV, ‖19.2.3
kyeytan staircase (= chungchung-tali) 18.SV
...-kyo bridge 26.2
kyōcang school principal ‖28.7
kyōhoy church 3.SV
kyohwan telephone exchange ‖27.10
kyohwan-swu telephone operator ‖27.10; 29.29
kyohyang-ak symphony 12.SV
kyohyang aktan symphony orchestra 12.SV
kyōkwa-se textbook 11.SV
kyōpha (religious) denomination 17.SV
kyōsil classroom 3.4
kyōswu professor 7.21
kyouy chair (= uyca) 3.21
kyōyuk education ‖28.7
kyul orange 18.44
kyumo scale (of size etc.), scope ‖28.7

...-l(q) [prospective modifier after vowel base] see ...-ul(q)
...'l(q) ... see ... il(q) ...
...-la [plain-style command in quotations, after vowel base] ‖19.3 Cf. ...-ula, ...-e la
... la [command particle] see ...-e ~
...'la [quoted copula after vowel] see ... ila
... lak hay yo ‖28.4
latio radio 4.18
...-le [purposive after vowel base] 16.2, ‖24.9 Cf. ...-ule
leykhōtu phonograph, record player (= chwuk.um-ki); (= ~phan) a record 11.SV
leykhōtu phan phonograph record 11.SV
leykhōtu um.ak recorded music 12.SV
leysutholang restaurant 13.SV
leytio = latio (radio)
...-lla [prospective adjunctive after vowel base] ‖24.10
...-llay = ...-lye (ko) hay to ‖24.9
... lo [particle after vowel or l] ‖4.9, ‖13.10, ‖19.8, ‖26.4, ‖27.6 Cf. ... ulo
... lul [direct object particle after vowel] ‖4.5, ‖22.9, ‖27.3 Cf. ... ul
...-lye [intentive after vowel base] ‖24.9 Cf. ...-ulye
...-lyo charge, fee, cost, rate; see ipcang ~ Cf. ˡyōkum, ...ˡyo
...-m [substantive after vowel base] see ...-um
...'m see ... im
...-m a ‖23.6
mā' see -ci ~
mā'ca see -ca ~
mac.e yo [mac-] meets up with, faces, confronts, has, gets, suffers, receives 12.33, 19.SV
machan-kaci the same thing, an identical thing 17.22 [< machi han kaci]
machi just, as though, as if 28.9
machye yo [machi-] finishes, completes 9.27
macimak the end 7.11
mac.un ... facing, opposite; (...) ~ phyen ey in the opposite (or facing) direction, across from (...) 3.26
mahun forty (= sā-sip) 6.SV
'mak-nay the lastborn, the youngest of the family [< macimak nan ay lastborn child] 7.11
mal end (= kkuth) 26.8
māl language, talk, words; ~ (ul) hay yo talks, speaks, says 1.28, 1.31; māl halq swu ēps.i indescribably, beyong words 18.26; tasi māl hamyen in other words 23.8; (sālam uy) ~ (ul) tul.e yo [tu-l-] obeys (a person) 28.17
māl(q) ... prospective modifier < mal.e yo
mal.e yo [mā-l-] avoids, desists, does not ‖18.2; ...-ci māsipsio (māsey yo) please do not ...; ...-ci mā(si)psita let's not (do) ...; ...-e ~ ends up doing, finally does 1.27, 7.32, ‖26.1; ...-ko (ya) ~, -ko mālko (yo) ‖18.2
... mali [counter for animals, fish, birds] 4.13
... māl ia I mean ..., you know ..., you see, uh, that is ... ‖28.5
mālko [gerund < mal.e yo]; not being ‖18.2
malle yo [malu-] gets dry ‖8.7, 26.SV
mallye yo [malli-] prevents/stops one from doing; dissuades 26.1
mallye yo [malli-] dries it, makes it dry ‖26.1
māl-ssum (esteemed person's) speech, language, words 1.15
malwu living room of Korean-style house; (= ~q patak) floor 3.SV, 16.28c
mālm substantive < mal.e yo
māma smallpox (= son nim) 19.SV
... man only, just 1.26, ‖6.3, ...-ci ~ but ‖7.2; ...-ki ~ ‖13.5
mān ten thousand (= il-mān); payk ~ a million; ~-nyen 10,000 years 6.SV
mān ... modifier < mal.e yo
mān-... fully, a full ... ‖28.7
... manchi = ... mankhum (‖24.15)
mang = neythu (net) 14.SV
... man hay yo ‖27.7
mānh.e to even though (there are) many; at most 8.21
mānh.e yo [mānh-] there is a lot, is much, are many 4.10, 12.29
mānh.i a lot, much, a great deal 1.14, ‖17.6
mān-il if, in the event that, if by any chance 9.19, 24.25 [< mān uy il one in ten thousand = a long-shot]
... mankhum to the same extent as ..., as much as ... 24.8, ‖24.15
manna yo [manna-] meets, sees (a person) 4.SV
mānnyen-phil fountain pen 2.SV
mānnyen tāyhak-sayng perpetual college student 7.13
mantwu meat-stuffed bun 16.SV
mantul.e yo = mayntul.e yo
manul garlic 18.37

mānwula an old hag; one's wife [vulgar] 28.17

mas taste, flavor 4.SV; mas i iss.e(y) yo, mas i 'ss.e(y) yo it has taste, it is delicious 18.23

masye yo [masi-] drinks 4.22

... mata each ..., every ...; achim ~ every morning 6.6, ‖6.3

math.e yo [math-] undertakes, assumes (a responsibility, a task) 24.20

maul village 28.12

maum mind, heart, spirit, feelings 7.23, 14.21, ‖18.7 ...uy ~ ey tul.e yo [tu-l-] pleases, appeals to 23.34

māycem a shop, a stand 8.SV

māyil every day (= nal mata) 6.7

māyn ... way, far (opposite of palo); ~ wi way above 3.36

māyn ... modifier < māy yo

mayntule yo [mayntu-l-] makes, achieves 13.32

maywe yo [mayw-] is hot(ly seasoned), spicy, highly seasoned 18.39

māy yo [māy-] ties; puts on, wears (tie, shoelaces, etc.) 8.3

me (= mwe = mues) what 22.SV

mek.e yo [mek-] eats 4.22; nai lul ~ acquires age; ... sal ul mek.ess.e(y) yo is ... years old; kwi ka ~ goes deaf 22.SV

mek.ye yo [mek.i-] feeds, makes one eat; syassu ey phul ul ~ starches a shirt 29.26

mēl(q) ... prospective modifier < mel.e yo

mel.e yo [mē-l-] is far, distant, a long way (off) 8.10; nwun i ~ goes blind, loses one's eyesight 22.SV

meli head ‖4.4; (= ~ thel) hair (on the head) 8.2

meli-khal(ak) a hair (of one's head) 22.SV

mēlli far 18.11, ‖17.6

mēlm substantive < mel.e yo

mēn ... modifier < mel.e yo

mence first (of all), to begin with 4.SV

menci dust 16.SV

mēng hay yo looks blank (vacant, expressionless); ~ hani (= ~ hakey) blankly 28.36

meych how many, several, some, a certain number; ~ hay how many years; ~ nyen how many years or what year; ~ si what time; ~ sālam how many people; several (some) people; ~ wel what month? 6.6, 6.SV

mēnun processive modifier < mel.e yo (goes blind)

meykye yo [meyki-] = mek.ye yo

meychil how many days; what date; some (several) days 6.2

meynuli = myenuli (daughter-in-law) 7.SV

mī-... not yet, un-, in- ‖28.7

Mi = Mikwuk (America); ~ Kongkwun American Air Force 17.C

mian hay yo is uneasy; is sorry or grateful, is obliged 1.12, 24.7; Mian hap.nita Excuse me or Thank you.

micang-wen beauty parlor 12.SV

micikun hay yo is lukewarm, tepid 29.SV

miin beautiful woman 19.19

mikki bait; nakk.si ~ fishing bait 28.SV

mikkulewe yo [mikkulew-] is slippery 19.7

Mikwuk America; ~ salam an American 2.28

mil wheat ‖27.SV

mīlay the future 26.SV

milq kalwu wheat flour ‖27.SV

milkhu = wuyu (cow's milk) 16.SV

mīl mul high tide; ~ i tul.e wa yo the tide comes in 28.13

min.e (sea)perch 28.SV

misa (Catholic) mass; ~ (lul) pwa yo says (reads) mass 17.SV

miswul-kwan museum of fine arts, art gallery 3.SV

mit.e yo [mit-] believes (in), trusts, has faith (in) 17.9

mith the place under(neath); ... ~ ey beneath, below ...; the bottom 3.12

mit.um belief, faith (= sīn.ang) 17.SV, ‖26.3

mo rice seedlings; ~ lul nāy yo [nāy-] transplants (sets out) rice seedlings 27.SV

moa yo [mou-] gathers, accumulates ‖8.7

moca hat 8.4

mōchin mother [impersonal] 19.18 Cf. emeni

mokcang stock-farm, ranch 27.SV

mokcek purpose, aim, goal 27.3

moksa minister, pastor; Kim moksa Reverend Kim 2.31

Mok-yoil Thursday 4.SV

mok.yok a bath, bathing; ~ (ul) hay yo bathes, takes a bath 8.SV

mok.yok-sil bath(ing) room ‖27.10

mokyok-thong bathtub 8.SV

moley day after tomorrow 9.27

mōlla yo [molu-] does not know (or un-

derstand) 1.34; ... ci to ~ maybe ‖21.3
mom body (= sinchey); ~ cōsim taking care of oneself 19.SV
mom-sal indisposition, slight illness; fatigue 28.27
mom-ttwungi body 22.11
mopsi awfully, terribly, very; hard, harshly 29.33
mos pond 28.SV
mōs not possibly, cannot; emphatically (definitely, absolutely) not, not at all; ~ hay yo (or haci ~ hay yo) cannot do, definitely does not 4.5
mōs-na yo is ugly; is stupid 28.35
mōsye yo [mōsi-] escorts/accompanies (someone esteemed), waits upon, attends; mōsiko ka yo takes (an esteemed person); mōsiko wa yo brings (an esteemed person) 12.36A
mo-thwungi corner 3.C
mōtun ... all ...; ~ kes everything 13.1
motwu all, everyone 18.9
mo.yang appearance, seeming 14.15, ‖14.9
...-m sey ‖23.6
mu-... lacking, without, -less ‖28.7
mū = muwu (giant white radish)
mues what (thing); something, anything 1.40, 2.1
mukewe yo [mukew-] is heavy 13.SV
mul water 3.32
mul dyed color; ~ (i) tul.e yo [tu-l-] gets dyed; ~ (ul) tul.ye yo [tul.i-] dyes; ~ (ul) ppāy yo [ppāy-] bleaches 29.SV
mul(q) ... prospective modifier < mul.e yo (bites)
mul.e yo [mūl-; mūt.ko, mūt.nunta] asks, inquires (= mul.e pwa yo [po-]) 1.44
mul.e yo [mu-l-] bites 26.SV
mulken things, goods 8.9
mullon of course 8.31
mulm substantive < mul.e yo (bites)
mul.um substantive < mul e yo (asks)
mul.un modifier < mul.e yo (asks)
muluph knee 22.SV
mun door; cip ~ door of the house 3.14
mun (= munhak) literature 19.17
mun ... modifier < mul.e yo (bites)
mūn.an sending regards 18.SV
mūncey problem, topic, question 13.SV, 23.7
mun.e octopus 28.SV
mungchye yo [mungchi-] packs, lumps together 22.10
munhak literature, letters 19.17
munq-kwa course (or department) of literature 19.17
munqpep grammar 24.30
munun processive modifier < mul.e yo (bites)
museng hay yo is rich (with verdure), grows thickly 12.17
musun ... what ... 2.3; ~ tal what month 6.SV Cf. etten
mūtay stage 12.SV
mūt.nun processive modifier < mul.e yo (asks)
muwu giant white radish 18.36
myech(il) = meych(il)
myelmang hay yo perishes 17.27
...-myen [conditional after vowel base] see ...-umyen
... myeng [impersonal counter for people] twū ~ two people; meych ~ how many people, several persons 6.18, 6.SV Cf. sālam, pun
myengseng fame 12.5
myengso famous place (= myengsung-ci) 26.SV
myengsung-ci famous place (= myengso) 26.SV
myengthay pollack 28.SV Cf. puk.e
myēnto shaving; ~ (lul) hay yo shaves 8.1
myenuli daughter-in-law 7.SV
...-n [modifier after vowel base] see ...-un
...'n ... see ... in ..., han ...
...-na [familiar-style question] ‖28.1
...-na [adversative after vowel base] but ‖18.3 Cf. ...-una
... na [softening particle] see ...-key ~
... 'na = ... ina [after a vowel]
na I/me 2.23; infinitive < na yo
naa yo [nā(s)-] recovers, gets better ‖11.6; is well (after having been sick) 11.32, pyēng i ~ sickness gets better 19.SV; is better, is preferable 19.SV
nac daytime 4.SV
nac.e yo [nac-] is low 12.17
nācwung (ey) in the end, at last, finally 17.15, 27.21
nah.a yo [nah-] gives birth to, produces 8.SV, 11.30, ‖11.6
nahul four days 6.SV
nai age; ~ ka mānh.e yo is old 7.23; ~ ka tul.e yo [tu-l-] grows old(er), acquires age 24.12 Cf. ⁿyensey, ⁿyen.lyeng, chwunchwu
nailon, nai(l)long nylon 29.SV
nakci a small octopus 28.SV

nakk.e yo fishes (with a hook), angles for 28.SV
nakk.si fish-hook (= ~q panul) 28.SV
nakk.si cil fishing, angling; ~(ul) ka yo goes fishing 28.3
nakk.siq cwul fishing line 28.SV
nakk.siq kwun a fisher, an angler 28.SV
nakk.siq pap fishing bait 28.SV
Cf. mikki
nakk.siq pay fishing boat 28.SV
nakk.siq tay fishing pole 28.SV
nal day; (= ~-ssi) weather 9.5
nal(q) ... prospective modifier < na yo, < nal.e yo
nala country 2.26; (= kwuk.ka) nation 27.13
nalq-ca (agreed-on) date 21.5
nal.e yo [na-l-] flies 26.SV, ‖26.1
nalk.e yo [nalk-] (a thing) grows old 23.23, ‖7.10 Cf. nulk.e yo
nalk.un ... old ‖7.10 Cf. hēn ..., nulk.un ...
nalle yo [nalu-] carries, loads 26.SV
nallye yo [nalli-] lets it fly, flies it ‖26.1
nalm substantive < nal e yo
nal-ssi weather (= nal) 9.5A
...-na-ma [extended adversative after vowel base] but anyway ‖18.3 Cf. ...-una-ma
nam substantive < na yo
namca man, male (opposite of ^{n}yeca) 3.SV, ‖27.10
nam.e yo [nām-] remains, stays, is left (over) 26.20, ‖26.1
namkye yo [namki-] leaves it (behind) ‖26.1
nammay brothers and sisters 7.SV
Cf. hyengcey
namphyen husband, a woman's spouse 2.SV, 7.SV
nam-tongsayng younger brother 7.11
namu tree, plant; wood, firewood 3.9
namul salad; sprouts 16.30
...-nam.un, -nam.u ... odd (number) ‖27.8
nan-... difficult ‖28.7
nan ... modifier < na yo, < nal.e yo
na'nal-i every day ‖17.6
^{l}nāngtok reading aloud; ~(ul) hay yo reads aloud 21.3, 21.SV
nanun processive modifier < na yo, < nal.e yo
nanwe yo [nanwu-] divides it ‖8.7
nappe yo [nappu-] is bad 4.SV
nās.nun processive modifier < naa yo

natha-nāy yo [-nāy-] expresses, shows (= phyo hay yo) 27.10
na-tul.i going out for a while (to be back later) 28.4
nay 1. [abbreviation of na uy] my; ~kes my thing, mine 2. [abbreviation of ~ ka] I (as subject) 2.6, 23.31 3. yep, yes 1.2A
^{l}nay-... the coming ..., next ... ‖28.7
nāy ... internal, inside, interior 19.15
nāy infinitive < nāy yo
^{l}naycwu next week 23.11
^{l}nayil tomorrow 6.28
naylye yo [nayli-] descends, goes down, gets off or out of (a vehicle), leaves; naylye ('ta) pwa yo looks down 8.SV, 16.39, 18.6
^{l}nay-^{l}naynyen year after next ‖28.7
nāy noh.a yo puts it out (for later) 29.22
^{l}naynyen next year 6.23
...-na yo [question] ‖16.7
na yo [na-] emerges, comes/goes out, exits, happens, is produced, gets born; sinmun ey ~ appears in the newspaper 8.SV, 11.29, ‖11.6. <u>See also</u> kkuth ~, kōcang (i) ~ , pyēng i ~
nāy-oy married couple, husband and wife [humble] (= pupu) 17.13
nāypok underwear (= sōk os) 8.SV
nāyq-kwa internal medicine; (= ~ uysa) a specialist in internal medicine, a physician 19.15
nāyuy underwear (= sōk os) 8.SV
nāy yo [nāy-] puts/lets out; pays, contributes; (= puchye yo) mails 11.SV, ‖21.SV; makes (a record) 13.32; mo lul ~ transplants rice seedlings 27.SV; nāy 'ta pwa yo looks out(side) ‖16.3
ne you (to a child) 22.7 Cf. ney
neh.e yo [neh-] puts in(side), inserts 16.SV
ne-huy you all, you people 22.27
nēk ... four [before certain counters] 6.SV
nēl(q) ... prospective modifier < nel.e yo
nel.e yo [nē-l-] spreads it out (to sun or air); os ul cwul ey ~ puts clothes out on the line (to dry) 29.SV
nēlm substantive < nel.e yo
nelp.e yo [nelp-] is wide, broad ‖26.1
nelp.hye yo [nelp.hi-] widens it, broadens it ‖26.1
nelp.i width ‖17.6
nemkye yo [nemki-] puts it over/across; nemkye ('ta) pwa yo looks over/across 16.40
nēn modifier < nel.e yo
nemu too, excessively, overly 9.12, 12.27

nengkye yo = nemkye yo
nēnun processive modifier < nel.e yo
nepchi flounder (= totali) 28.SV
netes, nete ... about four ‖27.8
ne(te)-tāys about four or five ‖27.8
...-ney [familiar-style statement] ‖28.1
nēy ... four 6.20
ney 1. [abbreviation of ne uy] your (to child); ~kes your thing, yours. 2. [abbreviation of ~ka] you (as subject—to child) 22.34
nēy yes, yep, yeah 1.2
nēy-keli crossroads, intersection 4.C, ‖21.5
neykthai necktie 8.3
nēys four (= sā) 1.19 See also nēy ..., nēk ...
neythu net 14.SV, ‖16.6
...-ni [plain-style question] ‖22.3
...-ni [sequential after vowel base] ‖18.1 Cf. ...-uni
...-ni-kka (n') [extended sequential after vowel base] ‖18.1 Cf. ...-uni-kka (n')
... nim [makes honorific titles] 1.1
noh.a yo [noh-] puts, sets, places 16.30; ...-e ~(does it) for later, (gets it done) in advance
noh.ye yo [noh.i-] gets put ‖26.1
no-kkun string 16.SV
nōl(q) ... prospective modifier < nol.a yo; abbreviation < noh.ul(q) ...
nolay song, singing; ~(lul) hay yo sings 9.16
nol.a yo [nō-l-] plays, has fun, amuses oneself, visits 4.17
nōlay yo [nōla(h)-] is golden yellow 26.SV
nol.i game, amusement ‖17.6
nollye yo [nolli-] lets one play; gives one a day off ‖26.1
nolyek effort, endeavor; ~(ul) hay yo, tries, makes an effort 24.SV
nōlm substantive < nol.a yo
nom [abusive word for person] See totwuk ~
[1]Noma-kyo the Roman (Catholic) faith 17.SV
non (lowland) rice field, paddy 27.28
nōn ... modifier < nol.a yo; abbreviation < noh.un ...
nongcak kikwu farm machinery or equipment 27.SV
nongcang farm 27.SV
nongchon farm village 27.5; ~saynghwal farm life 27.SV
nongka farmhouse 27.SV
nongmin farmers, peasants, the farm populace 27.SV
nongpu farmer 2.SV
[1]nōngtam joke, joking, kidding; ~(ul) hay yo, jokes, kids around 24.29
noph.a yo [noph-] is high or tall; is at the top 12.16, 19.3
noph.i height; (= noph.key) highly ‖17.6
noph.ye yo [noph.i-] raises it (up) ‖26.1
[1]Nosea Russia; ~mal Russian (language); ~q salam Russian (person) 2.SV
[1]notong labor ‖28.7
[1]notong-ca worker 3.SV
nōy yo = noh.ye yo
nuc.chwe yo [nuc.chwu-] postpones; loosens ‖26.1
nuc.e yo [nuc-] is/gets late; is loose, slack; nuc.e to even though it is/gets late, at the latest ‖4.7; 8.16
nuc.key late 4.SV
nul always; often 4.14
nul(q) ... prospective modifier < nul.e yo
...-nula [adjunctive] ‖24.10
nul.e yo [nu-l-] it lengthens, increases, grows, spreads, progresses 27.12
nulk.e yo (a person) grows old 23.23, ‖7.10 Cf. nalk.e yo
nulk.un i old person ‖7.10
nulm substantive < nul.e yo
...-nun [processive modifier] ... that does ‖12.2; ~ci ‖21.1-3; ~cwung/sai/tong-an ‖12.6, ‖16.1; ~ ka yo ‖16.6; ~ kes ul, ~ ke l' ‖22.9; ~ tey ‖21.5-6; ~ ya ‖19.3
nun ... modifier < nul.e yo
... nun [topic particle after vowel] as for ... ‖2.1, ‖3.6, ‖23.4; ...-ki ~ ‖13.4; ...-ko ~ ‖21.4 Cf. ...un
nunun processive modifier < nul.e yo
nwue yo [nwu-] voids (urine or feces); ocwum/sōpyen ul ~ urinates; ttong/tāypyen ul ~ defecates 19.SV
nwui-tongsayng a male's younger sister 7.SV
nwu' ka who (as subject) 2.16 Cf. nwukwu
nwukwu who/whom: someone; ~uy whose, someone's; ~ 'tun ci whoever (it might be), anyone at all 17.27 Cf. nwu' ka
nwūlay yo [nwūle(h)-] is yellow 26.SV
nwul.e yo [nwūl-; nwūt.ko, nwūt.nunta] gets scorched 29.33
nwūlule yo [nwūlu-] is yellow (= nwūlay yo) 26.SV
nwul.un modifier < nwul.e yo

nwūlun modifier < nwūlule yo

nwum substantive < nwue yo

nwun eye 22.13; ~i mel.e yo [mē-l-] goes blind, loses one's eyesight 22.SV; ~ul puth.ye yo closes one's eyes (= dozes off) 24.7

nwun ... modifier < nwue yo

nwūn snow; ~i wa yo [o-] it snows 9.SV; abbreviation < nwuwun

nwūna a male's older sister 7.SV

nwū'nim the esteemed older sister of a male 7.SV Cf. nwūna

nwun mul tear(s) 22.19

nwūnq salam . snow man 22.3

nwunq-sep (or nwun-ssep) eyebrow 22.SV

nwūnq tengeli snow ball 22.9

nwunq-tongca pupil (of eye) 22.SV

nwun-ttakpuli Goggle-Eyes 22.28

nwūt.nun processive modifier < nwul.e yo

nwuwe yo [nwuw-; nwupko, nwup.nunta] lies down; nwuwe iss.e(y) yo is lying down, is recumbent 8.SV

... nyen year(s) 6.35, 6.SV

Nyū-Yok si New York City 17.C

...-o [authoritative style after vowel bases] ‖29.1 Cf. ...-so

ō five (= tases) 6.SV

oa yo = wa yo

ōcen morning, forenoon, a.m. 6.10

ocing-e squid; (ppye~) cuttlefish 28.SV

ocwum urine (= sōpyen); ~ul nwue yo, ~ul ssa yo urinates 19.SV

ohilye rather, preferably 27.SV [Also oylye, oyley]

ōhwu afternoon, p.m. 4.15

ol(q) ... prospective modifier < wa yo

olapeni(m) a female's older brother 7.SV

olay for a long time [= olay(q) tong-an] 16.37; ~ka yo lasts long 19.28; ~ tōy yo becomes/is a long time ‖21.1

olay yo [olay-] is long (in duration) 16.37A

olh.a yo [olh-] is right; is correct 22.SV

olh.i rightly, correctly ‖17.6

olh.ci that's right! OK! 22.SV, 28.37

ol(h.)un phyen right side (= palun phyen) 16.32

olla yo [olu-] raises, goes up ‖26.1

ollye yo [olli-] raises, lifts; (= tulye yo, pachye yo) presents, gives ‖26.1

olun = ol(h.)un 3.20; [modifier < olla yo]

om substantive < wa yo

on modifier < wa yo

onul today 4.SV

onun processive modifier < wa yo

ō-payk five hundred 6.SV

opheyla opera (= kakuk) 12.SV

oppa a female's older brother (= olapeni) 7.3

os clothes, a garment ‖4.7, ‖7.10, 8.2

Ō-wel(q tal) May 6.23

oy ... single, lone, only; ~atul an (only) son 17.31

ōy-cōpu mother's father 24.27

... ōy-ey outside of ..., in addition to ..., except for ...; (+ NEGATIVE) only ... (+ AFFIRMATIVE) ‖23.5, 24.8 Cf. pakk

ōykwuk foreign country 23.21, ‖27.10

ōykwuk-cey foreign-made 23.21

ōykyo-kwan diplomat 21.29

oyley = ohilye (rather)

oylye = ohilye (rather)

ōythwu overcoat 8.SV

Ōymu Cāngkwan Minister of Foreign Affairs 21.SV

Ōymu Pu Ministry of Foreign Affairs (of the Republic of Korea) 21.SV

ōyn ... left (as opposed to right), ~ phyen/ccok left side (direction) 3.20; modifier < ōy yo

ōy yo [ōy-] = oywe yo [oywu-] 28.30

ō-[l]yuk five or six [pronounced ō.yuk or ōlyuk or ōnyuk] ‖27.8

pachye yo [pachi-] presents, submits, gives, hands over, hands in 13.11, 14.22

paci trousers 8.SV, ‖10.2

paio(l)lin violin (= ceykum) 12.SV

pakk (the place) outside; ...~-ey outside (of) ..., except for ..., (+ NEGATIVE) only ... (+ AFFIRMATIVE) 3.8, 8.21, ‖8.1, ‖23.5 Cf. ... ōy-ey

pakkwe yo [pakkwu-] exchanges; A lul B lo ~ exchanges A for B 13.SV

pak.mul-kwan museum 3.SV

paksa doctor, holder of a doctor's degree; Kim~ Dr. Kim 19.14

pal foot 8.SV, ‖10.2

palam wind 9.5; (...-nun)~ey under the influence of, in the midst of (...-ing) 28.30

pala yo [pala-] hopes for; looks forward to 13.29

palq-kalak toe 22.SV [in Seoul also -kwulak]

palk.e yo [palk-] is/gets bright; nal i~ the day breaks 28.SV

palle yo [palu-] is right ‖4.6-7

palmyeng invention ‖28.7
palo right, just, directly 3.35, ‖4.6-7
pālp.e yo [pālp-] steps on 26.SV
palp.hye yo [palp.hi-] gets stepped on ‖26.1
palun ... right (as opposed to left) (= olun ...) 3.20
pam night(time) 4.SV
pam-nac night and day; all the time 7.21
pān-... anti-, counter- ‖28.7
pan class 13.18
pān half; (... pān) and a half 6.14
panana banana ‖3.8
panchan dishes served to go with the rice, side dishes 16.SV, ‖20.1
panci (finger) ring 8.SV
pancwu hay yo plays an accompaniment; phiano ~ plays a piano accompaniment 12.6
pang room 3.SV
pānghak vacation (from school), school holidays 9.33
pāngmun a visit, a call; ~ (ul) hay yo makes a call, pays a visit, visits 19.5
pangmyen direction ‖28.7
pangpep method, way 27.30
pānki half-year term ‖28.7
pānmyen the other side, the opposite, the reverse 24.24
pānsin half of the body ‖28.7
pāntay opposite (thing) 24.16; ~ lo opposite(ly) 24.17; opposition; ~ (lul) hay yo opposes 17.12
pantusi inevitably, unfailingly, without exception, by all means, be sure to 12.SV
panu' cil sewing, needlework; ~ (ul) hay yo sews, does needlework 16.20
panul needle (for sewing) 16.20; hand (of timepiece) 23.SV
pap cooked rice; (= ūmsik) food ‖4.4; (= siksa) a meal; ~ (ul) hay yo prepares a meal 16.1 Cf. cīnci
pappe yo [pappu-] is busy 13.37, 14.11
pappi busily ‖17.6
passo = pēysu (bass, basso)
pata sea, ocean 3.28
pataq ka seashore 28.SV
patak ground, bottom; (= malwuq ~) floor 16.28c; (bottom) surface 22.SV
pat.e yo [pat-] receives, gets; wūsan ul ~ opens (or carries open) an umbrella 8.SV Cf. et.e yo
path field, garden 3.17
patha see (p)patha

pāy-... anti- ‖28.7
pay boat 3.29
pay stomach; ~ ka kopha yo is/gets hungry; ~ ka pull.e yo [pulu-] is full, replete 18.28, 18.SV, 22.SV
pāy (a) double (amount), twice as much 29.16
pāychwu (Chinese) cabbage 18.36
payk hundred, (= il-~) one hundred 6.SV
payk-man million 6.SV
payk.muk chalk 2.SV
paykwu volleyball 14.SV
pāym snake; ~ cange eel 28.SV
paypin other guests (besides the guest of honor) 18.SV
pāysang recompense, compensation (for damage) 29.35
pay thāl a stomach upset 18.32
paywe yo [paywu-] learns 4.6
pec = pecci a cherry 21.8A
pec kkoch cherry blossoms 21.8
pec namu cherry tree 21.8
... pel [counter for suits of clothes] 29.8
pelsse already; by now, before this 7.7
pelye yo [peli-] throws away, discards; ...-e ~ does completely 18.32, 28.30
pēm hay yo transgresses; cōy lul ~ commits a sin, sins 17.SV
... pen time(s); han ~ once, one time; han ~ te once more, again; meych ~ how often, how many times, a few times; i ~ this time('s); i ~ kaul this autumn 1.35, 6.SV, 7.26
pengeli mute person 22.SV
pen.yek translation, translating; ~ (ul) hay yo translates 21.SV
pep (= pangpep) method, way 27.30
pēs comrade, friend, pal 9.28
pesen (Korean) socks 8.SV
pes.e yo [pes-] removes, takes off, sheds; os ul ~ gets undressed, takes off one's clothes 8.SV
pes.kye yo [pes.ki-] undresses a person, has a person undress ‖26.1
pethe see (p)pethe
peykay pillow 29.SV
peykayq is pillow slip (case, cover) 29.SV
pēysu bass, basso (= passo) 12.SV
pēy yo [pēy-] cuts (into, off, or out) 4.SV
pha scallion, onion 18.37
pha group, branch, sect 17.SV Cf. kyōpha
phal arm 8.SV; eight (= yetelp) 6.SV
phal(q) ... prospective modifier < phal.e yo
phalay yo [phala(h)-] is bright blue 26.SV
phal.e yo [pha-l-] sells 8.SV

phal-kwu eight or nine ‖27.8
phalm substantive < phal.e yo
phal-mok wrist; ~ sikyey wrist watch 23.3
phal-payk eight hundred 6.SV
Phal-wel(q tal) August 6.SV
phan modifier < phal.e yo
phanun processive modifier < phal.e yo
phāthi a party 18.SV
phāy hay yo loses, is defeated (= cie yo) 14.SV
phek very 21.13
phelay yo [phele(h)-] is green or blue (= phulule yo) 12.18, ‖26.SV
pheyici page 1.24
pheyn pen 2.SV
phi blood (= hyel.ayk) 19.SV
phiano piano (= yangkum) 12.6, 12.SV
phiano pancwu piano accompaniment; ~ (lul) hay yo plays a piano accompaniment 12.6
phie yo [phi-] spreads it open, opens (a book) 1.22; blooms, blossoms 21.SV
phi'e yo [phi'-] = phiwe yo (smokes)
phikon fatigue, tiredness, weariness, exhaustion; ~ hay yo is tired 9.12
phil(q) ... prospective modifier < phie yo
phim substantive < phie yo
phin pin; ~ ul kkoc.a yo puts on (or wears) a pin 8.SV
phin ... modifier < phie yo
phingkyey excuse, pretext; ~ (lul) hay yo makes excuses 14.19
phingphong pingpong (= thak.kwu) 14.SV
phipu skin 22.SV
phiwe yo [phiwu-] smokes 4.SV
phokheys, phokheythu pocket (= ho-cwumeni) 3.SV
phokpho falls, waterfall 26.34
phul grass; plant 3.9
phul (laundry) starch 29.26
phulule yo [phulu-] is green or blue (= phelay yo) 12.18, 26.SV
...-phum goods, articles ‖27.10
phungsok custom 27.13
... phyen side, direction (= ccok); ōyn ~ (ey) (on) the left 3.20
phyēnci letter 4.24; ~ neh.nun kos mail box 12.SV
phyengkyun (on) the average 6.12
phyengtung equality ‖28.7
phyenki = pyenki
phyen.li hay yo is convenient 23.21A
phyēy lungs 19.SV
phyēyq-pyeng lung trouble, tuberculosis 19.SV
phyē yo = phie yo, phi'e yo
phyēyyem [pronounced /phyēylyem/] pneumonia 19.SV
phyo ticket 12.SV
phyo hay yo expresses, shows (= natha-nāy yo) 27.10
...-pi fee, expense ‖27.10
pi-... not (being), non-, un- ‖28.7
pi rain; ~ ka wa yo it rains 9.3
pich, pich-(k)kal color [= sayk(-kal) 26.SV
pie yo [pī-] is/gets empty 28.7
pi'e yo [pī'-] = piwe yo (empties it)
pihayng flying a plane ‖27.10
pihayng-cang airport 8.SV
pihayng-ki airplane ‖4.9, ‖12.4
pihayng-sa aviator, plane pilot ‖27.10
pī hay yo compares 27.16
pīl(q) ... prospective modifier < pie yo, < pil.e yo
pil.e yo [pī-l-] prays for, begs, asks; pok ul ~ asks a blessing 17.SV
pillye cwu.e yo [cwu-] lends 9.20
pillye yo [pilli-] borrows 9.20
pīlm substantive < pil.e yo
pīlyo fertilizer (= kelum)
pīm substantive < pie yo
pīn ... modifier < pie yo, < pil.e yo
pinge surf smelt 28.SV
pingsang kyēngki ice events (contests) 14.SV, ‖16.7
pinwu soap 8.SV
pin.yak hay yo is meager, insignificant 26.16
pipimq pap rice hash (cooked rice with other things mixed in) 16.SV
pipye yo [pipi-] rubs 29.SV
pis.e yo [pis-] combs (one's hair) 8.2
pis.kye yo [pis.ki-] combs (someone's hair), has someone comb his hair ‖26.1
pissa yo [pissa-] is expensive 9.18
pitwulki pigeon 3.13
piwe yo [piwu-] makes/leaves it empty, empties it 28.7
...-p.nita [formal statement after vowel base] ‖17.1 Cf. ...-sup.nita
poa yo see pwa yo
pocung-kum security, guarantee fund 18.SV
pok blessing; ~ ul pil.e yo asks a blessing 17.SV
pōko report 21.SV
poktek-pang house broker's office, real estate agent 18.SV

pol cheek (= ppyam) 22.SV

pol(q) ... prospective modifier < pwa yo

poli barley; ~ pap cooked barley 27.SV

poli pap cooked barley 27.SV

pom spring(time) 9.7; substantive < pwa yo

pon ... original, main 24.28; modifier < pwa yo

ponay yo [ponay-] sends ‖4.4, 17.11

poncek(-ci) ancestral home 11.SV

ponkwuk homeland, native country 11.SV

pon.lay basically, fundamentally 13.23

ponun processive modifier < pwa yo

pōsek jewel 23.28

pōsek-sang jewelry shop 23.SV

... pota (more/rather) than ... 21.16, ‖21.8, ‖27.5

pōthong usual, ordinary, regular; ~ (ulo) usually 4.23

pōthong hak.kyo elementary school (= kwuk.min hak.kyo) 13.SV

poye yo = pōy yo = po.ye yo

po.ye yo [poi-] shows it, makes it visible 12.15; it is visible, it can be seen ‖26.1

pōywe yo [pōyw-] sees, meets (someone esteemed) 1.18

pōy yo [pōy-] = po.ye yo

ppal(q) ... prospective modifier < ppal.e yo

ppal.e yo [ppa-l-] launders, washes 29.13

ppallay laundry (to be washed), laundering; ~ (lul) hay yo launders, does laundry, washes clothes 16.27

ppallayq cwul laundry line, clothesline 29.SV

ppalle yo [ppalu-] is fast ‖4.6-7

ppalli fast; (= ese, kot) right away 4.SV, ‖17.6, 18.4

ppalm substantive < ppal.e yo

ppan ... modifier < ppal.e yo

ppang bread 16.SV

ppanun ... processive modifier < ppal.e yo

ppappi busily ‖17.6

ppata, (p)patha butter 16.SV

ppāy yo [ppāy-] removes, takes out; os ey mul ul ~ bleaches clothes, removes dye from clothes 29.SV

(p)pesu bus 8.SV; ~ cengke-cang, ~ thanun kos bus stop 12.SV

(p)pethe butter 16.SV

ppop.a yo [ppop-] extracts, pulls/draws out; i lul ~ extracts a tooth 16.13

ppulye yo [ppuli-] sprinkles it (onto) 18.36

ppyam cheek 22.SV

ppye bone 22.SV

...-psita [formal proposition after vowel base] ‖17.1 Cf. ...-upsita

...-psiyo [formal command after honorific ...-usi-] ‖17.1 Cf. ...-siyo, ...-usiyo

...-ptikka [formal retrospective question after vowel base] ‖23.1 Cf. ...-suptikka

...-ptita [formal retrospective statement after vowel base] ‖23.1 Cf. ...-suptita

pu-... not, un-, in- [= pul-... (before vowel-followed t or c)]

pū-... assistant; side, by-, subsidiary ‖28.7

pu a government ministry (department) 21.SV

pu-ca.yen unnatural(ness) ‖28.7

pu-ca.yu discomfort ‖28.7

pu-cektang hay yo is inappropriate, unsuitable 29.35

puchin father [impersonal] 19.17 Cf. apeci

puchye yo [puchi-] mails it 11.SV

pucilen hay yo is diligent, hard-working 13.17

pucok hay yo is scarce, is in short supply, is insufficient 27.21

pu-cwuuy hay yo is careless, commits a careless act 29.36

puekh kitchen 18.10

Pūhwal(q cel) (Resurrection =) Easter 17.SV

puin married woman, wife; Madam(e); lady; Mrs. 1.2, 2.SV

puin-hoy women's club 21.1

puinq-kwa gynecology 19.SV

puk.e dried pollack 28.SV

pūkyel (ul) hay yo decides against, votes it down 21.SV

pul light; fire 3.SV

pul-... not, in-, un- ‖28.7 [pu-... before vowel-followed t or c]

pūl(q) ... prospective modifier < pul.e yo

pul.e yo [pū-l-] blows 9.5

pul-chincel unkind(ness) ‖28.7; ~ hay yo is unkind, inconsiderate 16.14

pulhayng unhappiness, misfortune; ~ hay yo is unhappy, unfortunate, unlucky 24.22

pul-hwal.yak inactive(ness) ‖28.7

pulk.e yo [pulk-] is red 26.18

pulkhway hay yo is unpleasant; am displeased 29.34

Pulkyo Buddhism 17.10

pulle yo [pulu-] calls 8.24; nolay lul ~ sings 12.SV

pulle yo [pulu-] is/gets full; pay ka ~ (stomach) is full, replete 18.SV

pullye yo [pulli-] has someone call ‖26.1

pūlm substantive < pul.e yo

pulphyen hay yo is inconvenient; is uncomfortable, unwell 23.21

pulphyeng trouble, disturbance, dissatisfaction; indisposition, ailment 29.SV

pul-phyengtung inequality 28.7

pulqsin-ca unbeliever, heathen 17.SV

pumo parents; ~ nim esteemed parents 4.13

...-pun minute; ilkop si sip-pun 7:10 o'clock 1.54, 6.7, 6.SV

... pun (counter for esteemed persons) 6.SV, ‖6.1 Cf. sālam, myeng

pūn indignation, anger; ~ (i) na yo = ~ (ul) nāy yo gets angry 24.SV

pūn ... modifier < pul.e yo

punchim minute hand (of a timepiece) 23.SV

puncwu hay yo is busy (= pappe yo) 13.37

pūnun processive modifier < pul.e yo

...-pun uy ... [fractions] 23.28

punye woman 27.5

pupu married couple, husband and wife ‖17.13A

pus'e yo [pus'u-] = puswe yo

pusok attachment; addenda ‖27.10

pusok-phum (mechanical) parts 23.8, ‖27.10

puswe cye yo [ci-] it breaks, crumbles 16.SV

puswe ttulye yo [ttuli-] = puswe yo (breaks it)

puswe yo [puswu-] breaks it 16.SV

pūthak a request; requesting; ~ (ul) hay yo makes a request, asks, begs, requests 29.47

... puthe from (...) 1.25, ‖6.4

puth.ye yo [puth.i-] attaches it, sticks it on, makes it adhere, puts (something onto something) 22.21; nwun ul ~ closes one's eyes (= dozes off) 24.7

pūti without fail, for sure, certainly, be sure to ... 27.33

pu-tonguy disagreement ‖28.7

pwa yo [po-] sees, looks at, (= ilk.e yo) reads 1.23; looks after, takes care of, does; cang (ul) ~ does the marketing 16.2; sihem ul ~ takes a test 13.SV; sang ul ~ sets the table, waits on the table; (= nwue yo) voids (urine or feces) 19.SV; ...-e ~ tries ...-ing ‖8.11, ‖16.8; ...-ulq ka ~ seems to ..., looks as if ... 24.7

pwāy yo = pōy yo

pye rice plants, unthreshed rice 27.SV

pyek wall (interior) 3.28 Cf. tam

pyel ... special 24.16, 27.14

pyēl star 13.SV

pyelqcang summer cottage 18.SV

pyelqsey hay yo (an esteemed person) dies [literary] 11.SV

pyen = tāypyen (feces; bowel movement)

pyēng sickness, illness 11.31; disease 19.24; ~ i na yo gets sick, falls ill 19.SV

pyēngca a patient, a sick person (= hwānca) 19.SV

pyengceng soldier 2.SV

pyēngchang (vocal) duet (= īcwung-chang) 12.SV

pyēngmyeng the name of a disease 19.24

pyēng mūn.an a sick call (visit) 19.SV

pyēngsil hospital room, sick-room(s), sick ward 19.20

pyēngwen hospital 19.1

pyēnho pleading ‖27.10

pyēnho-sa lawyer 2.SV

pyenki chamberpot, bed-pan ‖19.SV

pyēnkyeng a change, a shift; ~ (ul) hay yo changes, shifts 21.5

pyenso toilet (= twīq-kan); swusey-sik ~ western-style toilet; ~q congi toilet paper 3.SV

pyeth sunshine (= hayq pyeth) 29.SV

pyē yo = pie yo, pi'e yo

...-sa scholar, person ‖27.10

...-sa person, master ‖27.10

sa infinitive < sa yo

sā four (= nēys) four 6.28

sā-chon cousin 7.SV

sacin photograph 3.SV

sācwung-chang (vocal) quartet 12.SV

sācwung-cwu (instrumental) quartet 12.SV

sāep undertaking, job, business ‖28.7

sāhang items; thōuy ~ items for discussion, agenda 21.SV

sahoy presiding; (= ~-ca) chairman, master of ceremonies; ~ lul hay yo presides 21.SV

sāhoy society, group, community 27.11
sahul three days 6.SV
sāhwa historical stories 26.SV
sai intervening space, interval (of space or time — cf. tong-an); while; A hako B sai (ey) between A and B 3.27, ‖12.6, ‖16.1
sakwa apple 18.44
sākwa apology; ~ lul tulye yo gives/offers an apology 29.38
sākwan officer ‖28.7
sakwie yo [sakwi-] is/gets acquainted 24.18
... sal years of age; meych sal how many years old 6.SV
sal flesh 22.SV
sal(q) ... prospective modifier < sa yo
sāl(q) ... prospective modifier < sal.e yo
sālam people, person, man 2.27; [counter for people] 6.17, 6.SV
salang love; ~ hay yo loves 17.27
salang guest room (= room for entertaining guests) 21.11
sal.e yo [sā-l-] lives 4.12
salq kyel (texture of) skin, complexion 22.SV
sallim household; housekeeping; livelihood 24.18, ‖26.3
sallye yo [salli-] makes/lets one live; saves, revives ‖26.1
sālm life [substantive < sal.e yo] ‖26.3
sālm.e yo [sālm-] boils; ppallay lul ~ boils the wash 29.SV
sam three (= sēys) 6.27, sam-pun uy il one-third 23.28; substantive < sa yo
sāmang ... deceased; ~ (ul) hay yo dies [impersonal] 11.SV, ‖13.1
samci-chang fork 18.16
samcwung-chang (vocal) trio 12.SV
samcwung-cwu (instrumental) trio 12.SV
samo (nim) one's teacher's wife; Mrs., Madam ‖1.4
sam-payk three hundred 6.SV
sam-sā three or four ‖27.8
sāmu business affairs ‖27.10
sāmu-ka businessman (= sil.ep-ka) 2.SV
sāmu-sil office 3.SV, 29.2
sāmu-wen (office) clerk 8.SV
sāmu-yong for business (use) ‖27.10
sam-wel(q tal) March 6.SV
san mountain 12.15
san ... modifier < sa yo
sān ... (which is) live, living [modifier < sal.e yo]
sanay man, male (= namca); (= namphyen) (married) man, husband 24.21
sān-cek egg-dipped shish kebab 16.SV
...-sang -wise, with respect to ‖27.10
sāng-... upper, higher, top; first of two or three; earlier ‖28.7
sang table 3.24 Cf. chayk-sang
sangca box 3.SV
sangcem shop, store 3.SV
sangcing symbol; ~ (ul) hay yo symbolizes 26.31
sange shark 28.SV
sangin merchant, shopkeeper 2.SV
sāngkhway hay yo is refreshing, exhilarating 14.21
sāngko archaic times 26.SV
sangkwan concern, involvement, relevance; ~ (i) ēps.e(y) yo it doesn't matter, it makes no difference, it is of no concern 24.SV
sangq-po tablecloth 18.SV
sangtang hi quite, considerably, rather, very 23.33
sangtay opposite number, counterpart; punye lul ~ lo with women as opposite numbers 27.29
sangtay pang/phyen the other side, the opposing side 14.SV
sāngyen performance 12.SV, ‖16.7
sānq-kwa obstetrics 19.SV
sānmul product ‖28.7
sānqpo a walk, a stroll; ~ (lul) hay yo takes a walk 4.16
sanun processive modifier < sa yo
sānun processive modifier < sal.e yo
sā-o four or five ‖27.8
sapal porcelain rice bowl 18.SV; ~ sikyey bowl-shaped alarm clock 23.SV
sā-payk four hundred 6.SV
sāsil truth, fact; ~ māl hamyen = ~ un to tell the truth 13.26, 26.6
sa(tak)-tali ladder 18.SV
Sāwel(q tal) April 6.SV
sawi son-in-law 7.SV
say ... new (= say-lowun) ‖7.10, 8.5
sāy = sai (interval)
sāy bird 3.10
sa.yang hay yo declines one thing in favor of another; gives way to (another); makes room for 18.21
sayk(-kal) = pich(-kal) color 26.SV
sāyksi girl 19.19
say-lowa yo [-low-] it is new ‖7.10
...-sayng student ‖27.10

saynghwal life 7.15; living 23.27
saynghwal-pi living expenses ‖27.10
saynghwal-nan economic hardship, trouble earning a living 23.27
sayngil birthdate 6.28
sayngkak thought, idea, thinking; ~(ul) hay yo thinks 9.15; ~... uy sayngkak ey nun in ...'s opinion 13.17; ~(i) na yo remembers 21.10; ...-ulq sayngkak iey yo intends to do ..., is thinking of doing ... 27.2
sayngkye yo [sayngki-] happens, occurs, arises 29.48
sayngsen fish (as food) 18.SV Cf. (mulq) koki
sa yo [sa-] buys 6.35, 19.11, 23.31
saypyek dawn, sunrise; ~ puthe since dawn, at/from dawn 28.4
saywu shrimp 28.SV
... se (= ey~) from ..., (happening) at ... 4.14; ... hanthey/eykey ~ from (a person); ... kkey ~ from (an esteemed person), (= i/ka) an esteemed person as subject 7.20; ...-e ~ and (so/then), (goes) to do ‖16.1
se infinitive < se yo
secem bookshop 3.SV
secay one's study, (home) library 13.SV, ‖16.7
... sek jewel(s) (= pōsek) 23.28
seki secretary 21.27A
seki-kwan (official) secretary 21.27
sekk.e yo [sekk-] mixes it (together), combines them 18.37
...-sel version, story; (= haksel) theory; ilq ~ one version 26.27
selkec.i dishwashing; cleaning up after a meal; ~(lul) hay yo washes dishes, does dishwashing 16.25
selkyo sermon 17.SV
selmyeng explanation; ~(ul) hay yo explains 17.25
selo each other, mutually 1.42
selthang sugar 16.SV
selun thirty (= sam-sip) 6.SV
Sencwuk-kyo Sencwuk Bridge 26.1
sene-netes, sene-nete ... about three or four ‖27.8
senes, sene ... about three ‖27.8
sēng anger; ~(i) na yo = ~(ul) nāy yo gets angry 24.SV
sengak vocal music 12.3
sengak-ka vocalist, singer 12.3
sengcek records (of one's activities); school grades 13.30; ~ ul nāy yo makes a record 13.SV
sēngcil temper, disposition 28.33
sēngham esteemed name 11.SV, ‖16.7
sēngka Catholic hymn(s) 17.SV
sēngka-tay (Catholic) choir 17.SV
sengkong success; ~(ul) hay yo succeeds 24.15
sēng-manchan(q) sik Communion Service 17.SV
Sēngkyeng Bible 17.37
sēngmyeng name [impersonal] 11.SV
sengnyang matches 2.SV
Sēngthan (cel) (Holy Birth=) Christmas 17.SV
sēnke election 21.SV
senkyo spreading the faith ‖27.10
senkyo-sa missionary 2.SV
sēnmul gift, present 9.SV
sensayng teacher (= hak.kyo sensayng); gentleman, sir; you; Mister; Kim ~ Mr. Kim; Kim ~ puin Mrs. Kim 1.1
sēnswu athlete, champion 14.7, 14.SV, ‖15.1
senul hay yo is cool 9.SV, ‖10.1
sen.wen crewman, sailor 2.SV
Sēse Switzerland; ~q-cey Switzerland-made, Swiss make 23.15
Sēt-tal December (= Sip.i-wel) 6.SV
Sewul Seoul (capital of the Republic of Korea) 9.32
...-sey [familiar-style suggestion] ‖28.1
sēy ... three 6.9
sēy rent, cip ~ (house) rent, talq ~ monthly rent 18.SV; infinitive < sēy yo
se.yang the West, the Occident (opposite of tongyang the East, the Orient) 19.18A
sēyq cip rented house, house for rent 18.SV
sēykey strongly, so that it is strong [< sēy yo] 29.26
sēyl(q) ... prospective modifier < sēy yo
sēykyey world (= sēysang) 21.26
sēylyey baptism [usually Protestant]; ~(lul) cwue yo baptizes; ~(lul) pat.e yo gets baptized 17.SV Cf. chim.lyey
sēym substantive < sēy yo
sēyn ... modifier < sēy yo
sēynun ... processive modifier < sēy yo (counts)
sēyq pang rented room 18.SV
se yo [su- but often spelled se-] stands 8; (a timepiece) stops 23.5
sēys three (= sam) 1.19, 6.SV Cf. sēy ..., sēk ...
sēysang (= sēykyey) world 17.27

sēyswu washing oneself, washing up; ~ (lul) hay yo washes up 8.1
sēyswuq tayya wash basin 8.SV
sēythak wash, laundry 29.1
sēythak kikyey, sēythak-ki washing machine 29.SV
sēythak-mul laundry, things to be laundered 29.18
sēythak pinwu laundry soap 29.SV
sēythak-so laundry (establishment) 29.3
sēythakq-[l]yo laundry rate 29.16
seywe yo [seywu-] stands it up, erects, builds ‖26.1
...'sey yo [...'si-] (someone esteemed) is (= ... isey yo) 2.22
sēy yo [sēy-] is strong 29.26
... si ... o'clock; meych ~ what time 6.6
sī city (= tosi); Nyū-Yok ~ New York (City), Wasingthon ~ Washington (D.C.)
si-apeci, si-ape'nim a female's father-in-law, the husband's father 7.SV
sīcak start, beginning; ~ (ul) hay yo begins, starts 1.21, 6.4, ‖13.5
sīcang market (= cang)
sīcang mayor (of a city) 19.19
sīcheng city hall 19.12
si-emeni, si-eme'nim a female's mother-in-law, the husband's mother 7.SV
sīhap game, match 14.7
sihem test, examination; ~ (ul) hay yo gives a test 13.37, 13.SV
sihem-kwan official examiner ‖27.10
sika a woman's inlaws, the husband's family 28.26
siqka current price 23.28
sīqka market price 23.28A
sikan time 1.20; hour's time 6.11; meych ~ how many hours, a few hours; tases ~ five hours
sikan phyo timetable, schedule 23.SV
sikhye yo [sikhi-] orders (food, a meal), orders someone to do something; has/lets one do 22.36, ‖22.10, ‖26.1
sik.kwu family member(s) 7.1
sikol country (as opposed to city), rural area 11.19, 14.7, 14.SV
siksa a meal; eating (a meal) 18.SV ‖18.2
siktang dining room 18.18
siktang-cha diner, dining car 23.SV
sikyey timepiece, clock, watch 12.30
sikyey-cem watch shop 23.18
...-sil room ‖27.10
sīl thread, yarn 16.SV
sil.ep-ka businessman 2.SV
silhwa actual stories, true accounts 26.SV
silh.e yo [silh-] is disliked; I dislike; silh.e hay yo hates, dislikes 7.29
sillok annals, chronicles, historical records 26.SV
sillyey discourtesy; ~ (lul) hay yo commits a discourtesy 1.1
silmul real thing, actual object 26.5
silphay failure; ~ (lul) hay yo fails 24.SV
silqsup-sayng an intern, an apprentice 19.SV
silqswu mistake, error, blunder 29.42
silye yo [sili-] is cold (of the body or parts of the body) 22.4
sil'ye yo = silh.e yo
sim.e yo [sīm-] plants ‖8.3, 9.1, 27.SV
sīmpang a call, a visit; ~ (ul) hay yo visits, calls at, calls on 17.5
simphoni a symphony 12.SV
sim-sim hay yo is bored, is lonely 12.12
sin shoe(s) 8.7
sin-... new ‖28.7
sīn.ang belief, faith (= mit.um) 17.SV
sīnay down town 14.SV
sī'-nay(q mul) stream 14.SV, 28.SV
sīnca believer 17.SV
sinchey body (= mom) 19.SV, ‖19.7
sinchey kēmsa physical examination 19.SV
sin.e yo [sin-] puts on or wears (shoes, socks) on the feet 8.5
sinhwa myth 26.SV
sin-kilok a new record ‖28.7
sin kkun shoelaces, shoestrings; ~ ul māy yo ties, puts on, or wears shoelaces 8.SV
sinkye yo [sinki-] puts (footgear) on a person, has/lets one wear (shoes, socks) ‖26.1
Sinkyo Protestant(ism) 17.SV
sinmun newspaper 2.SV, ‖2.5
sin-palmyeng new invention ‖28.7
sinpu priest, a (Catholic) Father; Kim ~ Father Kim 2.31, 17.SV
sin-seykyey the new world ‖28.7
sinthong hay yo is marvelous, wonderful 16.28
Sin-yak New Testament 17.SV
sīn.yong faith, trust, dependability; ~ (i) iss.e(y) yo is trustworthy, dependable 23.18
sip ten (= yel) 1.51, 6.7

... siph.e yo [siph-] wants to, would like to 8.5, ‖8.6
Sip.i-wel(q tal) December 6.SV
Sip.il-wel(q tal) November 6.SV
sip-man hundred thousand 6.SV
siqka current price 23.28
sīqka market price 23.28A
sitay time, period, era 27.17
Sī'-wel(q tal) October 6.27
...-siyo [formal command after vowel base other than ...-usi-] ‖17.1 Cf. ...-usiyo, ...-psiyo
...-so [authoritative style after consonant bases] ‖29.1 Cf. ...-o
...-so place ‖27.10
sō-... small ‖28.7
so ox(en), cow, cattle 16.SV, ‖6.1
sōaq-kwa pediatrics 19.SV
sōcey (house)cleaning; ~(lul) hay yo cleans house, does housecleaning 16.27; sikyey lul ~ hay yo cleans a watch 23.6
sohwa digestion 19.SV
sohwaq pyeng dyspepsia, indigestion 19.SV
sōk the inside (of something rather full); ... sōk (ey) inside ... 3.5
so koki beef (= so 'y koki) 16.SV, ‖16.6
sōk nwunq-sep eyelash 22.SV
sōk os underwear (= nāypok, nāyuy) 8.SV, 29.8
sokum salt 18.36
sōkyeng blindman, blind person (= cāng nim) 22.SV
sol = so' namu pine (tree) 12.18
sōl a brush; ~ cil brushing; ~ cil (ul) hay yo brushes 29.SV Cf. chi-sol, iq-sol
soli noise, sound; (= māl) words 12.SV, 27.14
Solyen, Ssolyen Soviet Union 2.SV
somun rumor, hearsay 27.16
son hand 8.SV, ‖10.2
sonaki, sonak pi shower 14.28
so' namu pine (tree) (= sol) 12.18
sonayki = sonaki
sonca grandson 7.SV
soncwu (ai) grandchild 7.SV
songe trout 28.SV
sōngpyel farewell, send-off; ~ (ul) hay yo says/bids farewell to, sends (someone) off 21.SV
sōngpyel-hoy farewell party, farewell meeting 21.SV
Songto (a city of old Korea) 26.7
sōnhay damage, injury, harm 29.35
sonq-kalak finger 22.SV [in Seoul also -kwulak]
son nim guest 6.30; (= māma) smallpox 19.SV
sonnye granddaughter 7.SV
sonq patak palm (of hand) 22.SV
sonq swuken handkerchief 8.SV, ‖14.7
sonq tung back of the hand 22.SV
son-thop fingernail 22.SV
sophulano soprano (= koum) 12.SV
sōpyen urine (= ocwum); ~ ul nwue yo, ~ ul pwa yo urinates 19.SV
sōpyen kēmsa urine test 19.SV
sōpyen-ki urinal 19.SV
sōsel fiction 11.23
sōsel chayk novel (= book of fiction) 11.23
sōwi 2nd lieutenant; (hāykwun ~) ensign 2.SV
soy iron; (= yēlq ~) key; (= cam'ulq ~) lock 28.SV
so 'y koki = so koki (beef) 16.SV
syassu [syatsu] shirt (= waisyassu) 8.SV, 29.27
syawā shower (bath) 8.SV
ssa yo [ssa-] wraps up, envelops 26.3
ssa yo [ssa-] is inexpensive, cheap 9.19
ssal hulled rice, grain 16.SV
ssal(q) ... prospective modifier < ssa yo
ssam substantive < ssa yo
ssan ... modifier < ssa yo
ssa.ye yo [ssai-] gets wrapped/enveloped (= ssāy yo) 26.3
ssāy yo [ssāy-] gets wrapped/enveloped (= ssa.ye yo) 26.3
sse infinitive < sse yo; ... ulo ~ ‖19.8
ssek greatly, exceedingly, quite 22.18
ssēl(q) ... prospective modifier < ssel.e yo
ssel.e yo [ssē-l-] slices, cuts up 18.36
ssēlm substantive < ssel.e yo
ssēn ... modifier < ssel.e yo
ssēnun ... processive modifier < ssel.e yo
ssēpisu service (tennis or restaurant) 14.SV, ‖21.5
sse yo [ssu-] uses; spends (money) 8.SV; ay (lul) ~ tries, endeavors, does one's best 13.7
sse yo [ssu-] writes 4.24
sse yo [ssu-] puts on or wears (on or over the head) 8.4, 8.SV
... ssi Mr.; Mrs., Madame [impersonal] 19.17
... ssik apiece, each 6.11, ‖6.3
ssis.e yo [ssis-] washes; kulus ul ~

washes the dishes 8.SV, 16.23, 16.28

ssul(q) ... prospective modifier < sse yo, < ssul.e yo

ssul.e yo [ssu-l-] sweeps; patak ul ~ sweeps the floor 16.28c

ssulm substantive < ssul.e yo

ssum substantive < sse yo

ssun ... modifier < sse yo, < ssul.e yo

sul(q) ... prospective modifier < se yo

sum substantive < se yo

sumul, sumu ... twenty (= ī-sip) 6.SV

sumu'-nam.un, -nam.u ... twenty odd ‖27.8

sun ... modifier < se yo

sungkang-ki elevator 18.SV, ‖18.1

su'-nim Buddhist priest (= cwūng); [title of Buddhist Priest] 17.SV

supkwan habit 27.13

...-sup.nita [formal statement after consonant base] ‖17.1 Cf. ...-p.nita

...-suptikka [formal retrospective question after consonant base] ‖23.1 Cf. ...-ptikka

...-suptita [formal retrospective statement after consonant base] ‖23.1 Cf. ...-ptita

swī, swii soon; easily 11.30

swie yo [swī-] rests 1.54, 6.25

swīl(q) ... prospective modifier < swie yo

swīm substantive < swie yo

swīn fifty (= ō-sip) 6.SV

swīn ... modifier < swie yo

swīpkey easily, effortlessly 13.34; simply 17.30

swiwe yo [swīw-] is easy 13.1

...-swu hand, person, operator ‖27.10

swū-... a number of, several ‖27.8

swuce set of spoon and chopsticks 16.33

swucen offering (= hēnkum) 17.SV

swuch charcoal 22.12

swuep-lyo tuition (= welqsa-kum) 13.SV

swuq-kal(ak) spoon 16.SV

swukcey homework 3.SV, ‖4.4

swūken towel 8.SV

swūko trouble, care 1.14; ~(lul) hanta goes to trouble, shows care (in doing) 29.47; Swūko hasip.nita Hello! (to someone working), Swūko hasipsio Goodbye! (to someone working) 1.SV

swul wine, liquor 7.17

swu'l = swuq-kal(ak) spoon 16.SV

swulq can wine cup 18.SV

swulq cip wine house, bar

... swulok to the degree that ... 27.12

swunkwan policeman 3.SV

swunkyeng policeman 3.SV, ‖14.6

swūnse order, order of events, program 17.SV

swunye nun, Sister 17.SV

swuph forest, woods 3.18

swupyeng (naval) enlisted man, sailor 2.SV

swusen repair(ing), restoration; ~(ul) hay yo repairs, does repairing 23.1

swusen-kong repairman 23.SV

swusen-so repair shop 23.SV

swusenq-ˡyo repair charge 23.12

swuswul (surgical) operation; ~(ul) hay yo, has/performs an operation; hwānca lul ~ hay yo operates on a patient 19.SV

swuswulq-sil operating room 19.SV, ‖27.10

swut-kal(ak) = swuq-kal(ak)

swuto capital (city) 26.7

swuto ascetic exercise ‖27.10

swuto-wen monastery ‖27.10

Swu-yoil Wednesday 4.SV

syassu [syatsu] shirt (= waisyassu) 8.SV, 29.8

...-ta [plain-style statement] ‖19.2

...-ta [transferentive] see ...-ta (ka)

... 'ta [plain-style copula after vowel] see ... ita

ta-... many, poly-, multi- ‖28.7

tā all, all the way 1.20, 9.26; twūl(q) ~ both 1.45; ~ hay yo exhausts, uses up, pushes to the limit ‖18.7, 24.15

tā hay yo see tā

...-ta (ka) [transferentive] ‖16.2-3

takchye yo [takchi-] it impends, it draws near, it faces one 24.19

takk.e yo [takk-] polishes, shines; i lul ~ brushes one's teeth 8.SV

tal moon; month meych ~ how many months, several months 6.33

talam-cwi squirrel 3.11

talang-e tuna 28.SV

tali bridge 18.SV, 22.2; leg 8.SV, ‖10.2

talimi see ta(y)limi

talk chicken 11.34

talk koki chicken (meat) 16.SV

talkyal chicken egg (= kyeylan) 11.34

tālla ‖29.3

talle yo [talu-] is different (from), other 12.24

talm.e yo [talm-] resembles, takes after (a person) in appearance 24.26

talq sēy monthly rent 18.SV
talun ... different, other [modifier < talle yo] 12.24
talye yo [tali-] see ta(y)lye yo
tam wall (exterior) 16.40 Cf. pyek
tā-man only, just; but 24.2
tam.e yo [tām-] puts (into), stuffs/crams (into) 18.37
tam.im [often mispronounced tanim] charge, responsibility; person in charge 19.15
tāmpay cigarettes; tobacco 2.SV, ‖2.5
tāmq yo blanket 29.SV
tān-... short ‖28.7
tānchim the minute hand (of a timepiece) 23.SV
tanchwu = taynchwu (button)
tang hay yo undergoes, sustains, suffers 26.8, ‖26.1
Tang myen "nylon" noodles (= thin transparent noodles made of potato-flour or cornstarch) 18.25
tangpun-kan for the present; temporarily 23.25
tangsin you; ~uy your 2.10
tanim see tam.in
tān-keli short distance ‖28.7
tankol regular patronage; (= ~ cip) one's usual establishment/shop; (= ~ son nim) a regular customer/patron 29.3
tān-sikan short time ‖28.7
tanye yo [tani-] goes (regularly, back and forth); commutes; attends (school) 11.13
tao ‖29.3
tapang teahouse, teashop 12.10
tases five (= ō) 1.19, 6.SV
tas-say five days 6.SV
ta'tal-i every month ‖17.6
tat.e yo [tat-] closes it 4.21
tat.hye yo [tat.hi-] it closes ‖26.1
taum the next, (what is) adjacent 1.29; (next) after ‖12.5
ta-umcel polysyllable ‖28.7
tawu = tao
tāy-... great, big, major ‖28.7
... tay [counter for vehicles and mounted machines] 6.SV, ‖6.1
... tāy see ... tāy lo
tay bamboo
tāycep = ceptay 18.SV
tāychey substance, main points, outline; (= ~ lo) in general, by and large, on the whole, generally speaking; just (who, what, etc.) on earth?! 13.3
tāyhak university, college 6.3
tāyhak-wen graduate school ‖27.10
(...ey) tāy hay yo concerns, is about 27.19
tāyhoy a match, a tournament; a mass meeting 14.SV
tāy-hwal.yak great activity ‖28.7
tayk house (of an esteemed person), your house 3.14
tāykwel palace (= kwungkwel) 26.34
ta(y)lim cil (some) ironing, the ironing; ~(ul) hay yo does the ironing 29.42, 29.SV
ta(y)limi iron (for pressing) 29.SV
ta(y)limi phan ironing board 29.SV
... tāy lo ‖27.6
ta(y)lye yo [ta(y)li-] irons (clothing) 29.13
tāymun entrance gate; (= aph ~) front gate 12.31, 16.41
tay namu bamboo tree; bamboo wood 26.26
taynchwu button (= tanchwu); ~ lul kkie yo [kki-], ~ lul chaywe yo [chaywu-] buttons a button 8.SV
tāyphil writing on behalf of another 12.SV
tāypyen excrement, feces (= ttong); ~ ul nwue yo [nwu-], ~ ul pwa yo [po-] has a bowel movement 19.SV Cf. twī, pyen
tāys about five ‖27.8
tāysa ambassador 3.SV
tāysa-kwan embassy 3.SV
tāyse (= tāyphil) writing on behalf of another; (= tāyse-in) a letter writer (for the uneducated), a scrivener 12.SV
tāyse-so a scrivener's (office) 12.SV
tāysin stead, lieu; substitute, representative; (...-nun) ~ ey instead (of doing ...) 12.30, ‖12.7; 29.44
tāytan hi very, extremely, quite 7.23, 29.3
tāytap answer(ing); ~ (ul) hay yo answers 1.45
tāywi (army) captain; (hāykwun ~) navy lieutenant 2.SV
tāy-yes(es) about five or six ‖27.8
te more; han pen ~ again, once more 1.35 1.35
tekthayk ulo by (your) favor
tekwuna moreover, furthermore 17.14
... tele to (usually an inferior—in a command) 19.11, ‖19.5; 29.40
tēlewe yo [tēlew-] is dirty, untidy, messy 18.13, 29.SV
teng(el)i lump, mass, ball, piece; nwunq ~ snow ball 22.9

teph.e yo [teph-] puts (a lid on), uses (a cover) to cover it 18.38; chayk ul ~ closes a book 1.48

tew.e yo [tēw-] is warm, hot 9.8, 13.4; tewun mul warm/hot water 8.SV

tewi heat, hot spell ‖17.6

...-tey [familiar-style retrospective statement] ‖28.1

... tey [post-modifier] ‖21.5–7

... tey place that ... 29.43; talun ~ another place, somewhere else, elsewhere 17.C

teylye yo [teyli-] escorts, accompanies; teyliko wa yo brings (a person); teyliko ka yo takes (a person) 12.36

teywe yo [teywu-] heats/warms it ‖26.1

tha infinitive < tha yo

thak.a-so day nursery 27.27

thak.kwu table tennis, pingpong (= phingphong) 14.SV, ‖14.8

thāl something wrong/amiss, a hitch, a disorder; (= pyēng) an illness; pay ~ a stomach upset, stomach trouble; ~ i na yo gets out of order, (= pyēng i na yo) falls ill 18.34

thal(q) ... prospective modifier < tha yo

tham substantive < tha yo

than ... modifier < tha yo

thān(sayng)-il birthday of a king or saint

thānsayng hay yo (a saint) is born 11.SV, ‖13.1

thayk hay yo chooses, selects 27.15

tha yo it burns, gets burned 16.17

tha yo [tha-] rides; ... ul thako ka yo goes riding in/on ..., goes by ... 8.17

thāyto attitude 13.19

thaywe yo [thaywu-] burns/smokes it ‖26.1

thāy yo [thāy-] = thaywe yo

the place, site (for something); īl ~ work(ing) place, place to work 27.15

thek chin 22.SV

thel hair, fur; meli ~ hair (on the head) 8.2A, 22.SV

theyipul table (= sang) 3.SV

theyne tenor 12.SV

theynisu tennis (= cengkwu) 14.2

thīm team 14.SV

thiphusu typhus 19.SV

thong hay yo gets through, penetrates, gets understood 27.6

thongyek interpreting; ~ (ul) hay yo interprets 21.30

thōuy discussion, debate; ~ sāhang items for discussion, agenda 21.SV

Tho-yoil Saturday 4.24

thōywen discharge (from a hospital) 19.25

thukpyel special, particular 8.30, 24.27; ~ hi especially, particularly, in particular 24.27

thwuphyo balloting; ~ kākyel affirmative decision by ballot 21.SV; ‖21.3

... to also, even ‖4.10, ‖7.6; both ... and ..., neither ... nor ... ‖7.5; ...-e ~ although ‖8.13, ‖21.3; ...-ki ~ ‖13.3

tocwung in the midst of (= cwung) 21.26

tohoy city (= tosi) 27.SV

tokchang vocal solo; ~ (ul) hay yo sings a solo 12.4

tokchang-hoy vocal recital 12.SV, ‖12.8

tokpon reader, book of readings 24.30

toksayng-ca only son 17.27

tokse-sil reading room, study hall 13.SV

toksin (being) solitary, alone, single 7.15

toksup self-teaching; ~ (ul) hay yo studies without a teacher, teaches oneself 24.30

tōl stone 19.12

tōl(q) ... prospective modifier < tol.a yo

tol.a yo [tō-l-] it turns 8.14, ‖26.1

tol.a ka yo goes back; (= cwuk.e yo) dies 11.SV

tol.a wa yo comes back, returns 8.14

tollye yo [tolli-] turns it, makes it go around ‖26.1

tōlm substantive < tol.a yo

...-tolok [projective] to the point that ..., so that ... ‖24.8

tōm(i) sea bream 28.SV

tomuci (not) at all, all in all, totally 12.SV

tōn money 4.26

tōn ... modifier < tol.a yo

tong a period, an interval 6.22A

tong-an length/duration of time, interval, while; elmaq ~ how long, how much (length of) time 6.22, ‖12.6, ‖16.1

tōngca child, boy 22.SV

tōnghwa children's story (of ancient times), fable 26.SV

tōngki motive, reason 27.15

tōng.li = tōngney (village)

tongmu friend, companion, pal; comrade 9.28

tōngmul animal 21.3A

tōngmul-wen zoo 21.3

tōngney community, village 17.3

tongsayng younger brother and/or sister, younger sibling 7.10, ‖7.SV tonguy agreement ‖28.7

tōnguy (parliamentary) motion 21.SV

tongyang the East, the Orient (opposite of se.yang the West, the Occident) 19.18

tongyang-hwa Oriental art 19.18

tōp.nun ... processive modifier < towa yo

tose (a library of) books ‖27.10

tose-kwan library (building) 3.SV

tose-sil library (room) 13.SV

tosi city 12.SV, 14.SV; ~ saynghwal city life 27.SV

tot.a yo [tot-] rises; hay ka ~ the sun rises 28.SV

totali flounder (= nepchi) 28.SV

totwuk thievery, theft; (= ~ nom) thief, robber, burglar; ~ cil (ul) hay yo steals, burglarizes 12.28, 12.30

towa yo [tōw-; tōpko, tōp.nunta] helps; towa cwue yo helps one out 8.29

to.yaci = twāyci

tōy yo [toy-] becomes, gets to be; turns into; amounts to, is, consists (of), forms; is made, accomplished, completed, done, serves the purpose, will do, is all right; ...-key ~ it happens so that, it is arranged so that ‖17.5; toynun tāy lo ... as ... as possible ‖29.20

ttal, tta' nim daughter 7.7

ttan-ttan hay yo is firm, tight 22.10

ttattus hay yo is warm 9.SV, ‖10.2

ttay time, occasion; etten ~ certain times, sometimes 13.37, 16.14

ttaymun cause, reason; ...-ki ~ (ey) because ... ‖13.9

ttaynsu-hol dance hall 7.17

ttek rice cake 16.SV

ttel.e cye yo [ci-] it drops 16.SV

ttel.e ttulye yo [ttuli-] drops 16.SV

tte-na yo [na-] goes away, leaves, departs 8.SV, 27.1

tte yo [ttu-] is slow, sluggish 23.4; becomes detached, leaves, floats 8.SV; hay ka ~ (= tot.a yo) the sun rises 28.SV

tti belt; ~ lul ttie yo puts on (wears) a belt 8.SV

ttie yo [tti-] puts on <u>or</u> wears (a belt) 8.SV

tto again, and, too, also; ~ nun or (else) ...; nor ... (either); ~ eti where else 1.18, 3.33, ‖7.6

ttok-ttok hay yo is bright, smart, clever 7.8

ttong feces; defecating, a bowel movement; ~ ul nwue yo [nwu-], ~ ul ssa yo [ssa-] defecates, has a bowel movement 19.SV

ttukew.e yo [ttukew-] is hot 9.SV

ttukey ka yo goes late, (a timepiece) runs slow 23.4

ttul yard, grounds 3.16, 16.42

ttul(q) ... prospective modifier < tte yo

ttum substantive < tte yo

ttun ... modifier < tte yo

ttus meaning, significance 13.13, 26.26; ~ i iss.ey yo is meaningful, makes sense 27.21

ttwie yo [ttwi-] jumps; kēnne ~ jumps across 28.22

ttwukkeng lid, cover 18.38

ttwung-ttwung hay yo is fat 22.32

ttwungttwung-po fat fellow, fatso 22.27

ttyē yo [tti-] = ttie yo

...-tukwu(me)n = ...-tu' kwu(me)n [apperceptive retrospective] ‖23.3

... tul ...s [plural], group ‖3.7

tul(q) ... prospective modifier < tul.e yo (lifts etc.; enters etc.)

...-tula [plain-style retrospective statement] ‖23.1

tulai khullining dry cleaning; ~ (ul) hay yo dry cleans it, gets it dry cleaned 29.4

tul.e ka yo [ka-] goes in, enters 8.SV

tul.e wa yo [o-] comes in, enters 8.SV

tul.e yo [tu-l-] lifts it up; holds, has; partakes, drinks, eats 16.SV

tul.e yo [tu-l-] enters, comes/goes in 8.SV; costs 8.20; cam i ~ falls asleep 24.SV; maum ey ~ pleases one, appeals to one 23.34; mul i ~ is dyed, takes color 29.SV; nai ka ~ grows older 24.12

tul.e yo [tul-; tut.ko, tut.nunta] listens (to), hears; heeds, minds 1.30, 7.32

tulle yo [tullu-] = tullye yo (stops in, drops by) 16.3

tulye yo [tuli-] gives (to a superior); ...-e ~ does as a favor (for a superior) 8.30, ‖8.11; sākwa lul ~ offers an apology 29.38

tul.ye yo [tul.i-] puts/lets in; os ey mul ul ~ dyes clothes; tul.ye ('ta) pwa yo looks/peeks in 16.41, 29.SV

tullye yo [tulli-] (= tulle yo) stops in, drops by 16.3

tullye yo [tulli-] it sounds, is heard, is audible ‖26.1

tullye yo [tulli-] is attacked (by), is seized (afflicted) with; kāmki (ey) ~ catches a cold 19.SV

tulm substantive < tul.e yo (lifts etc.; enters etc.)

tul.um, tul.un < tul.e yo (listens)

...-tun [retrospective modifier] ‖23.2; ~ ci ‖24.4-5

tun ... modifier < tul.e yo (lifts etc.; enters etc.)

... tūng and so on, et cetera 26.34

... tūng-tung etc. etc. 26.34A

tung the back (= can-tung) 22.SV

...-tuni [retrospective sequential] ‖24.6

tunun processive modifier < tul.e yo (lifts etc.; enters etc.)

tut.nun processive modifier < tul.e yo (listens)

twāyci pig (= to.yaci); ~ koki pork 16.SV

twī (the place) behind, in back 3.16; (= hwū) after(ward), later 12.5; (= tāypyen) feces, bowel movement 19.SV, ~ ul pwa yo [po-] has a bowel movement

twī-ci toilet paper (= twīq congi, pyensoq congi) 3.SV

twīq kan toilet (= pyenso) 3.SV

twū ... two 6.SV

twues, twue ... about two, a couple 29.13

twue yo [twu-] puts (away), leaves it (somewhere); keeps, stores; maintains, has in one's house(hold); (does) and gets it over with; ku man ~ puts aside, leaves alone, discontinues 17.35, 18.36, 23.9, 28.8

twunun processive modifier < twue yo

twukkewe yo [twukkew-] is thick (through) 22.SV

twūl two (= ī), 1.19; 6.14, 6.SV

twul(q) ... prospective modifier < twue yo

twum substantive < twue yo

twun ... modifier < twue yo

twungkul.e yo [twungku-l-], twungkulewe yo [twungkulew-] is round 22.21

twu-seys, twu-sey ..., twu-sek ... two or three ‖27.8

twu-senes, twu-sene ... about two or three ‖27.8

...-ul(q) [prospective modifier after consonant base] ... that is to do/be ‖14.2-3; ~ cakceng ‖27.8; ~ ka ‖14.5, ‖16.6; ~ kes ‖14.7-8, 23.38; ~ (l)ak hay yo ‖28.4; ~ man hay yo ‖27.7; ~ pen hay yo ‖24.12; ~ sayngkak ‖27.2; ~ swu ‖14.6; ~ swulok ‖27.4; ~ they ‖27.2; ~ ttay ‖14.4, ‖16.1; ~ yeyceng ‖27.2

... ul [direct object particle after consonant] ‖4.5, ‖22.9, ‖27.3 Cf. ... lul

...-ula [plain-style command in quotations, after consonant base] ‖19.3 Cf. ...-la, ...-e la

...-ule [purposive after consonant base] Cf. ...-le

...-ulla [prospective adjunctive after consonant base] ‖24.10 Cf. ...-lla

...-ullay = ...-ulye (ko) hay to ‖24.9

... ulo [particle after consonant other than l] ‖4.9, ‖19.8, ‖26.4, ‖27.6 Cf. ... lo

...-ulye [intentive after consonant base] ‖24.9 Cf. ...-lye

...-um [substantive after consonant base] ‖26.3; ~ a ‖23.6; ~ ey ‖26.5; ~ sey ‖23.6; ~ ulo ‖26.4 Cf. ...-m

...-um a ‖23.6

um.ak music 7.18

um.ak-ka musician 12.2

um.ak-hoy concert 7.18

umcel syllable ‖28.7

ūm.lyo-swu drinking water 16.SV

umphan a phonograph record 11.SV

...-um sey ‖23.6

ūmsik food 4.SV, ‖4.4; ~ (ul) hay yo prepares food 16.26

ūmsik-cem restaurant 13.SV

ūmsik cēn fried food 16.SV

...-umyen [conditional after consonant base] if, when ‖9.4-5, ‖16.1, ‖27.4; as for ‖9.7; ~ se (to) while ‖9.6, ‖16.1 Cf. ...-myen

...-un [modifier after consonant base] ... that did; ... that is ‖12.1; ~ ci ‖21.1 3, ‖22.6; ~ ya ‖19.3

... un [topic particle after consonant] as for ... ‖2.1, ‖3.6 Cf. ... nun

un silver 12.30

...-una [adversative after consonant base] but ‖18.3 Cf. ...-na

...-una-ma [extended adversative after consonant base] but anyway ‖18.3 Cf. ...-na

un.e sweet smelt, sweetfish 28.13

ung mmh 22.2; yeah 22.25

ūngcep-sil living room 18.SV

ūngkup chilyo first aid, emergency treatment 19.SV

ūngwen cheering, rooting; ~ (ul) hay yo cheers, roots 14.SV
unhayng bank 4.29
...-uni [sequential after consonant base] ‖18.1 Cf. ...-ni
...-uni-kka (n') [extended sequential after consonant base] ‖18.1 Cf. ...-ni-kka (n')
...-up.nikka = ...-sup.nikka (after iss-, ēps-, -ess-, keyss-)
...-up.nita = ...-sup.nita (after iss-, ēps-, -ess-, -keyss-)
...-upsita [formal proposition after consonant base] ‖17.1 Cf. ...-psita
...-uptikka = ...-suptikka (after iss-, ēps-, -ess-, -keyss-)
...-uptita = ...-suptita (after iss-, ēps-, -ess-, -keyss-)
...-usiyo [formal command after consonant base] ‖17.1 Cf. ...-siyo, ...-psiyo
... uy of ... ‖2.5
uyca chair (= kyouy) 3.21
uyhak medical science, medicine 19.14
uy(hak) hak.kyo medical school 19.SV
uyhak paksa doctor of medicine 19.14
uyhak-sayng medical student 19.SV
(...ey) uy hamyen if we rely on, according to (...) 26.19
uyq-kwa medical specialty, medical course 19.16
ūykyen opinion, view; advice 21.SV
ūymi meaning ‖28.7
uynon, uy[l]non discussion; ~(ul) hay yo discusses 17.SV
uysa doctor, physician 2.SV
ūysa intention(s), what is on one's mind; one's will, desire, inclination 27.10
uywen clinic, doctor's office 19.SV
... wa [after vowel] with, and ‖4.9 Cf. ... kwa
waisyassu [waisyatsu] shirt (= syassu) 8.SV, 29.8
wang king 26.22
wānkwu toy 22.SV
wānseng completion, perfection ‖28.7
way why 4.SV
wa yo, oa yo [o-] comes 4.32; pi ka ~ it rains 9.3, nwūn i ~ it snows 9.SV; cam i ~ gets sleepy 24.5
...-wel see ...-wel(q tal)
welkup salary ‖28.7
...wel(q tal) [makes month names] 6.23, 6.SV
welqsa-kum tuition (= swuep-lyo) 13.SV, ‖16.7
Wel-yoil Monday 4.SV
...-wen institution ‖27.10
...-wen garden, park, institute ‖27.10
wen (money unit) wen, yen, dollar 6.SV
wēncang head (of an institution), director, chief 19.14
wēn hay yo wants 9.20, ‖13.7
wenko manuscript 24.10
wen.lay originally, from the start 24.20
wēn.yu-hoy picnic (in a park); a garden party 21.1
wi the place above; the top, (= ~ chung) upstairs; senior, older 3.10, ‖7.10
... ~(ey) above ..., over ..., on (top of) ...
wi chung upstairs 18.SV
(...ul) wi hay yo does for the good (sake/benefit) of, does in favor of (in behalf of, in the interest of) 13.26
wihem danger; ~ hay yo is dangerous 29.48
wisayng health, hygiene 27.30
wiwen committee member(s); ~-hoy committee (meeting) 21.SV
wu = wi 3.10
wūl(q) ... prospective modifier < wul.e yo
wul.e yo [wū-l-] cries, weeps 22.17, 28.32
wuli we/us 2.32
wūlm substantive < wul.e yo
wūn modifier < wul.e yo
wūncen operation, driving; ~(ul) hay yo drives/operates (a vehicle) 18.3
wūncen-swu driver, operator (of a vehicle) 18.3
wūntong sport, athletics; ~(ul) hay yo engages in sports, goes out for sports 13.36
wūntong-cang gymnasium; playing field 14.3
wuphyen-kwuk post office 4.32
wuphyo postage stamp 29.SV
wūsan umbrella; ~ ul sse yo carries an open umbrella, walks under an umbrella 8.SV
wus.e yo [wūs-] laughs 22.17
wusung victory (= ikim) 14.SV
wusuwe yo [wusuw-] is funny, comical 22.SV
wutwu vaccination; ~ lul cwue/noh.a yo vaccinates; ~ lul mac.e yo gets vaccinated 19.SV
wuyu (cow's) milk 9.SV, 18.18

... ya [vocative-exclamatory particle after vowel] ‖22.8 Cf. ... a

... ya [particle after vowel] only if (it be) ‖8.12; ‖18.2; incey ~ (only) now 21.12 Cf. ... iya

... ya [question] ‖19.3

ya hey there! (= yāy) 22.26

yak medicine 3.SV

yakcey-sa pharmacist (= cēyyak-sa) 19.SV

yak.hon engagement, getting engaged 7.29

yak.hon-ca fiancé, fiancée 7.29

yak-pang pharmacy, drug store 3.SV

yaksok appointment, promise, commitment; ~ (ul) hay yo makes an appointment, promises, agrees, commits oneself; ~ i iss.ey yo has an appointment (an engagement) 21.SV, 29.43

yākwang sikyey clock with illuminated dial 23.SV

yākwu baseball 14.SV, ‖16.7

yalp.e yo [yalp-] is thin (and flat) 23.SV

yang-... Western-style, Occidental 27.30

[l]yāng ... both ..., two; ~ phyen both sides ‖6.1, 22.23

yanghwa = kwutwu (shoes) see ~ -cem

yanghwa-cem shoe store 12.SV

yāngkyey chicken (poultry) raising 27.SV

yangmal socks, stockings 8.SV

yangpok suit, dress (Western-style) 8.SV, 29.8

yangsan umbrella, parasol 8.SV, ‖14.8

yath.e yo [yath-] is shallow 12.SV; is light (in color) 26.SV

yāy hey there! (= ya) 22.26; you 22.SV, ~ ya hey you!

yāyki (= yēyki, iyaki) story, talk; ~ (ul) hay yo talks, tells a story 1.42

yā.yu-hoy a picnic 21.1

...-ye odd (tens, hundreds, etc.) ‖27.8

[n]yeca girl, woman 3.SV, 7.14

[n]Yeca Chengnyen Hoy-kwan YWCA (building) 17.SV, 20.1

[n]Yeca Chengnyen Hoy YWCA (the organization) 17.SV

[l]yehayng trip, journey; ~ (ul) hay yo takes a trip, makes a journey 21.26

[l]yehayng-pi traveling expenses ‖27.10

yek railroad station (= cengke-cang) 3.SV

yeki here, this place 1.25

[l]yeksa history 26.6

[l]yeksa-cek historic(al) 26.6, 26.SV

[l]yeksa-hak (the study of) history 26.SV

[l]yeksa-ka historian 26.SV

[l]yek.sa-sang from the viewpoint of history 27.23

yeksi also, too, as well 24.30

[l]yekwan hotel 3.SV

yel fever, temperature 19.3

yel ten (= sip) 1.19; 6.SV

yēl(q) ... prospective modifier < yel.e yo

yeles, yele ... several, various, many, all kinds of ...; yele pen many times 18.22; yele pun you all, ladies and/or gentlemen 18.18

yel.e yo [yē-l-] opens it 1.22, ‖26.1; (hōy lul ~) holds (a meeting) ‖21.SV; yēlq soy lo ~ unlocks it 28.SV

yel hana, yel han ... eleven (= sip-il) 6.SV

yelhul ten days 6.SV

yellye yo [yelli-] it opens ‖26.1

yēlm substantive < yel.e yo

yelqsim earnestness, enthusiasm, zeal; ~ hay yo is enthusiastic; ~ hi = ~ ulo earnestly, enthusiastically, with zeal, assiduously ‖4.9, 13.31, 24.1

yēlq soy key 28.SV

yelum summer 9.SV

yel.uy zeal, enthusiasm (= yelqsim) 13.31A

[n]yēm.lye worry, concern; ~ (lul) hay yo worries, is concerned 18.5

yēmsayk dyeing; ~ (ul) hay yo dyes 29.6

yēn ... modifier < yel.e yo

...-[n]yen year(s)

ye'-nam.un, -nam.u ... ten odd ‖27.8

yēncwu-hoy concert, recital 12.SV

Yenge English (language) 1.26

yenghwa movie, motion picture 4.23

yenghwa-kwan movie theater 3.SV

[l]yēngkam an elderly gentleman; ... ~ nim Mr. ... (of old man) 28.SV

Yengkwuk England; ~ salam English person 2.SV

[l]yengsa consul 21.SV

[l]yengsa-kwan consulate 21.SV

yēngsayng eternal life 17.27

[l]yengsey baptism (usually Catholic); ~ (lul) hay yo gets baptized 17.SV

yēngwen hi forever, eternally 17.32

yēn hay yo (color) is light; is soft, tender 26.SV

yēnhoy dinner party, banquet 18.SV

[n]yenhoy annual conference 17.SV

^{n}yenkap the age of an esteemed person [old-fashioned] 11.SV Cf. ^{n}yensey, nai

^{n}yen.lyeng age [impersonal] 11.SV Cf. nai

^{l}yen-mos lily pond 28.SV

yenphil pencil 2.SV

yēnpo offering (= hēnkum) 17.SV

yēnsel speech 24.31

^{n}yensey the age of an esteemed person 7.22, 11.SV Cf. nai

^{l}yēnsup exercise, practice; ~(ul) hay yo exercises, practices 1.48

^{n}yentay era 26.SV

yēnun processive modifier < yel.e yo

yeph the place next to or beside; ... ~ (ey) next to ..., beside ... 3.19

^{n}yephyenney wife 28.7

ye' po! look here! hello! hey there! say! waiter! clerk! [to spouse] Dear! [abbreviation < ye(ki) poo, authoritative style] 1.SV

ye' posio! [informal] = ye' po!

ye' posipsio! [formal] = ye' po!

ye' posey yo! [polite] = ye' po!

yepse postcard 27.13

^{n}yeseng women, womankind, a woman (as an example of womankind) 21.25

yeses six (= ^{l}yuk) 1.19, 6.SV

yes-say six days 6.SV

yet-ahop about eight or nine ‖27.8

yetel(p) eight (= phal) 1.19, 6.SV

yeth.e yo [yeth-] = yath.e yo

^{n}ye-tongsayng younger sister 7.11

yetuley eight days 6.SV

yetun eighty = phalq-sip 6.SV

yēyceng intention; ...-ul ~ iey yo intends to (do) ... 27.1

yēyki story, talk (= yāyki, iyaki); ~ (lul) hay yo talks, tells a story 1.42

yey-nilkop about six or seven ‖27.8

yēypang prevention, prophylaxis; ~ cwūsa vaccination ‖19.SV

^{l}yeypay (Protestant) service, worship; ~ (lul) hay/pwa yo worships, holds (Protestant) services 17.SV

^{l}yeypay-tang church 3.SV

yēys (nal) olden times, ancient 26.34

Yeyswu Jesus, Christ 17.9; ~-kyo Christianity 17.23

yeyswun sixty (= ^{l}yuk-sip) 6.SV

... 'ykey = eykey; ce ~, ne ~, na ~

...-^{l}yo charge, fee, cost, rate (= ^{l}yōkum) 23.12, 29.16 Cf. (ipcang)-lyo

... yo [polite particle after vowel] ...-e ~ ‖1.1, ‖17.2; ...-ci ~ ‖11.1, ‖17.2; ... ke(y) ~ ‖14.7–8; ... ka ~ ‖16.6; ...-na ~ ‖16.7 Cf. iyo

yo = i (this) ‖3.5

yo (quilted) mattress 29.SV

yo cen not long ago, just recently, the other day 29.26A

yo cenq pen last time (= the time before this) 29.26

yoil day of the week; musun ~ what day of the week 4.SV

yoq is sheet, mattress cover 29.SV

yoki = yeki (here) ‖3.5

^{l}yōkum fee, price, rate 29.13

yole = ile (like this) ‖11.5

^{l}yoli cooking 27.30

yoli = ili (this way) ‖11.5

^{l}yoli-cem restaurant (= ^{l}yoliq cip) 13.SV

...-yong for the use of ‖27.10

yongse excusing, pardoning; ~ (lul) hay yo excuses, pardons 1.11

yoq is sheet, mattress cover 29.SV

yo say lately, nowadays, these days 13.28

^{l}yuchang hi easily, fluently 24.2

yuchi hay yo is infantile ‖27.10

yuchi-wen kindergarten 22.SV, ‖27.10

yuil han ... unique 27.3

^{l}yuk six (= yeses) 6.SV

yuk.a child care 27.30

yuk.aq-pep child-care methods 27.30

^{l}yuk-chil six or seven ‖27.8

^{l}yuk.kwun army 2.SV

^{l}yuksang kyēngki field and track events 14.SV

yuli glass 3.8

yuli al (watch) crystal 23.SV

yuli can glass, (glass) tumbler 18.SV

yuli chang window 3.8

yūmyeng hay yo is famous 12.4

^{l}yuseng-ki phonograph, record player (= chwuk.um-ki) 11.1

^{l}Yu'-wel(q tal) June 6.SV

ENGLISH-KOREAN VOCABULARY

ability caycwu
about (= approximately) han ..., ... ccum, ... ina; (= concerning) ... ey tāy hay se, ... ey tāy han ...
above wi (ey)
is absent kyelqsek (ul) hay yo
accepts (= receives) cepswu (lul) hay yo
aches aphe yo [aphu-]
accompanies teylye yo [teyli-]; (= plays an accompaniement) pancwu (lul) hay yo
accompaniment pancwu
according to ... ey uy hamyen; ... tāy lo
is accurate cēnghwak hay yo
across kēnne(q) ...; goes ~ kēnne yo [kēnnu-]
is/gets acquainted sakwie yo [sakwi-]
action (= effect) cak.yong
active(ness) hwal.yak
actual object silmul
actual story silhwa
addenda pusok
admission: (to a hospital) ip.wen; ~ ticket ipcangq-kwen, ~ price (fee) ipcang-lyo
advice (= opinion) ūykyen
affair īl
is afraid kep (i) na yo [na-]
after (...-un) hwū/twī/taum (ey)
afternoon ōhwu
again (= further) tto; (= once more) han pen te; ~ and ~ (= repeatedly) cōng-cong
age nai, ^{n}yensey, ^{n}yenkap, chwunchwu, ^{n}yen.lyeng; (years of ~) ... sal
agenda thōuy sāhang
ah a! o!
aid see help; see first aid
air force kongkwun
airplane pihayng-ki
airport pihayng-cang
all tā; mōtwu; mōtun ...; cen-...
all day long congil
all of a sudden kkampak
is all right (= OK) cōh.a yo [cōh-], kwaynchanh.e yo, tōy(ss.ey) yo [toy-]
all together tā kath.i
all the time pam-nac
all the way tā; māyn ...

allows see lets
alone honca, toksin
almost keuy
already pelsse
also tto, yeksi, ...to
alto cēum, altho
alumnus col.ep-sayng
always nul, pam-nac, cāylay lo
am see is
ambassador tāysa
America Mikwuk
American Mikwuk salam
amuses oneself nol.a yo [nō-l-]
ancient yēys ...
ancient times cwungko, yēys (nal)
and ... hako, ... kwa/wa, tto ...; kuliko, ...-ko; kulay (se), ...-e (se); kulen tey
and so on ... tūng(-tung)
gets angry sēng/hwā/kol/pūn (i) na yo, sēng/hwā/kol/pūn (ul) nāy yo
animal tōngmul; (counter for animals) ... mali
annals sillok
annual conference ^{n}yenhoy
another: (= one more) tto hana, hana te; (= different) talun (kes); one ~ selo
answer tāytap; answers tāytap (ul) hay yo
anti- pān-..., pay-...
(not) any āmu ... (to)
anyhow ha.ye-kan
a lot see lot(s)
apiece ... ssik (ina)
apology sākwa
appearance mo.yang
appointment yaksok
appetite ip mas
apple sakwa
is appropriate cektang hay yo
approximately see about
April Sā-wel(q tal)
archaic times sāngko
architect kēnchwuk-ka
are see is
arm phal
army ^{l}yuk.kwun
around (= surrounding vicinity) . ... cwuwi (ey); (= approximately) see about
artist hwāka
as ... ulo/lo; ...-uni(-kka); see like

as much as ... mankhum; ~ possible toynun tāy lo
ascetic exercise swuto
asks mul.e yo [mūl-], mul.e pwa yo [po-]; (= requests, invites) cheng hay yo; (= beseeches) pil.e yo [pī-l-]; (= tells someone to give to oneself) tālla ko hay yo, tālla 'y yo
asleep <u>see</u> sleep
assassination āmsal; assassinates āmsal (ul) hay yo
assistant ... pū-...
at ... ey, ... (ey) se; at the latest nuc.e to; at least cek.e to; at last nācwung (ey); at most mānh.e to
athlete sēnswu
athletics wūntong
attachment pusok
attendance chwulqsek; is in ~ chwulqsek (ul) hāy yo
attitude thāyto
audience (of listeners) chengcwung; (of viewers) kwancwung
August Phal-wel(q tal)
aunt acwumeni
automatic clock catong sikyey
automobile catong-cha
autumn kaul
average, (on) the ~ phyengkyun
aviator pihayng-sa
avoids (doing) (...-ci) mal.e yo, (...-ci) anh.e yo
a while cāmqkan; in ~ iss.ta (ka)
baby ayki
back (of the body) (can-)tung; (= behind) twī; (= earlier) cen
bachelor chōngkak
is bad nappe yo [nappu-]; is too bad an tōy yo [toy-], an tōyss.ey yo
bag (= handbag) kapang; (= purse) cwumeni
ball kōng
balloting thwuphyo
bamboo tay (namu)
banana panana
band (of musicians) aktan
bank unhayng; (= riverbank) kangq ka
baptism sēylyey, ˡyengsey; (by immersion) chim.lyey
Baptist faith Chim.lyey-kyo
bar (= tavern) swulq cip
barber ˡīpal(q)-sa
barber shop ˡīpal(q)-so
barely kyewu
barks cic.e yo [cic-]
barley poli; (cooked) poli pap
baseball yākwu
basically pon.lay
bass(o) pēysu, passo
bathes (one's body) kam.e yo [kām-], mok.yok (ul) hay yo; (another person) kamkye yo [kamki-]
bathing mok.yok
bathroom mok.yok-sil
bathtub mok.yok-thong
battle cēnthwu
be <u>see</u> is
beautiful <u>see</u> pretty; ~ woman miin
becomes tōy yo [toy-]
because (...-ki) ttaymun ey, (...-nun) kkatalk ulo
bed chīm-sang; goes to ~ ca yo [ca-]
bedding chīmkwu, ipu'-cali
bedroom chīm-pang, chīmsil
beef so koki, so 'y koki
before (...-ki) cen (ey); (= in front) aph (ey)
begins (...-ki) sīcak hay yo; to begin with mence
beginning: in the ~ cheum ey; (= before anything else) mence
behind ... twī (ey)
believes (in) mit.e yo [mit-]
believer sīnca
below (...) alay (ey); (...) mith ey
belt tti
bends it kwup.hye yo [kwup.hi-]
is bent kwup.e yo [kwup-]
benediction chwukpok kito, chwukto
best: is ~ kacang cōh.a yo [cōh-]; does one's ~ āy (lul) sse yo [ssu-]
better: is ~ (te) cōh.a yo [cōh-]; is/gets ~ naa yo [nā(s)-]
Bible Sēngkyeng
bicycle cacen-ke
big <u>see</u> large
Big-Nose Kho-Cwupu
bill (for payment) chengkwu-se
bird sāy; (counter for birds) ... mali
birth, gives ~ to nah.a yo [nah-]
birthday sayngil; thān(sayng)-il
birthplace chwulqsayng-ci
bishop chōng.li(-sa), kamtok; (Catholic) cwukyo
bites mul.e yo [mu-l-]
black kemceng; is ~ kem.e yo [kēm-]
blackboard chilphan
blanket tamq-yo
bleaches clothes os ey mul ul ppāy yo [ppāy-]
blessing pok
blind: ~ person, blindman cāng nim,

sōkyeng; goes ~ nwun i mel.e yo [mē-l-]
blood phi, hyel.ayk
blooms phie yo [phi-]
blows pul.e yo [pū-l-]
is blue phulule yo [phulu-], phelay yo [phele(h)-]; (bright blue) phalay yo [phala(h)-]
boat pay
body mom(-ttwungi), sinchey
boils sālm.e yo [sālm-]
bone ppye
book chayk; tose
bookcase chayk-cang
bookshop chayk-pang, secem, chayk-sa
border (= edge) kā
is bored sim-sim hay yo
gets born na yo [na-], chwulqsayng hay yo; (a saint ~) thānsayng hay yo
boss cwuin
both twūl(q) tā; [1]yāng ...; ~ oidoo cwāwu (phyen), [1]yāng phyen
bottom mith; patak
bought see buy
bowel movement (tāy)pyen, twī, ttong
bowl kulus; (metal rice bowl used in winter) cwupal; (porcelain rice bowl used in summer) sapal
box sangca
boy sōnyen, tōngca; see also child, man
bread ppang
breaks: (= smashes it) kkay-ttulye yo [-ttuli-], (= it smashes) kkāy-cye yo [-ci-]; (= crumbles it) puswe ttulye yo [ttuli-], (= it crumbles) puswe cye yo [ci-]; (= snaps it in two) kkunh.e yo [kkunh-]; (= gets out of order) kōcang (i) na yo [na-]; the day breaks nal i palk.e yo [palk-]
breakfast achim(q pap), copan
bridge tali, ...-kyo
briefcase kapang
briefly ccalp.key (pronounced /ccalkkey/)
is/gets bright palk.e yo [palk-]; is bright (= intelligent) ttok-ttok hay yo
brings (a thing here) kacye/kaciko wa yo [o-], (a thing there) kacye/kaciko ka yo [ka-]; (a person here) teyliko wa yo [o-], (a person there) teyliko ka yo [ka-]; (an esteemed person here/ there) mōsiko wa/ka yo
broils kwuwe yo [kwūw-]
brook kaywul
brother: (male's older) enni, hyeng nim; (female's older) oppa, olape nim; (male's younger) tongsayng, awu; (female's younger) nam-tongsayng
brothers hyengcey; ~ and sisters nammay
brush sōl; brushing sōl cil; brushes sōl cil (ul) hay yo
Buddhism Pulkyo
Buddhist priest cwūng, su'-nim
Buddhist temple cel
building kēnmul, cip; ... chay; ...-kwan
builds (= constructs) cie yo [cī(s)-]; (= erects) seywe yo [seywu-]
bun (meat-stuffed) mantwu
burglar totwuk (nom); burglarizes totwuk cil (ul) hay yo
burns: (= it burns) tha yo [tha-]; (= burns it) thaywe yo [thayw-], thāy yo [thāy-]; (= smarts, tingles) ēl-el hay yo
bursts kkwēy cye yo [ci-]
bus (p)pesu; ~ stop (p)pesu thanun kos
business: (= trade) cangsa; (= something to do) lalq Il, ~ affairs samu
businessman sil.ep-ka, sāmu-ka; (= tradesman) cangswu, cangsaq kwun
is busy pappe yo [pappu-], puncwu hay yo
but ...ci man, ...-una, ...-e to, ...-(nu)n tey; kuleh.ci man, kulena, kulay to, kulen tey
button ta(y)nchwu; buttons a garment os uy ta(y)nchwu lul kkie yo [kki-] or chaywe yo [chaywu-]
buys sa yo [sa-]; kwu hay yo
by: (= beside) ...yeph (ey); (= before, until) kkaci (ey); by now pelsse; by oneself honca; by the way kulen tey
by-product pū-sanmul
cab thayksi, (catong-)cha; jitney ~ hapsung(thayksi)
cabbage (Chinese) paychwu
calls pulle yo [pulu-]
call: (a visit) sīmpang, pāngmun; (a phone call) cēnhwa; calls (= summons, hails) pulle yo [pulu-], (= telephones) cēnhwa (lul) hay yo or kel.e yo [kē-l-], (= visits) sīmpang/pāngmun (ul) hay yo, chac.e ka/wa yo; calls at (= drops in at) ... ey tullye yo [tulli-]
call: has someone call pullye yo [pulli-]
came see come
can ...-ulq swu iss.ey yo [iss-]; (= knows how to) ...-ulq cwul al.e yo [ā-l-]
cannot mōs ..., ...-ci mōs hay yo; ...-ulq swu ēps.ey yo [ēps-], (= does not know how to) ...-ulq cwul mōlla yo [molu-]
capital city swuto, sewul
captain (in the army) tāywi

car: (= vehicle) cha; (= automobile) catong-cha
care cwūuy, cōsim; (of one's health) cosep, coli; (of one's behavior or safety) (mom) cōsim
is careful (= exercises caution) cwūuy (lul) hay yo
carelessness pu-cwuuy
carries: (on one's person) cha yo [cha-]; (= holds) kacye yo [kaci-], (= brings/ takes) kacye/kaciko ka yo [ka-] or wa yo [o-]; (= loads) naile yo [nalu-]; ~ an umbrella (over one) wūsan ul sse yo [ssu-]
case (= briefcase) kapang; (= box) sangca; (= situation) kyengwu; in case see if
catches cap.e yo [cap-]; gets caught cap.hye yo [cap.hi-]; (= is infected by) catches a cold kāmki (ey) tullye yo [tulli-], kāmki (ka) tul.e yo, kāmki ey kellye yo [kelli-]
cattle so
Catholic(ism) Chencwu-kyo, Khathollik(-kyo)
cause [l]īyu, ... ttaymun, ... kkatalk; causes bother swūko lul kkichye yo [kkichi-]; causes one to do (= makes/ lets one do) sikhye yo [sikhi-], ...-key hay yo
caution see care
ceiling chenceng
censor kēm.yel-kwan
censorship kēm.yel
cent cēn
center (of attention) cwungsim; see middle
certainly: (hopes) cēypal; (= without fail) pūti; (= of course) mullon, ...-ko mālko
chair uyca, kyouy
chairman sahoy-ca
chance: (= opportunity) kihoy; if by chance mān.il
change (returned when paying for a purchase) kesulumq tōn
changes: (= exchanges) pakkwe yo [pakkwu-], kal.e yo [ka-l-]; (= shifts) pyēnkyeng (ul) hay yo; (= turns into) see becomes
character (written) ca, kul
charcoal swuch
charge: (= fee) [l]yōkum, ...-lyo, ...-[l]yo; (= responsibility) tam.im
is cheap ssa yo
checkup kēmsa
cheek ppyam, pol
cheer(ing for a team) ūngwen; cheers ūnwen (ul) hay yo
cherry: (the fruit) pec(ci); (the tree) pec namu; (the blossoms) pec kkoch
chest: (of the body) kasum; (for storage) cāng
chicken talk; (= ~ meat) talk koki; ~ raising yāngkyey
child ai, āy; elin ai/ay/i
child care yuk.a(q pep)
chin thek
China Cwungkwuk
Chinese: (person) Cwungkuk salam, (language) Cwungkwuk mal
choir chān.yang-tay, sēngka-tay
chooses thayk hay yo
chopsticks ceq-kal(ak), ce'l, ce; spoon and ~ swuce
chorus hapchang
Christ Yeyswu, Kitok
Christianity Yeyswu-kyo, Kitok-kyo
Christmas Sēngthan (cel)
church kyōhoy, [l]yeypay-tang
cigarette tāmpay
circumstance kyengwu; ... tey
city tosi, tohoy, sī; (= down town) sīnay, keli
city hall sīcheng
clam cokay
class pān; kongpu, sikan
classroom kyōsil
is clean kkaykkus hay yo, (= is white) huye yo [huy-]
cleans (house, watch, etc.) sōcey (lul) hay yo; (clothes) see dry cleaning
clerk (in store) cēm.wen; (in office) sāmu-wen
is clever ttok-ttok hay yo
clinic uywen
clock sikyey; alarm ~ kyengcong, camyeng-cong, sapal sikyey; wall ~ kwāycong; table ~ cwācong; ~ with illuminated dial yākwang sikyey
closes: (= closes it) tat.e yo [tat-], (= it closes) tat.hye yo [tat.hi-]; ~ a book chayk ul teph.e yo [teph-] or tat.e yo [tat-]; ~ one's eyes (= dozes off) nwun ul puth.ye yo [puth.i-]
closet (= storeroom) kwāng
clothes os
cloud kwulum
it clouds up kwulum i kkie yo [kkī-]
is cloudy hulye yo [huli-]
club (= social group) hōy
coach (athletic) khōchi

cold: (= virus infection) kāmki; is cold (to the touch) cha yo [cha-], (of weather) chwuwe yo [chwuw-], (a part of one's body feels cold) silye yo [sili-]
collar khalle
collects (= gathers up) ketwe yo [ketwu-]
college tāyhak, cenmun hak.kyo
college student tāyhak-sayng
concern kwansin, (= worry) ⁿyēm.lye; concerns kwankyey hay yo; concerning ...ey tāy/kwan hay se, ...ey tāy/kwan han ...
color pich, pich-(k)kal, sayk(-kal)
combs (one's hair) (meli lul) pis.e yo [pis-]; (another's hair) pis.kye yo [pis.ki-]
comes: (here) wa yo [o-], (there) ka yo [ka-]; comes in tul.e wa/ka yo, comes out na wa/ka yo; comes regularly (= commutes) tanye yo [tani-]; the coming ... ˡnay-...
command hōlyeng; commands hōlyeng (ul) hay yo
commemoration kinyem; commemorates kinyem (ul) hay yo
committee (= committee members) wiwen; (= committee meeting, group) wiwen-hoy
is common hun hay yo, hunh.e yo [hunh-]; commonly hun hi
Communion Service Sēng-manchan(q) sik
community (= village) tōngney, tōng.li
company hōysa
compares pī hay yo
competition kyēngki
complains: (= voices one's discontent) pulphyeng ul māl hay yo; (legally) kōso (lul) hay yo
completion wānseng
concern (= relevance) sangkwan, kwankyey; (= worry) ⁿyēm.lye, kekceng; is concerned with (= is about) ... ey kwan hay yo, ... ul tāy hay yo
concert um.ak-hoy; (= recital) yēncwu-hoy
concrete(ly) kwuchey-cek (ulo)
conductor: (of streetcar) chacang; (of orchestra) cihwi-ca
confession capayk, capok; (Catholic) kōhay
consul(ate) ˡyengsa(-kwan)
is contagious cen.yem (ul) hay yo; contagious disease cen.yemq pyeng
contest kyēngki
continuation kyēysok; continues kyēysok (ul) hay yo
continuously cakkwu, kyēysok hay se
is convenient phyen.li hay yo
conversation hōyhwa
conveys (= reports) cen hay yo
confronts mac.e yo [mac-]
is considerate chincel hay yo
convict (= prisoner) cōyswu
cooking ˡyoli
is cool senul hay yo
corner mo-thwungi; (= intersection) nēy-keli
corvenia (yellow fish) coki
cost (= price) kaps; it costs ... (i/ka) tul.e yo [tu-l-]
cough kichim; coughs kichim (ul) hay yo
counter- pān-...
country: (= nation) nala, kwuk.ka; (= rural area) sikol; native ~ ponkwuk
couple: (= two) twūl, twū ...; (= about two) twues, twue ...; (= husband and wife) pupu, nāy-oy
course (of subjects) kwa; kongpu
cousin sāchwun
cover: (= lid) ttwukkeng; (= covering sheet) is, (to cover a coverlet) ipulq is, (to cover a mattress) yoq is; covers it = uses ... as covering (on ...) (...ey) ... ul teph.e yo [teph-]
coverlet ipul
cow so
crab kēy
creek kaychen
cries wul.e yo [wū-l-]
crosses kēnne yo [kēnnu-], kēnne ka/wa yo
crossroads nēy-keli
crystal (of watch) yuli al
cup can
custom phungsok
is cute kwīyewe yo [kwīyew-]
cuts: (into, off, or out) pēy yo [pēy-]; (= trims, mows) kkakk.e yo [kkakk-]
cuttlefish (ppye) ocing-e
damage sōnhay
dance chwum; dances (chwum ul) chwue yo [chwu-]
dance hall ttaynsu-hol
danger wihem; is dangerous wihem hay yo
is dark etwuwe yo [etwuw-]; (in color) cin hay yo, cith.e yo [cith-]; it gets dark cemul.e yo [cemu-l-]
date nalq-ca; (= engagement) yaksok

daughter ttal, tta'nim
daughter-in-law myenuli, meynuli
dawn saypyek
day: nal, ...-il; (number of days—see 6.SV); ~ of the week yoil; every day māyil, nal mata
day after tomorrow moley
day before yesterday kucekkey
daytime nac
debate thouy
deaf: goes deaf kwi (ka) mek.e yo [mek-]; deaf person kwi-mekeli
December Sip.i-wel(q tal), Sēt-tal
decides kyelqsim (ul) hay yo, ceng hay yo, cakceng hay yo; decides for (in favor of) kākyel (ul) hay yo, decides against pūkyel (ul) hay yo
decision cakceng; kyelqsim; affirmative ~ kāyel, negative ~ pūkyel
is delicious mas (i) iss.ey yo [iss-], mas i 'ss.ey yo
denomination (of religion) kyōpha
is dense cith.e yo [cith-]
dentist chiq-kwa uysa; dentist's office chiq-kwa (uywen); dentistry chiq-kwa
department kwa; ~ head kwacang
descends naylye yo [nayli-]
desk chayk-sang
dessert hwūsik
detail: is detailed casey hay yo; in detail casey hi
diagnosis cīntan
diamond kumkang
did see does
dies cwuk.e yo [cwuk-]; tol.a kasey yo [kasi-], pyelqsey hay yo, samang hay yo; (perishes) myelmang hay yo
difference chai
is different talle yo [talu-]
is difficult elyewe yo [elyew-], him tul.e yo [tu-l-]; nan-...
difficulty elyewum
digestion sohwa
is diligent pucilen hay yo
dining room siktang
dinner (= evening meal) cenyek (pap)
diploma col.ep-cang
diplomat ōykyo-kwan
direction pangmyen, ... phyen, ... ccok
is dirty tēlewe yo [tēlew-]; (= black) kem.e yo [kēm-]
disburses chile yo [chilu-]
discards pelye yo [peli-]
discharge (from a hospital) thōywen
discomfort pu-ca.yu
discourtesy sillyey
discussion uynon, uy^{l}non; thouy
disease pyēng; (= ~ name) pyēngmyeng
dislikes (...i/ka) silh.e yo [silh-], (... ul/lul) silh.e hay yo
dish: (to eat out of) kulus; (to eat) ūmsik, (side dishes to go with the rice) panchan
dishwashing selkeci
disorder kōcang, thāl
is displeased pulkhway hay yo
dissatisfaction pulphyeng
distance kēli
is distant mel.e yo [mē-l-]
district superintendent kam.li-sa
disturbance pulphyeng
ditch kaychen
divides nanwe yo [nanwu-]
do see does
doctor (= physician) uysa, uysa paksa; (= holder of doctor's degree) paksa
doctor's office uywen
does hay yo [ha-]
dog kāy
dollar wen
domestic production kwuksan
domesticated animals kachwuk
don't ...-ci anh.e yo, ...-ci mōs hay yo; ...-ci mal.e yo [mā-l-], ...-ci māsey yo (or māsipsio)
door mun, cip mun
double (amount) pāy
down alay; gets down naylye yo [nayli-], goes/comes down naylye ka/wa yo, looks down naylye ('ta) pwa yo
downstairs alay chung, alay
dozes col.a yo [cō-l-]
draws: (a picture) kūlye yo [kūli-]; (= writes) sse yo [ssu-]
draws near takchye yo [takchi-]
dream kkwum; dreams (a dream) (kkwum ul) kkwue yo [kkwu-]
dress yangpok, os; gets dressed (os ul) ip.e yo [ip-], dresses (a person) (sālam hanthey os ul) ip.hye yo [ip.hi-]
dries mallye yo [malli-]
drinks masye yo [masi-]; mek.e yo [mek-]
drinking water ūm.lyo-swu
drives (a vehicle) wūncen (ul) hay yo
driver wūncen-swu
drug store yak-pang
gets dry malle yo [malu-]; makes it dry mallye yo [malli-]
drops: (= drops it) ttel.e ttulye yo [ttuli-]; (= it drops) ttel.e cye yo [ci-]
dry cleaning tulai khullining; dry cleans (or gets it dry cleaned) tulai khullining

(ul) hay yo
dues hōypi
duet (vocal) īcwung-chang, pyēngchang; (instrumental) īcwung-cwu
dust menci
duties chayk.im
dye mul, yēmsayk; dyes it yēmsayk (ul) hay yo, (os ey) mul ul tul.ye yo [tul.i-]; gets/is dyed mul i tul.e yo [tu-l-]
dyspepsia sohwaq pyeng
each ... mata, ... ssik; kak-...
each other selo
ear kwi
early ilccik(i); is early ille yo [ilu-]
earnestly yelqsim hi/ulo
earnestness yelqsim
the East (= Orient) tongyang
Easter Puhwal(q cel)
is easy swiwe yo [swīw-]; easily (= effortlessly) swīpkey, (= fluently) ˈyuohang hi
eats (pap ul) mek.e yo [mek-], (cīnci lul) capswusey yo [capsus(i)-]; gets eaten mek.hye yo [mek.hi-], has/lets one eat mek.ye yo [mek.i-]
edge kā
eel (pāym) cange
effect: (= action) cak.yong; (= effective results) hyōqkwa
effort nolyek; makes an effort nolyek (ul) hay yo
egg al; (= chicken egg) talkyal, kyeylan; lays an egg al ul nah.a yo [nah-]
eight yetel(p), yetelq ...; phal; ~ days yetuley
eighteen yel yetel(p)/yetelq ...; sip-phal
eighty yetun, phalq-sip
elder: (= older) nai ka wi ˈey yo; (an Elder of the church) cang.lo
elder brother/sister see brother, sister
election sēnke
electric(al), electricity cēnki
elevator sungkang-ki
eleven yel hana/han ...; sip-il
eliminates ēps.ay yo [ēps.ay-]
else see or; where ~ tto eti
embassy tāysa-kwan
emergency treatment ūngkup chilyo
emerges na yo [na-]; (comes/goes out) na wa/ka yo [o-/ka-]
empty: is/gets empty pie yo [pī-]; empties it piwe yo [piwu-] or piˈe yo [pī-]; (stomach) is/gets empty (pay ka) kopha yo [kophu-]
embodiment kwuchey, kwusang
encouragement cāng.lye; encourages cāng.lye (lul) hay yo
end kkuth, mal, macimak; (= bottom of garment) (os) calak; to the very end (kkuth.)kkuth-nay
ends (= it ends) kkuth na yo [na-], (= ends it) kkuth nāy yo [nāy-]; ends up doing ...-ko mal.e yo [mā-l-]; see also finishes
endeavor (= effort) nolyek; endeavors āy (lul) sse yo [ssu-]
engagement (to be married) yak.hon; (= appointment) yaksok
engine kikwan
engineer kikwan-sa
England Yengkwuk
English: (language) Yenge, (person) Yengkwuk salam
enters tul.e yo [tu-l-], (= goes/comes in) tul.e ka/wa yo [ka-/o-]; enters and leaves chwul.ip hay yo
enterprise kīep
entertains ceptay/tāycep (ul) hay yo
enthusiasm yelqsim
entire cen-...
entrance gate tāymun
equality phyengtung
...-er: (= professional) ...-ka, ...-sa; (= more) (com) te ...
era ⁿyentay
escorts mōsye yo [mōsi-]
et cetera tūng(-tung)
eternal life yēngsayng
evangelist (woman) centoq puin
even ... kkaci, ... to; even though ...-e to; even so kulay to
evening cenyek, (= night) pam
every ... mata; kak-...
every day māyil, nal mata
everyday (= mundane) il.yong
everyone mōtwu, tā, nwukwu ˈtun ci, nwukwu ˈna
ex-... cen-...
exactly kkok; ~ on the hour of ... cēngkak
examination sihem; (= inspection) kēmsa, (= medical diagnosis) cīnchal
examining room cīnchalq-sil
examiner (official) sihem-kwan
is excessive kwā hay yo
excessively kwā hi, nemu
exchanges (A for B) (A lul B lo) pakkwe yo [pakkwu-]
excrement ttong, twī, pyēn, tāypyen
excuse kwūsil, phingkyey

Excuse me. Mian hap.nita. or Yongse hasipsio. or Sillyey hap.nita (for what I am doing) /hayss.sup.nita (for what I did) /hakeyss.^{s}up.nita (for what I am about to do).
exercise: (= practice) ^{l}yēnsup; (= athletic activities) wūntong
exhausts tā hay yo
exists iss.ey yo [iss-]; does not exist ēps.ey yo [ēps-]
exits see emerges, leaves
expense ...-pi; (= money) tōn
is expensive pissa yo
experience kyenghem
explains selmyeng (ul) hay yo
explanation selmyeng
expresses natha-nāy yo [-nāy-], phyo hay yo
expressionless: looks ~ mēng hay yo
exterminates ēps.ay yo [ēps.ay-]
extremely tāytan hi
eye nwun
eyebrow nwunq-sep (or nwun-ssep)
eye glasses see glasses
eyelash sōk nwunq-sep
eye specialty (= ophthalmology) ānq-kwa
fable tonghwa
face elkwul
faces (= confronts) mac.e yo [mac-]; A is faced with X A eykey X ka takchye yo [takchi-]
fact sāsil; ... kes; ... cwul
factory kongcang
factory worker cik.kong
fails silphay (lul) hay yo; (= neglects to do) ...-ci anh.e yo [anh-]
failure silphay
faith mit.um, sīn.ang; faithful subject chwungsin
fall (= autumn) kaul
falls see drops
fame myengseng; (= one's name) ilum
famous: is famous yūmyeng hay yo; famous place myengsung-ci, myengso
family kacok; (= household) cip, cip-an; (= ~ members) sik.kwu
is far mel.e yo [mē-l-]; māyn ...
farewell sōngpyel; says/bids ~ sōngpyel (ul) hay yo; ~ party sōngpyel-hoy
farm nongcang; ~ house nongka, ~ life nongchon sayngh wal, ~ machinery or equipment nongcak kikwu; ~ slack season hānnong-ki; ~ village nongchon
farmer nongpu, nongmin
fast: (= speedily) ppalli; is fast ppalle yo [ppalu-]
is fat ttwung-ttwung hay yo
fatso, fat fellow ttwungttwung-po
father apeci, ape' nim. puchin
father-in-law (= wife's father) cāngin, (= husband's father) si-apeci, si-ape' nim
favor: by (your) ~ tekthayk ulo; does as a ~ ...-e cwue yo [cwu-] or tulye yo [tuli-]
fear kep; fears kep (i) na yo [na-]
February Ī-wel(q tal)
fee ^{l}yōkum, ...-lyo, ...-^{l}yo
feeds (someone) mek.ye yo [mek.i-]
fertilizer pīlyo, kelum
festival (of ...) ... cel
fetches (= goes and gets) chac.e wa yo [o-]
fever yel
are few cek.e yo [cēk-]
fiancé(e) yak.hon-ca
fiction sōsel
field path; (lowland rice ~) non
field events ^{l}yuksang kyēngki
fifteen yelq tases, sip-o
fifty swīn, ō-sip
fills in (a form) kiip hay yo
finally nācwung (ey)
finds chac.e yo [chac-]; finds out al.e kacye yo [kaci-], al.e yo [ā-l-]
(chopped) fine calkey
finger sonq-kalak
fingernail son-thop
finishes machye yo [machi-]; see also ends, eliminates
fire pul
firm: a firm (= company) hōysa; is firm (= tight) ttan-ttan hay yo
first ches (ccay), cēy-il; (of two or three) sāng-...; first of all (= before anything else) mence; first floor il-chung
first aid ūngkup chilyo
fish (mulq) koki; (as food) sayngsen; (counter for fish) ... mali
fisherman koki cap.i, epu; (= angler) nakk.siq kwun
fishes koki cap.i (lul) hay yo; (= angles) nakk.e yo [nakk-]
fish-hook nakk.si(q panul)
fishing koki cap.i; (= angling) nakk.si cil
fishing boat nakk.siq pay
fishing bait nakk.siq pap, (nakk.si) mikki
fishing line nakk.siq cwul
fishing net nakk.si kumul
fishing pole nakk.siq tay
five tases, ō; ~ days tas-say
flat objects (counter for ~) ... cang

flavor mas
flesh sal
flies: (= it flies) nal.e yo [na-l-];
(= flies it, lets it fly) nallye yo [nalli-]
floor malwu(q patak), patak; (= storey) ...-chung
florist (= flower shop) kkoch cip
flounder nepchi, totali
flower kkoch; ~(ing) tree or shrub kkoch namu; ~ garden kkoch path; ~ shop kkoch cip; ~ viewing kkoch kwūkyeng
fluently [l]yuchang hi
flying a plane pihayng; see flies
fog ānkay
it fogs up ānkay ka kkie yo [kkī-]
folds up (= furls) cep.e yo [cep-]
follows coch.a yo [coch-]; (goes/comes following) coch.a ka/wa yo [ka-/o-]
food ūmsik; pap, cīnci; (a meal) siksa
foot pal
for (a person) ... hanthey, ... eykey; (instead of) ... tāysin (ey); (for the sake of) ... ul wi hay se, ... ul wi han ...; does it (as a favor) for ... hanthey ...-e cwue/tulye yo [cwu-/tuli-]; (for the use of) ...-yong; what for see why; looks for, waits for, etc. see the verb
foreign: ~ country ōykwuk; ~ made ōykwuk-cey; Ministry of Foreign Affairs Ōymu Pu
forehead ima
forenoon ōcen
forest swuph
forever yēngwen hi
forgets ic.e yo [ic-], ic.e pelye yo [peli-]
forgives yongse hay yo
fork samci-chang
former cen(-...)
'y mahun; sā-sip
fountain pen mānnyen-phil
four nēys, nēy ... (or nēk ...); sā; ~ days nahul
fourteen yel nēys/nēy/nēk; sip-sā
freedom ca.yu
freezes (= it freezes) el.e yo [ē-l-]
is frequent cac.e yo [cac-]
frequently cacwu, cal
Friday Kum-yoil
fried (food) ... cēn
friend chinkwu, tongmu
from (a time) ... puthe; (a place) ... (ey) se, ... (ey) se puthe; (a person) ... hanthey/eykey se, ... kkey se
from now on incey
from time to time kakkum
front aph
fruit kwāil
is full (= replete with food) pay ka pull.e yo [pulu-]
full(y) mān-...
fun caymi; is fun caymi iss.ey yo [iss-]; has fun caymi (lul) pwa yo [po-], nol.a yo [nō-l-]
fundamentally pon.lay
furniture kakwu
furthermore tekwuna
future mīlay; aph
game: (sports match) sīhap; (competition) kyēngki; (amusement) cangnan; (sports) wūntong
garden path, ...-wen; (flower ~) kkoch path; (vegetable ~) chāyso path
garlic manwul
garment os; (counter) ... pel
gate mun; (front ~) tāymun
gathers: (= amasses) moa yo [mou-]; (= collects) ketwe yo [ketwu-]; (cloud, fog, etc. forms) kkie yo [kkī-]
gave see gives
gee! acha!
generally tāychey (lo)
gentleman sensayng (nim), [l]yēngkam; (ladies and) gentlemen yele pun
genuine (article) cincca
geography cili(-hak)
gets: (= receives) pat.e yo [pat-]; (= obtains) et.e yo [et-], kwu hay yo; (= buys) sa yo [sa-]; (= understands) al.e yo [ā-l-], (= hears) tul.e yo [tul-]; gets it for a person (and gives it to him) kac'ta cwue yo [cwu-]; gets (= goes/comes) to a place ka/wa yo [ka-/o-]; gets someone to do it CAUSATIVE VERB or ...-key hay yo, sikhye yo [sikhi-]; gets it done to one PASSIVE VERB or ...-um ul tang hay yo; gets to do it ...-key tōy yo [toy-]; gets to be (= becomes) + NOUN ... i/ka (or ulo/lo) tōy yo [toy-], + ADJECTIVE ...-key tōy yo, ...-e cye yo [ci-]
gets up il.e na yo
gift sēnmul
girl [n]yeca, sāyksi, sōnye
gives cwue yo [cwu-]; (to an esteemed person) tulye yo [tuli-], pachye yo [pachi-], ollye yo [olli-]
glass yuli; (tumbler) yuli can; (window) yuli chang; (= mirror) kyewul

glasses (= spectacles) ānkyeng; puts on (or wears) ~ ānkyeng ul sse yo [ssu-]
is glorious hwachang hay yo
gloves cāngkap; puts on (or wears) ~ cāngkap ul kkie yo [kkī-]
God Hanu'nim, Hana'nim (Protestant), Chencwu (usually Catholic)
goes ka yo [ka-], (on foot) kel.e ka yo; (regularly commutes) tanye yo [tani-]; goes in/out tul.e/na ka yo; goes up ollye yo [olli-], ollye ka yo; goes down naylye yo [nayli-], naylye ka yo; goes by cīna yo [cīna-], cīna ka yo; goes on (= continues) kyēysok hay se (... hay yo); Go on and cry! Wūlci wul.e!
going out for a while (to be back later) na-tul.i
Goggle-Eyes nwun-ttakpuli
gold kum
is good cōh.a yo [cōh-]
Goodbye! (to one who is staying) Annyeng hi kyēysipsio (or kyēysey yo). (to one who is leaving) Annyeng hi kasipsio (or kasey yo).
Good morning/afternoon/evening! (= Hello) Annyeng hasip.nikka? or Annyeng hasey yo?
goods mulken; ...-phum
gosh! acha!
government cengpu
grade (= score) cemqswu; (= school record) sengcek
gradually cha-cha
graduate col.ep-sayng (= one who has graduated)
graduate school tāyhak-wen
graduate student tāyhak-wen haksayng
graduates col.ep (ul) hay yo
graduation col.ep
grain ssal, koksik
grammar munqpep
grandchild soncwu (ai)
granddaughter sonnye
grandfather hal-apeci, hal-ape'nim; copu (nim)
grandmother hal-'meni, hal-'me'nim; como (nim)
grandparents co-pumo (nim)
grandson sonca
grass phul
gratitude kāmsa
gray hoysayk, cayq pich
great tāy-...; is great (= large) khe yo [khu-], (= good) cōh.a yo [cōh-]; a great deal mānh.i
green cholok sayk; is green phulule yo [phulu-], phelay yo [phele(h)-]
greetings: (= courtesies) insa; (= sending regards) mūn.an
ground patak
grounds (= yard) ttul
group ...tul, ... kkili; (= branch, sect) pha; (= class) pān; (= kind) kaci
grows cala yo [cala-]; ~ thickly museng hay yo; ~ old nai ka tul.e yo [tu-l-]; (= becomes) ...-key tōy yo [toy-], ...-e cye yo [ci-]
guards kyēngkyey (lul) hay yo
guest son nim; ~ of honor cwūpin, other guests paypin
guest room kayksil, salang
gym(nasium) wūntong-cang
gynecology puinq-kwa
ha ha! ha ha!
habit supkwan
had see has
hair thel; (on the head) meli (thel), (a hair of one's head) meli-khal(ak)
haircutting [l]īpal
half pān; and a half ... pān
hand son; (= person) ...-swu; (of timepiece) panul: hour ~ cangchim, minute ~ punchim or tānchim, second ~ chochim
hands in/over (= presents) pachye yo [pachi-]
handbag kapang
handkerchief sonq swuken
handles (= manages) kamtang (ul) hay yo
hangs: (= hangs it) kel.e yo [kē-l-], (= it hangs) kellye yo [kelli-]
happens (il.e) na yo, sayngkye yo [sayngki-]
happiness (= joy) kippum, (= good fortune) hāyngpok
is happy (= glad) kippe yo, kippe hay yo; (= fortunate) hāyngpok hay yo
is hard (= difficult) elyewe yo, him tul.e yo [tu-l-]; nan-...
harvest chwuswu
harvests ketwe yo [ketwu-]
has (= has got, possesses) (... i/ka) iss.ey yo [iss-], (... ul/lul) kacye yo [kaci-]; see also holds; has to see must; has done use PAST
hat moca; puts on (or wears) a ~ moca lul sse yo [ssu-]
hates silh.e hay yo
have see has
he ku (i/sālam/pun/āy)
head meli; (of an institution) wēncang, (of a company or society) hōycang
is healthy kēnkang hay yo

hears tul.e yo [tul-]
heart maum; with one's whole ~ cengseng kkes
heats teywe yo [teywu-]
heaven hanul, chentang; heavenly kingdom hanul nala, chenkwuk
is heavy mukewe yo; cwūng-...
height noph.i; (= stature) khi
hell ciok
helps towa yo [tōw-], towa cwue/tulye yo [cwu-/tuli-]
henpecked husband che-sika
her see she
here yeki, yoki; (this way) ili, yoli
herring chenge, piwus
hey! ye' po! ye'posio! ya! yāy!
is high noph.a yo [noph-]; highly noph.i
high school kotung hak.kyo; junior ~ cwung-hak.kyo
him see he
historian ˡyeksa-ka
historic(al) ˡyeksa cek; ~ spot kōcek(-ci); ~ stories sāhwa
history ˡyeksa(-hak)
hits chie yo [chi-]
hitch (= snag, something amiss) thāl, kōcang
hmph! hung!
hobby chwīmi
holds tul.e yo [tu-l-]; ~ a meeting hōy lul yel.e yo [yē-l-] or hay yo
hole kwumeng
home cip, kaceng; sallim; ancestral ~ poncek(-ci); homeland ponkwuk; home town kōhyang
homework swukcey
honey kkwul
hopes for pala yo [pala-]; hopes that ... ...-umyen cōh.keyss.ey yo
hospital pyēngwen; ~ room pyēngsil
is hot ttukewe yo [ttukew-], tewe yo [tēw-]; (= spicy) maywe yo [mayw-]
hotel ˡyekwan
hour (of time) sikan; (o'clock) ...si
house cip; tayk
housecleaning sōcey
housekeeping sallim
housewife kaceng puin
how etteh.key, ecci; it is how ettay yo [ette(h)-], does how eccay yo [ecce-]
How are you? Annyeng hasip.nikka (or hasey yo)?
how much elma ('na)
how many meych ...
how come etteh.key, way
how long elmaq tong-an
however kuleh.ci man; ~ much amman

hundred payk
is/gets hungry pay ka kopha yo [kophu-]
husband namphyen, cwuin, sanay
hygiene wisayng
hymn chānsong-ka; (Catholic) sēngka
I na, nay ka; (formal) ce, cey ka
ice el.um; ~ water el.um mul; ~ events pingsang kyēngki
idea sayngkak
identical machan-kaci
if ...-umyen, ...-tula'myen; (perchance) mān-il; if not kuleh.ci anh.umyen
is/gets ill alh.e yo [alh-], pyēng i na yo [na-]
illness pyēng
immediately kot, ellun
impends takchye yo [takchi-]
impromptu (speech) ˡimsi (yēnsel)
in ... ey; ... ey se; (inside) ... an (ey), ... sōk (ey); goes/comes in tul.e ka/wa yo [ka-/o-]; (among) ... cwung (ey); in English Yenge lo; in case mān-il, ... kyengwu (ey nun); in a little while iss.ta (ka)
inactive(ness) pul-hwal.yak
is inappropriate pu-cektang hay yo
(being) incomplete mī-wanseng
is inconvenient pulphyen hay yo
increases (= it increases) nul.e yo [nu-l-]
indecision mī-kyelqceng
indeed ... to; ha to; ...-ki to hay yo; accwu!
indescribably māl halq swu ēps.i
indigestion sohwaq pyeng
indisposition mom-sal
industry kongep
inequality pul-phyengtung
inevitably pantusi, kkok, halq swu ēps.i
is inexpensive ssa yo [ssa-]
is infantile yuchi hay yo
infirmary chilyo-so
informs allye yo [alli-], allye cwue yo [cwu-]; ille yo [ilu-], māl hay yo
injection cwūsa; gives an ~ cwūsa lul cwue/noh.a yo; gets an ~ cwūsa lul mac.e yo
inlaws (of a man) cheka; (of a woman) sika
inside an; (of something rather full) sōk
inspection kēmsa
institution kikwan, ...-wen
intention yēyceng, cakceng, ūysa; (...-ul) they, ...-ulye
interest (= concern) kwansim; (= fun) caymi, (= hobby) chwīmi
is interesting caymi (ka) iss.ey yo [iss-]
intern silqsup-sayng

internal nāy-...; ~ medicine nāyq-kwa
interprets thongyek (ul) hay yo
intersection nēy-keli
interval (of space or time) sai, sāy; (of time) tong-an
invention palmyeng
invites cheng hay yo
invitation chotay
iron: (the metal) soy; (for pressing clothes) ta(y)limi, (small heart-shaped ~ with handle) intwu; electric ~ cēnkiq ta(y)limi
irons: (= does the ironing) ta(y)lim cil (ul) hay yo; (= irons it) ta(y)lye yo [ta(y)li-]
ironing ta(y)lim cil; ~ board ta(y)limi phan
irrelevance mu-kwankyey
is: (= exists) iss.ey yo [iss-], (an esteemed person) kyēysey yo [kyēysi-]; (= it is [an instance of]) ... iey yo [i-]
is not: (= exists not) ēps.ey yo [ēps-], (an esteemed person) an kyēysey yo [kyēysi-] or kyēysici anh.e yo; (= it is not [an instance of]) ... i/ka ani 'ey yo (ani '-)
-ist ...-ka
is itchy kalyewe yo [kalyew-]
it ku (kes)
items: (for discussion) (thōuy) sāhang; (= objects) mulken, ... kes; (counter) ... kay
jail kam.ok
jacket (Korean) cekoli
January Il-wel(q tal), Cengwel
Japan Ilpon
Japanese (language) Ilpon mal; (person) Ilponq salam
Jesus Yēyswu
jewel pōsek, ... sek
jewelry shop kum-unq pang, pōsek-sang
jitney (taxi) hapsung (thayksi)
joke [l]nōngtam; jokes [l]nōngtam (ul) hay yo
journey [l]yehayng; makes a ~ [l]yehayng (ul) hay yo
July Chil-wel(q tal)
jumps ttwie yo [ttwi-]; jumps across kēnne ttwie yo
June [l]Yu'-wel(q tal)
junior (= younger) (nai ka) alay
junior high school cwung-hak.kyo
just: (= exactly) kkok; (= only) ... man, ku man, tā-man; (= as though, as if) machi; just now cikum (un), just recently yo cen
key (yēlq) soy
kid see child; see joke
kills cwuk.ye yo [cwuk.i-]
kind (= variety) kaci; all kinds of yele (kaci)
is kind (= considerate) chincel hay yo
kindergarten yuchi-wen
king wang
kipper mallin chenge
kitchen puekh
kitten see cat
knee muluph
knows al.e yo [ā-l-]; does not know mōlla yo [molu-]; lets one know allye yo [alli-]
knowledge ālm
Korea Hānkwuk; Cosen
Korean (language) Hānkwuk mal, Cosen mal; Hān-e, Cosen-e
Korean (person) Hānkwuk salam, Cosenq salam
labor [l]notong
lacks (... i/ka) ēps.ey yo [ēps-]
ladder sa(tak)-tali
lady puin, samo-nim; ladies (and gentlemen) yele pun
lake hoswu
landowner cicwu
language māl; māl-ssum
is large: (in size) khe yo [khu-]; (in quantity) mānh.e yo [mānh-]
last: ~ time cīnan pen, yo cenq pen; ~ year cak.nyen, cīnan hay; ~ night eceyq pam, cīnan pam; ~ week/month/spring cīnan cwuil/tal/pom; the last (= most recent) cīnan pen ..., yo cenq pen ..., (= final) macimak ...; at last nācwung (ey)
lastborn 'mak-nay
lasts: (= it lasts, goes on) ka yo [ka-]; (= it takes time) (sikan ul) kellye yo [kelli-]
late nuc.key; is/gets late nuc.e yo [nuc-]; at the latest nuc.e to; lately yo say; later on iss.ta (ka), hwū/twī (ey/lo)
the late (Mr. ...) kō ...
laughs wus.e yo [wūs-]
launders ppal.e yo [ppa-l-], ppallay (lul) hay yo
laundry: (to be washed) ppallay, sēythak(-mul); (establishment) sēythak-so; ~ soap sēythak pinwu; ~ line ppallayq cwul
lawyer pyēnho-sa
is lazy keyulle yo [keyulu-]
leads (= guides) īnto (lul) hay yo
learns paywe yo [paywu-]; (= finds out)

al.e yo [ā-l-], al.e kacye yo [kaci-];
learning (= schooling) haksik, kul

leaves: (= emerges) na yo [na-], (goes/comes out) na ka/wa yo [ka-/o-]; (becomes detached) tte yo [ttu-], (departs) tte-na yo [-na-]; (leaves it behind) namkye yo [namki-], is left (over) nam.e yo [nām-]

lecture kāngyen; kāngsup; ~ room kāngsup-so

left: (= lefthand) ōyn ..., ōyn phyen/ccok, ~ and right cwāwu (phyen); (= departed; remaining) see leave

leg tali

legation kōngsa-kwan

legend censel

lends pillye cwue yo [cwu-]

lesson kwa; kongpu

lets: (= permits) ...-key hay yo or CAUSATIVE VERB; sikhye yo [sikhi-]; lets in tul.ye yo [tul.i-], lets out nāy yo [nāy-]

let's ...-upsita, ...-usipsita; ...-ca, ...-sey; ...-ulq ka yo, ...-ci yo

let's not ...-ci māpsita/māsipsita; ...-ci mālca/māsey

let's see (now) eti popsita/posey/poca

letter: (= epistle) phyēnci; (= written character) ca, (= writing) kul

library: (building) tose-kwan, (room) tose-sil, (the books) tose

lid ttwukkeng

lies (down) nwuwe yo [nwuw-]; is lying down nwuwe iss.ey yo

lieutenant: second ~ (= navy ensign) sōwi, first ~ (= navy ~ junior grade) cwungwi, navy (full) ~ (= army captain) tāywi

life saynghwal, sālm

light (to see by) pul; (electric) cēnkiq pul

is light: (in weight) kapyewe yo [kapyew-], kyeng-...; (in color) yath.e yo [yath-], yeth.e yo [yeth-], yen hay yo; (= bright) palk.e yo [palk-]

like ... chelem, ... kath.i, ... kath.ey yo [kath-]

is like ... kath.ey yo [kath-]; (= resembles) tālm.e yo [tālm-]

likes cōh.a hay yo

line cwul

lip ip-swul

liquor swul

listens to tul.e yo [tul-], tut.ko iss.ey yo [iss-]

literature munhak, mun

little: a ~ com, cokum; is ~ (in size) cak.e yo [cāk-], (in quantity) cek.e yo [cēk-]

livelihood sallim

lives sal.e yo [sā-l-], (sālko) iss.ey yo [iss-]; makes/lets one live sallye yo [salli-]

living room ūngcep-sil

lock (cam'ulq) soy

locks (cam'ulq/yēlq soy lo) camke yo [camku-]

locomotive engineer kikwan-swu

loin heli

is long: (in space or time) kil.e yo [kī-l-], cang-...; (in duration) olay yo [olay-]; for a long time olay(q tong-an), becomes/is a long time olay tōy yo [toy-]; lasts a long time olay ka yo [ka-]

looks: (= looks at) pwa yo [po-], kwūkyeng (ul) hay yo; ~ up (= searches out) chac.e yo [chac-]; ~ up at chye 'ta pwa yo, ~ down at naylye ('ta) pwa yo, ~ out at nāy 'ta pwa yo, looks in at tul.ye ('ta) pwa yo, ~ over/across at nemkye ('ta) pwa yo

looks after pwa yo [po-]

looks as if = looks like

looks like ... mo.yang iey yo, ...-ulq ka pwa yo, ... kes kath.ey [kath-]; see also resembles, like

is loose nuc.e yo [nuc-]

loosens nuc.chwe yo [nuc.chwu-]

the Lord see God

loses ilh.e yo [ilh-], ilh.e pelye yo [peli-]; (= suffers defeat) cie yo [ci-], phāy hay yo

a lot, lots mānh.i, cal; is ~ mānh.e yo [mānh-], mānh.i iss.ey yo [iss-]

love salang; loves salang hay yo

loyalty chwunguy

is lukewarm micikun hay yo

lump teng(el)i

lunch cēmsim

lungs phyēy

machine(ry) kikyey

mackerel kotung-e

mad see angry

made see make

magazine capci

is magnificent hwullyung hay yo, koyngcang hay yo

mail box phyēnci neh.nun kos

mails puchye yo [puchi-], nāy yo [nāy-]

makes cie yo [cī(s)-]; ma(y)ntul.e yo [ma(y)ntu-l-]; (a record) nāy yo [nāy-]

male namca, sanay

mama emma

man (= person) sālam; (= male) namca, sanay; (= husband) namphyen
manuscript wenko
are many mānh.e yo [mānh-]; ta-...
March Sam-wel(q tal)
mark (= grade, score) cemqswu
market cang, sīcang; does the marketing cang (ul) pwa yo [po-]
marriage kyelhon
married couple pupu, nāy-oy
marries kyelhon (ul) hay yo
mass (Catholic) misa; says ~ misa (lul) pwa yo [po-]
match: (to strike fire) sengnyang; (athletic) tāyhoy
matter see thing, affair, trouble, concern; it doesn't ~ sangkwan (i) ēps.ey yo, kwaynchanh.e yo
mattress yo
May Ōwel(q tal)
may (= it is all right if) ...-e to cōh.a/kwaynchanh.e yo; (= perhaps) see maybe
maybe ama, ... ci to mōlla yo [molu-]
mayor sīcang
me see I
is meager pin.yak hay yo
meal siksa, pap
meaning ttus, ūymi
is meaningful ttus i iss.ey yo [iss-]
is meaningless ttus i ēps.ey yo [ēps-]; mu-uymi
measles hongyek
meat koki
meat-stuffed bun mantwu
mechanism kikyey
medical: ~ science uyhak, ~ school uy(hak) hak.kyo, ~ student uyhaksayng, ~ specialty uyq-kwa, ~ treatment chilyo, ~ examination cīnchal
medicine: (= drug) yak; (= medical science) uyhak; doctor of ~ uyhak paksa, uysa
medium(-size) cwung-...
meets manna yo [manna-]; (= confronts) mac.e yo [mac-]; (= holds a meeting) hōy lul yel.e yo [yē-l-] or hay yo
meeting hōy
member hōywen
memorizes ōywe yo [ōywu-]
mends: (= sews) kkwēy may yo; (= repairs) kochye yo [kochi-]
merchant sangin, cangswu
is messy tēlewe yo [tēlew-]
method pangpep, pep
Methodism, Methodist Kam.li-kyo
middle cwung; ~ ages cwungsey; ~ school cwung-hak.kyo
midst (to)cwung; (= under the influence of) ... palam (ey)
mile (Korean) ˡī, ...-li
milk wuyu
million payk-man
mind: (= feelings) maum; minds (= looks after) pwa yo [po-]; (= heeds) (...uy māl ul) tul.e yo [tul-]; Do you mind if ...? ...e to kwaynchanh.e/cōha yo?
mine (= my thing) nay kes
minister: (of a church) moksa; (to a foreign country) kongsa; (of a cabinet) cāngkwan
ministry (of the government) pu
minute (of time) pun; minutes (of a meeting) hōylok
misfortune pulhayng
missionary senkyo-sa
mist ānkay
mistake calmos, silqswu
mixes (it/them) sekk.e yo [sekk-]
mmh (= yeah) ung
mom(ma) emma
monastery swuto-wen
Monday Wel-yoil
money tōn
month tal, [number of months] ...-kaywel or ... tal; [name of month] ...-wel(q tal); what month meych wel, musun tal
more te, com te; is more (te) mānh.e yo
moreover tekwuna
morning achim; (= forenoon) ōcen
most kacang, ku-cwung, cēy-il; (= almost all) keuy (tā)
moth com; a garment gets moth-eaten os ey com i mek.e yo
mothball comq yak
mother emeni, eme' nim; mōchin
mother-in-law: (= wife's mother) cāngmo; (= husband's mother) si-emeni, si-eme' nim
motive tōngki
motion (parliamentary) tōnguy
mountain san
mouth ip
movie yenghwa; (= ~ theater) yenghwa-kwan)
mows kkakk.e yo [kkakk-]
Miss ... sensayng
Mr. ... sensayng; ... ssi; ... chemci
Mrs. ... sensayng puin; ... (sensayng) samō nim; ... ssi
much mānh.i, cal; is much mānh.e yo [mānh-]

music um.ak
musician um.ak-ka
must ...-e ya hay yo; ...-ci anh.umyen an tōy yo
must not ...-umyen an tōy yo
mute person pengeli
my nay ..., cey ...; wuli ...
my! ke!
myth sinhwa
name ilum; sēngham, sēngmyeng
nap (= sleep) cam
narrow: is narrow cop.a yo [cop-]; makes it narrow cop.hye yo [cop.hi-]
native (= natural) chen.yen
nation kwuk.ka
nature ca.yen
navy hāykwun
is near kakkawe yo [kakkaw-]
nearly keuy
necktie neykthai
needle panul
needlework panu'oil
nephew cokha
net neythu; mang; kumul
nevertheless kulay to; kuleh.ci man
new say ..., say kes; sin-...; is new say-lowa yo [-low-], say kes iey yo
newspaper sinmun
New Testament Sin-yak
next taum; (= beside) yeph; (= coming) [1]nay-...
niece cokha ttal
night pam; cenyek
nine ahop, kwu; ~ days ahuley
nineteen yel ahop; sip-kwu
ninety ahun; kwu-sip
no ani (yo)
is noble chak hay yo
nobody see no one
is no good an tōy(ss.ey) yo
non-... pi-...
none see nothing; has none ēps.ey yo [ēps-]
is nonexistent ēps.e yo [ēps-]
noodle kwukswu; Tang myen
no one (= nobody) āmu (sālam) to + NEGATIVE
nor ... to + NEGATIVE; tto nun
nose kho
nostril khoq-kwumeng
not ani; an/mōs ...; ...-ci an/mōs hay yo, ...-ci anh.e yo; pul-..., pu-...
not at all chen-man ey (yo), chen-man uy māl-ssum ip.nita
notebook kong-chayk
nothing āmu kes (to) + NEGATIVE
novel sōsel (chayk)
novelist sōsel-ka
November Sip.il-wel(q tal)
now cikum; (= starting now, from now on) incey, only ~ incey ya; (= already) pelsse; (= next) taum (ey); now! ca!
now and then kakkum
now (then) kulem
nowadays yo say
number swū; swū-...
nun swunye
nurse kanho-pu
nursery thak.a-so
nylon nailon, nai(l)long; "nylon" noodles Tang myen
obeys ... (uy) māl ul tul.e yo [tul-]
obstacle cangay
obstetrics sānq-kwa
obtains et.e yo [et-], kwu hay yo
occasion (= time) ttay
o'clock ...si
October Sī'-wel(q tal)
octopus mun.e
odd (tens, hundreds, etc.) ...-ye
of ... uy
of course mullon; ...-ko mālko (yo)
offering hēnkum; yēnpo, swucen
office sāmu-sil; doctor's ~ uywen
officer (military) cāngkyo; (staff member) īm.wen, cik.wen
official (being ~) kongsik; (an ~) ...-kwan
often cacwu, cal; mānh.i; nul
Oh? Kulay (yo)? Kuleh.sup.nikka?
Oh! O! A! Acha!
is OK tōy(ss.ey) yo, kwaynchanh.e yo, cōh.a yo [cōh-]
old: (= not new) hēn ..., nalk.un ..., hēn/nalk.un kes; kwū-...; is old (= not new) nalk.e yo, (= not young) nai ka mānh.e yo, nulk.ess.ey yo; grows old nulk.e yo [nulk-]
is older (= senior) (nai ka) wi 'ey yo
older brother/sister see brother, sister
old person nulk.un i
Old Testament Kwū-yak
on: (= at) ... ey, (= atop) ... wi (ey); (= about, concerning) ... ey tāy/kwan hay se, ... ey tāy/kwan han ...
once (= one time) han pen
one hana, han ...; il; ~ day halwu; ~ another selo
oneself caki; by ~ honca
onion pha
only ... man, ku man, tā-man; ... pakk-ey + NEGATIVE
only son toksayng-ca

opens: (opens it) yel.e yo [yē-l-], (opens a book) yel.e yo or phie yo [phi-]; (it opens) yellye yo [yelli-]
opinion ūykyen, sayngkak
opera kakuk, opheyla
operates: (machinery) wūncen (ul) hay yo; (on a patient) swuswul (ul) hay yo
operating room swuswulq-sil
operation (surgical) swuswul
operator (telephone) kyohwan-swu
ophthalmology ānq-kwa
opportunity kihoy
opposes pāntay (lul) hay yo
opposite (= facing) mac.un phyen (ey), mac.un ...; (= opposition) pāntay; ~ number (= counterpart) sangtay
or ... ina, ...-una; or (else) tto nun; or else (= if not) kuleh.ci anh.umyen
orange kyul
order: gets out of ~ thāl/kōcang i na yo [na-]
orders sikhye yo [sikhi-]; hōlyeng (ul) hay yo; cwūmun (ul) hay yo
ordinary, ordinarily pōthong
Orient tongyang
Oriental art tongyang-hwa
originally wen.lay; (= earlier) cen (ey)
orphan koa
orphanage koa-wen
other: (= different) talun ..., (= additional) te; the ~ side sangtay pang/phyen
otorhinolaryngology i-pi-inhwuq kwa
out: goes/comes out na ka/wa yo [ka-/o-], na yo [na-]
outside pakk (ey)
over see above, finish(ed)
overcoat ōythwu
overly kwā hi, nemu
owns kacye yo [kaci-]
oyster kwul
packs (snow) (nwūn ul) mungchye yo [mungchi-]
page pheyici
is painful aphe yo [aphu-]
painter hwāka
pair khyelley; see also couple
palace tāykwel, kwungkwel
palm (of hand) sonq patak
paper congi
parasol yangsan
parents pumo (nim)
pares kkakk.e yo [kkakk-]
particular thukpyel; particularly thukpyel hi
parts (mechanical) pusok-phum
party canchi
passes (= goes by) cīna yo, cīna ka yo
past (the ~) kwāke
pastor (= minister) moksa; (unordained) cento-sa
patches (by sewing) kkwēy may yo
patient: (= invalid) hwānca, pyēngca; is patient with cham.e yo [chām-]
pawns cap.hye yo [cap.hi-]
pawnshop cēntang-pho
pays nāy yo [nāy-]; chile yo [chilu-]
pediatrics sōaq-kwa
peels (with a knife) kkakk.e yo [kkakk-]
pencil yenphil
penetrates thong hay yo; cf. pierces
people sālam (tul); ... salam, ... pun
pepper (black) hwuchwu; (red) kochwu
perch (fish) min.e
performance sāngyen
perhaps see maybe
perishes myelmang hay yo; ēps.e cye yo [ci-]
perpetual ... mān-nyen ...
person sālam, ...-sa, ...-ka, ... cayngi; ... i, ... salam, ... myeng, ... pun
pharmacist yakcey-sa
pharmacy yak-pang
phonograph [l]yuseng-ki, chwuk.um-ki, leykhōtu; ~ record [l]yuseng-ki/chwuk.um-ki/lekhōtu phan
photograph sacin
physician (nāyq-kwa) uysa
piano phiano; plays the ~ phiano lul chie yo [chi-]
pickled vegetables kimchi
picnic wēn.yu-hoy
picture kūlim; (= movie) yenghwa
pierces kkwēy yo [kkwēy-]
pig twāyci
pigeon pitwulki
pillow peykay; ~ slip (case, cover) peykayq is
pine (tree) sol, so' namu
pingpong phingphong, thak.kwu
is pitiful hansim hay yo
place kos, ... tey; ...-so, ...-cang
places see puts
plan kyēyhoyk, cakceng; ...-ul they, ...-ulye
plant phul; (= shrub) namu
plants it sim.e yo [sīm-]
plate cepsi; kulus
plays nol.a yo [nō-l-], cangnan hay yo; (ball, a piano) chie yo [chi-], (a violin) khie yo [khi-]; lets someone play nollye yo [nolli-]
pleading pyēnho
please (com) ...-e cwusipsio (or

cwusey yo); pūti, cēypal; ca, ese
pleases (... uy) maum ey tul.e yo [tu-l-]
is plentiful (= common) hun hay yo
plows kal.e yo [kā-l-]
pocket ho-cwumeni, phokheythu, phokheys; (inside one's ~) hoycwung
point cem
pointlessly kongyen hi [often pronounced kwayni or koyni]
pole (for fishing) nakk.siq tay
police kyēngchal
policeman kyēngkwan, kyēngchal-kwan, swunkyeng
polishes takk.e yo [takk-]
pollack myengthay; dried ~ puk.e
poly-... ta-...
pond mos, [l]yen-mos
is poor kanan hay yo
pork twāyci koki
positively (= absolutely) celqtay lo
postcard yepse; picture ~ kūlimq yepse
post office wuphyen-kwuk
postpones nuc.chwe yo [nuc.chwu-]
pot hangali
power him
practice [l]yēnsup
prays for pil.e yo [pī-l-]
prayer kito
is precious kwīcwung hay yo
is precise cēnghwak hay yo
preparation cwūnpi
prepares cwūnpi (lul) hay yo; ~ food (a meal) ūmsik/pap ul hay yo
Presbyterian faith Cang.lo-kyo
present: (= a gift) sēnmul; (= at ~) hyēncay; for the ~ tangpun-kan; is present (in attendance) chwulqsek (ul) hay yo
presents (= gives) ollye yo [olli-], pachye yo [pachi-], tulye yo [tuli-], cwue yo [cwu-]
president (of a club or a company) hōycang
presides sahoy (lul) hay yo
pretext phingkyey
is pretty ippe yo [ippu-]
prevents mallye yo [malli-]
price kaps; kakyek
priest sinpu
primary school sō-hak.kyo
principal (of a school) kyocang
prison kam.ok
prisoner coyswu
probably ama
problem mūncey
produces nah.a yo [nah-]; is produced na yo [na-]
product sānmul
professor kyōswu
program (= order of events) swūnse
promise yaksok; promises yaksok (ul) hay yo
pronounces pal.um (ul) hay yo
pronunciation pal.um
pro(s) and con(s) kā-pu
Protestant(ism) Sinkyo
pseudonym ho
in public kongsek ey se
pulls: (= drags) kkul.e yo [kku-l-]; ~ (= extracts) a tooth i lul ppop.a yo
pupil (of the eye) nwunq-tongca
purpose mokcek; ...-ulye, ...-ule
purse cwumeni
puts (= places) noh.a yo [noh-]; gets put noh.ye yo [noh.i-]
puts away twue yo [twu-]
puts in neh.e yo [neh-]; tul.ye yo [tul.i-]; (= stuffs, crams) tam.e yo [tām-]
puts on (to wear) ip.e yo [ip-]; (headgear, glasses) sse yo [ssu-]; (footwear) sin.e yo [sin-]; (gloves, rings) kkie yo [kkī-]; (neckties, shoelaces) māy yo [māy-]; (watch, pin, etc.) cha yo [cha-]; (a belt) ttie yo [tti-]
puts out nāy yo [nāy-], nāy noh.a yo [noh-]
puts over nemkye yo [nemki-]
puts up = puts away; ~ with cham.e yo [chām-]
quartet (vocal) sācwung-chang; (instrumental) sācwung-cwu
question cilmun; asks a ~ cilmun (ul) hay yo, mul.e pwa yo [po-]
quickly ppalli; ese, kot, ellun
quietly kaman hi
quite sangtang hi; acwu
radio latio, leytio
radish (giant white) muwu
rain pi; it rains pi ka wa yo [o-]
raises (= grows, nurtures) kille yo [kilu-]; (= elevates) nop.hye yo [nop.hi-]; (= lifts) tul.e yo [tu-l-], ollye yo [olli-]
raising chickens (poultry) yāngkyey
raising one's hand kēswu
rat cwi
rate <u>see</u> fee
rather ohilye
reaction pān-cak.yong
reader (= book of readings) tokpon
reads ilk.e yo [ilk-]; pwa yo [po-]
realizes kkaytal.e yo [kkaytal-]

really cham mal lo; Really? Kulay yo? Kuleh.sup.nikka?
reason [l]īyu; kkatalk, ttaymun
recalls kiek hay yo; sayngkak (i) na yo
receives pat.e yo [pat-]; (= suffers, confronts) mac.e yo [mac-]
recent times kūnsey
recently see lately
recital yēncwu-hoy; (vocal) tokchang-hoy
recompense (for damage) pāysang
record: (phonograph) lekhōtu/chwuk.um-ki/[l]yuseng-ki phan, umphan; (sports etc.) kilok; (academic) sengcek, makes a (school) ~ sengcek ul nāy yo [nāy-]
recorded music leykhōtu um.ak
recovers naa yo [nā(s)-]
is red pulk.e yo [pulk-]
is refreshing sāngkhway hay yo
regards: sending ~ mūn.an
regrets hwūhoy; regrets hwūhoy (lul) hay yo
regular(ly) pōthong
relation(ship) kwankyey
relevance kwankyey
religion congkyo
remains nam.e yo [nām-]; (= stays) iss.ey yo [iss-]; (place where there are) historical ~ kōcek(-ci)
remembers kiek hay yo; sayngkak (i) na yo; (= commemorates) kinyem (ul) hay yo
remorse see regret
removes ppāy yo [ppāy-]; nāy yo [nāy-]; ēps.ay yo [ēps.ay-], pelye yo [peli-]
rent sēy; (house ~) cip sey, (monthly ~ talq sey); rented house, house for rent sēyq cip
repair(ing) swusen; repairs swusen (ul) hay yo
repairman swusen-kong
repair shop swusen-so
repeatedly cōng-cong, cakkwu
repentance hōykay; repents hōykay (lul) hay yo
report pōko
request for payment chengkwu-se
requests cheng hay yo
resembles talm.e yo [tālm-]
residence cwūthayk
resident in ... cāy-...
with respect to ... ... -sang
restaurant ūmsik-cem, [l]yoli-cem, [l]yoliq cip, leysutholang
rests swie yo [swī-]
result kyelkwa
returns (= comes/goes back) tol.a wa/ka yo [o-/ka-]
revolution hyek.myeng
rice: (unhulled) pye, (hulled but uncooked) ssal, (cooked) pap
rice plant pye, (young seedling) mo
rice cake ttek
rice field non
rice hash pipimq pap
is rich: (with money) tōn i mānh.e yo [mānh-]; (with verdure) museng hay yo; (of liquid) cin hay yo
rid: gets ~ of ēps.ay yo [ēps.ay-]; (= discards) pelye yo [peli-]
rides tha yo [tha-]
right (as opposed to left) (direction) palun ..., ol(h.)un ...; palun/ol(h.)un phyen; (= just, directly) palo; is right (= correct) olh.a yo [olh-]; is all right kwaynchanh.e yo, cōh.a yo [cōh-]
right away kot, ese, ellun, ppalli
ring panci
rips (= gets ripped) kkwēy cye yo
rises olla yo [olu-]; il.e na yo [na-]
river kang; (stream) sī'-nay(q mul)
riverbank kangq ka
road kil, hayng-kil (= han-kil)
roll (call) cemmyeng; calls the roll cemmyeng (ul) hay yo
rolls it up kwūllye yo [kwūlli-]
Roman (Catholic) faith [l]Noma-kyo
room pang, ...-sil
rope cwul
is round twungkul.e yo [twungku-l-], twungkulewe yo [twungkulew-]
rubs pipye yo [pipi-]
rumor somun
rural area sikol
Russia [l]Nosea
Russian: (language) [l]Nosea mal, (person) [l]Noseaq salam
sailor: (= crewman) sen.wen, (= navy enlisted man) swupyeng
salad namul
salary welkup
salt sokum
salvation kwūwen
same machan-kaci; kath.un kes
sardine cengeli
is satisfactory cōh.a yo [cōh-]
Saturday Tho-yoil
saves (= revives) sallye yo [salli-]
says (māl) hay yo; ... ko yo; ille yo [ilu-]
scale (= scope) kyumo
scallion pha

gets scared kep (i) na yo [na-]
is scarce pucok hay yo; cek.e yo [cēk-]
scholar hakca; ...-sa
school hak.kyo
science kwahak
scientific kwahak-cek
scissors kawi
scorches (= gets scorched) nwul.e yo [nwūl-]
scratches kulk.e yo [kulk-], kalk.e yo [kalk-]
scrivener tāyse(-iṇ)
sea pata
sea bream tōm(i)
sea perch min.e
seashore hāypyen, pataq ka
seat cali, cwāsek
seats anc.hye yo [anc.hi-]
second (= number two) twū ccay, cēy-i; (to a motion) cāycheng; seconds (a motion) cāycheng (ul) hay yo
second hand (of a timepiece) chochim
secretary seki; (official) seki-kwan
seedling mo
seems ... mo.yang iey yo, ... kes kath.ey yo, ... ka pwa yo
sees pwa yo [po-]; (= meets a person) manna yo [manna-]; (sees someone esteemed) pōywe yo [pōyw-]
self (= oneself) caki; ~ study toksup
sells phal.e yo [pha-l-]
sends ponay yo [ponay-]; ~ a person off sōngpyel (ul) hay yo
sentence kul
Seoul Sewul
September Kwu-wel(q tal)
is serious cwūng hay yo
sermon selkyo
service (tennis or restaurant) ssēpisu; (Protestant) ^{l}yeypay
serviceman kwun.in
sets see puts; see seats; ~ the table sang ul pwa yo [po-]; ~ out (= transplants) seedlings mo lul nāy yo [nāy-]
seven ilkop, chil; ~ days iley
seventeen yel ilkop, sip-chil
seventy ilhun, chilq-sip
several yeles, yele ...; meych; ~ days meychil
sewing (= needlework) panu' cil, caypong; ~ machine caypong-thul
sews (= does needlework) panu' cil hay yo; (= stitches) kkwēy may yo [may-]
shade kunul
is shallow yeth.e yo, yath.e yo
shampoos meli lul kam.e yo [kām-]
sharpens a pencil yenphil ul kkakk.e yo [kkakk-]
shaves myēnto (lul) hay yo
she ku ^{n}yeca/āy (or = he)
shift (= change) pyēnkyeng; shifts pyēnkyeng (ul) hay yo
shirt (wai)syassu [syatsu]
shoe kwutwu, sin; ~ store yanghwa-cem
shoelaces, shoestrings sin kkun
shop māycem
is short (in stature) khi ka cak.e yo [cāk-]; (in length) ccalp.e yo [ccalp-], tān-...; (= low) nac.e yo [nac-]
short fellow kkoma
show (= spectacle) kwūkyeng, (= movie) yenghwa; shows po.ye yo [poi-], pōy yo [pōy-]
shower sona(y)ki, sonak pi
shrimp saywu
shrub namu
shuts: (= closes) tat.e yo [tat-], (a book) teph.e yo [teph-]; ~ in (confines) katwe yo [katwu-], gets shut in kat.hye yo [kat.hi-]
gets sick pyēng i na yo [na-]; alh.e yo [alh-]
sick call pyēng mūn.an
sickness pyēng
side (= direction) ... phyen; ... ccok
side effect pū-cak.yong
silver un
is similar kath.ey yo [kath-]
is simple kāntan hay yo, (= easy) swiwe yo [swīw-]; simply swīpkey
sin cōy; commits ~ cōy lul cie yo [cī(s)-] or pēm hay yo
sincerity cengseng
singer sengak-ka
single oy ...; toksin
sings nolay (lul) hay yo
sister: (male's older) nwūna, nwū' nim; (male's younger) ^{n}ye-tongsayng, nwui-tongsayng; (female's younger) tongsayng
sisters camay
site the
sits anc.e yo [anc-]
situation kyengwu
six yeses, ^{l}yuk; ~ days yes-say
sixteen yel yeses, sip-^{l}yuk [simnyuk]
sixty yeyswun, ^{l}yuk-sip
skin phipu; (texture of ~) salq kyel
skirt chima
sky hanul
sleep cam; sleeps (cam ul) ca yo [ca-], cwumusey yo [cwumusi-]; gets sleepy

col.a yo [cō-l-], cam i wa yo [o-];
falls asleep cam i tul.e yo [tu-l-]
is slender kanul.e yo [kanu-l-]
slices ssel.e yo [ssē-l-]
is slippery mikkulewe yo [mikkulew-]
is slow chēn-chen hay yo; tte yo [ttu-];
(a timepiece) runs slow ttukey ka yo [ka-]
slowly chēn-chen hi; ttukey
is small (in quantity) cek.e yo [cēk-];
(in size) cak.e yo [cāk-], sō-...
smallpox māma, son nim
is smart ttok-ttok hay yo
is smarting ēl-el hay yo
smashes: (= ~ it) kkay-ttulye yo [-ttuli-];
(= it ~) kkāy-cye yo [-ci-]
smelt (surf) pinge; (sweet) un.e
smokes phiwe yo [phiwu-], phi'e yo [phi'-]
snake pāym
sneeze caychayki; sneezes caychayki (lul) hay yo
snow nwūn; ~ ball nwūnq tengeli; ~ man nwūnq salam; it snows nwūn i wa yo [o-]
so: is so kule hay yo, kulay yo [kule(h)-];
does so kule hay yo, kulay yo [kule-]
soap pinwu
soccer chwuk.kwu; plays ~ chwuk.kwu lul hay yo
society sāhoy; (= association) hōy
socks yangmal; (Korean) posen
is soft yen hay yo
soldier pyengceng
sole (fish) kacaymi
solitary toksin
some see several; (= a bit) com
sometimes kakkum
son atul, atu' nim
song nolay
son-in-law sawi
soon swii, swī; ese, ellun
soprano sophulano, koum
is sorry mian hay yo; see regrets
soup kwuk
Soviet Union Solyen, Ssolyen
soy sauce kan-cang
speaks māl hay yo
special thukpyel; specially thukpyel hi
speech yēnsel
spends (money) sse yo [ssu-]
spirit maum; hon; cengsin
is splendid hwullyung hay yo
spontaneously (ce-)cel lo
spoon swuq-kal(ak); ~ and chopsticks swuce

sport wūntong
spot cem
spouse see husband, wife
spreads it out (to sun or air) nel.e yo [nē-l-]
spring pom
sprinkles ppulye yo [ppuli-]
squash hō-pak; fried ~ hō-pak cēn
squid nakci
squirrel talam-cwi
staff īm.wen
stage mūtay
stairs, staircase chungchung-tali/-tay, kyeytan
stamp wuphyo
stand (= shop) māycem
stands se yo [su-]; (= stands it up) seywe yo [seywu-]
starch phul; starches a shirt waisyassu ey phul ul mek.ye yo [mek.i-]
starts see begins
starves (= goes hungry) kwulm.e yo [kwulm-]; (= lets someone go hungry) kwulm.kye yo [kwulm.ki-]
station (railroad) cengke-cang
stationed in ... cwu-...
stays iss.ey yo [iss-], kyēysey yo [kyēysi-]
stead tāysin
steals hwumchye yo [hwumchi-], totwuk cil (ul) hay yo
steps on pālp.e yo [pālp-]; gets stepped on palp.hye yo [palp.hi-]
sticks: (= it ~) puth.e yo [puth-]; (= ~ it) puth.ye yo [puth.i-]
still: (= yet) acik; (= more) tto; (= but) kulena
stitches kkwēy may yo [may-]
stomach pay; ~ upset pay thāl
stone tōl
stopping a vehicle cengke
stops: (= stops moving) se yo [su-];
(= stops doing) ku man ... (hay yo);
(= finishes it) kkuth nāy yo [nāy-],
(= it finishes) kkuth na yo [na-]; (= stops in, drops by) tullye yo [tulli-]
store sangcem
storeroom kwāng
story iyaki, yāyki, yēyki; (children's fable) tonghwa
is straight: (= unbent, direct) kot.a yo [kot-]; (= stiff, unbending) kkos-kkos hay yo
stream sī'-nay
street kil; hayng-kil, han-kil; keli
streetcar cēncha

strength him; (one's reservoir of ~) āy
strikes chie yo [chi-]
is strong sēy yo [sēy-], him (i) iss.ey yo, kang hay yo; (= strongly brewed) cin hay yo
student haksayng, ...-sayng; college ~ tāyhak-sayng; short-course ~ kāngsup-sayng; medical ~ uyhak-sayng
studies kongpu (lul) hay yo
study kongpu; ...-hak; (= home library) secay
subject (= theme) ceymok; (= course) kwa; faithful ~ (of the king) chwungsin
substance (= main points) tāychey
succeeds sengkong (ul) hay yo
success sengkong
suddenly kkampak
suit yangpok
summer yelum; ~ cottage pyelqcang
Sunday Il-yoil, Cwuil (nal); ~ school Cwuil hak.kyo
sun hay; the ~ sets hay ka cie yo [ci-], the ~ rises hay ka tot.a/tte yo [tot-/ ttu-], the ~ shines hay ka na yo [na-]
sunshine (hayq) pyeth
supper (= evening meal) cenyek (pap)
sure enough kwā.yen
sweeps ssul.e yo [ssu-l-]
sweetfish un.e
Swiss make Sēse-cey
Switzerland Sēse
syllable umcel
symbol sangcing; symbolizes sangcing (ul) hay yo
symphony kyohyang-ak, simphoni; ~ orchestra kyohyang aktan
table sang, chayk sang, theyipul
takes: (a thing) kacye/kaciko ka yo [ka-]; (a person) teyliko ka yo [ka-], (an esteemed person) mōsiko ka yo [ka-]; (time) (sikan i) kellye yo [kelli-]; (advice) ūykyen ul tul.e yo [tul-]
talent caycwu
talk iyaki, yāyki, yēyki; māl(-ssum)
is tall: (in stature) khi ka khe yo [khu-]; (= high) noph.a yo [noph-]
taste mas
taxi thayksi, (catong-)cha; jitney ~ hapsung (thayksi)
tea cha, (black) hong-cha
teaches kaluchye yo [kaluchi-]
teacup chaq can
teahouse, teashop tapang, chaq cip
team thīm
tear (from the eye) nwun mul
telephone (call) cēnhwa; ~ exchange kyohwan, ~ operator kyohwan-swu
telephones cēnhwa lul kel.e yo [kē-l-] or hay yo
tells: (= informs) ille yo [ilu-], allye yo [alli-]; (= conveys) cen hay yo; (= says) ... ko (māl) hay yo; ~ someone to do it ...-ula (ko) hay yo, ~ someone to do it for oneself ...-e tālla (ko) hay yo
temper sēngcil
temperature: (body ~) cheyon; (fevel) yel
temple (Buddhist) cel
temporarily tangpun-kan
ten yel, sip; ~ days yelhul
is tender yen hay yo
tennis cengkwu, theynisu; ~ court cengkwu-cang
tenor theyne
is tepid micikun hay yo
term: (= time limit) kihan; (= half-year ~) pānki
termination kkuth
test sihem; (= checkup) kēmsa
textbook kyōkwa-se
than ... pota
is thankful komawe (hay) yo [komaw-]
thanks (= gives thanks) kāmsa (lul) hay yo
Thank you. Komapsup.nita. or Kāmsa hap.nita. or Mian hap.nita.
that ku/ko (kes); (more remote) ce/co (kes)
theater kukcang; (= movie ~) yenghwa-kwan
their ku (i/sālam) tul uy
them see they
theme ceymok
then: (= at that time) ku ttay; (= next) ku taum; (= later) ku twī/hwū; (= and then) kulem, kulemyen, kulen tey
there (= that place) keki/koki, (more remote) cēki/coki; (= that way) kuli/koli, celi/coli
thermometer: (for weather) han.lan-kyey; (for body) cheyon-kyey
these see this; ~ days yo say
they ku (i/sālam/pun/āy) tul
is thick: (through) twukkewe yo [twukkew-], (around) kwulk.e yo [kwulk-]; (a liquid) cin hay yo; (fog or hair) cith.e yo [cith-]
is thin: (around or across) kanul.e yo; (through) yalp.e yo [yalp-]
thing ... kes; mulken
thinks sayngkak hay yo; ... cwul (lo) al.e yo [ā-l-]; ...-ulq ka hay yo
third (= number three) sēy ccay, cēy-sam; (one third) sam-pun uy il

thirteen yelq sēys/sēy/sēk; sip-sam
thirty selhun, sam-sip
this i/yo (kes)
thought sayngkak; see thinks
thousand chen; ten ~ mān
thread sīl; threads a needle panul ey sīl ul kkwēy yo [kkwēy-]
three sēys, sēy ..., sēk ...; sam; ~ days sahul
thrusts kkwēy yo [kkwēy-]
Thursday Mok-yoil
ticket phyo; admission ~ ipcangq-kwen
tide (= high tide) mīl mul
ties māy yo [māy-]
till ... kkaci
time sikan, (= a stretch of ~) tong-an, (= occasion) ttay, (in a sequence) pen, (= era) sitay, (= o'clock) ... si; what ~ meych si; this ~ i pen; all the ~ pam-nac; ~ after ~ cōng-cong
timepiece sikyey
timetable sikan phyo
is tired phikon hay yo
title ceymok
to ... ey, ... ulo; (up to) ... kkaci, (a person) ... eykey, ... hanthey; (an esteemed person) ... kkey; (commanding an inferior) ... tele
today onul
toe palq-kalak
together kath.i [kachi], hamkkey
toilet pyenso, twīq kan; ~ paper twī-ci, pyensoq congi
tomorrow ^{l}nayil; day after ~ moley
tongue hye
too: (= overly) nemu, kwā hi; (= also) yeksi, tto, ... to
is too bad an tōyss.ey yo
tooth i(q-pal)
top wi; sāng-...
gets torn kkwēy cye yo [ci-]
tournament tāyhoy
towel swūken
town: (= down ~) keli, sīnay; (= city) si, tosi, tohoy; (= village) maul, tōngney
toy cangnanq kām, wānkwu
tradition (= legend) censel
train kicha, (electric) cēncha; cha
translates pen.yek (ul) hay yo
transplants (rice seedlings) (mo lul) nāy yo [nāy-]
treasurer hōykyey
treatment (medical) chilyo
tree namu
tries (= makes an effort) nolyek (ul) hay yo, (...-ki ey) him/āy (lul) sse yo [ssu-]; ~ doing (= samples) ...-e pwa yo [po-]
trims kkakk.e yo [kkakk-]
trio (vocal) samcwung-chang, (instrumental) samcwung-cwu
trip ^{l}yehayng; takes a ~ ^{l}yehayng (ul) hay yo
trivial ku-kkacis...
trouble: (= disorder) kōcang; (= illness) thāl, alh.i, pyēng; (= bother caused someone) swūko; (= dissatisfaction) pulphyeng
trousers paci
trout songe
true see truth
trust sīn.yong
trusts mit.e yo [mit-]
is trustworthy sīn.yong i iss.ey yo [iss-]
truth sāsil, cham (mal); to tell the ~ sāsil māl hamyen, sāsil un
tuberculosis phyēyq-pyeng
Tuesday Hwā-yoil
tuition swuep-lyo, welqso-kum
tuna talang-c
turns: (= it ~) tol.a yo [tō-l-], (= ~ it) tollye yo [tolli-]
twelve yelq twūlq/twū ...; sip-i
twenty sumul, sumu ...; ī-sip
two twūl, twū ...; ī; ~ days ithul
typhoid fever cang-thiphusu
typhus thiphusu
is ugly mōs-na yo [-na-]
uh ce ..., cham ..., ... māl ia
umbrella wūsan, yangsan
umpire emphaie
un-: (= not yet) mī-...; (= not being) pi-..., (= not doing) pul-/pu-...
unbeliever pulqsin-ca
uncle acessi
under ... mith
understands: (= knows) al.e yo [ā-l-], (= comprehends) ^{l}īhay hay yo; (= hears, heeds) tul.e yo [tul-]
underwear sōk os, nāypok, nāyuy
gets undressed os ul pes.e yo; undresses (a person) (sālam hanthey) os ul pes.kye yo [pes.ki-]
is uneasy mian hay yo
uneducated mī-kyoyuk
unfailingly pantusi, kkok
is unfortunate pulhayng hay yo
unique yuil han ...
university tāyhak
unkind(ness) pul-chincel; is unkind pul-chincel hay yo

unlocks (yēlq/cam'ulq) soy lo yel.e yo [yē-l-]
unnatural(ness) pu-ca.yen
up wi (lo); gets ~ il.e na yo [na-], stands ~ se yo [su-], goes ~ ollye yo [olli-], looks ~ (at) chye 'ta pwa yo [po-]
upstairs wi chung
urinal sōpyen-ki
urinates sōpyen ul nwue/pwa yo [nwu-/po-], ocwum ul nwue/ssa yo [nwu-/ssa-]
urine sōpyen, ocwum
us wuli; ce-huy
use: for the ~ of ...-yong
uses sse yo [ssu-]
usual pōthong; cf. tankol
usually pōthong (ulo)
vacation (from school) pānghak
vaccinates wutwu lul cwue/noh.a yo [cwu-/noh-]; gets vaccinated wutwu lul mac.e yo [mac-]
vaccination wutwu
is valuable kwī hay yo; kachi ka iss.ey yo [iss-]
valuables kwīcwung-phum
value kachi
various yele (kaci) ...
vegetable chāyso
vehicle cha; (classifier) ... tay
version ...-sel
very tāytan hi, cham, phek, acwu, mopsi
vest cokki
vice-... pū-...
vicinity kūnche
victory ikim, wusung
view: (= opinion) ūykyen; viewing kwukyeng; views kwūkyeng (ul) hay yo
village tōngney, tōng.li; maul
violin paio(l)lin, ceykum
is visible = gets seen po.ye yo [poi-], pōy yo [pōy-]
visit sīmpang, pāngmun; visits sīmpang/pāngmun (ul) hay yo, chac.e yo [chac-], chac.e wa yo [o-] (= drops in) tullye yo [tulli-]
vocal: ~ duet īcwung-chang, pyēngchang, ~ music sengak; ~ quartet sācwung-chang; ~ recital tokchang-hoy; ~ solo tokchang
vocalist sengak-ka
volleyball paykwu
volume (counter) ... kwen
waist heli
waits for kitalye yo [kitali-]
wakes up: (= comes awake) kkāy yo [kkāy-], (= makes awake) kkaywe yo [kkaywu-]
walk: (= gait) kel.um; (= stroll) sānqpo, takes a ~ sānqpo (lul) hay yo
walks kel.e yo [kēl-], (= goes/comes on foot) kel.e ka/wa yo [ka-/o-], (= strolls) sānqpo (lul) hay yo; (= makes/has someone walk) kellye yo [kelli-]
wall: (exterior) tam, (interior) pyek
wants (...-ki lul) wēn hay yo; ...-ko siph.e yo [siph-]; ...-ulye hay yo
is warm tewe yo [tēw-], ttattus hay yo; (lukewarm) micikun hay yo
was see is
wash (= laundry) sēythak
washes: (one's face and hands) sēyswu (lul) hay yo; (one's body or head) kam.e yo [kām-]; (laundry) ppal.e yo [ppa-l-]; (dishes, objects) ssis.e yo [ssis-], (dishes) selkeci (lul) hay yo
washing machine sēythak kikyey, sēythak-ki
waste (= wasting) hepi; wastes hepi (lul) hay yo
watch (= timepiece) sikyey; (= guarding) kyēngkyey; (= looking at) kwūkyeng
water mul; drinking ~ ūm.lyo-swu
waterfall phokpho
we wuli; ce-huy
wears ip.e yo [ip-]; (headgear, glasses) sse [ssu-]; (footwear) sin.e yo [sin-]; (gloves, rings) kkie yo [kkī-]; (neckties, shoelaces) māy yo [māy-]; (watch, pin, etc.) cha yo; (a belt) ttie yo [tti-]
weather nal(-ssi)
Wednesday Swu-yoil
week cwukan, cwuil; day of the ~ yoil
welcome (= welcoming) hwan.yeng; welcomes hwan.yeng (ul) hay yo; welcoming party hwan.yeng-hoy; You're welcome! Chen-man uy māl-ssum ip.nita! or Chen-man ey (yo)!
well: (= nicely) cal; (= well now) kulem, (= come on) ca; (= well let me think) kulssey yo
wen (Korean money unit) wen
were see is
West (= Occident) se.yang; Western-style yang-...
wet: gets wet cec.e yo [cec-]; wets it ceksye yo [ceksi-], (= dampens it) chwuk.ye yo [chwuk.i-]
what mues, mue, m(w)e; (= which) enu (kes); ~ kind of musen, etten; ~ place eti; ~ time meych si; ~ day of the week musun yoil, ~ month musun tal; ~ way ecci, etteh.key; is like ~ ette hay yo,

ettay yo [ette(h)-], does like ~ ecci hay yo, ettay yo [ette-], eccay yo [ecce-]

when ēncey; (= and then) ...-umyen, ...-ta ka; (= while) ...-nun sai/ tōng-an/cwung (ey)

where eti

which etten, enu; (= ~ one) etten/enu kes

is white huye yo [huy-]

who nwukwu; nwu' ka

whoever (it may be) nwukwu 'tun ci

whole cen-...; on the ~ tāychey (lo)

whose nwukwu uy (kes), nwukwu ...

why way, etteh.key, ecci

is wide nelp.e yo [nelp-]

widens it nelp.hye yo [nelp.hi-]

wife ^{n}yephyenney; puin; (one's own) an(h)ay, an, [vulgar] mānwula

wiles kkoy

will ...-keyss-, ...-ulq ke(s ie)y yo; ...-um a/sey

wind palam

window (yuli) chang

wine swul

wins ikye yo [iki-]

winter kyewul

wipes hwumchye yo [hwumchi-]

...-wise ...-sang

with ... hako, ... kwa/wa; (= by means of) ... ulo, ... kaciko

woman ^{n}yeca; punye, ^{n}yeseng

won see win; see wen

is wonderful sinthong hay yo, koyngcang hay yo

word māl(-ssum)

work īl; (study etc.) kongpu

worker ^{l}notong-ca; (= workman) īlq-kwun; (factory) cik.kong

works īl (ul) hay yo; (study etc.) kongpu (lul) hay yo

world sēykyey; sēysang

worn see wear; gets worn out hel.e yo [hē-l-]

worries ^{n}yēm.lye/kekceng (ul) hay yo

worry ^{n}yēm.lye, kekceng

worship ^{l}yeypay; worships ^{l}yeypay (lul) hay yo or pwa yo [po-]

worth (= value) kachi; is worthwhile kachi ka iss.ey yo [iss-]; is worth ...-ing ...-ul man hay yo

wraps up ssa yo [ssa-]; gets wrapped ssa.ye yo [ssai-], ssāy yo [ssāy-]

wrings cca yo [cca-]

wrist phal-mok; ~ watch phal-mok sikyey

writes sse yo [ssu-]

wrong (= a mistake) calmos; does it wrong calmos hay yo

X-ray Eyksu-kwangsen

yard (= grounds) ttul

yawn haphum; yawns haphum i na yo

yeah ung

year hay, ...-^{n}yen; last ~ cīnan hay, cak.nyen; year before last kulekkey, cāy-cak.nyen, ci-cinan hay; next ~ ^{l}naynyen; ~ after next nay-^{l}naynyen; ~ after ~ after next hwū-hwunyen

is yellow nwūlule yo [nwūlu-] or nwūlay yo [nwūle(h)-], (golden) nōlule yo [nōlu-] or nōlay yo [nōle(h)-]

yellow corvenia coki

yen (money unit) wen

yes nēy, nay; kulay (yo), kuleh.sup.nita, kulem

yesterday ecey; day before ~ kucekkey

yet acik; (= but) kulena

YMCA Kitok Chengnyen Hōy(-Kwan)

you sensayng (nim); tangsin; ne, ney ka; caney

you people, you all yele pun

is young: (a child ~) elye yo [eli-]; (an adult ~) celm.e yo [celm-]

is younger nai ka alay 'ey yo

younger brother and/or sister tongsayng

youngest of the family 'mak-nay

your sensayng (nim) uy; tangsin uy; ney; caney uy

yours = your thing

YWCA ^{n}Yeca Chengnyen Hōy(-Kwan)

zoo tōngmul-wen

TABLE OF ROMANIZATION SYSTEMS

The following table shows how several systems differ in representing the Hankul symbols. Minor details in each system, such as the abbreviation of wu to u after labials in the Yale system, are not mentioned. "McCune-R." refers to the McCune-Reischauer system; "Lukoff" refers to the phonemic orthography used in Fred Lukoff's Spoken Korean; "1959—SK" refers to the system of the ROK Ministry of Education; "CK" refers to that of the North Korean Academy of Sciences (*Cosen kwahak-wen*), as reported in the 1957 Peking volume Pīnyīn wéncì xiĕfă gūicè pp. 210—5.

Hankul	Yale	McCune-R.	Lukoff	1959-SK	CK
ㅂ	**p**	p, b	p	b	p
ㅍ	**ph**	p'	ph	p	ph
ㅃ	**pp**	pp	pp	bb	pp
ㄷ	**t**	t, d	t	d	t
ㅌ	**th**	t'	th	t	th
ㄸ	**tt**	tt	tt	dd	tt
ㅅ	**s**	s	s	s	s
ㅆ	**ss**	ss	ss	ss	ss
ㅈ	**c**	ch, j	j	j	ts
ㅊ	**ch**	ch'	jh	ch	tsh
ㅉ	**cc**	tch	jj	jj	tss
ㄱ	**k**	k, g	k	g	k
ㅋ	**kh**	k'	kh	k	kh
ㄲ	**kk**	kk	kk	gg	kk
ㅁ	**m**	m	m	m	m
ㄴ	**n**	n	n	n	n
ㅇ	**-ng**	-ng	-ng	-ng	-ng
ㄹ	**l**	l, r	l	l, r	r
ㅎ	**h**	h	h	h	h
ㅣ	**i**	i	i	i	i
ㅟ	**wi**	wi	wi	wi	wi
ㅔ	**ey**	e	e	e	e
ㅖ	**yey**	ye	ye	ye	ye
ㅞ	**wey**	we	we	we	we
ㅚ	**oy**	oe	ö	oe	oi
ㅐ	**ay**	ae	ä	ae	ai
ㅒ	**yay**	yae	yä	yae	yai
ㅙ	**way**	wae	wä	wae	wai
ㅡ	**u**	ŭ	ʉ	eu	ŭ
ㅓ	**e**	ŏ	ø	eo	ɤ (?)
ㅕ	**ye**	yŏ	yø	yeo	yɤ (?)
ㅝ	**we**	wŏ	wø	weo	wo (?)
ㅏ	**a**	a	a	a	a
ㅑ	**ya**	ya	ya	ya	ya
ㅘ	**wa**	wa	wa	wa	wa
ㅜ	**wu**	u	u	u	u
ㅠ	**yu**	yu	yu	yu	yu
ㅗ	**o**	o	o	o	o
ㅛ	**yo**	yo	yo	yo	yo
ㅢ	**-uy**	ŭi	(ʉi)	eui	ŭi

From A Korean-English Dictionary by Samuel E. Martin, Yang Ha Lee, and Sung-Un Chang, Yale University Press, New Haven, 1967.